Ancient Egypt: Myth and History

Ancient Egypt:
Myth and History

Part One first published by The Gresham Publishing Company.
Part Two copyright 1997 Geddes & Grosset Ltd.
Copyright this edition 1997 Geddes & Grosset Ltd, David Dale House,
New Lanark, Scotland ML11 9DJ.

ISBN 1 85534 353 3

Printed and bound in China

Preface

This book is divided into two parts. In Part One, the myths and legends of ancient Egypt are embraced in an historical narrative that begins with the rise of the great civilisation of the Nile and ends with the Graeco-Roman age. The principal gods are dealt with chiefly at the various periods in which they came into prominence, while the legends are so arranged as to throw light on the beliefs and manners and customs of the ancient people. Metrical renderings are given of those representative folk songs and poems as can be appreciated in the modern world.

Part Two is a comprehensive dictionary of Egyptology, the study of ancient Egypt in all its aspects, and it contains its own Introduction on page 307.

Egyptian mythology has a highly complex character and cannot be considered apart from its racial and historical aspects. The Egyptians were, as a Hebrew prophet declared, a 'mingled people', and this view has been confirmed by ethnological research. The process of racial fusion begun in the Delta at the dawn of history,' wrote Elliot Smith, 'spread through the whole land of Egypt.' In localities the early Nilotic inhabitants accepted the religious beliefs of settlers and fused these with their own. They also clung tenaciously to the crude and primitive tribal beliefs of their remote ancestors and never abandoned an archaic belief, even when they acquired new and more enlightened ideas. They accepted myths literally and regarded with great sanctity ancient ceremonies and usages. They even showed a tendency to increase rather than reduce the number of their gods and goddesses by symbolising their attributes. As a result, we find it necessary to deal with a bewildering number of gods and a confused mass of beliefs, many of which are obscure and contradictory. But the average Egyptian was never dismayed by inconsistencies in religious matters – he seemed rather to be fascinated by them.

There was, strictly speaking, no orthodox creed in Egypt. Each provincial centre had its own distinctive theological system, and the religion of an individual appears to have depended mainly on his habits of life. 'The Egyptian,' as Professor Wiedemann wrote, 'never attempted to systematise his concepts of the different divinities into a homogeneous religion. It is open to us to speak of the religious ideas of the Egyptians, but not of an Egyptian religion.'

The differing character of some of the ancient myths is dealt with in this Introduction so as to simplify the study of a difficult but extremely fascinating subject. It is shown that one section of the people recognised a Creator like Ptah, who created himself and 'shaped his limbs' before he created the universe, while another section perpetuated the idea of a Creatrix, a female creator, who give birth to all things. At the dawn of history these rival concepts existed side by side, and they were perpetuated until the end. It is evident, too, that the theologies that were based on these fundamental ideas had undergone, before the fusion of peoples occurred, a sufficiently prolonged process of separate development to give them a racial or, at any rate, a geographical significance. This much is suggested by the differing ideas that obtained regarding the world. One section, for instance, conceived of a land surrounded by sky-supporting mountains, peopled by gods and giants, around which the sun ass galloped to escape the night serpent. Another section believed that the world was embraced by the 'great circle' – ocean – and that the Nile flowed from sea to sea. A third concept was of a heavenly and an underground Nile. There were also two paradises – the Osirian and the Ra (sun god's). Osiris judged men according to their deeds. He was an agricultural deity, and the early system of Egyptian ethics seems to have had its origin in the experiences enshrined in the text: 'Whatsoever a man soweth that shall he also reap'. Admission to the paradise of the sun cult was secured, on the other hand, by the repetition of magic formulae. Different beliefs also obtained regarding the mummy. In the *Book of the Dead*, it would appear that the preservation of the body was necessary for the continued existence of the soul. Herodotus, however, was informed that after a period of three thousand years the soul returned to animate the dead frame, and this belief in transmigration of souls is illustrated in the Anpu-Bata story (Chapter 4), and is connected with a somewhat similar concept that the soul of a father passed to a son, who thus became 'the image of his sire', as Horus was of Osiris, and 'husband of his mother'.

Of special interest in this connection are the various forms of the archaic chaos-egg myth associated with the gods Ptah, Khnum, Geb, Osiris and Ra. As the European giant hides his soul in the egg, which is within the duck, which is within the fish, which is within the deer, and so on, and Bata hides his soul in the blossom, the bull and the tree before he becomes 'husband of his mother', so does Osiris 'hide his essence in the shrine of Amun', while his manifestations include a tree, the Apis bull, the boar, the goose and the Oxyrhynchus fish. Similarly, when Seth was slain he became a 'raring serpent', a hippopotamus, a crocodile or a boar. The souls of Ra, Ptah and Khnum are in the chaos egg like two of the prominent Hindu and Chinese gods. Other Egyptian deities who are 'hidden' include Amun, Sokar and Neith. This persistent myth, which appears to have been associated with belief in the transmigration of souls, may be traced even in Akhenaten's religion. We have 'Shu [atmosphere god] in his Aten [sun disc]' and a reference in the famous hymn to the 'air of life' in the 'egg'. There can be little doubt that the transmigration theory prevailed at certain periods and in certain localities in ancient Egypt and that the statement made by Herodotus was well founded, despite attempts to discredit it.

It is shown that the concept of a Creator was associated with that form of earth, air and water worship that was perpetuated at Memphis, where the presiding god was the hammer god Ptah, who resembles the Chinese Pan-ku, Indra of the Aryans, Tarku and Sutekh of Asia Minor, Heracles, Thor, etc. The Creatrix, on the other hand, was more closely associated with lunar, earth and water worship and appears to have been the principal goddess of the Mediterranean race, which spread into Asia Minor and Europe. In Scotland, for instance, as is shown, she is called Cailleach Bheur and, like other archaic tribal deities and ghosts, she was the enemy of humankind. Similarly, the Egyptian goddesses Sekhmet and Hathor were destroyers and Tefnut was goddess of plagues. Even the sun god Ra 'produced calamity after your [Osiris's] heart', as one of the late temple chants puts it.

In the chapter dealing with animal worship (Chapter 5), the racial aspect of early beliefs, which were connected with fixed and definite ceremonies, is illustrated in the Horus-Seth myth. The 'black pig' was Seth (the devil) in Egypt. Pork was taboo, and the swineherd was regarded as 'an abomination' and not allowed to enter temples. The Gauls and Achaeans, on the other hand, honoured the swineherd and ate pork freely, while in the Teutonic Valhal and the Celtic (Irish) paradise, swine's flesh was the reward of heroes. In Scotland, however, the ancient prejudice against pork exists in some places even today, and the devil is the 'black pig'. In his *Celtic Folklore*, Professor Sir John Rhys recorded that in Wales the black sow of All-Hallows was similarly regarded as the devil. The Gaulish treatment of the boar appears to be Asiatic. Brahma, in one of the Hindu creation myths, assumes the form of a boar, the 'lord of creatures', and tosses up the earth with his tusks from the primordial deep.

Another myth that seems to have acquired a remote racial colouring is the particular form of the dragon story, which probably radiated from Asia Minor. The hero is represented in Egypt by Horus, with his finger on his lips, in his character as Harpokrates, as the Greeks named this mysterious form of the god. The god Sutekh of Rameses II was also a dragon slayer. So was Heracles, who fought with the Hydra, and Thor, who at Ragnarok overcame the Midgard serpent. Sigurd, Siegfried, the Germanic heroes, and the Celtic Finn mac Coul suck a finger or thumb after slaying the dragon, or one of its forms (the salmon in Finn mac Coul's case), and cooking part of it, to obtain 'knowledge' or understand 'the language of birds'. In an Egyptian folk tale, Ahura, after killing the 'deathless snake', similarly understands 'the language of birds, fishes', etc. Harpokrates appears to be the god Horus as the dragon-slaying Sutekh, the imported legend being preserved in the Ahura tale of the New Kingdom, when Egypt received so many Asiatic immigrants that the facial type changed, as the statuary shows. Elliot Smith considers that while the early Egyptian was 'the representative of his kinsman the Neolithic European . . . the immigrant population into both Europe and Egypt' represented 'two streams of the same Asiatic folk'. Racial myths appear to have followed in the tracks of the racial drift.

In the historical narrative the reader is kept in touch with the great civilisations of the Cretans, Hittites, Babylonians, Assyrians, etc, which influenced and were influenced by Egypt. Attention is also given to the great figures in Biblical narrative – Joseph, Moses, Isaiah, Jeremiah, Nahum, and the notable kings of Israel and Judah. There are numerous quotations from the Old Testament, and especially from the prophets who dealt with the political as well as the religious problems of their times. It is impossible to appreciate the power of Isaiah's utterances without some knowledge of the history of ancient Egypt.

Contents

PART ONE
EGYPTIAN MYTH AND LEGEND

Introduction

Cleopatra's Needle, on the Thames Embankment in London, affords us an introduction to ancient Egypt, 'the land of marvels' and of strange and numerous deities. This obelisk was shaped from a single block of red granite quarried at Aswan. It is 68 feet 5½ inches (20.87 metres) high and weighs 186 tons (170.7 tonnes). Like one of our own megalithic monuments, it is an interesting relic of stone worship. Primitive man believed that stones were inhabited by spirits that had to be propitiated with sacrifices and offerings, and, long after higher conceptions obtained, their crude beliefs survived among their descendants. This particular monument was erected as a habitation for one of the spirits of the sun god. In ancient Egypt the gods were believed to have had many spirits.

The Needle was presented to the British Government in 1820, and in 1877–78 was transported to London by Sir Erasmus Wilson at a cost of £10,000. For many centuries it had been a familiar object at Alexandria. Its connection with the famous Queen Cleopatra is uncertain. She may have ordered it to be removed from its original site on account of its archaeological interest, for it was already old in her day. It was first erected at Heliopolis by order of the Eighteenth-Dynasty Pharoah Thuthmosis III, but even then Egypt was a land of ancient memories, the great pyramids near Cairo having been begun in the Third Dynasty and the calendar having been in existence since the end of the Second Dynasty.

Heliopolis, 'the city of the sun', is called On in the Bible. It was there that Moses was educated and became 'mighty in words and in deeds'. Joseph had previously married, at On, Asenath, the daughter of Potipherah, a priest of the sun temple, the site of which, at modern Matarieh, is marked by an obelisk of greater age even than the Needle. Nearby are a holy well and a holy tree, long invested with great sanctity by local tradition. Coptic Christians and Muslims still relate that when the New Testament Joseph and Mary fled with the infant Christ into Egypt to escape King Herod, they rested under the tree and that Mary washed in the well the swaddling clothes of the holy child.

When Cleopatra's Needle was erected at On, which is also called Bethshemesh[1], 'the house of the sun god', in the Hebrew Scriptures, the priests taught classes of students in the temple colleges. For about thirty centuries the city was the Oxford of Egypt. Eudoxus and Plato, in the course of their travels, visited the

[1] The Babylonian form is 'shamash'.

13

priestly professors and heard them lecture. As ancient tradition has credited Egypt with the origin of geometry, Euclid, the distinguished mathematician who belonged to the brilliant Alexandria school, no doubt also paid a pilgrimage to the ancient seat of learning. When he was a student he must have been familiar with our Needle. Perhaps he puzzled over it as much as some of us have puzzled over his problems.

At On, the Egyptian students were instructed among other things to read and create the pictorial signs that appear on the four sides of the Needle. These are hieroglyphics, a term derived from the Greek words *hieros*, 'sacred', and *glypho*, 'sculpted', and first applied by the Greeks because they believed that picture writing was used only by Egyptian priests for religious purposes. Much of what we know regarding the myths, legends and history of the land of the pharaohs has been accumulated since modern linguists acquired the art of reading those pictorial inscriptions. The ancient system had passed out of human use and knowledge for many long centuries when the fortunate discovery was made of a slab of black basalt on which had been inscribed a decree in Greek and Egyptian. It is called the Rosetta Stone, because it was dug up at Rosetta (now Rashid) by a French officer of engineers in 1799, when Napoleon, who had invaded Egypt, ordered a fort to be rebuilt. It was afterwards seized by the British, along with other antiquities collected by the French, and was presented by George III to the British Museum in 1802.

Copies of the Rosetta Stone inscriptions were distributed by Napoleon, and subsequently by British scholars, to various centres of learning throughout Europe. It was found that the Greek section recorded a decree issued by the native priests to celebrate the first anniversary of Pharaoh Ptolemy V in 195 BC. The mysterious Egyptian section was rendered in hieroglyphics and also in demotic, a late form of the cursive system of writing called hieratic. In 1814 two distinguished linguists—Dr Thomas Young in Britain and Professor Champollion in France—engaged in studying the pictorial signs. The credit of having first discovered the method of reading them is claimed for both these scholars, and a heated controversy waged for long years over the matter. Modern opinion inclines to the view that Young and Champollion solved the secret simultaneously and independently of each other. The translation of other Egyptian texts followed in due course, and so great has been the skill attained by scholars that they are now able to detect blunders made by ancient scribes. Much uncertainty exists, however, and must always exist, regarding the proper pronunciation of the language.

Another source of knowledge regarding the civilisation of Egypt is the history of Manetho, an Egyptian priest who lived at the beginning of the third century BC. His books perished when Alexander the Great conquered Egypt, but summaries survive in the writings of Julius Africanus, Eusebius and Georgius

Syncellus, while fragments are quoted by Josephus. Manetho divided the history of his country into thirty dynasties, and his system constitutes a framework, albeit a confusing one, on which our knowledge of the Egyptian past has accumulated.

Differing views exist regarding the value of Manetho's history, and these are invariably expressed with point and vigour. Professor Breasted, an American Egyptologist, for instance, characterised the chronology of the priestly historian as 'a late, careless, and uncritical compilation', and he held that it 'can be proven wrong from the contemporary monuments in the vast majority of cases'. 'Manetho's dynastic totals,' he says, 'are so absurdly high throughout that they are not worthy of a moment's credence, being often nearly or quite double the maximum drawn from contemporary monuments. Their accuracy is now maintained only by a small and constantly decreasing number of modern scholars.' Breasted goes even further than that by adding: 'The compilation of puerile folk tales by Manetho is hardly worthy of the name history'.

Flinders Petrie, whose work as an excavator was epochmaking, was inclined, on the other hand, to attach much weight to the history of the native priest. 'Unfortunately,' he says, 'much confusion has been caused by scholars not being content to accept Manetho as being substantially correct in the main, though with many small corruptions and errors. Nearly every historian has made large and arbitrary assumptions and changes, with a view to reducing the length of time stated. But recent discoveries seem to prove that we must accept the lists of kings as having been correct, however they may have suffered in detail . . . Every accurate test that we can apply shows the general trustworthiness of Manetho apart from minor corruptions.'

Breasted, supported by other leading Egyptologists, accepted what is known as the 'Berlin system of Egyptian chronology', which favoured shorter chronology than that established by Petrie, which was very much influenced by Petrie. The Hyksos invasion took place, according to Manetho, at the beginning of the Fifteenth Dynasty, and he calculated that the Asiatic rulers were in Egypt for 511 years. Breasted's minimum was 100 years. Hall, like Newberry and Garstang, allowed the Hyksos a little more than 200 years, while Hawes, the Cretan explorer, whose dating came very close to that of Dr Evans, said that 'there is a growing conviction that Cretan evidence, especially in the eastern part of the island, favours the minimum [Berlin] system of Egyptian chronology'. Breasted allows 420 years for the period between the Twelfth and Eighteenth Dynasties, while Petrie gives 1820 – a difference of 1400 years. From 1580 BC onward, the authorities are in practical agreement; prior to that date the chronology is uncertain.

This confusion has been partly caused by the Egyptians having ignored the leap year addition of one day. Their calendar of 365 days lost about a quarter of a day each twelve months and about a whole day every four years. New Year's Day began with the rising of the star Sirius (Sothos) on 17 June, and it coincided with the beginning of the Nile inundation. But in a cycle of 1461 years Sirius rose in every alternate month of the Egyptian year. When, therefore, we find in the Egyptian records a reference, at a particular period, to their first month (the month of Thoth), we are left to discover whether it was our April or October; and in dating back we must allow for the 'wanderings of Sirius'. Much controversial literature has accumulated regarding what is known as the Egyptian Sothic cycle.

Throughout this volume the dates are given in accordance with the minimum system, on account of the important evidence afforded by the Cretan discoveries. We may agree to differ from Petrie on chronological matters and yet continue to admire his genius and acknowledge the incalculable debt that he is owed as one who reconstructed some of the most obscure periods of Egyptian history. The light he threw on early Dynastic and pre-Dynastic times, especially, has assured him an undying reputation, and he set an example to all who followed him by the thoroughness and painstaking character of his practical fieldwork.

It is chiefly by modern-day excavators in Egypt, and in those countries that traded with the Nilotic kingdom in ancient times, that the past has been conjured up before us. We know more about ancient Egypt now than did the Greeks or the Romans, and more about pre-Dynastic times and the early Dynasties than even those Egyptian scholars who took degrees in the Heliopolitan colleges when Cleopatra's Needle was first erected. But our knowledge is still fragmentary. We can trace only the outlines of Egyptian history. We do not have that unfailing supply of documentary material that is available, for instance, in dealing with the history of a European nation. Fragments of pottery, a few weapons, strings of beads, some rough drawings and tomb remains are all that we have at our disposal in dealing with some periods. Others are made articulate by inscriptions, but even after civilisation had attained a high level, it is occasionally impossible to deal with those great movements that were shaping the destinies of the ancient people. Obscure periods recur throughout ancient Egyptian history, and some periods, indeed, are almost quite blank.

When Cleopatra's Needle was erected by Thuthmosis III, the conqueror and the forerunner of Alexander the Great and Napoleon, Egyptian civilisation had attained its highest level. Although occasionally interrupted by internal revolt or invasions from north and south, it had gradually increased in splendour until Thuthmosis III extended the empire to the borders of Asia Minor. The Mediterranean Sea then became an 'Egyptian lake'. Peace offerings were sent to Thuthmosis from Crete and Cyprus. The Phoenicians owed him allegiance, and his favours were courted by the Babylonians and Assyrians. The Needle records the gifts that were made by the humbled king of the Hittites.

After the passing of Thuthmosis, who flourished in the Eighteenth Dynasty, decline set in, and, although lost ground was recovered after a time, the power of Egypt gradually grew less and less. Cleopatra's Needle may be regarded as marking the 'halfway house' of Egyptian civilisation. It was erected at the beginning of the New Kingdom. The chief periods before that, interspersed with phases of decline or degeneration, are known as the Pre-Dynastic, the Thinite Period, the Old Kingdom and the Middle Kingdom. After the end of the New Kingdom, in the Twentieth Dynasty, came another intermediate period and the Late Period with periods of Libyan, Nubian (Ethiopian) and Assyrian supremacy and then 'The Restoration', or Saite period (the Twenty-sixth Dynasty), which ended with the Second Persian Occupation. Subsequently the Greeks possessed the kingdom, which was afterwards seized by the Romans. Arabs and Turks followed, and lastly the British, before Egypt finally became an independent country. Not since the day when Ezekiel declared, in the Saite period: 'There shall be no more a prince of the land of Egypt' (Ezekiel 30:13) has a ruler of the old Egyptian race sat on the throne of the pharaohs.

The mythology of Egypt was formulated before the erection of the Needle. Indeed, in tracing its beginnings we must go back to the pre-Dynastic times, when the beliefs of the various peoples who shared the ancient land were fused and developed under Egyptian influences.

We are confronted by a vast multitude of gods and goddesses. Attempts to enumerate them result, as a rule, in compilations resembling census returns. One of the pharaohs, who lived about 4,000 years ago, undertook the formidable task of accommodating them all under one roof and caused to be erected for that purpose a great building that Greek writers called 'The Labyrinth'. He had separate apartments dedicated to the various deities, and of these it was found necessary to construct no fewer than 3,000. The ancient Egyptians lived in a world that swarmed with spirits, 'numerous as gnats upon the evening beam'. They symbolised everything; they gave concrete form to every abstract idea; they had deities that represented every phase and function of life, every act and incident of importance, and every hour and every month; they had nature gods, animal gods and human gods, and gods of the living and gods of the dead. And, as if they had not a sufficient number of their own, they imported gods and goddesses from other countries.

In the midst of this mythological multitude, which one French Egyptologist called 'the rabble of deities', a few, comparatively speaking, loom vast and great. But some of these are only differentiated forms of a single god or goddess, whose various attributes were symbolised, so that deities budded from deities. Others underwent separate development in different localities and assumed various names. If we these linking deities are gathered together in groups, the task of grappling with Egyptian mythology is greatly simplified.

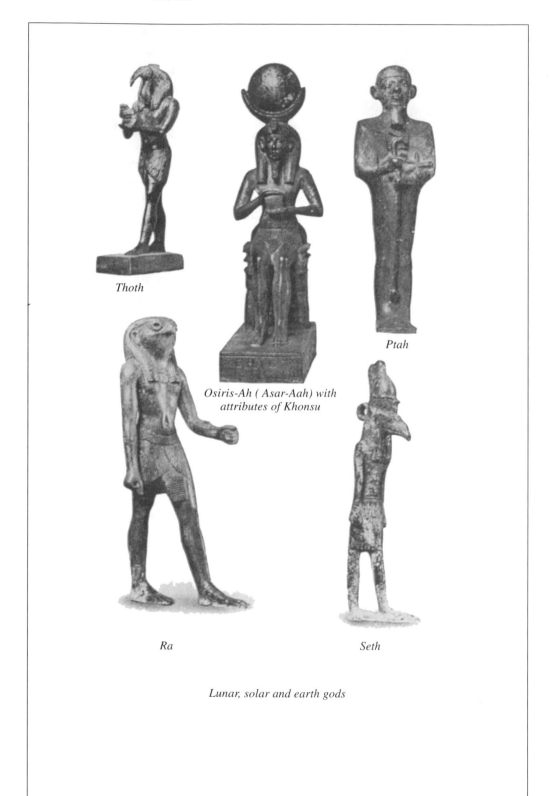

Thoth

Osiris-Ah (Asar-Aah) with
attributes of Khonsu

Ptah

Ra

Seth

Lunar, solar and earth gods

An interesting example of the separating process is afforded by Thoth of Hermopolis. That god of quaint and arresting aspect is most usually depicted with a man's body and the head of an ibis, surmounted by a lunar disc and crescent. As the divine lawyer and recorder, he checked the balance in the Judgment Hall of the Dead when the human heart was weighed before Osiris. As a Fate, he measured out at birth the span of human life on a rod with a serrated edge. He was also a patron of architects, a god of religious literature who was invoked by scribes, and a god of medicine. Originally he was a lunar deity, and was therefore of great antiquity, for, as Edward Payne emphasised in his *History of the New World*,[1] a connection is traced between lunar phenomena and food supply in an earlier stage of civilisation than that in which a connection is traced between food supply and solar phenomena.

The worship of the moon preceded in Egypt, as in many other countries, the worship of the sun. It still survives among primitive peoples elsewhere throughout the world. Even in highly civilised Europe we can still trace lingering evidence of belief in the benevolence of the lunar spirit, the ancient guide and protector of humankind.

The moon was believed to exercise a direct influence on Nature as a generative agency. Agriculturists were of the opinion that seeds sown during its waxing, its period of increase, had more prolific growth than those sown when it was on the wane. Pliny said that 'the blood of men grows and diminishes with the light of the moon, while leaves and herbage also feel the same influence'. Crops were supposed to receive greater benefit in moonlight than in sunshine. In one of the Egyptian temple chants, the corn god is entreated to 'give fertility in the nighttime'. The 'harvest moon' was 'the ripening moon', and many poets have sung its praises throughout the ages. It was followed in Scotland, where archaic Mediterranean beliefs appear to have survived a long time, by 'the badger's moon', which marked the period for laying in winter stores, and then by 'the hunter's moon', an indication that lunar worship prevailed in the archaeological 'hunting period'. Indeed, the moon bulks as largely in European as in ancient Egyptian folklore. It is still believed in certain areas to cure diseases and inspire love. Until comparatively recently, quaint ceremonies were performed in Scotland during its first phase by women who visited sculptured stones to pray for offspring.

Although the strictly lunar character of the Egyptian god Thoth is not apparent at first sight, it can be traced through his association with kindred deities. At Hermopolis and Edfu he was fused with Khonsu (or Khensu), who had developed from Ah, the lunar representative of the male principle, which was also 'the fighting principle'. Khonsu was depicted as a handsome youth, and he symbol-

---

[1] *History of the New World called America* by Edward John Payne (1844–1904), an account of its discovery and the ethnography, language, religion and social and economic condition of its indigenous peoples.

ised, in the Theban group of gods, certain specialised influences of the moon. He was the love god, the Egyptian Cupid, and the divine physician; he was also an explorer (the root *khens* signifies 'to traverse') and the messenger and hunter of the gods. Special offerings were made to him at the ploughing festival, just before the seed was sown, and at the harvest festival, after the grain was reaped, and he was worshipped as the increaser of flocks and herds and human families. Like Thoth, he was a 'measurer' and inspirer of architects, because the moon measures time. But in this direction Thoth had fuller development. He was a 'lawyer' because the orderly changes of the moon suggested the observance of well-defined laws, and a 'checker' and 'scribe' because human transactions were checked and recorded in association with lunar movements. Time was first measured by the lunar month.

Moon gods were also corn gods, but Thoth had no pronounced association with agricultural rites. That phase of his character may have been suppressed as a result of the specialising process. It is also possible that he was differentiated in the pastoral and hunting period when the lunar spirit was especially credited with causing the growth of trees. In the Nineteenth Dynasty, Thoth is shown recording the name of a pharaoh on the sacred sycamore. He must have been, therefore, at one time a tree spirit, like Osiris. Tree spirits, as well as corn spirits, were manifestations of the moon god.

Thoth also links with Osiris, and this association is of special interest. Osiris was originally an ancient king of Egypt who taught the Egyptians how to rear crops and cultivate fruit trees. He was regarded as a human incarnation of the moon spirit. As a living ruler he displayed his lunar qualities by establishing laws for the regulation of human affairs and by promoting agriculture and gardening. When he died, like the moon, he similarly regulated the affairs of departed souls in the agricultural paradise of the Egyptians. He was the great Judge of the Dead, and in the Hall of Judgment Thoth was his recorder.

Like Thoth, Osiris was identified with the tree spirit. His dead body was enclosed in a tree that grew round the coffin, and Isis voyaged alone over the sea to recover it. Isis was also the herald of the Nile inundation; she was, indeed, the flood. The myth, as will be seen, is reminiscent of archaic tree and well worship, which survived at Heliopolis, where the sacred well and tree were venerated in association with the Christian legend. In Ireland, the tree and corn god Daghda similarly has a wife who is a water goddess; she is called Boann and personifies the River Boyne.

Osiris had many manifestations, or, rather, he was the manifestation of many gods. But he never lost his early association with the moon. In one of the Isis temple chants, which details his various attributes and evolutionary phases, he is hailed as the god:

Who comes to us as a babe each month.

He is thus the moon child, a manifestation of the ever-young and ever-renewing moon god. The babe Osiris is cared for by Thoth:

> He lays your soul in the Maadit boat
> By the magic of your name of Ah [moon god].

Thoth utters the magic 'password' to obtain for Osiris his seat in the boat that will carry him over the heavens. This reference explains the line in the complex hymn to Osiris-Sokar:

> Hail, living soul of Osiris, crowning him with the moon.[1]

We have now reached a point where Thoth, Osiris, Khonsu, and Ah are one. They are various forms of the archaic moon spirit that was worshipped by primitive hunters and agriculturists as the begetter and guardian of life.

According to Wallis Budge, whose works on Egyptian mythology are as full of carefully compiled facts as were Joseph's great storehouses of grain, the ancient Egyptians, despite their crowded labyrinth, 'believed in the one great god, self-produced, self-existent, almighty and eternal, who created the "gods", the heavens, and the sun, moon and stars in them, and the earth and everything on it, including man and beast, bird, fish, and reptile. . . . Of this god,' Budge believed, 'they never attempted to make any figure, form, likeness, or similitude, for they thought that no man could depict or describe him, and that all his attributes were quite beyond man's comprehension. On the rare occasions in which he is mentioned in their writings, he is always called "Neter", i.e. God, and besides this he has no name. The exact meaning of the word "Neter" is unknown.'[2]

Budge explained the multiplication of Nilotic deities by saying that the behests of 'God Almighty . . . were performed by a number of gods, or, as we might say, emanations or angels', which were 'of African rather than Asiatic origin'. He preferred to elucidate Egyptian mythology by studying surviving African beliefs 'in the great forests and on the Nile, Congo, Niger, and other great rivers', and showed that in these districts the moon god was still regarded as the creator.

A distinction is drawn by Budge between the Libyan deities and those of Upper Egypt, and his theory of one god had forcible application when confined to the archaic lunar deity, referring to the period before the mingling of peoples and the introduction of Asiatic beliefs. But in dealing with historic Egyptian mythology, we must distinguish between the African moon spirit, which is still identified by some peoples with the creator god, and the representative Egyptian lunar deity, which symbolised the male principle and was not the 'first cause' but the

---

[1] *The Burden of Isis*, Dennis.
[2] Osiris-Sokar is also 'the mysterious one, he who is unknown to mankind', and the 'hidden god' (*The Burden of Isis*, Dennis).

son of a self-produced creating goddess. The difference between the two concepts is of fundamental character.

It is apparent that some of the great Egyptian deities, and especially those of Delta origin, or Delta characterisation, evolved from primitive groups of Nature spirits. At Heliopolis, where archaic Nilotic and other beliefs were preserved like flies in amber, because the Asiatic sun worshippers sought to include all existing forms of tribal religion in their own, a creation myth makes reference to the one god of the primordial deep. But associated with him, it is significant to note, were 'the Fathers and the Mothers'.

The Mothers appear to be represented by the seven Egyptian Fates who presided at birth. These were called 'the seven Hathors', but their association with the Asiatic Hathor, who was Ishtar, was evidently arbitrary. The Mediterranean people, who formed the basis of the Egyptian race, were evidently worshippers of the Mothers. In southern and western Europe, which they peopled in early times, various groups of Mothers were venerated. These included 'Proximae (the kinswomen), Dervonnae (the oak spirits), Niskai (the water spirits), Mairae, Matronae, Matres or Matrae (the mothers), Quadriviae (the goddesses of cross-roads). The Matres, Matrae and Matronae are often qualified by some local name. Deities of this type appear to have been popular in Britain, in the neighbourhood of Cologne, and in Provence. 'In some cases it is uncertain,' commented Professor Anwyl, in *Celtic Religion in Pre-Christian Times*, 'whether some of these grouped goddesses are Celtic or Teutonic.' They were probably pre-Celtic and pre-Germanic. 'It is an interesting parallel,' he added, 'to the existence of these grouped goddesses when we find that in some parts of Wales "Y Mamau" (the mothers) is the name for the fairies. These grouped goddesses take us back to one of the most interesting stages in the early Celtic religion, when the earth spirits or the corn spirits had not yet been completely individualised.'[1]

Representatives of the groups of Egyptian spirits called 'the Fathers' are found at Memphis, where Ptah, assisted by eight earth gnomes called Khnum, was believed to have made the universe with his hammer by beating out the copper sky and shaping the hills and valleys. This group of dwarfs resemble closely the European elves, or male earth spirits, who dwelt inside the mountains as the Khnum dwelt underground.

In the course of time the various groups of male and female spirits were individualised. Some disappeared, leaving the chief spirit alone and supreme. When Ptah became a great god, the other earth gnomes vanished from the Memphis creation myth. Other members of groups remained and were developed separately. This evolutionary process can be traced, we think, in the suggestive asso-

---

[1] Herodotus says: 'The Pelasgians did not distinguish the gods by name or surname. . . . They called them gods, which by its etymology means "disposers [Fates]"'.

ciation of the two sister goddesses Isis and Nephys. In one of the temple chants both are declared to be the mothers of Osiris, who is called:

> The bull, begotten of the two cows, Isis and Nephys . . .
> He, the progeny of the two cows, Isis and Nephys,
> The child surpassingly beautiful![1]

At the same time he is son of 'his mother Nut'. Osiris therefore has three mothers. The concept may be difficult to grasp, but we must remember that we are dealing with vague beliefs regarding ancient mythological beings. Heimdal, the Norse god, had nine mothers, 'the daughters of sea-dwelling Ran'.[2] The Norse god, Tyr's grandmother,[3] was a giantess with nine hundred heads. If we reduce that number to nine, it might be suggested that she represented nine primitive earth spirits, which were multiplied and individualised by the tellers of wonder tales of mythological origin. The Egyptian Great Mother deities had sons, and practically all of these were identified with Osiris. It is not improbable, therefore, that the Mediterranean moon spirit, whom Osiris represented, had originally as many mothers as he had attributes. The 'mothers' afterwards became 'sisters' of the young god. Nephys sings to Osiris:

> All your sister goddesses are at your side
> And behind thy couch.

The Heliopolitan reference to 'the Fathers' and the 'Mothers' indicates that fundamental beliefs of differing origin were fused by the unscientific but diplomatic priestly theorists of the sun cult. It is evident that the people who believed in 'Father spirits' were not identical with the people who believed in 'Mother spirits'.

We may divide into two classes the primitive symbolists who attempted to solve the riddle of the universe:

1 Those who believed that life and natural phenomena had female origin;
2 Those who believed that life and natural phenomena had male origin.

Both 'schools of thought' were represented in Egypt from the earliest times of which we have any definite knowledge, but it may be inferred that the two rival concepts were influenced by primitive tribal customs and habits of life.

---

[1] *The Burden Of Isis* (Wisdom of the East), James Teackle Dennis.
[2] See *Teutonic Myth and Legend.*
[3] There is no trace in Egypt of a 'grandmother' or of a 'great grandmother', like Edda of Iceland. With 'the mother', however, these may represent a triad of nature spirits. A basis of Mediterranean beliefs is traceable in Norse mythology.

It is possible that the theory of the female origin of life evolved in settled communities among large tribal units. These communities could not have come into existence, or continued to grow, without a system of laws. As much may be taken for granted. Now, the earliest laws were evidently those that removed the prime cause of rivalries and outbreaks in tribal communities by affording protection to women. As primitive laws and primitive religions were inseparable, women must have been honoured on religious grounds. In such communities the growth of religious ideas would tend in the direction of exalting goddesses or mother spirits, rather than gods or father spirits. The men of the tribe would be regarded as the sons of an ancestress, and the gods as the sons of a goddess. The Irish tribe known as 'Tuatha de Danann', for instance, were 'the children of Danu', the mother of the Danann gods.

The theory of the male origin of life, on the other hand, may have grown up among smaller tribal units of wandering or mountain peoples, whose existence depended more on the prowess and activities of the males than on the influence exercised by their females, whom they usually captured or lured away. Such nomads, with their family groups over which the fathers exercised supreme authority, would naturally exalt the male and worship tribal ancestors and regard gods as greater than goddesses.

In Egypt the 'mother-worshipping' peoples and the 'father-worshipping' peoples were mingled, as we have indicated, long before the dawn of history. Nomadic peoples from desert lands and mountainous districts entered the Delta region of the Mediterranean race many centuries before the Dynastic Egyptians made an appearance in Upper Egypt. The researches of Flinders Petrie proved conclusively that three or four distinct racial types were fused in pre-Dynastic times in Lower Egypt.

The evidence obtained from the comparative study of European mythologies tends to suggest that the 'mother' spirits and the Great Mother deities were worshipped by the Mediterranean peoples, who multiplied rapidly in their North African area of characterisation, and spread into Asia Minor and Europe and up the Nile valley as far as Nubia, where Thoth, the lunar god, was the son of Tefnut, one of the Great Mothers. But that matriarchal concept did not extend, as we have seen, into Central Africa. The evidence accumulated by explorers in the nineteenth century showed that the nomadic natives believed, as they had believed from time immemorial, in a Creator (god) rather than a Creatrix (goddess). Mungo Park found that the 'one god' was worshipped only 'at the appearance of the new moon'.[1] In Arabia, the 'mothers' were also prominent, and certain ethnologists have detected the Mediterranean type in that country. But, of course, all peoples who worshipped 'mother spirits' were not of Mediterranean origin. In this respect, however, the Mediterraneans, like other races that multi-

[1] The Akkadians also believed that the moon had prior existence to the sun.

plied into large settled communities, early on attained a comparatively high degree of civilisation on account of their reverence for motherhood and all that it entailed.

The Great Mother deity was believed to be self-created and self-sustaining. In the Isis chants addressed to Osiris we read:

> Your mother Nut comes to you in peace;
> She has built up life from her own body.
>
> There comes unto you, Isis, lady of the horizon,
> Who has begotten herself alone.[1]

According to the Greeks, the Great Mother Neith declared to her worshippers:

> I am what has been,
> What is,
> And what shall be.

A hymn to Neith contains the following lines:

> Hail! Great Mother, your birth has been uncovered;
> Hail! Great Goddess, within the underworld doubly hidden;
> Unknown one –
> Hail! divine one,
> Your garment has not has been unloosed.

The typical Great Mother was a virgin goddess who represented the female principle, and she had a fatherless son who represented the male principle. Like the Celtic Danu, she was the mother of the gods from whom humankind was descended. But the characteristics of the several mother deities varied in different areas, as a result of the separating and specialising process that we have illustrated in dealing with some of the lunar gods. One Great Mother was an earth spirit, another was a water spirit, and a third was an atmosphere or sky spirit.

The popular Isis ultimately combined the attributes of all the Great Mothers, who were regarded as different manifestations of her, but it is evident that each underwent, for prolonged periods, separate development and that their particular attributes were emphasised by local and tribal beliefs. An agricultural people, for instance, could not fail, in Egypt, to associate their Great Mother with the Nile flood. A pastoral people, like the Libyans, on the other hand, might be expected to depict her as an earth spirit who caused the growth of grass.

[1] *The Burden of Isis*, Dennis.

As a goddess of maternity, the Great Mother was given different forms. Isis was a woman, the Egyptianised Hathor was a cow, Apet of Thebes (Taweret) was a hippopotamus, Bastet was a cat, Tefnut was a lioness, Wadjet was a serpent, Hekt was a frog, and so on. All the sacred animals and reptiles were in time associated with Isis.

In Asia Minor the Great Mother was associated with the lioness. In Cyprus she was 'my lady of trees and doves'. In Crete she was the serpent goddess. In Rome, Bona Dea was an earth goddess, and the Norse Freyja was, like the Egyptian Bastet, a feline goddess – her chariot was drawn by cats.

One of the least known, but not the least important, of the Great Mothers of Europe is found in the Highlands of Scotland, where, according to ethnologists, the Mediterranean element bulks considerably among the racial types. She is called Cailleach Bheur and is evidently a representative survival of great antiquity. In Ireland she degenerated, as did other old gigantic deities, into a historical personage. An interesting Highland tale states that she existed 'from the long eternity of the world'. She is described as 'a great big old wife'. Her face was 'blue black',[1] and she had a single watery eye on her forehead, but 'the sight of it' was 'as swift as the mackerel of the ocean'.

Like the Egyptian Ptah, this Scottish hag engaged herself in making the world. She carried on her back a great creel filled with rocks and earth. In various parts of northern Scotland small hills were said to have been formed by the spillings of her creel. She let loose the rivers and formed lochs. At night she rested on a mountain top beside a spring of fresh water. Like the Libyan Neith, she was evidently the deity of a pastoral and hunting people, for she had herds of deer, goats and sheep, over which she kept watch.

In springtime, the Cailleach was associated with storms. When she sneezed, she was heard for miles. But her stormy wrath during the period in spring called *cailleach* in Gaelic was especially roused because her son fled away on a white horse with a beautiful bride. The Cailleach pursued him on a steed that leapt ravines as nimbly as the giant Arthur's[2] horse leapt over the Bristol Channel. But the son would not give up the bride, who was, it seems, in great dread of the terrible old woman. The Cailleach, however, managed to keep the couple apart by raising storm after storm. Her desire was to prevent the coming of summer. She carried in her hand a magic wand, or, as some stories have it, a hammer, which she waved over the earth to prevent the grass growing, but she could not baffle

---

[1] The Egyptians would have said 'true lapis lazuli'. The face of the Libyan goddess Neith was green. Isis was the 'green one whose greenness is like the greenness of the earth' (Brugsch).

[2] Arthur of 'the round table' was originally a giant, and, like other giants, became associated with the fairies. 'Arthur's Seat', Edinburgh, is reminiscent of his giant form. If there was once a king named Arthur, who was a popular hero, his name may have been given to a giant god originally nameless. The Eildon Hills giant was called Wallace.

Nature. She made a final attempt, however, to keep apart her son and the young bride, who was evidently the spirit of summer, by raising her last great storm, which brought snow and floods and was intended to destroy all life. Then her son fought against her and put her to flight. So 'the old winter went past', as a Gaelic tale has it.

One of the many versions of the Scottish Cailleach story makes her the chief of eight 'big old women' or witches. This group of nine suggests Ptah and his eight earth gnomes, the nine mothers of Heimdal, the Norse god, and the Ennead of Heliopolis.

An Egyptian Great Mother who was as much dreaded as the Scottish Cailleach, was Sekhmet, the lioness-headed deity, who was the wife of Ptah. In a Twelfth-Dynasty story she is referred to as the terrible goddess of plagues. All the feline goddesses 'represented,' says Wiedemann, 'the variable power of the sun, from genial warmth to scorching heat. Thus a Philae text states in reference to Isis-Hathor, who there personified all goddesses in one: "Kindly is she as Bastet, terrible is she as Sekhmet". As the conqueror of the enemies of the Egyptian gods, Sekhmet carried a knife in her hand, for she it was who, under the name of the "Eye of Ra", entered upon the task of destroying mankind. Other texts represent her as ancestress of part of the human race.'[1]

The oldest deities were evidently those of most savage character.[2] Sekhmet must, therefore, have been a primitive concept of the Great Mother who rejoiced in slaughter and had to be propitiated. The kindly Bastet and the lovable Isis, on the other hand, seem to be representative of a people who, having grown more humane, invested their deities with their own qualities. But the worship of mother goddesses was attended by rites that to us are revolting. Herodotus indicates the obscene character of those that prevailed in the Delta region. Female worshippers were unmoral (rather than immoral). In Asia Minor the festivals of the Great Mother and her son, who symbolised the generative agency in nature, were the scenes of terrible practices. Men mutilated their bodies and women became the 'sacred wives' of the god. There are also indications that children were sacrificed. In Israel large numbers of infants' skeletons have been found among prehistoric remains, and although doubt has been thrown on the belief that babies were sacrificed, we cannot overlook in this connection the evidence of Isaiah, who was an eyewitness of many terrible rites of Semitic and pre-Semitic origin. 'Against whom,' cried the Hebrew prophet, 'do ye sport yourselves? Against whom make ye a wide mouth and draw out the tongue? Are ye not chil-

---

[1] *Religion of the Ancient Egyptians*, A. Wiedemann. In old Arabia the sun deity was female, and there are traces of a sun goddess among the earlier Hittites (H. Winckler, *Mitteilungen der Deutschen Orient-Gesellschaft*).

[2] Ra, in one of the Isis temple chants, 'has produced calamity after the desire of your [Osiris's] heart', and Osiris-Sokar is 'the lord of fear who causes himself to come into being'. Sokar, who fused with Ra and Osiris, is one of the oldest Egyptian deities.

dren of transgression, a seed of falsehood, enflaming yourselves with idols under every green tree, slaying the children in the valleys under the clifts of the rocks' (Isaiah 57:4 and 5).

In Ireland similar rites obtained 'before the coming of Patrick of Macha', when the corn god, the son of the Great Mother, was dreaded and propitiated. He was called Cromm Cruaich and was probably Dagda, son of Danu.

> To him without glory
> They would kill their piteous, wretched offspring
> With much wailing and peril,
> To pour their blood around Cromm Cruaich.
>
> Milk and corn
> They would ask from him speedily
> In return for one-third of their healthy issue:
> Great was the horror and the scare of him.[1]

Neith, the Libyan Great Mother, was an earth goddess. Nut, on the other hand, was a sky goddess, and associated with her was an earth god called Geb. Sometimes she is depicted with Geb alone, and sometimes a third deity, the atmosphere god, Shu, is added. Shu separates the heavens from the earth and is shown as 'the uplifter', supporting Nut, as Atlas supports the world. Nut is also pictured with another goddess drawn inside her entire form. Within the second goddess a god is similarly depicted. This triad suggests Osiris and his two mothers. A mummy drawing of Nut, with symbols figured on her body, indicates that she was the Great Mother of the sun disc and lunar disc and crescent. In one of the myths of the sun cult, Ra, the solar god, is said to be 'born of Nut' each morning.

The most representative Egyptian Great Father was Ptah in his giant form and, in his union with Tanen, the earth god. He was self-created. 'No father begot you,' sang a priestly poet, 'and no mother gave you birth.' He built up his own body and shaped his limbs. Then he found 'his seat', like a typical mountain giant. His head supported the sky and his feet rested on the earth. Osiris, who also developed into a Great Father deity, was fused with Ptah at Memphis, and, according to the pyramid texts engraved on the pasage walls of pyramids at Saqqara, his name signifies 'the seat maker'. The sun and the moon were the eyes of the Great Father, the air issued from his nostrils and the Nile from his mouth. Other deities who link with Ptah include Khnum, Hershef and the great god of Mendes. These are dealt with in detail in Chapter 14.

It is possible that Ptah was imported into Egypt by an invading tribe in pre-Dynastic times. He was an artisan god, and his seat of worship was at Memphis,

---

[1] *Celtic Myth and Legend.*

the home of the architects and the builders of the pyramids and limestone mastabas. According to tradition, Egypt's first temple was erected to Ptah by King Meni.

The skilled working of limestone, with which Memphis was closely associated, made such a spontaneous appearance in Egypt as to suggest that the art was developed elsewhere. It is interesting to find, therefore, that in Israel a tall, pre-Semitic blonde race had constructed wonderful artificial caves. These were 'hewn out of the soft limestone,' wrote R. A. S. Macalister, 'with great care and exactness. . . . They vary greatly in size and complexity; one cave was found by the writer that contained no less than sixty chambers. This was quite exceptional; but caves with five, ten, or even twenty chambers large and small are not uncommon. The passages sometimes are so narrow as to make their exploration difficult; and the chambers are sometimes so large that it requires a bright light such as that of magnesium wire to illuminate them sufficiently for examination. One chamber, now fallen in, was found to have been 400 feet [122 metres] long and 80 feet [24 metres] high. To have excavated these gigantic catacombs required the steady work of a long-settled population.' They are 'immense engineering works'. The hewers of the artificial caves 'possessed the use of metal tools, as the pick marks testify'.

These caves, with their chambers and narrow passages, suggest the interiors of the pyramids. A people who had attained such great skill in limestone working were equal to the task of erecting mountains of masonry in the Nile valley if, as seems possible, they settled there in very early times. As they were of mountain characterisation, these ancient artisans may have been Ptah worshippers.

The pyramids evolved from mastabas.[1] Now in Israel there are, to the north of Jerusalem, 'remarkable prehistoric monuments'. These, Macalister wrote, 'consist of long, broad walls in one of which a chamber and shaft have been made, happily compared by Père Vincent to an Egyptian mastaba'.[2]

Legends regarding this tall people make reference to giants, and it is possible that, with other mountain folk, their hilltop deities, with whom they would be identified, were reputed to be of gigantic stature and bulk. They are also referred to in the Bible. When certain of the spies returned to Moses from southern Canaan 'they brought up an evil report of the land which they had searched'. They said: 'It is a land that eateth up the inhabitants thereof; and all the people that we saw in it are men of a great stature. And there we saw the giants, the sons of Anak, which come of the giants' (Numbers 13:32–33). In other words, they were 'sons of their gods'.

It is evident that this tall, cave-hewing people had attained a high degree of

[1] Oblong platform tombs that were constructed of limestone. The body was concealed in a secret chamber. See Chapter 8.
[2] *A History of Civilisation in Palestine*, R. A. S. Macalister.

civilisation, with a well-organised system of government, before they undertook engineering works on such a vast scale. Although they had established themselves in such close proximity to the Delta region, no reference is made to them in any surviving Egyptian records, so they must have flourished at a remote period. They preceded the Semites in southern Israel, and the Semites appeared in Egypt in Pre-Dynastic times. Macalister considers that they may be 'roughly assigned to 3000 BC'. A long period must be allowed for the growth of their art of skilled stone working.

When the mysterious cave-dwellers were at the height of their power, they must have multiplied rapidly, and it is not improbable that some of their surplus stock poured into the Delta region. Their mode of life must have particularly fitted them for residence in towns, and it may be that the distinctive character of the mythology of Memphis was because of their presence in no inconsiderable numbers in that cosmopolitan city.

There is no indication that the Dynastic Egyptians, who first made their appearance in the upper part of the Nile valley, utilised the quarries before their conquest of Lower Egypt. They were a brickmaking people, and their early tombs at Abydos were constructed of brick and wood. But after King Meni had united the two kingdoms by force, stoneworking was introduced into Upper Egypt. A granite floor was laid in the tomb of King Usephais of the First Dynasty. This sudden transition from brickmaking to granite-working is very remarkable. It is interesting to note, however, that the father of Usephais is recorded as having built a stone temple at Hierakonpolis. Probably it was constructed of limestone. As much is suggested by the finish displayed in the limestone chamber of the brick tomb of King Khasekhem of the Second Dynasty. Brick, however, continued in use until King Djoser of the Third Dynasty, which began about 2700 BC, had constructed of stone, for his tomb, the earliest Egyptian pyramid near Memphis.

It is highly probable that it was the experienced limestone workers of the north, and not the brickmakers of Upper Egypt, who first utilised granite. The pharaohs of the First Dynasty may have drafted southwards large numbers of the skilled workers who were settled at Memphis or in its vicinity. The presence of a northern colony in Upper Egypt can be traced by the mythological beliefs that obtained in the vicinity of the granite quarries at Aswan. The chief god of the First Cataract was Khnum, who bears a close resemblance to Ptah, the artisan god of Memphis. (See Chapter 14.)

Two distinct kinds of supreme deities have now been dealt with – the Great Father and the Great Mother with her son. It is apparent that they were conceived of and developed by peoples of diverse origin and different habits of life who mingled in Egypt under the influence of a centralised government. The ultimate result was a fusion of religious beliefs and the formulation of a highly complex mythology that was never thoroughly systematised at any period. The Great Father then became the husband of the Great Mother, or the son god was exalted as 'husband of his mother'. Thus Ptah was given for wife Sekhmet, the fierce lioness-headed mother, who resembles Tefnut and other feline goddesses. Osiris, the son of Isis and Nepthys, on the other hand, became 'husband of his mother', or mothers. He was recognised as the father of Horus, son of Isis, and of Anubis, son of Nepthys. Another myth makes him displace the old earth god Geb, son of Nut. Osiris was also a son of Nut, an earlier form of Isis. So was Geb, who became 'husband of his mother'. That Geb and Osiris were fused is evident in one of the temple chants, in which Isis, addressing Osiris, says: 'Your soul possesses the earth'.

In Asia Minor, where the broad-headed patriarchal alpine hill people blended with the long-headed matriarchal Mediterranean people, the Pappas[1] god (Attis, Adon) became likewise the husband of the Ma goddess (Nana). A mythological scene sculpted on a cliff at Ibreez in Cappadocia is supposed to represent the marriage of the two Great Father and Mother deities, and it is significant to find that the son accompanies the self-created bride. As in Egypt, the father and the son were fused and at times are indistinguishable in the legends.

The worship of the solar disc was unknown to the early Mediterranean people who spread through Europe and reached the British Isles and Ireland. Nor did it rise into prominence in the land of the pharaohs until after the erection of the Great Pyramids near Cairo. The kings did not become 'sons of the sun' until the Fifth Dynasty.

There is general agreement among Egyptologists that sun worship was imported from Asia and probably from Babylonia. It achieved its fullest development on Egyptian lines at Heliopolis, 'the city of the sun'. There, Ra, the sun god, was first exalted as the Great Father who created the universe and all the gods and goddesses, from whom men and animals and fish and reptiles were descended. But the religion of the sun cult never achieved the popularity of the older faiths. It was embraced chiefly by the pharaohs, the upper classes and the foreign sections of the trading communities. The great mass of the people continued to worship the gods of the moon, earth, atmosphere and water until the first Egyptian civilisation perished of old age. Osiris was always the god of the agriculturists, and associated with him, of course, were Isis and Nepthys. Seth, the red-haired god of prehistoric invaders, who slew Osiris, became the Egyptian Satan, and he was depicted as a black serpent, a black pig, a red mythical monster or simply as a red-haired man. He was also given half-animal and half-human form.

As has been indicated, the policy adopted by the priests of the sun was to ab-

---

[1] The Phrygian name of the father deity, also called Bagaios (Slav *bogu*, 'god'). The roots *pa*, *ap*, *da*, *ad*, *ta* and *at* signify 'father', while *ma*, *am*, *na* and *an* signify 'mother'.

sorb every existing religious cult in Egypt. They permitted the worship of any god, or group of gods, so long as Ra was regarded as the Great Father. No belief was too contradictory in tendency, and no myth was of too trivial a character, not to be embraced in their complex theological system. As a result, embedded like fossils in the religious literature of Heliopolis are many old myths that would have perished but for the acquisitiveness of the diplomatic priests of the sun.

The oldest sun god was Atum, and he absorbed a primitive myth about Khepera, the beetle god (scarab). After Ra was introduced into Egypt, the sun god was called Ra-Atum. A triad was also formed by making Ra the noonday sun, Atum the evening sun and Khepera the sun at dawn.

Khepera is depicted in beetle form, holding the sun disc between his two fore-legs. To the primitive Egyptians, the dung beetle was a sacred insect. Its association with the resurrected sun is explained by Wiedemann as follows: 'The female (*Ateuchus sacer*) lays her eggs in a cake of dung, rolls this in the dust and makes it smooth and round so that it will keep moist and serve as food for her young; and finally she deposits it in a hole which she has scooped out in the ground; and covers it with earth. This habit had not escaped the observation of the Egyptians, although they failed to understand it, for scientific knowledge of natural history was very slight among all peoples of antiquity. The Egyptians supposed the [scarab] to be male, and that it was itself born anew from the egg which it alone had made, and thus lived an eternal life. . . .'

The scarab became a symbol of the resurrection and the rising sun. The dawn god raised up the solar disc as the beetle raised up the ball containing its eggs before it set it rolling. Similarly, souls were raised from death to eternal life.

Another myth represented the newborn sun as the child Horus rising from a lotus bloom that expanded its leaves on the breast of the primordial deep. Less poetic, but more popular, apparently, was the comedy about the chaos goose, which was called 'great cackler' because at the beginning she cackled loudly to the chaos gander and laid an egg, which was the sun. Ra was identified with the historical egg,[1] but at Heliopolis the priests claimed that it was shaped by Ptah on his potter's wheel. Khnum, the other craftsman god, was similarly credited with the work. The gander was identified with Geb, the earth god, and in the end Amun-Ra, the combined deity of Thebes, was represented as the great chaos goose and gander in one. The 'beautiful goose' was also sacred to Isis.

Of foreign origin, probably, was the myth that the sun was a wild ass that was forever chased by the night serpent, Haiu, as it ran round the slopes of the mountains supporting the sky. These are probably the world-encircling mountains that, according to the modern Egyptians, are peopled by giants (genii). Belief in mountain giants survived for long among the hill people of Arabia, Syria, Asia Minor and Europe. The most popular old Egyptian idea was that the earth was

[1] The 'soul and egg' myth is dealt with in Chapter 5.

surrounded by the ocean, and the same opinion was held in Greece. The wild ass, as we have seen, was also Seth, the Nilotic Satan.

A similar myth represents the sun as a great cat, which was originally a female but was identified with Ra as a male. It fought with the serpent Apep below the sacred tree at Heliopolis and killed it at dawn. In this myth Seth is identified with the serpent.

The cat and the wild ass enjoyed considerable popularity at Heliopolis. In the *Book of the Dead* it is declared: 'I have heard the word of power [the magic word] which the ass spoke to the cat in the house of Hapt-ra,' but the 'password' that was used by the souls of the dead is not given.

Another belief regarding the sun had its origin apparently among the moon worshippers. It can be traced in one of the Nut pictures. Shu, the atmosphere god, stands beneath the curving body of the Great Mother and receives in one of his hands a white pool of milk, which is the sun. In the mummy picture, already referred to, the sun disc is drawn between the breasts of the sky goddess.

Nut is sometimes called the 'mother of Ra', but in a creation myth she is his wife, and her secret lover is Geb, the earth god.

It was emphasised at Heliopolis that Ra, as the Great Father, called Nut, Geb and Shu into being. Those deities that he did not create were either his children or their descendants.

The creation story in which the priests of Heliopolis fused the old myths will be found in Chapter 1. It familiarises the reader with Egyptian beliefs in their earliest and latest aspects.

The second chapter is devoted to the Osiris and Isis legends, which show that these deities have both a tribal and seasonal significance. In the chapters that follow, special attention is devoted to the periods in which the religious myths were formulated and the greater gods came into prominence[1], while light is thrown on the beliefs and customs of the ancient people of Egypt by popular renderings of representative folk tales and metrical versions of selected songs and poems.

---

[1] Aten worship is dealt with fully in its relation to primitive Egyptian myths in Chapter 26.

Chapter 1
Creation Legend of Sun Worshippers

The Primordial Deep – Ra's 'Soul Egg' arises – The Elder Gods – Isis and the Serpent – Plot to rival Ra – How his Magic Name was obtained – Ra seeks to destroy Mankind – An Avenging Goddess – The Deluge Worshippers are spared – Origin of Sacrifice – Ra ascends to Heaven – Earth God's Reptile Brood – Thoth the Deputy – The Sun God's Night Journey – Perils of the Underworld – Rebirth of Sun at Dawn.

The myths from which this chapter has been constructed date from the New Kingdom period, especially the Nineteenth and Twentieth Dynasties. Ra is the first human god (the pharaoh), then a world god like Ptah in his giant form and lastly a cosmic deity. The priests were evidently engaged in systematising the theology of the sun cult. Ra, the sun, is shown to be greater than his father, Nu, and a concession is made to the worshippers of Isis in the legend, which credits Ra with imparting to her the power she possessed. Horus is given recognition. He acquires the 'eyes' of Ra (the sun and moon). Thoth also, as Ah, has control of the moon. The result of the compromising process was to leave everything vague and even confused, but the greatness of Ra was made manifest.

At the beginning the world was a waste of water called Nu, and it was the home of the Great Father. He was Nu, for he was the deep, and he gave life to the sun god who said: 'Lo! I am Khepera at dawn, Ra at high noon and Atum at eventide.' The god of brightness first appeared as a shining egg that floated on the water's breast, and the spirits of the deep, who were the Fathers and the Mothers, were with him there, as he was with Nu, for they were the companions of Nu.

Now Ra was greater than Nu, from whom he arose. He was the divine father and strong ruler of gods, and those whom he first created, according to his wish, were Shu, the wind god, and his consort, Tefnut, who had the head of a lioness and was called The Spitter because she sent the rain. In afterlife these two deities shone as stars amidst the constellations of heaven and were called The Twins.

Then Geb, the earth god, came into being and Nut, the goddess of the firmament, who became the parents of Osiris and his consort, Isis, and also of Seth and his consort, Nephys.

Ra spoke at the beginning of Creation, and ordered the earth and the heavens to rise out of the waste of water. In the brightness of his majesty they appeared, and Shu, the uplifter, raised Nut on high. She formed the vault, which is arched over Geb, the god of earth, who lies prostrate beneath her from where, at the eastern horizon, she is poised on her toes to where, at the western horizon, bending down with outstretched arms, she rests on her fingertips. In the darkness are seen the stars that sparkle on her body and over her great unwearied limbs.

When Ra, according to his wish, uttered the deep thoughts of his mind, that which he named had being. When he gazed into space, that which he desired to see appeared before him. He created all the things that move in the waters and on the dry land. Now, mankind were born from his eye, and Ra, the Creator, who was ruler of the gods, became the first king on earth. He went about among people. He took a form like theirs, and to him the centuries were as years.

Ra had many names that were not known to gods or men, and he had one secret name that gave him his divine power. The goddess Isis, who dwelt in the world as a woman, grew weary of the ways of mankind. She sought rather to be among the mighty gods. She was an enchantress, and she wished greatly to have power equal with Ra in the heavens and on the earth. In her heart, therefore, she yearned to know the secret name[1] of the ruling god, which was hidden in his heart and was never spoken aloud.

Each day Ra walked out, and the gods in his train followed him, and he sat on his throne and uttered decrees. He had grown old, and as he spoke, moisture dripped from his mouth and fell on the ground. Isis followed him, and when she found his saliva she baked it with the earth on which it lay. She shaped the substance into the form of a spear, and it became a poisonous serpent. She lifted it up; she threw it from her, and it lay on the path along which Ra would travel when he went up and down his kingdom, surveying what he had made. Now the serpent that Isis had created was invisible to both gods and men.

Soon there came a day when Ra, the aged god, walked along the path, followed by his companions. He came near to the serpent, which was waiting for him, and the serpent stung him. The burning venom entered his body, and Ra was stricken with great pain. A loud and mighty cry broke from his lips, and it was heard in highest heaven.

Then the gods who were with him spoke, saying, 'What has happened to you?' and 'What thing is this?'

Ra did not answer. He shook, and all his body trembled and his teeth chattered, for the venom overflowed in his flesh as the Nile does when it floods the land of Egypt. But at length he controlled himself and subdued his heart and the fears of his heart. He spoke, and his words were:

'Gather about me, you who are my children, so that I may make known the

[1] The secret name was Ran; it was one of the god's spirits. See Chapter 7.

dreadful thing that has happened to me. I am struck with great pain by something I know not of . . . by something that I cannot see. Of that I have knowledge in my heart, for I have not done myself an injury with my own hand. Lo! I am without power to make known who has struck me so. Never before has such sorrow and pain been mine.'

He spoke further, saying: 'I am a god and the son of a god. I am the Mighty One, son of the Mighty One. Nu, my father, conceived my secret name, which gives me power, and he concealed it in my heart so that no magician might ever know it and, knowing it, be given power to work evil against me.

'As I went about even now, observing the world that I have created, a malignant thing bit me. It is not fire, yet it burns in my flesh; it is not water, yet cold is my body and my limbs tremble. Hear me now! My command is that all my children be brought near to me so that they may pronounce words of power that shall be felt on earth and in the heavens.'

All the children of Ra were brought to him, as was his wish. Isis, the enchantress, came in their midst, and they all sorrowed greatly, except her. She spoke mighty words, for she could utter charms to subdue pain and to give life to that from which life had departed. She spoke to Ra, saying:

'What ails you, holy father? You have been bitten by a serpent, one of the creatures that you created. I shall weave spells. I shall defeat your enemy with magic. Lo! I shall overwhelm the serpent utterly in the brightness of your glory.'

He answered her, saying: 'A malignant thing bit me. It is not fire, yet it burns my flesh. It is not water, yet cold is my body, and my limbs tremble. My eyes also have grown dim. Drops of sweat fall from my face.'

Isis spoke to the divine father and said: 'You must, even now, reveal your secret name to me, for, truly, you can be delivered from your pain and distress by the power of your name.'

Ra heard her in sorrow. Then he said:

'I have created the heavens and the earth. Lo! I have even framed the earth, and the mountains are the work of my hands. I made the sea, and I cause the Nile to flood the land of Egypt. I am the Great Father of the gods and the goddesses. I gave life to them. I created every living thing that moves on the dry land and in the sea depths. When I open my eyes there is light. When I close them there is thick darkness. My secret name is not known to the gods. I am Khepera at dawn, Ra at high noon and Atum at eventide.'

So spoke the divine father, but mighty and magic as were his words, they brought him no relief. The poison still burned in his flesh and his body trembled. He seemed ready to die.

Isis, the enchantress, heard him, but there was no sorrow in her heart. She wished above all other things to share the power of Ra, and to achieve this she must have revealed to her the sacred name that Nu had devised and uttered at the beginning. So she spoke to Ra, saying: 'Divine father, you have not yet spoken your name of power. If you shall reveal it to me I will have strength to give you healing.'

Hotter than fire burned the venom in the heart of Ra. Like raging flames it consumed his flesh, and he suffered fierce agony. Isis waited, and at length the Great Father spoke in majesty and said: 'It is my will that Isis be given my secret name and that it leave my heart and enter hers.'

When he had spoken thus, Ra vanished from before the eyes of the gods. The sun boat was empty, and there was thick darkness. Isis waited, and when the secret name of the divine father was about to leave his heart and pass into her own, she spoke to Horus her son and said:

'Now, compel the ruling god, by a mighty spell, also to yield up his eyes, which are the sun and the moon.'[1]

Isis then received in her heart the secret name of Ra, and the mighty enchantress said:

'Depart, O venom, from Ra. Come out from his heart and from his flesh; flow out, shining from his mouth. . . . I have worked the spell. . . . Lo! I have overcome the serpent and caused the venom to be spilled on the ground, because the secret name of the divine father has been given to me. . . . Now let Ra live, for the venom has perished.'

So the god was made whole. The venom departed from his body, and there was no longer pain in his heart or any sorrow.

As Ra grew old ruling over men, there were those among his subjects who spoke disdainfully about him, saying: 'Old, indeed, is King Ra, for now his bones are silver and his flesh is turned to gold, although his hair is still true lapis lazuli [dark].'

To Ra came knowledge of the words that were spoken about him, and there was much anger in his heart, because there were rebellious sayings on the lips of men and because they sought also to kill him. He spoke to his divine followers and said:

'Bring before me the god Shu and the goddess Tefnut, the god Geb and his consort, Nut, and the fathers and mothers who were with me at the beginning when I was in Nu. Bring Nu before me also. Let them all come in secret, so that men may not see them and, afraid, take sudden flight. Let all the gods assemble in my great temple at Heliopolis.'

The gods assembled as Ra wished, and they bowed before him. Then they said: 'Speak what you wish to say and we will hear.'

He addressed the gods, saying:

'O Nu, you, the eldest god, from whom I had my being, and you, ancestral gods, hear and know now that rebellious words are spoken against me by man-

---

[1] Hence the reference to 'Horus the Ra'.

kind, whom I created. Lo! They seek even to kill me. It is my desire that you should instruct me what you would do in this matter. Consider well among yourselves and guide me with wisdom. I have hesitated to punish mankind until I have heard from your lips what should now be done regarding them.

'For lo! I wish in my heart to destroy utterly that which I did create. All the world will become a waste of water through a great flood, as it was at the beginning, and I alone shall be left remaining, with no one else beside me except Osiris and his son Horus. I shall become a small serpent, invisible to the gods. To Osiris will be given power to reign over the dead, and Horus will be exalted on the throne that is set on the island of fiery flames.'

Then spoke Nu, god of primeval waters, and he said: 'Hear me now, O my son, you who are mightier far than I, although I gave you life. Steadfast is your throne; great is the fear of you among men. Let your eye go forth against those who are rebels in the kingdom.'

Ra said: 'Now do men seek to escape among the hills. They tremble because of the words they have uttered.'

The gods spoke together, saying: 'Let your eye go forth against those who are rebels in the kingdom and it shall destroy them utterly. When it comes down from heaven as Hathor, no human eye can be raised against it.'

Ra heard and, as was his will, his eye went forth as Hathor against mankind among the mountains, and they were speedily slain. The goddess rejoiced in her work and drove over the land, so that for many nights she waded in blood.

Then Ra repented. His fierce anger passed, and he sought to save the remnant of mankind. He sent messengers, who ran swifter than the storm wind, to Elephantine, so that they might speedily obtain many plants of virtue. These they brought back, and they were well ground and steeped with barley in vessels filled with the blood of mankind. So was beer made and seven thousand jars were filled with it.

Day dawned and Hathor[1] went upstream slaughtering mankind. Ra surveyed the jars and said: 'Now shall I give men protection. It is my will that Hathor may slay them no longer.'

Then the god commanded that the jars should be carried to the place where the vengeful goddess rested for the night after that day of slaughter. The jars were emptied out as was his wish, and the land was covered with the flood.

When Hathor awoke her heart was made glad. She stooped down and she saw her beautiful face mirrored in the flood. Then she began to drink eagerly, and she was made drunk so that she went to and fro over the land nor took any heed of mankind.

Ra spoke to her, saying: 'Beautiful goddess, return to me in peace.'

[1] The feline goddess Sekhmet is also given as the slaughterer. In one of the temple chants we read: 'Hathor overcomes the enemy of her sire by this her name of Sekhmet'.

Hathor returned, and the divine father said: 'Henceforth shall beautiful hand-maidens, your priestesses, prepare for you in jars, according to their number, draughts of sweetness, and these shall be given as offerings to you at the first festival of every New Year.[1]

So it came that from that day, when the Nile rose in red flood, covering the land of Egypt, offerings of beer were made to Hathor. Men and women took the draughts of sweetness at the festival and were made drunk like the goddess.

Now when Hathor had returned to Ra, he spoke to her with weariness, saying:

'A fiery pain torments me, nor can I tell from where it comes. I am still alive, but I am weary of heart and desire no longer to live among men. Lo! I have not destroyed them as I have power to do.'

The gods who followed Ra said: 'Be no longer weary. Power is yours according to your wish.'

Ra answered them, saying: 'Weary indeed are my limbs and they fail me. I shall go out no longer alone, nor shall I wait until I am struck again with pain. Help shall be given to me according to my desire.'

Then the ruler of the gods called to Nu, from whom he had being, and Nu bade Shu, the atmosphere god, and Nut, goddess of the heavens, to give aid to Ra in his distress.

Nut took the form of the Celestial Cow, and Shu lifted Ra on her back. Then darkness came on. Men came out from their hiding places in great fear, and when they saw Ra departing from them, they were sorrowful because of the rebellious words that had been spoken against him. Indeed they cried to Ra, beseeching him to kill those of his enemies who still remained. But Ra was borne through the darkness, and men followed him until he appeared again and shed light on the earth. Then his faithful subjects armed themselves with weapons, and they sallied forth against the enemies of the sun god and slaughtered them in battle.

Ra saw what his followers among men had done, and he was well pleased. He spoke to them saying: 'Now is your sin forgiven. Slaughter atones for slaughter. Such is sacrifice and the purpose thereof.'

When Ra had thus accepted in atonement for the sin of men the sacrifice of his enemies who wished to slay him, he spoke to the heavenly goddess Nut, saying:

'Henceforth my dwelling place must be in the heavens. No longer will I reign on the earth.'

So it happened, according to his divine will. The great god went on his way through the realms that are above, and these he divided and set in order. He spoke creative words and called into existence the field of Aalu, and there he caused to assemble a multitude of the beings that are seen in heaven, even the stars, and these were born of Nut. In millions they came to praise and glorify Ra.

[1] 20 July, when the star Sirius (Sothis) appears as the morning star, The Nile is at that time in full flood.

To Shu, the god of atmosphere, whose consort is Nut, was given the keeping of the multitude of beings that shine in thick darkness. Shu raised his arms, uplifting over his head the Celestial Cow[1] and the millions and millions of stars.

Then Ra spoke to the earth god, who is called Geb, and said:

'Many fearful reptiles live in you. It is my will now that they may have a fear of me as great as is my fear of them. You shall discover why they are moved with enmity against me. When you have done that, you shall go to Nu, my father, and bid him have knowledge of all the reptiles in the deep and on the dry land. Let it be made known to each one that my rays shall fall on them. By words of magic alone can they be overcome. I shall reveal the charms by which the children of men can defeat all reptiles, and Osiris, your son, shall favour the magicians who protect mankind against them.'

He spoke again and called forth the god Thoth who came into being by his word.

'For you, O Thoth,' he said, 'I shall make a resplendent abode in the great deep and the underworld, which is Duat. You shall record the sins of men and the names of those who are my enemies. In Duat you shall bind them. You shall be temporary dweller in my place. You are my deputy. Lo! I now give messengers to you.'

So came into being by his power the ibis, the crane and the dog ape,[2] the messengers of Thoth.

Ra spoke again, saying: 'Your beauty shall be shed through the darkness. You shall join night with day.'

So came into being the moon (Ah) of Thoth, and Ra said: 'All living creatures shall glorify and praise you as a wise god.'

When all the land is black, the sun barque of Ra passes through the twelve hour divisions of night in Duat. In the evening, when the god is Atum, he is old and very frail. Seventy-five invocations are chanted to give him power to overcome the demons of darkness who are his enemies. He then enters the western gate, through which dead men's souls pass to be judged before Osiris. In front of him goes the jackal god, Anubis, for he is 'Opener of the Ways'. Ra has a sceptre in one hand. In the other he carries the ankh, which is the symbol of life.

When the sun barque enters the River Urnes of the underworld, the companions of Ra are with him. Watchman is there and Striker, and Steersman is at the helm, and in the barque are also those divinities who are given power, by uttering magical incantations, to overcome the demons of evil.

The gloomy darkness of the first hour division is scattered by the brightness of Ra. Beside the barque gather the pale shades of the newly dead, but none of them

---

[1] Hathor the sky goddess, in her cow form, displaces Nut.

[2] Here the old lunar deity Thoth is associated with the dawn. The chattering of apes at sunrise gave origin to the idea that they worshipped the rising sun.

can enter it without knowledge of the magical formulae that it is given to few to possess.

At the end of the first hour division is a high and strong wall, and a gate is opened by incantations so that the barque of Ra may pass through. So from division to division, through the perilous night, the sun god proceeds, and the number of demons that must be defeated by magic and fierce fighting increases as he goes. Apep, the great serpent, always seeks to overcome Ra and devour him.

The fifth hour division is the domain of dreaded Sokar, the underworld god with three human heads, a serpent's body and mighty wings between which appears his hawk form. His abode is a dark and secret place guarded by fierce sphinxes. Near is the Drowning Pool, watched over by five gods with bodies like those of men and animals' heads. Strange and mysterious forms hover, and in the pool are demons in torture, their heads aflame with everlasting fire.

In the seventh hour division sits Osiris, divine judge of the dead. Fiery serpents, which are many-headed, obey his will. They have feet to walk on and hands, and some carry sharp knives with which to cut to pieces the souls of the wicked. Those whom Osiris deems to be worthy, he favours. They shall live in the Netherworld. Those whom he finds to be full of sin, he rejects, and these the serpents fall upon, dragging them away, while they utter loud and piercing cries of grief and agony, to be tortured and devoured. Lo! the wicked perish utterly. In this division of peril, the serpent Apep attacks the sun barque, curling its great body around the compartment of Ra with ferocious intent to devour him. But the allies of the god contend against the serpent. They stab it with knives until it is overcome. Isis utters mighty incantations that cause the sun barque to sail onward unscathed.

In the eighth division are serpents that spit forth fire to light the darkness, and in the tenth are fierce water reptiles and ravenous fishes. The god Horus burns great beacons in the eleventh hour division. Ruddy flames and flames of gold blaze on high in beauty – the enemies of Ra are consumed in the fires of Horus.

The sun god is reborn in the twelfth hour division. He enters the tail of the mighty serpent, which is named Divine Life, and issues from its mouth in the form of Khepera, which is a beetle. Those who are with the god are reborn also. The last door of all is guarded by Isis, wife of Osiris, and Nephtys, wife of Seth, in the form of serpents. They enter the sun barque with Ra.

Now Urnes, the river of Duat, flows into the primeval ocean in which Nu has his abode. And as Ra was lifted out of the deep at the beginning, so he is lifted by Nu at dawn. He is then received by Nut, goddess of the heavens. He is born of Nut and grows in majesty, ascending to high noon.

The souls of the dead utter loud lamentations when the sun god departs out of the darkness of Duat.

Chapter 2

The Tragedy of Osiris

Osiris the Wise King – Introduction of Agriculture – Isis the Strong Queen – Conspiracy of Seth – The Tragic Feast – Osiris is slain – The Quest of Isis – Seth the Oppressor – 'The Opener of the Ways' – Birth of Horus – Thoth the Healer – Tree encloses Osiris's Body – Isis as a Foster-mother – Her Swallow Guise – Flames of Immortality – Osiris brought back to Egypt – Torn in Pieces by Seth, the Boar Hunter – Isis recovers Fragments – Ghost of Murdered King – Horus as Hamlet – Succession of Uncle and Son – Agricultural Rites – The Inundation – Lamentations at Sowing Time and Harvest – Osiris and Isis as Corn Spirits – Haapi, the Nile Deity – Isis as a Male.

When Osiris was born, a voice from out of the heavens proclaimed: 'Now has come the lord of all things.' The wise man Pamyles had knowledge of the tidings in a holy place at Thebes, and he uttered a cry of gladness and told the people that a good and wise king had appeared among men.

When Ra grew old and ascended to heaven, Osiris sat in his throne and ruled over the land of Egypt. Men were but savages when he first came among them. They hunted wild animals, they wandered in broken tribes hither and thither, up and down the valley and among the mountains, and the tribes contended fiercely in battle. Evil were their ways and their desires were sinful.

Osiris ushered in a new age. He made good and binding laws, he uttered just decrees, and he judged with wisdom between men. He caused peace to prevail at length over all the land of Egypt.

Isis was the queen consort of Osiris, and she was a woman of very great wisdom. Perceiving the need of mankind, she gathered the ears of barley and wheat that she found growing wild, and these she gave to the king. Then Osiris taught men to break up the land that had been under flood, to sow the seed and, in due season, to reap the harvest. He instructed them also how to grind corn and knead flour and meal so that they might have food in plenty. At the behest of the wise ruler the vine was trained on poles, and he cultivated fruit trees and caused the fruit to be gathered. He was a father to his people, and he taught them to worship the gods, to erect temples and to live holy lives. The hand of man was no longer lifted against his brother. There was prosperity in the land of Egypt in the days of Osiris the Good.

When the king saw the excellent works that he had accomplished in Egypt, he went forth to travel the whole world with the purpose of teaching wisdom to all men and prevailing on them to abandon their evil ways. He achieved his triumphs not by battle conquest but by reason of gentle and persuasive words and by music and song. Peace followed in his footsteps, and men learned wisdom from his lips.

Isis reigned over the land of Egypt until his return. She was stronger than Seth, who regarded the good works of his brother with jealous eyes, for his heart was full of evil and he loved warfare better than peace. He wished to stir up rebellion in the kingdom. The queen frustrated his wicked designs. He sought in vain to prevail in battle against her, so he plotted to overcome Osiris by guile. His followers were seventy-two men who were subjects of the queen of Ethiopia.[1]

When Osiris returned from his mission, there was great rejoicing in the land. A royal feast was held, and Seth came to make merry, and with him were his fellow conspirators. He brought a handsome decorated chest, which he had had made according to the measurements of the king's body. All the people at the feast praised it, admiring its beauty, and many wished greatly to own it. When all hearts had been made glad with beer drinking, Seth proclaimed that he would give the chest to him whose body fitted its proportions with exactness. There was no suspicion of evil design among the faithful subjects of Osiris. The guests spoke lightly, making jests against one another, and all were eager to try the chest as Seth had desired. So it happened that one after another got in the chest on that fateful night, until it seemed that no man could be found to win it for himself. Then Osiris came forward. He lay down in the chest, and he filled it in every part. But dearly was his triumph won in that dark hour, which was his hour of doom. Before he could raise his body, the evil followers of Seth suddenly sprang forward and shut down the lid, which they nailed fast and soldered with lead. So the richly decorated chest became the coffin of the good king Osiris, from whom departed the breath of life.

The feast was broken up in confusion. Merrymaking ended in sorrow, and blood flowed after that instead of beer. Seth commanded his followers to carry away the chest and dispose of it secretly. As he commanded them, so did they do. They hastened through the night and flung it into the Nile. The current bore it away in the darkness, and when morning came it reached the great ocean and was driven hither and thither, tossing among the waves. So ended the days of Osiris and the years of his wise and prosperous reign in the land of Egypt.

When the sad tidings were borne to Isis, she was stricken with great sorrow and refused to be comforted. She wept bitter tears and cried aloud. Then she uttered a binding vow, cut off a lock of her shining hair, and put on the garments of

---

[1] After the period of Ethiopian supremacy (Twenty-fifth Dynasty) Seth was identified with the Ethiopians.

mourning. Thereafter the widowed queen wandered up and down the land, seeking for the body of Osiris.

Nor would she rest nor stop until she found what she sought. She questioned each one she encountered, and one after another they answered her without knowledge. At length she made search in vain, but at last she was told by shoreland children that they had seen the chest floating down the Nile and entering the sea by the Delta mouth that takes its name from the city of Tanis.[1]

Meanwhile Seth, the usurper, ascended the throne of Osiris and reigned over the land of Egypt. Men were wronged and deprived of their possessions. Tyranny prevailed, and the followers of Osiris suffered persecution. The good Queen Isis became a fugitive in the kingdom, and she sought concealment from her enemies in the swamps and deep jungle of the Delta. Seven scorpions followed her, and these were her protectors. Ra, looking down from heaven, was moved to pity because of her distress, and he sent to her aid Anubis, 'the opener of the ways', who was the son of Osiris and Nepthys, and he became her guide.

One day Isis sought shelter at the house of a poor woman who was stricken with such great fear when she saw the fearsome scorpions that she closed the door against the wandering queen. But a scorpion gained entrance and bit her child so that he died. Then loud and long were the lamentations of the stricken mother. The heart of Isis was touched with pity, and she uttered magical words that caused the child to come to life again, and the woman ministered to the queen with gratitude while she remained in the house.

Then Isis gave birth to her son Horus, but Seth came to know where the mother and babe were concealed, and he made them prisoners in the house.[2]

It was his desire to put Horus to death, lest he should become his enemy and the claimant of the throne of Osiris. But wise Thoth came out of heaven and warned Isis, and she fled with her child into the night. She took refuge in Buto, where she gave Horus into the keeping of Wadjet, the virgin goddess of the city, who was a serpent,[3] so that he might have protection against the jealous wrath of Seth, his wicked uncle, while she went in search of the body of Osiris. But one day, when she came to gaze on the child, she found him lying dead. A scorpion had bitten him, nor was it in her power to restore him to life again. In her bitter grief she called on the great god Ra. Her voice ascended to high heaven, and the sun boat was stayed in its course. Then wise Thoth came down to give aid. He worked a mighty spell. He spoke magic words over the child Horus, who was immediately restored to life again.[4] It was the will of the gods that he should grow into strong manhood and then smite his father's slayer.

---

[1] Tanis was during the later dynasties associated with the worship of Seth (Sutekh).
[2] Another version of the myth places the birth of Horus after the body of Osiris was found.
[3] She took the form of a shrew mouse to escape Seth when he searched for Horus.
[4] Thoth in his Lunar character as divine physician.

Osiris

Isis, winged, in the attitude of
protecting Horus

Horus (as
Harpokrates)

Osiris, Isis and Horus

The coffin of Osiris was driven by the waves to Byblos, in Syria, and it was cast on the shore. A sacred tree sprang up and grew around it, and the body of the dead ruler was enclosed in its great trunk. The king of that alien land marvelled greatly at the wonderful tree, because it had had such rapid growth, and he commanded that it should be cut down. As he wished, so it was done. Then the trunk was erected in his house as a sacred pillar, but to no man was given knowledge of the secret that it contained.

A revelation came to Isis, and she set out towards Byblos in a ship. When she reached the Syrian coast she went ashore clad in ordinary clothes, and she sat beside a well, weeping bitterly. Women came to draw water, and they spoke to her with pity, but Isis did not answer, nor cease to grieve, until the handmaidens of the queen drew near. She greeted them kindly. When they had spoken gently to her, she braided their hair and into each lock she breathed sweet and alluring perfume. So it happened that when the maidens returned to the king's house, the queen smelt the perfume and commanded that the strange woman should be brought before her. Then Isis found favour in the eyes of the queen, who chose her to be the foster-mother of the royal baby.

But Isis refused to suckle the child, and to silence his cries for milk she put her finger into his mouth. When night came she caused fire to burn away his flesh, and she took the form of a swallow and flew, uttering broken cries of sorrow, round about the sacred pillar that contained the body of Osiris. It happened that the queen came near and saw her baby in the flames. She immediately plucked him out, but although she rescued his body she caused him to be denied immortality.[1]

Isis again assumed her normal form, and she confessed to the queen who she was. Then she asked the king that the sacred pillar be given to her. The gift was granted, and she cut deep into the trunk and took out the chest, which was concealed therein. Embracing it tenderly, she uttered cries of lamentation that were so bitter and keen that the royal baby died with terror. Then she consecrated the sacred pillar, which she wrapped in linen and anointed with myrrh, and it was afterwards placed in a temple that the king caused to be erected to Isis, and for long centuries it was worshipped by the people of Byblos.

The coffin of Osiris was borne to the ship in which the queen goddess had sailed to Syria. Then she went aboard and took with her Maneros, the king's first-born, and put forth to sea. The ship sped on, and the land faded from sight. Isis yearned to behold once again the face of her dead husband, and she opened the chest and kissed his cold lips passionately, while tears streamed from her eyes. Maneros, son of the king of Byblos, came stealthily behind her, wondering

---

[1] We have here a suggestion of belief in cremation, which was practised by the cave-dwellers of southern Palestine. The ghost of Patroklos says: 'Never again will I return from Hades when I receive from you my meed of fire' – The *Iliad* 23, 75.

what secret the chest contained. Isis looked round with anger, her bright eyes blinded him, and he fell back dead into the sea.

When Isis reached the land of Egypt she concealed the body of the dead king in a secret place and hastened towards the city of Buto to embrace her son Horus; but her triumph was short-lived. It happened that Seth came hunting the boar[1] at full moon in the Delta jungle, and he found the chest that Isis had brought back from Syria. He caused it to be opened, and the body of Osiris was taken out and torn into fourteen pieces, which he cast into the Nile, so that the crocodiles might eat them. But these reptiles feared of Isis and did not touch them, and they were scattered along the river banks.[2] A fish (Oxyrhynchus) swallowed the phallus.

The heart of Isis was filled with grief when she learned what Seth had done. She had made for herself a papyrus boat and sailed up and down the Delta waters, searching for the fragments of her husband's body, and at length she recovered them all, except the part that had been swallowed by the fish. She buried the fragments where they were found, and for each she made a tomb. In later days temples were erected over the tombs, and in these Osiris was worshipped by the people for long centuries.

Seth continued to rule over Egypt, and he persecuted the followers of Osiris and Isis in the Delta swamps and along the sea coast to the north. But Horus, who was rightful king, grew into strong manhood. He prepared for the coming conflict and became a strong and brave warrior. Among his followers were cunning workers in metal who were called mesniu (smiths), and bright and keen were their weapons of war. The sun hawk was blazoned on their battle banners.

One night there appeared to Horus in a dream a vision of his father, Osiris.[3] The ghost urged him to overthrow Seth, by whom he had been so treacherously put to death, and Horus vowed to drive his wicked uncle and all his followers out of the land of Egypt. So he gathered his army together and went off to battle. Seth met him at Edfu and slew many of his followers. But Horus secured the aid of the tribes who remained faithful to Osiris and Isis, and Seth was again attacked and driven towards the eastern frontier. The usurper uttered a great cry of grief when he was forced to take flight. He rested at Zaru, and there the last battle was fought. It was waged for many days, and Horus lost an eye. But Seth was even more badly wounded,[4] and he was at length driven out of the kingdom with his army.

It is told that the god Thoth descended out of heaven and healed the wounds of Horus and Seth. Then the slayer of Osiris appeared before the divine council and claimed the throne. But the gods gave judgment that Horus was the rightful king,

[1] The Osiris boar. See Chapter 5.
[2] The crocodile worshippers held that their sacred reptile recovered the body of Osiris for Isis.
[3] This is the earliest known form of the Hamlet myth.
[4] He was mutilated by Horus as he himself had mutilated Osiris.

and he established his power in the land of Egypt and became a wise and strong ruler like his father Osiris.

Another version of the legend relates that when the fragments of the body of Osiris were recovered from the Nile, Isis and Nepthys lamented over them, weeping bitterly. In one of the temple chants Isis exclaims:

> Gods, and men before the face of the gods, are weeping for
> you at the same time when they behold me!
> Lo! I invoke you with wailing that reaches high as heaven—
> Yet you hear not my voice. Lo! I, your sister, I love you more
> than all the earth—
> And you love not another as you do your sister!

Nepthys cries:

> Subdue every sorrow that is in the hearts of us your sisters . . .
> Live before us, desiring to behold you.[2]

The lamentations of the goddesses were heard by Ra, and he sent down from heaven the god Anubis, who, with the assistance of Thoth and Horus, united the severed portions of the body of Osiris, which they wrapped in linen bandages. Thus had origin the mummy form of the god. Then the winged Isis hovered over the body, and the air from her wings entered the nostrils of Osiris so that he was imbued with life once again. He afterwards became the Judge and King of the Dead.

Egyptian burial rites were based on this legend. At the ceremony enacted in the tomb chapel two female relatives of the deceased took the parts of Isis and Nepthys, and recited magical formulae, so that the dead might be imbued with vitality and enabled to pass to the Judgment Hall and Paradise.

Osiris and Isis, the traditional king and queen of ancient Egyptian tribes, were identified with the deities who symbolised the forces of Nature, and were accordingly associated with agricultural rites.

The fertility of the narrow strip of country in the Nile valley depends on the River Nile, which overflows its banks every year and brings down fresh soil from the hills. The river is at its lowest between April and June, the period of winter. Fed by the melting snows on the Abyssinian hills, and by the equatorial lakes, which are flooded during the rainy season, the gradual rise of the river becomes perceptible about the middle of June. The waters first assume a reddish tint on account of the clay that they carry. For a short period they then become greenish and unwholesome. Before that change took place, the Ancient Egyptians would store water for domestic use in large jars. By the beginning of August the Nile runs high. It was then that the canals were opened in ancient days so that the waters might fertilise the fields.

'As the Nile rose,' wrote Wilkinson,[1] 'the peasants were careful to remove the flocks and herds from the lowlands; and when a sudden irruption of the water, owing to the bursting of a dike, or an unexpected and unusual increase of the river, overflowed the fields and pastures, they were seen hurrying to the spot, on foot or in boats, to rescue the animals and to remove them to the high grounds above the reach of the inundation. . . . And though some suppose the inundation does not now attain the same height as of old, those who have lived in the country have frequently seen the villages of the Delta standing, as Herodotus describes them, like islands in the Aegean Sea, with the same scenes of rescuing the cattle from the water.' According to Pliny, 'a proper inundation is of 16 cubits . . . in 12 cubits the country suffers from famine, and feels a deficiency even in 13; 14 causes joy, 15 scarcity, 16 delight; the greatest rise of the river to this period was of 18 cubits' (a cubit is approximately 18 inches (46 centimetres).

When the river rose very high in the days of the pharaohs, 'the lives and property of the inhabitants,' wrote Wilkinson, 'were endangered.' In some villages the houses collapsed. Hence the legend that Ra sought to destroy his enemies among mankind.

The inundation is at its height by the end of September, and continues stationary for about a month. Not until the end of September does the river resume normal proportions. November is the month for sowing. The harvest is reaped in Upper Egypt by March and in Lower Egypt by April.

It was believed by the ancient agriculturists that the tears of Isis caused the river to increase in volume. When Sirius rose before dawn about the middle of July it was identified with the goddess. In the sun-cult legend this star is Hathor, 'the eye of Ra', who comes to slaughter mankind. There are evidences that human sacrifices were offered to the sun god at this period.

E. W. Lane, in his *Manners and Customs of the Modern Egyptians*, wrote that the night of 17 June was called Leylet-en-Nuktah, 'the night of the drop', because 'it is believed that a miraculous drop then falls into the Nile and causes it to rise'. An interesting ceremony used to be performed at 'the cutting of the dam' in old Cairo. A round pillar of earth was formed, and it was called the 'bride', and seeds were sown on the top of it. Lane wrote that an ancient Arabian historian 'was told that the Egyptians were accustomed, at the period when the Nile began to rise, to dress a young virgin in colourful apparel, and throw her into the river, as a sacrifice to obtain a plentiful inundation'.

When the ancient Egyptians had ploughed their fields they held a great festival at which the moon god, who, in his animal form, symbolised the generative principle, was invoked and worshipped. Then the sowing took place, amidst lamentations and mourning for the death of Osiris. The divine being was buried in the earth, the seeds being the fragments of his body. Reference is made to this old

[1] *The Ancient Egyptians*, Sir J. Gardner Wilkinson.

custom in Psalm 146: 'They that sow in tears shall reap in joy. He that goes forth and weeps, bearing precious seed, shall doubtless come again with rejoicing, bringing his sheaves with him.'

When harvest operations began, the Egyptians mourned because they were killing the corn spirit. Diodorus Siculus wrote that when the first handful of grain was cut, the Egyptian reapers beat their breasts and lamented, calling on Isis. When, however, all the sheaves were brought in from the fields, they rejoiced greatly and held their 'harvest home'.

Both Osiris and Isis were originally identified with the spirits of the corn. The former represented the earth god and the latter the earth goddess. But after the union of the tribes who worshipped the human incarnations of ancient deities, the rival concepts were fused. As a result, sometimes the inundation is symbolised as the male principle and at other times as the female principle. The Nile god, Haapi, is depicted as a man with female breasts. In an Abydos temple chant Isis makes reference to herself as 'the woman who was made a male by her father, Osiris'.[1]

The Scottish Osiris
(John Barleycorn)

There were three kings into the east,
   Three kings both great and high,
And they hae sworn a solemn oath
   John Barleycorn should die.

They took a plough and plough'd him down
   Put clods upon his head,
And they hae sworn a solemn oath
   John Barleycorn was dead.

But the cheerful spring came kindly on,
   And show'rs began to fall;
John Barleycorn got up again,
   And sore surpris'd them all.

The sultry suns of summer came,
   And he grew thick and strong,
His head weel arm'd wi' pointed spears,
   That no one should him wrong.

[1] *The Burden of Isis*, Dennis.

The sober autumn enter'd mild,
  When he grew wan and pale;
His bending joints and drooping head
  Show'd he began to fail.

His colour sicken'd more and more,
  He faded into age;
And then his enemies began
  To show their deadly rage.

They've ta'en a weapon long and sharp,
  And cut him by the knee;
Then ty'd him fast upon a cart,
  Like a rogue for forgerie.

They laid him down upon his back,
  And cudgell'd him full sore;
They hung him up before the storm,
  And turn'd him o'er and o'er.

They fillèd up a darksome pit
  With water to the brim,
They heaved in John Barleycorn—
  There let him sink or swim.

They laid him out upon the floor,
  To work him farther woe;
And still, as signs of life appear'd,
  They tossed him to and fro.

They wasted, o'er a scorching flame,
  The marrow of his bones;
But the miller us'd him worst of all,
  For he crush'd him between two stones.

And they hae ta'en his very heart's blood.
  And drank it round and round;
And still the more and more they drank
  Their joy did more abound.

John Barleycorn was a hero bold
  Of noble enterprise;

For if you do but taste his blood,
 'Twill make your courage rise.

'Twill make a man forget his woe;
 'Twill heighten all his joy;
'Twill make the widow's heart to sing,
 Tho' the tear were in her eye.

Then let us toast John Barleycorn,
 Each man a glass in hand;
And may his great posterity
 Ne'er fail in old Scotland.

Robert Burns

Chapter 3

Dawn of Civilisation

Early Peoples – The Mediterranean Race – Blonde Peoples of Morocco and Southern Palestine – Fair Types in Egypt – Migrations of Mediterraneans – They reach Britain – Early Nilotic Civilisations – Burial Customs – Osiris Invasion – The Seth Conquest – Sun Worshippers from Babylonia – Settlement in North – Coming of Dynastic Egyptians – The Two Kingdoms – United by Meni – The Mathematicians of the Delta – Introduction of Calendar – Progressive Pharaohs – Early Irrigation Schemes.

In the remote ages, before the ice cap had melted in northern Europe, the Nile valley was a swamp with a growth of jungle like the Delta. Rain fell in season, so that streams flowed from the hills, and slopes that are now barren wastes were green and pleasant grassland. Tribes of Early Stone Age peoples hunted and herded there, and the flints they chipped and splintered so rudely are still found in mountain caves, on the surface of the desert and embedded in mud washed down from the hills.

Other peoples of higher development appeared in time,[1] and after many centuries elapsed they divided the valley between them, increasing in numbers and breaking off into tribes. Several small independent kingdoms were thus formed. When government was ultimately centralised after conquest, these kingdoms became provinces, called nomes,[2] and each had its capital, with its ruling god and local theological system. The fusion of peoples that resulted caused a fusion of religious beliefs, and one god acquired the attributes of another without complete loss of identity.

The early settlers came from North Africa, which was occupied by tribes of the Mediterranean race. They were light-skinned 'long heads' of short stature, with slender bodies, aquiline noses, and black hair and eyes. In the eastern Delta they were the Archaic Egyptians; in the western Delta and along the coast, which suffered from great subsidence in later times, they were known as the Libyans. Tribes of the latter appear to have mingled with a blonde and taller stock.[3] On the

---

[1] The early Palaeolithic men were probably of Bushman types, and the later of Mediterranean. Evidence of development from the Palaeolithic to the Neolithic Age has been forthcoming.

[2] The Greek name; the old Egyptian name was 'hesp'.

[3] There were Libyans in the western Delta; on its border were the 'Tehenu', and beyond these the 'Lebu', and still farther west were the 'Meshwesh', the Maxyes of the Greeks. All were referred to as Libyans.

northern slopes of the Atlas Mountains this type has still survived. A similar people occupied southern Palestine in pre-Semitic times. Blue-eyed and light-haired individuals thus made an appearance in the Nile valley at an early period. They were depicted in tomb paintings, and, although never numerous, were occasionally influential. There are fair types among modern-day Berbers. The idea that these are descendants of Celts or Goths no longer obtains.

As they multiplied and prospered, the Mediterranean peoples spread far from their North African area of characterisation. Their migration southward was arrested in Nubia, where the exploring tribes met in conflict hordes of Bushmen, with whom they ultimately blended. Fusion with taller Africans followed in later times. Thus began the virile Nubian people, who were always a menace to the Dynastic pharaohs.

But the drift of Mediterranean peoples appears to have been greater towards the north than the south. Branching eastward, they poured into Palestine and Asia Minor. They were the primitive Phoenicians, who ultimately fused with Semites, and they were the Hittites, who blended with Mongols and Alpine (or Armenoid) 'broad heads'. Taking possession of large tracts of Italy and Greece, they became known to history as the Italici, Ligurians, Pelasgians, etc, and they founded a great civilisation in Crete, where evidence has been forthcoming of their settlement as early as 10,000 BC.

The western migration towards Morocco probably resulted in periodic fusions with blonde mountain tribes, so that the people who entered Spain across the Straits of Gibraltar may have been more akin in physical type to the Libyans than to the Archaic Egyptians. The early settlers spread through western Europe and are known to history as the Iberians. They also met and mingled with the tribes branching along the sea coast from Greece. Moving northwards through the river valleys of France, the Iberians crossed over to Britain, absorbing everywhere, it would appear, the earlier inhabitants who survived the conflict. These were the people of the Late Stone Age, which continued through vast intervals of time.

A glimpse of the early Mediterranean civilisation is obtained in the Delta region. The dwellings of the very early Egyptians were of mud-plastered wickerwork and grouped in villages, around which they constructed strong stockades to ward off the attacks of desert lions and leopards, and give protection to their herds of antelopes, goats and ostriches. The cat and the dog were already domesticated. Men tattooed their bodies and painted their faces. They wore slight garments of goatskin and adorned their heads with ostrich feathers. The women, who affected similar habits but had fuller attire, set decorated combs in their hair, and they wore armlets and necklets of shells, painted pebbles and animals' teeth, which were probably charms against witchcraft.

These early settlers were herdsmen and hunters and fishermen, and among them were artisans of great skill who chipped from splintered flint sharp lances and knives and keen arrowheads, while they also fashioned artistic pottery and hollowed out shapely stone jars. In their small boats they sailed and rowed on the Nile. They caught fish with bone hooks and snared birds in the Delta swamps. Their traders bartered goods constantly among the tribes who dwelt on the river banks. They were fierce and brave warriors, as fearless when hunting as in battle, for they not only slew the wild ox but also attacked crocodile and hippopotamus with lance and bow, and hunted wild boar and desert lion in moonlight.

As day followed night, so they believed that life came after death. They buried their dead in shallow graves, clad in goatskin, crouched as if taking a rest before setting forth on a journey, while beside them were placed their little palettes of slate for grinding face paint, their staffs and flint weapons and vessels of pottery filled with food for sustenance and drink for refreshment.

Long centuries went past, and a new civilisation appeared in Lower Egypt. Tribes from the east settled there and conquered, introducing new arts and manners of life and new beliefs. The people began to till the soil after the Nile flood subsided, and they raised harvests of barley and wheat. It was the age of Osiris and Isis.

Each king was an Osiris, and his symbols of power were the shepherd's staff and the flail. The people worshipped their king as a god, and, after thirty years' reign, devoured him at their Sed festival[1] with cannibalistic ceremonial, so that his spirit might enter his successor, and the land and the people have prosperity. The gnawed bones of monarchs have been found in tombs.[2]

Laws, which were stern and inexorable as those of nature, disciplined the people and promoted their welfare. Social life was organised under a strict system of government. Industries were fostered and commerce flourished. Traders went farther afield as the needs of the age increased, and procured ivory from Nubia, silver from Asia, and from Arabia its sweet perfumes and precious stones, and for these they bartered corn, linen and oil. There was also constant exchange of pottery and weapons and ornaments. Centuries went past, and this civilisation at length suffered gradual decline, probably because of the weakening of the central power.

Then followed a period of anarchy, when the kingdom, attracting plunderers, sustained the shock of invasion. Hordes of Semites, mingled probably with northern mountaineers, poured in from Syria and the Arabian steppes and overthrew the power of the Osirian ruler. They were worshippers of Seth (Sutekh), and they plundered and oppressed the people. Their sway, however, was only slight in the region of the western Delta, where frequent risings occurred and rebellion was forever fostered. Warfare disorganised commerce and impoverished the land. Art declined and an obscure period ensued.

---

[1] Petrie's view. See *Researches in Sinai*.

[2] Maspero. This opinion, however, has been sharply challenged.

But the needs of a country prevail in the end, and the north flourished once again with growing commerce and revived industries. On their pottery the skilled artisans painted scenes of daily life. Men and women were, it appears, clad in garments of white linen, and the rich had belts and pouches of decorated leather and ornaments of silver and gold set with precious stones. Tools and weapons of copper had come into use, but flint was also worked with consummate skill, unsurpassed by any other people.

The land was a veritable hive of industry. Food was plentiful, for the harvests yielded corn, and hunters found wild animals more numerous as beasts of prey were driven from their lairs and lessened in number. Great galleys were built to trade in the Mediterranean, and each was propelled by sixty oarsmen. The ships of other peoples also visited the ports of Egypt, probably from Crete and the Syrian coast, and caravans crossed the frontier going eastward and north, while alien traders entered the land and lived in it. Battle conflicts with various races were also depicted on the pottery, for there was much warfare from time to time.

Growing communities with Babylonian beliefs settled in the north. These were the sun worshippers whose religion ultimately gained ascendancy all over Egypt. From primitive Pithom (house of Atum) they may have passed to On (Heliopolis), which became sacred to Ra-Atum and was the capital of a province and probably, for a period, of the kingdom of Lower Egypt.

A masterful people also appeared in Upper Egypt. They came from or through Arabia, and had absorbed a culture from a remote civilisation, which cannot be located, in common with the early Babylonians. Crossing the lower end of the Red Sea, they entered the green valley of the Nile over a direct desert route, or through the highlands of Abyssinia. They were armed with weapons of copper, and made their earliest settlement, it would appear, at Edfu. Then by gradual conquest they welded together the various tribes, extending their sway over an ever-increasing area. New and improved methods of agriculture were introduced. Canals were constructed for purposes of irrigation. The people increased in number and prosperity, and law and order were firmly established in the land.

These invaders were sun worshippers of the Horus hawk cult, but they also embraced the religious beliefs of the people with whom they mingled, including the worship of the corn god Osiris. From Edfu and Hierakonpolis they pressed northward to sacred Abydos, the burial place of kings, and to Thinis, the capital of four united provinces. Several monarchs, who wore with dignity the white crown of Upper Egypt, reigned and 'abode their destined hour'. Then arose a great conqueror who was named Zaru, 'the scorpion'. He led his victorious army down the Nile valley, extending his kingdom as he went, until he reached the frontier of the Faiyum province, which was then a great swamp. There his progress was arrested. But a new era had dawned in Egypt, for there then remained only two kingdoms – the Upper and the Lower.

King Zaru was not slain at the Sed festival in accordance with the suggested ancient custom. He impersonated Osiris, throned in solitary dignity and wearing his crown, within a small curtained enclosure that opened at the front, and he held the crook in one hand and the flail in the other. The people made obeisance before him. It is not possible to follow the details of the ceremony, but from pictorial records it appears that large numbers of captives and oxen and cattle were offered up in sacrifice, so that slaughter might be averted by slaughter. The monarch was believed to have died a ceremonial death and to have come to life again with renewed energy that prolonged his years. An Abydos inscription declares of an Osiris ruler in this connection: 'You begin your days anew; like the holy moon child you are permitted to prosper . . . you have grown young and you are born to life again.'[1] An important event at the festival was the appearance before the pharaoh of his chosen successor, who performed a religious dance; and he was afterwards given for wife a princess of the royal line, so that his right to the throne might be secured.

The closing years of Zaru's reign were apparently occupied in organising and improving the conquered territory. As befitted an Osirian king, he devoted much attention to agriculture, and land was reclaimed by irrigation. An artist depicted him in the act of digging on the river bank with a hoe, as if performing the ceremony of 'cutting the first sod' of a new canal. The people are shown to have had circular dwellings, with fruit trees protected by enclosures. Their square fields were surrounded by irrigation ditches.

When the king died he was buried at Abydos, like other rulers of his line, in one of the brick tombs of the time. The investigation of these by Flinders Petrie has made possible the reconstruction in outline of the history of Egypt immediately prior to the founding of the First Dynasty. It is significant to note that the dead were buried at full length instead of in contracted posture as in Lower Egypt.

The next great monarch was Narmer, who is believed by certain authorities to have been Meni. Petrie, however, holds that they were separate personalities. Another view is that the deeds of two or three monarchs were attributed to Meni, as in the case of the Sesostris of the Greeks. Evidently many myths attached to the memory of the heroic figure who accomplished the conquest of the northern kingdom and founded the First Dynasty of united Egypt. Meni was represented, for instance, as the monarch who taught the people how to gorge luxuriously while he lay on a couch and slaves massaged his stomach, and tradition asserted

---

[1] The Horus worshippers had evidently absorbed the beliefs of the Nilotic moon cult. Some authorities credit the Dynastic Egyptians with the introduction of Osiris worship. The close resemblance of Osiris to similar deities in Asia Minor and Europe favours the view that Osiris first entered Lower Egypt. See *The Golden Bough* – Adonis Attis, Osiris volume The Osirian heaven was of Delta character.

that he met his death, apparently while intoxicated, by falling into the Nile, in which he was devoured by a hippopotamus. But these folk tales hardly accord with the character of a conqueror of tireless energy, who must have been kept fully occupied in organising his new territory and stamping out the smouldering fires of rebellion.

The initial triumph of the traditional Meni, in his Narmer character, was achieved in the swampy Faiyum, the buffer state between Upper and Lower Egypt. It had long resisted invasion, but in the end the southern forces achieved a great victory. The broad Delta region then lay open before them, and their ultimate success was assured. King Meni is shown on a slate palette clutching with one hand the headlocks of the Faiyum chief – who kneels in a helpless posture – while with the other he swings high a mace to smite the final blow. A composed body servant waits upon the conquering monarch, carrying the royal sandals and a water jar. The hawk symbol is also depicted to signify that victory was attributed to Horus, the tribal god. Two enemies take flight beneath, and above the combatants are two cow heads of the pastoral and sky goddess Hathor.

This great scene was imitated, in the true conservative spirit of the ancient Egyptians, on the occasion of similar acts of conquest in later times. Indeed, for a period of 3,000 years each succeeding pharaoh who achieved victory in battle was depicted, like Meni, smiting his humbled enemy, and his importance was always emphasised by his gigantic stature. It was an artistic convention in those ancient days to represent an Egyptian monarch among his enemies or subjects like a Gulliver surrounded by Lilliputians.

After the conquest of the Faiyum, the Libyans appear to have been the dominant people in Lower Egypt. Their capital was at Sais, the seat of their goddess Neith. The attributes of this deity reflect the character of the civilisation of her worshippers. Her symbol was a shield and two arrows. She was depicted with green hands and face, for she was an earth spirit who provided vegetation for the flocks of a pastoral people. A weaver's shuttle was tattooed on her body to indicate, apparently, that she imparted to women their skill at the loom.

Meni conquered the Libyans in battle, and many thousands were slain, and he extended his kingdom to the shores of the Mediterranean. Then he assumed, in the presence of his assembled army, the red crown of Lower Egypt. He appears also to have legitimatised the succession by taking as his wife Neithhotep, 'Neith rests', a princess of the royal house of Sais.

So the Horus tribe was united with the Libyans who worshipped a goddess. In later times the triad of Sais was composed of Osiris, Neith and Horus. Neith was identified with Isis.

The race memory of the conquest of Lower Egypt is believed to be reflected in the mythical tale of Horus overcoming Seth. The turning point in the campaign was the Faiyum conflict where the animal gods of Seth were slain. Petrie urges with much circumstantial detail the striking view that the expulsion of Seth from Egypt signifies the defeat of the military aristocracy of 'Semites'[1] by the Horus people, who, having espoused the religion of Osiris, also espoused the cause of the tribe who introduced his worship into the land. It is evident, from an inscription on a temple of southern Edfu, that many conquests were effected in the Delta region before the union was accomplished. One version of the great folk tale states that when Horus overcame Seth he handed him over to Isis bound in chains. She failed, however, to avenge her husband's death and set her oppressor free. In his great wrath Horus then tore the crown from her head. This may refer particularly to the circumstances that led to the Libyan conquest. 'We can hardly avoid,' wrote Petrie, 'reading the history of the animosities of the gods as being the struggles of their worshippers.'

The Libyans were always a troublesome people to the pharaohs, whose hold on the western district of the Delta was never certain. Meni apparently endeavoured to break their power by taking captive no fewer than 120,000 prisoners. His spoils included also 400,000 oxen and 1,420,000 goats.

This displacement of so large a proportion of the inhabitants of the north was not without its effect in the physical character of the Nile-valley peoples. The differences of blend between north and south were well marked before the conquest. After the union of the two kingdoms, the ruling classes of Upper Egypt approximated closely to the Delta type. It is evident that the great native civilisation that flourished in the Nile valley for over forty centuries owed much to the virility and genius of the Mediterranean race, which promoted culture wherever its people settled. One is struck, indeed, to note in this connection that the facial characteristics of not a few pharaohs resemble those of certain leaders who have achieved distinction among European nations.

The culture of the Horus-worshipping conquerors was evidently well adapted for the Nile valley. It developed there rapidly during the three centuries that elapsed before the Delta was invaded and assumed a purely Egyptian character. Hieroglyphics were in use from the beginning. Copper was worked by 'the smiths', and superior wheel-turned pottery made its appearance. But the greatest service rendered to ancient Egypt by the Horus worshippers was the ultimate establishment of settled conditions over the entire land in the interests of individual welfare and national progress.

The contribution of the north to Dynastic culture was not inconsiderable. In fact, it cannot really be overestimated. The Delta civilisation was already well developed before the conquest. There was in use among the people a linear script that resembled closely the systems of Crete and the Aegean and those also that appeared later in Karia and Spain. Its early beginnings may be traced, perhaps, in

---

[1] It is possible that Seth (Sutekh) was the god of a pre-Semitic people whose beliefs were embraced by certain Semitic tribes.

those rude signs that the pioneers of the Late Stone Age in western Europe scratched on the French dolmens. Archaic Phoenician letters show that the great sea traders in later times simplified the system and diffused it far and wide.[1] Our alphabet is thus remotely North African in origin.

It was in the Delta also that the calendar was invented by great mathematicians who recognised that an artificial division of time was necessary for purposes of accurate record and calculation. At first it was based on the phases of the moon, but from around the end of the Second Dynasty they began their year with the rising of the star Sirius (Sothis) at the height of the Nile inundation, and it was divided into twelve months of thirty days each, five extra days being added for religious festivals associated with agricultural rites. This calendar was ultimately imported and adjusted by the Romans, and it continues in use, with subsequent refinements, all over the world.

Under Meni's rule there is evidence of the progress that is always fostered when ideas are freely exchanged and a stimulating rivalry is promoted among the people. The inventive mind was busily at work. Pottery improved in texture and construction, and was glazed in colours. Jewellery of great beauty was also produced, and weapons and tools were fashioned with artistic design. Draught-boards and sets of ninepins were evidently in demand among all classes for recreation in moments of leisure.

Meanwhile the administration of the united kingdom was thoroughly organised. Officials were numerous and their duties strictly defined. Various strategic centres were garrisoned so as to prevent outbreaks and to secure protection for every industrious and law-abiding citizen. Memphis became an important city. According to tradition it was built by Meni, but the local theological system suggests that it existed before his day. It is probable that he erected buildings there, including a fortification, and made it a centre of administration for the northern part of his kingdom.

When Meni died he was buried at Abydos, and he was succeeded by his son Aha, 'the fighter'. Under the new monarch a vigorous military campaign was conducted in the south, and another province was placed under the sway of the central government. The peaceful condition of the north is emphasised by his recorded visit to Sais, where he made offerings at the shrine of Neith, the goddess of his mother's people.

Meanwhile the natural resources of the Nile valley were systematically developed. Irrigation works were undertaken everywhere. Jungle was cleared away, and large tracts of land were reclaimed by industrious toilers. These activities were promoted and controlled by royal officials. King Den, a wise and progressive monarch, inaugurated the great scheme of clearing and draining the Faiyum,

[1] Professor Macalister was inclined to credit the Philistines instead of the Phoenicians with the work of systematising the script.

which was later to become a fertile and populous province. The surveyors set to work and planned the construction of a canal, and the scheme was developed and continued by the monarchs who followed. It was as shrewdly recognised in the time of the First Dynasty, as it is in our own day, that the progress and welfare of the Nile-valley people must always depend on the development of the agricultural resources of the country. The wealth of Egypt is drawn from the soil. All the glory and achievements of the dynasties were made possible by the systems of government that afforded facilities and protection for the men who 'cast their bread upon the waters' so that abundant return might be secured 'after many days'. When we are afforded, therefore, a glimpse of daily life on the land, as is given in the ancient and treasured folk tale that follows,[1] we are brought into closer touch with the people who toiled in contentment many thousands of years ago in the land of Egypt than is possible when we contemplate with wonder their exquisite works of art or great architectural triumphs. The spirit that pervaded the ancient peasantry of the Nile valley is reflected in the faithful and gentle service and the winning qualities of poor Bata, the younger brother. It gives us pause to reflect that the story of his injured honour and tragic fate moved to tears those high-born women whose swaddled mummies now lie in our museums to be stared at by visitors who wonder how they lived and what scenes surrounded their daily lives.

[1] It assumed its final form in the New Kingdom and is evidently of remote antiquity.

Chapter 4

The Peasant who became King

The Two Brothers – Peasant Lifes – The Temptresss – Wrath of Anpus – Attempt to slay his Brothers – Flight of Batas – Elder Brother undeceiveds – Kills his Wifes – Bata hides his Soul – His Wife – Sought by the Kings – Bata's Soul Blossom destroyeds – Wife becomes a Queens – Recovery of Lost Souls – Bata as a Bulls – Slaughtered for the Queens – Bata a Trees – Bata reborn as Son of his Wifes – The King who slew his Wife-mothers – Belief in Transmigration of Souls.

There were once two brothers, and they were sons of the same father and of the same mother. Anpu was the name of the elder, and the younger was called Bata. Now Anpu had a house of his own, and he had a wife. His brother lived with him, as if he were his son, and made garments for him. It was Bata who drove the oxen to the field. It was he who ploughed the land, and it was he who harvested the grain. He laboured continually on his brother's farm, and his equal was not to be found in the land of Egypt. He was imbued with the spirit of a god.

In this manner the brothers lived together, and many days went past. Each morning the younger brother went out with the oxen, and when evening came on, he drove them again into the byre, carrying on his back a heavy burden of fodder that he gave to the animals to eat, and he brought with him also milk and herbs for Anpu and his wife. While these two ate and drank together in the house, Bata rested in the byre with the cattle and he slept beside them.

When day dawned, and the land grew bright again, the younger brother was first to rise up, and he baked bread for Anpu and carried his own portion to the field and ate it there. As he followed the oxen he heard and he understood their speech. They would say: 'Yonder is sweet grass, and he would drive them to the place of their choice, at which they were well pleased. They were indeed noble animals, and they increased greatly.

The time of ploughing came on, and Anpu spoke to Bata, saying: 'Now get ready the team of oxen, for the Nile flood is past and the land may be broken up. We shall begin to plough tomorrow, so carry seed to the field that we may sow it.'

As Anpu wished, so did Bata do. When the next day dawned, and the land grew bright, the two brothers laboured in the field together, and they were well pleased with the work that they accomplished. Several days went past in this manner, and it happened that one afternoon the seed was finished before they had completed their day's task.

Anpu thereupon spoke to his younger brother saying: 'Hurry to the granary and fetch more seed.'

Bata ran towards the house and entered it. He saw his brother's wife sitting on a mat, languidly pleating her hair.

'Arise,' he said, 'and fetch corn for me, so that I may hasten back to the field with it. Do not delay me.'

The woman sat still and said: 'Go you yourself and open the storeroom. Take whatever you wish. If I were to rise for you, my hair would fall in disorder.'

Bata opened the storeroom and went in. He took a large basket and poured into it a great quantity of seed. Then he came out, carrying the basket through the house.

The woman looked up and said: 'What is the weight of that great burden of yours?'

Bata answered: 'There are two measures of barley and three of wheat. I carry, in all, on my shoulders five measures of seed.'

'Great indeed is your strength,' sighed the woman. 'Ah, how I contemplate and admire you each day!'

Her heart was moved towards him, and she stood up saying: 'Stay here with me. I will clothe you in fine raiment.'

The lad was made as angry as the panther, and said: 'I regard you as a mother, and my brother is like a father to me. You have spoken evil words and I do not wish to hear them again, nor will I repeat to any man what you have just spoken.'

He departed abruptly with his burden and hurried to the field, where he resumed his work.

At eventide Anpu returned home and Bata prepared to follow after him. The elder brother entered his house and found his wife lying there, and it looked as if she had suffered violence from an evildoer. She did not give him water to wash his hands, as was her custom. Nor did she light the lamp. The house was in darkness. She moaned where she lay, as if she were sick, and her garment was beside her.

'Who has been here?' asked Anpu, her husband.

The woman answered him: 'No one came near me save your younger brother. He spoke evil words to me, and I said: "Am I not as a mother, and is not your elder brother as a father to you?" Then he was angry and he struck me until I promised that I would not inform you. . . . Oh! if you allow him to live now, I shall surely die.'

The elder brother became like an angry panther. He sharpened his dagger and went out and stood behind the door of the byre with the intention of slaying young Bata when he came home.

The sun had gone down when the lad drove the oxen into the byre, carrying on his back fodder and herbs, and in one hand a vessel of milk, as was his custom each evening.

The first ox entered the byre, and then it spoke to Bata, saying: 'Beware! For your elder brother is standing behind the door. In his hand is a dagger, and he wishes to slay you. Do not draw near to him.'

The lad heard with understanding what the animal had said. Then the second ox entered and went to its stall, and likewise spoke words of warning, saying: 'Take speedy flight.'

Bata peered below the byre door, and he saw the legs of his brother, who stood there with a dagger in his hand. He at once threw down his burden and made a hurried escape. Anpu rushed after him furiously with the sharp dagger.

In his distress the younger brother cried to the sun god Ra-Harmachis, saying: 'O blessed lord! You are he who distinguishes between falsehood and truth.'

The god heard his cry with compassion and turned round.[1] He caused a wide stream to flow between the two brothers and, behold! it was full of crocodiles. Then it came that Anpu and Bata stood confronting one another, one on the right bank and the other on the left. The elder brother twice smote his hands with anguish because he could not slay the youth.

Bata called out to Anpu, saying: 'Wait where you are until the earth is made bright once again. Lo! when Ra, the sun god, rises up, I shall reveal in his presence all that I know, and he shall judge between us, discerning what is false and what is true. . . . Know that I may not dwell with you any longer, for I must depart to the fair region of the flowering acacia.'

When day dawned, and the sun god Ra appeared in his glory, the two brothers stood gazing at each other across the stream of crocodiles. Then the lad spoke to his elder brother, saying: 'Why did you come against me, wishing to slay me with treachery before I had spoken for myself? Am I not your younger brother, and have you not been as a father and your wife as a mother to me? Hear and know now that when I hurried to fetch seed your wife spoke, saying: "Stay with me." But this happening has been related to you in another manner.'

So spoke Bata, and he told his brother what was true regarding the woman. Then he called to witness the sun god, and said: 'Great was your wickedness in wishing to murder me by treachery.' As he spoke he cut off a piece of his flesh and flung it into the stream, where it was devoured by a fish.[2] He sank fainting on the bank.

[1] Ra is here in his human form, walking through Egypt.
[2] He was thus mutilated like Osiris, Attis, Adonis and other gods.

Anpu was stricken with anguish; tears ran from his eyes. He wished greatly to be beside his brother on the opposite bank of the stream of crocodiles.

Bata spoke again, saying: 'Truly did you wish an evil thing, but if your wish now is to do good, I shall instruct you what you should do. Return to your home and tend your oxen, for know now that I may not dwell with you any longer, but must depart to the fair region of the flowering acacia. What you shall do is to come to seek for me when I need your aid, for my soul shall leave my body and have its dwelling in the highest blossom of the acacia. When the tree is cut down, my soul will fall on the ground. There you may seek it, even if your quest be for seven years, for, truly, you shall find it if such is your desire. You must then place it in a vessel of water, and I shall come to life again and reveal all that has happened and what shall happen thereafter. When the hour comes to set out on the quest, behold! the beer given to you will bubble and the wine will have a foul smell. These shall be signs to you.'

Then Bata took his departure, and he went into the valley of the flowering acacia, which was across the ocean.[1] His elder brother returned home. He lamented, throwing dust on his head. He slew his wife and cast her to the dogs, and abandoned himself to mourning for his younger brother.

Many days went past, and at length Bata reached the valley of the flowering acacia. He dwelt there alone and hunted wild beasts. At eventide he lay down to rest below the acacia, in whose highest blossom his soul was concealed. In time he built a dwelling place and he filled it with everything that he desired.

Now it chanced that on a day when he went forth he met the nine gods who were surveying the whole land. They spoke one to another and then asked of Bata why he had forsaken his home because of his brother's wife, for she had since been slain. 'Return again,' they said, 'for you did reveal to your elder brother the truth of what happened to you.'

They took pity on the youth, and Ra spoke, saying: 'Fashion now a bride for Bata, so that he may not be alone.'

Then the god Khnum[2] fashioned a wife whose body was more beautiful than any other woman's in the land, because she was imbued with divinity.

Then came the seven Hathors[3] and gazed upon her. In one voice they spoke, saying: 'She shall surely die a speedy death.'

Bata loved her dearly. Each day she remained in his house while he hunted wild beasts, and he carried them home and laid them at her feet. He warned her each day, saying: 'Do not walk outside, lest the sea may come up and carry you away. I could not rescue you from the sea spirit,[4] against whom I am as weak as

---

[1] Probably in Syria.

[2] A creative god who resembled Ptah.

[3] The seven Fates.

[4] A non-Egyptian concept apparently.

you are, because my soul is concealed in the highest blossom of the flowering acacia. If another should find my soul I must needs fight for it.'

Thus he opened to her his whole heart and revealed its secrets.

Many days went past. Then on a morning when Bata had gone out to hunt, as was his custom, his girl wife went out to walk below the acacia, which was near to the house.

Lo! the sea spirit saw her in all her beauty and caused his billows to pursue her. Hastily she fled away and returned to the house, at which the sea spirit sang to the acacia: 'Oh, would she were mine!'

The acacia heard and cast to the sea spirit a lock of the girl wife's hair. The sea bore it away towards the land of Egypt and to the place where the washers of the king cleansed the royal garments.

Sweet was the fragrance of the lock of hair, and it perfumed the linen of the king. There were disputes among the washers because the royal garments smelt of ointment, nor could anyone discover the secret. The king rebuked them.

Then was the chief washer in distress because of the words that were spoken daily to him regarding this matter. He went down to the seashore. He stood at the place that was opposite the floating lock of hair, and at length he saw it and caused it to be carried to him. Sweet was its fragrance, and he hastened with it to the king.

Then the king summoned before him his scribes, and they spoke, saying:

'Lo! this is a lock from the hair of the divine daughter of Ra, and it is gifted to you from a distant land. Command now that messengers be sent abroad to seek for her. Let many men go with the one who is sent to the valley of the flowering acacia so that they may bring the woman to you.[1]

The king answered and said: 'Wise are your words and pleasant to me.'

So messengers were sent abroad to all lands. But those who journeyed to the valley of the flowering acacia did not return because Bata slew them all. The king had no knowledge of what happened to them.

Then the king sent forth more messengers and many soldiers also, so that the girl might be brought to him. He sent also a woman, and she was laden with rare ornaments—and the wife of Bata came back with her.

Then was there great rejoicing in the land of Egypt. Dearly did the king love the divine girl, and he exalted her because of her beauty. He prevailed upon her to reveal the secrets of her husband, and the king then said: 'Let the acacia be cut down and splintered in pieces.'

Workmen and warriors were sent abroad, and they reached the acacia. They severed the highest blossom from it, in which the soul of Bata was concealed. The petals were scattered, and Bata dropped down dead.[2]

---

[1] An early version of the Cinderella story.

[2] Like the typical giant of European folklore, who conceals his soul and is betrayed by his wife.

A new day dawned, and the land grew bright. The acacia was then cut down.

Meanwhile Anpu, the elder brother of Bata, went into his house, and he sat down and washed his hands.[1] He was given beer to drink, and it bubbled, and the wine had a foul smell.

He seized his staff, put on his shoes and his garment, armed himself for his journey and departed to the valley of the flowering acacia.

When he reached the house of Bata, he found the young man lying dead on a mat. Bitterly he wept because of that. But he went out to search for the soul of his brother at the place where, below the flowering acacia, Bata was accustomed to lie down to rest at eventide. For three years he continued his search, and when the fourth year came his heart yearned greatly to return to the land of Egypt. At length he said: 'I shall depart at dawn tomorrow.'

A new day came, and the land grew bright. He looked over the ground again at the place of the acacia for his brother's soul. The time was spent thus. In the evening he continued his quest, and he found a seed, which he carried to the house, and, lo! the soul of his brother was in it. He dropped the seed into a vessel filled with cold water, and sat down as was his custom at evening.

Night came on, and then the soul absorbed the water. The limbs of Bata quivered, and his eyes opened and gazed on his elder brother, but his heart was without feeling. Then Anpu raised the vessel that contained the soul to the lips of Bata, and he drank the water. Thus did his soul return to its place, and Bata was as he had been before.

The brothers embraced and spoke to one another. Bata said: 'Now I must become a mighty bull with every sacred mark. None will know my secret. Ride on my back, and when the day breaks I shall be at the place where my wife is. To her must I speak. Lead me before the king, and you shall find favour in his eyes. The people will wonder when they see me, and shout welcome. But you must return to your own home.'

A new day dawned, and the land grew bright. Bata was a bull, and Anpu sat on his back and they drew near to the royal dwelling. The king was made glad, and he said: 'This is indeed a miracle.' There was much rejoicing throughout the land. Silver and gold were given to the elder brother, and he went away to his own home and waited there.

In time the sacred bull stood in a holy place, and the beautiful girl wife was there. Bata spoke to her, saying: 'Look upon me where I stand, for, lo! I am still alive.'

Then said the woman: 'And who are you?'

The bull answered:

'Truly, I am Bata. It was you who caused the acacia to be cut down. It was you who revealed to pharaoh that my soul dwelt in the highest blossom, so that it

[1] The Egyptians always washed their hands before and after meals.

might be destroyed and I might cease to be. But, lo! I live on, and I am become a sacred bull.'

The woman trembled; fear possessed her heart when Bata spoke to her in this manner. She at once went out of the holy place.

It chanced that the king sat by her side at the feast, and made merry, for he loved her dearly. She spoke, saying: 'Promise before the god that you will do what I ask of you.'

His majesty took a vow to grant her the wish of her heart, and she said: 'It is my desire to eat of the liver[1] of the sacred bull, for he is nothing to you.'

Sorrowful was the king then, and his heart was troubled, because of the words that she spoke. . . .

A new day dawned, and the land grew bright. Then the king commanded that the bull should be offered in sacrifice.

One of the king's chief servants went out, and when the bull was held high on the shoulders of the people he smote its neck and it cast two drops of blood[2] towards the gate of the palace, and one drop fell on the right side and one on the left. There grew up in the night two stately Persea trees[3] from where the drops of blood fell down.

This great miracle was told to the king, and the people rejoiced and made offerings of water and fruit to the sacred trees.

A day came when his majesty rode forth in his golden chariot. He wore his collar of lapis lazuli, and round his neck was a garland of flowers. The girl wife was with him, and he caused her to stand below one of the trees, and it whispered to her:

'You false woman, I am still alive. Lo! I am Bata, whom you did wrong. It was you who caused the acacia to be cut down. It was you who caused the sacred bull to be slain, so that I might cease to be.'

Many days went past, and the woman sat with the king at the feast, and he loved her dearly. She spoke, saying: 'Promise now before the god that you will do what I ask of you.'

His Majesty made a vow of promise, and she said: 'It is my wish that the Persea trees be cut down so that two fair seats may be made of them.'

As she wished, so was it done. The king commanded that the trees should be cut down by skilled workmen, and the fair woman went out to watch them. As she stood there, a small chip of wood entered her mouth, and she swallowed it.

After many days a son was born to her, and he was brought before the king, and one said: 'Unto you a son is given.'

A nurse and servants were appointed to watch over the babe.

[1] It was believed that the soul was in the liver.
[2] The belief that the soul was in the blood.
[3] One tree for the spirit and one for the soul.

The Girl Wife and the Bata Bull
From the painting by Maurice Greiffenhagen

There was great rejoicing throughout the land when the time came to name the girl wife's son. The king made merry, and from that hour he loved the child, and he appointed him Prince of Ethiopia.

Many days went past, and then the king chose him to be heir to the kingdom.

In time his majesty fulfilled his years, and he died, and his soul flew to the heavens.

The new king (Bata) then said: 'Summon before me the great men of my court so that I may now reveal to them all that has befallen me and the truth concerning the queen.'

His wife[1] was then brought before him. He revealed himself to her, and she was judged before the great men, and they confirmed the sentence.[2]

Then Anpu was summoned before his majesty, and he was chosen to be the royal heir.

When Bata had reigned for thirty years,[3] he came to his death, and on the day of his burial his elder brother stood in his place.

Egyptian Love Songs

(Collected by scribes over 3,000 years ago, and laid in tombs so that they might be sung by departed souls in paradise.)

The Wine of Love

Oh! when my lady comes,
    And I with love behold her,
I take her to my beating heart
    And in my arms enfold her;
My heart is filled with joy divine
For I am hers and she is mine.

Oh! when her soft embraces
    Do give my love completeness,
The perfumes of Arabia
    Anoint me with their sweetness;
And when her lips are pressed to mine
I am made drunk and need not wine.

---

[1] Who was also his mother. Bata was reborn as the son of his wife. The tale is based on belief in the transmigration of souls.

[2] The sentence is not given but is indicated by the prophecy of the seven Hathors, who said she would die 'a speedy death' (a death by violence).

[3] This suggests that he was sacrificed at the Sed festival.

The Snare of Love
(Sung by a girl snarer to one she loves)

With snare in hand I hide me,
    I wait and will not stir;
The beauteous birds of Araby
    Are perfumed all with myrrh—
Oh, all the birds of Araby,
    That down to Egypt come,
Have wings that waft the fragrance
    Of sweetly smelling gum!

I would that, when I snare them,
    Together we could be,
I would that when I hear them
    Alone I were with thee.
If you will come, my dear one,
    When birds are snared above,
I'll take thee and I'll keep thee
    Within the snare of love.

The Sycamore Song

A sycamore sang to a lady fair,
    And its words were dropping like honey dew
'Now ruby red is the fruit I bear
    All in my bower for you.

'Papyri green are my leaves arrayed,
    And branch and stem like to opal gleam;
Now come and rest in my cooling shade
    The dream of your heart to dream.

'A letter of love will my lady fair
    Send to the one who will happy be,
Saying: 'Oh, come to my garden rare
    And sit in the shade with me!

'"Fruit I will gather for your delight,
    Bread I will break and pour out wine,
I'll bring you the perfumed flow'rs and bright
    On this festal day divine."

'My lady alone with her lover will be,
    His voice is sweet and his words are dear—
Oh, I am silent of all I see,
    Nor tell of the things I hear!'

The Dove Song

I hear thy voice, O turtle dove—
    The dawn is all aglow—
Weary am I with love, with love,
    Oh, whither shall I go?

Not so, O beauteous bird above,
    Is joy to me denied. . . .
For I have found my dear, my love;
    And I am by his side.

We wander forth, and hand in hand
    Through flow'ry ways we go—
I am the fairest in the land,
    For he has called me so.

Jealousy

My face towards the door I'll keep
    Till I my love behold,
With watching eyes and list'ning ears
    I wait . . . and I turn cold,
        I sigh and sigh;
        He comes not nigh.

My sole possession is his love
    All sweet and dear to me;
And ever may my lips confess
    My heart, nor silent be.
        I sigh and sigh;
        He comes not nigh.

But now . . . a messenger in haste
    My watching eyes behold . . .
He went as swiftly as he came.
    'I am delayed', he told.
        I sigh and sigh;
        He comes not nigh.

Alas! confess that thou hast found
    One fairer far than me.
O thou so false, why break my heart
    With infidelity?
        I sigh and sigh;
        He'll ne'er come nigh.

The Garden of Love

Oh! fair are the flowers, my beloved,
  And fairest of any I wait.
A garden art thou, all fragrant and dear,
  Thy heart, O mine own, is the gate.

The canal of my love I have fashioned,
  And through thee, my garden, it flows –
Dip in its waters refreshing and sweet,
  When cool from the north the wind blows.

In our beauteous haunt we will linger,
  Thy strong hand reposing in mine –
Then deep be my thoughts and deeper my joy,
  Because, O my love, I am thine.

Oh! thy voice is bewitching, beloved,
  This wound of my heart it makes whole—
Ah! when thou art coming, and thee I behold,
  Thou'rt bread and thou'rt wine to my soul.

Love's Pretence

With sickness faint and weary
    All day in bed I'll lie;
My friends will gather near me
    And she'll with them come nigh.
She'll put to shame the doctors
    Who'll ponder over me,
For she alone, my loved one,
    Knows well my malady.

Chapter 5

Racial Myths in Egypt and Europe

Worship of Animals – Possessed by Spirits of Good and Evil – Reptiles as Destroyers and Protectors – Pigs of Seth and Osiris – The Moon Eater – Horus Solar and Storm Myth – The Devil Pig in Egypt and Scotland – Contrast with Gaulish, Irish and Norse Beliefs – Animal Conflicts for Mastery of Herd – Love God a Pig – Why Eels were not eaten – The Sacred Bull – Irish and Egyptian Myths – Corn Spirits – The Goose Festival in Europe – The Chaos Egg – Giant's Soul Myth – Nilotic and other Versions – Wild Ass as Symbol of Good and Evil.

One of the most interesting phases of Nilotic religion was the worship of animals. Juvenal ridiculed the Egyptians for this particular practice in one of his satires, and the early fathers of the Church regarded it as proof of the folly of pagan religious ideas. Some modern-day apologists, on the other hand, have leapt to the other extreme by suggesting that the ancient philosophers were imbued with a religious respect for life in every form, and professed a pantheistic creed. Our task here, however, is to investigate rather than to justify or condemn ancient Egyptian beliefs. We wish to get, if possible, at the Egyptian point of view. That being so, we must recognise at the outset that we are dealing with a confused mass of religious practices and conceptions of Egyptian and non-Egyptian origin, which accumulated during a vast period of time and were perpetuated as much by custom as by conviction. The average Egyptian of the later Dynasties might have been as little able to account for his superstitious regard for the crocodile or the serpent as is the person today who dreads being one of a dinner party of thirteen or of spilling salt at table. He worshipped animals because they had always been worshipped, and, although originally only certain representatives of a species were held to be sacred, he was not unwilling to show reverence for the species as a whole.

We obtain a clue that helps to explain the origin of animal worship in Egypt in an interesting Nineteenth-Dynasty papyrus preserved in the British Museum. This document contains a calendar in which lucky and unlucky days are detailed in accordance with the ideas of ancient seers. Good luck, we gather, comes from the generous deities and bad luck is caused by the operations of evil spirits. On a particular date demons are let loose, and the peasant is warned not to lead an ox with a rope at any time during the day, lest one of them should enter the animal and cause it to gore him with its horns. An animal, therefore, was not feared or worshipped for its own sake but because it was liable to be possessed by a good or evil spirit.

The difference between good and evil spirits was that the former could be propitiated or bargained with, so that benefits might be obtained, while the latter remained ever insatiable and unwilling to be reconciled. This primitive conception is clearly set forth by Isocrates, the Greek orator, who said:

'Those of the gods who are the sources to us of good things have the title of Olympians; those whose department is that of calamities and punishments have harsher titles. To the first class both private persons and states erect altars and temples; the second is not worshipped either with prayers or burnt sacrifices, but in their case we perform ceremonies of riddance.'

'Ceremonies of riddance' are, of course, magic ceremonies. It was by magic that the Egyptians warded off the attacks of evil spirits. Ra's journey in the sun boat through the perilous hour divisions of night was accomplished with the aid of spells that defeated the demons of evil and darkness in animal or reptile form.

In Egypt both gods and demons might possess the same species of animals or reptiles. The ox might be an incarnation of the friendly Isis or of the demon that might gore the peasant. Serpents and crocodiles were at the same time the protectors and the enemies of mankind. The dreaded Apep serpent symbolised everything that was evil and antagonistic to human welfare, but the mother goddess Wadjet of Buto, who shielded Horus, was also a serpent, and serpents were worshipped as defenders of households. Images of them were hung up for 'luck' or protection, as horseshoes are in our own country even today. The serpent amulet was likewise a protective device, like the serpent stone of the Gauls and the 'lucky pig' that was worn as a charm.

In certain parts of Egypt the crocodile was also worshipped, and was immune from attack.[1] In others it was ruthlessly hunted down. As late as Roman times, the people of one nome waged war against those of another because their sacred animals were being slain by the rival religious organisation.

Here we touch on the tribal aspect of animal worship. Certain animals or reptiles were regarded as the protectors of certain districts. A particular animal might be looked on by one tribe as an incarnation of their deity and by another as the incarnation of their Satan. The black pig, for instance, was associated by the Egyptians with Seth, who was the god of a people who conquered and oppressed them in pre-Dynastic times. Horus is depicted standing on the back of the pig

---

[1] Snake worshippers in India are careful not to injure or offend a serpent and believe that 'the faithful' are never stung.

Uraeus, | Shrine with | Ape | Ibis
Cat (Bastet) | with horns | Sokar hawk | (Thoth) | (Thoth)

Apis Bull   Fish   Jackal   Snake   Ichneumon (form   Cat with
                (Lepidotus)   (Anubis) (Wadjet)   of Wadjet)   kittens (Bastet)

Sacred Animals

and piercing its head with a lance; its legs and jaws are fettered with chains. But the pig was also a form of Osiris, 'the good god'.

Seth was identified with the Apep serpent of night and storm, and in certain myths the pig takes the place of the serpent. It was the Seth pig, for instance, that fed on the waning moon, which was the left eye of Horus. How his right eye, the sun, was once blinded is related in a Heliopolitan myth. Horus sought, it appears, to equal Ra and wished to see all things that had been created. Ra delivered him a salutary lesson by saying: 'Behold the black pig'. Horus looked, and immediately one of his eyes (the sun) was destroyed by a whirlwind of fire. Ra said to the other gods: 'The pig will be abominable to Horus'. For that reason pigs were never sacrificed to him.[1] Ra restored the injured eye and created for Horus two horizon brethren who would guard him against thunderstorms and rain.

The Egyptians regarded the pig as an unclean animal. Herodotus relates that if they touched it casually, they at once plunged into water to purify themselves.[2] Swineherds lost caste and were not admitted to the temples. Pork was never included among the meat offerings to the dead. In Syria the pig was also 'taboo', and in the Highlands of Scotland there was a strong prejudice against pork, and the black pig was identified with the devil.

[1] Evidently because the sun cult was opposed to lunar rites, which included the sacrifice of pigs.
[2] Before the Greeks sacrificed a young pig, in connection with the mysteries of Demeter and Dionysius, they washed it and themselves in the sea – Plutarch.

On the other hand, the Gauls, who regarded the pig as sacred, did not abstain from pork. Like their kinsmen, the Achaeans, too, they regarded swineherds as important personages; these could even become kings. The Scandinavian heroes in Valhalla feast on swine's flesh, and the boar was identified with Frey, the corn god. In the Celtic (Irish) Elysium presided over by Dagda, the corn god, as the Egyptian-Paradise was presided over by Osiris, there was always 'one pig alive and another ready roasted'.[1] Dagda's son, Angus, the love god, the Celtic Khonsu, had a herd of swine, and their chief was the inevitable black pig.

In *The Golden Bough*, Professor Frazer shows that the pig was tabooed because it was at one time a sacred animal identified with Osiris. Once a year, according to Herodotus, pigs were sacrificed in Egypt to the moon and to Osiris. The moon pig was eaten, but the pigs offered to Osiris were slain in front of house doors and given back to the swineherds from whom they were purchased.

Like the serpent and the crocodile, the pig might be either the friend or the enemy of the corn god. At sowing time it rendered service by clearing the soil of obnoxious roots and weeds which retard the growth of crops. When, however, the agriculturists found the –

Snouted wild boar routing tender corn,

they apparently identified it with the enemy of Osiris – it slew the corn god. The boar hunt then ensued as a matter of course. We can understand, therefore, why the Egyptians sacrificed swine to Osiris because, as Plutarch says, 'not that which is dear to the gods but that which is contrary is fit to be sacrificed'. The solution of the problem may be that at sowing time the spirit of Osiris entered the boar, and that at harvest the animal was possessed by the spirit of Seth.

This conclusion leads us back to the primitive conception of the Great Mother Deity. In the archaic Scottish folk tale, which is summarised in the Introduction, she is the enemy of mankind.[2] But her son, the lover of the spirit of summer – he is evidently the prototype of the later love god – is a charitable giant. He fights against his mother, who separated him from his bride and sought to destroy all life. Ra similarly desired to slay 'his enemies', because he created evil as well as good. Geb, the Egyptian earth god, was the father of Osiris, 'the good god', and of Seth, the devil; they were 'brothers'. Osiris was a boar, and Seth was a boar. The original 'battle of the gods' may, therefore, have been the conflict between the two boars for the mastery of the herd – a conflict that also symbolised the

---

[1] *Celtic Myth and Legend*. This is a tribe phase of pig worship, apparently, of different character from that which obtained in Egypt. It may be that the reverence for the good pig was greater than the hatred of the black and evil pig.

[2] Ghosts also were enemies A dead wife might cause her husband to be stricken with disease. Budge's *Osiris and the Egyptian Resurrection*.

warfare between evil and good, winter and summer. Were not the rival forces of Nature created together at the beginning? The progeny of the Great Father, or the Great Mother, included evil demons as well as good gods.

The Greek Adonis was slain by a boar; Osiris was slain by Seth, the black boar; the Celtic Diarmid was slain by a boar that was protected by a hag who appears to be identical with the vengeful and stormy Scottish earth mother. The boar was taboo to the worshippers of Adonis and Osiris; in Celtic folklore 'bonds' are put on Diarmid not to hunt the boar. Evidently Adonis, Osiris and Diarmid represented the 'good' boars.

These three deities were love gods; the love god was identified with the moon, and the primitive moon spirit was the son of the Great Mother; the Theban Khonsu was the son of Mut; the Nubian Thoth was the son of Tefnut. Now Seth, the black boar of evil, devoured the waning moon, and in doing so he devoured his brother Osiris. When the Egyptians, therefore, sacrificed a pig to the moon and feasted on it like Seth, they ate the god. They did not eat the pig sacrificed to Osiris, because apparently it represented the enemy of the god; they simply slew it and thus slew Seth.

It would appear that there were originally two moon pigs – the 'lucky pig' of the waxing moon and the black pig of the waning moon. These were the animal forms of the moon god and of the demon who devoured the moon – the animal form of the love god and the thwarted rebel god. They also symbolised growth and decay – Osiris was growth, and Seth symbolised the slaughter of growth: he killed the corn god.

The primitive lunar myth is symbolised in the legend that tells that Seth hunted the boar in the marshes of the Delta region. He set out at the time of the full moon, just when the conflict between the demon and the lunar deity might be expected to begin, and he found the body of Osiris, which he broke up into fourteen parts – a suggestion of the fourteen phases of lunar decline. We know that Seth was the moon-eating pig. The black boar of night therefore hunts, slays and devours the white boar of the moon. But the phallus of Osiris is thrown into the river and is swallowed by a fish – similarly Seth flings the wrenched-out 'eye' of Horus into the Nile.

Now the fish was sacred in Egypt. It had a symbolic significance; it was a phallic symbol. The Great Mother of Mendes, another form of Isis, is depicted with a fish on her head. Priests were not permitted to eat fish, and food that was taboo to the priests was originally taboo to all the Egyptians. In fact, certain fish were not eaten during the Eighteenth Dynasty and later, and fish were embalmed. Those fish that were allowed were brought to the table with fins and tails removed. The pig, which was eaten sacrificially once a year, similarly had its tail cut off. Once a year, on the ninth day of the month of Thoth, the Egyptians ate fried fish at their house doors: the priests offered up their share by burning them. Certain fish were not eaten by the ancient Britons. The eel was abhorred in Scotland, and it was sacred and tabooed in Egypt also.[1]

Osiris was worshipped at Memphis in the form of the bull Apis, Egyptian Hapi, which was known to the Greeks as Serapis, their rendering of Asar-Hapi (Osiris-Apis), hence the name Serapeum given to the place of worship. This sacred animal was reputed to be of miraculous birth, like the son of the Great Mother deity. 'It was begotten,' Plutarch was informed, 'by a ray of generative light flowing from the moon.' 'Apis,' wrote Herodotus, 'was a young black bull whose mother can have no other offspring.' It was known by its marks; it had 'on its forehead a white triangular spot, on its back an eagle, a beetle lump under its tongue, while the hair of its tail was double'. Plutarch wrote that 'on account of the great resemblance that the Egyptians imagine between Osiris and the moon, its more bright and shining parts being shadowed and obscured by those that are of darker hue, they call the Apis the living image of Osiris'. The bull, Herodotus says, was 'a fair and beautiful image of the soul of Osiris'. Diodorus similarly states that Osiris manifested himself to people through successive ages as Apis. 'The soul of Osiris migrated into this animal', he explains.

That this bull represented the animal that obtained mastery of the herd is suggested by the popularity of bull fights at the ancient sports. On ancient tombs there are several representations of Egyptian peasants, carrying staves, urging bulls to battle against one another. Worshippers appear to have perpetuated the observance of the conflict between the male animals in mock fights at temples. Herodotus related that when the votaries of the deity presented themselves at the temple entrance they were armed with staves. Men with staves endeavoured to prevent their admission, and a combat ensued between the two parties, 'in which many heads were broken, and, I should suppose,' added Herodotus, 'many lives lost, although this the Egyptians positively deny.' Apparently Seth was the thwarted male animal – that is, the demon with whom the Egyptianised Seth (Sutekh) was identified.

The sacred Apis bull might either be allowed to die a natural death or it was drowned when its age was twenty-eight years – a suggestion of the twenty-eight phases of the moon and the violent death of Osiris. The whole nation mourned for the sacred animal. Its body was mummified and laid in a tomb with much ceremony. Auguste Mariette, the French archaeologist, discovered the Eighteenth-Dynasty tombs of the Memphite bulls in 1851. The sarcophagi that enclosed the bodies weighed about 59 tonnes each. One tomb that he opened had been undisturbed since the time of the burial, and the footprints of the mourners were discoverable after a lapse of 3000 years.[2]

After the burial the priests set out to search for the successor of the old bull,

---

[1] The Egyptian sacred fish were the Oxyrhinchus, Lepidotus, Latus and Phagrus.

[2] Apis worship was of great antiquity. Reference is made to the Apis priests in the Fourth Dynasty.

and there was great rejoicing when one was found, its owner being compensated with generous gifts of gold. In the Anpu-Bata story, which is evidently a version of the Osiris myth, the elder brother is honoured and becomes rich after he delivers the Bata bull to the pharaoh. It will be noted that the Osiris soul was believed to be in the animal's liver, which was eaten – here we have again the ceremony of eating the god. Before the bull was transferred to its temple, it was isolated for forty days and was seen during that period by women only.

At Heliopolis the soul of Osiris entered the Mneuis bull. This sacred animal was evidently a rival to Apis. Ammianus Marcellinus said that Apis was dedicated to the moon and Mneuis to the sun.

In Upper Egypt the sacred bull was Bakh (Bacis), a form of Mentu. It was ultimately identified with Ra.

The worship of Apis ultimately triumphed and in Roman times became general all over Egypt.

Like the Osiris boar, the Osiris bull was identified with the corn spirit. But its significance in this regard is not emphasised in the Egyptian texts. That may have been because different tribes regarded different animals as harvest deities. The association of Apis with Ptah is therefore of interest. It has been suggested that Ptah was originally worshipped by a people of mountain origin. In the great caves of southern Palestine there survive primitive drawings of cows and bulls, suggesting that this pastoral people venerated their domesticated animals. In Europe the corn spirit was identified with the bull and cow, principally by the Hungarians, the Swiss and the Prussians, and by some of the French, for the 'corn bull' was slain at Bordeaux. On the other hand, it may be that in the Irish legend regarding the conflict between the Brown Bull of Ulster and the White-horned Bull of Connacht there is a version of a very ancient myth that was connected with Osiris in Egypt. Both Irish animals were of miraculous birth – their mothers were fairy cows.

Like the Egyptian Anpu-Bata story, the Irish legend is characterised by belief in the transmigration of souls. It relates that the rival bulls were originally swineherds. One served Bodb, the fairy king of Munster, who was a son of Dagda, the Danann corn god. The other served Ochall Ochne, the fairy king of Connacht, the province occupied by the enemies of the good Danann deities. The two herds fought one against another. 'Then, the better to carry on their quarrel, they changed themselves into two ravens and fought for a year; next they turned into water monsters, which tore one another for a year in the Suir and a year in the Shannon; then they became human again, and fought as champions; and ended by changing into eels. One of these eels went into the River Cruind in Cualgne in Ulster, where it was swallowed by a cow belonging to Daire of Cualgne; and the other into the spring of Uaran Garad, in Connacht, where it passed into the belly of a cow of Queen Medb's. Thus were born those two famous beasts, the Brown

Figure of the Apis bull with a king making an offering

Bull of Ulster and the White-horned Bull of Connacht.'[1] The brown bull was victorious in the final conflict. It afterwards went mad, burst its heart with bellowing and fell dead. In this myth we have the conflict between rival males, suggested in the Osiris-Seth boar legend and the mock fights at the Egyptian bull temple.

The sacred cow was identified with Isis, Nepthys, Hathor and Nut. Isis was also fused with Taweret, the female hippopotamus, who was goddess of maternity and was reputed to be the mother of Osiris. Even the crocodile was associated with the worship of the corn god. In one of the myths this reptile recovers the body of Osiris from the Nile.

Bastet, another Great Mother who was regarded as a form of Isis, was identified with the cat, an animal that was extremely popular as a household pet in Egypt. Herodotus related that when a house went on fire the Egyptians appeared to be occupied with no thought but that of preserving their cats. These animals were prone to leap into the flames, and when a family lost a cat in such circumstances there was universal sorrow. A Roman soldier was once mobbed and slain because he killed a household cat.[2] The cat was identified in France with the corn spirit: the last portion of grain that was reaped was called 'the cat's tail'.[3]

In the Introduction mention is made of the goose that laid the sun egg. Apparently this bird was at one time sacred. Although it was a popular article of diet in

[1] *Celtic Myths and Legends.*

[2] Similarly, British soldiers once got into trouble for shooting sacred pigeons.

[3] In Ireland the cat deity was the god Cairbre *cinn cait*, 'of the cat's head'. He was a god of the Fir Bolg, the enemies of the Gaulish Danann people.

ancient Egypt, and was favoured especially by the priests, it was probably eaten chiefly in the winter season. The goose and the duck were sacred in Abyssinia, where the Mediterranean type has been identified in fusion with Semitic, Negroid and other types. In the Highlands of Scotland the goose was eaten, until recently, on Christmas Day only. Throughout England it was associated with Michaelmas. 'If you eat goose at Michaelmas,' runs an old saying, 'you will never want money all the year round.' The bird was evidently identified with the corn spirit. In Shropshire the shearing of the last portion of grain was referred to as 'cutting the gander's neck'. When all the corn was gathered into a stackyard in Yorkshire, an entertainment was given that was called 'The Inning Goose'. During the reign of Henry IV, the French subjects of the English king called the harvest festival the 'Harvest Gosling'. The Danes also had a goose for supper after harvest.

The sun god Ra, of Egypt, was supposed to have been hatched from the egg that rose from the primordial deep. This belief is reminiscent of the folk tale of the European giant who hid his soul in an egg, as Anpu hid his soul in the blossom of the acacia.

In one Scottish version of the ancient mythical story, the giant's soul is in a stump of a tree, a hare, a salmon, a duck and an egg; in another it is in a bull, a ram, a goose and an egg. Ptah was credited with making the sun egg that concealed his own soul, or the soul of Ra. So was Khnum. These craftsmen gods appear to be of common origin (see Chapter 14). They became giants in their fusion with the primitive earth god, who was symbolised as a gander, while they were also identified with the ram and the bull. Khnum received offerings of fish, so that a sacred fish might be added. Anpu's soul passed from the blossom to a bull and then to a tree. It may be that in these folk tales we have renderings of the primitive myths of a pastoral people, which gave rise to the Egyptian belief in the egg associated with Ra, Ptah and Khnum. In the *Book of the Dead* reference is made to the enemies of Ra, 'who have cursed that which is in the egg'. The pious were wont to declare: 'I keep watch over the egg of the Great Cackler' (the chaos goose) or, according to another reading: 'I am the egg which is in the Great Cackler' (Budge). Seth, the earth deity, was believed to have flown through the air at the beginning in the form of the chaos goose. The Celtic deities likewise appeared to humankind as birds.

The hare was identified with a god of the underworld. Doves and pigeons were sacred; the ibis was an incarnation of Thoth, the hawk of Horus, and the swallow of Isis. The mythical phoenix, with wings partly of gold and partly of crimson, was supposed to fly from Arabia to Heliopolis once every five hundred years. It was reputed to spring from the ashes of the parent bird, which thus renewed its youth.

The frog was sacred, and the frog goddess Hekt or Heket was a goddess of maternity. Among the gods identified with the ram were Amun and Min and the group of deities resembling Ptah. Anubis was the jackal. Mut, the Theban Great Mother, and the primitive goddess Nekhebat were represented by the vulture. The shrew mouse was sacred to Wadjet, who escaped from Seth in this form when she was the protector of Horus, son of Isis. The dog-faced ape was a form of Thoth; the lion was a form of Aker, an old, or imported, earth god.

There were two wild asses in Egyptian mythology, and they represented the good and evil principles. One was Seth, and the other the sun ass, which was chased by the night serpent. Although the souls of the departed, according to the *Book of the Dead*, boasted that they drove back the 'eater of the ass' (the serpent that devoured the sun), they also prayed that they would 'smite the ass' (the devil ass) 'and crush the serpent'. When Seth was driven out of Egypt, he took flight on the back of the night ass, which was another form of the night serpent. Seth was also the Apep serpent and the 'roaring serpent', which symbolised the tempest.

Herodotus recorded that although the number of beasts in ancient Egypt was comparatively small, both those that were wild and those that were tame were regarded as sacred. They were fed on fish and ministered to by hereditary lay priests and priestesses. 'In the presence of the animals,' the Greek historian wrote, 'the inhabitants of the cities perform their vows. They address themselves as supplicants to the deity who is believed to be manifested by the animal in whose presence they are. . . . . It is a capital offence to kill one of these animals.'

Chapter 6

The City of the Elf God

The London of Ancient Egypt – Ptah Chief of Nine Earth Spirits – God of a Military Aristocracy – Palestine Cave-dwellers and Alpine 'Broad Heads' – Creation Crafstmen of Egyptians, Europeans, Indians and Chinese – Sun Egg and Moon Egg – The Later Ptah – Neith as a Banshee – Sokar, God of the Dead – Earliest Memphite Deity – Ptah and Osiris – Manetho's Folk Tales – A Famous Queen – The First Pyramid.

Now, when there was corn in Egypt 'as the sand of the sea', traders from foreign countries crossed the parched deserts and the perilous deep, instructed, like the sons of Jacob, to 'get you down thither and buy for us from thence'. So wealth and commerce increased in the Nile valley. A high civilisation was fostered, and the growing needs of the age caused many industries to flourish.

The business of the country was controlled by the cities, which were nursed into prosperity by the wise policy of the pharaohs. Among these cities, Memphis looms prominently in the history of the early Dynasties. Its ruling deity was, appropriately enough, the craftsman god Ptah, for it was not only a commercial but also an important industrial centre. Indeed, it was the home of the great architects and stone builders whose activities culminated in the erection of the pyramids, the most sublime achievements in masonry ever accomplished by man.

Today the ruins of Old Memphis lie buried deep in the sand. The peasant tills the soil and reaps the harvest in season above its once busy streets and stately temples, its clinking workshops and noisy markets. 'I have heard the words of its teachers whose sayings are on the lips of men. But where are their dwelling places? Their walls have been cast down and their homes are not, even as though they had never been.' Yet the area of this ancient city was equal to that of modern London from Bow to Chelsea and the Thames to Hampstead, and it had a teeming population.

> O mighty Memphis, city of 'White Walls',
> The habitation of eternal Ptah,
> Cradle of kings . . . on you the awful hand
> Of Vengeance has descended. . . . . Nevermore
> Can bard acclaim your glory; nevermore

Shall harp, nor flute, nor timbrel, nor the song
Of maids resound within your ruined halls,
Nor shouts of merriment in you be heard,
Nor hum of traffic, nor the eager cries
Of merchants in your markets murmurous;
The silence of the tomb has fallen on you,
And you are faded like a lovely queen,
Whom loveless death has stricken in the night,
Whose robe is rent, whose beauty is decayed –
And nevermore shall princes from afar
Pay homage to your greatness, and proclaim
Your wonders, nor in reverence behold
Your sanctuary glories . . .
                              Are your halls
All empty, and your streets laid bare
And silent as the soundless wilderness?
O Memphis, mighty Memphis, has the morn
Broken to find you not?

Memphis was founded by Meni and named by King Pepy I,[1] and is called Noph in the Old Testament. Its early Dynastic name was 'White Walls', the reference being probably to the fortress erected there soon after the conquest. Of its royal builder we know little, but his mother, Queen Shesh, enjoyed considerable repute for many centuries afterwards as the inventor of a popular hair wash that is referred to in a surviving medical papyrus.

After Egypt was united under the double crown of the Upper and the Lower Kingdoms, and the pharaoh became 'Lord of the Two Lands', the seat of government remained for a long period at Thinis, in the south. The various nomes, like the present-day states of the United States of America, each had its centre of local administration. Pharaoh's deputies were nobles who owed him allegiance, collected the imperial taxes, supplied workmen or warriors as required, and carried out the orders of the court officials regarding the construction and control of canals. The temple of the nome god adorned the provincial capital.

Ptah, the deity of Memphis, is presented in sharp contrast to the sun god Ra, who was of Asiatic origin, and the deified King Osiris, whose worship was associated with agricultural rites. He was an earth spirit, resembling closely the European elf. The concept was evidently not indigenous, because the god also had a giant form, like the hilltop deities of the mountain peoples (see Chapter 12). He

---

[1] The Greek rendering of 'Menefer', the name of Pepy's pyramid. Another Egyptian name was Hikuptah, or, according to Budge, 'Het-Ka-Ptah, "house of the double of Ptah", from which the Greek name of Egypt is derived'.

was probably imported by the invaders who constituted the military aristocracy at Memphis in pre-Dynastic times. These may have been the cave-dwellers of Southern Palestine, or tall and muscular 'broad heads' of Alpine or Armenoid type who, prior to the Conquest, appear to have pressed southward from Asia Minor through the highlands of Palestine, and, after settlement, altered somewhat the physical character of the 'long heads' of the eastern Delta. Allowance has to be made for such an infusion in accounting for the new Dynastic type as well as for the influence exercised by the displacement of a great proportion of the mingled tribes of Libyans. The Palestine cave-dwellers may have been partly of Alpine origin.

A people seldom remember their early history, but they rarely forget their tribal beliefs. That being so, the god Ptah is of special interest in dealing with the tribal aspect of mythology. Among all the gods of Egypt, his individuality is perhaps the most pronounced. Others became shadowy and vague, as beliefs were fused and new and greater conceptions evolved in the process of time. But Ptah never lost his elfin character, even after he was merged with deities of different origin. He was the chief of nine earth spirits (that is, eight and himself added) called Khnum, 'the modellers'. Statuettes of these represent them as dwarfs, with muscular bodies, bent legs, long arms, big broad heads and faces of intelligent and even benign expression. Some wear long moustaches,[1] so unlike the shaven or smooth-skinned Egyptians.

At the beginning, according to Memphite belief, Ptah shaped the world and the heavens, assisted by his eight workmen, the dwarfish Khnum. He was also the creator of mankind, and in Egyptian tombs are found numerous earthenware models of these 'elves', who were believed to have had power to reconstruct the decaying bodies of the dead. As their dwellings were underground, they may have also been 'artisans of vegetation', like the spirits associated with Tvashtar, the 'master workman' of the Rig-Veda hymns and the 'black dwarfs' of Teutonic mythology. A particular statuette of Ptah, wearing a tight-fitting cap, suggests the familiar 'wonder smith'[2] of the Alpine 'broad heads' who were distributed along Asiatic and European mountain ranges from Hindu Kush to Brittany and the British Isles and mingled with the archaic Hittites in Asia Minor. The Phoenician sailors carried figures of dwarfs in their ships and worshipped them. They were called *pataikoi*. In the Far East a creation craftsman who resembles Ptah is Pan Ku, the first Chinese deity, who emerged from a cosmic egg.

Like Ra, Ptah was also believed to have first appeared as an egg, which, ac-

---

[1] The suggestion that these represented serpents is not supported by anything we know about Ptah worship. There was a winged serpent goddess in the Delta named Wadjet. The Greeks called her Buto and identified her with their Leto.

[2] Ptah has been compared to the Greek Hephaestus (Vulcan). He was not a fire god. His consort, Sekhmet, symbolised fire and sun heat, but his association with her was arbitrary.

cording to one of the many folk beliefs of Egypt, was laid by the chaos goose that came to be identified with Geb, the earth god, and afterwards with the combined deities Amun-Ra. Ptah, as the primeval 'craftsman god', was credited with making 'the sun egg' and also 'the moon egg', and a bas-relief at Philae shows him actively engaged at the work, using his potter's wheel.

A higher and later conception of Ptah[1] represents him as a sublime creator god who has power to call into existence each thing he names. He is the embodiment of mind from which all things emerge, and his ideas take material shape when he gives them expression. In a philosophic poem a Memphite priest eulogises the great deity as 'the mind[2] and tongue of the gods', and even as the creator of other gods as well as of 'all people, cattle and reptiles', the sun and the habitable world. Thoth is also credited with similar power, and it is possible that in this connection both these deities were imparted with the attributes of Ra, the sun god.

According to the tradition perpetuated by Manetho, the first temple in Egypt was erected at Memphis, that city of great builders, to the god Ptah at the command of King Meni. It is thus suggested that the town and the god of the ruling caste existed when the Horus sun worshippers moved northwards on their campaign of conquest. As has been shown, Meni also gave diplomatic recognition to Neith, the earth goddess of the Libyans, 'the green lady' of Egypt, who resembles somewhat the fairy, and especially the banshee, of the Iberians and their Celtic conquerors.

The Ptah worshippers were probably not the founders of Memphis. An earlier deity associated with the city is the dreaded Sokar (Seker). He was a god of the dead, and in the complex mythology of later times his habitation was located in the fifth hour division of night.[3] When sun worship became general in the Nile valley, Sokar was identified with the small winter sun, as Horus was with the large sun of summer. But the winged and three-headed monster god, with serpent body, suffers complete loss of physical identity when merged with the elfin deity of Memphis. Ptah-Sokar is depicted as a dwarf and one of the Khnum. Another form of Sokar is a hawk, of different aspect to the Horus hawk, which appears perched on the Ra boat at night with a sun disc on its head.[4]

Ptah-Sokar was in time merged with the agricultural Osiris whose spirit passed from pharaoh to pharaoh. Ptah-Osiris was depicted as a human-sized mummy, swathed and mute, holding firmly in his hands before him the Osirian *dadu* (pil-

---

[1] Eighteenth Dynasty.

[2] The poet says 'heart', which was believed by the Egyptians to be the seat of intelligence. At the judgment of the dead the heart is weighed in the balance.

[3] See Chapter 1.

[4] Osiris-Sokar is 'the brilliant one', 'lord of great fear and trembling', 'the mysterious one, he who is unknown to mankind' and 'enlightener of those who are in the underworld'.—*The Burden of Isis*, Dennis (Hymn to Osiris-Sokar).

lar) symbol. The triad, Ptah-Sokar-Osiris, gives us a combined deity who is a creator, a judge of the dead and a traditional king of Egypt. The influence of the sun cult prevailed when Sokar and Osiris were associated with the worship of Ra.

Memphis, the city of Ptah, ultimately became the capital of a united Egypt. It was then at the height of its glory; a great civilisation had evolved. Unfortunately, however, we are unable to trace its progress, because the records are exceedingly scanty. Fine workmanship in stone, exquisite pottery, etc, indicate the advanced character of the times, but it is impossible to construct from these alone an orderly historical narrative. We have also the traditions preserved by Manetho. Much of what he tells us, however, belongs to the domain of folklore. We learn, for instance, that for nearly a fortnight the Nile ran with honey, and that one of the pharaohs, who was a giant about 9 feet (3 metres) high, was 'a most dangerous man'. It is impossible to confirm whether a great earthquake occurred in the Delta region, where the ground is said to have yawned and swallowed many of the people, or whether a famine occurred in the reign of one pharaoh and a great plague in that of another, and if King Meni really spent his leisure moments compiling works on anatomy. The story of a Libyan revolt at a later period may have had foundation in fact, but the explanation that the rebels broke into flight because the moon suddenly attained enormous dimensions shows how myth and history were inextricably intertwined.

Yet Manetho's history contains important material. His list of early kings is not imaginative, as was once supposed, although there may be occasional inaccuracies. The Palermo Stone, so called because it was taken to the Sicilian city of that name by some unknown curio collector, has inscribed on it in hieroglyphics the names of several of the early kings and references to notable events that occurred during their reigns. It is one of the little registers that were kept in temples. Many of these, no doubt, existed, and some may yet be brought to light.

Four centuries elapsed after the conquest before Memphis became the royal city. We know little, however, regarding the first three hundred years. Two dynasties of Thinite kings ruled over the land. There was a royal residence at Memphis, which was the commercial capital of the country – the marketplace of the northern and southern peoples. Trade flourished and brought the city into contact with foreign commercial centres. It had a growing and cosmopolitan population, and its arts and industries attained a high level of excellence.

The Third Dynasty opens with King Djoser, who reigned at Memphis. He was the monarch for whom the first pyramid was erected. It is situated at Saqqara, in the vicinity of his capital. The kings who reigned before him had been entombed at Abydos, and the new departure indicates that the supremacy of Memphis was made complete. The administrative, industrial and religious life of the country was for the time centred there.

The Step Pyramid of Saqqara (Tomb of Djoser, of which Imhotep was the architect)

Djoser's preference for Memphis had, perhaps, a political bearing. His mother, the wife of Khasekem,[1] the last of the Thinite kings, was probably a daughter of the ruling noble of 'White Walls'. It was the custom of monarchs to marry the daughters of nome governors and also to give their sons his daughters in marriage. The aristocracy was thus closely connected with the royal house. Indeed, the relations between the pharaoh and his noblemen appear to have been intimate and cordial.

The political marriages, however, were the cause of much jealous rivalry. As the pharaoh had more than one wife, and princes were numerous, the choice of an heir to the crown was a matter of great political importance. The king named his successor, and in the royal harem there were occasionally plots and counterplots to secure the precedence of one particular prince or another. Sometimes methods of coercion were adopted with the aid of interested noblemen whose prestige would be increased by the selection of a near relative – the son, perhaps, of the princess of their nome. In one interesting papyrus roll that survives there is a record of an abortive plot to secure the succession of a rival to the pharaoh's favourite son. The ambitious prince was afterwards disposed of. In all probability he was executed along with those concerned in the household rebellion. Ad-

---

[1] This king's brick tomb at Abydos contains a limestone chamber, which suggests the employment of the Memphite craftsmen.

dressing his chosen heir, the monarch remarks that 'he fought the one he knew, because it was unwise that he should be beside your majesty'.

It may be that these revolts explain the divisions of the lines of early kings into dynasties. Djoser's personality stands out so strongly that it is evident he was a prince who would brook no rival to the throne. His transference of the seat of power to the city of Ptah suggests, too, that he found his chief support there.

With the political ascendancy of Memphis begins the great Pyramid Age; but before we look at the industrial and commercial life in the city and survey the great achievements of its architects and builders, we shall deal with the religious beliefs of the people so that it may be understood why the activities of the age were directed to making such elaborate provision for the protection of the bodies of dead monarchs.

Chapter 7

Death and the Judgment

The Human Triad – Ghosts – Spirits of the Living – Why the Dead were given Food – Souls as Birds – The Shadow and the Name – Beliefs of Diverging Origin – Burial Customs – The Crouched Burial – Secondary Interment – Extended Burials – Mummies – Life after Death – Two Conceptions – Souls in the Sun Boat – The Osirian Paradise – Journey to the Other World – Perils on the Way – Conflicts with Demons – The River of Death – The Judgment Hall – Weighing the Heart – The Happy Fields.

In the maze of Egyptian beliefs there were diverging views regarding the elements that constitute the human personality. One triad was a unity of the *ka* (spirit), the *khu* (soul) and the *khat* (the body). Another grouped *khaybet* (the shadow) with ka (the spirit) and *sahu* (the mummy). The physical heart was called *hati* – it was supposed to be the seat of the intelligence, and its 'spirit' was named *ab*, which signified the will and desires. The 'vital spark', or controlling force, was symbolised as the *sekhem*, and the *ran* was the personal name.

The ka of the first triad is the most concrete conception of all. It was probably, too, the oldest. The early people appear to have believed that the human personality combined simply the body and the spirit. In those tomb scenes that depict the birth of kings, the royal baby is represented by two figures – the visible body and the invisible 'double'. The ka began to be at birth; it continued to live on after death.

But a human being was not alone in possessing a ka. Everything that existed was believed to have its 'double'. A fish or other animal had a ka; so also had a tree; and there were spirits in water, in metals, in stone, and even in weapons and other manufactured articles. These spirits were invisible to all except seers, who were those individuals able to exercise on occasion the 'faculty' that Scottish Highlanders call 'second sight'.

It was conceived that the ka could leave the human body during sleep or while the subject lay in a trance. It then wandered about and visited people and places, and its experiences survived in the memory. Dreams were accounted for in this way as actual happenings. When a man dreamt of a dead friend, he believed that his ka had met with the ka of the dead, talked with it and engaged in the performance of some Otherworld duty. Sometimes the wandering ka could be observed

91

at a distance from where the sleeper lay. It had all the appearance of the individual, because it was attired in the 'doubles' of his clothing and might carry the 'double' of his staff. Ghosts, therefore, included 'the spirits of the living', which were not recognised to be spirits until they vanished mysteriously. They might also be simply heard and not seen.

In the story of Anpu and Bata (Chapter 4) is contained the belief that the ka could exist apart from the body. Its habitation was a blossom, and when the petals were scattered the younger brother fell dead. He revived, however, when the seed was placed in a vessel of water. This concept was associated with belief in the transmigration of souls. Bata entered a new state of existence after he left his brother.

During normal life the ka existed in the human body. It was sustained by the 'doubles' of everything that was partaken of. After death it required food and drink, and offerings were made to it at the grave.

In ancient times a cult believed that the ka could be fed by magic. Mourners or ancestor worshippers who visited the tomb simply named the articles of food required, and these were immediately given existence for the spirit. The 'good wishes' were thus considered to be potent and practical.

It was essential that the dead should receive the service of the living, and those who performed the necessary ceremonies and made the offerings were called the 'servants'. Thus the Egyptian word for 'priest' signified a 'servant'. But the motive that prompted the mourners to serve the departed was not necessarily sorrow or undying affection but rather genuine fear. If the ka or ghost were neglected and allowed to starve, it could leave the grave and haunt the offenders. Primitive people had a genuine dread of spirits, and their chief concern was always to propitiate them, no matter how great might be the personal sacrifice involved.

Sometimes a small 'soul house' was provided by the wayside for the wandering ka, but more often an image of wood or stone was placed for its use in the grave. The statues of kings, which have been found in their tombs, were constructed so that their disembodied spirits might be given material bodies, and those that they caused to be built in various parts of the kingdom were primarily intended for a similar purpose and not merely to perpetuate their fame, although the note of vanity is rarely absent in the inscriptions.

The khu, or 'soul', was a vague concept. It was really another form of the ka, but it was the 'double' of the intellect, will and intentions rather than the 'double' of the physical body. The khu was depicted as a bird,[1] and was called 'the bright one' or 'the glorious one'.

The *ba* of the second triad was a concept uniting both the ka and the khu. It is

---

[1] According to Celtic folk belief, the dead sometime appear as birds. This idea may be a survival of the transmigration-of-souls concept; the soul passed through many animals before re-entering a human body.

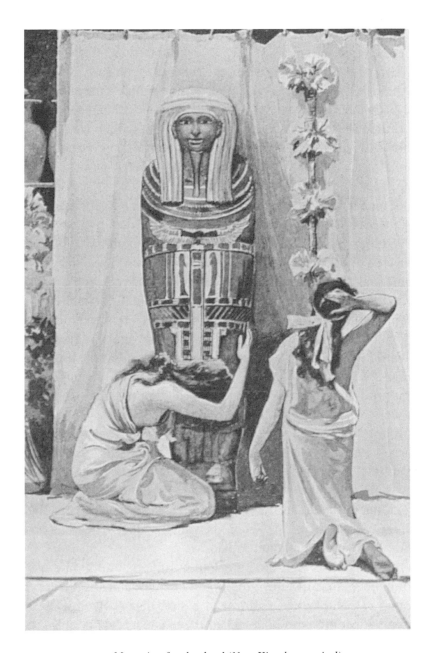

Mourning for the dead (New Kingdom period)
From the drawing by J. R. Weguelin RWS

represented in bird form with a human head hovering over the sahu, or mummy, on which it gazes wistfully, always seeking to re-enter the bandaged form. Like the ka, it required nourishment, which was provided, however, by the goddess of the consecrated burial ground.

The khaybet, or shadow, is evidently the survival of an early belief. It is really another manifestation of the ka. Like all primitive peoples, the ancient Egyptians believed that their shadows were their souls. Higher concepts evolved in time, but their cultured descendants clung to the old belief, which was perpetuated by folk customs associated with magic practices. Spells were wrought by casting shadows on a man, and he might be insulted or injured if an offence were committed against his shadow.

The ran, or name, was also a manifestation of the ka. Power could be exercised by uttering the name, because there was magic influence in those words, which were believed to have spiritual 'doubles'. A personal name was the spirit identified; its service was secured when the name was uttered. The spirit was the name and the name was the spirit. If a magician wished to work evil against an individual, he made use of the name when uttering potent magical formulae. The dead were similarly conjured up when their names were spoken in invocations; evil spirits were cast out by those who knew their names.[1] To guard himself against wizards who uttered 'words of power', or verbal spells, the Egyptian therefore considered it necessary to have two names – the big name and the little name, or the true name and the good name. He kept his 'big, true name' secret because it was the ran; his 'good little name' was his nickname and was not a part of his living being.

The naming ceremony was conducted in secret. The child's fate was bound up in the true name and his character was influenced by it. After it was conferred, a nickname was used, but the true name was the grave name and was uttered when the welfare of the spirit was secured by the utterance of magic spells that 'opened the way' in the land of the dead. The gods had rans also. When Isis obtained the secret name of Ra, she became his equal.

The diverging concepts regarding the soul in Egyptian religion arose from the mingling of beliefs caused by the mingling of peoples, and also the Egyptian tendency to cling to every belief, or form of belief, that evolved in the course of time in Egypt. A people who believed in the existence of 'doubles' and in the transmigration of souls had many vague and complex concepts. Incoherencies were a feature of their religious beliefs. It must be borne in mind, at the same time, that this review covers a vast period of time, during which various religious cults exercised supreme influence in moulding Egyptian thought. One cult predominated at one period; another cult arose in turn to teach its own peculiar tenets, with the result that all beliefs were ultimately accepted. This process is

[1] The 'ceremony of riddance' referred to by Isocrates.

clearly indicated by the various burial customs and the complex religious ceremonies that prevailed in different ages.

As has been seen, the early people buried their dead crouched up in shallow graves with due provision of nourishment and implements.[1] They appear to have believed that the ka remained beside the body until the flesh decayed. Then it either ceased to be or it haunted the cemetery. Among primitive peoples much concern was evinced regarding the ghosts of the newly dead.

The Egyptian tree worshippers conceived a tree goddess who gave food cakes and poured out drink to disembodied kas. The influence of this ancient cult is traced in the Osiris and Bata folk tales. In late Dynastic times, tree worship was revived when the persisting beliefs of the common people gained ascendancy, and it took a long time to disappear in the Delta region, where the sacred tree and the holy well were regarded with reverence.

The Horus-worshipping, or Dynastic, Egyptians who pressed northwards on their gradual campaign of conquest, introduced a new burial custom. Instead of digging shallow graves, they erected brick-lined tombs in which the dead were laid on their backs, fully extended, clad in state and adorned with articles of jewellery. In the inscriptions, the ka and khu are referred to, but no attempt was made, even in the First and Second Dynasties, to preserve the body from decay, and sumptuous offerings were placed in the tombs.

Another burial custom involved secondary interment, as was the case in those European districts where early graves have been found to contain disconnected skeletons. In Egypt attempts were sometimes made to arrange the bones in proper position, but they were often heaped in confusion. It appears that temporary interment was a ceremony of riddance, the object being probably to hasten the departure of the ka. Dismemberment was also practised, and many graves show that decapitation was carried out after death.

In one of the sacred books of ancient Egypt, the mutilation of dead bodies is referred to with horror. 'I shall not be destroyed,' it records, 'my head will not be cut off, nor my tongue taken out, nor will the hair of my head or my eyebrows be shaved off. My body will endure for all time.'

The revolt against dismemberment took place at the beginning of the Third Dynasty, about 2700 BC. Massive stone tombs were then constructed and the bodies of the dead were mummified. The idea was either that the ka would ultimately return and cause the dead to live again or that the existence of the soul in the nether world depended on the existence of the body upon earth. The embalming of the dead ultimately became general throughout Egypt, but the belief in dismemberment survived in the practice of disjointing one of the mummy's feet. During the Middle Kingdom period, the dead were laid on their left sides, as if to

[1] This burial custom survived at least as late as the Fifth Dynasty, when mummification was well established.

peer through the Osiris or Horus eyes that were depicted outside the mummy cases.

Herodotus, who visited Egypt in the fifth century BC, found the people 'adhering contentedly to the customs of their ancestors, and averse to foreign manners'. He related that when an influential man died, the women of the household smeared their hands and faces with dirt, and ran through the streets with their clothes in disorder, beating their bodies and lamenting aloud. The men behaved in a similar manner after the corpse was removed from the house.

Embalmers were licensed to practise their profession, and they displayed much ingenuity and surgical skill. When a body was taken to them, they produced models of mummies and arranged a price. The quality of their work depended on the amount of money spent by the dead person's friends.

The costliest method of embalming was as follows. The brain was extracted through the nostrils with the aid of instruments and after the infusion of a chemical preparation. Then a stone knife was used to make an incision on one side of the body. The liver, heart, lungs and intestines were immediately drawn out, and, after being cleansed, they were steeped in palm wine and sprinkled with rich perfume. The body was dried, and stuffed with powdered myrrh, cassia, etc, and sewn up. It was afterwards covered with nitre for seventy days. Then it was washed all over and carefully wrapped in bandages that had been dipped in a strong gum. As soon as it was carried back to the home, it was placed in a large coffin, shaped like a human form, that was inscribed with magic charms and decorated with sacred symbols and figures of gods and goddesses. The face of the dead was carved on the lid; in the Roman period it was painted.

A cheaper method of embalming was to inject a chemical preparation before the body was covered with nitre. At the end of seventy days, the intestines were drawn out. Nothing then remained except the skin and bones; the flesh had been eaten away by the nitre. Poor people could only afford to have a cheap preservative injected into the veins, after which the body was left in nitre for the usual period.

The intestines were placed in four canopic jars, on the lids of which were often shaped the heads of the four protecting gods, who were the sons of Horus and represented the north, south, east and west. These were Amset, with a human face, who guarded the stomach and large intestines; Haapi, with a dog's head, who guarded the small intestines; Duamutef, with a jackal's head, who guarded lungs and heart; and Kebeh-senuf, the hawk-headed, who guarded the liver and gall bladder. These jars were placed in a chest and deposited in the tomb. The organs they contained were those that were believed to have caused the various sins to be committed.

The funeral procession was a solemn and touching spectacle. All the family were present, and women mourners wailed aloud on the way to the cemetery on the western bank of the Nile. The mummy was drawn along on a sledge. When the tomb was reached, the coffin was set up on end, facing the south, and an elaborate ceremony was gone through. It was conducted by the chief mourner, who recited the ritual from a papyrus roll while responses were made by the relatives. Two females represented Isis and Nepthys, for a part of the ceremony was a reproduction of the scene enacted around the body of Osiris when it was restored and prepared for burial. The dead had also to be instructed how to reach the Egyptian heaven. The journey could not be accomplished in safety without the aid of magic formulae. So these were spoken into the ears of the corpse, as was probably the custom in the days of crouched burials. But the danger was ever present that the dead would fail to remember all the priestly instructions which were repeated over them. The formulae were therefore inscribed on the coffin and on the walls of the tomb, and as time went on it became customary to prepare rolls of papyrus, which were ultimately collected into the *Book of the Dead*. This papyrus might be wrapped under the mummy bandages or else laid within the coffin. A bull was slaughtered to provide food for the sustenance of the ka and as a sacrifice to the gods.

The coffin was afterwards lowered down the grave shaft to the secret chamber in which had been placed the image of the dead, his or her weapons and clothing, ornaments and perfumes and, perhaps, several articles of furniture. Then the entrance was closed up with stonework. A funeral feast in the antechamber concluded a ceremony that grew more and more elaborate as time went on. Food offerings were afterwards brought at intervals by faithful mourners.

There were two distinct concepts of the afterlife, and these became confused in the ages that followed. The sun worshippers believed that the souls of the dead passed to the first division of night, where those who were privileged to utter the magic spells that could compel the obedience of the gods were permitted to enter the barque of Ra. In their tombs were placed models of the sun boat.

The Otherworld concept of the Osirian cult made more permanent appeal to the Egyptian mind. Heaven is pictured as the 'double' of the Delta region, where apparently the concept had its origin. But, before it can be reached, the soul must travel a long and weary way that is beset by many perils. The paradise of Aalu is situated in the west. Bleak and waterless deserts have to be crossed, and these are infested by fierce reptiles. Boiling streams also intercept the pilgrim, who is always in danger of being compelled to turn back.

When the soul sets out, he takes with him his stave and his weapons and also food for nourishment. He climbs the western mountains and then enters the Kingdom of the Dead. An immense sycamore tree towers before him with great clusters of fruit amidst its luxuriant foliage. As he approaches it, a goddess leans out from the trunk, as from a window, displaying the upper part of her body. In her hands she holds a tray heaped with cakes and fruit. She also has a pot of clear fresh water. The soul must eat the magic food and drink the magic water, and thus become a servant of the gods if he is to proceed farther. If he rejects the hospitality of the tree goddess, he will have to return again to the dark and narrow tomb from which he came and lead forever there a solitary and joyless existence.

The soul of he who is faithful eats and drinks as desired, and then proceeds on the journey, facing many perils and enduring great trials. Evil spirits and fierce demons surround him, desiring that he should die a second death and cease to be. A gigantic tortoise rises against him. He must fight against it with his lance. Serpents are poised to strike, and they must be overcome. The very insects have poisonous stings and must be driven away. But his most formidable enemy is the fierce god Seth, the murderer of Osiris, the terror of the good gods and of men, who appears as an enormous red monster with a head like a camel and the body of a hound, his long and forked tail erect and venomous, eager to devour the pilgrim on his way.

When the evil god is overcome and driven back, the soul goes forward until he reaches the bank of a wide river. There a magic boat awaits him. The crew consist of silent divinities who give him no aid. But before he can embark he must answer each question that the boat addresses to him. He must know and tell how it is constructed in every part, and if the papyrus roll that was laid beside his mummy contains the secrets of the boat and the magic formulae that must also be repeated, he will be ferried over the river and taken to the Osirian kingdom. The sulky 'ferryman' is called Turnface – his face is always turned away from the dead who call to him.

After entering the boat the soul's journey is not yet near to its end. He wishes greatly to join those happy beings who have their dwellings in the blessed fields of Aalu, but he must first be tried before Osiris, the King of the Dead and Judge of All. The only approach to paradise is through the hall of justice, which rises before him, stupendous and dark and full of mystery. The gate is shut fast. No man can draw the bolts or enter without the permission of the king.

Alone, and trembling with fear, the pilgrim soul stands before the gate with both hands uplifted in adoration. He is beheld by the shining god who is inside. Then, in a clear, full voice the soul cries out in the deep silence:

> Hail, unto you, O great god, you who are lord of truth!
> Lo! I draw nigh to thee now, O my lord, and my eyes behold you beauty.
> You I know, and I know also the two-and-forty gods assembled with you in
>   the hall of justice;
> They observe all the deeds of the wicked;
> They devour those who seek to do evil;
> They drink the blood of those who are condemned before you, O just and
>   good king.

Judgment Scene; Weighing the heart
The judge is Osiris, behind whom stand Isis and Nepthys. Horus and Anubis lead in two forms
of deceased. Thoth makes the record, another form of Anubis adjusts the balance, and the
monster waits to destroy the deceased if the verdict is unfavourable. On the upper part of the
picture, the deceased salutes some of the forty-two gods who surround the Judgment Hall.
From Book of the Dead *papayrus.*

Hail! Lord of Justice; you I know,
I come before you even now to speak what is true;
I will not utter what is false, O Lord of All.

The soul then recites the ritual confession in which he claims to be guiltless of
the offences that are punishable:

I have done no evil against any man.
I have never caused my kinsfolk to be put to death,
I have not caused false witnesses to speak in the hall of justice.
I have not done that which is hated by the gods.
I am not a worker of wickedness.
I have never oppressed a servant with too much work.
I have not caused men to hunger nor to weep.
I have not been devoid of good works, nor have I acted weakly or with
    meanness.
I am not a murderer.
I have not conspired to have another put to death.
I have not plotted to make another grieve.

I have not taken away temple offerings.

I have not stinted the food offered to the gods.

I have not despoiled the dead.

I have never committed adultery.

I have not failed to keep myself pure as a priest.

I have not lessened the corn measure.

I have not shortened the hand measure.

I have not tampered with the balance.

I have not deprived children of milk.

I have not stolen cattle from the meadows.

I have not snared the birds consecrated to the gods.

I have not taken fish from holy lakes.

I have not prevented (Nile) water from running (in channels).

I have not turned aside the water.

I have not stolen water from a channel.

I have not put out the fire when it should burn.

I have never kept from the Nine Gods what was their due.

I have not prevented the temple cattle from grazing on my land.

I have not obstructed a god (his image) when he came forth (in a festival procession).

The soul concludes by declaring that he is sinless and expresses the hope that no ill will befall him in the hall of judgment.

The jackal-headed god Anubis, 'opener of the ways', then strides from the hall and leads the soul by the hand before Osiris, who had heard the confession in silence. No word is uttered as the dead man enters. The King of the Dead sits on his high throne within a dim pavilion. His crown is on his head. In one hand he holds the crook and in the other the flail. He is the supreme judge of the dead. Before him stands the sure balance on which the heart of the dead man will be weighed. Thoth, the recording god, is beside it, and Horus and Maat, goddess of truth and justice, are there also. The guardian of the balance is a monster, which is ready to fall upon sinners who are condemned before the great god. Around the dread hall crouch the forty-two animal gods who tear the wicked to pieces.

In the tingling silence that prevails, the pilgrim again recites the confession. Osiris makes no comment. Then, quivering with fear, the soul watches the gods deliberately weighing his heart in the balance, while Maat, the goddess of truth and justice, or her symbol, an ostrich feather, occupies the opposite scale.

The trembling soul cries out to his heart not to witness against him. 'O heart that was mine,' he says, 'do not say "Behold the things he has done." Permit me not to be wronged in the presence of the great god.'

If the heart is found to be neither too heavy nor too light, the dead man is acquitted. Thoth makes known the result of the weighing to Osiris, who then orders the heart to be restored to the man on trial. 'He has won the victory,' the King of the Dead exclaims. 'Now let him dwell with the spirits and the gods in the fields of Aalu.'

Released and rejoicing, the dead man goes forth to gaze on the wonders of the nether world. The divine kingdom is a greater and more glorious Egypt in which the souls work and hunt and combat against their enemies as in other days. To each man is allotted his task. He must till the soil and reap the grain that grows in abundance and to a great height. The harvest never fails, and famine and sorrow are unknown.

When the soul wishes to return to visit familiar scenes on earth, it enters the body of a bird or an animal, or perhaps it blossoms as a flower. It may also visit the tomb as the ba and reanimate the mummy and go forth to gaze on scenes that were familiar and dear in other days.

The souls of dead men whom Osiris condemns, because of sins committed on earth, are subjected to terrible tortures before they are devoured by the animal gods who crouch, waiting, in the silent and awful hall of judgment.

Chapter 8
The Religion of the Stone Workers

Memphite Religion – The Cult of Ptah – Ethical Beliefs – Pharaoh worshipped as a God – 'Husband of his Mother' – Magical Incantations – 'Mesmerising the Gods' – The Earliest Mastabas – Endowment of Tomb Chapels – The Servants of the Dead – Scenes of Everyday Life – Djoser's Two Tombs – The First Pyramid – An Architect who became a God – Inspiration of Egyptian Religion – How it promoted Civilisation – Mythology of the Stone Builders – Ptah and Khnum – The Frog Goddess – A Prototype of Isis – A Negroid Deity – Khnum associated with Khufu (Cheops).

When Old Memphis became the leading city of the united Egypt, the religious beliefs of the mingled peoples were in the process of fusion and development. Commerce was flourishing, and ideas were being exchanged as freely as commodities. In the growing towns men of many creeds and different nationalities were brought into close personal contact, and thought was stimulated by the constant clash of opinions. It was an age of change and marked progress. Knowledge was being rapidly accumulated and more widely diffused. Society had become highly organised, and archaic tribal beliefs could no longer be given practical application under the new conditions that obtained throughout the land. A new religion became a necessity – at any rate existing beliefs had to be unified and systematised in the interests of peace and order, especially in a city like Memphis with its large and cosmopolitan population.

The cult that began to mummify the dead had evidently formulated a creed that appealed to the intellectual classes. Beliefs regarding the afterlife took definite shape. The 'land of shades' was organised like the land of Egypt. Ideas of right living and good government prevailed, and the growth of ethical thought was reflected in the conception of a judge of the dead who justified or condemned people after consideration of their actions during life. The attributes of the principal gods were defined. Their powers and their places were adjusted. They were grouped in triads and families, and from the mass of diverging beliefs was evolving a complex mythology that was intended not only to instruct but to unite the rival beliefs prevailing in a community.

Egyptian religion as a whole, however, was never completely systematised at this or any subsequent period. Each locality had its own theological system. The old tribal gods remained supreme in their nomes and when they were grouped with others; the influence at work was more political than intellectual in character. The growth of culture did not permeate through all classes of society, and the common people, especially in rural districts, clung to the folk beliefs and practices of their ancestors. A provincial nobleman, supported by the priests, secured the loyalty of his followers, therefore, by upholding the prestige of their ancient god, who could be linked, if needs be, with the deity of another tribe with whom a union had been brought about. If the doctrines of a rival creed influenced the beliefs of the people of a particular district, the attributes of the rival god were then attached to their own. When Ptah, for instance, ceased to make an intellectual appeal as a creation craftsman, he was exalted above Ra and the other gods, whom he was considered to have brought into existence by uttering magic words.

Ptah, as we have seen, was linked with Osiris. The combined deity was at once the god of the industrial and agricultural classes and the judge of the dead. He was the chief deity of the new religion that controlled the everyday life of the people. He was the Revealer who made city life possible by promoting law and order as a religious necessity, and by instructing the people how to live honourably and well. He ordained the fate of all. He rewarded the virtuous and punished the sinners. Masters were required to deal humanely with their servants and servants to perform their duties with diligence and obedience. Children were counselled to honour their parents lest they might complain to the god and he should hear them.

The supremacy of Ptah was not yet seriously threatened by the sun god Ra, whose cult was gathering strength at Heliopolis. For a full century the ascendancy of the Memphite cult was complete and unassailable. The influence of the north was thus predominant. The Horite religion, which was a form of sun worship, had been displaced. It was overshadowed by the Ptah-Osiris creed. Apparently the people of Lower Egypt had achieved an intellectual conquest of their conquerors. The Osirian paradise was a duplicate of the Delta region, and the new creed was strongly influenced by Osirian beliefs that had prevailed before Meni's day.

Although great rivalry existed between the various cults throughout the land, the people were united in revering the pharaoh. He was exalted as a god. Indeed he was regarded as an incarnation of the ruling deity. Until the Fourth Dynasty the monarch was the living Osiris. Then he became the earthly manifestation of Ra, the sun god. The people believed that a deity must needs take human form to associate with mankind. His ka, therefore, entered the king's body as the king's ka entered his statue. In temple scenes we find the people engaged in worshipping pharaoh. In fact, the pharaoh might worship himself—he made offerings to his ka, which was the ka of a god.

The idea of the divinity of kings was, no doubt, a survival of ancestor worship. Families worshipped the spirit of their dead father and tribes that of their departed leader. But the pharaoh was not like other men, who became divine after death. He was divine from birth. His father had been the ruling god and his mother the god's wife. On the walls of temples elaborate scenes were carved to remind the people of the divine origin of their ruler. At the marriage ceremony the king impersonated the god, and he was accompanied by his divine attendants. As Ptah Tanen he wore 'the high feathers' and two ram's horns, and carried the holy symbols. As Osiris he appeared with crook and flail. As Ra he was crowned with the sun disc. The queen was thus married to the god within his temple. In sculptured scenes depicting royal births we see goddesses in attendance as midwives, nurses and foster mothers. This close association with deities was supposed to continue throughout the pharaoh's life. He was frequently shown in company of gods and goddesses.

When the king died, the spirit of the god passed to his successor. The son, therefore, according to Egyptian reasoning, became his own father, and, in the theological sense, 'husband of his mother'. Horus, who was born after Osiris was slain, was 'the purified image of his sire'. In one of the religious chants the same idea is given expression when it is declared that 'the god Geb was before his mother'. The new pharaoh, on ascending the throne, became doubly divine, because both ideas regarding the divinity of kings were perpetuated at the same time.

The worship of a particular pharaoh did not cease when he died. Like other departed souls, he required the service of the living. His priests must assist him to reach the Osirian paradise of Aalu, or the sun barque of Ra. Even Ra had to be assisted to pass through the perilous hour divisions of the night. Indeed all the good forces of Nature had to be continually prompted by men who desired to be benefited by them. Similarly the evil forces had to be thwarted by the performance of magic ceremonies and the repetition of magic formulae. Egyptian religion was based on belief in magic.

Pharaoh's body was therefore mummified, so that his soul might continue to exist and be able to return to reanimate the bandaged form. Food offerings were given regularly for the sustenance of the ka. Magic ceremonies, which were religious ceremonies, were performed to cause the gods to act and to speak as was desired—to imitate those who impersonated them upon earth. The priests were supposed, as it were, to mesmerise the gods when they went through their elaborate ceremonies of compulsion and their ceremonies of riddance.

It was considered necessary to provide secure protection for the pharaoh's mummy, as his enemies might seek to dismember it with the purpose of termi-

Servitors bringing their offerings
From the bas-relief in the mastaba of Ti, Saqqara

nating the life of the soul. Substantial tombs were therefore erected, and the old brick and wood erections that were constructed for the kings at Abydos went out of fashion.

A tomb chamber was hewed out of solid rock, and over it was built an oblong platform structure of limestone, called a mastaba. The mummy was lowered down the shaft, which was afterwards filled up with sand and gravel and closed with masonry. This low and flat-roofed building was large enough to accommodate at least a hundred bodies, but it was made solid throughout with the exception of the secret shaft. Robbers would have to wreck it completely before the hiding place of the body could be discovered. On the east side there was a false door through which the ka could pass when it came from, or departed towards, the western land of shades. In time a little chapel was provided, and the false door was placed at the end of it. This apartment was used for the performance of the ceremonies associated with the worship of the dead. Mourners came with offerings and met in the presence of the invisible ka.

The statue was concealed in an inner chamber, which was built up, but occasionally narrow apertures were constructed through which food and drink were given to the ka. But only to kings and rich men could this service be rendered for a prolonged period, so the practice ultimately evolved of providing the dead with models of offerings, which by a magic process gave sustenance to the hungry spirit.

Mortuary chapels were endowed as early as the First Dynasty. Priests were regularly engaged in worshipping dead kings and princes who had made provision in their wills for the necessary expenses. The son of one monarch in the Fourth Dynasty devoted the revenues of a dozen towns to maintain the priesthood attached to his tomb. This custom created grave financial problems.

In a few generations the whole land might be mortgaged to maintain mortuary chapels, with the result that a revolution involving a change of dynasty became an economic necessity.

> Hearken! you kings, while horror stalks the land,
> Lo! your poor people fall a ready prey
> Made weak by your oppression, even in death—
> Burdened and bruised and terrorised; their lands
> Tax-ridden for these temples you endowed,
> That fawning priests might meek obeisance make
> And render ceaseless homage to your shades.

The walls of the chapel were either sculpted in low relief or painted with scenes of daily life, and from these we gather much of what we know regarding the manners and customs of the ancient people. But such works of art were not intended merely to be decorative or to perpetuate the fame of the dead. It was desired that those scenes should be duplicated in paradise. The figures of farm servants sowing and reaping corn, of artisans erecting houses, and cooks preparing meals, were expected to render similar services to the departed soul. Magic texts were inscribed with the purpose of ensuring this happy condition of affairs. Others called down curses on the heads of tomb robbers.

Kings and nobles had no pleasure in the prospect that they would have to perform humble tasks in the nether world. There they wished to occupy the exalted stations that they had enjoyed on earth. It was necessary, therefore, to have numerous employees so that their mansions might be erected, their fields cultivated and their luxuries provided as of old.

The custom at first obtained of slaying a number of servants to accompany the great dignitary to paradise. These poor victims were supposed to be grateful because they were to be rewarded with assured immortality. But the shedding of blood was rendered unnecessary when the doctrine obtained that substitutes could be provided by sculptors and painters.

Another mortuary custom was to provide little figures, called *ushebtiu*, 'the answerers', inscribed with magic formulae, which would obey the dead and perform whatever duties he desired of them in paradise. These were ultimately shaped in mummy form, and in the later dynasties were made of glazed ware because wooden figures suffered from the ravages of the white ant.

Many toy-like figures of servants are found in early tombs. Here we discover, perhaps, the model of a nobleman's dwelling. An ox is being slain in the

Ushebtiu figures of various periods
1 Limestone, made for Ahmosis I (Eighteenth Dynasty). 2 Limestone (Twelfth Dynasty.
3 Painted alabaster, about 1100 BC. 4 Porcelain, inscribed for an official (Twenty-sixth Dynasty).
5 Zoned alabaster, probably made for a king, about 1200 BC. 6 Limestome, about 800 BC.
7 Painted limestone, about 550 BC. (British Museum)
Figures 1 and 6 are inscribed with versions of Chapter 6 of Book of the Dead.

backyard. In the kitchen members of the staff are engaged in cooking an elaborate meal; one man devotes himself entirely to a goose that he turns on a spit before the fire. We have a glimpse of high life in another scene. The nobleman has feasted, and he sits at ease in a large apartment listening to singers and harpists. A dancing girl comes out to whirl before him, while her companions keep time to the music by clapping their hands. Meanwhile artisans are busy in their workshops. We see a potter moulding a vessel of exquisite shape, while near at hand a carpenter saws wood with which he intends to construct an elaborate piece of furniture. Boats are rocking at a pier, for the soul may desire to sail down the Nile of the nether world. Here, in fact, is a boat pursuing its way. A dozen strenuous oarsmen occupy the benches, while the steersman stands erect at the helm with the guiding rope in his hands. Armed men are on guard, and the nobleman sits with a friend below an awning on a small deck in the centre of the boat, calmly engaged in playing a game of draughts.

King Djoser had two tombs erected for himself. One is a great brick mastaba at Abydos, which may have been a 'soul house', in the chapel of which his 'double' was worshipped. The other, which is made of limestone, is situated in the desert behind Memphis. The latter is of particular interest to students of Egyptian history. It is a terraced structure nearly 200 feet (61 metres) in height, formed by a series of mastabas of decreasing size superimposed one above another. This wonderful building is called the Step Pyramid of Saqqara. It is not only the first pyramid that was erected in Egypt but the earliest great stone structure in the world.

So much attention is paid to the three pyramids at Giza that Djoser's limestone tomb is apt to be overlooked. Yet it is of marked importance in the history of the country. It was constructed nearly a hundred years before Khufu (Cheops) ascended the throne, and the experience gained in undertaking a work of such vast dimensions made possible the achievements of later times. The architect was the famous Imhotep, vizier of the Third-Dynasty pharaoh, Djoser. His fame was perpetuated in Egypt until the Saite or Restoration period, when he was worshipped as the god called Imuthes by the Greeks. He was an inventive and organising genius, and a statesman who exercised much influence at the court of Djoser. Like Solomon, he was reputed to be the wisest man of his age. He was the author of a medical treatise, and he left behind him a collection of proverbs that endured as long as the old Egyptian language. As a patron of learning, his memory was revered by the scribes for over two thousand years, and it was their custom before beginning work to pour out a libation to his spirit from their jars.

The Step Pyramid was Imhotep's conception. He prepared the plans and overlooked the work of construction. No doubt, too, he was responsible for the organisation of the army of labourers and artisans who were employed for a prolonged period in erecting this enduring memorial of a great monarch.

Such a vast undertaking is a sure indication of the advanced character of the civilisation of the times. Much wealth must have accumulated in the royal exchequer. The country was in a settled and prosperous condition owing to the excellent system of government and the activity of administrators. It was no small task to bring together thousands of workmen, who had to be housed and fed and kept under control. Skilled tradesmen were employed, who had been trained in quarrying and dressing stone. Evidently masonry had flourished in Memphis for a considerable period. There were hundreds of overseers experienced in the organisation of labour, and large numbers of educated scribes conversant with the exact keeping of accounts.

Education was no longer confined to the ruling classes. We know that there were schools in Memphis. Boys were instructed in 'the three Rs', and in a papyrus of maxims it was quaintly remarked that they could 'hear with their backs', an indication as to the manner in which corporal punishment was inflicted. The system of writing was the cursive style called hieratic, which originated in pre-Dynastic times as a rough imitation in outline of hieroglyphics. A knowledge of elementary arithmetic was required in the ordinary transactions of business. Some corrected exercises have survived. Advanced pupils were instructed in geometry – which had its origin in Egypt – in measurement and in the simpler problems of algebra.

As the Egyptians were an intensely practical people, school studies were specialised. Boys were trained for the particular profession in which they were to be employed. If they were to become businessmen, they attended commercial classes. The number of 'trial pieces' that have been found show that young sculptors attended technical schools, as did also artists and metal workers. In the temple colleges the future officials and lawyers and doctors were made conversant with the accumulated knowledge and wisdom of the age. Education was evidently controlled by the priests.

Memphis was a hive of organised industry. The discipline of business pervaded all classes, and everywhere law and order were promoted. Pharaoh was no idler. His day was fully occupied in the transaction of public business, and to every prince was allotted a responsible post, and his duties had to be efficiently performed. The nation was in its youth: the foundations had been securely established of a great civilisation that was to endure for some thirty centuries.

It may be said that the royal house of the Old Kingdom was established on a rock. When the pharaoh's builders discarded brick and began to quarry and hew stone, Egyptian civilisation made rapid progress. It had its beginnings in the struggle with Nature in the Nile valley. An increasing population was maintained under peaceful conditions when the problem of water distribution was solved by the construction of canals. These had to be controlled, and the responsibility of a regulated flow was imposed on the pharaoh. Good government, therefore, became a necessity; a failure of water caused famine and insurrection. To those who toiled and those who protected the toiler, Nature gave a bountiful reward. More food was produced than was required for home consumption. The surplus yield of corn was, as we have seen, the means of promoting trade, which made Egypt a wealthy country. As capital accumulated, the progress of knowledge was assured, and men entered on those higher pursuits that promote moral and intellectual advancement.

Egypt might have continued happily on the even tenor of its way as an agricultural and trading country but its civilisation could never have attained so high a degree of perfection if its arts and industries had not been fostered and developed. We may not think highly of Egyptian religion, of which, after all, we have but imperfect knowledge, but we must recognise that it was the inspiration of the architects and craftsmen whose achievements we regard with wonder and admiration after the lapse of thousands of years. It was undoubtedly a civilising agency. It promoted culture and refinement and encouraged people to love beauty for its own sake. Egyptian art flourished because it was appreciated and was in demand.

The surplus wealth of Egypt was expended largely for religious purposes. Temple building kept architects and sculptors constantly engaged; an ever-increasing class of skilled workers had also to be trained, disciplined and organised. Men of ability were brought to the front and were judged on their own merits. There is no place for pretenders in the world of art. When the pharaohs, therefore, undertook the building of temples and tombs they not only ensured regularity of labour but also stimulated intellectual effort, with results that could not have been otherwise than beneficial to society at large.

We may well regard the conquest of stone as one of the greatest conquests that the Egyptians achieved. In the Introduction it was suggested that the new industry may have been introduced by the cave-hewing pre-Semitic inhabitants of southern Palestine. The remarkable skill manifested by the earliest stone workers of Egypt with almost dramatic suddenness was evidently the result of long experience. Deft workmanship was accomplished from the outset; stones were measured and dressed with accuracy and skill. The changes that took place in burial customs during the early dynasties also suggest that influences from without were being felt in the ancient kingdom.

Whatever the origin of the stone workers may have been, it is evident that they were closely associated with Memphis at a very early period. As we have seen, the art of stone working and stone building on a grand scale was first displayed by the worshippers of Ptah, the craftsman god. It is of special interest to find, therefore, that Manetho has preserved those persistent Egyptian traditions that connect Memphis with the new industry. He credited Djoser, the builder of the Step Pyramid at Saqqara, with the introduction of stonework. He also recorded that the first temple in Egypt was erected to Ptah at Memphis by King Meni. The city's name of White Walls suggests that the fortress was constructed of lime-stone.

We know now that stone was used at Abydos before Djoser's day – not, however, until after the conquest of the north – but the traditional association of Memphis with the new industry is none the less significant. The probability that a colony of Memphite artisans settled in the vicinity of the Aswan quarries and introduced stone working into Upper Egypt is emphasised by the worship of Khnum, the god of the First Cataract, who bears so striking a resembling to Ptah. He was similarly regarded as the modeller of the world. Like Ptah, he was associated with the chaos egg, and he is depicted shaping the first man on his potter's wheel.

Khnum was merged at an early date with the ram god Min, for he is invariably shown with ram's horns or a ram's head. He was a Great Father, and represented the male principle. His consort is Hekt, the frog-headed goddess, who is evidently of great antiquity. The Egyptians believed that frogs were generated spontaneously from Nile-fertilised mud, and they associated Hekt with the origin of life. This quaint goddess was one of the 'mothers' who was supposed to preside at birth, and so persistent was the reverence shown her by the great mass of the people that she was ultimately fused with Hathor. In Coptic times Hekt was a symbol of the resurrection.

Another goddess associated with Khnum was named Sati. Her title, Lady of the Heavens, links her with Nut and Hathor. She is usually depicted as a stately woman wearing a cow's horns and the crown of Upper Egypt. She is 'the queen of the gods'.

An island goddess, called Anukt, belongs to the same group. She is dark-skinned and wears a crown of feathers.

It is apparent that this arbitrary grouping of deities at the First Cataract was the direct result of the mingling of peoples of different origin. Hekt represents a purely Egyptian cult, while Sati is evidently one of the forms of the Great Mother deity of the earliest civilised people in the Nile valley. She resembles closely the historic Isis. Anukt, on the other hand, was probably of Nubian origin and may have been introduced by those settlers from the south whose aggressive tendencies caused so much concern at the royal court from time to time. The theory that Khnum was the god of the quarries, and builders especially, is supported not only by his resemblance to Ptah but also by the fact that the pharaoh who erected the greatest pyramid at Giza was called Khnum Khufu – this is the monarch whom the Greeks called Cheops.

Chapter 9

A Day in Old Memphis

In the Streets – The Temple of Ptah – Glimpses of Life – A Dispute – Old Age is honoured – A Dignified Nobleman – High-born Women – Racial Types – Bearers of Temple Offerings – In the Slums – Crafttsmen at Work – The Marketplace – Fresh Fish on Sale – On the Quays – Sailors from Crete – Pharaoh's Soldiers – Arrest of the Tax Collectors – A Significant Folk Tale – The Wronged Peasant – His Appeal to the Judge – Eloquent Speeches – Honoured by His Majesty.

As we look at the scenes depicted in tombs, read the inscriptions and piece together fragments of papyri containing old legends, we are afforded vivid glimpses of life in the Old Kingdom. The great city of Memphis is conjured up before us. Its gates lie open, and armed guards permit us to enter. We walk through the crowded streets, pausing now and again to look at the people as they come and go, or, perhaps, we loiter in front of a yard or workshop, watching the busy craftsmen plying their trades.

We pass through a main thoroughfare. Most of the houses are built of brick. The dwellings of the poor are of wattles daubed with clay. Now we enter a spacious square, in the centre of which towers a huge statue of the pharaoh. The sun is hot, although it is still early morning, and we seek the shadow of that vast dominating building around which the city has grown up. It is the stone temple of the god Ptah, grandly severe in outline and fronted by two noble pylons of massive proportions. We peer through the gateway as we pass. A procession of priests is crossing an inner court, across which fall the broad shadows of great square pillars that are set widely apart and support immense blocks of limestone. One is impressed by the air of mystery and solemnity that pervades the temple interior.

We can seat ourselves here on the stone bench and watch the crowds pouring in from the streets. Memphis is a wonderfully quiet city. There is a constant hum of voices. It murmurs like a great beehive, but there is no clatter of traffic, for the streets are devoid of vehicles, and horses are as yet unknown in Egypt. Peasants from the countryside are leading their asses laden with salt, corded bales, rushes for basket-makers, bundles of papyrus stalks and hard stones. Great burdens are carried on the shoulders of labourers. Even boys stagger under heavy loads.

Everyone is scantily clad. Men of the lower classes wear only a loincloth, while those of higher social rank have short kilts of linen, which are strapped around their waists with leather belts. Women of all ranks are gowned to the ankles, and ladies have skirts so narrow that they walk with short steps but yet gracefully.

Half-naked the men may be, yet it is not difficult to distinguish the various classes. There is no mistaking the labourer, even although his burden has been delivered, or the tradesman, for he carries his tools. Here is a busy merchant knitting his brows, and there a bland-faced scribe with dry, pouting lips and peering eyes set in cobwebs of wrinkles. A few merry students are walking leisurely towards the temple with papyrus rolls under their arms.

A loud clamour of voices in dispute has broken out at a street corner. Two carriers have collided, and the one who has fallen is an Egyptian, the other being a tall African. The smaller man leaps to his feet. Insult has been added to injury, for the alien is a slave, and, fuming with anger, the Egyptian throws himself on the African, who is hampered by his load, and beats him with his fists. A crowd collects, its sympathy evidently with the Egyptian, but suddenly a few city guards rush forward. They hit the combatants with their staves, force them apart and cause them to hasten away. The crowd disperses speedily, and order is again restored.

Note the studied politeness of the greater number of pedestrians. Age is highly honoured. Young men stand aside to allow their seniors to pass; three lads have risen from a shaded seat to make room for an old man who is frail and breathless and wishes to rest a little before he enters the temple.

Now the moving crowd breaks apart, for somebody of importance is coming up the street. He is a nobleman and a royal official of high rank. In the court he is Keeper of the Royal Robes and Sandal-bearer to the Pharaoh. He is also one of those great judges who sit in the Hall of Justice. In his youth he was a college friend of the monarch's and is now privileged at court ceremonies to kiss the royal toe instead of the dust on which it trod. He owns a large estate and has much wealth and influence. As he walks past, the pedestrians salute him respectfully with uplifted arms. He makes no response; he appears to be oblivious to their presence. Mark his imperious air and lordly gait. His kilt is finely embroidered; the upper part of his body is bare; on his head he wears a great stiff wig that falls down behind over his shoulders, protecting his neck from the hot sun. He is square-chested and muscular; he walks erect, with tilted chin. His face is drawn and severe; he has firmly set, drooping lips, and his eyes are stern and proud. He is obviously a man accustomed to command and to be obeyed. A servant shuffles after him carrying his sandals and water bottle.

He has just acknowledged with a curt bow the deep bow of that rich merchant. But now he meets an equal in the middle of the square – Imhotep, chief architect to the king. Before they speak, they both bow gravely, bending their backs, with hands reaching to their knees. Then they converse for a few moments, salute one another again and turn gravely away.

Some high-born ladies have gathered in the shade. Two carry bunches of lotus flowers, and the others smell them with appreciation. Their faces are refined and vivacious, and one is 'black but comely', for she is a Nubian by birth. How they chatter as they flicker their broad fans! Their white gowns are elaborately embroidered in colours, and they all wear sandals, for the builders have left much grit in the streets. Their wigs are drawn low on their foreheads, round which they are held by engraved bands of silver and gold. Gems sparkle in their necklaces, which are of elaborate design, and one or two wear their wigs set well back to display heavy earrings, which are becoming fashionable. A handsome girl is wearing a broad gold armlet that came from Crete. The others examine it with interest, and when they break into laughter, displaying gleaming white teeth, the girl looks sideways in confusion, for they tease her about her far-travelled lover who gave her that rare ornament. Now they saunter in pairs across the square. They are going down to the quays to sail on the Nile.

There is a variety of racial types about us. The southern Egyptians are almost black, those from the centre of the kingdom are brown, and the Delta people have yellow skins. That bearded man who has just gone past is a Semite from Arabia, and here comes a soft-featured Syrian, walking with an oblique-eyed Sumerian from Babylonia. These tall Africans are Nubian mercenaries who were taken captive in a frontier war. Of late the stone builders have been buying them in large numbers, for they have great muscular strength and make excellent labourers.

There is no mistaking the awkward, wide-eyed peasant who came to the market with salt and is now surveying the great city of wonderful buildings and endless streets. That red-haired man who is hurrying past is an Amorite; he came south to barter rugs for corn. He looks behind with an ugly scowl – a carrier has shouted something after him, because an Egyptian peasant dislikes a man who reminds him of red-haired Seth, the slayer of Osiris.

Now here comes a handsome stranger who is exciting much interest. Men and women turn round to look after him. Children regard him with wonder. Not only is he taller than the majority of Memphites, but he is distinguished by his lightly coloured hair and his strange blue eyes. Some would wish to know if his cheeks are a natural red or smeared with face paint. No one doubts from where he came. He is one of the fair Libyans, and he is evidently a man of some importance, for even royal officials acknowledge his salutations. Before we turn away, let us watch that little procession of young peasants walking past. They are carrying offerings and are going to the temple. One lad has shouldered a live calf, another brings a bundle of papyrus stalks, and a third has a basket of flour on his head. The girls carry bunches of flowers, doves in pairs and tame pelicans. One or two

A seated scribe
From the limestone statue in the Louvre, Paris

calves are led by boys. Little notice is taken of the peasants. Processions of similar character are seen daily in Memphis.

We had better cross over quickly, for here comes a great herd of unwilling goats driven by shouting peasants who wield their staves rather freely and do not care whether they miss a goat and strike a pedestrian. The city guards are watching them with interest, for they know their men.

Now turn down this narrow twisting street. Houses are lower here, and some are built with brick, but most of them are constructed of clay-plastered wickerwork. Why not enter this little dwelling? The door lies open, and there is nobody inside. Man and wife labour in a potter's yard. The furniture consists of one or two rough stools, a low bed over which hangs a gnat-protecting net, and here and there are a few jars and pots of coarse pottery. Within the window frame a bunch of lotus leaves is drying in the sun; a cut of salted fish hangs on the wall; a flint knife lies on the floor. The house is used mainly as a sleeping apartment, and if there is a baby it is near the mother in the potter's yard.

Outside, a few children are playing a curious game, which appears to be an imitation of a temple ceremony. Wives of artisans sit gossiping in the shade of a brick building. Some are sewing, and others are cutting vegetables that they have brought from the market. Two girls go past with water pots on their heads.

We have glimpses, as they walk on, of long narrow lanes of small and low-roofed houses. There is evidently much congestion in the poorer quarters of the city. Look through that open door and you will see a busy family. A widow and her three daughters are spinning and weaving fine linen, which might well be mistaken for silk.

Here is a brickyard. Labourers are mixing the clay. Others shape the bricks with a binding of straw and lay them out to dry. Carriers come for those that are ready and take heavy loads in two slings suspended from poles, which they lift on to their shoulders. An overseer hastens them on, for the builders cannot be kept waiting.

Farther on is a stone-worker's yard. Under an awning squat several skilled workers who are engaged in making vessels of alabaster and porphyry. The process is slow and arduous. One has shaped and polished a handsome jar with a fluted lip and narrow neck, and is hollowing it out with a copper-tipped drill that is fed with ground emery. He pauses for a moment to wipe the perspiration from his forehead, and remarks to a fellow: 'This is certainly a handsome vessel.' The other looks up and surveys it critically. 'It is your masterpiece,' he remarks with a smile, and then goes on drilling a large shallow milk bowl.

Two men are cutting a block of porphyry with a copper saw, while an apprentice supplies the emery and relieves them in turn. See how skilfully those labourers are levering a granite boulder into position. It is mounted on a rounded wooden cradle, and slewed this way and that. A lad is gathering wedges with which to raise it up. One or two naked boys, squatting in a shady corner, are watching the proceedings with interest. They are going to saw stone, too, when they grow strong.

We enter another street and our ears are assailed by the clamour of metal workers. It is a noisy quarter. Bang, bang go the hammers on a large sheet of copper. The noise is deafening. Passers-by twitch their eyes and foreheads and hurry on. Look at these naked men kneeling round the blazing furnace, puffing their cheeks and blowing through long pipes. No Egyptian inventor has yet contrived a mechanical bellows. Now the glowing metal is pulled from the furnace, and a

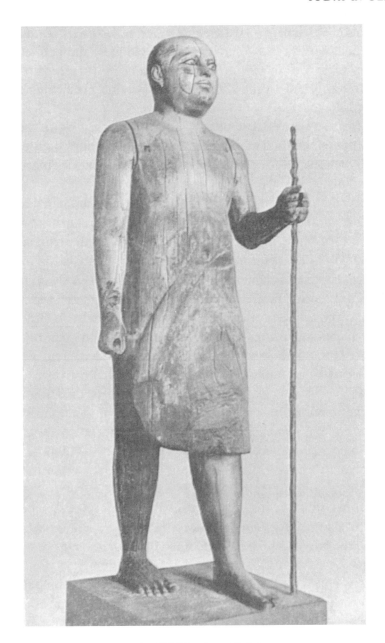

An Old Kingdom official
The name Sheikh-el-Beled (mayor) was given to the statue by the Arabs on account of its
resemblance to a familiar specimen of that modern functionary
From a wooden statue in the Cairo Museum

dozen exhausted workers rise, with their blowpipes in their hands, coughing and rubbing their eyes, to wait until the hammermen need them again.

Here are goldsmiths at work. A man is weighing precious metal in a balance, and a scribe sits in front of him, making careful records on a sheet of papyrus.

117

Nearby are men with clever fingers and keen eyes, who engrave and pierce little pieces of gold and silver, shape earrings and necklaces, and hammer out sheets of gold that are to be inscribed with hieroglyphics. An overseer moves to and fro from bench to bench and worker to worker, surveying everything that is being done with critical eyes.

So we pass from street to street, here watching potters at work, there sculptors and carvers of wood and ivory, and sandal makers and those deft leather cutters who provide gentlemen with a slitted network to suspend on the back of their kilts for sitting on.

Now we reach the principal marketplace. The scene is animated and intensely human. Merchants are squatted beside their stalls, some drowsing in the heat while they wait for buyers, and others gesticulating excitedly while they bargain. There is a good deal of wrangling, and voices are often raised in dispute, while friends gather in knots and chatter and laugh or engage in lively argument. Some make purchases with ring money, but the majority engage in barter. Here a merchant has displayed a fine collection of vases and bowls. A lady surveys his wares critically and shakes her head over the prices he demands; but he waits patiently, for he knows she is tempted to buy and notes that she always returns to a particular porphyry jar of exquisite design.

A woman of the working class leans over a basket of fish and doubts if they are quite fresh. The vendor lifts one, presses it with his fingers and smiles at her. 'Caught this morning,' he says. She decides to have it for her husband's dinner and gives in exchange a piece of red pottery. Another woman barters a small carved box for ointment and perfume, while a man gives a fan for a bundle of onions.

A steward from a nobleman's house passes from stall to stall, accompanied by two servants, making numerous purchases, because several guests of note are coming to the evening meal. He is welcomed, although a hard bargainer, for he pays with money.

We catch, as we turn away, a soothing glimpse of the broad blue river and turn towards it, for the streets are dusty and hot, and we know the air is cooler beside the quays. We cross an open space in which are piled up the cargoes of unloaded boats. Here come half a dozen foreign sailors who are going sightseeing. They also intend to make private purchases for their friends at home. You can tell by their pants and characteristic 'wasp waists' that they are Cretans. They are short of stature and slim and have sharp features like the Delta coast dwellers, and their movements are active. Their dark hair is pleated in three long coils that fall over their shoulders, and they affect small coloured turbans. They all wear armlets, which are greatly favoured in the distant island kingdom.

A company of the pharaoh's soldiers is marching towards the great limestone fortress. They are naked, save for their loincloths, and about half of them are archers. The others are armed with long spears and carry wooden shields, square at the bottom and arching to a point at the top. They go past with a fine swing, although they have been drilling all morning on an open space two miles south of the city.

Over there are boat builders at work. The Cretan traders have brought them a fresh supply of seasoned timber as well as a raft of drifted logs from Lebanon. Wood is scarce and dear in Egypt, and watchmen are on duty in the yard day and night.

Three roomy river boats are being built. The work is well advanced, for the carpenters are fitting in the benches, which are being pierced and prepared for jointing on trestles by men who sit astride them. The workers are skilled and active, and the overseers who direct operations are easily recognised – they carry long staffs in their right hands and constantly urge on the men.

But what is happening over there in front of the government buildings? A large crowd has assembled, and the jeers and roars of laughter indicate that something amusing is going on. We press forward to find that the city guards have made several arrests and are hauling their protesting prisoners through the doorway. The spectators are delighted to see 'the tables turned', for these are their oppressors – the tax collectors – who are being taken before the pharaoh's accountants so that their accounts may be audited. There have been several complaints of late of extortionate dealings and dishonest transactions. In a large hall inside we see the stern auditors kneeling at their low desks, on which are piled the official records. Scribes record the proceedings. Each arrested man crouches on his knees and is held firmly by a guard while he is sharply questioned and his accounts are checked. All his private papers have been seized. He must explain every entry and prove that he is a man above suspicion. It is a rough-and-ready, but effective, manner of doing business. Punishments for dishonesty or oppression are sharp and peremptory.

The pharaoh is the protector of all his subjects, great and small. A poor man may suffer a great wrong and find himself unable to have it put right even in the hall of justice, but if the monarch is appealed to, he will prove to be no respecter of persons and will give the wrongdoer a punishment of great severity.

A tale has come down the ages which was often related in the dwellings of poor and great alike to show how the pharaoh might espouse the cause of the humblest man in the kingdom. Scribes recorded it on papyri, and fragments of these still survive.

Once upon a time a peasant had his dwelling in the Faiyum, and it was his custom to load his ass with nitre and reeds, salt and stones, and seeds and bundles of wood, and drive it to a town in the south, where in the marketplace he exchanged what he had brought for other things that he and his family required. He began to be prosperous.

One day, when it was near harvest time, he journeyed to the town and reached the estate of a great royal official named Meritensa. As he passed through it, he came to the farm of Hamti, a feudal tenant. The farmer saw him approach, and said to himself: 'May the god permit me to rob the peasant of his ass and its burden. I have need of salt.'

The path along the river bank was very narrow, for Hamti had sowed much land. Between his corn and the water there was scarcely the breadth of a man's body.

The farmer said to one of his servants: 'Bring me a rug from inside.' The man ran to Hamti's house and came back with a rug, which was spread out on the path, and it reached from the corn to the river edge.

The peasant drove his ass along the narrow way, past the corn, and when he drew near, the farmer called to him, saying: 'Watch where you are going. Do not soil my rug.'

'I will do as you will,' remarked the peasant, 'and avoid troubling you.'

So he hit his ass and turned it inland to pass round the field. But the farmer was not satisfied with even that. He shouted with an angry voice, saying: 'Do you dare to trample on my corn? There is no path that way.'

'What else can I do?' argued the peasant. 'You prevent me from using the path by laying a rug on it.'

As he spoke, his ass began to eat the grain, and the farmer seized it and said: 'I will take this animal in payment for the damage it has done.'

The peasant cried indignantly: 'What? First you close the path against me, and now you seize my ass because it has taken a few ears of barley. Do not dare to do me wrong on this estate. It belongs to the just Meritensa, the great judge, who is a terror to all evildoers in the kingdom. You know well that I speak the truth. Do not imagine that you can hurt me on the land of such a good and high nobleman.'

But the farmer laughed. 'Have you not heard,' he asked, 'the maxim that says: "A peasant is esteemed only by himself?" Know now, too, that I am Meritensa, the judge, of whom you have spoken. I will deal with you here and now.'

Having spoken thus, the farmer seized a whip and lashed the peasant fiercely, seeking to drive him away. But the wronged man refused to leave. His body ached with many wounds. He waited about all day, but neither by threat nor tearful appeal could he prevail upon the farmer to give him back his ass and the burden it carried.

Then the peasant hurried to the house of Meritensa. He waited for the great lord to come out, sitting patiently beside the wall gate. Hours went past, and at length he saw Meritensa walking out to step into a boat at the river side.

'Hail, my lord!' he called. 'Ask one of your servants to hear the tale of my wrong.'

The farmer plunders the peasant
From the painting by Maurice Greiffenhagen

As the man wished, so did the nobleman do. He asked a scribe to talk to the peasant, who related how he had been done wrong by Hamti.

So it happened that, when sitting in the hall of justice next morning, Meritensa repeated the accusations that the peasant had made against the farmer. The other judges heard, and then said:

'It is our rule here that these peasants should bring witnesses. We know their ways. If it is proved that the farmer stole some nitre and salt, he can be ordered to make payment, or else he can be whipped. But we must first hear evidence to confirm what is said by this peasant fellow.'

Meritensa made no reply. He was indignant at the other judges and refused to discuss the matter with them any further. He decided to advise the wronged man what to do.

But the peasant could not find witnesses, and again he waited for the good judge to come out. Then he praised him with a loud voice, saying: 'You are mighty among the mighty ones and the good friend of poor men. May fair winds carry you on the lake of truth. May no wave hit you or any terror come near. You are a father to the fatherless, and a husband to the widow, and a brother to the girl in need. I praise you name, for you give excellent counsel without wish of reward. You are the enemy of the wrongdoer and the lover of justice. You heard my cry and you permitted me to speak. You are esteemed by those who are worthy. Now show me mercy and right my wrong. Hear my prayer. Ask about me, and you will find that I have been robbed.'

Meritensa was on his way to the palace, and he repeated to pharaoh what the peasant had said, and related how he had been robbed by the farmer.

His majesty said: 'This man has great eloquence. See that his wrong is not righted for a little time yet, and arrange that all his fine speeches are recorded by your scribes. I should like to hear them word by word. Meantime see that his wife and his children do not lack food.'

The peasant was given a supply of bread each day, and Meritensa arranged that his wife and children should also be supplied with food in abundance.

Every day the wronged man waited for the nobleman to come out and addressed him with great eloquence and poetic fervour. The scribes recorded all his words, but Meritensa pretended not to notice him, and he even had him beaten.

Nine times the peasant appealed to the judge, and at length two servants went and spoke to the man, who, when he saw them approach, feared that he was about to be whipped once again. But the words that they spoke for their lord were:

'You have no cause to be afraid because you addressed the judge these many times. The pharaoh has read your speeches and has praised them, and you will be rewarded.'

Meritensa then caused his scribes to take down the evidence of the peasant regarding the robbery of his ass and its burden of nitre and salt, and he laid the document before his majesty.

Pharaoh said: 'I cannot attend to this matter. Take care of it yourself and see that justice is done.'

Meritensa then dispatched his officers to the farm, and he caused Hamti's house and all his goods to be confiscated and given to the peasant.

All that was done was confirmed and approved by the pharaoh, who commanded that the eloquent peasant should be brought to the palace. His majesty took delight in his speeches and honoured him greatly, for he caused rich delicacies from the royal table to be sent to the man and his family.

Chapter 10

The Great Pyramid Kings

Djoser and Snofru – Their Great Tombs – Snofru's Battles with Invaders – Mastabas of Officials – The Grand Vizier – A New Dynasty – Khufu the Tyrant King – His Great Pyramid – The World's Greatest Stone Structure – An Army of Workers – How the Pyramids were built – Rocking Machines – A Religious Revolution – The Gods of the Sun Cult – Ptah excluded – King Khafra— Menkaure the Just King – The Sacred Heifer – Khufu's Line overthrown.

When the great pyramids were being erected, Egypt was already a land of ancient memories. Some of the royal tombs at Abydos were a thousand years old. Folk tales had gathered round the memories of notable kings. Their order was confused, and not a few were quite forgotten.

Djoser of the Third Dynasty and Snofru of the Fourth are really the first Egyptian monarchs of whom we obtain any accurate idea. They were forceful personalities. We trace Djoser's activities in Sinai, where he continued to work the copper mines from which several of his predecessors had obtained supplies of the indispensable metal. He waged war on the southern frontier, which he extended below the first cataract, and he imposed his rule firmly over the north. That peace prevailed all over the kingdom is evident; otherwise he could not have devoted so much time to the erection of his great tomb, at which a great army of workmen were kept continuously employed.

Snofru, whose very name suggests swiftness of decision and unswerving purpose, impressed himself on the imagination of the Egyptians for many generations. When a great national achievement was accomplished it became customary to remark that no such success had been attained 'since the days of Snofru'. He battled against Asian hordes who invaded the Delta region, and erected forts, like a chain of blockhouses, across the frontier, and these were associated with his name for over ten centuries. In Sinai there was trouble regarding the copper mines. Other people had begun to work them and disputed right of possession with the Egyptians. Snofru conducted a vigorous and successful campaign, and so firmly established his power in that region that his spirit was worshipped generations afterwards as the protecting god of the mines. His ambitions were not confined to land, for he had great ships built and he traded with Crete and along the Syrian coast. The cedars of Lebanon were then cut and drifted to the Nile by

Egyptian sailors. In the south Nubia was dealt with firmly. We gather that thousands of prisoners were captured and taken north as slaves to be employed, apparently, at the building of temples and tombs. Three pyramids are attributed to Snofru, the greatest of which is situated at Maidum.

The power and wealth of the officials had increased greatly. Their mastabas, which surround the royal tombs, are of greater and more elaborate construction. Pharaoh was no longer hampered with the details of government. A grand vizier controlled the various departments of state, and he was the supreme judge to whom final appeals were made by the courts. There were also a 'chancellor of the exchequer' and officials who controlled the canals and secured an equitable distribution of water. There were governors of nomes and towns, and even villages had their 'mayor'. To secure the effective control of the frontier, always threatened by raids from Nubia, a local vizier was appointed to quell outbreaks, and troops were placed at his disposal. These high offices were usually held by princes and noblemen, but apparently it was possible for men of humble rank to attain distinction and be promoted, like Joseph, to positions of responsibility. In mastaba chapels there are records of promotion acquired by capable and successful officials who began life as scribes and were governors before they died.

lAfter Snofru, the next king of the Fourth Dynasty begins with Khufu, the Cheops of the Greeks, who erected the largest pyramid in Egypt. His relationship to Snofru is uncertain. He was born in the Beni Hasan district and was probably the son of a nobleman of royal birth. Snofru may have left no direct heir or one who was a weakling. There is no record or tradition of a revolution, and it may be that Khufu was already a prominent figure at the court when he seized the crown. In his harem was a woman who enjoyed the confidence of his predecessor, and it is possible that matters were arranged in his interests in that quarter.

No statues of Khufu survive. These were probably destroyed when, a few centuries after his death, his tomb was raided and his mummy torn to pieces, for he was remembered as a great tyrant. So much was he hated that Herodotus was informed by the priests that he 'degenerated into the extremest profligacy of conduct'. He barred the avenues to every temple and forbade the Egyptians to offer sacrifices. He proceeded next to make them labour as slaves for himself. Some he compelled to hew stones in the quarries of the Arabian mountains and drag them to the banks of the Nile. Others were selected to load vessels. 'A hundred thousand men were employed.' But the memory of ancient wrongs was perpetuated by the priests not merely in sympathy for the workers and those who had to bear the burdens of taxation. A religious revolution was imminent. The sun worshippers at Heliopolis were increasing in numbers and power, and even in Khufu's day their political influence was being felt. In fact, their ultimate ascendancy may have been because of the public revolt against the selfish and tyrannical policy of the pyramid-building kings.

We enjoy a privilege not shared by Greeks or Romans, who heard the Egyptian traditions regarding the masterful monarch. Petrie discovered an ivory statue of Khufu, which is a minute and beautiful piece of work. The features occupy only a quarter of an inch, and are yet animate with life and expression. Khufu's face suggests that of the Duke of Wellington. The nose is large and curved like an eagle's beak; the eyes have a hard and piercing look. The cheekbones are high, the cheeks drawn down to knotted jaws. The chin is firmly cut and the hard mouth has an uncompromising pout. The brows are lowering. The face is that of a thinker and man of action – an idealist and an iron-willed ruler of men:

> whose frown
> And wrinkled lip and sneer of cold command
> Tell that the sculptor well those passions read
> Which still survive

stamped on the statuette of the greatest of the pyramid builders. There is also an air of self-consciousness, and we seem to hear, 'My name is Khufu':

> . . . King of Kings;
> Look on my works, ye mighty, and despair.

Petrie, the great archaeologist of Egypt, calculated that Khufu's vast pyramid is composed of some 2,003,000 blocks of limestone averaging about $2^1/_2$ tonnes each. It occupies an area of 13 acres (5.26 hectares). Each side of the square base originally measured 768 feet (234 metres), but the removal of the coating, which left the sides smooth, caused a shrinkage of about 18 feet (5.5 metres). The height is now roughly 450 feet (137 metres), 30 feet (9 metres) less than when it was completed.

This pyramid is the greatest pile of masonry ever built by man. Not only is it a monument to a mighty ruler and his great architects and builders, but also to the stone workers of Memphis. Many of the great stones have been cut and dressed with amazing skill and accuracy, and so closely are they placed together that the seams have to be marked with charcoal to be traced in a photograph. Blocks of limestone weighing tons are finished with almost microscopic accuracy, 'equal,' says Petrie, 'to optician's work of the present day.'

Volumes have been written to advance theories regarding the purpose of this and other pyramids. The orientation theory has been especially keenly debated, but it no longer obtains among prominent Egyptologists. A pyramid has no astronomical significance whatsoever. The Egyptians were not star worshippers. It is simply a vast burial cairn and an architectural development of the mastaba, which had been growing higher and higher until Djoser's architect conceived the

The Great Pyramid of Khufu (Cheops)
The two insets show front and side views of the small ivory statue of Khufu,
now in the Cairo Museum

idea of superimposing one upon the other until an effect was obtained that satisfied his sense of proportion. Geometricians decided its final shape rather than theologians.

There are several chambers in the interior of Khufu's pyramid, and his mummy reposed in a granite sarcophagus in the largest, which is 19 feet high (5.8 metres), 34¼ feet (10.5 metres) in length and 17 feet (5.2 metres) in breadth. The entrance is from the north.

Herodotus was informed by the Egyptian priests that 100,000 workers were employed and were relieved every three months. The limestone was quarried on the eastern side of the Nile, below Cairo, and drifted on rafts across the river. The low ground was flooded, so that the high ground was made an island. We are informed that ten years were spent in constructing a causeway up which the blocks were hauled. A considerable time was also spent in preparing the rocky foundations. The pyramid itself was the work of twenty years.

When the base was completed, the same writer explains, the stones were raised by the aid of 'machines' made of 'short pieces of wood'. Models have been found in tombs of wooden 'cradles' – flat on the top and rounded off so that they could be rocked – on which boulders were evidently poised and then slewed into position by haulage and leverage. The cradles were raised by wedges. When the block was lifted high enough, it could be tilted and made to slide down skids into position. Herodotus says that, according to one account, the stones were elevated by the numerous 'machines' from step to step, and to another they were lifted into position by one great contrivance. This process was continued until the summit was reached. Then a granite casing was constructed downward to the base, and it was covered over with hieroglyphics that recorded the various sums of money spent on food supplied to the workers. 'Cheops (Khufu) exhausted his wealth,' adds Herodotus.

The royal exchequer does not appear to have been depleted, because Khufu also erected three smaller pyramids for members of his family, and his successor afterwards undertook the construction of a vast tomb also.

Apart from his pyramid work we know little or nothing regarding the events of Khufu's reign. Snofru's military activities had secured peace on the frontiers, and neither Nubian nor Asiatic dared enter the land to plunder or despoil. That the administration was firm and perfectly organized under the iron-willed monarch may be taken for granted.

But a great change was impending, which could not be controlled by the will of a single man. Prolonged peace had promoted culture, and the minds of men were centred on the great problems of life and death. Among the educated classes a religious revolution was imminent. Apparently Khufu was raised to power on an early wave of insurrection. It was a period of transition. The downfall of the Ptah cult as a supreme political force was in progress, and the rival cult of Ra, at Heliopolis, was coming into prominence. Already in Snofru's reign, a sun worshipper, one Ra-hotep, occupied the influential position of Superintendent of the South. It remained for the priests of the sun to secure converts among the members of the royal family, so as to obtain political and religious ascendancy, and it can be understood that those who were educated at their temple college were likely to embrace their beliefs. If they failed in that direction, the combined influence of priests and nobles was sufficient to threaten the stability of the throne. A strong ruler might delay, but he could not thwart, the progress of the new movement.

The king's name, as we have stated, was Khnum Khufu, which means: 'I am guarded by the god Khnum'. That 'modeller' of the universe may have closely resembled Ptah, but the doctrines of the two sects developed separately, being subjected to different racial influences. Khnum was ultimately merged with the sun god, and his ram became 'the living soul of Ra'. Khnum was regarded at Heliopolis as an incarnation of Osiris, whose close association with agricultural rites perpetuated his worship among the great mass of the people. In the theological system of the sun cult, Osiris became a member of the Ra family and succeeded to the throne of the 'first king' who ruled over Egypt. But Ptah, significantly enough, was never included among the sun god's companions, and the idea that he created Ra was confined to Memphis, and evolved at a later date.

The rivalry between the two powerful cults must have been bitter and pronounced.

If Ptolemaic tradition is to be relied on, Khufu constructed a temple to the goddess Hathor, who was merged with the frog goddess Hekt. Indeed Hekt came to be regarded as a form of Hathor.

King Khufu's son and successor must have come under the influence of the Ra cult, for his name, Khafra, signifies 'Ra is my glory' or 'My brightness is Ra'. The sun cult had received their first great concession from the royal house, but not until the following dynasty did the priests of Heliopolis obtain supreme power and compel the pharaoh to call himself 'son of the sun', a title that afterwards remained in use. Sun worship then became the official religion of Egypt – it gradually coloured every other cult. When the Osirian religion was revived, under the Libyan monarchs, the old deified king, who was an incarnation of the corn god, was also identified with the sun.

King Khafra did not, it would appear, satisfy the ambitions of the Ra worshippers, who desired more than formal recognition. A legend that survives only in fragmentary form relates that 'the gods turned away from Khufu and his house'. The powerful cult became impatient, and 'hope deferred' made them rebels. A political revolution was fostered, and Khufu's dynasty was doomed.

Khafra, the Chephren of Herodotus, who says Khufu was his brother rather than his father, erected the second great pyramid, which is only about 30 feet (9 metres) lower than the other. The remains of his temple still survive. It is built of granite, and although the workmanship is less exact, as if the work were more hastily performed than in Khufu's day, the architecture is austerely sublime. Immense square pillars support massive blocks; there are great open spaces, and one is impressed by the simplicity and grandeur of the scheme.

Seven statues of Khafra were discovered by Mariette, so that his ka was well provided for. The great diorite statue preserved in the Cairo museum is one of the enduring triumphs of Egyptian art. The concept is at once grand and imposing. The king is seated on the throne, but he wears the wig of the great ruling judge. At the back of his head is the figure of the protecting Horus hawk. His face is calmer than Khufu's – resolution is combined with dignity and patience. He seems to be imbued with the spirit of Old Kingdom greatness.

Although cut from so hard a material as diorite, there is much muscular detail in the figure, which is that of a strong and vigorous man. His throne is straight-backed, but the stately floral design of the sides and the lions' heads and fore paws in front are in keeping with the naked majesty of the whole statue, which was originally covered with a soft material.

Again the reign is a blank. The priests informed Herodotus that Khafra's conduct was similar to that of Khufu. 'The Egyptians had to endure every species of oppression and calamity, and so greatly do they hate the memories of the two

Khafra (Fourth Dynasty)
Who built the second Great Pyramid
From the statue in diorite in Cairo Museum

monarchs that they are unwilling to mention their names. Instead they called their pyramids by the name of the shepherd Philitis, who grazed his cattle near them.'

The great Sphinx was long associated with Khafra, whose name was carved on it during the Eighteenth Dynasty, but it is believed to be of much later date. It is

fashioned out of the rock and is over 60 feet (18 metres) in height. The body is a
lion's, and the face was a portrait of a pharaoh, but it has been so much disfigured that it cannot be identified with certainty. Nor is there complete agreement
as to the significance of the Sphinx. Centuries after its construction, the Egyptians regarded it as a figure of the sun god, but more probably it was simply a
symbol of royal power and greatness.

There were kindlier memories of Menkaure, the Mycerinus of Herodotus, who
said that this king was a son of Khufu. He erected the third great pyramid, which
is only 218 feet (66.5 metres) high, and three small ones for his family. He was
reputed, however, to have eased the burden of the Egyptians and especially to
have allowed the temples to be reopened so that the people might offer sacrifices
to the gods. As a just monarch he excelled all his predecessors, and his memory
was long revered. Not only did he deliver equitable judgements, but he was always ready to hear appeals when complaints were made against officials and
willing to remove and redress wrongs. His statue shows us a less handsome man
than either Khufu or Khafra, and the expression of the face accords with his traditional character. Indeed, it is not only unaffected but melancholy.

A story was told to Herodotus that the king was greatly stricken by the death of
his daughter. He had her body enclosed in a heifer made of wood, which was
covered over with gold. It was not buried but placed in a palace hall at Sais. Incense was burned before it daily, and at night it was illuminated. The heifer re-
clined on its knees. A purple robe covered the body, and between the gilded
horns blazed a great golden star. Once a year, in accordance with the request of
the dying princess, the image was carried outside so that she might behold the
sun. The occasion was an Osirian festival, and the heifer, it is believed, represented Isis.

We know definitely that a daughter of Menkaure was given in marriage to
Ptah-shepses, a high official, who became the priest of three obelisks. The appointment is full of significance, because these obelisks were erected to Ra. Sun
worship was evidently gaining ground.

The mummy of the king was enclosed in a great sarcophagus of basalt but was
destroyed with the others. Mention is also made of a Fourth-Dynasty monarch
named Radadef, but he cannot be placed with certainty. Khufu's line flourished
for about a century and a half and then was overthrown. A new family of kings,
who were definitely Ra worshippers, sat on the throne of the united Egypt. In the
folk tales that follow are interesting glimpses of the life and beliefs of the times.

Chapter 11

Folk Tales of Fifty Centuries

A Faithless Lady – The Wax Crocodile – Pharaoh's Decree – Story of the Green Jewel – A Sad-hearted King – Boating on the Lake – How the Waters were divided – Dedi the Magician – His Magical Feats – A Prophecy – Khufu's Line must fall – Birth of the Future Kings – Goddesses as Dancing Girls – Ghostly Music and Song – Tale of a King's Treasure – Fearless Thieves – A Brother's Bravery – Pharaoh's Soldiers are tricked – How a Robber became a Prince – King visits the Underworld.

King Khufu sat to hear tales told by his sons regarding the wonders of other days and the doings of magicians. The Prince Khafra stood before him and related the ancient story of the wax crocodile.

Once upon a time a pharaoh went towards the temple of the god Ptah. His counsellors and servants accompanied him. It chanced that he paid a visit to the villa of the chief scribe, behind which there was a garden with a stately summer house and a broad artificial lake. Among those who followed the pharaoh was a handsome youth, and the scribe's wife looked on him with love. Soon afterwards she sent gifts to him, and they had secret meetings. They spent a day in the summer house, and feasted there, and in the evening the youth bathed in the lake. The chief butler then went to his master and informed him what had happened.

The scribe told the servant to bring a certain magic box, and when he received it he made a small wax crocodile, over which he muttered a spell. He placed it in the hands of the butler, saying: 'Throw this image into the lake behind the youth when next he bathes himself.'

On another day, when the scribe dwelt with the pharaoh, the lovers were together in the summer house, and in the evening the youth went to bathe in the lake. The butler stole through the garden, and stealthily he threw into the water the wax image, which immediately was given life. It became a great crocodile that seized the youth suddenly and took him away.

Seven days passed, and then the scribe spoke to the pharaoh regarding the miracle that had been done, and requested that his majesty should accompany him to his villa. The pharaoh did so, and when they both stood beside the lake in the garden the scribe spoke magic words, bidding the crocodile to appear. As he commanded, so did it do. The great reptile came out of the water carrying the youth in its jaws.

The scribe said: 'Lo! it shall do whatever I command to be done.'

The pharaoh said: 'Tell the crocodile to return at once to the lake.'

Before he did that, the scribe touched it, and immediately it became a small image of wax again. The pharaoh was filled with wonder, and the scribe told him all that had happened, while the youth stood waiting.

The pharaoh said to the crocodile: 'Seize the wrongdoer.' The wax image was again given life and, clutching the youth, leaped into the lake and disappeared, and it was never seen after that.

Then the pharaoh gave a command that the wife of the scribe should be seized. On the north side of the house she was bound to a stake and burned alive, and what remained of her was thrown into the Nile.

Such was the tale told by Khafra. Khufu was pleased and ordered that offerings of food and refreshment be placed in the tombs of the pharaoh and his wise servant.

Prince Khafra stood before his majesty and said: 'I will relate a marvel that happened in the days of King Snofru, your predecessor.' Then he told the story of the green jewel.

Snofru was one day disconsolate and weary. He wandered about the palace with a desire to be cheered, but there was nothing to take the gloom from his mind. He ordered that his chief scribe be brought before him, and he said to him: 'I would like to have entertainment, but I cannot find any in this place.'

The scribe said: 'Your Majesty should go boating on the lake, and let the rowers be the prettiest girls in your harem. It will delight your heart to see them splashing the water where the birds dive and to gaze on the green shores and the flowers and trees. I myself will go with you.'

The king consented, and twenty virgins who were fair to behold went into the boat, and they rowed with oars of ebony that were decorated with gold. His majesty took pleasure in the outing, and the gloom passed from his heart as the boat went to and fro, and the girls sang together with sweet voices.

It chanced, as they were turning round, an oar handle brushed against the hair of the girl who was steering and shook from it a green jewel, which fell into the water. She lifted up her oar and stopped singing, and the others grew silent and ceased rowing.

Snofru said: 'Do not pause. Let us go on still farther.'

The girls said: 'She who steers has lifted her oar.'

Snofru said to her: 'Why have you lifted your oar?'

'Alas, I have lost my green jewel!' she said. 'It has fallen into the lake.'

Snofru said: 'I will give you another. Let us go on.'

The girl pouted and answered: 'I would rather have my own green jewel again than any other.'

His majesty said to the chief scribe: 'I am given great enjoyment by this novelty. Indeed my mind is much refreshed as the girls row me up and down the lake. Now one of them has lost her green jewel, which has dropped into the water, and she wants it back again and will not have another to replace it.'

The chief scribe at once muttered a spell. Then by reason of his magic words the waters of the lake were divided like a lane. He went down and found the green jewel that the girl had lost and came back with it to her. When he did that, he again uttered words of power, and the waters came together as they were before.

The king was well pleased, and when he had had full enjoyment with the rowing on the lake he returned to the palace. He gave gifts to the chief scribe, and everyone wondered at the marvel that he had accomplished.

Such was Khafra's tale of the green jewel, and King Khufu commanded that offerings should be laid in the tombs of Snofru and his chief scribe, who was a great magician.

Next Prince Hordadef stood before the king, and he said: 'Your Majesty has heard tales regarding the wonders performed by magicians in other days, but I can bring forth a worker of marvels who now lives in the kingdom.'

King Khufu said: 'And who is he, my son?'

'His name is Dedi,' answered Prince Hordadef. 'He is a very old man, for his years are a hundred and ten. Each day he eats a joint of beef and five hundred loaves of bread, and drinks a hundred jugs of beer. He can smite off the head of a living creature and restore it again. He can make a lion follow him, and he knows the secrets of the habitation of the god Thoth, which Your Majesty has desired to know so that you may design the chambers of your pyramid.'

King Khufu said: 'Go now and find this man for me, Hordadef.'

The prince went down to the Nile, boarded a boat and sailed southwards until he reached the town called Dedsnefru, where Dedi had his dwelling. He went ashore and was carried in his chair of state towards the magician, who was found lying at his door. When Dedi was awakened, the king's son saluted him and told him not to rise up because of his years. The prince said: 'My royal father wishes to honour you and will provide for you a tomb among your people.'

Dedi blessed the prince and the king with thankfulness, and he said to Hordadef: 'Greatness be yours; may your ka have victory over the powers of evil, and may your khu follow the path that leads to paradise.'

Hordadef helped Dedi to rise up and took his arm to help him towards the ship. He sailed away with the prince, and in another ship were his assistants and his magic books.

'Health and strength and plenty be yours,' said Hordadef, when he again stood before his royal father, King Khufu. 'I have come downstream with Dedi, the great magician.'

His Majesty was well pleased and said: 'Let the man be brought into my presence.'

Dedi came and saluted the king, who said: 'Why have I not seen you before?'

'He that is called comes,' answered the old man. 'You have sent for me and I am here.'

'It is told,' King Khufu said, 'that you can restore the head that is taken from a live creature.'[1]

'I can indeed, Your Majesty,' answered Dedi.

The king said: 'Then let a prisoner be brought forth and decapitated.'

'I would rather it were not a man,' said Dedi. 'I do not deal even with cattle in such a manner.'

A duck was brought forth and its head was cut off, and the head was thrown to the right and the body to the left. Dedi spoke magic words. Then the head and the body came together, and the duck rose up and quacked loudly. The same was done with a goose.

King Khufu then caused a cow to be brought in, and its head was cut off. Dedi restored the animal to life again, and caused it to follow him.

His Majesty then spoke to the magician and said: 'It is told that you possess the secrets of the dwelling of the god Thoth.'

Dedi answered: 'I do not possess them, but I know where they are concealed, and that is within a temple chamber at Heliopolis. There the plans are kept in a box, but it is no insignificant person who shall bring them to Your Majesty.'

'I would gladly know who will deliver them to me,' King Khufu said.

Dedi prophesied that three sons would be born to Rud-dedit, wife of the chief priest of Ra. The eldest would become chief priest at Heliopolis and would possess the plans. He and his brothers would one day sit on the throne and rule over all the land.

King Khufu's heart was filled with gloom and alarm when he heard the prophetic words of the great magician.

Dedi then said: 'What are your thoughts, O King? Behold your son will reign after you, and then his son. But next one of these children will follow.'

King Khufu was silent. Then he spoke and asked: 'When shall these children be born?'

Dedi informed his majesty, who said: 'I will visit the temple of Ra at that time.'

Dedi was honoured by his majesty and afterwards dwelt in the house of the Prince Hordadef. He was given daily for his portion an ox, a thousand loaves of bread, a hundred jugs of beer, and a hundred bunches of onions.

The day came when the sons of the woman Reddedet were to be born. Then the

[1] This trick was performed by Egyptian conjurors.

high priest of Ra, her husband, prayed to the goddess Isis and her sister Nepthys, to Meskhent, goddess of birth, and to the frog goddess Hekt, and to the creator god Khnum, who gives the breath of life. These he entreated to take care of the three babies who were to become three kings of Egypt, one after the other.

The deities heard him. Then came the goddesses as dancing girls, who went about the land, and the god Khnum followed them as their burden bearer. When they reached the door of the high priest's dwelling, they danced before him. He entreated them to enter, and they did as he wished, and shut themselves in the room with the woman Reddedet.

Isis called the first child who was born Userkaf, and said: 'Let no evil be done by him.' The goddess Meskhent prophesied that he would become king of Egypt. Khnum, the creator god, gave the child strength.

The second baby was named Sahure by the goddess Isis. Meskhent prophesied that he also would become a king. Khnum gave him his strength.

The third was called Kakai. Meskhent said: 'He shall also be a king,' and Khnum gave him strength.

Before the dancing girls took their departure, the high priest gave a measure of barley to their burden bearer, and Khnum carried it away on his shoulders.

They all went on their way, and Isis said: 'Now let us work a wonder on behalf of these children, so that their father may know who has sent us to his house.'

Royal crowns were made and concealed in the measure of barley that had been given to them. Then the deities caused a great storm to arise, and in the midst of it they returned to the dwelling of the high priest, and they put the barley in a cellar and sealed it, saying they would return again and take it away.

It came to pass that after fourteen days Reddedet asked her servant to bring barley from the cellar so that beer might be made.

The girl said: 'There is none left except the measure that was given to the dancing girls.'

'Bring that then,' said Reddedet, 'and when the dancing girls return I will give them its value.'

When the servant entered the cellar she heard the low sounds of sweet music and dancing and song. She went and told her mistress of this wonder, and Reddedet entered the cellar and at first could not discover from where the mysterious sounds came. At length she placed her ear against the sack that contained the barley given to the dancing girls and found that the music was within it. She at once placed the sack in a chest and locked it, and then told her husband, and they rejoiced together.

Now it happened that one day Reddedet was angry with her servant, and hit her heavily. The girl vowed that she would be avenged and said: 'Her three children will become kings. I will inform King Khufu of this matter.'

So the servant went away and visited her uncle, who was her mother's eldest brother. She told him all that had happened and all she knew regarding the children of her mistress.

He was angry with her and spoke, saying: 'Why come to me with this secret? I cannot consent to make it known as you wish.'

Then he struck the girl, who went afterwards to draw water from the Nile. On the bank a crocodile seized her, and she was devoured.

The man then went towards the dwelling of Reddedet, and he found her mourning with her head on her knees. He spoke, saying: 'Why is your heart full of gloom?'

Reddedet answered him: 'Because my servant girl went away to reveal my secret.'

The man bowed and said: 'Behold! She came to me and told me all things. But I struck her, and she went towards the river and was seized by a crocodile.'[1]

So the danger was averted. Nor did King Khufu ever discover the babies regarding whom Dedi had prophesied. In time they sat on the throne of Egypt.

A folk tale regarding the king who reigned in Egypt before Khufu was related by a priest to Herodotus, the Greek historian.

The monarch was called Rhampsinitus. He built the western portion of the temple of Ptah. He also erected two statues – one to Summer, which faced the north and was worshipped, and the other to Winter, which faced the south but was never honoured. The king possessed great wealth, and he caused to be constructed beside the palace a strong stone chamber in which he kept his riches. One of the builders, however, contrived to place a stone in such a way that it could be removed from the outside.

It chanced that, after the king had deposited his treasure in the chamber, this builder was stricken with illness and knew his end was near. He had two sons, and he told them his secret regarding the stone and gave them the measurements so that they might locate it.

After the man died, the sons went out in the darkness of night, and when they found the stone they removed it. Then they entered the chamber and carried away much treasure, and before they departed they closed up the wall again.

The king was greatly puzzled when he discovered that his riches had been plundered, for the seals of the door were unbroken, and he did not know whom to suspect. Again and again the robbers returned, and the treasure diminished greatly. At length the king caused traps to be laid in the chamber, for his guards, who kept watch at the entrances, were quite unable to prevent the mysterious robberies.

---

[1] The manuscript, which is part of the Westcar Papyrus, ends here. It was purchased in Egypt by a Miss Westcar and is now preserved in Berlin. The beginning and end had been torn off. The children referred to become the first three kings of the Fifth Dynasty, which marks the political ascendancy of the Ra cult.

Soon afterwards the brothers returned. They removed the stone, and one of them entered stealthily. He went towards the treasure, as was his custom, but was suddenly caught in a trap. In a moment he realised that escape was impossible, and he reflected that he would be put to death the next day, while his brother would be seized and similarly punished. So he said to himself: 'I alone will die.'

When he had thus resolved to save his brother, he called to him softly in the darkness, bidding him to enter cautiously. He made known his great misfortune, and said: 'I cannot escape, nor dare you wait long in case you are discovered. When they find me here I will be recognised, and they will seize you and put you to death. Cut off my head at once, so that they may not know who I am, and thus save your own life.'

With a sad heart the brother did as he was told and carried away the head. Before he escaped in the darkness he replaced the stone, and no one saw him.

When morning came, the king was more astounded than ever to find a headless body trapped in the treasure chamber, for the door had not been opened, and yet two men had entered and one had escaped. He commanded that the corpse should be hung on the palace wall, and stationed guards at the place, bidding them to keep strict watch so that they might discover if anyone came to sorrow for the dead man. But no one came near.

Meanwhile, the mother grieved in secret. Her heart was filled with anger because the body was exposed in such a manner, and she threatened to inform the king regarding all that had happened if her other son would not contrive to carry away the corpse. The young man attempted to dissuade her, but she only repeated her threat, and that firmly. He therefore made preparations to obtain possession of the corpse.

He hired several asses, and on their backs he put many skins of wine. In the evening he drove them towards the palace. When he drew near to the guards who kept watch over his brother's body, he removed the stoppers of some of the skins. The wine ran out on to the highway, and he began to lament aloud and beat his head as if he were in sore distress. The soldiers ran towards the asses and seized them, and caught the wine in vessels, claiming it for themselves. At first the brother pretended to be angry and abused the men, but when they had calmed him down, as they thought, he spoke to them pleasantly and began to make secure the stoppers of all the skins.

In a short time he was chatting with the guards, and pretended to be much amused when they teased him about the accident. Then he invited them to drink, and they filled their flasks readily. So they began, and the young man poured out wine until they all became very drunk. When they fell asleep, the cunning fellow took down his brother's body, and laid it on the back of one of the asses. Before he went away he shaved the right cheeks of the soldiers. His mother welcomed him on his return in the darkness and was pleased.

The king was very angry when he discovered how the robber had tricked the guards, but he was still determined to have him taken. He sent forth his daughter in disguise, and she waited for the criminal. She spoke to several men, and at length she found him, because he came to know that he was sought and wished to deal cunningly with her. So he addressed her, and she offered to be his bride if he would tell her the most artful thing and also the most wicked thing he had ever done.

He answered readily: 'The most wicked thing I ever did was to cut off my brother's head when he was caught in a trap in the royal treasure chamber, and the most artful was to deceive the king's guards and carry away the body.'

The princess tried to seize him, but he thrust forth his brother's arm, which he carried under his robe, and when she clutched it he made speedy escape.

Great then was the astonishment of the king at the cunning and daring of the robber. He caused a proclamation to be made, offering him a free pardon and a generous reward if he would appear at the palace before him. The man went readily, and his majesty was so delighted with his speeches and great ingenuity that he gave him his daughter in marriage. There is no more artful people than the Egyptians, but this man had no equal in the land.

It was told that this same king journeyed to the land of Death, where he played dice with the goddess Isis[1] and now won and now lost. She gave him a napkin embroidered with gold, and on his return a great festival was held, and it was repeated every year thereafter. On such occasions it was customary to blindfold a priest and lead him to the temple of Isis, where he was left alone. It was believed that two wolves met him and conducted him back to the spot where he was found. The Egyptians esteemed Isis and Osiris[2] as the greatest deities of the underworld.

[1] Herodotus gives Demeter (Ceres).
[2] Ceres and Bacchus.

Chapter 12

Triumph of the Sun God

Rival Cults – Ptah as a Giant – His Mountain 'Seat' – Paradise of Osiris – Paradise of Sun Worshippers – Ideas of Hades – The Devil Serpent – The Great Worm of the Bible – The Nine Gods of Heliopolis – Stone and Sun Worship – The Horus Cult – Various Concepts of the God – Union with other Deities – Legend of the Winged Disc – Ra's Enemies slain – Seth as the 'Roaring Serpent' – Sun Worshippers as Kings – Ptah Worshippers as Grand Viziers – Unas the Eater of Gods – The Egyptian Orion

The rise of the sun god had both theological and political significance. Ra was elevated as the Great Father of a group of cosmic and human deities, and his high priest, who was evidently of royal descent, sat on the throne of a united Egypt. The folk tale about the prophecy of Dedi and the birth of three children who were to become kings appears to have been invented in later times to give divine origin to the revolution that abruptly terminated the succession of Khufu's descendants.

An interesting contrast is afforded by the two great rival religions of this period of transition. While the theology of Heliopolis was based on sun worship, that of Memphis was based on earth worship. Ptah, the creation elf of the latter city, had been united with Tanen (or Tatunen), the earth giant,[1] who resembles Geb. The dwarfish deity then assumed gigantic proportions and became a 'world god' or Great Father. A hymn addressed to Ptah Tanen declares that his head is in the heavens while his feet are on the earth or in Duat, the underworld. 'The wind,' declared the priestly poet, 'issues from your nostrils and the waters from your mouth. Upon your back grows the grain. The sun and the moon are your eyes. When you sleep it is dark, and when you open your eyes it is bright again.'

Ptah Tanen was lauded as 'a perfect god' who came forth 'perfect in all his parts'. At the beginning he was all alone. He built up his body and shaped his limbs before the sky was fashioned and the world was set in order, and before the waters issued forth. Unlike Ra, he did not rise from the primordial deep. 'You did discover yourself,' sang the Memphite poet, 'in the circumstance of one who made for himself a seat and shaped the Two Lands' (Upper and Lower Egypt).

[1] The lion Aker was another earth god.

The suggestion is that, therefore, of a mountain giant with his 'seat' or 'chair' on some lofty peak, an idea that only a hill folk could have imported.

'No father begot you and no mother gave you birth,' the poet declared. 'You did fashion yourself without the aid of any other being.'

The further union of Ptah with Osiris is reflected in the concept of a material paradise, where the souls of the dead were employed in much the same way as the workers in Egypt. Ethical beliefs pervaded this religious system, as we have seen. People were judged after death; their future happiness was the reward of right conduct and good living. Thus we find people declaring in tomb inscriptions:

'I have constructed this tomb by honest means. I have never stolen from another. . . . I have never seized by force what belonged to another. . . . I was never whipped before an official [for law breaking] since I was born. My conduct was admired by all men. . . . I gave food to those who hungered, and those who were destitute I did clothe. . . . No man ever cried out to the god complaining against me as an oppressor.'

Men died believing that Osiris would justify their actions. 'I shall live like Osiris. He perished not when he died, neither shall I perish when I die.'

These professions continued to be recorded after the rise of the sun god. The new religion was embraced mainly by the royal and aristocratic families and the Asiatic element in the population. It was infused by magic rather than ethical beliefs; a man's future happiness depended wholly on his knowledge of magic formula: and his devotion to religious rites.

The paradise of the sun worshippers was of a more spiritual character than that believed in by the cult of Ptah-Osiris. Their great hope was to find a place in the sun barque of Ra. The chosen among the dead became shining spirits who accompanied their god on his safe journey through the perils of darkness, and they ate his celestial food and shared his celestial drink. They became one with Ra and yet did not suffer loss of identity.

It was taught by the priests of Heliopolis that after death the souls of human beings travelled towards the west and entered the first hour division of the dark underworld Duat. There, in Amenti, 'the hidden region', they awaited the coming of the barque of Ra. Those who could repeat the necessary magic 'passwords' were permitted to enter, and they journeyed onward in the brightness diffused by the god until they reached the eastern horizon at dawn. Then they ascended the heavens and passed through happy fields. They could even visit old friends and old haunts on earth, but they had to return to the sun barque in the evening, because evil spirits would devour them in the darkness. So they sailed each night through the underworld. They lived in eternal light.

Less fortunate souls resided in the various hour divisions of Duat. Some were left in the first; others were allowed to enter the sun barque until they reached the particular divisions to which the power of their magic formulae extended. These remained in darkness, faintly lit up by the fire that serpents spat out and the flames of the torture pools, except for one of the twenty-four hours, when the sun barque appeared. Then they enjoyed the blessings of sunlight and the special benefits conferred by Ra. Assembling on the river banks they adored the passing deity, and when he departed their voices were raised in lamentation. They enjoyed the privilege of having food supplied without labour.

The supernatural enemies of Ra were slain nightly by spears, which were sun rays, and knives, which were flames of fire, as well as by powerful magic spells. When the god had passed by, all the demons came to life again. Ra's human enemies were those, apparently, who had not worshipped him on earth. Such were consigned to torture in lakes of everlasting fire.

Later Egyptian beliefs retained the memory of this ancient belief. The Copts peopled hell with demons who had the heads of serpents, crocodiles, lions and even bears. After death these 'avengers' seized the doomed person and wrenched the soul from the body with much violence. Then they stabbed and hacked it with knives, and thrust goads into its sides, and carried it to a river of fire and plunged it in. Afterwards the tortured soul was cast into outer darkness, where it gnashed its teeth in the bitter cold. It might also be consigned to a place of horror that swarmed with poisonous reptiles. But although it could be wounded and hacked to pieces it did not perish. In time the soul passed to the first hour division of Duat.

Egypt swarmed with snakes in early times, and they were greatly dreaded by the people. Even Ra feared them. He was bitten by the snake that Isis created, and when he left the earth and ascended to heaven, after reigning over men, he spoke of them as his enemies and provided magic spells so that they might be overcome. Snake charmers have not yet entirely disappeared in Egypt, and they had great fame in ancient days. Symbolic reference is made to their powers in the Bible. 'Their poison,' declared the Psalmist, 'is like the poison of a serpent; they are like the deaf adder that stoppeth her ear, which will not hearken to the voice of charmers' (Psalm 58:4-5). In Jeremiah 8:17, we read: 'I will send serpents, cockatrices, among you, which will not be charmed, and they shall bite you.' And in Ecclesiastes 10:11: 'Surely the serpent will bite without enchantment'. Those who watched the genuine serpent charmers at work in Egypt testified to the efficacy of their powers.[1]

In ancient Egypt serpents were believed, especially by the sun worshippers, to be incarnations of evil spirits.[2] Darkness, the enemy of light, was symbolised as the Apep serpent, which is also referred to as the Great Worm. It rose up each night in the realms of Duat to destroy the sun barque and devour Ra. Occasion-

---

[1] Lane's *Manners and Customs of the Modern Egyptians.*
[2] See Chapter 5.

ally it issued forth in daylight and appeared in darkening thunder clouds, when a dread battle was waged and lightning spears were hurled against it. At dreaded eclipse it seemed to achieve temporary triumph. In this respect the Apep serpent resembled the Chinese dragon.

When Ra was in peril the priests chanted powerful spells to assist him, and the people assembled and shouted together to scare away the monster of darkness and evil. The ordinary ritual of the sun worshippers provided magical formulae that were recited to render service to the god at regular intervals. Written spells were also considered to be efficacious, and these were inscribed with green ink on new papyrus, which was burned. Belief in sympathetic magic is reflected in the ceremony of making and destroying a green wax figure of the great serpent. At midnight, when Ra began his return journey and the power of evil was strongest, the wax figure was placed in a fire and spat upon. As it melted, the pious worshippers of the sun god believed that the Apep serpent suffered loss of power. The ashes of the figure and of the papyrus were afterwards mixed with filth and committed to the flames a second time. It was also customary to make wax models of the serpent fiends that assisted Apep, and they were given the heads of black and white cats, crocodiles and ducks.[1] Stone knives were stuck in their backs, and they were thrown in the dust and kicked with the left foot.[2]

Symbolic references are also made in the Bible to the great Egyptian serpent. In Isaiah 66:24, we read: 'Their worm shall not die, neither shall their fire be quenched, and they shall be an abhorring unto all flesh,' and also: 'The worm shall eat them like wool' (51:8). In Coptic literature the Apep serpent is a monster that lies in outer darkness, encircling the world and clutching its tail between its jaws, like the Midgard serpent of Norse mythology. From its mouth issues forth 'All ice,[3] dust, cold, disease, and sickness' (*Pistis Sophia*).

The idea that the sun was an incarnation of the Creator was imported from Asia, but the concept of Duat, with its lakes of fire, is of Egyptian origin. In the Babylonian Hades, to which Ishtar descended, eternal darkness prevailed, and doomed souls ate filthy food and drank unclean waters. They were not tortured by flames but by pestilent odours and by diseases.[4]

---

[1] The duck-headed serpent recalls the fire drake of the Beowulf poem. Giants with cats' heads and dogs' heads are found in Celtic folklore.

[2] King James in his *Demonology* says: 'The devil teacheth how to make pictures of wax or, that by roasting thereof, the person that they bear the name of may be continually melted or dried away by continual sickness.'

[3] In the reign of Rameses II, Khattusil, the Hittite king, visited Egypt. An inscription at Abu Simbel expresses the hope that on his journey homeward he will not be delayed by snow and ice on the mountains. Isaiah makes symbolic reference to the serpent: 'In that day the Lord with his sore and great and strong sword shall punish leviathan the piercing (or stiff) serpent, even leviathan that crooked serpent; and he shall slay the dragon that is in the sea' (Isaiah 27:1).

[4] As in the Nifel-hel of Germanic mythology.

Ra theology developed along Egyptian lines and was fused with pre-existing local beliefs. The sun barque, which was called the 'barque of millions of years', sailed on an underworld Nile by night and a celestial Nile by day, and the seasonal changes of its course over the heavens were accounted for by the celestial inundation. Ra occupied the Maadit barque in the morning and the Sekti barque in the afternoon. The change was effected at noon, when special magical formulae were chanted.[1]

As the theology of the sun worshippers developed at Heliopolis, other gods, which were imported or had their origin in Egypt, were included in the divine family. The number three and its multiple had evidently magic significance. Ra, Khepera, and Atum formed the sun triad. The sun god and his children and descendants: Nut, the heavens, Shu, the air, Geb, the earth, with the lioness-headed Tefnut, 'the spitter', Osiris, the deified king and corn spirit, Isis, the Delta Great Mother, and her sister Nepthys, and the Semitic Seth, formed the ennead of Heliopolis. The group of nine gods varied at different periods. In one, Horus displaces Seth, and in another Osiris is absent and his place is occupied by Khepera, the beetle god. The inclusion of Horus probably marks the union of the Horite creed with that of Ra. Attempts were frequently made by kings and priests to absorb the Osirian cult at Heliopolis, but they were never successful. A compromise was evidently effected in time, for in Duat a 'division' was allocated to Osiris, and there he judged his followers. Ultimately the two ideas of paradise were confused rather than fused, and in the end the earlier faith achieved the victory after centuries of repression. We have already noted that Ptah was rigidly excluded from the ennead of the sun worshippers.

Archaic religious beliefs also received recognition at Heliopolis. The priests of the sun were evidently prepared to recognise any god so long as Ra was acknowledged as the Great Father. They not only tolerated but perpetuated the worship of trees and wells, and of stones and sacred mounds. Reverence is still shown for the well in which Ra was accustomed to wash his face daily, and it is called by the Arabs 'the spring of the sun'. A sycamore near it is also regarded with veneration. Sacrifices were offered up on a holy sand mound, and the custom prevailed at funeral services in tombs of setting up the mummy case in erect position on a heap of sand. One of the spirits[2] of the sun god was believed to inhabit a great block of stone. Indeed, On, the Egyptian name of the sacred 'city of the sun', signifies 'stone pillar'. In the Fifth Dynasty the Ra kings erected roofless temples in which there towered great broad obelisks surmounting mastaba-like square platforms. One of these stone idols at Abusir measured 138 feet (42 metres) at the base, and was 111 feet (34 metres) high. Outside the temple was a brick sun barque over 90 feet (27 metres) in length.

[1] The Muslim noonday prayer is probably a survival of the sun worshippers' custom.
[2] Gods and Pharaohs had several kas. Ra had fourteen and he had also seven bas (souls).

This form of temple was discontinued after the Sixth Dynasty, when the political power of the Ra priests was undermined. The tradition of stone worship survived, however, in the custom of erecting in front of temples those shapely obelisks similar to Cleopatra's Needle on the Thames Embankment in London. One still remains erect at Matarieh (Heliopolis) to mark the site of a vanished temple. It bears the name of Sesostris I of the Twelfth Dynasty.

The religion of the Horite sun worshippers, which was introduced by the Dynastic Egyptians who pressed northwards and conquered the whole land, appears to have differed from that of the Ra cult. It is not possible now to distinguish the original form of the tribal god or to discover what particular religious rites were associated with him. There are several forms of Horus. The most familiar is the hawk, which symbolised the spirit of the sun. It protected the early kings, who were 'the priests or descendants of Horus' – a royal title that continued in use ever afterwards. Like the Ra cult, the cult of Horus absorbed Egyptian beliefs, and the concept of the hawk god varied accordingly in different districts.

The two outstanding Horuses are the elder and the younger – the Horus who was the brother of Osiris and the Horus child who was the son of Osiris and Isis.

Horus of Letopolis, near Memphis, was a hawk-headed man and the son of Hathor, the sky goddess. In Upper Egypt he was similarly represented or simply as a hawk. At Edfu in particular he has the attributes of a sky god, and at Shedenu, a city in Lower Egypt, he was Horus of the Two Eyes, the sun being one and the moon another, thus resembling the concept of Ptah Tanen. He was also Harmakhis, Horus of the Two Horizons, and in this character became one of the chief forms of Ra. As the 'golden Horus' he was a dawn god, and in this character received the dead in the Judgment Hall of Osiris. The planet Saturn was Horus the Bull, Mars was Red Horus, and Jupiter 'Horus, revealer of secrets'. At Letopolis a temple was erected to Horus of Not Seeing. In this form he is supposed to have represented the sun at solar eclipse, but he may have simply represented the firmament at night. It is possible that Hathor, as the 'chaos cow', was originally the Great Mother and that the sky, sun, moon and stars were the various forms assumed by her son Horus or her various Horus sons.

When the child Horus became the son of Isis, there may have been simply a change of mother. Isis and Hathor are similar concepts; indeed, the deities were ultimately confused. Both also resemble Nut as Great Mothers, but Nut represented Mother Heaven and Isis Mother Earth, while Hathor was the World Cow, representing fertility in that form. Nut was also represented as a cat. In her human form she gave birth to the sun daily and the moon every month, and in another concept the sun and moon were her eyes. Before Ra became the Great Father he was born of Nut.

The tribal aspect of the Osiris, Isis and Horus myth is dealt with in a previous chapter. There is abundant evidence in Egyptian mythology that the union of deities signified the union of the tribes that worshipped them. The multiplicity of deities was due to the fact that an original concept remained in its old tribal form and was perpetuated alongside the new concept. Two gods might be fused into one, but Egypt retained not only the new deity but the two old deities as well, and thus instead of one god we have three. We need not be surprised, therefore, to find more than one Horus. The name alone may survive in some cases, for the process of blending varied in districts and at various periods. Egyptian religion is made up of many forms of faith.

Horus was united with Ra as Harmakhis, and the sun god of Heliopolis became Ra Harmakhis. The hawk god was thus symbolised as the winged sun disc. The legend that was invented to account for the change can be summarised.

When Ra reigned as king over Egypt he sailed up the Nile towards Nubia, because his enemies were plotting against him. At Edfu Horus entered the barque of the great god and hailed him as father. Ra greeted the hawk god and entreated him to slay the rebels of Nubia. Then Horus flew up to the sun as a great winged disc, and he was afterwards called 'the great god, the lord of the sky'. He perceived the enemies of Ra, and went against them as a winged disc. Their eyes were blinded by his brightness, and their ears were made deaf, and in the confusion they slew one another. Not a single conspirator remained alive.

Horus returned to the barque of Ra, and from that day he became Horus, god of Edfu, in the form of a winged sun disc. Ra embraced him and said: 'You have made the water wine-red with blood, and my heart is glad.'

Ra afterwards visited the battlefield and, when he saw the dead bodies of his foes, he said: 'Life is pleasant.' The name of the place thus became Horbehudti, which means 'pleasant life'.

The slain men were covered by water (at inundation) and became crocodiles and hippopotami. Then they attacked Horus as he sailed past, but his servants slew them with iron lances. Thoth rejoiced with a glad heart when he saw the enemies of Ra lying dead.

The legend continues in this strain and relates that Horus pursued the enemies of the god Ra downstream. Apparently Egypt was full of these enemies. We then learn that they were the followers of Seth, who was driven towards the frontier. He was afterwards taken prisoner and, with manacled hands and a spear stuck in his neck, he was brought before Ra. Then we find that there are two Horuses. The elder Horus is commanded by the sun god to deliver Seth to Horus, son of Isis. The younger Horus cuts off the head of Seth, and the slayer of Osiris becomes a roaring serpent that seeks refuge in a hole and is commanded to remain there.

Osiris is not mentioned in the legend, and Ra refers to the younger Horus as his own son. Apparently the theorists of Heliopolis wished Ra to supplant Osiris. Place names are played upon so that their origin may be ascribed to something said by the sun god, and grammatical construction is occasionally ignored with this end in view.

Horus worship never became popular in Egypt. It was absorbed by the various cults so that, as we have indicated, its original form is confused. The religion of the sun cult at Heliopolis, which was imported by the Asiatic settlers, was the religion that received prominence at the beginning of the Fifth Dynasty. A new title was given to the pharaoh. He became the 'son of the sun' as well as 'priest of Horus', 'priest of Seth', 'lord of the north and south', etc.

The rise of the sun god involved far-reaching political issues. Although the high priest of Ra sat on the throne, he did not become a tyrannical dictator like a Fourth-Dynasty king. A compromise had to be effected with the powerful faction at Memphis, and the high priest of Ptah became the vizier, a post previously held by the pharaoh's chosen successor. Nome governors were also given extended powers as administrators, as a reward probably for the share they had taken in the revolution, or at any rate to conciliate them and secure their allegiance. This decentralising process weakened the ruling power, but Egypt appears to have prospered as a whole, and the peaceful conditions that prevailed imparted activity to its intellectual life, as we shall see. Small and roughly constructed pyramid tombs were erected by the monarchs, who could no longer command an unlimited supply of labour.

The Fifth Dynasty began with Userkaf, the first babe mentioned in the Dedi folk tale, and he was succeeded in turn by the other two, who were not, however, his brothers. The ninth and last king of the dynasty was Wenis. In the so-called Pyramid Texts, in his own tomb and that of Teti, the first king of the Sixth Dynasty, who had married the daughter of Wenis, the monarch was deified as a star god and has been identified with the constellation of Orion. The concept is a remarkable one. It smacks of absolute savagery, and we seem to be confronted with a symbolic revival of Pre-Dynastic cannibalistic rites, which are suggested, according to Maspero, by the gnawed and disconnected bones found in certain early graves. At the original Sed Festival the tribal king, as Flinders Petrie suggests, appears to have been sacrificed and devoured, so that his people might derive from his flesh and blood the power and virtues that made him great. The practice was based on belief in contagious magic. Bulls and boars were eaten to give men strength and courage, deer to give fleetness of foot, and snakes to give cunning. The blood of wounded warriors was drunk so that their skill and bravery might be imparted to the drinkers.[1] King Wenis similarly feasts after death on 'the spirits' known at Heliopolis as 'the fathers and the mothers' and on the bodies of men and gods. He swallows their spirits, souls and names, which are contained in their hearts, livers and entrails, and consequently becomes great and

---

[1] In the *Nibelungenlied* the Burgundians drink the blood of fallen heroes and are refreshed and strengthened. See *Teutonic Myth and Legend*.

all-powerful.[1] The resemblance to the man-eating giants of Europe is extremely striking.

The rendering that follows of the remarkable Wenis hymn is fairly close. It is in metrical form in an endeavour to reproduce the spirit of the original.

Orion[2] in Egypt

Now heaven rains, and trembles every star
With terror; bowmen scamper to escape;
And quakes old Aker, lion of the earth,
While all his worshippers betake to flight,
For Wenis rises and in heaven appears
Like to a god who lived upon his sires
And on his mothers fed.

                         Wenis the lord
Of wisdom is; the secret of his name
Not e'en his mother knows. . . . His rank is high
In heaven above; his power is like to Atum's,
His sire divine . . . Greater than Atum is he.

His shadowy doubles follow him behind
As he comes forth. The uraeus on his brow
Uprears; the royal serpent guides him on;
He sees his ba[3] a flame of living fire.

The strength of Wenis shields him . . . He is now
The Bull of Heaven, doing as he wills,
Feeding on what gives life unto the gods –
Their food he eats who would their bellies fill
With words of power from the pools of flame.

Against the spirits shielded by his might,
Wenis arises now to take his meal –

---

[1] Budge is of the opinion that human beings were sacrificed to the sun god. The practice was 'of vital importance'. Referring to the Ra obelisk in the early sun temples, he says that 'the size and number of conduits to carry away blood bears evidence of the magnitude of the slaughterings' (*Osiris and the Egyptian Resurrection* and *Gods of the Egyptians*).

[2] Osiris, in his fusion with Ra, is addressed as 'you first great sun god', and Isis says 'There proceeds from you the strong Orion in heaven at evening, at the resting of every day' – *The Burden of Isis* ('Wisdom of the East' Series), translated by Dennis.

[3] The soul.

Men he devours; he feasts upon the gods
This lord who reckons offerings: he who makes
Each one to bow his forehead, bending low.

Amkenhuu is snarer; Herthertu
Has bound them well; and Khonsu killer is
Who cuts the throats and tears the entrails out –
'Twas he whom Wenis sent to drive them in . . .
Divided by Shesemu, now behold
The portions cooking in the fiery pots.

Wenis is feasting on their secret names;
Wenis devours their spirits and their souls –
At morn he eats the largest, and at eve
The ones of middle girth, the small at night:
Old bodies are the faggots for his fire.

Lo! Mighty Wenis makes the flames to leap
With thighs of aged ones, and into pots
Are legs of women flung that he may feast.

Wenis, the Power, is the Power of Powers!
Wenis, the mighty god, is god of gods!
Voraciously he feeds on what he finds,
And he is given protection more assured
Than all the mummies 'neath the western sky.

Wenis is now the eldest over all –
Thousands he ate and hundreds he did burn;
He rules o'er Paradise. . . . Among the gods
His soul is rising up in highest heaven –
The Crown is he as the horizon lord.

He reckoned livers as he reckoned knots;
The hearts of gods he ate and they are his;
He swallowed up the White Crown and the Red,
And fat of entrails gulped; the secret names
Are in his belly and he prospers well –
Lo! He devoured the mind of every god,
And so shall live for ever and endure
Eternally, to do as he desires.

The souls of gods are now in his great soul;
Their spirits in his spirit; he obtains
Food in abundance greater than the gods –
His fire has seized their bones, and lo! their souls
Are Wenis's; their shades are with their forms.

Wenis ascends. . . . Wenis ascends with these –
Wenis is hidden, is hidden[1]. . . . An One
For him has ploughed. . . . The seat of every heart
Is Wenis's among all living men.

---

[1] 'Hail, hidden god, Osiris in the underworld.'—*The Burden of Isis*.

Chapter 13

Fall of the Old Kingdom

Nobles become Little Pharaohs – The Growth of Culture – Temple Building – Maxims of Ptah-hotep – Homely Superstitions – Charms to protect Children – Fear of the Evil Eye – Seth and Red-haired Babes – Gruesome Ghosts – Feudal Lords assert Themselves – A Strong Monarch – Military Expeditions – The Promotion of Weni – Coming of the Deng – A Queen's Vengeance – Revolt of Feudal Lords – Pyramids raided.

During the Fifth Dynasty the power of the nobles gradually increased until they became little pharaohs in their own provinces. Even at the court they could make their influence felt, and when they set out on expeditions their successes received personal acknowledgement and were not recorded to the credit of an overshadowing monarch. They recognised the official religion but fostered the local religious cult, and in their tombs related the stories of their own lives, boasting of their achievements and asserting the ethical principles that justified them before Osiris. The age thus became articulate. Education was spreading, and the accumulation of wealth promoted culture. The historic spirit had birth, and the scribes began to record the events of the past and compile lists of kings. Among the tomb pictures of everyday life were inscribed fragments of folk song, and it is evident that music was cultivated, for we find groups of harpists and flautists and singers.

The religious energies of the pharaohs were devoted more to the building of temples than to the erection of tombs. Ra worship introduced elaborate ceremonials, and large numbers of priests were engaged at Heliopolis. At a later period we learn that over 12,000 persons were directly connected with the temples there. The pharaohs continued to reside in the vicinity of Memphis, and the court was maintained with great splendour. Their tombs were erected at Abusir, farther south than those of the Khufu line of kings.

No wars of any consequence occurred during the Fifth Dynasty, but exploring expeditions were fitted out, and in the time of Sahure, the second monarch, the coast of what is now Somalia, which was called Punt, was visited, and there were large imports of gum and resins for incense in the temples, and of wood and precious metals.

The quarries in Sinai continued to be worked, and the name of Pharaoh Isesi is associated with the working of black granite at Wadi Hammamat. We know little or nothing regarding the personalities of the kings. They appear to have reigned with discretion and ability, for the age was one of political progress and extending culture.

In the reign of King Dedka Ra Isesi – to give him his full name – a famous collection of maxims, 'The Instruction of Ptahhotep', was compiled. This collection survives in the Prisse Papyrus, which was called after the French archaeologist who purchased it from an Egyptian in 1847. The author was Isesi's grand vizier, and he was evidently of Memphite birth and a Ptah worshipper, for his name signifies 'Ptah is well pleased'. He lived over a thousand years before Hammurabi, the wise king of Babylon, and long ages before Solomon collected his proverbs at Jerusalem.

The maxims of Ptahhotep were for centuries copied by boys in the schools of ancient Egypt. In their papyrus 'copybooks' they would inscribe the following phrases:

> It is excellent for a son to obey his father.
> He that obeys shall become one who is obeyed.
> Carelessness today becomes disobedience tomorrow.
> He that is greedy for pleasure will have an empty stomach.
> A loose tongue causes strife.
> He that rouses strife will inherit sorrow.
> Good deeds are remembered after death.

The maxims afford us interesting glimpses of the life and culture of the times. Old Ptahhotep is full of worldly wisdom, and his motto is: 'Do your duty and you will be happy'. He advises his son to acquire knowledge and to practise the virtues of right conduct and right living. His precepts are such as we would expect to find among a people who conceived of an Osirian Judgment Hall in the next world.

The 'Instruction' is dedicated to Isesi. The vizier feels the burden of years and laments his fate. He opens in this manner:

> O King, my lord, I draw nigh to life's end,
> To me the frailties of life have come
> And second childhood. . . . Ah! the old lie down
> Each day in suffering; the vision fails,
> Ears become deaf and strength declines apace,
> The mind is ill at ease. . . . An old man's tongue
> Has naught to say because his thoughts have fled,
> And he forgets the day that has gone past. . . .

Meanwhile his body aches in every bone;
The sweet seems bitter, for all taste is lost –
Ah! such are the afflictions of old age,
Which work for evil. . . . Fitful and weak
His breath becomes, standing or lying down.

Ptahhotep then proceeds to petition the king to be released from his duties so that his son may succeed him. He desires to address to the young man the words of wisdom uttered by sages of old who listened when the gods spoke to them.

His majesty at once gives his consent and expresses the hope that Ptahhotep's son will listen with understanding and become an example to princes.

'Speak to him,' adds the king, 'without making him feel weary.'

The 'Instruction' is fairly long – over 4000 words – so that it was necessary to have it copied out. Here are a few of the most representative maxims:

Do not be vain although you are well educated; speak to an illiterate man as you would to a wise one. After all, there is a limit to cleverness; no worker is perfect. Courteous speech is more uncommon than the emeralds that girl slaves find among the stones.

If you speak with an argumentative man who really knows more than you do yourself, listen respectfully to him and do not lose your temper if he differs from you.

If, however, an argumentative man knows less than you do, correct him and show him that you are the wiser of the two; others will approve of you and give you an excellent reputation.

If a man of low rank argues without knowledge, be silent. Do not speak angrily to him. It is not very creditable to put such an one to shame.

When you become a leader, be courteous and see that your conduct is exemplary. . . . Do not tyrannise over men. . . . It is he who gives to those who are in need that prospers; not the man who makes others afraid. . . . Listen graciously to one who appeals to you. Let him speak frankly, and be ever ready to put an end to a grievance. If a man is not inclined to tell everything he knows, it is because he to whom he speaks has the reputation of not dealing fairly. A mind that is well controlled is always ready to consider. . . . See that your employees are adequately rewarded, as is proper on the part of one to whom the god has given much. It is well known that it is no easy thing to satisfy employees. One says today: 'He is generous; I may get much', and tomorrow: 'He is a mean, exacting man'. There is never peace in a town where workers are in miserable circumstances.

That man is never happy who is always engaged reckoning his accounts, but the man whose chief concern is to amuse himself does not provide for his household. . . . If you become rich after having been poor, do not bind your heart with your wealth; because you are the administrator of what the god has given you. Remember that you are not the last, and that others will become as great as you. . . . Enjoy your life, and do not occupy the entire day at your work. Wealth is no use to a worn-out man.

Love your wife; feed her and clothe her well; make her happy; do not deal sternly with her; kindness makes her more obedient than harshness; if she yearns for something that pleasures her eye, see that she gets it. . . . Do not be jealous, or despondent, or cross if you have no children. Remember that a father has his own sorrows, and that a mother has more troubles than a childless woman. . . . How beautiful is the obedience of a faithful son. The god loves obedience; he hates disobedience. A father rejoices in a son's obedience and honours him. A son who listens to counsel guards his tongue and conducts himself well. A disobedient son is foolish and never prospers. He blunders continually. . . . In the end he is avoided because he is a failure. . . . A father should teach wisdom to his sons and daughters so that they may be of good repute. When others find them faithful and just, they will say: 'That father has trained them well'. . . . A good son is a treasure given by the god.

Ptahhotep reminds his son that when he goes to dine with a great man he should take what is given to him. A nobleman gives the daintiest portions to those he likes best. He must not keep staring at his host, or speak until he is spoken to; then he should answer. . . . When he is sent with a message from one nobleman to another he should take care not to say anything that will cause strife between them. He should not repeat what a nobleman said when in a temper.

'Let your heart be more generous than your speech,' advises Ptahhotep as he draws his 'Instruction' to a close. He hopes that his son will prosper as well as he himself has prospered, and that he will satisfy the king by his actions. 'I have lived,' he adds, 'for a hundred and ten years, and have received more honours from his majesty than did any of my ancestors, because I have been just and honourable all through life.'

Such was the ethical, but there was also a superstitious element in Egyptian domestic life. The people believed that the world swarmed with spirits that were continually desiring to inflict injuries on living beings, and were abroad by day as well as by night. An amulet on which was depicted a human hand was considered to be efficacious, and the Egyptian mother suspended it from a cord that was put round the baby's neck. She tied a knot in the morning and another in the evening until there were seven knots in all. On each occasion she repeated a formula over a knot, which was to the following effect: 'Isis has twisted the cord. Nepthys has smoothed it, and it will guard you, my bonnie child, and you will become strong and prosper. The gods and the goddesses will be good to you, and the evil ones will be thwarted. The mouths of those who utter spells against you will be closed. . . . I know all their names, and may those, whose names I know not, suffer also, and that quickly.'[1]

Erman, a German Egyptologist, translated an interesting papyrus by an unknown scribe, which contained the formulae used to protect children. Some children were more liable to be attacked by evil spirits than others. In Europe pretty children required special protection against the evil eye. Red-haired youngsters were disliked because the wicked god Seth was red-haired and was likely to carry them away. Their mothers, therefore, had to exercise special care with them, and there was a particular charm for their use. In Russia red-haired people were believed to have more knowledge of magic than others and were disliked on that account.

The Egyptian ghosts, the enemies of the living, like the archaic deities, were of repulsive aspect. They came from tombs in mummy bandages with cheeks of decaying flesh, flat noses, and eyes of horror, and entered a room with averted faces,[2] which were suddenly turned on children, who at once died of fright. They killed sleeping babes by sucking their breath[3] when they kissed, or rather smelled, them, and if children were found crying they rocked them to sleep – the sleep of death.

When an infant was being hushed to sleep the Egyptian mother sang a ditty to scare away the ghosts of dead men and then made a protecting charm with lettuce, garlic, tow, bones and honey. The following is a rendering of one of the old 'sleepy songs':

> Oh, depart! you ghosts of night,
>> Nor do my baby harm;
> You may come with steps so light,
>> But I'll thwart you with my charm.
>
> For my babe you must not kiss,
>> Nor rock if she should cry –
> Oh! if you did ought amiss,
>> My own, my dear, would die.

---

[1] The knotted cord was in general use throughout Europe. In the Highlands of Scotland red neck cords were used to protect children against the evil eye, while sprains, etc, were cured by knotted cords, a charm being repeated as each knot was tied.

[2] Like Turnface in the boat of the dead.

[3] Cats were credited in Europe with taking away life by sucking children's breath as they lay asleep.

O you dead men, come not near –
  Now I have made the charm –
There's lettuce to prick you here,
  Garlic with smell to harm;

There 's tow to bind like a spell,
  The magic bones are spread;
There 's honey the living love well –
  'T is poison to the dead.

According to tradition, the Sixth-Dynasty kings were not descendants of Meni. Teti, the first king, may have come to the throne as a result of a harem conspiracy. He was a Ra worshipper, and probably a powerful nobleman, supported by a well-organised military force that held the balance of power. The kingdom was in a state of political unrest. In every nome the hereditary chieftains clamoured for concessions from the royal house, and occasionally their requests were couched in the form of demands. Pepy I, the third king of the line, who was a strong monarch, appears to have secured the stability of the throne by promoting a policy of military aggression, which kept the ambitious nobles fully engaged on the northern and southern frontiers. Nubia was invaded with success, and expeditions visited the land of Punt.

The Egyptians had imagined that the edge of the world was somewhere a little beyond the first cataract, and that the intervening space was peopled by demigods, called Manes. Now the horizon was considerably widened. The heavenly Nile was believed to descend in a cascade much farther south than had hitherto been supposed, and the region of mystery was located beyond the area occupied by the too human and ever-aggressive Nubians.

Pepy I selected capable officials of proven loyalty to hold the noblemen in check and secure the equitable distribution of water throughout the kingdom. These were liberally rewarded and were privileged to erect elaborate tombs, like the nome governors, and in these they had their biographies inscribed.

On an Abydos tomb wall are recorded the achievements of Weni, who rose from humble official rank to be the pharaoh's intimate confidant and counsellor. He was, he says, Pepy's 'guardian of heart', and he 'knew everything that happened and every secret affair'. Although he was only 'superintendent of irrigated lands', he exercised more influence over the kingdom than any other dignitary. Royal journeys were arranged by him, and at court ceremonies he marshalled the nobles, which was, no doubt, a delicate task. The perils that continually beset the throne are indicated in his reference to a harem conspiracy. 'When one visited the palace to give secret information against the great royal wife Ametsi, his majesty selected me to enter the harem to listen to business. No scribe was called, nor any other except me alone. I was selected because of my probity and discretion. I recorded everything.'

He was only, he repeats, 'superintendent of irrigated lands'. It was the first occasion on which a man of his rank had listened to harem secrets. Weni tells us no more. We do not even know what fate befell the plotting queen.

When military campaigns were carried out, Weni was placed in command of the army. He tells that there were generals in it, Mamelukes from Lower Egypt, friends of the king, and princes from the north and south, besides a host of officials of high rank. But they had all to obey the man who was only the superintendent of irrigated lands. Evidently the commissariat arrangements were of a simple character. Each man carried his own supply of bread. The inhabitants of the towns they passed through had to supply the soldiers with beer and 'small animals'.

Several campaigns were successfully conducted by Weni, and on each occasion large numbers of the enemy were slain, while 'fig trees were cut down and houses burned'. So firmly was peace established in the south that Merenra, the next monarch, was able to visit the first cataract, where he received the homage of the nobles.

After Weni's death, the chief of a warlike tribe at Elephantine, who was a veritable Rob Roy, came into royal favour. He made several raids into Nubia, and brought back ivory and ebony and gold. On one occasion he returned with a pygmy or Deng. It was a great triumph, for Dengs belonged to the land of the Manes (demigods) and were able to charm even the sulky ferryman who transported the dead over the river of Hades. King Merenra had just died, and his successor, Pepy II, a young man, was greatly excited over the coming of the Deng. Orders were sent to guard the pygmy carefully, and those who slept beside him in the boat were changed ten times each night. The little fellow was welcomed like royalty at Memphis, and he delighted the pharaoh with his strange antics, boisterous manners and war dances. It was the desire of everyone who watched him to be transformed into a Deng after death, so that the ferryman of Hades might come to the bank at once to transport the waiting soul to the other side.

These military expeditions taught the Nubians to respect the power of Egypt, and they subsequently became subjects of the pharaohs.

The Sixth Dynasty, however, was doomed. Conspiring nobles regarded one another with suspicion and cast ambitious eyes on the throne. Local religious cults also gathered strength, and the political influence exercised by the priests of Heliopolis suffered decline. For about three centuries Ra had remained supreme; now his power was being suppressed. Serious revolts occurred. Merenra II – the successor of Pepy II, who is credited with a reign of over ninety years – was deposed twelve months after he ascended the throne. According to Herodotus, who is supported in this connection by Manetho, his queen immediately seized the reins of power. The Egyptian priests informed the Greek historian that Merenra was murdered and that the queen, Nitocris, avenged his death in the following manner. She caused a large subterranean hall to be made for the purpose of celebrating festivals, as she pretended, and invited a number of noblemen to visit it. As the conspirators sat feasting, the waters of the Nile flooded the artificial cave through a secretly constructed canal, and the guests were all drowned. Great indignation was aroused throughout the kingdom, and the queen committed suicide by suffocation in an apartment filled with the fumes of burning wood. The story appears to be more mythical than historical.

At the close of the Sixth Dynasty, the kingdom was plunged into anarchy. The nobles attempted to establish a government in which they were to hold power in rotation. It was impossible for such an arrangement to succeed, because the interests of each feudal lord were centred in his own particular nome, and so the Old Kingdom, which had existed from the time of Meni, came to an end and what is called the First Intermediate Period began. The Seventh Dynasty was brief. According to tradition there were 'seventy kings in seventy days'. Egypt was then divided into a number of small separated states, which were administered by the hereditary owners of the soil; and we find one of them declaring, significantly enough, in his tomb inscription that he had 'freed his city in a time of war from the oppression of the king'.

During the Old Kingdom a great civilisation had evolved. It had grown rich in art and architecture. Indeed, the artistic achievements of the Old Kingdom were never afterwards surpassed, either in technique or naturalism. The grandeur of its architectural triumphs is emphasised by the enduring pyramids, and especially Khufu's great tomb with its finely wrought stonework, which remains unequalled to the present day.

The people, too, had prospered and made great progress. Refined and cultured faces appear in the surviving statuary; indeed, many of the men and women look much like those of the present day. Agriculture flourished, the industries developed, and commerce made the people prosperous. Formal education appears to have been thorough – within its limits – and had gradually become more widespread.

Although the power of the monarchy declined in the First Intermediate Period, the people as a whole did not lapse back into a state of semi-savagery. The nomes were well governed by the nobles, but a system of detached local administration was foredoomed to failure on account of the physical conditions of the country. Egypt required then, as now, a strong central government to promote the welfare of the entire country. A noble might continue to cut canals, but there was no guarantee that he would receive an equitable and regular supply of water. In a country that has to be irrigated, water laws must be strictly observed, otherwise the many will suffer because of the heedlessness or selfishness of the few. When

Nefert, a royal princess of the Old Kingdom period
From the limestone statue in the Cairo Museum

the power of the pharaoh was shattered, the natural resources of Egypt declined and a great proportion of the people were threatened with periodic famines.

The demands of the court when it was at the height of its power may have seemed oppressive to the feudal lords. The pharaoh required a proportion of their crops and livestock, much free labour and many fighting men, because he gave them water and protected them against the inroads of invaders. He also had private ambitions and wished to erect a great tomb for himself. Yet he governed Egypt for the good of the greater number, and the conflicts between the court and the feudal lords were really conflicts between national and local interests. The country as a whole suffered from the effects of extreme governmental decentralisation – a policy inaugurated by priestly pharaohs, who were, perhaps, too greatly concerned about promoting a national religion based on sun worship.

The ascendancy of the nobles was impossible so long as the pharaohs were, in a practical sense, the chief priests of each particular cult. Diplomatic rulers honoured local gods and looked after the building and endowment of temples. They wedged themselves in between the hereditary chieftains and the priests who exercised so powerful an influence over the people. When, however, the nobles became the sole patrons of their nome cults, they were able to defy the court openly.

So, when the throne tottered, a plague of anarchy fell on Egypt, and the forces of reaction were let loose. Nome warred against nome, and the strong prevailed over the weak. Temples were ruthlessly pillaged, and tombs were raided by robber bands. The mummies of hated kings were torn from the pyramids. Statuary was shattered and inscriptions were destroyed. Only in those provinces where good government was maintained did the old order of things remain. But Egypt was so thoroughly disorganised as a whole that several centuries had to elapse before the central government could be once again firmly established in the interests of progress and the welfare of the great mass of the people.

Occasionally a strong pharaoh arose to compel rival lords to make truce with each another, but such successes were only temporary. The feudal system was deeply rooted, and all a king could do was to organise a group of nobles to deal with those who threatened to grow too powerful. He could not raise or maintain a standing army, for each lord commanded all the fighting men in his own nome, and they owed allegiance to him alone; nor could the pharaoh employ mercenaries, because the resources of the royal treasury were strictly limited.

Chapter 14

Father Gods and Mother Goddesses

An Obscure Period – Popularity of Osiris Worship – A Mythical Region – The Lake of Fire – Hershef, who resembles Ptah – Links with Khnum – A Wind God and Earth God – Giants and Elves – The God of Mendes – The Ram a Corn Spirit – Deities fused with Osiris – Feline Goddesses – Flying Serpents The Mother of Mendes – Abydos, the Egyptian Mecca – Foreign Invaders – A Buffer State – North and South in Revolt.

The First Intermediate Period was an obscure and disturbed time. The petty states of Egypt continued to wage sporadic wars of conquest one against another, and a prolonged struggle was in progress for supreme power. In time the political units grew less numerous and several federated tribes were ruled over by powerful feudal lords. The chief centres of government in Upper Egypt were established at Thebes and Herakleopolis. Memphis was for a time the capital of a group of allied nomes in middle Egypt, and at Sais in the north there was a reigning family of whom we know nothing except from casual references in later times. The eastern Delta lay open to invaders, and it is believed that foreign settlements were made there. Ultimately, Egypt was divided into two great states. The southern group of allies was governed by the Theban power, and the northern by the Herakleopolitan. Then history repeated itself, and the kingdom was once again united by a conqueror who pressed northwards from Upper Egypt.

The Eighth-Dynasty kings claimed to be descended from those of the Sixth, but although they reigned at Memphis, their control of the disordered kingdom was so slight that they were unable to erect any monuments. No royal inscriptions survive at the quarries. After a quarter of a century of weak Memphite rule, the powerful nome governor of Herakleopolis Magna seized the throne and established the Ninth Dynasty. The kings of the Tenth Dynasty are also believed to have been his descendants.

Manetho calls the new king Akhthoes, and his name in the hieroglyphs is usually rendered as Kheti. He is also known as Abmerira. Like Khufu, he was reputed in the traditions of later times to have been a great tyrant, who in the end went mad and was eaten by a crocodile. He seems to have held in check for a period the ambitious feudal nobles whose rivalries so seriously retarded the agricultural prosperity of the kingdom. No doubt famines were common.

Each nome promoted its own theological system, and that of Herakleopolis now assumes special interest because of its association with the monarchy. The political influence of the priests of Heliopolis had passed, but the mark of their culture remained. Osiris worship continued to be popular on account of its close association with agriculture. A Horus temple had existed at Herakleopolis from early Dynastic times, but the identity of the god does not appear to have survived the theological changes of the intervening period.

Herakleopolis, which the Egyptians called Khenensu, is of special mythological interest. It came to be recognised as the scene of the great creation myth of the sun worshippers. There Ra, at the beginning, rose from the primeval deep in the form of the sun egg or the lotus flower:

> He who opens and he who closes the door;
> He who said: 'I am but One'.
> Ra, who was produced by himself;
> Whose various names make up the group of gods;
> He who is Yesterday [Osiris] and the Morrow [Ra].

Khenensu district was the scene of the 'war of the gods', who contended against one another at Ra's command – a myth that suggests the everlasting struggle between the forces of nature, which began at Creation's dawn and is always controlled by the sun. Somewhere in the nome were situated the two mythical lakes, 'the lake of natron' and 'the lake of truth', in which Ra cleansed himself, and there, too, at the height of their great struggle – symbolised as the struggle between good and evil – Seth flung filth in the face of Horus, and Horus mutilated Seth. The ultimate victory was due to Ra, who, in the form of the Great Cat that haunted the Persea tree at Heliopolis, fought with the Apep serpent and overcame it. 'On that day,' according to the *Book of the Dead*, 'the enemies of the inviolable god [Osiris] were slain.'

In the vicinity of Khenensu was the fiery region. At the entrance crouched the demon, who had human skin and the head of a greyhound. He was concealed by the door and pounced unexpectedly on 'the damned'; he tore out their hearts, which he devoured, and he swallowed their spirits. So the faithful sun worshippers would pray:

> O Ra-Atum give me deliverance from the demon who devours those who are condemned – he who waits at the door of the fiery place and is not seen. . . . Save me from him who clutches souls, and eats all filth and rottenness by day and by night. Those who dread him are helpless.

At Khenensu lived the Phoenix[1] – the Great Bennu. It resembled an eagle and had feathers of red and gold. Some authorities identified this mythical bird with the planet Venus, which, as the morning star, was 'the guide of the sun god'.

The religion of Herakleopolis was, no doubt, strongly tinged by the theology of the sun worshippers. It seems also to have been influenced by Memphite beliefs. The chief god was Hershef, who bears a stronger resemblance to Ptah Tanen than to Horus. He was a self-created Great Father, whose head was in the heavens while his feet rested on the earth. His right eye was the sun and his left the moon, while his soul was the light that he shed over the world. He breathed from his nostrils the north wind, which gave life to every living being.

'Wind' and 'breath' and 'spirit' were believed by many primitive peoples to be identical.[2] Hershef was therefore the source of universal life. As a 'wind god' he resembles the southern deity Khnum, who was also called Knef (the Kneph of the Greeks). The Egyptian *knef* means 'wind', 'breath' and 'spirit' – 'the air of life'. In Hebrew *nephesh ruach* and in Arabic *ruh* and *nefs* have similar significance.

Ptah Tanen, Khnum and Hershef, therefore, combined not only the attributes of the earth giant Geb but also those of Shu, the wind god, whose lightness is symbolised by the ostrich feather but who had such great strength that he was the 'uplifter' of the heavens. Both Geb and Shu are referred to as self-created deities.

It has been suggested that the elfin Khnum, of whom Ptah was the chief, had a tribal origin and were imported into Egypt. In European lore, dwarfs and giants are closely associated and are at times indistinguishable. The fusion of the dwarf Ptah with the giant Tanen is thus a familiar process, and in the concept we may trace the intellectual life of a mountain people whose giants, or genii, according to Arabian folk belief, dwell in the chain of world-encircling hills.

In what we call Germanic or Teutonic lore, which has pronounced Asiatic elements, the giant is the Great Father, and in what we call Celtic, in which the Mediterranean influence predominates, the giantess is the Great Mother. The Delta Mediterranean people had Great Mother goddesses like Isis, Neith, the virgin deity of Buto, and Bastet. At Mendes there was a Great Father deity who links with Ptah, Hershef and Khnum. He is called Banebtettu, the ram god and 'lord of Tettu', and he became, in the all-embracing theology of Heliopolis, 'the breath [life] of Ra'. In the *Book of the Dead* there is a reference to Ra as 'the lord of air who gives life to all mortals'.

The god of Mendes was reputed to have made 'the wind of life' for all men and was called 'chief of the gods', 'ruler of the sky' and 'monarch of all deities'. The

---

[1] At a later date it was located in Arabia.

[2] 'Spirit' is derived from *spiro*, 'I breathe'. The Aryan root *an* also signifies 'wind' and 'spirit' and survives in words like 'animal' and 'animate', etc.

earth was made fertile by his influence, and he was the origin of the passion of love. He caused the fertilising Nile flood. Like Ptah Tanen, from whose mouth issued forth the waters, and like Ptah, Khnum and Shu, he was the pillar (*dad*) of the sky. Osiris is also associated with the sky prop or props. All these deities appear to have had their origin in crude concepts that survive in various stages of development in European lore.[1]

Like Banebtettu, the Mendes Great Father, Hershef of Herakleopolis was also a ram god, symbolising the male principle; so was Khnum of the first cataract district. In some representations of Ptah, the ram's horns appear on his head. The ram was the primitive Min, who was worshipped throughout Egypt and was absorbed by all the Great Father deities, including Ra. Min was honoured at harvest festivals and was therefore a corn god, a character assumed by the deified King Osiris.

One of the figures of Hershef of Herakleopolis is almost as complex as that of Sokar, the Memphite god of the dead. He is shown with four heads – a ram's head, a bull's head and two heads of hawks. The bull was Mentu, who, like Min, represented the male principle and was also a war god, the epitome of strength and bravery.

All the Great Fathers – Hershef, Ptah, Khnum and Banebtettu – were fused with Osiris. Ptah united with Osiris as ruler of the dead, Khnum became a form of Osiris at Heliopolis, Banebtettu of Mendes was also Banebded, another name for Osiris, and Hershef of Herakleopolis was 'he on the sand', a form of Osiris, who is called 'the god on the sand'.

Hershef is usually represented as a ram-headed man, wearing the white crown with plumes, surmounted by two discs (sun and moon) and two serpents with discs on their heads. Plutarch regarded him as the symbol of 'strength and valour', a concept that accords with the military reputation of at least some of the kings of Herakleopolis, who lived in stormy times.

The goddess associated with Hershef was Atet, who was also call Mersekhnet, a Great Mother deity similar to Hathor, Isis, Neith, and others. She was a cat goddess, and in her cat form was called Maau, an appropriate name. She slew the Apep serpent – a myth that, as we have seen, was absorbed by Ra. Other feline deities are Bastet of Bubastis, Sekhmet, wife of Ptah, and Tefnut.[2]

---

[1] In Scottish archaic lore the mountains are shaped by the wind hag, the mother of giants. The Irish Anu or Danu, associated with the Paps of Anu, has the attributes of a wind goddess and is the mother of deities; the Irish hag Morrigan and her two sisters are the storm hags and war hags. On Jochgrimm Mountain in Tyrol three hags brew the breezes. The Norse Angerboda is an east-wind hag and the enemy of the gods of Asgard. The gods who are wind deities include Zeus and Odin, the 'wild huntsman in the raging host'. The Germanic hags are evidently of pre-Germanic origin; they are what the old Irish mythologists called in Gaelic 'non gods'.

[2] The Norse Freyja, goddess of love, is also a cat goddess. In the Empire period Astarte was added to the Egyptian collection of feline deities.

*Isis and the child Horus
(British Museum)*

*Sekhmet, lion-headed goddess,
wife of Ptah ('Sekhmet, the
destroyer') (British Museum)*

*Bastet, the cat goddess,
holding a Hathor-headed
sistrum and an aegis
(British Museum)*

Three typical Great Mother deities

At Herakleopolis there was a shrine to Neheb-Kau, who, like the virgin deity of Buto in the Delta, was a serpent goddess, symbolising the female principle. She is represented as a flying serpent,[2] a reptile that Herodotus heard much about in Egypt but searched for in vain. She also appears as a serpent with human head, arms and legs. She was worshipped at the ploughing festival before the seed was sown. Like the sycamore goddess, she was believed to take a special interest in the souls of the dead, whom she supplied with celestial food and drink.

Another Herakleopolitan deity was the vine god Heneb, who suggests an Egyptian Bacchus. He was probably a form of Osiris.

The female counterpart of the northern god, Banebtettu, was Herupa-Kaut, Mother of Mendes, who was represented as a woman with a fish on her head. She was in time displaced by Isis, as her son was by Horus. The ceremonies associated with all the mother goddesses were as elaborate as they were indecent.

Osiris worship flourished at Abydos, which became an Egyptian Mecca with its holy sepulchre. The tomb of King Djer, of the First Dynasty, was reputed to be that of the more ancient deified monarch Osiris, and it was visited by pious pilgrims and heaped with offerings. Elaborate religious pageants, performed by priests, illustrated the Osiris-Isis story. Seth, the fearful red demon god, was execrated, and the good Osiris revered and glorified. Isis, mother of the god Horus, was a popular figure. 'I who let fall my hair, which hangs loosely over my forehead, I am Isis when she is hidden in her long tresses.'

Pious worshippers sought burial at Abydos, and its cemetery was crowded with the graves of all classes. Nome governors, however, were interred in their own stately tombs, like those at Beni Hasan and elsewhere, but their mummies were often carried first to Abydos, where the Judgment of the Dead was enacted. The pharaohs appear to have clung to the belief in the Ra barque, which they entered, as of old, by uttering the powerful magic formula. The victory of the early faith was, however, complete among the masses of the people. With the exception of the Ra believers, the worshippers of every other deity in Egypt rested their faith in Osiris, the god of the dead.

Some Egyptologists regard the Herakleopolitans as foreign invaders. Their theology suggests that they were a mountain people of similar origin to the Memphite worshippers of Ptah, but no records survive to afford us definite information on this point. The new monarchs were evidently kept fully engaged by their military operations, and not until nearly the close of the Tenth Dynasty do we obtain definite information regarding the conditions that prevailed during the First Intermediate Period.

There then came into prominence a powerful nome family, who remained faithful to the royal house and kept at bay the aggressive Thebans. In their cliff

---

[2] Isaiah refers to Egypt as 'the land of troubles and anguish, from whence come the young and old lion, the viper and fiery flying serpent' (Isaiah 30:6; see also Isaiah 14:29).

tombs we read inscriptions that indicate that, for a period at least, the pharaohs were able to maintain peace and order in the kingdom. One of these records that the royal officials performed their duties effectively and that war had ceased. Children were no longer killed in their mother's arms, nor were men cut down beside their wives. The rebels were suppressed, and people could sleep out of doors in perfect safety, because the king's soldiers were the terror of all doers of evil. Further, we learn that canals were constructed and that there were excellent harvests – a sure indication that a degree of order had been restored. A standing army was in existence and could be dispatched at short notice to a disturbed area. The nobles appear to have been the pharaoh's generals. They enjoyed intimate relations with the ruling house. One, Tefaba, reduced the south by military force and won a great naval battle on the Nile. His son was a vigorous governor. He stamped out another southern rebellion and made a great display with his fleet, which stretched for miles. But although southern Egypt was temporarily pacified, a rebellion broke out in the north, and Pharaoh Kheti III was suddenly driven from Herakleopolis. His army, however, pressed northwards and won a decisive victory, and he was again placed on the throne, but his reign was brief, and he was the last king of the Tenth Dynasty.

The Delta was now in a state of aggressive revolt, and the power of the Theban house was growing in Upper Egypt. Ultimately the Tenth Dynasty fell to the southern forces, and a new official god and a new royal family appeared as the Middle Kingdom began.

Chapter 15

The Rise of Amun

The Theban Rulers – Need for Centralised Government – Temple Building – The first Amun King – Various Forms of Amun – The Oracle – Mentu the War God – Mut, Queen of the Gods – The Egyptian Cupid – Story of the Possessed Princess – God casts out an Evil Spirit – A Prince's Dream – The God of Spring – Amenemhet's Achievements – Feudal Lords held in Check – The Kingdom United – A Palace Conspiracy – Selection of Sesostris – The First Personality in History.

Inyotef, the feudal lord of the valley of Thebes, was the next pharaoh of Egypt. With him begins the Eleventh Dynasty, the first of the Middle Kingdom. His power was confined chiefly to the south, but he exercised considerable influence over the whole land by gaining possession of sacred Abydos. The custodians of the holy sepulchre were assured of the allegiance of the great mass of the people at this period of transition and unrest.

The new royal line included several King Inyotefs and King Mentuhoteps, but little is known regarding the majority of them. Iyontef I, who was descended from a superintendent of the frontier, probably had royal blood in his veins and a remote claim to the throne. He reigned for fifty years and appears to have consolidated the power of his house. Mentuhotep II, the fifth king, was able to impose his will upon the various feudal lords and secured their allegiance partly, no doubt, by force of arms, but mainly, it would appear, because the prosperity of the country depended on the establishment of a strong central government that would secure the distribution of water for agricultural purposes. Famine may have accomplished what the sword was unable to do. Besides, the road to sacred Abydos had to be kept open. The political influence of the Osirian cult must therefore have been pronounced for a considerable time.

Under Mentuhotep II the country was so well settled that a military expedition was dispatched to quell the Nubian warriors. Commerce had revived, and the arts and industries had begun to flourish again. Temples were built under this and the two succeeding monarchs of the line. The last Mentuhotep was able to organise a quarrying expedition of ten thousand men.

Meanwhile, the power of the ruling house was being securely established throughout the land. The pharaoh's vizier was Ammenemes, and he made vigorous attacks on the feudal lords who pursued a policy of aggression against their neighbours. Some were deposed, and their places were filled by loyal supporters of the pharaoh. After a long struggle between the petty 'kings' of the nomes and the royal house, Ammenemes I founded the Twelfth Dynasty, under which Egypt became once again a powerful and united kingdom. He was probably a grandson of the vizier of the same name.

A new god – the chief god of Thebes – has now risen into prominence. His name is Amun or Amen. The earliest reference to him appears in the pyramid of the famous King Wenis of the Fifth Dynasty, where he and his consort are included among the primeval gods associated with Nu – 'the fathers and mothers' who were in 'the deep' at the beginning. We cannot, however, attach much importance to the theorising of the priests of Wenis's time, for they were busily engaged in absorbing every religious myth in the land. Amun is evidently a strictly local god, who passed through so many stages of development that it is impossible to grasp the original tribal concept, which may, perhaps, have been crude and vague enough. His name is believed to signify 'the hidden one' – he concealed his 'soul' and his 'name', like the giant who hid his soul in an egg.[1] Sokar of Memphis was also a 'hidden' god and was associated with the land of the dead. Amun may have been likewise a deity of Hades, for he links with Osiris as a moon deity (Chapter 22). In fact, as Amun-Ra he displaced Osiris for a time as judge of the dead.

Amun is represented in various forms:

1 as an ape;[2]
2 as a lion resting with head erect, like the primitive earth lion Aker;
3 as a frog-headed man accompanied by Ament, his serpent-headed female counterpart;
4 as a serpent-headed man, while his consort is cat-headed;[3]
5 as a man god with the royal sceptre in one hand and the symbol of life (*ankh*) in the other;
6 as a ram-headed man.

In the Twelfth Dynasty a small temple was erected to Amun in the northern part of the city, which was called Apet, after the mother goddess of that name who ultimately was fused with Hathor. 'Thebes' is believed to have been derived from her name, the female article 'T', being placed before 'Ape', Tap or Tape being pronounced Thebai by the Greeks, who had a town of that name.[4] The sa-

---

[1] Osiris Sokar 'hides his essence in the great shrine of Amun' – *The Burden of Isis*.

[2] Osiris Sokar is addressed: 'Hail, you who grow like unto the ape of Tehuti' (Thoth). The Thoth ape appears to be a dawn god.

[3] Geb is depicted with a serpent's head. The cat goddess is Bastet, who links with other Great Mothers.

[4] Budge's *Gods of the Egyptians*.

cred name of the city was Nu or Nu-Amun. 'Are you better than populous No?' cried the Hebrew prophet, denouncing Nineveh. 'Ethiopia and Egypt were her strength and it was infinite.'

Amun, the ram god, was the most famous oracle in Egypt. Other oracles included the Apis bull; Sebek, the crocodile; Wadjet, the serpent goddess of Buto; and Bes, the grotesque god who comes into prominence later. Revelations were made by oracles in dreams, and when Thuthmosis IV slept in the shadow of the Sphinx it expressed its desire to him that the sand should be cleared from about its body. Worshippers in a state of religious ecstasy were also given power to prophesy.

The oracle of Amun achieved great fame. The god was consulted by warriors, who were duly promised victory and great spoils. Wrongdoers were identified by the god, and he was even consulted regarding affairs of state. Ultimately his priests achieved great influence owing to their reputation as foretellers of future events, who made known the will of the god. A good deal of trickery was evidently indulged in, for we gather that the god signified his assent to an expressed wish by nodding his head or selected a suitable leader of men by extending his arm.

Amun was fused with several deities, as his various animal forms indicate. The ram's head comes, of course, from Min, and it is possible that the frog's head was from Hekt. His cult also appropriated the war god Mentu, who is depicted as a bull. Mentu, however, continued to have a separate existence, owing to his fusion with Horus. He appears in human form wearing a bull's tail with the head of a hawk, which is surmounted by a sun disc between Amun's double plumes. He is also depicted as a hawk-headed sphinx. As a bull-headed man he carries bow and arrows, a club, and a knife.

In his Horus form, Mentu stands on the prow of the sun barque on the nightly journey through Duat and slays the demons with his lance. He was appropriated, of course, by the priests of Heliopolis and became the 'soul of Ra' and 'bull of heaven'. A temple was erected to him near Karnak, and in late times he overshadowed Amun as Mentu-Ra.

Amun was linked with the great sun god in the Eleventh Dynasty, and as Amun-Ra he ultimately rose to the supreme position of national god, while his cult became the most powerful in Egypt. In this form he is dealt with in a later chapter.

Amun's wife was the Theban Mut, whose name signifies 'the mother', and she may be identical with Apet. She was 'queen of the gods' and 'lady of the sky'. Like Nut, Isis, Neith, and others, she was the Great Mother who gave birth to all that exists. She is represented as a vulture and also as a lioness. The vulture is Nekhebet, 'the mother', and the lioness, like the cat, symbolises maternity. Mut wears the double crown of Egypt, which indicates that she absorbed all the Great

Mother goddesses in the land. Her name, in fact, is linked with Isis, with the female Atum, with Hathor, the Buto serpent, etc. In the *Book of the Dead* she is associated with a pair of dwarfs who each have the face of a hawk and the face of a man. It was to Mut that Amenophis III, the father of Akhenaten, erected the magnificent temple at Karnak with its great avenue of ram-headed sphinxes. Queen Tiy's lake in its vicinity was associated with the worship of this Great Mother.

The moon god Khonsu was regarded at Thebes as the son of Amun and Mut. At Hermopolis and Edfu he was linked with Thoth. In the Wenis hymn he is sent out by Orion to drive in and slaughter the souls of gods and men – a myth that explains why stars vanish before the moon. His name means 'the traveller'.

As a moon deity Khonsu caused the crops to spring up and ripen. He was also the Egyptian Cupid, who touched the hearts of lads and girls with love. The oracle of Khonsu was consulted by those who prayed for offspring. Agriculturists praised him for increasing their flocks and herds.

This popular god also gave 'the air of life' to the newly born and was thus a wind god like Hershef and Khnum. As ward of the atmosphere, he exercised control over the evil spirits that caused the various diseases and took possession of human beings, rendering them epileptic or insane. Patients were cured by Khonsu, 'giver of oracles', whose fame extended beyond the bounds of Egypt.

An interesting papyrus of the Ramessid period relates the story of a miraculous cure effected by Khonsu. It happened that the pharaoh, 'the Horus, he who resembles Atum, the son of the sun, the mighty with scimitars, the smiter of the nine-bow barbarians', etc, was collecting the annual tribute from the subject kings of Syria. The Prince of Bakhten,[1] who brought many gifts, 'placed in front of these his eldest daughter'. She was very beautiful, and the pharaoh immediately fell in love with her, and she became his 'royal wife'.

Some time afterwards the Prince of Bakhten appeared at Uas (Thebes) with an envoy. He brought presents to his daughter and, having prostrated himself before the 'son of the sun', announced:

'I have travelled hither to plead with Your Majesty for the sake of Bentrash, the younger sister of your royal wife. She is stricken with a grievous malady that causes her limbs to twitch violently. I entreat Your Majesty to send a learned magician to see her, so that he may give her aid in her sore distress.'

Pharaoh said: 'Let a great magician who is learned in the mysteries be brought before me.'

As he wished, so was it done. A scribe of the House of Life appeared before him, and his majesty said: 'It is my will that you should travel to Bakhten to see the younger daughter of the royal wife.'

The magician travelled with the envoy, and when he arrived at his journey's

---

[1] Identified with the king of the Hittites who became the ally of Rameses II.

end he saw the Princess Bentrash, whom he found to be possessed of a hostile demon of great power. But he was unable to draw it out.

Then the Prince of Bakhten appeared at Uas a second time, and addressing the pharaoh said: 'O King, my lord, let a god be sent to cure my daughter's malady!'

His majesty was compassionate, and he went to the temple of Khonsu and said to the god: 'Once again I have come on account of the little daughter of the Prince of Bakhten. Let your image be sent to cure her.'

Khonsu, 'giver of oracles' and 'expeller of evil spirits', nodded his head, assenting to the prayer of the king, and caused his fourfold divine nature to be imparted to the image.

So it happened that the statue of Khonsu was placed in an ark, which was carried on poles by twelve priests while two chanted prayers. When it was carried from the temple, pharaoh offered up burning incense, and five boats set out with the ark and the priests, accompanied by soldiers, a chariot and two horses.

The Prince of Bakhten came forth from his city to meet the god, accompanied by many soldiers, and prostrated himself.

'So you have indeed come,' he cried. 'You are not hostile to us. The goodwill of the Pharaoh has caused you to come here.'

Khonsu was then carried into the presence of the Princess Bentrash, who was immediately cured of her malady. The evil demon was cast out, and it stood before the god and said: 'Peace be with you, O mighty god. The land of Bakhten is your possession, and its people are your slaves. I am your slave also. As you wish, I will return again to the place whence I came. But first let the Prince of Bakhten hold a great feast that I may partake thereof.'

Khonsu then instructed a priest, saying: 'Command the Prince of Bakhten to offer up a great sacrifice to the evil spirit whom I have expelled from his daughter.'

Great fear fell upon the prince and the army and all the people when the sacrifice was offered up to the demon by the soldiers. Then amidst great rejoicings that spirit of evil took its departure and went to the place from where it had come, according to the wish of Khonsu, 'the giver of oracles'.

Then the Prince of Bakhten was joyful of heart, and he desired that Khonsu should remain in the land. As it happened, he kept the image of the god for over three years.

One day the prince lay asleep on his couch, and a vision came to him in a dream. He saw the god rising high in the air like a hawk of gold and taking flight towards the land of Egypt. He awoke suddenly, trembling with great fear, and he said: 'Surely the god is angry with us. Let him be placed in the ark and carried back to Uas.'

The prince caused many rich presents to be laid in the temple of the god when his image was returned.

Courtyard of an Egyptian temple (restored)

One of Khonsu's popular names was 'the beautiful one at rest'. He was depicted, like the Celtic love god Angus, 'the ever-young', as a handsome youth. The upper part of a particularly striking statue of this handsome deity was found in the ruins of his temple at Karnak.

As a nature god, Khonsu was a hawk-headed man, crowned with a crescent moon and the solar disc; he was a sun god in spring. Like Thoth, he was also an architect, 'a deviser of plans' and a 'measurer', for he measured the months. Both the lunar deities are evidently of great antiquity. The mother-goddess-and-son concept is associated with the early belief in the female origin of the world and of life. The Great Mother was self-created, as the Great Father was, and the strange Egyptian idea that a god became 'husband of his mother' arose from the fusion of the conflicting ideas regarding creation.

Ammenemes I, the first great ruler who promoted the worship of Amun, was also assiduous in honouring the other influential deities. From Tanis in the Delta, southwards into the heart of Nubia, he has left traces of his religious fervour, which had, of course, a diplomatic motive. He erected a red granite altar to Osiris at sacred Abydos, a temple to Ptah at Memphis. He honoured the goddess Bastet with monuments at Bubastis and duly adored Amun, of course, at Thebes. His ka statues were distributed throughout the land, for he was the 'son of Ra' and had therefore to be worshipped as 'the god' – the human incarnation of the sun god.

Ammenemes was an active military ruler. Not only did he defeat the Syrians and the Nubians, but he also punished the rebellious feudal lords who did not bend to his will. New and far-reaching changes were introduced into the system of local, as well as central, government. The powers of nome governors were restricted. When one was forcibly deposed, an official took his place and the appointment of town rulers and mayors of villages became once again vested in the crown. This policy was followed by Ammenemes's successors, until ultimately the feudal system, which for centuries had been a constant menace to the stability of the throne, was finally extinguished. The priestly allies of the provincial nobles were won to the crown by formal recognition and generous gifts, and all the chief gods, with the exception of Ptah, were included in the 'family' of Amun-Ra.

Ammenemes gathered about him the most capable men in the kingdom. Once again it was possible for humble officials to rise to the highest rank. The industries of the country were fostered, and agriculture received special attention, so that harvests became plentiful again and there was an abundance of food in Egypt.

When the king was growing old, he selected his son Sesostris to succeed him. Apparently the choice did not please some of the influential members of the royal house. In the 'Instruction of Ammenemes', a metrical version of which is given at the end of the next chapter (page 182), we learn that a harem conspiracy was organised to promote the claims of a rival to the throne. A band of conspirators gained access to the palace through a tunnel that had been secretly constructed and burst in upon the old monarch as he lay resting after he had eaten his evening meal. He 'showed fight', although unarmed, and in the parley that ensued was evidently successful. It appears to have been accepted that the succession of Sesostris was inevitable.

How the conspirators were dealt with we have no means of knowing. It is possible that the majority of them were pardoned. So long as Ammenemes remained alive, they were safe, but they must have feared the vengeance of Sesostris, who was a vigorous and warlike prince and eminently worthy to succeed his father. The papyrus story of 'The Flight of Sinuhe' is evidently no mere folk tale but a genuine fragment of history. It is possible that Sinuhe was one of the sons of Ammenemes. At any rate, he appears to have been compromised in the abortive palace conspiracy. When the old king died at Memphis, where he appears to have resided most often, a messenger was hurriedly dispatched to Sesostris, who was engaged in leading an army against the troublesome Libyans. None of the other princes was informed, and Sinuhe, who overheard the messenger informing the new king of his father's death, immediately fled towards Syria. He found that other Egyptians had taken refuge there.

After many years had elapsed, his whereabouts were revealed to King Sesostris, who was evidently convinced of his innocence. Sinuhe was invited to return to Egypt and was welcomed at the palace by his royal kinsman.

The narrative has a homely and graceful character, and affords us more intimate knowledge of the life of the period than can be obtained from tomb inscriptions and royal monuments. Sinuhe is one of the earliest personalities in history. We catch only fleeting glimpses of the man Ammenemes in his half-cynical 'Instruction', with its vague references to a palace revolt. In the simple and direct narrative of the fugitive prince, however, we are confronted by a human being whose emotions we share and with whom we are able to sympathise. The latter part of the story has some of happy touches. Our old friend rejoices because he is privileged once again to sleep in a comfortable bed after lying for long years in the desert sand. He throws away his dirty rustic clothing and dresses himself in perfumed linen, and feels young when his beard is shaved off and his baldness is covered by a wig. He is provided with a mansion that is newly decorated, but what pleases him most is the presence of the children who come to visit him. He was fond of children. . . . Our interest abides with a man who was buried, as he wished to be, after long years of wandering, in the land of his birth, some forty centuries ago!

Chapter 16

Tale of the Fugitive Prince

A Libyan Campaign – Death of King Ammenemes – The Prince's Flight – Among the Bedouins – An Inquisitive Chief – The Prince is honoured – A Rival Hero – Challenge to Single Combat – Sinuhe victorious – Egyptian Love of Country – Appeal to Pharaoh – Prince returns Home – Welcome at the Court – A Golden Friend – An Old Man made Happy.

Sinuhe, 'son of the sycamore', was a hereditary prince of Egypt. When war was waged against the Libyans, he accompanied the royal army, which was commanded by Sesostris, the chosen heir of the great Ammenemes. As it happened, the old king died suddenly on the seventh day of the second month of Shait. Like the Horus hawk, he flew towards the sun. Then there was great mourning in the palace. The gates were shut and sealed, and noblemen prostrated themselves outside. Silence fell on the city.

The campaign against the Libyans was being conducted with much success. Many prisoners were taken and large herds of cattle were captured. The enemy were scattered in flight.

Now the nobles, who had taken possession of the palace, met in together, and they dispatched a trusted messenger to Prince Sesostris, so that he might be secretly informed of the death of his royal father. All the king's sons were with the army, but none of them was called when the messenger arrived. The messenger spoke to no man of what had happened except Sesostris alone.

Now it happened that Sinuhe was concealed near to the new king when the secret tidings were brought to him. He heard the words that the messenger spoke, and immediately he was stricken with fear. His heart shook and his limbs trembled, but he retained his presence of mind. His first thought was for his own safety, so he crept quietly away until he found a safe hiding place. He waited until the new king and the messenger walked on together, and they passed very close to him as he lay concealed in a thicket.[1]

No sooner had they gone out of hearing than Sinuhe hurried to escape from Egypt. He made his way southwards, wondering greatly as he went if civil war had broken out. When night was far spent, he lay down in an open field and slept. In the morning he hurried along the highway and overtook a man who

[1] No reason is given in the story for Sinuhe's sudden alarm.

176

showed signs of fear. The day passed, and in the evening he crossed the river on a raft to a place where there were quarries. He was then in the region of the goddess Hirit of the Red Mountains, and he turned northwards. On reaching a frontier fortress, which had been built to repel the raiding Bedouin archers, he concealed himself lest he should be observed by the guards.

As soon as it grew dark, he continued his journey. He travelled all night long, and when dawn broke he reached the Qumor valley. . . . His strength was nearly spent. He was tortured by thirst, his tongue was parched and his throat was swollen. Greatly he suffered, and he moaned to himself: 'Now I begin to taste of death.' Yet he struggled on in his despair, and suddenly his heart was cheered by the sound of a man's voice and the sweet lowing of cows.

He had arrived among the Bedouins. One of them spoke to him kindly, and first gave him water to drink and then some boiled milk. The man was a chief, and he perceived that Sinuhe was an Egyptian of high rank. He showed him much kindness, and when the fugitive was able to resume his journey the Bedouin gave him safe conduct to the next camp. So from camp to camp Sinuhe made his way until he reached the land of the Edomites, and then he felt safe there.

About a year went past, and then Amuanishi, chief of Upper Tonu, sent a messenger to Sinuhe, saying: 'Come and reside with me and hear the language of Egypt spoken.'

There were other Egyptians in the land of Edom, and they had praised the prince highly, so that the chief desired greatly to see him

Amuanishi spoke to Sinuhe, saying: 'Now tell me frankly why you have fled to these parts. Is it because someone has died in the royal palace? Something appears to have happened of which I am not aware.'

Sinuhe made an evasive answer: 'I certainly fled here from the country of the Libyans, but not because I did anything wrong. I never spoke or acted treasonably, nor have I listened to treason. No magistrate has received information regarding me. I really can give no explanation why I came here. It seems as if I obeyed the will of King Ammenemes, whom I served faithfully and well.'

The Bedouin chief praised the great king of Egypt, and said that his name was dreaded as greatly as that of Sekhmet, the lioness goddess, in the time of famine.

Sinuhe again spoke, saying: 'Know now that the son of Ammenemes sits on the throne. He is a just and tactful prince, an excellent swordsman, and a brave warrior who has never yet met his equal. He sweeps the barbarians from his path; he hurls himself upon robbers; he crushes heads and strikes down those who oppose him, for he is indeed a valiant hero without fear. He is also a swift runner when pursuing his foes, and he smites them with the claws of a lion, for they cannot escape him. Sesostris rejoices in the midst of the fray, and none can withstand him. To his friends he is the essence of courtesy, and he is much loved throughout the land. All his subjects obey him gladly. Although he extends his southern frontier he has no desire to invade the land of the Bedouins. If it happens, however, that he should come here, tell him that I live among you.'

The chief heard and then said: 'My wish is that Egypt may flourish and have peace. As for yourself, you will receive my hospitality so long as you please to live here.'

Then Sinuhe was given as his wife the eldest daughter of the chief of Upper Tonu. He was also allowed to select for himself a portion of land in that excellent country which is called Aia. There was an abundance of grapes and figs. Wine was more plentiful than water. The land flowed with milk and honey. Olives were numerous, and there were large supplies of corn and wheat, and many cattle of every kind.

The chief honoured Sinuhe greatly and made him a prince in the land so that he was a ruler of a tribe. Each day the Egyptian fared sumptuously on cooked meat and roasted fowl and on the game he caught, or which was brought to him, or was captured by his dogs, and he always had bread and wine. His servants made butter and gave him boiled milk of every kind as he wished.

Many years went past. Children were born to him, and they grew strong and, in time, each ruled over a tribe. When travellers were going past, they turned aside to visit Sinuhe, because he showed great hospitality. He gave refreshment to those who were weary, and if it happened that a stranger was plundered, he chastised the wrongdoers; he restored the stolen goods and gave the man safe conduct.

Sinuhe commanded the Bedouins who fought against invaders, for the chief of Upper Tonu had made him general of the army. Many and great were the successes he achieved. He captured prisoners and cattle and returned with large numbers of slaves. In battle he fought with much courage with his sword and his bow. He displayed great cunning on the march and in the manner in which he arranged the plan of battle The chief of Tonu loved him dearly when he saw how powerful he had become, and elevated Sinuhe to still higher rank.

There was a mighty hero in Tonu who had achieved much fame, and he was jealous of the Egyptian. The man had no other rival in the land. He had killed all who had dared to stand up against him. He was brave and he was bold, and he said: 'I must needs combat with Sinuhe. He has not yet met me.'

The warrior wished to slay the Egyptian and win for himself the land and cattle that he owned.

When the challenge was received, the chief of Tonu was much concerned and spoke to Sinuhe, who said:

'I do not know this fellow. He is not of my rank, and I do not associate with his kind. Nor have I ever done him any wrong. If he is a thief who wishes to obtain my goods, he had better be careful how he behaves himself. Does he think I am a steer and that he is the bull of war? If he wishes to fight with me, let him have the opportunity. As it is his will, so let it be. Will the god forget me? Whatever happens will happen as the god wishes.'

Having spoken thus, Sinuhe retired to his tent and rested. Then he prepared his bow and made ready his arrows, and he saw that his arms were polished.

When dawn came, the people assembled around the place of combat. They were there in large numbers; many had travelled from remote parts to watch the duel. All the subjects of the chief of Tonu greatly wished that Sinuhe should be the victor. But they feared for him. Women cried 'Ah!' when they saw the challenging hero, and the men said one to another: 'Can any man prevail over this warrior? See, he carries a shield and a lance and a battle-axe, and he has many javelins.'

Sinuhe came out. He pretended to attack, and his adversary first threw the javelins; but the Egyptian turned them aside with his shield, and they fell harmlessly to the ground. The warrior then swung his battle-axe, but Sinuhe drew his bow and shot a swift arrow. His aim was sure, for it pierced his opponent's neck so that he gave a loud cry and fell forward on his face. Sinuhe seized the lance and, having thrust it through the warrior's body, he raised a shout of victory.

Then all the people rejoiced together, and Sinuhe gave thanks to Mentu, the war god of Thebes, as did also the followers of the slain hero, for he had oppressed them greatly. The chief ruler of Tonu embraced the victorious prince with a glad heart.

Sinuhe took possession of all the goods and cattle that the boastful warrior had owned and destroyed his house. So he grew richer as time went on. But old age was coming over him. In his heart he wished greatly to return to Egypt again and to be buried there. His thoughts dwelt on this matter, and he decided to appeal to King Sesostris. Then he drew up a petition and dispatched it in the care of a trusted messenger to the royal palace. Addressing his majesty as 'the servant of Horus' and 'son of the sun', Sinuhe wrote:

> I have put my faith in the god, and lo! he has not failed me. . . . Although I fled away from Egypt my name is still of good repute in the palace. I was hungry when I fled and now I supply food to others. I was naked when I fled and now I am clad in fine linen. I was a wanderer and now I have many followers. I had no riches when I fled and now possess land and a dwelling. . . . I entreat of Your Majesty to permit me to sojourn once again in the place of my birth, which I love dearly, so that when I die my body may be embalmed and laid in a tomb in my native land. I, who am a fugitive, entreat you now to permit me to return home. . . . To the god I have given offerings so that my desire may be fulfilled, for my heart is full of regret – I who took flight to a foreign country.

May Your Majesty grant my request to visit once again my native land so that I may be your favoured subject. I humbly salute the queen. It is my desire to see her once again and also the children so that life may be renewed in my blood. Alas! I am growing old; my strength is diminishing; my eyes are dim; I totter when I walk, and my heart is feeble. Well I know that death is at hand. The day of my burial is not far off. . . . Before I die, may I gaze on the queen and hear her talk about her children so that my heart may be made happy until the end.

King Sesostris read the petition that Sinuhe had sent to him and was graciously pleased to grant his request. He sent presents to his fugitive subject, and messages from the princes, his royal sons, accompanied his majesty's letter, which declared:

These are the words of the King. . . . What did you do, or what has been done against you, that you fled away to a foreign country? What went wrong? I know that you never calumniated me, but although your words may have been misrepresented, you did not speak next time in the gathering of the lords even when called upon. . . . Do not let this matter be remembered any longer. See, too, that you do not change your mind again. . . . As for the queen, she is well and receives everything she wishes. She is in the midst of her children. . . .

Leave all your possessions, and when you return here you may live in the palace. You will be my closest friend. Do not forget that you are growing older each day now; that the strength of your body is diminishing and that your thoughts dwell on the tomb. You will be given seemly burial; you will be embalmed; mourners will wail at your funeral; you will be given a gilded mummy case, which will be covered with a cypress canopy and drawn by oxen; the funeral hymn will be sung and the funeral dance will be danced; mourners will kneel at your tomb crying with a loud voice so that offerings may be given to you. Lo! all shall be as I promise. Sacrifices will be made at the door of your tomb; a pyramid will be erected and you will lie among princes. . . . You must not die in a foreign country. You are not to be buried by Bedouins in a sheep skin. The mourners of your own country will smite the ground and mourn for you when you are laid in your pyramid.

When Sinuhe received this message he was overcome with joy and wept. He threw himself on the sand and lay there. Then he leapt up and cried out: 'Is it possible that such good fortune has befallen an unfaithful subject who fled from his native land to a hostile country? Great mercy is shown to me this day. I am delivered from the fear of death.'

Sinuhe slays the warrior of Tonu
From the painting by Maurice Greiffenhagen

Sinuhe sent an answer to the king saying:

> You mighty god, what am I that you should favour me thus? . . . If Your Majesty will summon two princes who know what occurred they will relate all that came to pass. . . . It was not my desire to flee from Egypt. I fled as in a dream. . . . I was not followed. I had not heard of any rebellious movement, nor did any magistrate receive my name. . . . I fled as if I had been ordered to flee by His Majesty. . . . As you have commanded, I will leave my riches behind me, and those who are my heirs here will inherit them. . . . May Your Majesty have eternal life.

When he had written this to his majesty, Sinuhe gave a great feast, and he divided his wealth among his children. His eldest son became the leader of the tribe, and he received the land and the corn fields, the cattle and the fruit trees, in that pleasant place. Then Sinuhe turned his face towards Egypt. He was met on the frontier by the officer who commanded the fort, who sent tidings to the palace of Sinuhe's approach. A boat laden with presents went to meet him, and the fugitive spoke to all the men who were in it as if he were of their own rank, for his heart was glad.

A night went past, and when the land grew bright again he drew near to the palace. Four men came out to conduct him, and the children awaited his coming in the courtyard, as did also the nobles who led him before the king.

His majesty sat on his high throne in the great hall, which is adorned with silver and gold. Sinuhe prostrated himself. The king did not at first recognise him, yet he spoke kindly words; but the poor fugitive was unable to make answer. He grew faint; his eyes were blinded and his limbs were without strength. It seemed as if he were about to die.

The king said: 'Help him to rise up so that we may converse one with another.'

The courtiers lifted Sinuhe, and his majesty said: 'So you have returned again. I perceive that in skulking about in foreign lands and playing the fugitive in the desert you have worn yourself out. You have grown old, Sinuhe. . . . But why do you not speak? Have you become deceitful like the Bedouin. Declare your name. What causes you to feel afraid?'

Sinuhe found his tongue and said: 'I am unnerved, Your Majesty. I have naught to answer for. I have not done that which deserves the punishment of the god. . . . I am faint, and my heart has grown weak, as when I fled. . . . Once again I stand before Your Majesty. My life is in your hands. Do with me according to your will.'

As he spoke, the royal children entered the great hall, and his majesty said to the queen:

'This is Sinuhe. Look at him. He has come like a desert dweller in the dress of a Bedouin.'

The queen uttered a cry of astonishment, and the children laughed, saying: 'Surely it is not him, Your Majesty?'

The king said: 'Yes, it is Sinuhe.'

Then the royal children decked themselves with jewels and sang before the king, each tinkling a sweet sistrum. They praised his majesty and called upon the gods to give him health and strength and prosperity, and they pleaded for Sinuhe, so that royal favours might be conferred on him.

> Mighty your words and swift your will!
>> Then bless your servant in your sight –
> With air of life his nostrils fill,
>> Who from his native land took flight.
> Your presence fills the land with fear;
>> Then marvel not he fled away –
> All cheeks grow pale when you are near;
>> All eyes are stricken with dismay.

The king said: 'Sinuhe must not tremble in my presence, for he will be a golden friend and chief among the courtiers. Take him hence that he may be attired as befits his rank.'

Then Sinuhe was conducted to the inner chamber, and the children shook hands with him. He was given apartments in the house of a prince, the son of the king, in which he obtained dainty things to eat. There he could sit in a cool chamber; there he could eat refreshing fruit; there he could dress himself in royal garments and anoint his body with perfumes; and there courtiers waited to converse with him and servants to obey his will.

He grew young again. His beard was shaved off, and his baldness was covered with a wig. The smell of the desert left him when his rustic garments were thrown away, and he was dressed in linen garments and anointed with perfumed oil. Once again he lay on a bed – he who had left the sandy desert to those accustomed to it.

In time Sinuhe was provided with a house in which a courtier had dwelt, when it had been repaired and decorated. He was happy there, and his heart was made glad by the children who visited him. The royal children were continually about his house.

King Sesostris caused a pyramid to be erected for Sinuhe. His statue was also carved at his majesty's command, and it was decorated with gold.

'It was for no ordinary man,' adds the scribe, who tells us that he copied the story faithfully, 'that the king did all these things. Sinuhe was honoured greatly by his majesty until the day of his death.'

The Instruction of Ammenemes

Be in splendour like the god, my son . . .
Hearken and hear my words, if you would reign
In Egypt and be ruler of the world,
Excelling in your greatness. . . . Live apart
In stern seclusion, for the people heed
The man who makes them tremble; mingle not
Alone among them; have no bosom friend,
Nor intimate, nor favourite in your train –
These serve no goodly purpose.

                    Before to sleep
You lie down, prepare to guard your life –
A man is friendless in the hour of trial. . . .
I to the needy gave, the orphan nourished,
Esteemed alike the lowly and the great;
But he who ate my bread made insurrection,
And those my hands raised up, occasion seized
Rebellion to create. . . . They went about
All uniformed in garments that I gave
And deemed me but a shadow. . . . Those who shared
My perfumes for anointment, rose betimes
And broke into my harem.

                    Through the land
Beholden are my statues, and men laud
The deeds I have accomplished . . . yet I made
A tale heroic that has ne'er been told,
And triumphed in a conflict no man saw. . . .

Surely these yearned for bondage when they smote
The king who set them free. . . . Methinks, my son,
Of no avail is liberty to men
Grown blind to their good fortune.

                    I had dined
At eve and darkness fell. I sought to rest
For I was weary. On my bed I lay

And gave my thoughts release, and so I slept. . . .
The rebels 'gan to whisper and take arms
With treacherous intent . . . I woke and heard
And like the desert serpent waited there
All motionless but watchful.

                      Then I sprang
To fight and I alone. . . . A warrior fell,
And lo! he was the captain of my guard.
Ah! had I but his weapons in that hour
I should have scattered all the rebel band –
Mighty my blows and swift! . . . but he, alas!
Was like a coward there. . . . Nor in the dark,
And unprepared, could I achieve renown.

Hateful their purpose! . . . I was put to shame.
You were not near to save. . . . Announced I then
That you did reign, and I had left the throne.
And gave commands according to your will. . . .
Ah! as they feared me not, 'twas well to speak
With courtesy before them. . . . Would I could
Forget the weakness of my underlings!

My son, Sesostris, say – are women wont
To plot against their lords? Lo! mine have reared
A brood of traitors and assembled round
A rebel band forsworn. They did deceive
My servants with command to pierce the ground
For speedy entry.

                    Yet to me from birth
Misfortune has a stranger been. I ne'er
Have met my equal among valiant men . . .
Lo! I have set in order all the land.
From Elephantine adown the Nile
I swept in triumph: so my feet have trod
The outposts of my kingdom. . . . Mighty deeds
Must now be measured by the deeds I've done.

I loved the corn god. . . . I have grown the grain
In every golden valley where the Nile

Entreated me; none hungered in my day,
None thirsted, and all men were well content –
They praised me, saying: 'Wise are his commands'.

I fought the lion and the crocodile,
I smote the dusky Nubians, and put
The Asian dogs to flight.

                                        My house I built
Gold-decked with azure ceilings, and its walls
Have deep foundations; doors of copper are,
The bolts of bronze. . . . It shall endure all time.
Eternity regards it with dismay!
I know each measurement, O Lord of All!

Men came to see its beauties, and I heard
In silence while they praised it. No man knew
The treasure that it lacked. . . . I wanted you,
My son, Sesostris. . . . Health and strength be yours!
I lean upon you, O my heart's delight;
For you I look on all things. . . . Spirits sang
In that glad hour when you were born to me.

All things I've done, now know, were done for you;
For you must I complete what I began
Until the end draws near. . . . O be my heart
The isle of your desire. . . . The white crown now
Is given you, O wise son of the god –
I'll hymn your praises in the barque of Ra. . . .
Your kingdom at Creation was. 'Tis yours
As it was mine – how mighty were my deeds!
Rear your statues and adorn your tomb. . . .
I struck your rival down. . . . 'Twould not be wise
To leave him near you. . . . Health and strength be yours!

Chapter 17

Egypt's Golden Age

A Leader of Men – Gloomy Prophecy – Agriculture flourishing – The Chief Treasurer and his Auditors – Great Irrigation Scheme – Lake Moeris formed – Military Expeditions – A Murdered King – Disturbing Race Movements – First Mention of Hittites – Abraham in Egypt – Syria invaded – The Labyrinth – Like Mazy Cretan Palace – Fall of Knossos – Bronze in Egypt – Copper and Iron – Trade in Tin – The British Mines – Spiral Ornament in Egypt and Europe.

The Twelfth Dynasty in the Middle Kingdom, which embraces just over two centuries, was a period of industrial and intellectual activity and is appropriately called the Golden Age of Egypt. It was ushered in, as we have seen, by Ammenemes I, whose name signifies 'Amun leads'. The king was, in a true sense, a leader of men. He displayed great military and administrative genius, and proved to be a saviour of the people. He rose to power at a time when a great crisis was approaching. The kingdom had grown weak as a result of prolonged internal dissension, and its very existence as a separate power was being threatened by invaders on the northern and southern frontiers. The hour had come, and with it the man.

Ammenemes subdued the Nubians, who were warlike and aggressive. He cleared the eastern Delta of hordes of Asiatics, attracted there by prospects of plunder and the acquisition of desirable territory, and he reduced by shattering blows the growing power of the Libyans. His administrative reforms were beneficial to the great mass of the people, for the establishment of a strong central government protected them from brigands and the periodic visitations of devastating famines. Agriculture was promoted, and the revival of trade ensured a more equitable distribution of wealth. As the influence of the feudal lords declined, it became possible for capable men of humble rank to attain high official positions.

In a striking literary production of the age, a prophetic scribe, named Apura, stands before his king, uttering grave warnings of approaching national disaster. He pictures Egypt in the throes of revolution – brothers contend against brothers; men cease to till the soil. The prophet exclaims:

In vain will the Nile rise in flood, for the land will lie barren. Men who were wont to plough will say: 'What is the good of it? We know what is coming.' No children will be born in Egypt. Poor people will seize on treasure. A man hitherto unable to purchase sandals will obtain possession of much grain. Diseases will decimate all classes; a terrible plague will smite the land; there will be war and much shedding of blood. Rich men will sorrow and poor men will laugh. All the cities will desire to throw off the yoke of their rulers. . . . Slaves will plunder their masters, and their wives will be decked with fine jewellery. Royal ladies will be driven from their homes; they will sit in the dust, wailing: 'Oh! that we had bread to eat.'

Thus, he declared, Egypt would suffer from the Conquest of Evil. But a more terrible conquest would immediately follow. Suddenly foreigners would enter the land to set up barbarous rule. Then all classes of Egyptians would endure great afflictions.

Having drawn this dark and terrible picture, the prophet foretells that a great deliverer is to arise. He will 'cool the fire of oppression' and will be called 'the shepherd of his people'. He will gather together his wandering flocks. He will defeat the wrongdoer. He will stir up enthusiasm in the hearts of the men of Egypt and become their leader. 'May he indeed be their deliverer!' exclaims the scribe. 'Where is he to be found? Is he already here, waiting among the people?'

It is possible that at this period contemporary historical events were narrated in the prophetic manner and that the scribe was eulogising the reigning pharaoh and justifying his reforms. In the 'Instruction of Ammenemes' the old king reflects with astonishment that those he set free should rise up against him. A more literal rendering of his remark is: 'He struggles for an ox that is bound who has no memory of yesterday'. Ammenemes had set the people free, and those who had received benefits showed that they failed to appreciate them by espousing the cause of their old oppressors. Was it their desire to become serfs again?

The condition of the past is reflected in the tomb inscription of one of the nome lords whose family owed its rise to its loyalty to the monarch. He boasts that every available piece of land under his jurisdiction was thoroughly cultivated. He protected the lives of the people. None starved, for he saw that all received food. A widow was treated in the same manner as a woman whose husband was alive, and when relief was given the poor received the same treatment as the powerful. Financial embarrassment is not a modern phenomenon. The problem is one of long standing, for this governor – Ameni of the Gazelle nome – states that when the river rose high, and there was an abundance of produce, he 'did not oppress the peasant because of his arrears'.

It was the duty of the chief treasurer to see that the various nomes were administered in such a manner that they yielded adequate surpluses. A 'sinking fund' was instituted for bad years, and relief was given in those localities where harvests were insufficient. The problem of irrigation received constant attention, and it became customary to measure the rise of the Nile on the rocks of the second cataract. The statistics thus obtained made possible the calculation of the probable yield of grain, so that the assessments might be fixed in the early part of each year. The royal auditors were constantly engaged throughout the land 'taking stock' and checking the transactions of those who collected taxes 'in kind', and references are made to their operations in tomb inscriptions. Their returns were lodged in the office of the chief treasurer at Memphis, who was always therefore in a position to advise the pharaoh regarding the development of a particular district and, in times of distress, to know where to find supplies to relieve the needy.

During the reign of Ammenemes III, the sixth monarch of the dynasty, a great water storage and irrigation scheme was successfully carried out. The possibilities of the swampy Faiyum had been recognised by certain rulers. King Den, of the First Dynasty, began the work of reclamation there, and some of his successors continued to deal with the problem. Ammenemes' operations were conducted on a grand scale. Lake Moeris was formed by the erection of a reclaiming wall that extended for nearly 30 miles (48 kilometres). It was connected with the Nile by a broad canal, and its largest circumference was 150 miles (240 kilometres), while its area was about 750 square miles (1,942 square kilometres). It served the same purpose as Lake Nasser and the Aswan dam of the present day, but of course benefited only the province of the Faiyum and the district below it. Strabo, writing long centuries after it was constructed, said: 'The Lake Moeris, by magnitude and depth, is able to sustain the superabundance of water that flows into it when the river rises, without overflowing the inhabited and cultivated parts of the country. When the river falls, the lake distributes the excess of water through its canal, and both the lake and the canal retain a remainder which is used for irrigation. . . . There are locks on both mouths of the canal, and the engineers use these to store up and distribute the water.'

When the scheme was completed, the area of land reclaimed embraced, according to one estimate, about 27,000 acres (11,000 hectares). It has been calculated that a sufficient quantity of water was conserved to double the flow of the Nile during the period between April and July, when it is very low. The extension of the cultivable area increased greatly the revenue of the chief treasurer. The pharaoh, in a generous moment, being, no doubt, well pleased with the success of the scheme, made over the revenue from the fishing rights of the lake to his queen, so that she might provide luxurious dresses and jewellery for herself and her train.

Sesostris I, the friend of Sinuhe, was an able and vigorous ruler. During his reign of over thirty years he appears to have engaged himself mainly in carrying out the policy inaugurated by his father, Ammenemes. The results were eminently satisfactory. Peace was maintained with a firm hand on the northern frontier, and the Libyans were kept at bay. He found it necessary, however, to lead in person a strong army into Nubia. There does not appear to have been much fighting, for in the tomb of his general, the favoured Ameni, it is recorded that the losses were insignificant. Apparently the most notable event of the campaign was the capture of an elephant. Other expeditions followed, the last being in the year before the king's death. The Nubians never ceased to give trouble.

Sesostris restricted at every opportunity the powers of the feudal lords and pursued the diplomatic policy of conciliating the various religious cults. He erected a great temple at Heliopolis, and its site is marked today by an obelisk that bears his name. He also repaired or extended temples at Abydos, Koptos, Hierakonpolis and Karnak, and his monuments were judiciously distributed throughout the land.

Two years before his death, Sesostris appointed as regent his son, who became the second Ammenemes. After reigning for over thirty years, Ammenemes II lost his life, according to Manetho, in a palace revolution. Sesostris II, who followed, appears to have resided chiefly at Illahun, a town that is of special interest because a plan of it was discovered by Petrie in the royal tomb. The accommodation provided for the great mass of the inhabitants is not impressive. The workers resided in narrow slums. Many of the living rooms in the blocks run one into another, so that there could not have been either great comfort or much privacy.

A new type of face begins to appear in the royal house, as is shown by the smaller sculptural work of the time. This is dealt with in the next chapter. Nomadic tribes were also settling in Egypt. In the Beni-Hasan tomb of the loyal nome governor Khnumuhotep ('the god Khnum is satisfied') appears an interesting wall painting of a company of Semites, who are presenting gifts of perfumes to the pharaoh. They are accompanied by their wives and families, as if they wished to become loyal subjects in the land of prosperity and good government.

Syria at this period was in a state of constant unrest. Great race movements were in progress over a considerable area in Asia and Europe. These were caused by one of those periodic waves of migration from Arabia, the southward and westward pressure of hill tribes in middle Asia, and by the aggressive tendencies of the Hittites. The earliest mention of the latter is made in the reign of Ammenemes I. Their seat of power was at Boghaz-Koi in Asia Minor, and they were raiding Mesopotamia and gradually pressing down through northern Syria. The smaller tribes were displaced by the larger, and migrations by propulsion were in consequence frequent and general. Many privations were endured by the scattered people, and of course agricultural operations must have been completely suspended in some districts.

About this time Abraham sojourned in Egypt, because 'the famine was grievous in the land' (Canaan). After he returned, he purchased from Ephron, the Hittite, the cave of Machpelah in which to bury his dead. This landowner was evidently a pioneer settler from Asia Minor. He was friendly to the patriarch, whom he addressed as 'a mighty prince among us'. The Hittites may have penetrated Canaan as far south as Jerusalem.

Owing to the unrest on his northern frontier, Sesostris III found it necessary to invade Syria. A stele of his has been found. It is recorded at Abydos that a battle was fought in which the Asiatics were defeated, and Sebek-khu, an Egyptian dignitary to whom we are indebted for this scrap of interesting history, boasts of the gifts he received from the pharaoh for his bravery on the field. Nubia was also giving trouble again during this reign. A vigorous campaign against the restless warriors resulted in the extension of the Egyptian frontier to the third cataract. Two great forts were afterwards erected and garrisoned. It was also decreed that no Africans with cattle or merchandise should pass northwards by land or water beyond a certain point. Traders were followed by colonists, and then fighting men desired to take forcible possession of territory. A second campaign was conducted against the Nubians eight years after the first, and three years later there was another. The flesh pots of Egypt were attracting all sorts and conditions of peoples.

The interests of the next king, Ammenemes III, were centred chiefly in the Faiyum, where he saw completed the great Lake Moeris scheme. His reign, which lasted for nearly half a century, was peaceful and prosperous. He was one of the great pharaohs of Egypt. Under his jurisdiction the country developed rapidly, commerce increased, and industries were fostered. Instead of sending periodic expeditions to Sinai for copper and turquoise, as had been the custom hitherto, he established a colony there. A reservoir was constructed and a temple built to the goddess Hathor. The colonists suffered greatly from the heat during the summer months. A nobleman recorded on a stele the hardships endured by a pioneer expedition that visited the mines at an earlier date than usual, before permanent settlement was made in that tropical land. 'The mountains are hot,' he said, 'and the rocks brand the body.' He endured his hardships with exemplary fortitude and expressed the hope that others would similarly show their readiness to obey royal commands.

It was a building age, and Ammenemes honoured the gods and at the same time humoured the growing communities of priests by erecting and enlarging temples. He gave special recognition to Osiris at sacred Abydos, where many Egyptians of all ranks continued to seek to put their tombs, and to Amun, the family deity at Karnak, and to Hershef at Herakleopolis. Ptah, the god of the artisans, appears to have been neglected, which seems to indicate that he had absorbed, or was absorbed by, Hershef, whom he so closely resembles.

This Ammenemes is credited with having erected the great labyrinth in the vi-

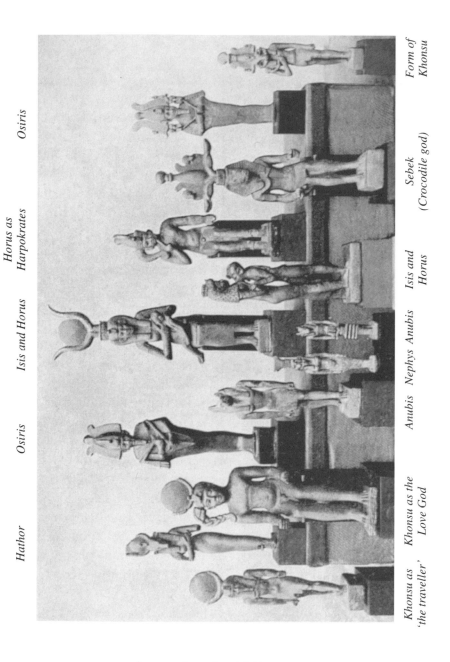

A group of prominent deities

cinity of Lake Moeris. The mosque-building Arabs must have used it as a quarry, for no trace of it remains. It appears to have been an immense temple, with apartments for each of the Egyptian gods. 'All the works of Greece,' declared Herodotus, 'are inferior to it, both in regard to workmanship and cost.' The Greek historian was of the opinion that it surpassed even the pyramids. There were twelve covered courts with entrances opposite to each other – six to the north and six to the south – and the whole was enclosed by a wall. Of the three thousand apartments, half were underground. 'The numerous winding passages through the various courts,' Herodotus wrote, 'aroused my warmest admiration. I passed from small apartments to spacious halls, and from these to magnificent courts, almost without end. Walls and ceilings were of marble, the former being sculpted and painted, and pillars of polished marble surrounded the courts.' At the end of the labyrinth stood pharaoh's pyramid, with figures of animals carved on its casement. 'No stranger,' Strabo informs us, 'could find his way in or out of this building without a guide.' The brick pyramids of the Twelfth Dynasty were also constructed with winding passages to baffle the tomb robbers, but they were 'jerry-built', compared with those of the Khufu type and survive in various stages of decay.

The idea of a labyrinth may have come from Crete. The palaces of that island kingdom were of maze-like character, and the earliest at Knossos and Phaestos were erected in the First Middle Minoan period, which is parallel with the Egyptian Eleventh Dynasty. Their fame must have reached the Nile valley, for the influence of the island kingdom's architecture is traceable in the construction of Mentuhotep's complicated temple at Deir el-Bahri. A people who appear to have been 'broad-headed' mountaineers invaded Crete at the close of its Second Middle Minoan period, which is parallel with the Egyptian Twelfth Dynasty. Their success culminated in the destruction of the earlier palace of Knossos. At a later age, when a similar invasion occurred, large numbers of Cretans fled to Asia Minor, and it is possible that in the time of Ammenemes III many of the island refugees settled in the Nile valley. If these included architects and skilled artisans, they must have received a most hospitable welcome.

Egypt, we know, was at this period in close touch with Crete. The numerous relics of the Twelfth Dynasty that have been found in the palace ruins of the island show how free and continuous was the sea trade between the two kingdoms. No doubt it was greatly stimulated by the Egyptian demand for tin. We find that bronze came into more general use during the Twelfth Dynasty than had previously been the case. In Old-Kingdom times tools were made chiefly of copper, and occasionally of iron. The latter was called 'the metal of heaven', and is referred to in the Pyramid Texts of King Wenis. If it was obtained originally from meteorites, as has been suggested, it is understandable why, in Egypt as elsewhere, it was supposed to possess magic qualities. It does not seem to have been excavated in great quantities by the early Egyptians – the difficulty of smelting it must have been great because of the scarcity of timber.

Copper was used in the late Pre-Dynastic period, when expeditions from the southern kingdom began to visit the mines of the Sinai Peninsula. The Delta people may have also obtained it from Cyprus, where the earliest weapons and pottery resemble Egyptian forms. At the close of the Third Dynasty, bronze was introduced or manufactured. The bronze 'rod of Maidum' was found deeply embedded in the fillings of a mastaba associated with the pyramid of King Snofru. A bronze socketed hoe of the Sixth Dynasty bears a resemblance to examples from Cyprus and southern Russia in the British Museum in London. Trade with the copper island did not assume any dimensions, however, until the Eighteenth Dynasty, and the Cypriot weapons that were imported into the Nile valley before that period may have come along the trade route through Syria, if they were not captured in frontier conflicts with invaders.

Egypt manufactured its own bronze, and a suggestion that certain figures on a Sixth-Dynasty relief are 'Aegeans bringing tin into Egypt' is therefore of special interest. If such a trade existed, it must have been hampered greatly, if not entirely cut off, during the First Intermediate Period, before the rise of Ammenemes I.

From where were the liberal supplies of bronze obtained by the Egyptians in the Twelfth Dynasty? The unrest in Asia must have interrupted trade along the great caravan routes to the ancient tin mines of Khorassan in Persia, from which Babylonia received its supplies. The Phoenician mariners had scarcely yet begun to appear in the Mediterranean. Tin must have come mainly through Crete therefore. Indeed, the island traders could not have had anything more valuable to offer in exchange for the corn of Egypt.

Crete had long been familiar with bronze. The First Early Minoan period, which marks the transition from stone, began in Egypt's Third Dynasty, or slightly earlier. Was its tin obtained from central Europe or Brittany? Duncan Mackenzie, the archaeologist, said in this connection: 'By the beginning of the Bronze Age [in Crete] the valley of the Rhone must have played a dominant role of communication between the great world of the Mediterranean and the north; by that time it was probably the high continental trade route towards the tin mines of Britain.' If so, the tin-mining industry of Cornwall and the Scilly islands must have been increased greatly by the demand created by the tin-importing and temple-building pharaohs of the Twelfth Dynasty, who flourished long before Joseph appeared in the land of Egypt.

Another link between ancient Britain and the Nile valley is the spiral ornament that appears in 'degenerate form' on the so called 'spectacle stones' of Scotland. The spiral is common on Egyptian scarabs of the Twelfth Dynasty. We find that it passed to Crete and then along the Danube trade route to Denmark, where the ornaments on which it appeared were possibly given in exchange for the much-sought-for Baltic amber. It spread in time through Scandinavia. The spiral must also have followed the Rhone-valley route, for it was passed on from France to the British Isles, through which it was widely diffused in the Bronze Age. In Ireland it was carved on the stones of the famous New Grange barrow in County Meath.

The brilliant Twelfth Dynasty came to an end soon after the death of the great Ammenemes III. His closing years were shadowed by domestic grief, for his favourite son, Ewib-Ra, predeceased him. A wooden statue of the prince is preserved in Cairo and is that of a handsome and dignified youth. The next king, Ammenemes IV, ruled for about seven years. He left no son and was succeeded by his sister, Sobekneferu, a daughter of Ammenemes III and the last of her 'line', who sat on the throne for five years. With her passed away the glory and grandeur of the Golden Age, the latter half of which had special features of much interest. These are dealt with in the next chapter.

Chapter 18

Myths and Lays of the Middle Kingdom

Foreign Brides – Succession by Male and Female Lines – New Religious Belief – Sebek the Crocodile God – Identified with Seth and Sutekh – The Crocodile of the Sun – The Friend and Foe of the Dead – Sebek Kings – The Tame Crocodile – Usert, the Earth Goddess – Resemblance to Isis and Neith – Sutekh and Baal – Significance of Dashur Jewellery – The Great Sphinx – Literary Activity – Egyptian Folk songs – Dialogue of a Man with his Soul – 'To be or not to be' – Sun Cult Doctrines – 'The Lay of the Harpist'.

During the Twelfth Dynasty, Babylon fell and Crete was invaded. Egypt alone among the older kingdoms successfully withstood the waves of aggression that were passing over the civilised world. It was not immune, however, to foreign influence. A controlling power in Syria had evidently to be reckoned with, for raiding bands were constantly hovering on the frontier. It has been suggested that agreements were concluded, but no records of any survive. There are indications, however, that diplomatic marriages took place, and these may have been arranged for purposes of conciliation. At any rate, foreign brides were entering the royal harem, and the exclusive traditions of Egypt were being set at defiance.

Sesostris II had a favourite wife called Nefert, 'the beautiful', who appears to have been a Hittite. Her son, Sesostris III, and her grandson, Ammenemes III, have been referred to as 'new types'.[1] Their faces, as is shown plainly in the statuary, have distinct non-Egyptian and non-Semitic characteristics. They are long and angular – the third Sesostris's seems quite Mongoloid – with narrow eyes and high cheek bones. There can be no doubt about the foreign strain.

It is apparent that Sesostris III ascended the throne as the son of his father. This fact is of special interest, because, during the Twelfth Dynasty, succession by the female line was generally recognised in Egypt. Evidently Sesostris II elevated to the rank of crown prince the son of his foreign wife. Ammenemes III appears to have been similarly an arbitrary selection. No doubt the queens and dowager queens were making their presence felt and were responsible for innovations of far-reaching character, which must have aroused considerable opposition. It may

[1] Newberry and Garstang, and Petrie.

be that a legitimist party had become a disturbing element. The high rate of mortality in the royal house during the latter years of the dynasty suggests the existence of a plot to remove undesirable heirs by methods not unfamiliar in other early courts.

Along with the new royal faces new religious beliefs also came into prominence. The rise of Sebek, the crocodile god, may have been a result of the tendency shown by certain of the pharaohs to reside in the Faiyum. The town of Crocodilopolis was the chief centre of the hitherto obscure Sebek cult. It is noteworthy, however, that the reptile deity was associated with the worship of Seth – not the familiar Egyptian Seth, but rather his prototype, Sutekh of the Hittites. Apparently an old tribal religion was revived in new and developed form.

In the texts of Wenis, Sebek is referred to as the son of Neith, the Libyan 'earth mother', who personified the female principle and was believed to be self-sustaining, as she had been self-produced. She was 'the unknown one' and 'the hidden one', whose veil had never been lifted. Like other virgin goddesses, she had a fatherless son, the 'husband of his mother', who may have been identified with Sebek as a result of early tribal fusion.

It is suggested that in his crocodile form Sebek was worshipped as the snake was worshipped, on account of the fear he inspired. But, according to Diodorus, crocodiles were also regarded as protectors of Egypt because, although they devoured the natives occasionally, they prevented robbers from swimming over the Nile. Opinions, however, differed as to the influence exercised by the crocodile on the destinies of Egypt. Some Indian tribes worshipped snakes and did everything they could to protect even the most deadly specimens. In Egypt the crocodile was similarly protected in particular localities, while in others it was hunted down by sportsmen.[1] We also find that in religious literature the reptile is now referred to as the friend and now as the enemy of the good Osiris. He brings ashore the dead body of the god to Isis in one legend,[2] and in another he is identified with his murderers. In the 'Winged Disc' story the followers of Seth are crocodiles and hippopotami and are slain by Horus because they are 'the enemies of Ra'. Yet Sebek was, in the revolutionary Sixth Dynasty, identified with the sun god, and in the *Book of the Dead* there is a symbolic reference to his dwelling on Sunrise Hill, where he was associated with Hathor and Horus – the Great Mother and son.

Sebek-Atum-Ra ultimately became the crocodile of the sun, as Mentu became 'bull of the sun', and he symbolised the power and heat of the orb of day. In this form he was the 'radiant green disc' – 'the creator', who rose from Nu 'in many shapes and in many colours'.

---

[1] Herodotus wrote 'Those who live near Thebes and the Lake Moeris hold the crocodile in religious veneration. . . . Those who live in or near Elephantine make the beast an article of food.'

[2] This is of special interest, because Hittite gods appear on the backs of animals.

At Ombos, Sebek was a form of Geb, the earth giant, the son of Nut, and 'husband of his mother'. He was called the 'father of the gods' and 'chief of the Nine Bow Barbarians'.

In his Seth form, Sebek was regarded in some parts as an enemy and devourer of the dead. But his worshippers believed that he would lead souls by 'short cuts' and byways to the Egyptian paradise. In the Pyramid Texts he has the attributes of the elfin Khnum, whose dwarfish images were placed in tombs to prevent decay, for he renews the eyes of the dead, touches their tongues so that they can speak and restores the power of motion to their heads.

The recognition that Sebek received at Thebes may have been the result of the influence of the late kings of the Twelfth Dynasty and those of the Thirteenth who had Sebek names. The god is depicted as a man with a crocodile's head, and he sometimes wears Amun plumes with the sun disc. He is also shown simply as a crocodile. He was familiar to the Greeks as Sukhos. Strabo, who visited Egypt in the Roman period, relates that he saw a sacred crocodile in an artificial lake at Crocodilopolis in the Faiyum. It was quite tame[1] and was decorated with gold earrings, set with crystal, and wore bracelets on its fore paws. The priests opened its jaws and fed it with cakes, flesh and honey wine. When the animal leapt into the water and came up at the other side, the priests followed it and gave it a fresh offering. Herodotus tells that the fore feet of the sacred crocodile that he saw were secured by a chain. It was fed not only with choice food, but with 'the flesh of sacred victims'. When the reptile died, its body was embalmed and, having been deposited in a sacred chest, was laid in one of the lower chambers of the labyrinth. These subterranean cells were reputed to be of great sanctity, and Herodotus was not permitted to enter them.

The deity Usert, whose name is associated with the kings Sesostris (also rendered Usertesen), was an earth goddess. She is identified with Isis and closely resembles Neith – the Great Mother with a son whose human incarnation is the pharaoh. Usert worship may have been closely associated, therefore, with Sebek worship, because Sebek was the son of an earth goddess. He rose from Nu, the primordial deep, as the crocodile rose from Lake Moeris, the waters of which nourished the 'earth mother', and caused green vegetation to spring up where formerly there was only sandy desert.[2] Sebek was thus in a new sense a form of Ra and a 'radiant green sun disc'. His association with Seth was probably the result of Asiatic influence, and the foreign strain in the royal house may have come from a district where Seth was worshipped as Sutekh. The Egyptian Seth developed from an early concept of a tribal Sutekh as a result of Asiatic settlement in the eastern Delta in Pre-Dynastic times. The Hittite Sutekh was a sun

[1] The god was not feared. It had been propitiated and became the friend of man.
[2] When the Nile rises it runs, for a period, green and foul, after running red with clay. The crocodile may have been associated with the green water also.

Khnum (ram-headed)

Sebek,
crocodile god

Min

Bes

Anubis

Local gods with added solar and other attributes

god and a weather god. But there were many Sutekhs, as there were many Baals. Baal signifies 'lord' or 'chief god', and in Egypt he was identified with Seth and with Mentu, the bull of war. At Tanis he was 'lord of the heaven'. Sutekh, also a 'baal' or 'lord', appears to have been similarly adaptable in tendency. If it was because of his influence that the crocodile god of the Faiyum became a solar deity, the foreign women in the pharaoh's harem must have been Hittites, whose religious beliefs influenced those of their royal sons.

Exquisite jewellery has been found at Dahshur, where Ammenemes II and his grandson, Sesostris III, lived and erected their pyramids – two diadems of princesses of the royal house, the daughters of the second Sesostris's foreign wife, at Dahshur. One is a mass of little gold flowers connected by gold wires, which recalls the reference, in Exodus 39:3, to the artisans who 'did beat the gold into thin plates, and cut it into wires'. The design is strengthened by large 'Maltese crosses' set with gems.[1] Other pieces of Twelfth-Dynasty jewellery are similarly 'innovations' and of the character that, long centuries afterwards, became known as Etruscan. But they could not have come from Europe at this period. They resemble the work for which the Hittites were famous.

The great sphinx may also have owed its origin to the influence exercised by the Hittites, whose emblem of power was a lion. Certain Egyptologists[2] are quite convinced that it was sculpted during the reign of Ammenemes III, whose face they consider it resembles. Nile gods had animal heads with human bodies. The sphinx, therefore, could not have been a god of Egypt. Scarab beetle seals were also introduced during the Twelfth Dynasty. The dynastic civilisation of Egypt began with the use of the Babylonian seal cylinder.

The Golden Age is distinguished not only for its material progress but also for its literary activity. In this respect it may be referred to as the 'Elizabethan Age' of ancient Egypt. The compositions appear to have been numerous, and many were of high quality. During this dynasty the kingdom was 'a nest of singing birds' and the home of storytellers. There are snatches of song even in tomb inscriptions, and rolls of papyri have been found in mummy coffins containing love ditties, philosophic poems and tales of wonder, which were provided for the entertainment of the dead in the next world.

It is exceedingly difficult for us to enter into the spirit of some of these compositions. There are baffling allusions to unfamiliar beliefs and customs, while our ignorance of the correct pronunciation of the language makes some ditties seem absolutely nonsensical, although they may have been regarded as gems of wit. Such quaint turns of phrase, puns and odd mannerisms as are recognisable are entirely lost when attempts are made to translate them. The Egyptian poets liked

---

[1] The Maltese cross is believed to be of Elamite origin. It is first met with in Babylon on seals of the Kassite period. It appears on the Neolithic pottery of Susa.
[2] Newberry and Garstang.

to play upon words. In a Fifth-Dynasty tomb inscription this tendency is apparent. A shepherd drives his flock over the wet land to tramp down the seed, and he sings a humorous ditty to the sheep. We gather that he considers himself to be in a grotesque situation, for he 'salutes the pike', and is like a shepherd among the dead, who converses with strange beings as he converses with fish. 'Salutes' and 'pike' are represented by the same word, and it is as if we said in English that a fisherman 'flounders like flounders' or that joiners 'box the box'.

A translation is therefore exceedingly bald:

> The shepherd is in the water with the fish;
> He converses with the sheath fish;
> He salutes the pike;
> From the West – the shepherd is a shepherd from the West.

'The West' is, of course, the land of the dead.

Some of the Twelfth-Dynasty 'minor poems' are, however, of universal interest because their meaning is as clear as their appeal is direct. The two that follow are close renderings of the originals:

The Woodcarver

> The carver grows more weary
>   Than he who hoes all day,
> As up and down his field of wood
>   His chisel ploughs away.
> No rest takes he at even,
>   Because he lights a light;
> He toils until his arms drop down
>   Exhausted, in the night.

The Smith

> A smith is no ambassador –
>   His style is to abuse;
> I never met a goldsmith yet
>   Able to give one news.
> Oh, I have seen a smith at work,
>   Before his fire aglow –
> His 'claws' are like a crocodile;
>   He smells like fish's roe.

The Egyptian peasants were great talkers. Life was not worth living if there was nothing to gossip about. A man became exceedingly dejected when he had to work in solitude. He might even die from sheer boredom. So we can understand the ditty that tells of a brick-maker who is puddling all alone in the clay at the time of inundation and has to talk to the fish. 'He is now a brick-maker in the West.' In other words, the lonely task has been the death of him.

This horror of isolation from sympathetic companionship pervades the wonderful composition that has been called 'The Dialogue of a Man with his Soul'. The opening part of the papyrus is lost, and it is uncertain whether the lonely Egyptian was about to commit suicide or was contemplating with feelings of horror the melancholy fate that awaited him when he would be laid in the tomb. He appears to have suffered some great wrong. His brothers have deserted him, his friends have proved untrue, and – terrible fate! – he has nobody to speak to. Life is, therefore, not worth living, but he dreads to die because of the darkness and solitude of the tomb that is waiting for him. The fragment opens at the conclusion of a speech made by the soul. Apparently it has refused to accompany the man, so that he is faced with the prospect of not even having his soul to converse with.

'In the day of my sorrow,' the man declares, 'you should be my companion and my sympathetic friend. Why scold me because I am weary of life? Do not compel me to die, because I take no delight in the prospect of death; do not tell me that there is joy in the "aftertime". It is a sorrowful thing that this life cannot be lived over again, for in the next world the gods will consider with great severity the deeds we have done here.'

He calls himself a 'kindly and sympathetic man', but the soul thinks otherwise and is impatient with him. 'You poor fool,' it says, 'you dread to die as if you were one of these rich men.'

But the Egyptian continues to lament his fate; he has no belief in joy after death. The soul warns him, therefore, that if he broods over the future in such a spirit of despondency he will be punished by being left forever in his dark solitary tomb. The implication appears to be that those who lack faith will never enter paradise.

'The thought of death,' says the soul, 'is sorrow in itself, it makes men weep; it makes them leave their homes and throw themselves in the dust.'

Men who display their unbelief never enjoy, after death, the light of the sun. Statues of granite may be carved for them, their friends may erect pyramids that display great skill of workmanship, but their fate is like that of 'the miserable men who died of hunger at the riverside, or the peasant ruined by drought or by the flood – a poor beggar who has lost everything and has none to talk to except the fishes'.

The soul counsels the man to enjoy life and to banish care and despondency. He is a foolish fellow who contemplates death with sorrow because he has grown weary of living. The one who has cause to grieve is he whose life is suddenly cut short by disaster. Such appears to be the conclusion that should be drawn from the soul's references to some everyday happenings of which the following is an example:

'A peasant has gathered in his harvest; the sheaves are in his boat; he sails on the Nile, and his heart is filled with the prospect of making merry. Suddenly a storm comes on. He is compelled to remain beside his boat, guarding his harvest. But his wife and his children suffer a melancholy fate. They were coming to meet him, but they lost their way in the storm, and the crocodiles devoured them. The poor peasant has good cause to lament aloud. He cries out, saying:

"'I do not sorrow for my beloved wife, who has gone hence and will never return, so much as for the little children who, in the dawn of life, met the crocodile and perished."'

The man is evidently much impressed by the soul's reasoning. He changes his mind and praises the tomb as a safe retreat and resting place for one who, like himself, cannot any longer enjoy life. Why he feels so utterly dejected we cannot tell; the reason may have been given in the lost portion of the old papyrus. There is evidently no prospect of enjoyment before him. His name has become hateful among men. He has been wronged. The world is full of evil as he is full of sorrow.

At this point the composition becomes metrical in construction:

> Hateful my name! . . . more hateful is it now
> Than the rank smell of ravens in the heat;
> Than rotting peaches, or the meadows high
> Where geese are wont to feed; than fishermen
> Who wade from stinking marshes with their fish,
> Or the foul odour of the crocodile;
> More hateful than a husband deems his spouse
> When she is slandered, or his gallant son
> Falsely accused; more hateful than a town
> Which harbours rebels who are sought in vain.
>
> Whom can I speak to? . . . Brothers turn away;
> I have no friend to love me as of yore;
> Hearts have turned cold and cruel; might is right;
> The strong are spoilers, and the weakly fall,
> Stricken and plundered. . . . Whom can I speak to?
> The faithful man gets sorrow for reward –
> His brother turns his foe – the good he does,
> How swiftly 'tis undone, for thankless hearts
> Have no remembrance of the day gone past.

Whom can I speak to? I am full of grief –
There is not left alive one faithful man;
The world is full of evil without end.

Death is before me like a draught prepared
To banish sickness; or as fresh, cool air
To one who, after fever, walks abroad.
Death is before me sweet as scented myrrh;
Like soft repose below a shelt'ring sail
In raging tempest. . . . Death before me is
Like perfumed lotus; like a restful couch
Spread in the Land of Plenty; or like home
For which the captive yearns, and warriors greet
When they return. . . . Ah! death before me is
Like to a fair blue heaven after storm –
A channel for a stream – an unknown land
The huntsman long has sought and finds at last.

He who goes Yonder rises like a god
That spurns the sinner; lo! his seat is sure
Within the sun barque, who has offered up
Choice victims in the temples of the gods;
He who goes Yonder is a learned man,
Whom no one hinders when he calls to Ra.

The soul is now satisfied, because the man has professed his faith in the sun god. It promises, therefore, not to desert him. 'Your body will lie in the earth,' it says, 'but I will keep you company when you are given rest. Let us remain beside one another.'

It is possible that this composition was intended to make converts for the sun cult. The man appears to dread the judgment before Osiris, the King of the Dead, who reckons up the sins committed by men in this world. His soul approves of his faith in Ra, of giving offerings in the temples and of becoming a 'learned man' – one who has acquired knowledge of the magic formulae that enable him to enter the sun barque. This soul appears to be the man's conscience. It is difficult to grasp the Egyptian ideas regarding the soul which enters Paradise, the soul which hovers over the mummy, and the conscious life of the body in the tomb. These were as vague as they appear to have been varied.

One of the most popular Egyptian poems is called 'The Lay of the Harpist'. It was chanted at banquets given by wealthy men. 'Before the company rises,' wrote Herodotus, 'a small coffin that contains a perfect model of the human body is carried round and is shown to each guest in rotation. He who bears it exclaims: "Look at this figure. . . . After death you will be like it. Drink, therefore, and be merry." The Lay in its earliest form was of great antiquity. Probably a real mummy was originally hauled through the banquet hall.

Lay Of The Harpist

'Tis well with this good prince; his day is done,
His happy fate fulfilled. . . . So one goes forth
While others, as in days of old, remain.
The old kings slumber in their pyramids,
Likewise the noble and the learned, but some
Who builded tombs have now no place of rest,
Although their deeds were great. . . . Lo! I have heard
The words Imhotep and Hordadaf spoke –
Their maxims men repeat. . . . Where are their tombs? –
Long fallen . . . e'en their places are unknown,
And they are now as though they ne'er had been.

No soul comes back to tell us how he fares –
To soothe and comfort us ere we depart
Whither he went betimes. . . . But let our minds
Forget of this and dwell on better things. . . .
Revel in pleasure while your life endures
And deck your head with myrrh. Be richly clad
In white and perfumed linen; like the gods
Anointed be; and never weary grow
In eager quest of what your heart desires –
Do as it prompts you . . . until that sad day
Of lamentation comes, when hearts at rest
Hear not the cry of mourners at the tomb,
Which have no meaning to the silent dead . . .
Then celebrate this festal time, nor pause –
For no man takes his riches to the grave;
Yea, none returns again when he goes hence.

Chapter 19

The Island of Enchantment

A Sailor's Story – Shipwrecked – The Sole Survivor – A Lonely Island – A Voice like Thunder – The Giant Serpent God – A Threat – Sailor given Protection – Sacrifice of Asses – Rescued by a Ship – The Parting – A Man of Wisdom.

Once upon a time a ship set forth on a voyage to the mines of Sinai, and it was swamped in a storm. All the sailors were drowned except one, who swam to the Isle of Enchantment, which was inhabited by the 'manes' – serpent gods who have heads and arms like human beings and are able to talk.

When this man returned to Egypt, he related his story to his lord, saying: 'Now, be well satisfied that I have come back, although alone. Your ship on which I have returned is safe, and no men arc missing. I was rescued by it, and I had no other means of escape. When you have cleansed your limbs, I pray you to inform the pharaoh of the things that have happened to me.'

The master said: 'So you persist in repeating this tale of yours. But speak on. I will hear you to the end, and, perhaps, your words will betray the truth. But lower your voice and say what you have to say without excitement.'

The sailor said: 'I will begin at the beginning, and tell what happened to myself. I voyaged towards the mines in your great ship, in which were 150 of the finest sailors in Egypt. They were all stout-hearted men. Now, some said that the wind would be unfavourable, and others said that there would be no wind at all. As it happened, a great storm arose, and the ship was tossed about in the midst of high waves so that it was swamped. When I found myself in the angry waters, I clung to a floating spar. All the others were drowned. In time I was cast ashore, and I found myself on a lonely island, where I lay helplessly for three days and three nights. Then I began to revive. I was faint with hunger and thirst, and went in search of food, and I found fruit and birds and fishes, and ate them. I gave thanks to the god because I was alive and offered up a sacrifice.

'No sooner had I given thanks in this manner than I heard a loud noise like thunder, and the earth trembled beneath me and the trees were stricken as with tempest. I hid my face with terror, and after I had lain a time on the ground I looked up and saw a giant serpent god with a human face and arms. He wore a long beard, and his body was golden and blue.

'I prostrated myself before him, and he spoke, saying: "Speak and tell, little fellow, speak and tell why you have come here. If you do not speak without delay, I will cause your life to end. If you do not tell me what I have not heard and what I do not know,[1] I will cause you to pass out of existence like a flame that has been extinguished."'

'Before I answered him he carried me inland and set me down without injury, whereupon I said that I had come from the land of Egypt in a great ship that perished in the storm, and that I had clung to a spar and was washed ashore.'

'The serpent god heard, and said: "Do not be terrified, little fellow, do not be terrified, and be cheerful, for it is the god who sent you to me. Here you may dwell until four moons wax and wane; then a ship will come, and you will depart in it and return once again to the land of Egypt. . . . It is pleasant to have a conversation. Know, then, that I dwell here with my kind, and I have children, and there is also a girl who perished by accident in a fire. I will take you to my home, and you will return to yours again in time."'

'When the giant serpent god had spoken thus, I prostrated myself before him, and I said: "To the King of Egypt I will tell the things I have seen. I will praise your name, and offerings of oil and perfumes will be made to you. Asses[2] and birds will I sacrifice to you, and the king will send you rich offerings because you are a benefactor of mankind."'

'"I do not need your perfumes," answered the serpent god. "I am a ruler of Punt, and these I possess in abundance, but I have no oil of Egypt here. But know that when you go away this island will never again be seen by any man; it will vanish in the midst of the sea."'

'When four moons had waxed and waned, a ship appeared as the serpent god had foretold. I knelt down and bade farewell to the inhabitants of the island of enchantment, and the great god gave me gifts of perfumes and ivory and much treasure, and he also gave me rare woods and baboons. I took my leave with a grateful heart, and I thanked the god because of my deliverance. Then I went to the shore and hailed the ship and was taken aboard it.'

'These are the things that happened to me, my lord and master. Now conduct me, I pray you, before his majesty that I may present him with the gifts of the serpent god. . . . Look upon me, for I have returned to tell of the wonders I did see with my own eyes. . . . In my youth I was instructed to acquire wisdom so that I might be highly esteemed. Now I have become a wise man indeed.'

Apparently 'the master' was convinced by this wonderful story, which was duly recorded by a scribe of the temple of Amun.

---

[1] The Norse giant Vafthrudner similarly puts to death those who cannot tell him something he does not know.

[2] The reference is unique. Seth is associated with the wild ass, but except in this tale there is no indication that asses were sacrificed in Egypt. The Aryans sacrificed the horse.

Chapter 20

The Hyksos and their Strange God

The Sebek-Ra Rulers – A Great Pharaoh – The Shadow of Anarchy – Coming of the 'Shepherd Kings' – Carnival of Destruction – A Military Occupation – Causes of World-wide Unrest – Dry Cycles – Invasions of Pastoral Peoples History in Mythology – Tribal Fathers and Mother Deities – Sutekh, Thor, Hercules – Mountain Deities and Cave Demons – Hyksos Civilisation – Trade with Europe and Asia – The Horse – Hittite Influence in Palestine – Raid on Babylon – Kassites and Aryans – Aryan Gods in Syria – Mitanni Kingdom.

After the end of the Twelfth Dynasty and the close of the Golden Age, the materials for Egyptian history become somewhat scanty. The Thirteenth Dynasty opened peacefully, and the Sebek-Ra names of its kings indicate that the cults of the crocodile and the sun held the balance of power. The influence exercised by the pharaohs, however, appears to have been strictly circumscribed. Some of them may have reigned in Crocodilopolis or its vicinity, but Thebes ultimately became the capital, which indicates that the Delta region, with its growing foreign element, was considered insecure for the royal house. The great kings of the Twelfth Dynasty had established their power in the north, where they found it necessary to keep watchful eyes on the Libyan and Syrian frontiers.

Succession to the throne appears to have been regulated by descent in the female line. Evidently the legitimists were resolved that alien influence should not predominate at court, and in this regard they must have received the support of the great mass of the Egyptian people, of whom Herodotus said: 'They contentedly adhere to the customs of their ancestors, and are averse to foreign manners'. It is significant to find that the father of one of the Sebekhotep kings was a priest who achieved greatness because he married a princess. This Sebekhotep was followed by his son, who had a Hathor name, but he was dethroned after a brief reign. The next pharaoh was the paternal uncle of the fallen monarch. His royal name was Neferkhara-Sebekhotep, and he proved to be the greatest ruler of this obscure period.

He controlled the entire kingdom, from the shores of the Mediterranean to the second cataract, where records were made of the rise of the Nile. On the island of

Argo, near the third cataract, he erected two granite statues over 20 feet (6 metres) in height, which stood in front of a large temple. Nubian aggression must have been held firmly in check by a considerable garrison, but not for long. After two weak kings had reigned, the throne was seized by Neshi, 'the Negro', a worshipper of Ra and Seth. His colossal statue of black granite testifies to the supremacy achieved by the Nubian raiders. In the north another usurper of whom we have trace is Mermenfatiu, 'commander of the soldiers'.

The shadow of anarchy had again fallen on Egypt. Once more, too, the feudal lords asserted themselves, and the kingdom was broken up into a number of petty states. A long list of monarchs is given by Manetho for this Second Intermediate Period, and these may include many of the hereditary nome governors who became pharaohs in their own domains and waged war against their neighbours. Thebes remained the centre of the largest area of control, which may have enjoyed a measure of prosperity, but the rest of Egypt must have suffered greatly on account of the lack of supervision over the necessary distribution of water. Peasants may well have neglected to till the soil in districts always open to the raids of plunderers, exclaiming, in the words of the Twelfth-Dynasty prophet: 'What is the good of it? We know what is coming.'

Egypt was thoroughly disorganised and unable to resist its enemies, who were ever watchful for an opportunity to strike. The Nubians had already achieved some success, although they were ultimately expelled by the Thebans; the Libyans must have been active in the north, while Asiatic tribes were pouring over the Delta frontier and taking possession of great tracts of territory. Then came the Hyksos invaders, regarding whose identity much controversy has been waged. They were evidently no disorganised rabble, and there are indications that under their sway Egypt became, for an uncertain period, a part of a great empire of which, as yet, we know little.

Josephus, the patriotic Jewish historian, who believed that the Hyksos were 'the children of Israel', quoted Manetho as saying that 'they were a people of ignoble race who had confidence to invade our country, which they subdued easily without having to fight a battle. They set our towns on fire; they destroyed the temples of the gods, and caused the people to suffer every kind of barbarity. During the entire period of their dynasty they waged war against the people of Egypt, wishing to exterminate the whole race. . . . The foreigners were called Hyksos, which signifies "shepherd Kings".'

Manetho's reference to a carnival of destruction is confirmed by the inscription of Queen Hatshepsut of the Eighteenth Dynasty, who declared with characteristic piety:

> I have restored what was cast down,
> I have built up what was uncompleted,

Since the Asiatics were in Avaris of the north land,
And the barbarians were among them, destroying buildings,
While they governed, not knowing Ra.

But if the hated Hyksos were wreckers of buildings, so were the Egyptians, who were always prone to obliterate all records of unpopular rulers. Khufu's enduring pyramid defied them, but they destroyed his mummy and perpetuated his memory in a spirit of undeniable bitterness, although he was one of their greatest men. He was an enemy of their gods, which means that he laid too firm a hand on the ambitious and acquisitive priests. Thuthmosis III and Akhenaten also undertook in their day the vengeful work of erasing inscriptions, while Rameses II and others freely appropriated the monuments of their predecessors. It is not surprising, therefore, to find that few traces of the Hyksos rulers survive, and that, in a folk tale, they are referred to as 'the impure'. They ruled 'not knowing Ra', and were therefore consigned to oblivion. Manetho, who compiled his history about a thousand years after they were driven from the country, was unable to ascertain much about them. Only a few of the kings to whom he makes reference can be identified, and these belong to the Fifteenth Dynasty. Of the Sixteenth Dynasty he knew little or nothing, but in dealing with the Seventeenth he was on surer ground, because Upper Egypt had then regained its freedom and was gradually reconquering lost territory in the north.

The Hyksos overwhelmed the land at the close of the Fourteenth Dynasty. Then they chose for a king 'one of their own people'. According to Manetho, his name was Salatis, and with him begins the Fifteenth Dynasty. He selected Memphis as his capital, and there 'he made Upper and Lower Egypt pay tribute', while he left garrisons at places that were 'considered to be proper for them'. Did the Hyksos, therefore, merely undertake a military occupation of Egypt and compel the payment of tribute to a controlling power in Asia? On this point we obtain no clear idea from Manetho, who proceeds to state that the foreigners erected a strongly fortified town called Avaris – afterwards destroyed by the Egyptians – and there they kept a garrison of 240,000 men so as to secure the frontier from the attacks of the Assyrians, 'who, they foresaw, would invade Egypt'. Salatis held military reviews to overawe all foreigners.

Whatever enemy the Hyksos feared, or prepared to meet, it was certainly not the Assyrians, who were at the time fully occupied with their own affairs. They had not yet acquired the military strength that subsequently caused the name of their god Assur to be dreaded even in the Nile valley.

The reference, however, may be to Babylonia, where an aggressive people had made their appearance.

In the absence of reliable records regarding the Hyksos people, or perhaps we should say peoples, for it is possible that there was more than one invasion, we must cross the frontier of Egypt to obtain some idea of the conditions prevailing in Asia during this obscure but fascinating period.

Great changes were passing over the civilised world. Old kingdoms were being broken up and new kingdoms were in the process of formation. The immediate cause was the outpourings of pastoral peoples from steppes and plateaux in quest of 'fresh woods and pastures new', because vegetation had grown scanty during a prolonged dry cycle in countries like Arabia and Turkestan and on the Iranian plateau. Once these migrations by propulsion began, they were followed by migrations caused by expulsion. The movements were in some districts accompanied by constant fighting, and a people who displayed the best warlike qualities ultimately became conquerors on a gradually increasing scale. Another cause of migration was the growth of population. When an ancestral district became crowded, the surplus population broke away in waves. But movements of this kind invariably followed the line of least resistance and did not necessarily involve marked changes in habits of life, for pastoral peoples moved from upland to upland, as did agriculturists from river valley to river valley and seafarers from coast to coast. When, however, peaceful settlements were made by nomads in highly civilised areas, an increased impetus must have been given to migration from their native country, where their kindred, hearing of their prosperity, began to dream dreams of the land of plenty. Nomads who entered Babylonia or Egypt became 'the outposts' of those sudden and violent migrations of wholesale character, which occurred during prolonged periods of drought. The Hyksos conquest of Egypt is associated with one of these dry cycles.

In Chapter 3 reference was made to the gradual expansion from North Africa of the early Mediterranean 'long heads', who spread themselves over the unoccupied or sparsely populated valleys and shores of Palestine, Asia Minor and Europe. Simultaneously, or not much later, Asiatic 'broad heads' moved in successive waves along the mountain ranges. These are the people called Alpine by ethnologists, and they are traced from the the Himalayas to Brittany and the British Isles. The beliefs and tribal customs of the Mediterranean peoples appear to have been mainly of a matriarchal character, while those of the Alpine folk were mainly patriarchal.

The mixture of these peoples caused the development of a great civilisation in Asia Minor, and so, it is believed, the origin of the Hittite kingdom. Other races were embraced, however, in the Hittite confederacy. Mongols from Turkestan apparently moved southwards during a dry period and became a strong element in the Hittite area of control, while Semites from Arabia, who appeared at very early times in Syria, became allies of the rising people, with whom they fused in some districts. The eagle-nosed, bearded Alpine Hittites are believed to be represented by the present-day Armenians and the Mongolian Hittites by the Kurds. Some ethnologists are of the opinion that the characteristic Jewish nose indicates an early fusion of Hittites and Syrians. There was also an Alpine blend in Assyria, where the Semites had facial characteristics that distinguished them from the ancestral population in Arabia.

Hittite theology is of special interest to us because its influence can be traced in Egypt immediately before and especially during the Hyksos period. Some of the tribes of Asia Minor worshipped the Great Mother deity Ma or Ammas, who, like the Libyan Neith and other virgin goddesses of the Delta, was self-created and had a fatherless son. She was essentially an earth goddess, and of similar character to Astarte, Aphrodite, the Cretan serpent goddess, Our Lady of Doves in Cyprus, the Celtic Anu or Danu in Ireland, and the Scottish Cailleach Bheur who shaped the hills, let loose the rivers and waved her hammer over the growing grass.

In Cilicia the male deities predominated, and in southern Cappadocia, where primitive tribal beliefs appear to have fused early, we find a great rock sculpture depicting, it is believed, the marriage of the Great Father and Great Mother deities of the Alpine and Mediterranean peoples.

The Great Father god of the Hittites is Pappas or Attis ('father'), who was best known to the Egyptians as Sutekh. He is identified with Baal, 'the lord,' a deity no longer regarded as Semitic in origin. It was the moon god Sin, for instance, who gave his name to Sinai, and the Arabian sun deity was female.

Sutekh is depicted on a cliff near Smyrna as a bearded god with curly hair and a high, curving nose. He looks a typical mountaineer, clad in a tunic that is tightened round the waist by the 'hunger belt' so familiar in Scottish hill lore, and wearing boots with turned-up toes, specially suited for high snow-covered altitudes.

Sutekh was a sky and atmosphere deity who caused the storms and sent thunder. He was a god of war and wore goat's horns to symbolise fertility and the male principle. As Tark or Tarku he is depicted carrying in one hand a hammer and in the other three wriggling flashes of lightning, suggesting the Germanic Thor. He is also shown grasping a mace and trident or a double battle-axe. As Ramman,[1] with double horns, and bearing his axe and three thunderbolts, he received adoption in Babylon after the Hittite conquest.

When the Great Mother was wedded to the Great Father, her son may have been regarded as the son of Tarku also. It was probably the younger deity who was identified by the Greeks with Heracles, son of Zeus. But we need not expect a continuity of well-defined ideas regarding deities of common origin who have developed separately. These two gods, the Great Father and the son of the Great Mother, are sometimes indistinguishable. They not only varied in different districts but also at different periods. In the latest phase of Hittite religion, the Great

---

[1] 'When I bow down myself in the house of Rimmon, the Lord pardon thy servant in this thing' – 2 Kings 5:18.

Father, the conquering war god of the Alpine people, predominated, and he absorbed the attributes of other deities in localities where Hittite influence became supreme.

The Hittite deities were associated with mountains and mysterious caves, which indicates that in their earliest stages they were giants and hags of the type familiar among the Tyrol mountains, in the Scottish highlands and in Scandinavia. They had also their animal affinities and were depicted standing on the backs of lions and lionesses. The double-headed eagle and the three-legged symbol also had religious significance.

In addition to the deities, there were fearful demons. The Hittite Typhoon, like the Egyptian Seth and Apep serpent, warred against the gods. He was half-human and half-reptile – the upper part of his body was that of a man and the lower that of a serpent. He lived in a cave that was connected by an underground passage with the cave of the gods. Tempests issued from his jaws, and lightning flashed from his terrible flaming eyes. He was slain by Tarku, as the Hydra was slain by Heracles, and the various dragons of European story were slain by heroes of popular romance.

Egypt also had its somewhat colourless dragon legend, which was probably imported. In one of the Horus stories, Seth became a 'roaring serpent', and in this form he concealed himself in a hole (a cave) which, by command of the ubiquitous Ra, he was not permitted to leave. He thus became identified with the Apep serpent. Sutekh, the later Seth, who was regarded in the Delta as the true sun god, displaced Ra and Horus and figured as the 'dragon slayer'. The earlier Seth was not originally a demon. He was, it would appear, the god of a foreign people who entered Egypt in Pre-Dynastic times and were ultimately associated with all that was evil and impure, like the later Hyksos who worshipped Sutekh.

In Syria and Mitanni, prior to the Hyksos period, the Great Father deity of the Hittites became the supreme god. The most reasonable inference is that he was the divine representative of the conquering people in Asia Minor. He bore several territorial names: Hadad or Dad in Syria and Teshub (or Teshup) in Mitanni; he was Tarku farther north. But of the fact that he was identical with Sutekh there can be little doubt, for when Rameses II entered into a treaty with the Hittites, Sutekh and Amun-Ra were referred to as the chief representative gods of the two great empires.

Now it is a significant fact that the Hittite war god was the chief deity of the Hyksos. Like Ra-Atum of Heliopolis and Horus of Edfu, his appearance in Egypt points to a definite foreign influence. He was the deity of a people who exercised control over subject states – a strange god who was adopted by compulsion because he represented the ruling power. The Hyksos kings endeavoured to compel the Egyptians to recognise Sutekh, their official non-Arabian god – an indication that their organisation had a religious basis.

From Manetho's references to this obscure period we gather that the invaders of Egypt were well organised indeed. Their raid was not followed by those intertribal feuds that usually accompanied forcible settlement in a country by Semitic hordes from Arabia. They did not break up into warring factions, like the early invaders of Palestine. Before reaching Egypt, they must have come under the influence of a well-organised state. They had attained, at any rate, that stage of civilisation when a people recognise the necessity for establishing a strong central government.

The Hyksos must be credited with military and administrative experience, since they garrisoned strategic points and maintained a standing army like the greatest of the pharaohs. The collection of tribute is also significant. In a similar manner the later Egyptian emperors extracted revenue from the petty kings of subject states in Syria. What power received the tribute gathered by the Hyksos? All the indications point to the Hittites. If the Hyksos people were not wholly from Asia Minor, it is highly probable that the army of occupation was under Hittite control.

It may be that the invading forces included Semites from Arabia, plundering Bedouins, Amorites, and even Phoenicians who had migrated from the north of the Persian Gulf to the Palestine coast, and that assistance was given by the Libyans, reinforced by mercenaries from Crete or the Aegean Peninsula. But it is inconceivable that a hungry horde of desert dwellers, or an uncontrolled and homogeneous rabble from Arabia, could have maintained firm control of Egypt for a prolonged period. The nomads, however, who accompanied the Hyksos forces, may have been 'the barbarians in the midst of them', who are referred to in the inscription of Hatshepsut. No doubt the invaders were welcomed and assisted by those troublesome alien peoples, who, during the Twelfth Dynasty, had settled in Egypt and absorbed its civilisation. But the army of occupation was always regarded as a foreign element, and in all probability it was reinforced mainly from outside. The country must have been well governed. Hatshepsut admits as much, for she condemns the Hyksos chiefly on religious grounds. They destroyed the temples – perhaps some were simply allowed to fall into disrepair – and they ruled 'not knowing Ra'. Had the foreign kings followed the example of some of the most popular pharaohs, they might have purchased the allegiance of the priests of the various cults, but their desire was to establish the worship of the Hittite Sutekh, as a result, it may be inferred, of political influence exercised by the foreign power that received the tribute. One or two of the Hyksos kings affected a preference for Egyptian gods.

We must take at a discount the prejudiced Egyptian reference to the hated alien rulers. During the greater part of the Hyksos period, peaceful conditions prevailed not only in Egypt but over a considerable area in Asia. The great trade routes were reopened, and commerce appears to have been in a flourishing con-

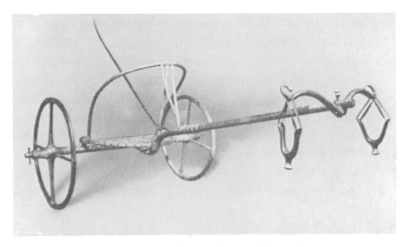

Egyptian chariot (Florence Museum)

Egyptian king (Sethos 1) mounted on chariot
From the bas-relief on the great temple at Karnak

dition. Agriculture, therefore, must have been fostered – a surplus yield of corn was required not only to pay tribute but also to offer in exchange for the commodities of other countries. We meet, in Manetho's King Ianias, a ruler who was evidently progressive and enterprising. He is identified with Ian, or Khian, whose name appears on Hyksos relics that have been found at Knossos in Crete and Baghdad in Persia. His non-Egyptian title, 'ank adebu', which signifies 'embracer of countries', suggests that he was a representative of a great power that controlled more than one conquered kingdom. Breasted, the American Egyptologist, translated Hyksos as 'rulers of countries', which means practically the same thing, although other authorities show a preference for Manetho's rendering, 'shepherd kings', or its equivalent, 'princes of desert dwellers'. It may be, of course, that 'Hyksos' was a term of contempt for a people whom the proud Egyptians made scornful reference to as 'the polluted' or 'the impure'.

We regard the Hyksos period as a dark age, mainly because of the absence of those records that the Egyptians were at pains to destroy. Perhaps we are also prone to be influenced by their denunciations of the foreigners. We have no justification for assuming, however, that progress was arrested for a prolonged period extending over about two centuries. The arts did not suffer decline, nor did the builders lose their skill. So thoroughly was the kingdom reorganised that the power of the feudal lords was completely shattered. Even the Twelfth-Dynasty kings were unable to accomplish as much. The Hyksos also introduced the domesticated horse into Egypt, but at what date we are unable to ascertain. Manetho makes no reference to it in his brief account of the invasion. If, however, there were charioteers in the foreign army when it swept over the land, they could not have come from Arabia, and Bedouins were not likely to be able to manufacture or repair chariots. Only a rich country could have obtained horses at this early period. They had newly arrived in western Asia and must have been scarce and difficult to obtain.

From where, then, came the horse, which shattered and built up the great empires? It was first tamed by the Aryans, and its place of origin is signified by its Assyrian name, 'the ass of the East'. How it reached western Asia and subsequently made its appearance in the Nile valley is a matter of special interest to us in dealing with the Hyksos problems.

We must first glance, however, at the conditions that prevailed in the immediate neighbourhood of Egypt prior to the invasion. During the Golden Age, the pharaohs were much concerned about maintaining a strongly defended northeastern frontier. No Egyptian records survive to throw light on the relations between Egypt and Syria, but the large number of Twelfth-Dynasty ornaments, scarabs and amulets, bearing hieroglyphic inscriptions, that have been excavated indicate that trade was brisk and continuous. A great change had meantime passed over Palestine. 'Sometime about 2000 to 1800 BC,' wrote R. A. S. Macalister, the Palestinian explorer, 'we find a rather sudden advance in civilisation to have taken place. This, like all the other forward steps of which recent excavation in the country has revealed traces, was due to foreign interference. The Semitic nations, Amorite, Hebrew or Arab, never invented anything; they assimilated all the elements of their civilisation from without.'

During the Twelfth Dynasty, therefore, Palestine came under the sway of a people who had attained a high degree of culture. But they could not have been either Assyrian or Babylonian, and Egypt exercised no control beyond its frontier. The great extending power at the time was the Hittite in the north. Little is known regarding the early movements of its conquering peoples, who formed small subject states that were controlled by the central government in Asia Minor. That they penetrated into southern Palestine as traders and made, at least, a social conquest, is certain, because they were known to Ammenemes I, although he never crossed the Delta frontier. The northern war god was established at an early period in Syria and in Mitanni, and Biblical references indicate that the Hittites were prominent landowners. They were probably the people who traded with Egypt at Gezer and with whom the Twelfth-Dynasty pharaohs arrived at some understanding. It is unlikely that the influential foreign princesses who were thought worthy to be introduced into the royal harem were the daughters of rough desert dwellers. The Dahshur jewellery suggests that they were women of refined tastes and accustomed to luxurious living.

We have no means of ascertaining why Sesostris III, the son of one of the alien wives, invaded Syria and fought a battle at Gezer. It may be that the Hittites had grown restless and aggressive, and it is also possible that he co-operated with them to expel a common enemy – perhaps Semites from Arabia.

Some time prior to the Hyksos invasion, the Hittites raided Babylon and overthrew the Hammurabi dynasty. But they were unable to enjoy for long the fruits of conquest. An army of Kassites pressed down from the mountains of Elam and occupied northern Babylonia, apparently driving the Hittites before them. The Kassites are a people of uncertain origin, but associated with them were bands of Aryans on horseback and in chariots. This is the first appearance in history of the Indo-European people.

A westward pressure of tribes followed. The Kassites and Aryans probably waged war against the Hittites for a period, and the Hyksos invasion of Egypt may have been an indirect result of the migrations from the Iranian plateau and the conquest of Babylonia. At any rate, it is certain that the Aryans continued to advance, for, prior to the close of the Hyksos period, they had penetrated Asia Minor and reached the Syrian coast. Whether or not they entered Egypt we have no means of knowing. All foreigners were Hyksos to the Egyptians at this time, as all northern barbarians were Celts to the Greeks at a later period. Some change occurred, however, for there was a second Hyksos dynasty. What we know for certain is that a military aristocracy appeared in Mitanni, where Tushratta, who had an Aryan name, subsequently paid tribute to Egypt in the time of Amenophis III and his son, Akhenaten. He is believed to have been educated in the land of the pharaohs, and his ancestors must have been the expellers from Mesopotamia of the Hittite rulers; the Mitanni rulers were for a period overlords of Assyria. In addition to the Hittite Sutekh-Teshub, the Mitanni pantheon then included Indra,

Mithra and Varuna, the well-known Iranian gods. These had been introduced into the Punjab by an earlier wave of Aryans that swept towards India about the beginning of the Twelfth Dynasty in Egypt.

It may also be noted here that when the Egyptians expelled the weakened Hyksos army of occupation, they possessed horses and chariots. They afterwards pressed into Syria, but the danger of subsequent invasion was not secured until Thuthmosis III overcame the Mitanni power, which apparently was not unconnected with the later Hyksos overlordship of Egypt.

During the Hyksos period the children of Israel appear to have settled in Egypt.

Chapter 21

Joseph and the Exodus

Biblical References to Hyksos Period – Joseph as Grand Vizier – His Sagacity – Reorganising the Kingdom – Israelites in Goshen – A Jacob King – Period of the Exodus – Egyptian References to Hebrew – A Striking Folk Tale – Cause of Theban Revolt – A National Hero – A Famous Queen Mother – A Warrior King – 'Battles Long Ago' – Expulsion of Foreigners – Unrest in Syria – New Methods of Warfare.

In the familiar Bible story of Joseph, the young Hebrew slave who became grand vizier in the land of the Nile, there is a significant reference to the nationality of his master, Potiphar. Although that dignitary was 'an officer of pharaoh, captain of the guard', he was not of alien origin. We are pointedly informed that he was 'an Egyptian'. We also gather that Hyksos jurisdiction extended beyond the Delta region. During the dry cycle, when the great famine prevailed, Joseph 'gathered up all the money that was found in the land of Egypt and in the land of Canaan' for the corn that the people purchased. Then he proceeded to acquire for the crown all the privately owned estates in the Nile valley and Delta region, with the purpose, it would appear, of abolishing the feudal system. An exception was made, however, of the lands attached to the temples. Apparently pharaoh wished to conciliate the priests, whose political influence was very great, because we find that he allowed them free supplies of corn. Indeed, he had previously selected for Joseph's wife, 'Asenath, the daughter of Potiphera, priest of On', an indication that he specially favoured the influential sun cult of Heliopolis. Hatshepsut's assertion that the foreign kings ruled in ignorance of Ra was manifestly neither strictly accurate nor unbiased.

The inference drawn from the Biblical narrative that the Hyksos pharaohs adopted a policy of conciliation is confirmed by the evidence gleaned amidst the scanty records of the period. We find that some of these rulers assumed Ra titles, although they were also 'beloved of Seth' (Sutekh), and that one of them actually restored the tomb of Queen Apuit of the Sixth Dynasty. The Egyptians apparently indulged in pious exaggerations. That the Hyksos' influence was not averse to culture is evident by the fact that the name of King Apepa Ra-aa-user is associated with a mathematical treatise that is preserved in the British Museum.

If learning was fostered, the arts and industries could not have been neglected.

The Egyptian iconoclasts systematically destroyed practically all the monuments of the period, so we have no direct evidence to support the assumption that it was characterised by a spirit of decadence because of the influence of uncultured desert dwellers. The skill displayed at the beginning of the Eighteenth Dynasty was too great to be of sudden growth and certainly does not suggest that for about two centuries there had existed no appreciation of, or demand for, works of art. Although sculpture had grown mechanical, there had been, apparently, progressive development in other directions. We find, for instance, a marked and increased appreciation of colour, suggesting influence from a district where Nature presents more variety and distinguishing beauty than the somewhat monotonous valley of the Nile. Pottery was being highly glazed and tinted with a taste and skill unknown in the Twelfth Dynasty, and painting had become more popular.

But, perhaps, it was in the work of administration that the Egyptians learned most from their Hyksos rulers. Joseph, who was undoubtedly a great statesman, must have impressed them greatly with his sound doctrines of political economy. That sagacious young vizier displayed an acute and far-sighted appreciation of the real needs of Egypt, a country that cannot be made prosperous under divided rule. No doubt he was guided by experienced councillors at court, but had he not been gifted with singular intelligence and strong force of character, he could never have performed his onerous duties with so much distinction and success. He fostered the agricultural industry during the years of plenty and 'gathered corn as the sand of the sea, very much, until he left numbering; for it was without number'.

Then came the seven years of famine. 'And when all the land of Egypt was famished, the people cried to Pharaoh for bread. . . . And Joseph opened all the storehouses and sold unto the Egyptians.' Much wealth poured into the imperial exchequer. 'All countries came into Egypt to Joseph for to buy corn.' The dry cycle prevailed apparently over a considerable area, and it must have propelled the migrations of pastoral peoples, which subsequently made so great a change in the political conditions of Asia.

It is interesting to note that at this period the horse was known in Egypt. On the occasion of Joseph's elevation to the post of grand vizier, pharaoh 'made him to ride in the second chariot which he had'. Then when the Egyptians, who found it necessary to continue purchasing corn, cried out 'the money faileth', the young Hebrew 'gave them bread in exchange for horses', etc.

The wholesale purchase of estates followed. 'Buy us and our land for bread,' said the Egyptians, 'and we and our land will be servants unto Pharaoh. . . . So the land became Pharaoh's. . . . And as for the people, he [Joseph] removed them to cities from one end of the borders of Egypt even to the other end thereof.'

The work of reorganisation proceeded apace. Joseph in due season distributed seed and made it conditional that a fifth part of the produce of all farms should be paid in taxation. A strong central government was thus established on a sound economic basis, and it may have flourished until some change occurred of which we have no knowledge. Perhaps the decline of the Hyksos power was not wholly the result of a revolt in the south; it may have been contributed to as well by interference from outside.

Meanwhile the children of Israel 'dwelt in the land of Egypt, in the country of Goshen; and they had possessions therein and multiplied exceedingly'. Josephus's statement that they were identical with the Hyksos hardly accords with the evidence of the Bible. It is possible, however, that other Semites besides Joseph attained high positions during the period of foreign control. In fact, one of the pharaohs was named Jacob-her, or possibly, as Breasted suggested, Jacob-El. Such a choice of ruler would not be inconsistent with the policy of the Hittites, who allowed subject peoples to control their own affairs so long as they adhered to the treaty of alliance and recognised the suzerainty of the supreme power.

It is impossible to fix with any certainty the time at which the Israelites settled in Egypt. They came, not as conquerors, but after the Hyksos had seized the crown. Apparently, too, they had no intention of settling permanently, because the bodies of Jacob and Joseph, having been embalmed, were carried to the family cave tomb 'in the land of Canaan', which Abraham had purchased from 'Ephron the Hittite'.

No inscription regarding Joseph or the great famine has survived, but the Egyptians were not likely to preserve any record of a grand vizier who starved them into submission. A tablet that makes reference to a seven years' famine during the Third Dynasty has been proved to be a pious fraud of the Roman period. It was based, in all probability, on the Joseph story. The alleged record sets forth that King Djoser, who was greatly distressed regarding the condition of the country, sent a message to the governor of Nubia asking for information regarding the rise of the Nile. Statistics were duly supplied according to his desire. Then pharaoh 'dreamed a dream' and saw the god Khnum, who informed him that Egypt was being afflicted because no temples had been erected to the gods. As soon as he woke up, his majesty made gifts of land to the priests of Khnum and arranged that they should receive a certain proportion of all the fish and game caught in the vicinity of the first cataract.

There is no agreement as to when the exodus of the Israelites took place. Some authorities are of the opinion that it coincided with the expulsion of the Hyksos. Such a view, however, conflicts with the Biblical reference to a period of bondage. The pharaoh of the oppression was a 'new king' and he 'knew not Joseph'. He enslaved and oppressed the Israelites, who had been so singularly favoured by the foreign rulers. According to tradition, he was Rameses II, during whose reign Moses acquired 'all the wisdom of the Egyptians' and became 'mighty in words and deeds'. The next king was Meneptah, but he cannot be regarded as the pharaoh of the exodus. He reigned little over ten years, and one of his inscriptions makes reference to the Israelites as a people resident in Canaan, where they were attacked by the Egyptian army during a Syrian campaign. It is probable that the Hebrews were the Khabri mentioned in the Amarna Letters, two centuries before Meneptah's time. They were then waging war against Canaanitish allies of Egypt, and the prince of Gezer sent an urgent but ineffectual appeal to Pharaoh Akhenaten for assistance. The exodus must have taken place in the early part of the Eighteenth Dynasty and possibly during the reign of Thuthmosis I – about a generation after Ahmosis expelled the Asiatics from Avaris.

During the latter part of the Hyksos period, the Theban princes, whom Manetho gives as the kings of the Seventeenth Dynasty, were tributary rulers over a goodly part of Upper Egypt. Reinforced from Nubia and aided by the princes of certain of the nomes, they suddenly rose against their oppressors and began to wage the war of independence, which lasted for about a quarter of a century and ended the Second Intermediate Period.

An interesting papyrus, preserved in the British Museum in London, contains a fragmentary folk tale that indicates that the immediate cause of the rising was an attempt on the part of the Hyksos overlord to compel the Egyptians to worship the god Sutekh.

'It came to pass,' it reads, 'that Egypt was possessed by the impure, and there was no lord and king.'

This may mean that either the Hyksos rule had limited power in Upper Egypt or was subject to a higher authority in Asia. The folk tale proceeds:

'Now King Seqenenre was lord of the south. . . . Impure Asiatics were in the cities [as garrisons?], and Apepa was lord in Avaris. They worked their will in the land and enjoyed all the good things of Egypt. The god Sutekh was Apepa's master, for he worshipped Sutekh alone, and erected for him an enduring temple. . . . He sacrificed and gave offerings every day to Sutekh. . . .'

The tale then goes on to relate that Apepa sent a messenger to Seqenenre, the lord of Thebes, 'the city of the south', with an important document that had been prepared after lengthy consultation with a number of learned scribes.

Seqenenre appears to have received the messenger with undisguised alarm. He asked: 'What order do you bring? Why have you made this journey?'

The document was read and, as far as can be gathered from the blurred and mutilated papyrus, it was something to the following effect:

> The King Ra Apepa sends to you to say: Let the hippopotami be put out of the pool in the city of Thebes. I cannot get sleep, either by day or by night, because their roaring is in my ear.

No wonder that 'the lord of the south' was astounded. The sacred animals at Thebes could not possibly be disturbing the slumbers of a monarch residing on the Delta frontier. Apepa was evidently anxious to pick a quarrel with the Thebans, for his hypocritical complaint was, in effect, an express order to suppress a popular form of worship. He would know well that he could not adopt a more direct means to stir up a spirit of rebellion among his Egyptian subjects. Possibly the growing power of the Theban ruler may have caused him to feel somewhat alarmed, and he wished to shatter it before it became too strong for him.

Seqenenre was unable for a time to decide what reply he should make. At length, having entertained the messenger, he asked him to convey the following brief but pointed answer to Apepa: 'I intend to do as is your wish'.

Apparently he wished to gain time, for there could remain no doubt that a serious crisis was approaching. No sooner had the messenger made his departure than the Theban ruler summoned before him all the great lords in the district and related to them 'what had come to pass'. These men were likewise 'astounded'. They heard what Seqenenre had to tell them 'with feelings of sorrow, but were silent, for none knew what to say'.

The fragmentary tale then ends abruptly with the words: 'The King Ra Apepa sent to——'

We can infer, however, that his second message roused a storm of opposition and that whatever demand it contained was met with a blank refusal. King Ra Apepa must have then sent a strong army southwards to enforce his decree and subdue the subject princes who dared to have minds of their own.

If we identify Seqenenre with the Theban king of that name, whose mummy was found at Deir el-Bahri and is now in the Cairo, we can conclude that the ancient folk tale contained a popular account of the brief but glorious career and tragic death of a national hero, who, like the Scottish Sir William Wallace, inspired his countrymen with the desire for freedom and independence.

Seqenenre died on the battlefield. We can see him pressing forward at the head of the Egyptian army, fighting with indomitable courage and accomplishing mighty deeds. Accompanied by his most valiant followers, he hews his way through the Hyksos force. But 'one by one they fall around him'. . . . Now he is alone. He is surrounded. . . . The warriors in front of him are mowed down, for none can withstand his blows. But a Hyksos soldier creeps up on his left side, swings his battle-axe and smites a glancing blow. Seqenenre totters, his cheek bone and teeth laid bare. Another soldier on his right leaps up and stabs him on the forehead. Before he falls, his first successful assailant strikes again, and the battle-axe crashes through the left side of the hero's skull. The Hyksos shout triumphantly, but the Egyptians are not dismayed. Clamouring in battle fury, they rush on to avenge the death of Seqenenre. . . . That hero has not died in vain.

A platoon (troop) of Egyptian spearmen
From the bas-relief in the temple at Deir el-Bahri

The mummy of the great prince bears the evidence of the terrible wounds that he received. In his agony he had bitten his tongue between his teeth. But it is apparent that before he fell he turned the tide of battle and that the Hyksos were compelled to retreat, for his body was recovered and carried back to Thebes, where it was embalmed after putrefaction had set in.

Seqenenre appears to have been a handsome and dashing soldier. He was tall, slim and active, with a strong, refined face of dark Mediterranean type. Probably he was a descendant of one of the ancient families that had taken refuge in the south after the Hyksos invaders had accomplished the fall of the native monarchy.

His queen, Ahhotep, who was a hereditary princess in her own right, lived until she was a hundred years old. Her three sons reigned in succession and continued the war against the Hyksos. The youngest of these was Ahmosis, and he was the first pharaoh of the Eighteenth Dynasty, the first dynasty of the New Kingdom. Ahhotep must have followed his career with pride, for he drove the Asiatics across the frontier. She survived him and then lived through the reign of Amenophis I also, for she did not die until Thuthmosis I ruled in splendour over a united Egypt and caused its name to be dreaded in western Asia.

Ahmosis, like the heroic Seqenenre, received the support of the El Kab family, which was descended from one of the old feudal lords. His successes are recorded in the tomb of his namesake, the son of Ebana, a princess, and of Baba, the lord of El Kab, who had served under Seqenenre. This El Kab Ahmosis was quite a youth – he tells us that he was 'too young to have a wife' – when he fought on foot behind the chariot of the pharaoh. He was afterwards promoted to the rank of admiral and won a naval victory on a canal. So greatly did the young nobleman distinguish himself that he received a decoration – a golden collar, the equivalent of our Victoria Cross. Indeed he was similarly honoured for performing feats of valour on four subsequent occasions, and he also received gifts of land and of male and female slaves who had been taken captive.

The progress northwards of Ahmosis, with army and river fleet, was accompanied by much hard fighting, but at length he compelled the Hyksos force, which had suffered heavily, to take refuge in the fortified town of Avaris. After a prolonged siege the enemy took flight, and he pursued them across the frontier.

We have followed, so far, the narrative of Ahmosis, son of Ebana. According to Manetho's account of the expulsion, as quoted by Josephus, who, perhaps, tampered with it, King Ahmosis was unable to do more than shut up the Hyksos in Avaris. Then Thuthmosis, successor of Ahmosis, endeavoured to seize the town by assault but failed in the attempt. Just when he was beginning to despair of accomplishing his purpose, the enemy offered to capitulate if they would be allowed to depart in peace. This condition was accepted, whereupon 240,000 men, women and children evacuated Avaris and crossed the frontier into Syria. Manetho adds that they migrated to the district afterwards known as Judea and built Jerusalem, because 'they were in dread of the Assyrians'. But, as we have seen, the Assyrians were not at this period the predominant power in the east. Manetho (or Josephus) was plainly wrong. A new and hostile enemy, however, had appeared at Mitanni – the dreaded Aryans, who worshipped the strange gods Indra, Mithra and Varuna.

After clearing the Delta of Asiatic soldiers, Ahmosis turned his attention to Nubia. He did not meet with much opposition and succeeded in extending the southern frontier to the second cataract, thus recovering the area that had been controlled by the great pharaohs of the Twelfth Dynasty. He had afterwards to suppress two abortive risings in the heart of the kingdom, which may have been engineered by Hyksos sympathisers. Then he devoted himself to the work of restoring the monuments of his ancestors and the temples of the gods. After a strenuous reign of over twenty years, he died in the prime of life, lamented, no doubt, by the people whom he had set free and especially by the queen mother, Ahhotep, that wife of a mighty leader and nurse of valiant heroes – one of the first great women in history.

The military successes of the Egyptians were largely contributed to by their use of the horse, which the Aryans had introduced into the West.

New methods of fighting had also been adopted by the Egyptians. When the Eighteenth-Dynasty soldiers were depicted on monuments and in tombs the artists had for their models highly disciplined and well-organised bodies of men who had undergone a rigorous training. The infantry were marshalled in regular lines and on battlefields made vigorous and orderly charges. Charioteers gathered into action with the dash and combination of later cavalry. Had this new military system evolved in Upper Egypt as a result of the example shown by the Hyksos? Or had the trade in horses brought into the Nile valley Aryan warriors who became the drill sergeants and adjutants of the army that drove the Hyksos from the land of the pharaohs?

Chapter 22

Amun, the God of the New Kingdom

Lunar Worship – The Great Mother of Darkness – Amun as a Moon God – Fusion with Ra – Ptah a Form of the Theban Deity – 'Fenkhu' and 'Fenish' Artisans Osiris and Amun – Veneration of Religious Pharaohs – Amun's Wife and Concubine – Conquests of Thuthmosis I – Rival Claimants to the Throne – Queen Hatshepsut – Her Famous Expedition – Rise of Thuthmosis III – A Great Strategist – His Conquests – The Egyptian Empire – Amun's Poetic Praise – The Emperor's Buildings and Obelisks.

The moon god Ah comes into prominence during the war of independence. This ancient deity must have been closely associated with the Theban religious cult which Ra Apepa, the Hyksos king, singled out for attack, because the name of the queen mother, Ahhotep, signifies 'Ah is satisfied', and that of her victorious son Ahmosis, 'born of Ah'.

It is highly probable that Ah was the son of the great Mother deity Apet, who was identified with the female hippopotamus Taweret, 'the mighty one', goddess of maternity and 'mother of the gods'. At Thebes and Ombos, Osiris was regarded as the son of the sacred hippopotamus. As we have seen in the Introduction, he was, like Ah, identified with the moon spirit, which symbolised the male principle. The Apet hippopotamus was the animal incarnation of the Great Mother. As a water goddess, therefore, Apet links with Nut, who rose from the primordial deep and was 'the waters above the firmament'.

At the beginning there was nothing save darkness and water. The spirit of the night was the Great Mother, and her first-born was the moon child. Life came from death and light from darkness. Such appears to have been the belief of the worshippers of the sky-and-water goddess and the lunar god.

On the other hand, the worshippers of the male earth spirit believed that the firmament was made of metal that was beaten out by the Great Father, Ptah, at the beginning. Before metal came into use, it may have been believed that the sky was made of stone. Hathor, the sky goddess, was significantly enough 'the lady of turquoise', and Ra, the sun god, was in the Fifth Dynasty symbolised by an obelisk.

Osiris, the human incarnation of primitive Nile deities, absorbed the attributes of the moon spirit and the male earth spirit. Isis, on the other hand, apparently absorbed those of Nut, the sky-and-water goddess, and of Neith, the earth goddess, who symbolised growth.

As moon worship was of greater antiquity in Egypt than sun worship and was associated with agricultural rites, the Theban cult must have held popular appeal and helped to rally the mass of the people to throw off the yoke of the Hyksos Ra and Sutekh worshippers. The political significance of Apepa's order to slay the hippopotami is therefore apparent.

When the influence of the southern conquerors extended to Hermopolis, Ah was merged with Thoth, who was originally a lunar deity. In fact, as we have seen in the Introduction, he was another form of Khonsu. With Mut, 'the mother', who is indistinguishable from Apet, Khonsu and Thoth formed a Theban triad. In Nubia, where archaic Mediterranean beliefs appear to have been persistent, Thoth was the son of Tefnut, the lioness-headed goddess, who was given arbitrary association with Shu, the atmosphere god, by the theorists of Heliopolis. Mut was also depicted at Thebes with the head of a lioness.

As has been already suggested, it is possible that Amun was originally the son of Mut-Apet. He may have developed as a symbolised attribute of Ah. Fragments of old hymns make reference to him as a lunar deity, and as a 'traverser' of space, like Khonsu-Thoth. Indeed, even in his hawk-headed form, he retains his early association with the moon, for he wears the solar disc with the lunar crescent.[1]

Amun, like the sons of all the Great Mother deities, represented in his animal forms the male principle and the fighting principle. He became 'the husband of his mother' when the Great Father and Great Mother beliefs were fused. This process is illustrated in the triad formed by Ptah, the father, Mut, the mother, and Thoth, the son. Ptah's wife, Sekhmet, with the head of a lioness, is indistinguishable from Mut, Tefnut and Bastet.

As a Great Father deity, Amun, 'husband of his mother', became 'king of the gods'[2] and lost his original lunar character. His fusion with the sun god of Heliopolis, which was accomplished for political purposes, made the change complete, for he became Amun-Ra, the great representative deity of Egypt, who combines the attributes of all other gods.

Amun-Ra was depicted as a great bearded man, clad in a sleeveless tunic that was suspended from his shoulders, with the tail of an animal hanging behind. His headdress of high double plumes, with lunar and solar symbols, was coloured in sections red and blue, and red and green, as if to signify an association with the

[1] In an Amun-Ra hymn the deity is called 'maker of men, former of the flocks, lord of corn' (*Religion of the Ancient Egyptians*, Wiedemann).

[2] 'The gods gather as dogs round his feet.' – *Hymn to Amun-Ra*.

Haapi, god of the Nile

Amun-Ra, king of the gods

Mut 'the mother'

Deities of the New Kingdom

river flowing between its banks and the growth of vegetation. Sometimes he is shown with Min's ram's horns curving downwards round his ears and sometimes with those of Khnum spreading outward.[1] He wore a collar and armlets and bracelets.

As a god of war he rose into great prominence during the Eighteenth Dynasty. The victorious kings, who became owners of all the land in Egypt and returned with great spoils from many battlefields, were lavish in their gifts to his temple, and his priests became exceedingly wealthy and powerful. There never was in Egypt a more influential cult than that of Amun-Ra.

His solar attributes, however, were not so prominent in the Eighteenth as in the Nineteenth and Twentieth Dynasties. The influence of the moon cult remained for a considerable period. As much is suggested by the names of the kings. Ahmosis I, 'born of Ah', was followed by four rulers called Amenophis (Amenhotep), 'Amun is satisfied', and four called Thuthmosis, 'born of Thoth'.

The influence of the Ra cult at Heliopolis was tempered by that of the Amun cult at Thebes, with the result that the old Egyptian lunar gods came into prominence. Nor were Ptah and other kindred deities excluded from the group of official gods, as in the Fifth Dynasty. At Memphis Amun-Ra was worshipped as Ptah. In a hymn addressed to the great Theban deity it was declared:

> Memphis receives thee in the form of Ptah –
> He who is the first-born of all gods;
> He who was at the beginning.

It would appear that the Memphites had combined with the Thebans to drive the Hyksos out of Egypt. When Ahmosis began the work of reconstructing the temples, the first gods he honoured were Amun and Ptah. In the limestone quarries near Cairo two tablets record that stone was excavated for the great temples at Memphis and Thebes. No reference is made to Heliopolis. It is of special interest to find that the workmen who were employed were of the Fenkhu, a Syrian tribe. There can be no doubt that these quarriers were foreigners. In an Aswan inscription of Thuthmosis II, it is stated that the boundary of the Egyptian empire on the north extended to the Syrian lakes and that the pharaoh's arms were 'not repulsed from the land of the Fenkhu'. A stele erected by Thuthmosis III at Wadi Halfa records a victory during a Syrian campaign over 'the Fenkhu'. Ahmosis must have obtained these skilled quarriers from the Fenkhu for the purpose of hastening on the work of restoring the temples in return for some favour conferred, for he did not wage war against the tribe, which remained powerful at the time of Thuthmosis III. It is impossible, however, to identify them with certainty. To this day the inhabitants of Palestine still credit all the surviving works of an-

[1] 'Amun of the two horns.'

tiquity to the 'Fenish', and although the reference is evidently to the Philistines and Phoenicians as well as to the hewers of the great artificial caves, it is possible that the latter, who are referred to in the Bible as the Rephaim or Anakim, were originally the 'Fenish' and the Egyptian 'Fenkhu'. Ahmosis may have followed the example of his temple- and pyramid-building predecessors in drawing fresh supplies of skilled stone-workers from southern Palestine.

Osiris worship was combined with that of Amun at Thebes, but, as we have seen, Osiris and Amun had much in common, for both gods had lunar attributes. Osiris 'hides his essence in the great shrine of Amun'.[1] The Amun ram was an animal incarnation of the corn spirit. It is significant to find in this connection that the priests of Amun for a long period sought to be buried at sacred Abydos, which had become closely associated with Osirian worship. But there was a strange fusion of beliefs regarding the other world. Men died believing that they would enter the barque of Ra and also reach the Osirian paradise. Ultimately the Heliopolitan belief in the efficacy of magical formulae impaired the ethical character of the Ptah-Osirian creed.

Although Ahmosis was the liberator of Egypt, his memory was not revered so greatly as that of his son and successor, Amenhotep I (Amenophis). The great pharaohs of the records were the religious pharaohs. If a monarch was assiduous in venerating the gods, and especially in erecting and endowing temples, his fame was assured – the grateful priests 'kept his memory green'. Amenophis I and his wife, Aahmes-Nefertari, were, after their deaths, revered as deities. References are made to them as protectors and punishers of men in the Nineteenth Dynasty.

Nefertari was during her life 'Amun's wife'. She slept in the temple, and her children were reputed to be the sons and daughters of the god. The high priest's wife was 'the concubine of Amun'. It was Amenophis I who founded the endowments of the Amun cult at Thebes, which ultimately became so wealthy and powerful. He also began the erection of the magnificent buildings at Karnak, which were added to by his successors. His reign, which lasted for about twenty years, was occupied chiefly in reorganising the kingdom and in establishing the new national religion. Assisted by the veteran military nobles of El Kab, he waged war against the Libyans on the north and the Nubians on the south. He appears also to have penetrated Syria, but no records of the campaign survive. His successors, however, before he invaded Asia, claimed to hold sway as far north as the Euphrates.

The next king, Thuthmosis I, came to the throne as the husband of a princess of the royal line. He found it necessary to invade Nubia. Ahmosis of Ebana, who accompanied him, recorded in his tomb that a battle was fought between the sec-

---

[1] That is, the soul of Osiris is in Amun, as the soul of the giant is in the egg, the ram, etc, 'doubly hidden'. Amun-Ra is addressed in a temple chant: 'Hidden is your abode, lord of the gods'.

ond and third cataract. The pharaoh slew the Nubian leader who opposed him and, on his return, had the body suspended head downwards at the bow of the royal ship. Thuthmosis penetrated Nubia beyond the third cataract and reached the island of Argo, where Sebekhotep had undertaken the erection of his great statues. A fortress was erected and garrisoned on an island at the third cataract. Nubia thus became once again an Egyptian province.

A campaign of conquest was next waged in Syria, where Egyptian dominance was continually challenged by the rival powers in Asia Minor and Mesopotamia. 'It was probably,' wrote Hall and a colleague, 'with the Iranian kingdom of Mitanni, between Euphrates and Tigris, that the Dynasty carried on its struggle for Syria.' No royal records of the campaign of Thuthmosis I survive, but tomb inscriptions tell of a great victory won in Naharina, 'the land of the rivers', which secured Egyptian supremacy. The king was afterwards able to boast that the northern boundary of the empire extended 'as far as the circuit of the sun' – it was believed that the world's edge was at the source of the Euphrates, on the north, and of that of the Nile, on the south, and that both rivers flowed from the ocean, 'the great circle' surrounding the earth, in which lay the great serpent.

Thuthmosis I made an addition to the Karnak temple and erected two great pylons on the thirtieth anniversary of his reign, when, at the Sed Festival, he appears to have selected his successor. On one of the pylons he recorded that he had established peace in Egypt, ended lawlessness and stamped out impiety, and that he had subdued the rebels in the Delta region. He also implored Amun to give the throne to his daughter, Hatshepsut.

The closing period of the king's reign is obscure, and there is no agreement as to the events that occurred in connection with the family feud that ensued. Thuthmosis III dated his reign from the year before the death of Thuthmosis I, but in the interval Thuthmosis II and Hatshepsut sat on the throne.

The children of the royal princess who was the wife of Thuthmosis I included two sons and two daughters, but they all died young, with the exception of the Princess Hatshepsut. Another wife was the mother of Thuthmosis II, while a concubine gave birth to Thuthmosis III.

Such is Breasted's reading of the problem, which is made difficult on account of the mutilation of inscriptions by the rival claimants. Other Egyptologists suggest that Thuthmosis III was the son of Thuthmosis II.

Thuthmosis III was a priest in the temple of Amun. He secured his succession by marrying either Hatshepsut or her daughter. According to Breasted, he superseded Thuthmosis I at a festival at which the oracle of Amun proclaimed him as the pharaoh. Thuthmosis III then began his reign, and the old king lived in retirement. After a time the usurping prince had to recognise the co-regency of Hatshepsut, but before long he was thrust aside, and the queen reigned alone as 'the female Horus'. Thuthmosis II then seized the throne on his own and his fa-

Queen Aahmes-Nefertari (wife of Thuthmosis I), mother of the famous Hatshepsut
The face is of Mediterranean type. She represents the royal line, which soon
afterwards fused with a foreign strain so that the facial type changed
From a plaster cast of the relief on the wall of the temple at Deir el-Bahri

ther's behalf, and when Thuthmosis I died, Thuthmosis II allied himself with Thuthmosis III. When they had reigned about two years, Thuthmosis II died, but Thuthmosis III was not able to retain his high position. Once again Hatshepsut, who had evidently won over a section of the priesthood, seized the reins of government and Thuthmosis III was once again 'relegated to the background'. At the festivals he appeared as a priest.

Hatshepsut must have been a woman of great ability and force of character to have displaced such a man as Thuthmosis III. She ruled alone and engaged herself chiefly in restoring the religious buildings that had either been demolished or had fallen into disrepair during the Hyksos period. She completed the great mortuary temple at Deir el-Bahri, which had been begun under Thuthmosis II. It was modelled on the smaller temple of Mentuhotep. Situated against the western cliffs at Thebes, it was constructed in three terraces with sublime colonnades, finely proportioned and exquisitely wrought. An inner chamber was excavated from the rock. On the temple walls the mythical scenes in connection with the birth of the queen were sculpted in low relief, and to get over the difficulty of being recognised as a 'son of the sun', Hatshepsut was depicted in the company of her male 'double'. On state occasions she wore a false beard.

The queen's most famous undertaking was to send an expedition of eight ships to the land of Punt to obtain myrrh trees, incense, rare woods and sacred animals for the temple. It was her pious wish that Amun should have a garden to walk in.

To celebrate her jubilee, Hatshepsut had erected two magnificent obelisks, nearly 100 feet (30 metres) high, in front of the Karnak temple in which Thuthmosis III was a priest. One of these still stands erect and is greatly admired by visitors. The obelisks, like the temple, were designed by the much favoured architect Senmut, an accomplished artist and scheming statesman, who was a prominent figure in the party that supported the queen.

But so deeply was Hatshepsut concerned in devoting the revenues of the state to religious purposes that the affairs of empire were neglected. The flame of revolt was spreading through Syria, where the tribal chiefs scorned to give allegiance to a woman, especially as she neglected to enforce her will at the point of the sword. Apparently, too, the Mitanni power had recovered from the blows dealt by the military pharaohs of a previous generation and had again become aggressive. Then Hatshepsut died. She may have been a victim of a palace revolt of which no record survives. Her mummy has never been discovered. When the deep tunnel that she had had constructed for her tomb was entered, it was found to have been despoiled. It may be that her body was never deposited there. After her death no more is heard of her favourite, Senmut, or her daughter, whom she had selected as her successor. Her name was ruthlessly erased from her monuments. All the indications point to a military revolt, supported by a section of the priesthood, at a time of national peril.

Ruins of the temple of Deir el-Bahri

Thuthmosis III, who immediately came to the throne, lost no time in raising an army and pressing northwards to subdue the Syrian rebellion. Although he has been referred to as 'this little man with coarse features, as we know from his mummy', it would be a mistake to retain the impression that he was of repulsive aspect. He died when he was an old man. His jaw was not tied up before embalming, which was not highly successful, for his nose was disfigured and has partly crumbled away. The statues of the king present the striking face of a vigorous and self-contained man. In one he has a nose that rivals that of the Duke of Wellington, and an air of dignity that accords with what we know of his character, for, not only was he a great leader who, as his grand vizier has informed the ages, knew all that happened and never failed to carry out a matter he took in hand, he was also a man of artistic ability, accustomed, in Breasted's view, to spend his leisure time 'designing exquisite vases'.

The hour had come and the man! With a well-organised army, in which he had placed the most capable men in command, he swept his victorious way through Syria and struck terror into the hearts of the rebels. His name – Manakhpirria (Men-kheper-ra) Thuthmosis – was dreaded long after his death and may have been the origin of the Semitic title 'pharaoh', which was never used by the native kings of Egypt.

The greatest triumph of the various Syrian campaigns conducted by Thuthmosis III was the capture of Megiddo, in the Hebrew tribal area of Issachar. That fortified stronghold, situated on the plain of Jezreel, was a point of great strategic importance – 'the key', indeed, of northern Palestine. It had to be approached over the ridge of Carmel and was partly surrounded by the tributary known as 'the brook Kina', which flows into the Kishon River. Two highways leading to Megiddo lay before the Egyptian army, like the legs of inward-curving callipers, and between these a narrow mountain pass cut in an almost straight and direct line into the town.

The Egyptian generals intended to advance along the northern curving highway, but Thuthmosis III was a great strategist who always did the unexpected. He decided to push through the pass, although along the greater part of it his horsemen would have to advance in Indian file. To inspire his followers with his own great courage, the fearless monarch rode in front. His daring manoeuvre was a complete success. Before it was comprehended by the enemy, his army was pouring down upon the plain.

He completely upset the plans of the Asiatic allies, who had divided their forces to await the advance of the Egyptians by the north and the south, occupying the while, no doubt, strong positions.

The battle took place next day on the river bank. Thuthmosis led a victorious charge and scattered the enemy so that they retreated in confusion and took refuge in the city. Had the Egyptians not been too eager to secure the spoils of victory, they might have captured Megiddo, as Thuthmosis informed them afterwards. A long siege followed, but at length the town was starved into submission, and the princes came out to swear allegiance to the pharaoh. They also made payment of the tribute that they had withheld during the closing years of Hatshepsut's reign. Thuthmosis took the eldest sons of the various rebel princes as hostages and deported them to Thebes. The spoils of victory included over 900 chariots and 200 coats of mail and much gold and silver. Before he returned home, he captured three towns in Lebanon and reorganised the administration of northern Palestine.

Other campaigns followed. On one of these Thuthmosis made a swift attack on some rebel princes by crossing the sea and landing on the Phoenician coast. The Hittites gave trouble in the north, and he pushed on to Carchemish, their southern capital, and captured it. At Kadesh, on the Orontes, he also dealt a shattering blow against the Hittites and their allies from Mitanni. He had previously subdued the Libyans and conducted a successful campaign into Nubia. Thus he built up a great empire and made Egypt the foremost power in the world. Tribute poured into the royal exchequer from the various subject states, and peace offerings were made by the Hittites and even by the rulers of Cyprus and Crete. Both Assyria and Babylon cultivated friendly relations with Thuthmosis III, who appears to have been as distinguished a diplomatist as he was a conqueror.

The priests of Amun composed a great hymn in his honour, which, they pretended, had been recited by their god:

I have come, I have given to you to smite the land of the Syrians-
Under your feet they lie through the length and breadth of the god's
    land;
I have made them see your might like to a star revolving
When it sheds its burning beams and drops its dew on the meadows.

I have come, I have given to you to vanquish the Western peoples
Crete is stricken with fear, terror is reigning in Cyprus;
Like to a great young bull, I have made them behold your power,
Fearless and quick to strike, none is so bold to resist you.

I have come, I have given to you to conquer the folk of the marshes,
The terror of you has fallen over the lands of Mitanni;
Like to a crocodile fierce they have beheld you in glory;
O monarch of fear at sea, none is so bold to approach you.

The chief buildings of Thuthmosis III were erected to Amun at Thebes, but he did not fail to honour Ra at Heliopolis, Ptah at Memphis and Hathor at Dendera. One of his jubilee obelisks, which he erected at Thebes, now stands in Istanbul; another is in Rome. The pair set up at Heliopolis have been given prominent sites on either side of the Atlantic Ocean – one in New York and the other on the Thames Embankment, London. His reign, which he dated from his first accession prior to the death of Thuthmosis I, extended over a period of fifty-four years. He was buried in the Valley of the Kings.

Chapter 23

Tale of the Doomed Prince

Pharaoh's Heir – Decree of the Fates – Son must die a Sudden Death – His Lonely Childhood – The Dog – Prince goes on his Travels – The Lady of the Tower – Won by the Disguised Prince – An Angry Father – Prince returns Home – Perils of Darkness – The Giant and the Crocodile – The Serpent slain – Mystery of the Prices Fate – Resemblances to European Stories – An Unsolved Problem

Now hear the tale of the doomed prince. Once upon a time there was a king in Egypt whose heart was heavy because he had no son. He called upon the gods, and the gods heard, and they decreed that an heir should be born to him. In time came the day of the child's birth. The seven Hathors (Fates) greeted the prince and pronounced his destiny. They said he would meet with a sudden death, either by a crocodile or a serpent or a dog.

The nurses informed the king what the Hathors had said, and the heart of his majesty was troubled. He commanded that a house should be erected in a lonely place so that the child might be guarded well, and he provided servants and all kinds of luxuries and gave orders that the prince should not be taken outside his safe retreat.

It came to pass that the boy grew strong and big. One day he climbed to the flat roof of the house. Looking down, he saw a dog, which followed a man, and wondered greatly about it.

Then he spoke to one of the servants, saying: 'What is that which follows the man walking along the road?'

'That,' answered the servant, 'is a dog.'

The boy said: 'I should like to have one for myself. Bring a dog to me.'

When he spoke thus, the servant informed the king. His majesty said: 'Let him have a young boar hunter, so that he may not fret.'

So the prince was given a dog as he had wished.

The boy grew into young manhood, and his limbs were stout; he was indeed a prince of the land. He grew restless in the lonely house and sent a message to his royal father, saying: 'Hear me. Why am I kept a prisoner here? I am destined to die, either by a crocodile, a serpent or a dog; it is the will of the gods. Then let me go forth and follow my heart's desire while I live.'

His Majesty considered the matter and said he would grant the lad's wish. So he caused him to be provided with all kinds of weapons and consented that the dog should follow him.

A servant of the king conducted the young prince to the eastern frontier[1] and said: 'Now you may go wherever you wish.'

The lad called his dog and set his face towards the north. He hunted on his way and fared well. In time he reached the country of Naharina (Mitanni) and went to the house of a chief.

Now the chief had no son, and he had only one daughter and she was very fair. He had caused to be erected for her a stately tower with seventy windows, on the summit of a very tall cliff. The fame of the girl went abroad, and her father sent for all the sons of chiefs in the land and said to them:

'My daughter will be given in marriage to the youth who can climb up to her window.'

Day after day the lads endeavoured to scale the cliff, and one afternoon when they were so engaged the young prince arrived and saw them. He was given a hearty welcome. They took him to their house, they cleansed him with water and gave him perfumes, and then they set food before him and gave fodder to his horse. They showed him great kindness, and brought sandals to him.

Then they said: 'Whence come you, young man?'

The prince answered: 'I am the son of one of the pharaoh's charioteers. My mother died, and my father then took another wife, who hates me. I have run away from home.'

He said no more. They kissed him as if he were a brother and prevailed upon him to wait with them a while.

'What can I do here?' asked the prince.

The young men said: 'Each day we try to scale the cliff and reach the window of the chief's daughter. She is very fair and will be given in marriage to the fortunate one who can climb up to her.'

On the next day they resumed their usual task, and the prince stood apart, watching them. Then day followed day, and they endeavoured in vain to reach the window, while he looked on.

Then at length that the prince said to the others: 'If you consent, I will endeavour also. I should like to climb among you.'

The young men gave him leave to join them in the daily task. Now it happened that the beautiful daughter of the chief in Naharina looked down from her window in the high tower, gazing on the youths. The prince saw her, and he began to climb with the sons of the chiefs, and he went up and up until he reached the window of the great chief's daughter, the fair one. She took him in her arms, and she kissed him.

[1] Apparently the prince was safe from attack so long as he was away from Egypt.

Then one who had looked on, sought to gladden the heart of the girl's father, and hurried to him and spoke, saying:

'At last one of the youths has reached the window of your daughter.'

'The great chief asked: 'Whose son is he?'

He was told: 'The youth is the son of one of the pharaoh's charioteers, who fled from Egypt because of his stepmother.'

Then the great chief was very angry, and he said: 'Am I to give my daughter in marriage to an Egyptian fugitive? Order him to return at once to his own land.'

Messengers were sent to the youth in the tower, and they said to him: 'Begone! You must return to the place from where you came.'

But the fair maid clung to him. She called upon the god and swore an oath, saying: 'By the name of Ra Harmakhis, if he is not to be mine, I will neither eat nor drink again.'

When she had spoken thus she grew faint, as if she were about to die.

A messenger hastened to her father and told him what the girl had vowed and how she sank fainting.

The great chief then sent men to put the stranger to death if he remained in the tower.

When they came near the girl, she cried: 'By the god, if you slay my chosen one, I will die also. I will not live a single hour if he is taken from me.'

The girl's words were repeated to her father, and he, the great chief, said: 'Let the young man, this stranger, be brought into my presence.'

Then the prince was taken before the great chief. He was stricken with fear, but the girl's father embraced him and kissed him, saying: 'You are indeed a noble youth. Tell me who you are. I love you as if you were my own son.'

The prince answered: 'My father is a charioteer in the army of the pharaoh. My mother died, and my father then took another wife, who hates me. I have run away from home.'

The great chief gave his daughter to the prince for wife, and provided a goodly dwelling, with servants, a portion of land and many cattle.

It came to pass some time after this that the prince spoke to his wife, saying:

'It is my destiny to die one of three deaths, either by a crocodile or a serpent or a dog.'

'Let the dog be slain at once,' urged the woman.

Said the prince: 'I will not permit that my dog be slain. Besides, he would never do me harm.'

His wife was much concerned for his safety. He would not let the dog go out unless he went with it.

It came to pass that the prince travelled with his wife to the land of Egypt and visited the place in which he had formerly dwelt. A giant was with him there. The giant would not allow him to go out after dark, because a crocodile came up

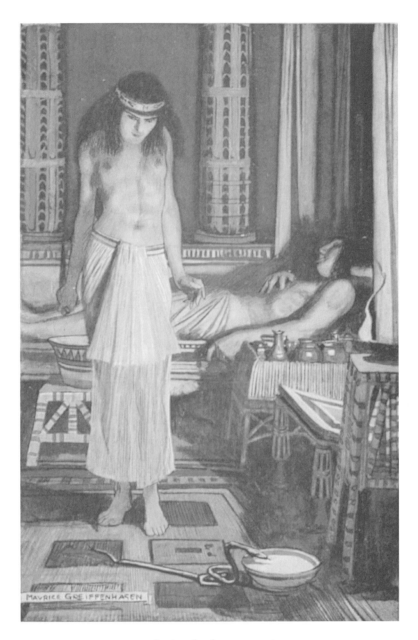

Luring the doom serpent
From the painting by Maurice Greiffenhagen

from the river each night. But the giant himself went out, and the crocodile sought in vain to escape him. He bewitched it.

He continued to go out each night, and when dawn came the prince went abroad, and the giant lay down to sleep. This continued for the space of two months.

It came to pass on a certain day that the prince made merry in his house. There was a great feast. When darkness fell he lay down to rest, and he fell asleep. His wife busied herself cleansing and anointing her body. Suddenly she saw a serpent that had crept out of a hole to sting the prince. She was sitting beside him, and she called the servants to fill a bowl with milk and honeyed wine for the serpent, and it drank the drink and was intoxicated. Then it was rendered helpless and rolled over. The woman seized her dagger and slew the serpent, which she flung into her bath.

When she had finished, she woke the prince, who marvelled greatly that he had escaped, and his wife said: 'Behold the god has given me the chance to remove one of your dooms. He will let me strike another blow.'

The prince made offerings to the god and prostrated himself, and he continued so to do every day.

It came to pass many days afterwards that the prince went out to walk some distance from his house. He did not go alone, for his dog followed him. It chanced that the dog seized an animal in flight, and the prince followed the chase, running. He reached a place near the bank of the river and went down after the dog. Now the dog was beside the crocodile, who led the prince to the place where the giant was. The crocodile said: 'I am your doom and I follow you . . . [I cannot contend] with the giant, but, remember, I will watch you. . . . You may bewitch me [like] the giant, but if you see [me coming once again you will certainly perish].'

Now it came to pass, after the space of two months, that the prince went . . .

Note: Here the British Museum papyrus, which contains several doubtful sentences, is mutilated and ends abruptly. The conclusion of the story is left, therefore, to our imaginations.

One cannot help being struck with certain resemblances in the ancient narrative to a familiar type of Celtic story, which relates the adventures of a king's son who goes forth disguised as 'a poor lad' to seek his fortune and win a bride by performing some heroic deed in a foreign country. The lady in the lofty tower is familiar. In Irish mythology she is the daughter of Balor, King of Night, who had her secluded in this way because it was prophesied that her son would slay him. But the Cyclopean smith, Mackinley, won her, and her son, Lugh, the dawn god, killed Balor with the 'round stone', which was the sun. The mother of the Greek Hermes, who slew his grandson, Argus, with the 'round stone', was concealed in a secret underground chamber from which her lover rescued her.

Apparently the Egyptian prince was safe so long as he resided in a foreign country, and that may be the reason why his father had him conducted to the frontier. It would appear also that he has nothing to fear during the day. The crocodile is bewitched so long as the giant lies in slumber. In certain European stories a man who works a spell must similarly go to sleep. When Sigurd (the Norse Siegfried) roasts the dragon's heart, Regin lies down to sleep, and when Finn-mac-Coul (the Scottish Finn) roasts the salmon, Black Arky, his father's murderer, lies asleep also. In a Sutherland story a magician goes to sleep while snakes are being boiled to obtain a curative potion.

The Egyptian protecting giant (also translated 'mighty man') is likewise familiar in a certain class of Scottish (Mediterranean?) folk tales.

In our Northern legends that relate the wonderful feats of the disguised son of a king he invariably lies asleep with his head on the knees of the fair lady who 'combs his hair'. She sees 'the beast' (or dragon) coming against her and wakens him. In this Egyptian tale the woman, however, slays the serpent, which comes against the man instead.

Readers will naturally ask: 'Was the prince killed by the crocodile or by the dog? Or did he escape? Was his wife given the opportunity to strike a blow?'

In Celtic stories the 'first blow' is allowed, and it is invariably successful. One relates that a woman saved a hero's life by striking, as was her privilege, the first blow, and, as she used a magic wand, she slew the sleeping giant who was to strike the next 'trial blow'.

Was the crocodile slain in the end, and did the dog kill his master by accident? This faithful animal is of familiar type. He is one of the dogs 'which has its day'. In Northern tales the dog is sometimes slain by its master after it has successfully overcome a monster of the night. The terrible combat renders it dangerous afterwards. Besides, 'it had its day'.

Did the Egyptian dog kill the crocodile? Or did the prince's wife slay the dog, thinking the crocodile was unable to injure her husband? And was the spell then broken, and the crocodile permitted to slay the prince?

The problem may be solved if, and when, another version of this ancient story is discovered.

Chapter 24

Changes in Social and Religious Life

Wealth and Luxury – Gaiety of Town Life – Social Functions – Ancient Temperance Lectures – The Judges – Mercenary Soldiers – Foreign Brides and their Influence – Important Deities worshipped – Sutekh and Baal – The Air God – The Phoenician Thor – Voluptuous Goddesses Ashtoreth of the Bible – References to Saul and Solomon – The Strange God Bes – Magic and Ethics – New Ideas of the Judgment – Use and Significance of Amulets – Jacob's Example – New Burial Customs.

In less than a century after the expulsion of the Hyksos, a great change passed over the social conditions of Egypt. The kingdom was thoroughly organised under the supreme control of the court. Every inch of land that the pharaohs had reconquered was vested in the crown. The estates of the old nobility who had disappeared under the regime of Joseph were administered by officials. All the peasants became serfs of the king and paid a proportion of their produce in rent and taxation. The law was firmly administered, and the natural resources of the country were developed to the utmost.

When the arms of the pharaoh secured settled conditions in Syria, the trade routes were reopened and the merchant class increased and prospered. There was no lack of employment. Temple building nursed the various industries into prosperity, and careers were opened for capable men in the civil service and the army. When the wealth of Asia poured into Egypt, not only through the ordinary channels of commerce but also in tribute from the dependencies, the nation assumed the air of comfort and prosperity that we find reflected in the artistic productions of the time. The tomb scenes no longer reveal a plain-living, scantily attired people or dignified and barefooted noblemen and pharaohs amidst scenes of rural simplicity. Egypt of the Eighteenth Dynasty has a setting of oriental splendour. Its people are gaily attired and richly bejewelled, and the luxurious homes of the wealthy resound with music and song and the clatter of wine cups.

When the Egyptian nobles of the Old and Middle Kingdoms had carved in their tombs the scenes of everyday life that they wished to be repeated in paradise, they were content to have ploughmen and builders and domestic servants to

244

provide them with the simple necessities of life. The leisured classes of the New Kingdom sought more after amusements. They could not be happy without their society functions, their merry feasts and rich attire, their troops of singers and dancers, their luxurious villas with elaborate furnishings, and their horses and chariots and grooms.

Town life was full of gaiety. Wealthy people had large and commodious houses and delighted to entertain their friends, who drove up in chariots, attended by servants, and clad in many-coloured and embroidered garments. As the guests gathered and gossiped in these ancient days, hired musicians played harps and lyres, guitars, flutes and double pipes. The lords and ladies seated themselves on single and double chairs, and wine and fruits were brought in by slaves, who also provided garlands and bouquets of scented flowers, perfumes and oil for anointment. The drinking cups were of artistic shape and might be either of glass or porcelain, or of silver or gold, finely engraved and perhaps studded with precious stones.

The dinner consisted of many courses. These Eighteenth-Dynasty guests ate the flesh of the ox, the wild goat or the gazelle, and certain fish, but never the tabooed eel, and they partook of geese and ducks and other birds in season. Pork and mutton were rigidly excluded.[1] A variety of vegetables, and fruit and pastries, were included in the menu. In fact all classes feasted well. It is not surprising to find that when the Israelites were starving in the deserts of Arabia they sighed for the food of Egypt and said: 'Who shall give us flesh to eat? We remember the fish which we did eat in Egypt freely; the cucumbers, and the melons, and the leeks, and the onions, and the garlick' (Numbers 11:4 and 5). They also longed for Egyptian bread (Exodus 16:3).

The society guests of Egypt were served at little tables, or as they sat in rows according to rank, by the nude or scantily attired servants, who handed round the dishes and napkins. All the guests ate with their fingers. They used knives for cutting and spoons for liquids. They washed before and after meals.

Before wine drinking was resumed, the model of a mummy, or perhaps a real mummy, was drawn round the feasting hall, while the musicians chanted 'The Lay of the Harpist' (Chapter 18). Then came a round of amusements. Jugglers and acrobats performed feats, nude girls danced, and songs were sung. Again and again the drinking cups were replenished with wine. Many drank heavily. It was no uncommon thing in ancient Egypt to see intoxicated people. Even in the Middle Kingdom tombs at Beni Hasan there is evidence that the priestly exhortations to live temperate lives were made necessary by the habits of the time. Servants are depicted carrying home their masters in various stages of intoxication.

---

[1] Sheep and pigs were 'taboo' because they were sacred animals that were eaten sacrificially only. Shepherds appear to have been shunned like swineherds. Joseph informed his brethren that 'every shepherd is an abomination unto the Egyptian' (Genesis 46:34) (See Chapter 5).

Pastime in ancient Egypt three thousand years ago
After the painting by Sir Lawrence Alma-Tadema RA in Preston Art Gallery

Nor were the women guiltless in this respect. In the empire tomb scenes at Thebes, tipsy women are seen supported by servants or attended with bowls when they turn sick and their embroidered robes slip from their shoulders.[1]

A temperance advocate in ancient Egypt, who lamented the customs of his age, addressed his friends as follows: 'Do not drink beer to excess. . . . When you are intoxicated you say things that you are unable to recall; you may trip and break your limbs, but no one goes to your assistance, and your friends who continue to drink despise you and call out: "Put this fellow away; he is drunk!" If, perchance, someone desires to ask your advice when you are intoxicated, you are found lying in the dust like a senseless child.'

A teacher once wrote to his pupil, saying: 'I am told that you are neglecting your studies, and that you are giving yourself up to enjoyment. It is said that you wander about through the streets of an evening smelling of wine. The smell of wine will make men avoid you. Wine will destroy your soul; you will become like a broken oar that cannot steer on either side; like a temple in which there is no god, or like a house without bread. Wine is an abomination.'

In sharp contrast to the merrymakers of the empire period are the stern and just administrators of the law. Judges were expected to make no distinction between rich and poor, and exemplary punishments were meted out to those who, by showing favour or accepting bribes, were found to be unworthy stewards. Daily courts were held, at which the evidence was taken down by scribes. Cases were debated, the forty law rolls were always referred to and consulted, and decisions were enforced by the officers of the court. The king boasted not only of the victories he achieved on foreign campaigns; he desired also to have his memory revered as 'the establisher of law'. When ineffectual appeal was made to him as the supreme judge, he 'spoke not; the law remained'.

But although Egypt was being governed by men of high ideals, influences were at work that were sapping the vitality of the nation. The accumulation of wealth and the increasing love of luxury made men less prone to undertake severe and exacting duties. It was ultimately found impossible to recruit a large army in Egypt. The pleasure-loving gentlemen preferred the excitement of the chase to the perils of the battlefield, and the pleasures of cities to the monotony of garrison life and the long and arduous marches on foreign campaigns. 'Soldiers of fortune' were accordingly enlisted, so that a strong standing army might be maintained. The archers known as the 'Nine-bow Barbarians' came from Nubia, and from Europe were obtained the fierce Shardana, the Mycenaean people who gave their name to Sardinia. Ultimately Libyans, and even Asiatics, were recruited. One of the regiments that followed Rameses II in his Syrian cam-

---

[1] Hebrew women were also addicted to drinking. 'Now Hannah, she spake in her heart; only her lips moved, but her voice was not heard; therefore Eli thought she had been drunken. And Eli said unto her, "Put away thy wine from thee"' (1 Samuel 1:13-14)

paign was named after the alien god Sutekh. The foreign section of the Egyptian army was acknowledged to be the best. Its loyalty, however, depended on the condition of the imperial exchequer, and it ultimately became a menace instead of a support.

Foreign traders were also being attracted to Egypt, while the kings and the noblemen showed such a decided preference for handsome alien wives that a new type of face appeared in society, as may be seen in the pictures and statuary of the times. Instead of the severe and energetic faces of the Old and Middle Kingdoms, we find among the upper classes effeminate-looking noblemen with somewhat languid expressions, and refined ladies with delicately cut features, languorous eyes and sensitive lips. Occasionally, however, a non-Egyptian face is at once cultured and vigorous.

The foreign elements in society exercised a marked influence on the religious beliefs of the age. Strange gods were imported, and the voluptuous worship of the goddesses of love and war became increasingly popular. The former included Baal, Sutekh and Reshep, and the latter Astarte, Anath and Kadesh. Before we deal with the changes that were brought about by foreign influence in the Egyptian religion, we will pass these deities briefly under review.

Baal signifies 'the god', 'the lord' or 'the owner' and was a term applied to the chief or ruler of one of the primitive groups of nameless deities[1]. His spouse was called 'Baalath', 'the lady'. The Baal of Tyre was Melkarth; the Baal of Harran was Sin, the moon god; the Baal of Tarsus was an atmospheric or wind god; the Baal of Heaven was the sun god.[2] There were as many Baals in Asia as there were Horuses in Egypt.

Sutekh and Baal were generic terms. As already indicated, Sutekh was the prototype of the Egyptianised Seth, the terminal *kh* signifying 'majesty'. Indeed, Seth and Sutekh were identified in the Nineteenth Dynasty. The 'roaring Seth' was the atmospheric or storm god Sutekh, the 'Baal' or 'lord' of all other deities. Possibly the Egyptian 'Neter' was similarly a term applied originally to the nameless chief god of primitive belief.

Baal and Sutekh were, like Ptah and Khnum, the Great Father deities of the tribes who conceived that life and the world were of male origin. Some people identified the Great Father with the earth or water, as others identified him with the sun or the moon. The Baal and Sutekh worshippers, on the other hand, believed that the 'air god' was the originator of life; he was the 'soul' of the world. Like the Egyptian Shu, he was 'the uplifter'. According to Wiedemann, the root 'shu' signifies 'to uplift oneself'. As the 'uplifter' of himself and the heavens, Shu was 'the Baal'. Primitive peoples all over the world have identified 'air' and 'breath' with 'spirit'. As has been shown in Chapter 14, Khnum's name 'Kneph'

---

[1] Nameless deities are the oldest.
[2] Philo of Byblus.

signifies 'wind' and 'spirit' – the 'air of life'. The Aryan root *an*, 'to blow' or 'breathe', is found in the Latin *anima*, 'air' and 'breath'; the Gaelic *anal*; the Greek *anemos*; and in English words like 'animate', etc. The significance of Baal and Sutekh as atmospheric or wind gods is thus quite apparent – they were the sources of 'the air of life'.

As 'the creator god' was the originator of both good and evil, he was worshipped as the giver of food, the nourisher of crops and the generative principle in nature and was also propitiated as a destroying and blighting and avenging influence. His wrath was made manifest in the storm; he was then 'the roaring Seth', or the thunder god, like the Norse Thor. In the Bible the God of Israel is contrasted with 'the Baal' when Elijah, after exposing and slaying Baal's false prophets (1 Kings 18), took refuge in a cave:

> Behold, the Lord passed by, and a great and strong wind rent the mountains and brake in pieces the rocks before the Lord; but the Lord was not in the wind; and after the wind an earthquake; but the Lord was not in the earthquake; and after the earthquake a fire; but the Lord was not in the fire; and after the fire a still small voice (1 Kings 19:11-12).

Baal was thus 'the lord' of wind, earthquake and fire. 'In Egypt,' says Wiedemann,[1] 'Baal was regarded as a god of the sky – a conception which fairly corresponds to his original nature – and as a great but essentially a destructive deity.' He was 'a personification,' says Budge,[2] 'of the burning and destroying sun heat and the blazing desert wind'. Similarly Shu, 'the uplifter', was identified with the hot desert winds, while his consort, Tefnut, symbolised the blazing sunlight and was the bringer of the pestilence. She was also 'the spitter' who sent the rain.

Baal was worshipped in Egypt at Tanis (Zoan). A temple was also erected to him at Memphis. Rameses II boasted that he was a warrior lord like Baal and showed much respect for the imported deity.

Sutekh, 'lord of heaven', was the 'Sutekh of Kheta' (the Hittites), the god of the North Syrian allies of the Hittites, the god of the Hyksos, and the god of the early invaders who attacked the Osirian people of Pre-Dynastic Egypt. As has been shown in Chapter 18, Sutekh came into prominence as a great god during the Twelfth Dynasty in connection with the worship of the crocodile. Sethos I, father of Rameses II, was named after Sutekh, and a temple was erected for his worship by Rameses III at Thebes.

Sutekh is shown on a scarab with wings and a horned cap, standing on the back of a lion. He was respected by the Egyptians because he represented the Hittite

---

[1] *Religion of the Ancient Egyptians.*
[2] *Gods of the Egyptians.*

power; he was the giver of victory and territory.[1] As Seth, he was despised in Egypt during the period that he represented a repulsed and powerless enemy.

Another Asiatic deity who was honoured in Egypt was Reshep (or Reshpu), the Resef of the Phoenicians. He was another form of Baal, a 'heaven lord', 'lord of eternity', 'governor of the gods', etc. His name signifies 'lightning' or 'he who shoots out fire'. As the thunder god he was the god of battle. The Egyptians depicted him as a bearded man with Semitic profile, carrying a club and spear, or a spear and the symbol of life (ankh). From his helmet projects the head and neck of a gazelle, one of the holy animals associated with Astarte. A triad was formed in Egypt of Min, Reshep and Kadesh.

Astarte was the most popular of the imported deities. Her worship became widespread during the later dynasties. At Memphis she was adored with the moon god, Ah, and when Herodotus visited the city he found a small temple dedicated to 'the strange Aphrodite' (Venus). She was the goddess of the eastern part of Tanis (Zoan). Astarte is the goddess of ill repute referred to in the Bible as Ashtaroth and Ashtoreth 'of the Zidonians'. Solomon 'went after Ashtoreth' (1 Kings 11:5). The Israelites were condemned when 'they forsook the Lord and served Baal and Ashtaroth' (Judges 2:13). Samuel commanded: 'Put away the strange gods and Ashtaroth from among ye'. This goddess was worshipped both by the Phoenicians and the Philistines, and when the latter slew Saul, they hung his armour in her temple (1 Samuel 31:10). Temples were erected to her in Cyprus and at Carthage. As Aphrodite she was the spouse of Adonis, and at Apacha in Syria she was identified with the planet Venus as the morning and evening star; she fell as a meteor from Mount Lebanon into the River Adonis. As a goddess of love and maternity she links with Isis, Hathor, Ishtar, 'Mother Ida', Mylitta and Baalath. Among the mountains this Mother Goddess had herds of deer and other animals, like the Scottish hag, Cailleach Bheur.

Astarte was worshipped in Egypt early in the Eighteenth Dynasty and was a lunar deity and goddess of war. She appears to have been introduced into the Nile valley with the horse. Like Tefnut, and other Egyptian feline goddesses, she was depicted with the head of a lioness. As the 'lady of horses' she stands in a chariot driving four horses over a fallen foe.

There were many local types of this Great Mother deity in Asia. Another who was honoured in Egypt was Anthat (Anta), who was associated in ancient Arabia with the moon god Sin and in Cappadocia, Asia Minor, with Ashir (Ashur). Several towns in northern and southern Syria bear her name. Thuthmosis III erected a shrine to her at Thebes, and in a treaty between Rameses II and the Hittites, she and Astarte are paired like Isis and Nepthys. Anthat is also the spouse of Sutekh. She is depicted on the Egyptian monuments as a goddess of battle, holding a

---

[1] This belief is emphasised in Judges 11:24: 'Wilt not thou possess that which Chemosh thy god giveth thee to possess?' Chemosh was the god of the Moabites.

Fowling scene
(fresco from tomb at Thebes, Eighteenth Dynasty, about 1580–1350 BC, now
in the British Museum)
The deceased, accompanied by his wife and daughter, stands in a reed canoe
in a marsh filled with large papyrus reeds and is occupied in knocking down
birds with a stick, which is made in the form of a snake. In front of him is his
hunting cat, which has seized three birds, one with its hind claws, one with
its fore claws and one by the wings with its mouth. Numerous butterflies are
represented, and the lake is well stocked with fish. The line of hieroglyphics
at the back of the deceased indicates that the scene is supposed to represent
the state of happiness that he will enjoy in the next world.

spear in one hand and swinging a battle-axe in the other, seated on a throne or armed with shield and club, riding on a horse in her Aasith form, favoured by Sethos I. Rameses III named a favourite daughter Banth-anth, 'daughter of Anthat'.

Kadesh (Quedesh), 'the holy one', was another form of Astarte. As the 'mistress of all the gods', and the patroness of the 'unmoral' women connected with her temples, she emphasised the licentious phase of the character of Ashtoreth, which was so warmly denounced by the Hebrew prophets. The Egyptians depicted her as a moon goddess, standing nude on the back of a lioness, which indicated that she was imported from the Hittites. In one hand she carries lotus flow-

Farm scene: the counting and inspection of geese
(fresco from tomb at Thebes, about 1580–1350 BC)
In the upper register, the seated scribe is preparing to make a list of the geese,
which are being marshalled before him. Below is a group of goose herds with
their flock, who are prostrating themselves before him while one of their number
places the birds in baskets. The scribe has risen and is engaged in unrolling a
new papyrus on which to inscribe his list. The horizontal line of hieroglyphics
above the geese contains an exhortation of one goose herd to another to 'make
haste' so that he may bring his flock before the scribe. In front of the scribe is a
red leather sack or bag in which he kept his clothes, etc, and round it is rolled
the mat on which he sat.

ers and what appears to be a mirror, and in the other two serpents. As 'the eye of Ra' she links with Hathor and Sekhmet.

The grotesque god Bes also came into prominence during the Eighteenth Dynasty, and it is possible that he was introduced as early as the Twelfth. Although his worship spread into Syria he appears to have been of African origin and may have been imported. Like the Deng, he was a dwarf with long arms and crooked legs. His nose was broad and flat. His ears projected like those of a cat. He had bushy hair and eyebrows and a beard. His lips were thick and gross. Over his back he wore the skin of a wild animal, the tail trailing behind. He was always drawn full face, like Kadesh and unlike typical Egyptian deities. He was a war god, a god of music playing a harp and a love god. The oldest surviving representation of Bes is found in the Deir el-Bahri temple of Amun, where he attends at the birth of Hatshepsut. As late as Roman times he was known by his oracle at

Abydos. Absorbed by the sun worshippers, he became the nurse of Harpokrates (Horus) whom he nourished and amused. He also guarded the child god against the attacks of serpents, which he tore to pieces between his teeth. As Sepd he was given a handsome body and a leonine face.

The luxury-loving and voluptuous worshippers of the New Kingdom found the ethical principles of the Ptah-Osirian creed little to their taste. They appear to have argued that if men and women were to be judged by the King of the Dead, according to the deeds they committed upon earth, there was little hope of the rich ever entering paradise. Apparently belief in the heaven of the sun worshippers had faded away. It was incomprehensible, especially to the foreign element, that generations of Ra believers could be accommodated in the sun boat, to which entry was obtained by uttering magic 'passwords'.

The priests of Amun-Ra, who combined the worship and beliefs of the sun and moon cults, solved the problem of securing admission to the happy fields of Osiris, in Nether Egypt, by the use of charms and formulae. It was unnecessary for worshippers who believed the priests either to live moral lives or to commit to memory the 'confession of faith' that they must repeat before Osiris. The necessary formulae were inscribed on the rolls of papyri that form the *Book of the Dead*, and when one of these was purchased, to be laid beside the mummy, the name of the dead was written in the spaces left blank for that purpose.

But another difficulty had to be surmounted. When the heart was weighed before Osiris, it made confession, according to the beliefs of the Old Kingdom, of the sins of which it was guilty. The priests effectively silenced the heart by using as a charm the scarab, the symbol of resurrection, on which was inscribed: 'Oh, my heart, confess not against me as a witness!' These words were believed to have magical potency, and the scarab and other amulets became increasingly popular during the New Kingdom. The tet amulet was a symbol of the blood of Isis and protected the dead against the demons. The dad amulet, a fourfold altar, symbolised the backbone of Osiris and gave strength to the body and secured entrance to paradise. The ankh was a symbol of life, renewed vitality. The oval-shaped cartouche, which gave magic protection to the names of monarchs on their monuments, was also used as an amulet – evidently to prevent the demons from devouring the name of the dead.

Among the numerous charms were the 'Horus eyes', which were always vigilant to detect evil influences. The right eye was the sun and the left the moon, so that protection was secured by day and by night.

Charms were in use from the earliest times, but the elaborate use of them in connection with burials begins with the Eighteenth Dynasty. They are, of course, relics of stone worship. Young and old in primitive times wore 'luck stones' to protect themselves against the 'evil eye', to prevent and cure diseases and to secure good fortune. Indeed all personal ornaments appear to have had origins as charms. That they were recognised by the Hebrews as having idolatrous significance is clearly indicated in the Bible. After Jacob had met Esau and slain the Hivites who desired to marry his daughters and female followers, he commanded his household to 'put away the strange gods that are among you'. Then we read: 'And they gave unto Jacob all the strange gods which were in their hand, and all their earrings which were in their ears; and Jacob hid them under the oak which was by Shechem' (Genesis 35:3, 4). Evidently the earrings were connected with pagan worship and were as unworthy of Israel as the idols.

The changes that passed over the religious beliefs of the Egyptians during the New Kingdom were accompanied by new burial customs. Instead of constructing pyramids and mastabas, the pharaohs and their lords had tomb chambers excavated among the hills. The cliffs opposite Thebes are honeycombed with the graves of the nobility. Behind them lies the lonely Valley of the Kings, the royal burial ground. Some of the royal tombs are of elaborate structure, with many chambers and long narrow passages, but none surpasses the greatest of the mysterious artificial caves that had been made in southern Palestine, on which they may have been modelled.

The splendour and wealth of this age is reflected in the elaborate furnishing of the tombs and the expensive adornment of mummies. Even among the middle and lower classes, comparatively large sums were expended on performing the last material services to the departed.

Chapter 25

Amenophis the Magnificent and Queen Tiy

Prejudice against Thuthmosis III – Religion of Amenophis II – Human Sacrifices in his Tomb – Thuthmosis IV and the Sphinx – Amenophis III half a Foreigner – Queen Tiy's Father and Mother – A Royal Love Match – Recreations of the King – Tiy's Influence upon Art – A Stately Palace – The Queen's Pleasure Lake – Royalty no longer exclusive – The 'Vocal Memnon' – King stricken with a Malady – Tiy's Powerful Influence – Relations with the Priests of Amun – Akhenaten's Boyhood.

For some unexplained reason, the memory of Thuthmosis III was not revered by the priests, although he had once been a priest himself and never failed, on returning from his victorious campaigns, to make generous gifts to Amun's temple at Karnak. No folk tales about his tyranny and impiety survive, as in the case of the great Khufu (Cheops), the pyramid builder. He has suffered more from a conspiracy of silence. The prejudice against him remained even until Roman times, when an elderly priest translated to Germanicus the annals of Egypt's greatest emperor and coolly ascribed them to Rameses II. This intentional confusion of historical events may have given origin to the legends recorded by Greek writers regarding a mythical Pharaoh Sesostris, to whom was credited, with exaggerations, not only the achievements of Thuthmosis III and Rameses II, but also those of Sesostris III, the first pharaoh to invade Syria. Herodotus believed that one of the sculpted representations of the Hittite Great Father deity in Lydia was a memorial of Sesostris.

It may be that Thuthmosis III and Hatshepsut were supported by rival sects of the Theban priesthood and that the disposal of Senmut and his friends, who were probably executed, was never forgiven. The obliteration of the great 'female king's' name from the monuments, as we have suggested, may have been associated with a revolt that was afterwards regarded as heretical. We know little regarding the religious beliefs of Thuthmosis, but those of his son, Amenophis II, were certainly peculiar, if not reactionary. He adored, besides Amun, Khnum, Ptah and Osiris, the crocodile god, Sebek, and the voluptuous goddess, Astarte (Ashtoreth), as well as Bastet and Sekhmet, the feline deities, and Wadjet, the virgin serpent, and two of the Hathors. In his tomb there is evidence that he revived human sacrifice, which was associated with sun worship in the Fifth Dynasty – the body of a man with a cleft in his skull was found bound to a boat, and the mummies of a woman and child in an inner chamber suggest that he wished to have the company in the Osirian paradise of his favourites in the royal household. Although he reigned for over twenty years, we know little about him. Possibly some of his greater monuments were either destroyed or appropriated by his successors. He conducted a campaign in Syria soon after he ascended the throne and returned in triumph with the bodies of seven rebel princes suspended, heads downward, at the prow of the royal barge. Six of these were afterwards exposed on the walls of Thebes, and one was sent to Napata in Nubia. He also conducted a military expedition as far south as Khartoum.

Another mysterious revolt, which may mark the return to power of the anti-Thuthmosis party, brought to the throne the next king, the juvenile Thuthmosis IV, who was not, apparently, the prince selected as heir by Amenophis II. The names of the half-dozen brothers of the new pharaoh were erased in the tomb of the royal tutor, and they themselves disappear from history. According to a folk tale, Thuthmosis IV was the chosen of the sun god – a clear indication of priestly intervention – who was identified for the first time, as Ra Harmakhis, with the great Sphinx at Giza. Thuthmosis had been out hunting and lay to rest at noon in the shadow of the Sphinx. He dreamt that the sun god appeared before him and desired that the sand should be cleared away from about his body. This was done, and a temple erected between the paws, which was soon afterwards covered over by the sand drift.

Thuthmosis IV was evidently favoured by the priests. His distinctly foreign face indicates that his mother was an Asiatic beauty – it is handsome but somewhat effeminate. He died when he was about thirty, after a reign about ten years. His royal wife was a daughter of Artatama I, the Aryan king of Mitanni. She was the mother of Amenophis III and grandmother of Akhenaten.

The third Amenophis had a distinctly non-Egyptian face but of a type somewhat different from that of his father. The cheeks are long, the nose curves upwards, and he has the pointed chin and slim neck that distinguished his favourite wife, Queen Tiy, and their son, Akhenaten.

Much controversy has been waged over the racial origin of Queen Tiy, who was one of Egypt's most notable women. While some authorities regard her as Asiatic – either Semitic, Hittite or Aryan – others believe her to be either an Egyptian or Libyan. It is impossible to confirm either of the conflicting views that she was a fair-haired, rosy-cheeked beauty with blue eyes, or that she was dark, with lustrous eyes and a creamy complexion, but there can be no doubt that she was a woman of great personal charm and intellectual power. One of her portraits, sculpted in low relief, is a delicately cut profile. Her expression combines

Amenophis III
From the colossal granite bust in the British Museum

sweetness with strength of will, and there is a disdainful pout in her refined and sensitive mouth; her upper lip is short, and her chin is shapely and protruding. Whether she was born in Egypt or not, there can be little doubt that she had alien blood in her veins. Her father, Yuaa, appears to have been one of those Asiatic noblemen who was educated in Egypt and settled there. He held the honorary, but probably lucrative, position of superintendent of Amun's sacred cattle. His mummy shows him to have been a handsome, lofty-browed man with a nose like that of the Victorian poet Lord Tennyson. He had also the short upper lip and chin of his daughter. Tiy's mother appears to have been Egyptian. The marriage of King Amenophis III to Tiy had no political significance; the boy and girl – they could not have been much more than sixteen – had evidently fallen in love with one another. The union proved to be a happy one, and their mutual devotion continued all through life. Tiy was no mere harem favourite. Although not of

257

royal birth, she was exalted to the position of queen consort, and her name was coupled with that of her husband on official documents.

Amenophis' reign of thirty-eight years was peaceful and brilliant, and he earned his title 'the magnificent' rather by his wealth and love of splendour than by his qualities as a statesman. The Asiatic dependencies gave no trouble. The grandsons of the martial princes whom Thuthmosis III had subdued by force of arms had been educated at Thebes and thoroughly Egyptianised. Amenophis would have, no doubt, distinguished himself as a warrior had occasion offered, for on the single campaign of his reign, which he conducted into Nubia, he displayed the soldierly qualities of his ancestors. He was a lover of outdoor life and a keen sportsman. During the first ten years of his life he slew 102 lions, as he recorded, and large numbers of wild cattle.

Queen Tiy, on the other hand, was a woman of intellectual attainments and artistic temperament. No doubt she was strongly influenced by her father. To look at the the proud face of Yuaa's invites the speculation that he was 'the power behind the throne'. The palace favourites included not only high-born men and women but scholars and thinkers to whom the crude beliefs and superstitious conventionalities associated with the worship of Amun and the practices of the worldly-minded priests had become distasteful and obsolete. Architects and artists and musicians also basked in royal favour. The influence of Queen Tiy on the art of the age was as pronounced as it was beneficial. She encouraged the artists to shake off the stiff mannerisms of the schools, to study nature and appreciate its beauties of form and colour, to draw 'with their eyes on the object'. And so Egypt had not only its 'revolution of artistic methods', but its 'renaissance of wonder'. No doubt the movement was stimulated by the art that had reached so high a degree of perfection in Crete. Egypt at the time was the most powerful state in the civilised world and was pulsating with foreign influences. The old giant, shackled by ancient customs and traditions, was aspiring to achieve intellectual freedom.

The new movement was accompanied by a growing love of luxury and display of oriental splendour, which appealed to the young king. To please his winsome bride, he caused to be erected a stately palace on the western bank of the Nile at Thebes. It was constructed of brick and rare woods. The stucco-covered walls and ceilings of its commodious apartments were decorated with paintings, which included nature studies, scenes of Egyptian life and glimpses of paradise, exquisitely drawn and vividly coloured. Here and there were suspended those beautiful woven tapestries that were not surpassed by the finest European productions of later times, and there was a wealth of beautiful vases in coloured glass, porcelain, and silver and gold. The throne room, in which Queen Tiy held her brilliant courts, was 130 feet (40 metres) long and 40 feet (12 metres) wide. Papyri- and lotus-bud pillars of haunting design supported the roof and blossomed against a sky-blue ceiling, with its flocks of pigeons and golden ravens in flight. The floor was richly carpeted and painted with marsh and river scenes – snarers capturing the 'birds of Araby', huntsmen slaying wild animals, and fish gaping wide-eyed in clear waters. Amidst the carved and inlaid furniture in this scene of beauty the eye was taken by the raised golden thrones of the king and queen, over which the great gleaming pinions of the royal vulture were displayed in noble proportions.

A shady balcony protruded from the outer decorated walls. It was radiant with greenery and brilliant flowers from Asia, covered with coloured rugs and provided with cushioned seats. When the invigorating wind from the north blew cool and dry over the desert, Queen Tiy and her artistic friends, lingering on the balcony, must have found much inspiration in the prospect unfolded before them. The grounds within the palace walls, basking in the warm sunlight, were agleam with Asian and Egyptian trees, shrubs and many-coloured flowers. On the west rose in light and shadow the wonderful Theban hills of every changing hue. Eastward, between the blue, palm-fringed Nile, with its green banks and background of purple hills, lay a great mile-long artificial lake, sparkling in sunshine and surrounded by clumps of trees and mounds ablaze with strange and splendid blossoms. On this cool stretch of restful water the king and queen were accustomed to be rowed in their gorgeous barge of purple and gold named *Beauties of Aton*, while girl voices rose bird-like in song and sweet music came from many stringed harps and lyres, and from guitars and lutes, and warbling double pipes. On nights of festival, religious mysteries were enacted on the illuminated waters, which reflected the radiance of many-coloured lights, the brilliant stars and the silver crescent of the moon.

In the vicinity of the palace were the luxurious villas and beautiful gardens, with bathing pools and summer houses, of the brilliant lords and ladies who attended the state banquets and entertainments organised by Queen Tiy.

Egypt's king and queen no longer held themselves aloof from the people with the exclusiveness of the Old and Middle Kingdoms. They were the leaders of social life; their everyday doings were familiar to the gossipers. No air of mystery and idolatrous superstition pervaded the court. Domestic life in its finest aspects was held up as an ideal to the people. Public functions were invested with great splendour. Royalty drove out in chariots of silver and gold, brilliantly costumed, and attended by richly attired lords and ladies and royal attendants and guards. The king was invariably accompanied by the queen.

Amenophis vied with his predecessors in erecting magnificent temples. His favourite architect was Amenhotep, a remarkable man whose memory was long venerated; by the common people he was regarded as a great magician. It must have been he who appealed to the vanity of the king by designing the two colossal royal statues that were erected on the western plain of Thebes. In the first century BC they were known as the 'vocal Memnon', because, following an earthquake cracks opened in the stone in which dew formed on chilly nights. In the heat of the day this evaporated and expanded, creating a moaning sound. These representations of Amenophis III rose to a height of 70 feet (21 metres) and guarded the entrance of the royal mortuary temple, which was demolished in the following dynasty. Amenophis was worshipped in his temple at Memphis, while Queen Tiy was similarly honoured in Nubia.

Great wealth accumulated in Egypt during this period. Tushratta, the subject king of Mitanni, writing to Amenophis, declared, when he asked for gold 'in great quantity', that 'in the land of my brother gold is as plentiful as dust'. The pharaoh had added to his harem a sister of Tushratta, his Asian cousin, named Gilu-khipa,[1] and she arrived with over three hundred ladies and attendants, but she did not displace Queen Tiy.

Much light has been thrown on the relations between Egypt and other countries by the Amarna Letters – a number of clay tablets inscribed in Babylonian script (the language of diplomacy at the time), which were discovered in 1887. In these we find rulers writing in affectionate terms to one another and playing the game of politics with astuteness and duplicity.

In the beautiful Theban palace was born to Queen Tiy, in the twentieth year of her husband's reign, the distinguished Akhenaten, who was to become the most remarkable pharaoh who ever sat on the throne of Egypt. He was the only son; several princesses had preceded him. The young heir of the favourite wife was called Amenophis, and when his father died he ascended the throne as Amenophis IV. He was then about fourteen years of age, but had already married Nerfertiti, an Asiatic princess, apparently a daughter of Tushratta.

The last half dozen years of the life of Amenophis III were clouded in gloom. He was disabled by some disease – either paralysis or insanity – which Tushratta of Mitanni sought to cure by sending on two occasions images of the goddess Ishtar.[2] Queen Tiy appears to have governed the kingdom in the interval, and it is possible that she inaugurated the religious revolt, which became so closely associated with the name of her son, to counteract not only the retrogressive tendencies of the priests of Amun but also, perhaps, to curb their political power, for, no doubt, they did their utmost to exercise a direct influence on the affairs of state. The existence of strained relations between the Amun temple and the royal palace during the boyhood of the future pharaoh may well have infused his mind with that bitterness against the great religious cult of Thebes which he afterwards did his utmost to give practical expression to by doctrinal teachings and open persecution.

[1] Her father was King Sutarna, whose sister was the wife of Thuthmosis IV. Sutarna's father was Artatama I, a contemporary of Thuthmosis III.

[2] The goddess of Nineveh Tushratta must therefore have held sway over part of Assyria. The Mitanni King Saushatar, great-grandfather of Tushratta, captured and plundered Ashur.

Chapter 26

The Religious Revolt of the Poet King

The Shelley of Egypt – King as a Prophet – The Need of the Empire – Disturbing Race Movements – Fall of Cretan Kingdom – Hittites press Southward – Khabri advance on Palestine – Akhenaten's War on Amun – The New Capital – A Poet's Dream – Empire going to Ruin – Aten the 'First Cause' – A Grand Theology – Origin of the New Deity – Shu in the Sun – The Soul in the Egg – The Air of Life – A Jealous God – The Future Life – Paradise or Transmigration of Souls – Death of Akhenaten – Close of a Brilliant Dynasty.

Herodotus was informed by the sages of Egypt that the souls of the dead passed through 'every species of terrestrial, aquatic and winged creatures', and, after a lapse of about three thousand years, 'entered a second time into human bodies'. If that belief were as prevalent now as it was in early Celtic times, we might be at pains to convince the world that Shelley was a reincarnation of Akhenaten. The English poet was born 3,130 years after the death of Egypt's 'heretic king', and both men had much in common. They were idealists and reformers at war with the world and 'beautiful but ineffectual angels'. With equal force these lines by William Watson may be applied to the one as to the other:

> Impatient of the world's fixed way,
> He ne'er could suffer God's delay,
> But all the future in a day
> Would build divine. . . .

Shelley's reference to himself in 'Adonais' is admirably suited for Akhenaten:

> Mid others of less note, came one frail form,
> A phantom among men; companionless
> As the last cloud of an expiring storm,
> Whose thunder is its knell; he, as I guess,
> Had gazed on Nature's naked loveliness,
> Actaeon-like, and now he fled astray
> With feeble steps o'er the world's wilderness. . . .

> A pard-like spirit beautiful and swift –
> A Love in desolation masked – a Power
> Girt round with weakness; it can scarce uplift
> The weight of the superincumbent hour;
> It is a dying lamp, a falling shower,
> A breaking billow – even whilst we speak
> Is it not broken? . . .

Like Shelley, too, Akhenaten appears to have resolved, while still a boy, to fight against 'the selfish and the strong', whom he identified particularly with the priests of Amun, for these were prone indeed to 'tyrannise without reproach and check'. The Egyptian prince, like the young English gentleman, began to 'heap knowledge from forbidden mines of lore' and 'from that secret store wrought linked armour for his soul'. He embraced and developed the theological beliefs of the obscure Aten cult and set forth to convince an unheeding world that:

> The One remains, the many change and pass,
> Heaven's light forever shines, Earth's shadows fly. . . .

From the point of view of the Egyptian imperialists, the reign of Akhenaten, like that of Hatshepsut, was a distinct misfortune. As it happened, the dreamer king ascended the throne with the noble desire to make all men 'wise, and just, and free, and mild', just when the empire was in need of another ruler like Thuthmosis III to conduct strenuous military campaigns against hordes of invaders and accomplish the subjection of the rebellious Syrian princes. Once again, as in the Twelfth Dynasty, the civilised world was being disturbed by the outpourings from mountainous districts of pastoral peoples in quest of 'fresh woods and pastures new'. Crete had been invaded during the reign of Amenophis III. The 'sack of Knossos' was already a thing of the past. The great civilisation of the island kingdom had received its extinguishing blow, and thousands of the Kheftiu were seeking permanent homes in the Aegean, Asia Minor, Phoenicia and Egypt. Before Akhenaten's father had died, Thebes received ominous intelligence of the southward pressure of the Hittites and also of the advance on Palestine of the Khabri (Hebrews?) – the first wave of the third great Semitic migration from eastern Arabia, known as the Aramaean. The days of the half-Iranian, half-Egyptian Tushratta were numbered; the civilisation of Mitanni was doomed to vanish like that of Crete.

Akhenaten began to reign as Amenophis IV. With the purpose, apparently, of effecting the immediate conversion of Thebes, he began the erection of a temple to Aten (or Aton) in close proximity to that of Amun. Before long an open rup

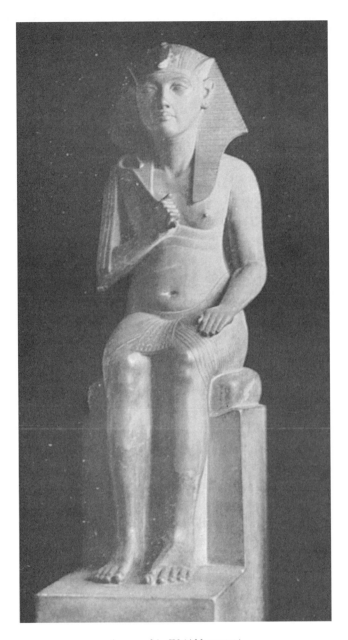

Amenophis IV (Akhenaten)
From the statuette in the Louvre, Paris

ture between the priesthood and the pharaoh became the chief topic of political interest. Amun's high priests had been accustomed to occupying high and influential positions at court; under Amenophis III one had been chief treasurer and another grand vizier. Akhenaten was threatening the cult with complete political extinction. Then something was done, or attempted to be done, by the priestly party, that roused the anger of the strong-minded young king, for he suddenly began to wage a war of bitter persecution against Amun. Everywhere the god's name was chipped from the monuments; the tombs were entered, and the young pharaoh did not spare even the name of his father. It was at this time that he himself became known officially as Akhenaten, 'the spirit of Aten'[1] – the human incarnation of the strange god. Then he decided to desert Thebes, and at Amarna, about 300 miles farther south, he caused to be laid out a 'garden city', in which were built a gorgeous palace, which surpassed that of his father, and a great temple dedicated to 'the one and only god'. Aten temples were also erected in Nubia, near the third cataract, and in Syria at a point that has not been located.

When he entered his new capital, which was called 'horizon of Aten', the young king resolved never to leave it again. There, dwelling apart from the unconverted world and associating with believers only, he dedicated his life to the service of Aten and the propagation of those beliefs, which, he was convinced, would make the world a paradise if, and when, mankind accepted them.

Meanwhile more and more alarming news poured in from Syria. 'Let not the king overlook the killing of a deputy,' wrote one subject prince. . . . 'If help does not come, Bikhura will be unable to hold Kumidi.' In a later communication the same prince 'begs for troops', but he begged in vain. 'If the king does not send troops,' he next informed Akhenaten, 'all the king's lands, as far as Egypt, will fall into the hands of the Khabri.' Another faithful ally wrote: 'Let troops be sent, for the king has no longer any territory; the Khabri have wasted all'. To this communication was added a footnote addressed to the royal scribe, which reads: 'Bring *aloud* before my lord, the king, the words, "*The whole territory of my lord, the king, is going to ruin.*"'[2]

In the stately temple at Amarna, made beautiful by sculptors and painters, and strewn daily with bright and perfumed flowers, the dreamer king, oblivious of approaching disaster, continued to adore Aten with all the abandon and sustaining faith of a cloistered medieval monk.

'You have made me wise in your designs and by your might,' he prayed to the god. . . . 'The world is in your hand.'

Akhenaten accounted it sinful to shed blood or to take away the life that Aten gave. No sacrifices were offered up in his temple – only the fruits of the earth were laid on the altars. He had already beaten the sword into a ploughshare. When his allies and his garrison commanders in Syria appealed for troops, he had little else to send them but a religious poem or a prayer addressed to Aten.

Hard things are often said about Akhenaten. One writer dismissed him as an 'aesthetic trifler'. Others regarded him as 'a half-mad king', but we must recognise that he was a profoundly serious man with a great mission, a high-souled prophet if an impractical pharaoh. He preached the gospel of culture and univer-

[1] Or, 'Aten is satisfied' (Sethe)
[2] 'Tel-el-Amarna Letters' in Professor Flinders Petrie's *History of Egypt*, Vol. 2.

sal brotherhood, and his message to mankind is the only vital thing that survives to us in Egypt amidst the relics of the past.

> 'Tis naught
> That ages, empires, and religions there
> Lie buried in the ravage they have wrought;
> For such as he can lend – they borrow not
> Glory from those who made the world their prey;
> And he is gathered to the kings of thought
> Who waged contention with their time's decay,
> And of the past are all that cannot pass away.

He remains to us as one of 'the inheritors of unfulfilled renown',

> Whose names on earth are dark
> But whose transmitted effluence cannot die
> So long as fire outlives the parent spark. . . .

He believed in the 'one and only god', Aten, whose power was manifested in the beneficent sun. The great deity was Father of all humankind and provided for their needs and fixed the length of their days. Aten was revealed in beauty, and his worshippers were required to live beautiful lives – the cultured mind abhorred all that was evil and sought after 'the things that are most excellent'. It shrank from the shedding of blood, promoted the idea of universal brotherhood and conceived of a beautiful world pervaded by universal peace.

No statues of Aten were ever made, as Akhenaten forbade idolatrous customs. Although Aten was a sun god, he was not the material sun; he was the First Cause manifested by the sun, 'from which all things came, and from which ever issued forth the life-giving and life-sustaining influence symbolised by rays ending in hands that support and nourish human beings'. 'No such grand theology had ever appeared in the world before, so far as we know,' wrote Flinders Petrie, 'and it is the forerunner of the later monotheist religions, while it is even more abstract and impersonal, and may well rank as scientific theism.'[1] The same writer also said: 'If this were a new religion, invented to satisfy our modern scientific conceptions, we could not find a flaw in the correctness of its view of the energy of the solar system. How much Akhenaten understood we cannot say, but he had certainly bounded forward in his views and symbolism to a position which we cannot logically improve upon at the present day. No rag of superstition or of falsity can be found clinging to this new worship evolved out of the old Aten of Heliopolis, the sole lord or Adon of the Universe'[2]

[1] *Religion of Egypt.*
[2] *A History of Egypt.*

The chief source of our knowledge of Akhenaten's religion is his great hymn, one of the finest surviving versions of which was found in the tomb of a royal official at Amarna. It was first published by Bouriant and has since been edited by Breasted, whose version became the recognised standard for translations.[1]

The development of the Aten religion may have been advanced by Yuaa, Queen Tiy's father, during the reign of Amenophis III, when it appears to have been introduced in court circles, but it reached its ultimate splendour as a result of the philosophical teachings of the young genius, Akhenaten. It has its crude beginnings in the mythological beliefs of those nature worshippers of Egypt and other countries who believed that life and the universe were of male origin. We can trace it back even to the tribal belief that the soul of the world-shaping giant was in the chaos egg. In the Theban recension of the *Book of the Dead*, Ra is addressed:

> O you are in your Egg, who shines from your Aten. . . .

> O you beautiful being, you renew yourself, and make yourself young again under the form of Aten. . . .

> Hail Aten, lord of beams of light; you shine and all faces [i.e. everybody] live.

There was an Aten cult at Heliopolis which taught that the creator Ra was 'Shu in his Aten'. Aten is the solar disc and Shu is the air god, the source of 'the air of life', the Great Father who is the soul of the universe. Like 'the Baal', Shu is also associated with the sun; the atmospheric god is manifested by lightning and fire as well as by tempest. Shu is thus not only 'air which is in the sun', but also, according to Akhenaten's religion, 'heat which is in Aten'. In the Amarna poem, Aten, who creates all things, 'makes the son to live in the body of his mother'. Then follows a reference to 'the egg':

> When the chick is in the egg and is making a sound within the shell,
> You give it *air* inside it so that it may keep alive.

An alternative version is:

> The small bird in the egg, sounding within the shell,
> You give to it *breath* within the egg
> To give life to that which you make.

And another:

---

[1] The most important of these appear in the following publications: Breasted's *A History of Egypt*, Petrie's *A History of Egypt* (version by Griffiths), Budge's *Gods of the Egyptians*, and Wiedemann's *Religion of the Ancient Egyptians*. In Naville's *The Old Egyptian Faith* (English translation by C. Campbell) the view is urged that Akhenaten's religious revolt was political in origin.

> When the chicklet cries in the egg-shell,
> You give him *breath* therein, to preserve him alive.[1]

When Akhenaten and his queen were depicted worshipping Aten, the rays that stretched out from the sun and ended in hands not only supported their bodies but pressed towards their nostrils and lips the ankh, the symbol of life. The air of life was the sun-heated air; life was warmth and breath.[2] Why the ankh touched the lips is clearly indicated in the great hymn. When the child is born, Aten:

> Opens his mouth that he may speak.

Aten was thus, like certain other Egyptian gods, 'the opener',[3] who gave power of speech and life to a child at birth or to the mummy of the dead. In this connection Wiedemann says that Ptah 'bore a name that is probably derived from the root *pth*, "to open", especially as used in the ritual term "opening of the mouth".' Porphyrius,[4] 'who was well informed in Egyptian matters', tells us that the god (Ptah) came forth from an egg that had issued from the mouth of Kneph (a word signifying 'air', 'breath' and 'spirit'). Kneph is Khnum in his character as an atmosphere god.

Some authorities identify Aten with the old Syrian god Adon. The root *ad* or *dad* signifies 'father'. As *ad* becomes *at* in 'Attis', it may be that, as a result of habitual phonetic conditions, Adon became Aten. But Akhenaten's Aten was a greater concept than Adon.

The marked difference between the various Egyptian and Asiatic Great Fathers and the god of Akhenaten lies in this – Aten was not the chief of a pantheon, he was the one and only god. 'The Aten,' says Professor Petrie, 'was the only instance of a "jealous god" in Egypt, and this worship was exclusive of all others, and claims universality.'[5] Had Akhenaten's religion been the same as that of the Aten cult at Heliopolis, we might expect to find him receiving direct support from that quarter. To the priests of Ra he was as great a heretic as he was to the priests of Amun, or Amun-Ra, at Thebes.

Akhenaten's concept of the material universe did not differ from that which generally obtained in his day in Egypt. There was a Nile in heaven and a Nile in the underworld. In rainless Upper Egypt he believed that:

> The Nile in heaven is for the strange people. . . .
> You [Aten] place a Nile in heaven that it may rain upon them.

---

[1] Amun-Ra also 'gives breath to that which is in the egg'.

[2] A ray of light from the moon gave origin to the Apis bull. See Chapter 5.

[3] Osiris Sokar is 'the opener of the mouth of the four great gods who are in the underworld' (*The Burden of Isis*).

[4] Eusebius, *Preparatio Evangelica*; Wiedemann, *Religion of the Ancient Egyptians*.

[5] *The Religion of Ancient Egypt*.

The Nile of the underworld was 'for the land of Egypt'.

> When you have made the Nile beneath the earth
> You bring it according to your will to make the people live. . . .
> That it may nourish every field.

Aten also made the firmament in which to rise:

> Rising in your forms as the living Aten,
> Shining afar off and returning . . .
> All eyes see you before them.

We do not obtain from the hymn any clear idea of Akhenaten's concept of evil. There is no reference to the devil serpent or to the war waged against the sun god in Heliopolitan myth. But it appears that as light was associated with life, goodness and beauty, darkness was similarly filled with death and evil. At night men lie down to sleep and 'their nostrils are stopped', or 'their breath is shut up'. Then creatures of evil are abroad; 'every lion comes from his den and serpents of every kind bite' Nor is there any reference to the afterlife. 'When you [Aten] set in the western horizon the earth is in darkness, and is like a being that is dead' or 'like the dead'. Akhenaten appears to have believed in the immortality of the soul – the bodies of Queen Tiy, his mother, and of his daughter and himself were embalmed – but it is not certain whether he thought that souls passed to paradise, to which there is no reference in the poem, or passed from egg, or flower, to trees, animals, etc, until they once again entered human bodies, as in the Anpu-Bata story and others resembling it, which survive in the folk tales of various ages and various countries.

Akhenaten's hymn to Aten is believed to have been his own composition. Its beauty is indicated in the following extracts:

> When you rise in the eastern horizon of heaven
> You fill every land with your beauty.

> When you set in the western horizon of heaven
> The world is in darkness like the dead.

> Bright is the earth when you rise in the horizon,
> When you shine as Aten by day.
> The darkness is banished, when you send forth your rays.

> How manifold are all your works,
> They are hidden from before us,
> O sole god, whose powers no other possesses,
> You did create the earth according to your desire
> While you were alone.

Akhenaten, his queen and their children
(The upper panel shows Aten, the solar disc, sustaining and
protecting royalty. The rays terminate in hands, some of
which hold the ankh symbols.)
From bas-reliefs in Berlin

The world is in your hand,
Even as you have made them.
When you have risen, they live.
When you set, they die.
For you are duration, beyond your mere limbs.
By you man lives,
And their eyes look upon your beauty
Until you set.

You make the beauty of form. . . .
You are in my heart.

The revolution in art that was inaugurated under Amenophis III is a marked feature of Akhenaten's reign. When sculptors and painters depicted the king, he posed naturally, leaning on his staff with crossed legs or accompanied by his queen and children. Some of the decorative work at Tel-el-Amarna will stand comparison with the finest of today,

The records that survive to us of the Akhenaten period are very scanty, for when the priests of the old faith again came to power they were at pains to obliterate them. Queen Tiy does not appear to have taken a prominent part in the new movement, which had developed beyond her expectations, and although she occasionally visited the city of Aten, her preference for Thebes, the scene of her social triumphs, remained to the end. Akhenaten's wife was a queen consort, as Tiy had been, and the royal couple delighted to appear among the people accompanied by their children.

The fall of the Amun party was complete. For several years the eight temples of Amun at Thebes lay empty and silent. Their endowments had been confiscated for Aten, to whom new temples were erected in the Faiyum and at Memphis, Heliopolis, Hermonthis and Hermopolis.

An endeavour was made to enforce the worship of Aten by royal decree all over Egypt, with the result that the great mass of the people, who appear to have shown little concern regarding the fall of the tyrannical Amun party, was aroused to oppose, with feelings of resentment, an uncalled-for interference with the immemorial folk customs and beliefs that were so closely associated with their habits of life. But still the power of the 'heretic king' remained supreme. The army remained loyal, although it had shrunk to an insignificant force, and when Akhenaten placed Horemheb in command it appears to have controlled the disturbed areas effectively.

Akhenaten died while still a young man and left no son to succeed him. Semenkh-ka-ra, who had married a princess, became the next pharaoh, but he appears to have been deposed by another son-in-law of the 'heretic', named Tutenk-aton, who returned to Thebes, allied himself with the priests and called himself Tutankhamun, 'image of Amun'. He was followed in turn by Ai (Eye), who called himself 'divine father', and then a military revolt, instigated by the priests, brought to the throne, after a brief period of anarchy, Horemheb, a member of the provincial nobility who secured his position by marrying a princess of the royal line. He popularised himself with the worshippers of the ancient cults by ruthlessly persecuting the adherents of the religion of Akhenaten, erasing the name of Aten everywhere. He appears to have re-established the power of Egypt over a part of Palestine, and he restored order in the kingdom. So the Eighteenth Dynasty came to an end about two and a half centuries after the expulsion of the Hyksos.

Chapter 27

The Empire of Rameses and the Homeric Age

Sectarian Rivalries – Struggles for Political Ascendancy – New Theology – The Dragon Slayer – Links between Sutekh, Horus, Sigurd, Siegfried, Finnmac-Coul, Dietrich, and Hercules – Rameses I and the Hittites – Break up of Mitanni Empire – Sethos's Conquests – War of Rameses II – Treaty with the Hittites – Pharaoh's Sublime Vanity – Sea Raids by Europeans on Egypt – The Last Strong Pharaoh – The Great Trojan War

The Nineteenth Dynasty opens with Rameses I, but no record survives to throw light on his origin or the political movement that brought him to the throne. He was elderly and does not appear to have been related to Horemheb. When he had reigned for about two years, his son Sethos was appointed co-regent.

But although history is silent regarding the intrigues of this period, its silence is eloquent. As the king's throne name indicates, he was attached to the cult of Ra, and it is of significance to note that among his other names there is no recognition of Amun.

The history of Egypt is the history of its religion. Its destinies were controlled by its religious cults and by the sects within the cults. Although Ra was fused with Amun, there are indications that rivalries existed not only between Heliopolis and Thebes but also between the sects in Thebes, where several temples were dedicated to the national god. The theological system that evolved from the beliefs associated with Amun, the old lunar deity, must have presented many points of difference from those that emanated from Heliopolis, the home of scholars and speculative thinkers. During the Eighteenth Dynasty the priesthood was divided into two great parties: one supported the claims of Hatshepsut, while the other espoused the cause of Thuthmosis III. It may be that Hatshepsut was favoured by the Ra section of the Amun-Ra cult and that her rival was the chosen of the Amun section. The Thuthmosis III party retained its political ascendancy until Thuthmosis IV, who worshipped Ra Harmakhis, was placed on the throne, although not the crown prince. It is possible that the situation created by the feuds that appear to have been waged between the rival sects in the priesthood facilitated the religious revolt of Akhenaten, which, it may be inferred, could have been stamped out if the rival sects had presented a united front and made common cause against him.

With the accession of Rameses I we appear to be confronted with the political ascendancy of the Ra section. It is evident that the priests brought about the change in the succession to the throne, for the building was at once undertaken of the great colonnaded hall at Karnak, which was completed by Rameses II. The old Amun party must have been broken up, for the solar attributes of Amun-Ra became more and more pronounced as time went on, while lunar worship was associated mainly with Khonsu and the imported moon goddesses of the type of Astarte and the 'strange Aphrodite'. To this political and religious revolution may be attributed the traditional prejudice against Thuthmosis III.

The new political party, as its 'new theology' suggests, derived its support not only from Heliopolis but also from half-foreign Tanis in the Delta. Influences from without were evidently at work. Once again, as in the latter half of the Twelfth Dynasty and in Hyksos times, the god Seth or Sutekh came into prominence in Egypt. The son of Rameses I, Sethos, was a worshipper of Seth – not the old Egyptianised devil Seth but the Seth who slew the Apep serpent and was identified with Horus.

The Seth of Rameses II, son of Sethos,[1] wore a conical hat like a typical Hittite deity, and from it was suspended a long rope or pigtail; he was also winged like the Horus sun disc. On a small plaque of glazed steatite this 'wonderful deity' is depicted 'piercing a serpent with a large spear'. The serpent is evidently the storm demon of one of the Corycian caves in Asia Minor – the Typhon of the Greeks, which was slain by the deity identified now with Zeus and now with Heracles. The Greek writers who have dealt with Egyptian religion referred to 'the roaring Seth' as Typhon also. The god Sutekh of Tanis combined the attributes of the Hittite dragon slayer with those of Horus and Ra.

It is possible that to the fusion of Horus with the dragon slayer of Asia Minor may be traced the origin of Horus as Harpokrates (Her-pe-khred), the child god who touches his lips with an extended finger. The Greeks called him 'the god of silence'. Egyptian literature throws no light on his original character. From what we know of Horus of the Osirian legends, there is no reason why he should have considered it necessary to preserve eternal silence.

In a particular type of the dragon-slaying stories of Europe,[2] which may have

---

[1] Griffiths in *Proceedings of the Society of Biblical Archaeology*.

[2] One must distinguish between the various kinds of mythical monsters lumped as 'dragons'. The fiery flying serpent' may resemble the 'fire drake', but both differ from the 'cave dragon', which does not spout fire, and the 'beast' of Celtic story associated with rivers, lakes and the sea. The latter is found in Japan and China as well as in Scotland and Ireland. In *Beowulf*, Grendel and his mother belong to the water 'beast' order; the dragon that causes the hero's death is a 'fire drake'. Egypt also has its flood and fire monsters. Thor slew the Midgard serpent at the battle of the 'Dusk of the Gods'.

gone north from Asia Minor with the worshippers of Tarku (Thor or Thunor), the hero – a humanised deity – places his finger in his mouth for a significant reason. After Siegfried killed the dragon, he roasted its heart, and when he tasted it he immediately understood the language of birds. Sigurd, the Norse dragon slayer, is depicted with his thumb in his mouth after slaying Fafner.[1] The Highland Finn, the slayer of Black Arky, discovered that he had a tooth of knowledge when he roasted a salmon and similarly thrust his burnt finger into his mouth.[2] In the Nineteenth-Dynasty fragmentary Egyptian folk tale, 'Setna and the Magic Book', which has been partially reconstructed by Professor Petrie,[3] Ahura relates: 'He gave the book into my hands; and when I read a page of the spells in it, I also enchanted heaven and earth, the mountains and the sea; I also knew what the birds of the sky, the fishes of the deep, and the beasts of the hill all said'. The prototype of Ahura in this 'wonder tale' may have been Horus as Harpokrates. Ahura, like Sigurd and Siegfried, slays a 'dragon' before he becomes acquainted with the language of birds; it is called 'a deathless snake'. 'He went to the deathless snake, and fought with him, and killed him; but he came to life again, and took a new form. He then fought again with him a second time; but he came to life again, and took a third form. He then cut him in two parts, and put sand between the parts, that he should not appear again' (Petrie). Dietrich von Bern experienced a similar difficulty in slaying Hilde, the giantess, so as to rescue Hildebrand from her clutches,[4] and Heracles was unable to put an end to the Hydra until Iolaus came to his assistance with a torch to prevent the growth of heads after decapitation.[5] Heracles buried the last head in the ground, thus imitating Ahura, who 'put sand between the parts' of the 'deathless snake'. All these versions of a well-developed tale appear to be offshoots of the great Cilician legend of 'The War of the Gods'. Attached to an insignificant hill cave at Cromarty, in the Scottish Highlands, is the story of the wonders of Typhon's cavern in Sheitandere (Devil's Glen), Western Cilicia. Whether it was imported from Greece or taken north by the Alpine people is a problem that does not concern us here.

At the close of the Eighteenth Dynasty, the Hittites were pressing southwards through Palestine and were even threatening the Egyptian frontier. Indeed, large numbers of their colonists appear to have settled at Tanis, where Sutekh and

[1] *Teutonic Myth and Legend.*

[2] *Finn and his Warrior Band.* The salmon is associated with the water 'dragon'; the 'essence' or soul, of the demon was in the fish as the 'essence' of Osiris was in Amun. It would appear that the various forms of the monster had to be slain to complete its destruction. This concept is allied to the belief in transmigration of souls.

[3] *Egyptian Tales* (second series), London, 1895.

[4] *Teutonic Myth and Legend.* In Swedish and Gaelic stories similar incidents occur.

[5] *Classic Myth and Legend.* The colourless character of the Egyptian legend suggests that it was imported, like Sutekh; its significance evidently faded in the new geographical setting.

Astarte had become prominent deities. Rameses I arranged a peace treaty[1] with their king, Sapalul (Shubiluliuma), although he never fought a battle, which suggests that the two men were on friendly terms. The mother of Sethos may have been a Hittite or Mitanni princess, the daughter or grandchild of one of the several Egyptian princesses who were given as brides to foreign rulers during the Eighteenth Dynasty. That the kings of the Nineteenth Dynasty were supported by the foreign element in Egypt is suggested by their close association with Tanis, which had become a city of great political importance and the chief residence of the pharaohs. Thebes tended to become more and more an ecclesiastical capital only.

Sethos was a tall, handsome man of slim build with sharp features and a vigorous and intelligent face. His ostentatious piety had, no doubt, a political motive. All over Egypt his name appears on shrines, and he restored many monuments that had suffered during Akhenaten's reign. At Abydos he built a great sanctuary to Osiris, which shows that the god Seth whom he worshipped was not the enemy of the ancient deified king, and he had temples erected at Memphis and Heliopolis, while he carried on the work at the great Theban colonnaded hall. He called himself 'the sun of Egypt and the moon of all other lands', an indication of the supremacy achieved by the sun cult.

Sethos was a dashing and successful soldier. He conducted campaigns against the Libyans in the north and the Nubians in the south, but his notable military successes were achieved in Syria.

A new Hittite king had arisen who either did not know the pharaoh or regarded him as too powerful a rival; at any rate, the peace was broken. The Hittite overlord was fomenting disturbances in northern Syria, and probably also in Palestine, where the rival Semitic tribes were engaged in constant and exhausting conflicts. He had allied himself with the Aramaeans, who were in possession of great tracts of Mesopotamia, and with Aryan-speaking invaders from Europe in the northwest of Asia Minor.

The Hittite empire had been broken up. In the height of its glory its kings had been overlords of Assyria. Tushratta's great-grandfather had sacked Ashur, and although Tushratta owed allegiance to Egypt he was able to send to Amenophis III the Nineveh image of Ishtar, a sure indication of his supremacy over that famous city. When the Mitanni power was shattered, the Assyrians, Hittites and Aramaeans divided among them the lands held by Tushratta and his Aryan ancestors.

Shubiluliuma was king of the Hittites when Sethos scattered hordes of desert robbers who threatened his frontier. He then pressed through war-vexed Palestine with all the vigour and success of Thuthmosis III. In the Orontes valley he met and defeated an army of Hittites, made a demonstration before Kadesh and

---

[1] It is referred to in the subsequent treaty between Rameses II and the Hittite king.

returned in triumph to Egypt. Sethos died in 1279, having reigned for over fifteen years.

His son, Rameses II, called 'the great' (by his own command), found it necessary to devote the first fifteen of the sixty-seven years of his reign to conducting strenuous military operations, chiefly against the Hittites and their allies. A new situation had arisen in Syria, which was being colonised by the surplus population of Asia Minor. The Hittite army followed the Hittite settlers, so that it was no longer possible for the Egyptians to effect a military occupation of the northern Syrian territory, held by Thuthmosis III and his successors, without waging constant warfare against their powerful northern rival. Rameses II appears, however, to have considered himself strong enough to reconquer the lost sphere of influence for Egypt. As soon as his ambition was realised by Mutallu, the Hittite king, a great army of allies, including Aramaeans and European raiders, was collected to await the ambitious pharaoh.

Rameses had operated on the coast in his fourth year, and early in his fifth he advanced through Palestine to the valley of the Orontes. The Hittites and their allies were massed at Kadesh, but the pharaoh, who trusted the story of two natives whom he captured, believed they had retreated northwards beyond Tunip. This seemed highly probable, because the Egyptian scouts were unable to get in touch with the enemy. But the overconfident pharaoh was being led into a trap.

The Egyptian army was in four divisions, named Amun, Ra, Ptah and Sutekh. Rameses was in haste to besiege Kadesh and pressed on with the Amun regiment, followed closely by the Ra regiment. The other two were, when he reached the city, at least a day's march in the rear.

Mutallu, the Hittite king, allowed Rameses to move round Kadesh on the western side with the Amun regiment and take up a position on the north. Meanwhile he sent round the eastern side of the city a force of 2,500 charioteers, which fell on the Ra regiment and cut through it, driving the greater part of it into the camp of Amun. Before long Rameses found himself surrounded, with only a fragment of his army remaining, for the greater part of the Amun regiment had fled with that of Ra and were scattered towards the north.

It was a desperate situation. But although Rameses was not a great general, he was a brave man, and fortune favoured him. Instead of pressing the attack from the west, the Hittites began to plunder the Egyptian camp. Their eastern wing was weak and was divided by the river from the infantry. Rameses led a strong force of charioteers and drove this part of the Hittite army into the river. Meanwhile some reinforcements came up and fell upon the Hittites in the Egyptian camp, slaying them almost to a man. Rameses was then able to collect some of his scattered forces, and he fought desperately against the western wing of the Hittite army until the Ptah regiment came up and drove the enemies of Egypt into the city.

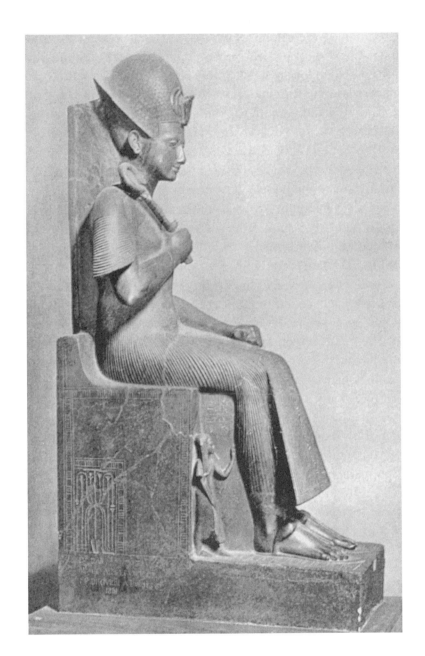

Rameses II
From a statue in black granite in Turin

Rameses had achieved a victory but at a terrible cost. He returned to Egypt without accomplishing the capture of Kadesh and created for himself a great military reputation by recording his feats of personal valour on temple walls and monuments. A poet who sang his praises declared that when the pharaoh found himself surrounded and, of course, 'alone', he called upon Ra, whereupon the sun god appeared before him and said: 'Alone are you not, for I, your father, am beside you, and my hand is more to you than hundreds of thousands. I who love the brave am the giver of victory.' In one of his inscriptions the pharaoh compared himself to Baal, god of battle.

Rameses delayed but he did not prevent the ultimate advance of the Hittites. In his subsequent campaigns he was less impetuous, but although he occasionally penetrated far northwards, he secured no permanent hold over the territory that Thuthmosis III and Amenophis II had won for Egypt. In the end he had to content himself with the overlordship of Palestine and part of Phoenicia. Mutallu, the Hittite king, had to deal with a revolt among his allies, especially the Aramaeans, and was killed, and his brother, Hattusilis (known to the Egyptians as Khetasar), who succeeded him, entered into an offensive and defensive alliance with Rameses, probably against Assyria, which had grown powerful and aggressive. The treaty, which was drawn up in 1271 BC, made reference to previous agreements, but these, unfortunately, have perished. It was signed by the two monarchs and witnessed by a thousand Egyptian gods and a thousand Hittite gods.

Several years afterwards Hattusilis visited Egypt to attend the celebration of the marriage of his daughter to Rameses. He was accompanied by a strong force and brought many gifts. He was regarded by the great mass of the Egyptians as a vassal of the pharaoh. He is believed to be the prince referred to in the folk tale that relates that the image of the god Khonsu was sent from Egypt to cure his afflicted daughter (see Chapter 15).

Rameses was a man of inordinate ambition and sublime vanity. He wished to be known to posterity as the greatest pharaoh who ever sat on the throne of Egypt, so he covered the land with his monuments and boastful inscriptions, appropriated the works of his predecessors, and even demolished temples to obtain building material. In Nubia, which had become thoroughly Egyptianised, he erected temples to Amun, Ra and Ptah. The greatest of these is the sublime rock temple at Abu Simbel, which he dedicated to Amun and himself. Beside it is a small temple to Hathor and his queen, Nefertari, 'whom he loves', as an inscription states. Four gigantic colossi were erected fronting the Amun temple. One of Rameses remains complete – he sits, hands on knees, gazing contentedly over the desert sands. That of his wife has suffered from falling debris but survives in a wonderful state of preservation.

At Thebes the pharaoh erected a large and beautiful temple of victory to Amun-

Ra, which is known as the Ramesseum, and he completed the great colonnaded hall at Karnak, the most vast structure of its kind the world has ever seen. On the walls of the Ramesseum is the well-known Kadesh battle scene, sculpted in low relief. Rameses is depicted like a giant, bending his bow as he drives in his chariot, scattering before him into the River Orontes hordes of Lilliputian Hittites.

But although the name of Rameses II dominates the Nile from Wadi Halfa down to the Delta, we know now that there were greater pharaohs than he and, in fact, that he was a man of average ability. His mummy has a haughty aristocratic face and a high curved nose that suggests that he was partly of Hittite descent. He lived until he was nearly a century old. A worshipper of voluptuous Asiatic goddesses, he kept a crowded harem and boasted that he had a hundred sons and a large, although uncertain, number of daughters.

His successor was Sethos Meneptah. Apparently Ptah, as well as Seth, had risen into prominence, for Rameses had made his favourite son, who predeceased him, the high priest of Memphis. The new king was well up in years when he came to the throne in 1212 BC and hastened to establish his fame by despoiling existing temples, as his father had done before him. During his reign of ten years, Egypt was threatened by a new peril. Europe was in a state of unrest, and hordes of men from 'the isles' were pouring into the Delta and allying themselves with the Libyans with the purpose of conquering and settling permanently in the land of the pharaohs. At about the same time, the Phrygian occupation of the north-western part of Asia Minor was in progress. The Hittite empire was doomed; it was soon to be broken up into petty states.

The raiders of Egypt appear to have been a confederacy of the old Cretan mariners, who had turned pirates, and the kinsfolk of the peoples who had overrun the island kingdom. Included among them were the Shardana[1] and Danauna (the 'Danaoi' of Homer?) who were represented among the mercenaries of pharaoh's army, the Akhaivasha, the Shakalsha and the Tursha. It is believed that the Akhaivasha were the Achaeans, the big, blonde, grey-eyed warriors identified with the Keltoi of the ancients, who, according to ethnologists, were partly of Alpine and partly of Northern descent. It is possible that the Shakalsha were the people who gave their name to Sicily and that they and the Tursha were kinsmen of the Lycians.

Pharaoh Meneptah was thoroughly alarmed, for the invaders penetrated as far as Heliopolis. But the god Ptah appeared to him in a dream and promised victory. Supported by his Shardana and Danauna mercenaries, who had no scruples about attacking their kinsmen, he routed the army of allies, slaying about 9,000 men and taking as many prisoners.

---

[1] The old Cretans, the Keftiu, were not referred to by the Egyptians after the reign of Amenophis III. These newcomers were evidently the destroyers of the great palace at Knossos.

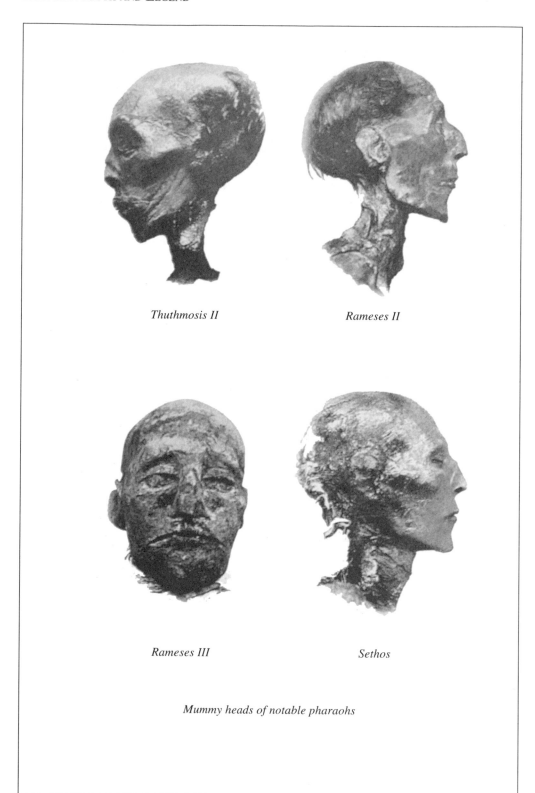

Thuthmosis II

Rameses II

Rameses III

Sethos

Mummy heads of notable pharaohs

A stele at Thebes makes reference to a campaign waged by Meneptah in Palestine, where the peoples subdued included the children of Israel.

Although the son of the great Rameses II boasted that he had 'united and pacified all lands', Egypt was plunged in anarchy after his death, which occurred in 1202 BC. Three claimants to the throne followed in succession in ten years, and then a Syrian usurper became the pharaoh. Once again the feudal lords asserted themselves, and Egypt suffered from famine and constant disorders.

The second king of the Twentieth Dynasty, Rameses III, was the last great pharaoh of Egypt. In the eighth year of his reign a second strong sea raid occurred. On this occasion the invading allies were reinforced by tribes from Asia Minor and northern Syria, which included the Tikkarai, the Muski (Moschoi of the Greeks?) and the Pulishta, or Pilesti, who were known among Solomon's guards as the Peleshtem. The Pulishta are identified as the Philistines from Crete who gave their name to Palestine, which they occupied along the seaboard from Carmel to Ashdod and as far inland as Beth-shan below the plain of Jezreel.

It is evident that the great raid was well organised and under the supreme command of an experienced leader. A land force moved down the coast of Palestine to co-operate with the fleet, and with it came the raiders' wives and children and their goods and chattels conveyed in wheel carts.[1] Rameses III was prepared for the invasion. A land force guarded his Delta frontier, and his fleet awaited the coming of the sea raiders. The first naval battle in history was fought within sight of the Egyptian coast, and the pharaoh had the stirring spectacle sculpted in low relief on the north wall of his Amun-Ra temple at Medinet Habu, on the western plain of Thebes. The Egyptian vessels were crowded with archers who poured deadly fusillades into the enemies' ships. An overwhelming victory was achieved by the pharaoh, and the sea power of the raiders was completely shattered.

Rameses then marched his army northwards through Palestine to meet the land raiders, whom he defeated somewhere in southern Phoenicia.

The final defeat of Troy after a ten-year siege took place about the time of this great attack on Egypt. Homer's Troy, the seventh city of the archaeologists, had been built by the Phrygians. Priam was their king, and he had two sons, Hector, the crown prince, and Paris. Menelaus had secured the throne of Sparta by marrying Helen, the royal heiress. When, as it happened, he went from home – perhaps to command the sea raid on Egypt – Paris carried off his queen and thus became, apparently, the claimant of the Spartan throne. On his return home Menelaus assembled an army of allies, set sail in a fleet of sixty ships and besieged the city of Troy. This war of succession became the subject of Homer's

---

[1] When the Philistines were advised by their priests to return the ark to the Israelites it was commanded: 'Now, therefore make a new cart and take two milch kine and tie the kine to the carts. – (1 Samuel 6:7).

great epic, the *Iliad*, which deals with a civilisation of the 'Chalkosideric' period – the interval between the Bronze and Iron Ages.[1]

Meanwhile Egypt had a rest from its enemies. Rameses reigned for over thirty years. He had curbed the Libyans and the Nubians as well as the sea and land raiders, and held sway over a part of Palestine. But the great days of Egypt had come to an end. It was weakened by internal dissension, which was only held in check and not stamped out by an army of foreign mercenaries, including Libyans as well as Europeans.

The national spirit flickered low among the half-foreign Egyptians of the ruling class. When Rameses III was laid in his tomb, the decline of the power of the pharaohs, which he had arrested for a time, proceeded apace. The destinies of Egypt were then shaped from without rather than from within.

---

[1] The Cuchullin saga of Ireland belongs to the same archaeological period; bronze and iron weapons were used. Cuchullin is the Celtic Achilles; to both heroes were attached the attributes of some old tribal god. The spot on the heel of Achilles is shared by the more primitive Diarmid of the Ossianic saga.

Chapter 28

Egypt and the Hebrew Monarchy

Isaiah foretells Egypt's fall – Priest Kings – Rise of the Libyans Philistines and Hebrews – A 'Corner' in Iron – Saul and David – Solomon's alliance with Pharaoh Shoshenq (Shisak) – Jeroboam's Revolt – Israel Worships the 'Lady of Heaven' – The Ethiopian Kings – Assyrian Great Empire – The 'Ten Lost Tribes' – Pharaoh Taharqa and Hezekiah – Assyrian Army destroyed – Isaiah a Great Statesman – Assyrian Conquest of Egypt – Sack of Thebes.

'The burden of Egypt. Behold, the Lord rideth upon a swift cloud, and shall come into Egypt: and the idols of Egypt shall be moved at his presence, and the heart of Egypt shall melt in the midst of it. And I will set the Egyptians against the Egyptians: and they shall fight every one against his brother, and every one against his neighbour; city against city, and kingdom against kingdom. And the spirit of Egypt shall fail in the midst thereof. . . . The brooks of defence shall be emptied and dried up; the reeds and flags shall wither. The paper reeds[1] by the brooks, by the mouth of the brooks, and everything sown by the brooks, shall wither, be driven away, and be no more. The fishers also shall mourn, and all they that cast angle into the brooks shall lament, and they that spread nets upon the waters shall languish. Moreover, they that work in fine flax, and they, that weave networks, shall be confounded. And they shall be broken in the purposes thereof, all that make sluices and ponds for fish' (Isaiah 19:1–10).

Ater the death of Rameses III came what is now called the Third Intermediate Period, about three and a half centuries of turbulence and change. The last great pharaoh of the Twentieth Dynasty was followed by eight weak rulers bearing the name of Rameses. Little is known, or is worth knowing, about them. They were puppets in the hands of the powerful priests of Amun-Ra, who had become the commanders of the army, the chief treasurers, grand viziers and high judges of Egypt. The oracle of Amun-Ra confirmed all their doings. In the end the great Theban god became the rival of Osiris as Judge of the Dead, and the high priest, Herihor, thrust aside Rameses XI and seized the crown. Another priest king reigned at Tanis (Zoan) in the Delta.

[1] Papyri

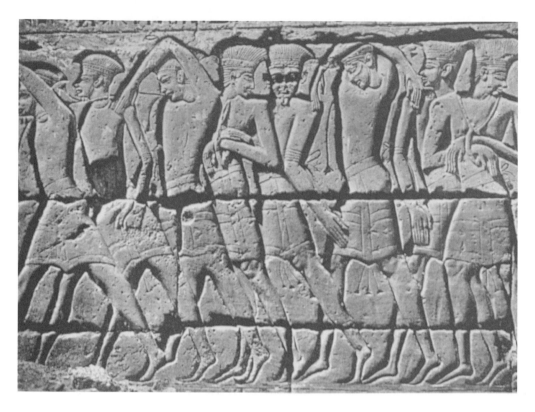

Great sea and land raid: Philistine prisoners
From the bas-relief on the gate of the temple of Rameses III at Medinet Habu

Egypt was thrown into confusion under ecclesiastical rule, and land fell rapidly in value. Robbery on the highways and especially in tombs became a recognised profession, and corrupt officials shared in the spoils. The mummies of great pharaohs, including Sethos and Rameses II, had to be taken by pious worshippers from the sepulchral chambers and concealed from the robbers. No buildings were erected, and many great temples, including the Ramesseum, fell into disrepair.

After the passing of an obscure and inglorious century, we find that the mingled tribes of Libyans and their western neighbours and conquerors, the Meshwesh, had poured into the Delta in increasing numbers and penetrated as far south as Herakleopolis. Egypt was powerless in Palestine. The Philistines had moved southwards and for a period were overlords of the Hebrews. They had introduced iron and restricted its use among their neighbours, as is made evident in the Bible:

Now there was no smith found throughout all the land of Israel: for the Philistines said, Lest the Hebrews make them swords or spears; but all the Israelites went down to the Philistines, to sharpen every man his share, and his coulter, and his axe, and his mattock. Yet they had a file for the mattocks, and for the coulters, and for the forks, and for the axes, and to sharpen the goads. So it came to pass in the day of battle, that there was neither sword nor spear found in the hand of any of the people that were with Saul and Jonathan; but with Saul and with Jonathan his son was there found (1 Samuel 13:19–22).

Thus the Hebrews at the very beginning of their history as a nation had experience of a commercial 'corner', which developed their business instincts, no doubt. Their teachers were Europeans who represented one of the world's oldest civilisations.[1] The oppression that they endured welded together the various tribes, and under Saul the Hebrews made common cause against the Philistines. When handsome, red-cheeked David,[2] who had probably a foreign strain in his blood, had consolidated Judah and Israel, the dominance of the Cretan settlers came to an end. They were restricted to the sea coast, and they ceased to have a monopoly of iron. Solomon, the chosen of the priests, was supported by a strong army, which included mercenaries, and became a great and powerful monarch, who emulated the splendour of the pharaohs of the Eighteenth Dynasty. His supremacy in southern Syria was secured by an alliance with Egypt:

And Solomon made affinity with Pharaoh king of Egypt, and took Pharaoh's daughter, and brought her into the city of David, until he had made an end of building his own house, and the house of the Lord, and the wall of Jerusalem round about (1 Kings 3:1).

The Pharaoh with whom Solomon had come to an understanding was Shoshenq (Shishak), a vigorous ruler and successful military leader, who established peace in his kingdom. He secured his Delta frontier from attack by laying a firm hand on the territory between Egypt and the 'buffer state' of the Hebrews. In time we read that he had 'taken Gezer [an independent city state] and burnt it with fire, and slain the Canaanites that dwelt in the city, and given it for a present unto his daughter, Solomon's wife' (1 Kings 9:16).

Shoshenq was the first king of the Libyan (Twenty-Second) Dynasty, which lasted for about 120 years. He was the descendant of a Meshwesh-Libyan mercenary who had become high priest of Hershef at Herakleopolis and the commander of the local troops. Under this foreign nobleman and his descendants, the nome flourished and became so powerful that Shoshenq was able to control the Delta region, where he allied himself with other Libyan military lords. In the end he married the daughter of the last weak priest king of Tanis and was proclaimed

---

[1] 'The remnant of the country of Caphtor' (Crete) – Jeremiah 47:4.
[2] 'A youth of ruddy and of fair countenance' (1 Samuel 17:42).

Amun presenting to Shoshenq a list of cities captured in Israel and Judah
From the bas-relief at the great temple at Karnak

pharaoh of Egypt. He made Bubastis his capital, and the goddess of the locality, the cat-headed Bastet, became the official deity of the kingdom. Amun was still recognised but at the expense of other Delta deities who shared in the ascendancy of 'the kindly Bastet'. Shoshenq held nominal sway over Thebes and appointed his son the high priest of Amun-Ra, and he was able to extract tribute from Nubia.

Shoshenq's chief need was money, for he had to maintain a strong standing army of mercenaries. He must have cast envious eyes on the wealth that had accumulated in Solomon's kingdom and, as it proved, was not slow to interfere in its internal affairs when the opportunity was offered. He extended his hospitality to Jeroboam, the leader of the Israelites, who desired to be relieved of the heavy taxes imposed by Solomon 'Solomon sought therefore to kill Jeroboam' (1 Kings, 11:40). When Rehoboam came to the throne, Jeroboam pleaded on behalf of the oppressed ten tribes of the north, but the new king was advised to say: 'My little finger shall be thicker than my father's loins'. A revolt ensued, and Jeroboam became king of the north, supported, evidently, by Shoshenq. The golden calf was then worshipped by Jeroboam's subjects. It was probably the symbol of the Hathor-like 'lady of heaven', whose worship was revived even in Jerusalem, when Jeremiah said: 'The children gather wood, and the fathers kindle the fire, and the women knead their dough, to make cakes to the queen of heaven, and to pour out drink offerings unto other gods' (Jeremiah 7:18). The religious organisation, based on the worship of the God of Israel, which had been promoted by

David, was thus broken up – 'there was war between Rehoboam and Jeroboam all their days' (1 Kings 14:30).

The opportunity afforded for invasion was quickly seized by Shoshenq. According to his own annals, he swept through Palestine, securing great spoils. Indeed, he claims that his mercenaries penetrated as far north as the River Orontes. It is stated in the Bible that he plundered Jerusalem and 'took away the treasures of the house of the Lord, and the treasures of the king's house; he even took away all; and he took away all the shields of gold that Solomon had made' (I Kings 14:25–6).

About a century after the death of Shoshenq, the power of the royal house is found to have declined, and the various hereditary Libyan lords showed only nominal allegiance to the crown. A rival kingdom had also arisen in the south. When the priest kings were driven from Thebes, they founded a theocracy in the Nubian colony, which later became known as Ethiopia, and there the oracle of Amun controlled the affairs of state.

In time the Ethiopian kingdom became strong enough to control a large part of Upper Egypt, and Thebes was occupied. Then Piankhy, the most capable of all the Nubian rulers, extended his conquests until he forced the princes of the north to acknowledge his supremacy.

Piankhy's most serious rival was Tefnakht, prince of Sais, who assembled an army of allies and fought his way southwards as far as Thebes. He was driven back by Piankhy, who ultimately swept in triumph to Sais and compelled the submission of Tefnakht and his allies. He did not, however, effect the permanent occupation of Lower Egypt.

Shabaka, the first pharaoh of the Nubian (Twenty-Fifth) Dynasty, ruled over all Egypt, having secured by force of arms the allegiance of the princes, or petty kings, of the north. He is believed to be the Biblical 'So, King of Egypt' (2 Kings 17:4). Syria and Palestine had become dependencies of the great empire of Assyria, which included Babylonia and Mesopotamia and extended into Asia Minor. Shabaka had either dreams of acquiring territory in southern Syria or wished to have buffer states to protect Egypt against Assyrian invasion, for he entered into an alliance with some of the petty kings. These included King Hoshea of Israel, who, trusting to Egypt's support, 'brought no present [tribute] to the King of Assyria as he had done year by year' (2 Kings 17:4). Sargon II of Assyria anticipated the rising and speedily stamped it out. He had Ilu-bi'-di of Hamath flayed alive. He defeated a weak Egyptian force and took Hanno, prince of Gaza, and King Hoshea prisoners. Then he distributed, as he has recorded, 27,290 Israelites – 'the ten lost tribes' – between Mesopotamia and the Median highlands.[1] Large numbers of troublesome peoples were drafted from Babylonia

---

[1] These tribes were worshippers of the 'golden calf'. There is no proof that they were not absorbed by the peoples among whom they settled.

into Samaria, where they mingled with the remnants of the tribes that remained. Thus came to an end the kingdom of the northern Hebrews. That of Judah – the kingdom of the Jews – remained in existence for another century and a half.

Taharqa, the third and last Nubian pharaoh, whose mother was a Negro, is referred to in the Bible as Tirhakah (Isaiah 37:9). Like Shabaka, he took an active part in Asian politics and allied himself with, among others, Luli, king of Tyre, and Hezekiah, king of Judah. Sargon, 'the later', as he called himself, had been assassinated, and his son, Sennacherib, had to deal with several revolts during the early years of his reign. Ionians had invaded Cilicia and had to be subdued. Many of the prisoners were afterwards sent to Nineveh. Trouble was constantly brewing in Babylonia, where the supremacy of Assyria was being threatened by a confederacy of Chaldeans, Elamites and Aramaeans. A pretender even arose in Babylon, and Sennacherib's brother, the governor, was murdered, and the city had to be besieged and captured. This 'pretender', Merodach-Baladan,[1] had been concerned in the Egypto-Syrian alliance, and Sennacherib found it necessary to push westwards, as soon as he had overrun Chaldea, to deal with the great revolt. He conquered Phoenicia, with the exception of Tyre, but King Luli had taken refuge in Cyprus. Hastening southwards, he scattered an army of allies, which included Pharaoh Taharqa's troops, and, having captured a number of cities in Judah, he laid siege to Jerusalem. Hezekiah held out but, according to the Assyrian account, made terms of peace with the emperor and afterwards sent great gifts to Nineveh. A later expedition appears to have been regarded as necessary, however, and, according to the Biblical account, it ended disastrously, for Sennacherib's army was destroyed by a pestilence. Isaiah, who was in Jerusalem at the time, said: 'Thus saith the Lord . . . Behold I will send a blast upon him, and he shall hear a rumour and shall return to his own land, and I will cause him to fall by the sword in his own land' (2 Kings 19:6, 7).

> And it came to pass that night, that the angel of the Lord went out, and smote in the camp of the Assyrians an hundred and four score and five thousand. . . . So Sennacherib, King of Assyria, departed (2 Kings 19:35, 36).

> The Assyrian came down like the wolf on the fold,
> And his cohorts were gleaming in purple and gold;
> And the sheen of their spears was like stars on the sea,
> When the blue wave rolls nightly on deep Galilee.

[1] He 'sent letters and a present to Hezekiah' (Isaiah 39:1). The shadow of the sundial of Ahaz has gone 'ten degrees backward'. According to an astronomical calculation, there was a partial eclipse of the sun – of the upper part – which was visible at Jerusalem on 11 January 689 BC, about 11.30 a.m. (See also 2 Chronicles 32).

Triumphant return of an Assyrian king from battle to the camp
(On the left are seen officials counting heads of the enemy)
From a tablet in the British Museum

Like the leaves of the forest when summer is green,
That host with their banners at sunset was seen:
Like the leaves of the forest when autumn hath blown,
That host on the morrow lay withered and strown.

For the angel of death spread his wings on the blast,
And breathed in the face of the foe as he passed;
And the eyes of the sleepers waxed deadly and chill,
And their hearts but once heaved – and for ever grew still!

And there lay the steed with his nostril all wide,
But through it there rolled not the breath of his pride;
And the foam of his gasping lay white on the turf,
And cold as the spray of the rock-beating surf.

And there lay the rider distorted and pale,
With the dew on his brow, and the rust on his mail:
And the tents were all silent – the banners alone –
The lances unlifted – the trumpet unblown.

And the widows of Ashur are loud in their wail,
And the idols are broke in the temple of Baal;
And the might of the Gentile, unsmote by the sword,
Hath melted like snow in the glance of the Lord.

Lord Byron.

Isaiah, statesman and scholar, had been no party to the alliance between Egypt and Judah and the other powers who trusted in the Babylonian pretender; in fact, he had denounced it at the very outset. He entertained great contempt for the Egyptians. 'Lo, thou trustest in the staff of this broken reed, on Egypt; whereon if a man lean, it will go into his hand and pierce it' (Isaiah 36:6) . . . 'The princes of Zoan [Tanis] are become fools, and the princes of Noph [Memphis [1]] are deceived' (Isaiah 19:13). He foretold the fall of Tyre and the subjection of Egypt, and admonished the pro-Egyptians of Judah, saying: 'Woe to the rebellious children . . . that walk into Egypt . . . to strengthen themselves in the strength of Pharaoh, and to trust in the shadow of Egypt' (Isaiah 30:1, 2). 'For the Egyptians,' he warned Hezekiah, 'shall help in vain and to no purpose . . . their strength is to sit still . . . write it before them in a tablet,' he added, 'and note it in a book' (Isaiah 30:7, 8). He had summed up the situation with characteristic sagacity.

Sennacherib's campaigns paralysed the kingdom of the Jews. Thousands of prisoners were deported, and when peace again prevailed Hezekiah had left only 'the remnant that is escaped of the house of Judah' (2 Kings 19:30).

After Sennacherib was murdered, as the result of a revolt that disturbed Babylon, his son, Esarhaddon (Assarhaddon), had to deal with another western rising fomented by that scheming Pharaoh Taharqa, who was riding speedily on the road to ruin.

About 671 BC the young Assyrian emperor conducted a vigorous campaign in Syria and struck at the root of his imperial troubles by invading Egypt, which he conquered and divided up between some twenty princes, the chief of whom was the half-Libyan Necho of Sais. Taharqa endeavoured to reconquer his kingdom, and Esarhaddon set out with a strong army to deal with him but died on the march.

A few years later, Assurbanipal, the new Assyrian emperor, defeated Taharqa at Memphis. Necho of Sais, who had been intriguing with the Nubian king, was pardoned and appointed chief agent of the emperor in Egypt, which had become an Assyrian province.

Taharqa gave no further trouble. When he died, however, his successor, Tantamini, king of Nubia, endeavoured to wrest Upper and Lower Egypt from the Assyrians. Necho marched southwards with a force of Assyrian troops but was defeated and slain at Memphis. But the triumph of Tantamini was short-lived. Assurbanipal once again entered Egypt and stamped out the last spark of Nubian power in that unhappy country. Thebes was captured and plundered. The images of the great gods were carried away to Nineveh, and the temples were despoiled of all their treasure. Half a century later, when Nahum, the Hebrew prophet, foretold the fall of Nineveh, 'the bloody city . . . full of lies and robbery

---

[1] Or Napata in Nubia.

. . . the noise of the whip, and the noise of the rattling of the wheels, and of the prancing horses, and of the jumping chariots' . . . he referred in his own graphic manner to the disaster that fell on Thebes at the hands of the vengeful Assyrians.

'Art thou better than populous No [Thebes] that was situate among the rivers,' cried the prophet, 'that had the waters round about it . . . Ethiopia and Egypt were her strength and it was infinite . . . Yet was she carried away, she went into captivity: her young children also were dashed in pieces at the top of all the streets; and they cast lots for her honourable men, and all her great men were bound in chains' (Nahum 3:8-10).

So the glory departed from Thebes, never again to return. Amun was cast down from his high place, the priesthood was broken up, and the political schemers who escaped the Assyrians found refuge in Ethiopia, where the kings submitted to their rule and became 'as clay in the hands of the potter', with the result that the civilisation of the Nubian power gradually faded away. Psammetichus, who, according to Herodotus, had fled to Syria on the death of his father, Necho, became Assyrian governor (Shaknu) in Egypt, and the country was left to settle down in its shame to produce the wherewithal demanded in tribute year by year by the mighty Emperor Assurbanipal of Assyria.

Chapter 29

The Restoration and the End

The God of the People – Egypt yearns for the Past – Rise of Saite Kings – Osiris as Great Father – Christianised Horus Legend – Scythians and Cimmerians – End of Assyrian Empire – Jeremiah and Pharaoh Necho – Surrender of Jerusalem – Early Explorers – Zedekiah and Pharaoh Hophra – Jerusalem sacked – Babylonian Captivity – Amasis and the Greeks – Coming of King Cyrus – Fall of Babylon – Persian Conquest of Egypt – Life in the Latter Days – Homely Letters – Cry of a Lost Soul

The civilisation of ancient Egypt began with Osiris and ended with Osiris. Although the deified king had been thrust into the background for long centuries by the noble and great, he remained the god of the common people.

'The dull crowd,' as Plutarch called them, associated the ideas about their gods 'with changes of atmosphere according to the seasons, or with the generation of corn and sowings and ploughings, and in saying that Osiris is buried when the sown corn is hidden by the earth, and comes to life and shows himself again when it begins to sprout. . . . They love to hear these things and believe them, drawing conviction from things immediately at hand and customary.' The peasant lived and died believing in Osiris. 'As Osiris lives, so shall he also live; as Osiris died not, so shall he also not die; as Osiris perished not, so shall he also not perish.'[1] Egypt was made prosperous by Osiris: he gave it the corn that brought all its wealth and power. The greatest pharaohs were those who, revering Osiris, cut new irrigation canals and boasted, like Ammenemes I:

> I loved the corn god . . . I have grown the grain
> In every golden valley where the Nile
> Entreated me. . . .

Egypt's Bata-like peasants constituted the strongest army commanded by the pharaohs. They won golden spoils from nature, which were of more account than the spoils from Syrian battlefields and the tribute of subject kings. Those con-

---

[1] Erman, *Handbuch*

THE RESTORATION AND THE END

stant toilers, who were innately conservative in their methods and customs and beliefs, bulk largely in the background of ancient Egyptian history. They were little affected by the changes that passed over the country century after century. Once a political storm died down, they settled back into their own habits of life; they were 'the nails that held the world (of Egypt) together'.

We have seen the pharaohs and their nobles going after strange gods, marrying foreign wives and adopting new manners and customs, forgetting those traditions that are the inspiration of national life and the essence of true patriotism. When Egypt fell and was ground under the heel of the Assyrian, it was from the steadfast, although unlettered, peasants that the strength of the restoration was derived; they remembered the days that were, and they remembered Osiris. 'Those Egyptians who live in the cultivated parts of the country,' wrote Herodotus, 'are of all I have seen the most ingenious, being attentive to the improvement of memory beyond the rest of mankind.'

The Assyrian conquest stirred Egypt to its depths. When Thebes was sacked and Amun-Ra cast down from his high place, the worshippers of Osiris were reviving the beliefs and customs of the Old Kingdom, for they had never gone wholeheartedly after Ra and Amun or Sutekh and Astarte. When Assurbanipal shattered the power of the Asiatic nobles of Egypt and drove out the Nubians, he rescued the Egyptian people from their oppressors and strengthened the restoration movement that had begun under the Nubian kings and led to the Late Period.

Assurbanipal was unable to retain for long his hold on the land of the pharaohs. Persistent revolts occupied his attention at the very heart of his empire. His brother, the subject king of Babylon, had secured the co-operation of the Elamites, the Aramaeans, the Chaldeans and the Arabians, and a fierce struggle ensued, until in the end Babylon was besieged and captured and Elam was devastated. Meanwhile Cimmerians were invading Asia Minor and the Aryan Medes were pressing into Elam. When peace was at length restored Assyria, although triumphant, was weakened as a result of its terrible struggles, and the empire began to go to pieces.

Assyria's misfortunes gave Psammetichus his opportunity. About two years after his rival, Tantamini, was driven out of Thebes, he had come to an understanding with King Gyges of Lydia, who, having driven off the first attack of Cimmerians, was able to send him Ionian and Carian mercenaries. This encouraged Psammetichus to cease to pay tribute to Assurbanipal, and he was proclaimed pharaoh of a united Egypt. As he had married a daughter of Taharqa, the Nubian, his succession to the throne was legalised according to the 'unwritten law' of Egypt. The Assyrian officials and soldiers were driven across the Delta frontier.

Herodotus relates an interesting folk tale regarding the rise of Psammetichus. He was informed that the Egyptians chose twelve kings to reign over them, and these 'connected themselves with intermarriages, and engaged to promote the common interest', chiefly because an oracle had declared that the one among them who offered a libation to Ptah in a brass vessel should become the pharaoh. One day in the labyrinth, eleven of the kings made offerings in golden cups, but the priest had brought out no cup for Psammetichus, who used his brass helmet. The future pharaoh was promptly exiled to a limited area in the Delta. He visited the oracle of the serpent goddess at Buto and was informed that his cause would prosper when the sea produced brass figures of men. Soon afterwards he heard that a body of Ionians and Carians, clad in brass armour, had come overseas and were plundering on the Egyptian coast. He immediately entered into an alliance with them, promising rich rewards, vanquished his rivals in battle and thus became sole sovereign of Egypt.

Sais was then the capital, and its presiding deity, the goddess Neith, assumed great importance, but she was regarded by the mass of the people as a form of Isis. The great city of Memphis, however, was the real centre of the social and religious life of the new Egypt, which was the old. Thebes had ceased to have any political significance. No attempt was made to restore its dilapidated temples, from which many of the gods had been deported to Assyria, where they remained until the Persian age. Amun had fallen from his high estate, and his cult was presided over by a high priestess, a sister of Psammetcihus's queen, the 'wife' of the god. With this queen was afterwards associated one of the daughters of Psammetchus, so that the remnant of the Amun endowments might come under the control of the royal house. Ra of Heliopolis shrank to the position of a local deity. The conservative Egyptians, as a whole, had never been converted to sun worship.

Osiris was restored as the national god in his Old Kingdom association with Ptah, the Great Father, the world deity, who had his origin on the earth – his right eye was the sun and his left eye was the moon. But although the sun was 'the eye of Osiris', the ancient deity was no more a sun god than Ra was an earth god. As Osiris-Ra he absorbed certain attributes of the solar deity, but as Ra had similarly absorbed almost every other god, the process was not one of change so much as adjustment.[1] Ra ceased to be recognised as the Great Father of the Egyptian pantheon. 'Behold, you (Osiris) are upon the seat of Ra.' Osiris was essentially a god of vegetation and the material world; he was the soul of Ra, but his own soul was the soul of Geb, the earth god, which was hidden now in a tree, now in an animal, now in an egg: the wind was the breath and spirit of Osiris, and his eyes gave light. He was not born from the sun egg like Ra. Geb, the earth giant, in his

---

[1] The various gods became manifestations of Osiris. In the Osirian hymns, which were added to from time to time, Osiris is addressed: 'You are Atum, the forerunner of Ra . . . the soul of Ra . . . the pupil of the eye that beholdest Atum . . . lord of fear, who causes himself to come into being' (*The Burden of Isis*, Dennis).

bird form was before the egg, and Osiris absorbed Geb. Osiris became 'the great egg', which was 'the only egg', for the Ra 'egg' had been appropriated from the earth worshippers. He was both Geb and the 'egg' – 'you egg who become as one renewed'. The father of Ra was Nu (water); the father of Osiris was Tanen (earth).[1]

But although he fused with Ptah-Tanen and became the Great Father, Osiris was not divested of his ancient lunar attributes. He was worshipped as the Apis bull; his soul was in the bull, and it had come from the moon as a ray of light. Here then we have a fusion of myths of diverging origin. Osiris was still the old lunar god, son of the Great Mother, but he had become 'husband of his mother' or mothers, and also his own father, because he was the moon that gave origin to the sacred bull. He was also the world giant whose soul was hidden. The Egyptian theologians of the Late Period clung to all the old myths of their mingled tribal ancestors and attached them to Osiris.

So Osiris absorbed and outlived all the gods. In early Christian times, the Serapeum, the earthly dwelling place of Serapis (Osiris-Apis), was the haunt of society. Hadrian, writing to the consul Servian, said that the Alexandrians 'have one god, Serapis, who is worshipped by Christians, Jews and Gentiles'. The half-Christianised Egyptians identified Christ with Horus, son of Osiris, and spoke of the Saviour as the young avenger in the 'Legend of the Winged Disc', who swept down the Nile valley driving the devil (Seth) out of Egypt. As early Gaelic converts said: 'Christ is my Druid', those of the land of the pharaohs appear to have declared similarly: 'Christ is my Horus'.

Horus and his mother, Isis, came into prominence with Osiris. Seth, as Sutekh, was banished from Egypt and was once again regarded as the devil. The cult of Isis ultimately spread into Europe.[1]

But not only were the beliefs of the Old Kingdom revived; even its language was imitated in the literature and inscriptions of the Saite period, and officials were given the titles of their predecessors who served Djoser and Khufu. Art revived, drawing its inspiration from the remote past, and once again the tomb scenes assumed a rural character and all the mannerisms of those depicted in Old Kingdom times. Egypt yearned for the glories of other days and became an imitator of itself. Everything that was old became sacred. Antiquarian knowledge was regarded as the essence of wisdom. Hieroglyphic writing was gradually displaced by demotic, and when the Greeks found that the learned priests alone were able to decipher the ancient inscriptions, they concluded that picture writing was a sacred art; hence the name 'hieroglyphics', derived from *hieros*, 'sacred', and *glypho*, 'I engrave'.

The excess of zeal displayed by the revivalists is illustrated in their deification

---

[2] *The Burden of Isis.*
[1] An image of Isis was found on the site of a Roman camp in Yorkshire.

of Imhotep, the learned architect of King Djoser of the Third Dynasty (see Chapter 8). His memory had long been revered by the scribes; now he was exalted to a position not inferior to that held by Thoth in the time of empire. As the son of Ptah, he was depicted as a young man wearing a tight-fitting cap, sitting with an open scroll on his knees. He was reputed to cure diseases by the power of spells and was a patron of learning, and he was a guide or priest of the dead, whom he cared for until they reached the Osirian paradise. In Greek times he was called Imuthes and identified with Asklepios.

Animal worship was also carried to excess. Instead of regarding as sacred the representative of a particular species, the whole species was adored. Cats and rams, cows and birds, and fishes and reptiles were worshipped wholesale and mummified. The old animal deities were given new forms; Khnum, for instance, was depicted as a ram -headed hawk, Bastet as a cat-headed hawk, and Anubis as a sparrow with the head of a jackal.

Psammetichus reigned for over fifty-four years and Egypt prospered. At Memphis he extended the temple of Ptah and built the Serapeum, in which the sacred bull was worshipped. He waged a long war in Philistia and captured Ashdod, and had to beat back from his frontier hordes of Scythians and Cimmerians, Aryan-speaking peoples, who had overrun Asia Minor and were pressing down through Syria like the ancient Hittites. During their reign of terror, King Gyges of Lydia was defeated and slain.

The Greeks were encouraged to settle in Egypt, and their folklore became current in the Delta region. Herodotus related a version of the tale of Troy that was told to him by the priests. It was to the effect that Paris fled to Egypt when Menelaus began military operations to recover Helen, and that he was refused the hospitality of the Pharaoh. In the *Odyssey* Menelaus says to Telemachus:

> Long on the Egyptian coast by calms confined,
> Heaven to my fleet refused a prosperous wind,
> No vows had we preferred, nor victim slain,
> For this the gods each favouring gale restrain.
> *Odyssey* 4, 473

When Psammetchus's son, Necho II, came to the throne, the Assyrian empire was going to pieces. Nahum was warning Nineveh:

> Behold, I am against thee, saith the Lord of hosts. . . . I will shew the nations thy nakedness and the kingdoms thy shame. . . . The gates of thy land shall be set wide open unto thine enemies; the fire shall devour thy bars. . . . Thy shepherds slumber, O King of Assyria: thy nobles shall dwell in the dust: thy people is scattered upon the mountains, and no man

Imhotep (Imuthes)
The architect of the first pyramid, who became a
god in the Late Period and 'son of Ptah or Ptah-
Osiris'

Painted and gilded figure of Ptah-
Seker-Asar (Ptah-Sokar-Osiris) on a
stand with a cavity containing a small
portion of a body

Deities of the Late Period

297

gathereth them. There is no healing of thy bruise; wound is grievous: all that hear the bruit of thee shall clap the hands over thee (Nahum 3:5–19).

After Assurbanipal had devastated Elam, it was occupied by the Aryan Medes. About 607 BC, Cyaxares, the Median king, who had allied himself with the rebel Babylonians, besieged Nineveh, which was captured and ruthlessly plundered. The last Assyrian king, Sinsharishkun, the second son of Assurbanipal, is identified with the Sardanapalus of legend who set fire to his palace and perished in its flames so that he might not fall into the hands of his enemies. Tradition attached to his memory the achievements of his father.

Pharaoh Necho took advantage of Assyria's downfall by seizing Palestine. King Josiah of Judah went against him at Megiddo and was defeated and slain. 'And his servants carried him in a chariot dead from Megiddo and brought him to Jerusalem' (2 Kings 23:30). Jehoahaz was selected as Josiah's successor, but Necho deposed him and made him a prisoner and, having fixed Judah's tribute at 'an hundred talents of silver and a talent of gold', he 'made Eliakim, the son of Josiah, king . . . and turned his name to Jehoiakim' (2 Kings 23:34), so making Jehoiakim a puppet king.

But Necho's triumph was short-lived. Less than four years later, Nebuchadnezzar, king of Babylon, who claimed Syria, routed Necho's army at Carchemish in 605 BC, and the Egyptians were forced to hasten back to their own land. 'This is the day of the Lord of hosts, a day of vengeance,' cried Jeremiah. . . . 'Come up ye horses; and rage ye chariots; and let the mighty men come forth: the Ethiopians and the Libyans, that handle the shield; and the Lydians [mercenaries] that handle and bend the bow. . . . The sword shall devour. . . . Let not the swift flee away, nor the mighty man escape. . . . The nations have heard of thy shame,' cried the Hebrew prophet to the escaping Egyptians (Jeremiah 46). 'And the King of Egypt came not again any more out of his land: for the King of Babylon had taken from the river of Egypt unto the River Euphrates all that pertained to the King of Egypt' (2 Kings 24:7).

Necho had come to an understanding with Nebuchadnezzar and interfered no more in Palestine. A few years later Jehoiakim rebelled against the king of Babylon, expecting that Necho II would support him, despite the warnings of Jeremiah, and Jerusalem was besieged and forced to surrender. Jehoiakim had died in the interval, and his son, Jehoiachin, and a large number of 'the mighty of the land' were deported to Babylon (2 Kings 24). Mattaniah, son of Josiah, was selected to rule over Jerusalem, his name being changed to Zedekiah.

Necho II, according to Herodotus, had undertaken the construction of a canal between the Mediterranean and the Red Sea but stopped after a time on account of a warning received from an oracle. He then devoted himself to building a large fleet. His father was reputed to have tried to discover the source of the Nile, and it was probably with a desire to have the problem solved that Necho sent an expedition of Phoenicians to circumnavigate Africa. When the vessels, which started out from the Red Sea, returned three years later by the Straits of Morocco, the belief was confirmed that the world was surrounded by the 'great circle' – the ocean.

Apries, the second king after Necho, is the Pharaoh Hophra of the Bible. He had dreams of conquest in Syria and formed an alliance that included the unfortunate Judah, so that 'Zedekiah rebelled against the King of Babylon' (Jeremiah 52:3). Nebuchadnezzar took swift and terrible vengeance against Josiah's unstable son. Jerusalem was captured after a two years' siege and laid in ruins (about 586 BC). Zedekiah fled but was captured, 'And the king of Babylon slew the sons of Zedekiah before his eyes. . . . Then he put out the eyes of Zedekiah; and the king of Babylon bound him in chains and carried him to Babylon, and put him in prison till the day of his death' (Jeremiah 52:10, 11). The majority of the Jews were deported; a number fled with Jeremiah to Egypt. So ended the kingdom of Judah.

> Oh! weep for those that wept by Babel's stream,
> Whose shrines are desolate, whose land a dream. . . .
> Tribes of the wandering foot and weary breast,
> How shall ye flee away and be at rest!
>
> Lord Byron.

Jeremiah proclaimed the doom of Judah's tempter, crying: 'Thus saith the Lord; Behold I will give Pharaoh Hophra, king of Egypt, into the hand of his enemies, and into the hand of them that seek his life; as I gave Zedekiah, king of Judah, into the hand of Nebuchadnezzar, king of Babylon, his enemy, and that sought his life' (Jeremiah 44:30).

Apries fell about 570 BC. According to Herodotus, the Egyptians revolted against him, apparently because of his partiality to the Greeks. His army of Ionian and Carian mercenaries was defeated by a native force under Amasis (Ahmosis II), whose mother was a daughter of Psammetichus II. A mutilated inscription at Babylon is believed to indicate that Nebuchadnezzar invaded Egypt about this time, but it is not confirmed by any surviving Nilotic record. Apries was kept a prisoner by the new king, but the Egyptians demanded his death, and he was strangled.

Amasis reigned for over forty years. He was well known to the Greeks. Herodotus says that he regulated his time in this manner: from dawn until the city square was crowded he gave audience to whoever required it; the rest of the day he spent making merry with friends who were people of not very high morals. Some of his nobles remonstrated with him because of his 'excessive and un-

Fine example of Restoration period coffin for priest of Amun and Bastet

Characteristic Graeco-Roman coffin with painted portrait

Mummy cases

becoming levities' and said he should conduct himself so as to increase the dignity of his name and the veneration of his subjects. Amasis answered: 'Those who have a bow bend it only when they require to; it is relaxed when not in use. And if it were not, it would break and be of no service in time of need. It is just the same with a man; if he continually engaged in serious pursuits, and allowed no time for diversion, he would suffer gradual loss of mental and physical vigour.'

Amasis 'was very partial to the Greeks, and favoured them at every opportunity' Herodotus says. He encouraged them to settle at Naucratis,[1] where the temple called Hellenium was erected and Greek deities were worshipped. Amasis erected a magnificent portico to Neith at Sais, had placed in front of Ptah's temple at Memphis a colossal recumbent figure 75 feet (23 metres) long and two erect figures 20 feet (6 metres) high, and caused to be built in the same city a magnificent new temple to Isis. To the Graeco-Libyan city of Cyrene, with which he cultivated friendly relations, he gifted 'a golden statue of Minerva'. He married a princess of the Cyrenians. Herodotus relates that during the wedding celebrations Amasis 'found himself afflicted with an imbecility that he experienced under no other circumstances' – probably he had been drinking heavily, as he was prone to do. His cure was attributed to Venus, who was honoured with a statue for reward.

Amasis was not over-popular with the Egyptians. Not only did he favour the Greeks, but he promulgated a law to compel every citizen to make known once a year the source of his earnings. It is not surprising to find that he had to send Greek soldiers to Memphis to overawe the offended natives, who began to whisper treasonably to one another.

His foreign policy was characterised by instability. Although he cultivated friendly relations for the purpose of mutual protection, he gave no assistance in opposing the Persian advance westwards.

About the middle of the reign of Amasis, a new power arose in the east that was destined to shatter the crumbling edifices of old-world civilisation and usher in a new age. 'Cyrus, the Achaemenian, King of Kings,' who was really a Persian, overthrew King Astyages (550 BC) of the Medes and founded the great Aryan Medo-Persian empire and pressed westwards to Asia Minor. Amasis formed alliances with the kings of Babylon, Sparta and Lydia, and occupied Cyprus, which he evacuated when the Persians overthrew the Lydian power. Egypt had become 'a shadow' indeed. Cyrus next turned his attention to Babylonia, besieging and capturing city after city. The regent, Belshazzar, ruled as king in Babylon, which, in 539 BC, was completely besieged. On the last night of his life, deeming himself secure, 'Belshazzar the king made a great feast to a thousand of his lords, and drank wine before the thousand' (Daniel 5:1).

---

[1] 'Mighty in ships.'

In that same hour and hall,
The fingers of a hand
Came forth against the wall,
And wrote as if on sand:
The fingers of a man –
A solitary hand
Along the letters ran,
And traced them like a wand.

'Belshazzar's grave is made,
His kingdom passed away,
He, in the balance weighed,
Is light and worthless clay;
The shroud his robe of state,
His canopy the stone;
The Mede is at his gate!
The Persian on his throne!'
Lord Byron

So Babylon fell. Cyrus, who was proclaimed its king, allowed the Jews to return home, and the first lot saw the hills of Judah in 538 BC, nearly half a century after Zedekiah was put to shame.

Cambyses succeeded Cyrus in 529 BC. Nine months after the death of Amasis, the ineffectual intriguer (526 BC), Cambyses moved westwards with a strong army and conquered Egypt, establishing the Twenty-seventh Dynasty, the first of Persian occupation. Psammetichus III, after the defeat of his army of mercenaries at Pelusium, on the east of the Delta, retreated to Memphis. Soon afterwards a Persian herald sailed up the Nile to offer terms, but the Egyptians slew him and his attendants and destroyed the boat. Cambyses took speedy revenge. He besieged Memphis, which before long surrendered. According to Herodotus, Cambyses committed gross barbarities, forcing the daughters of Amasis to fetch water like slaves and executing his son and two thousand Egyptian youths after marching them in procession with ropes around their necks. On his return from Nubia, where he had conducted a fruitless campaign, he is said to have slain a newly found Apis bull, perhaps because Amasis had 'loved Apis more than any other king'. At Sais the vengeful Persian, according to Egyptian tradition, had the mummy of Amasis torn to pieces and burned. Later history has been altogether kinder to Cambyses and, indeed, even credits him with supporting Egyptian cults.

With the conquest by Persia the history of ancient Egypt may be brought to an end. Before the coming of Alexander the Great, in 332 BC, the short-lived and weak Dynasties Twenty-eight to Thirty flickered like the last flames of smoul-dering embers. Then followed the Ptolemaic age, which continued until 30 BC, when, with the death of the famous Cleopatra, Egypt became 'the granary of Rome'.

Under the Ptolemies there was another restoration. It was modelled on the civi-lisation of the latter half of the Eighteenth Dynasty. A large proportion of the for-eign population embraced Egyptian religion, and the dead were given gorgeous mummy cases with finely carved or painted portraits.

Vivid glimpses of life in Egypt from the second to the fourth century AD, are afforded by papyri discovered at Oxyrhynchus, chiefly by Grenfell and Hunt. Wealthy and populous Alexandria had its brilliant and luxury-loving social groups. Invitations to dinner were sent out in much the same form as they were to be done later in the centuries. The following is dated second century AD:

Chaeremon requests your company at dinner at the table of the lord of Serapis in the Serapeum tomorrow, the 15th, at 9 o'clock.

The worship of Apis was fashionable. A lady wrote to a friend about the begin-ning of the fourth century:

Greeting, my dear Serenia, from Petosiris. Be sure, dear, to come up on the 20th for the birthday festival of the god, and let me know whether you are coming by boat or by donkey in order that we may send for you accord-ingly. Take care not to forget. I pray for your continued health.

There were spoiled and petted boys even in the third century. One wrote to his indulgent father:

Theon to father Theon, greeting. It was a fine thing of you not to take me with you to the city. If you won't take me with you to Alexandria I won't write you a letter, or speak to you, or say goodbye to you, and if you go to Alexandria I won't take your hand or ever greet you again. This is what will happen if you won't take me. Mother said to Archelaus: 'It quite up-sets me to be left behind'. It was good of you to send me presents. . . . Send me a lyre I implore you. If you don't, I won't eat, I won't drink – there now!

Alexandria was always a hotbed of sedition. A youthful citizen in good cir-cumstances wrote to his brother:

I learned from some fishermen that Secundus's house has been searched and my house has been searched. I shall therefore be obliged if you will write me an answer on this matter so that I may myself present a petition to the Prefect. . . . Let me hear about our bald friend, how his hair is growing again on the top; be sure and do.

Marriage engagements were dissolved when prospective sons-in-law were found to be concerned in lawless actions; prisoners were bailed out; improvident people begged for loans from friends to take valuables and clothing out of pawn; country folk complained that merchants sent large cheeses when they ordered small ones. Young men were expected to write home regularly. The following is a father's letter:

I have been much surprised, my son, at not receiving hitherto a letter from you to tell me how you are. Nevertheless, sir, answer me with all speed, for I am quite distressed at having heard nothing from you.

So the social life of an interesting age is made articulate for us, and we find that human nature has not changed much through the centuries.

In the Ptolemaic age a papyrus was made eloquent with the lamentation of a girl wife in her tomb. At fourteen she was married to the high priest of Ptah, and after giving birth to three daughters in succession she prayed for a son, and a son was born. Four brief years went past and then she died. Her husband heard her crying from the tomb, entreating him to eat and drink and be merry, because the land of the dead was a land of slumber and blackness and great weariness. . . . 'The dead are without power to move . . . sire and mother they know not, nor do they long for their children, husbands, or wives. . . . Ah, woe is me! would I could drink of stream water, would I could feel the cool north wind on the river bank, so that my mind might have sweetness and its sorrow an end.'

It is as if the soul of ancient Egypt, disillusioned in the grave, were crying to us in the darkness 'down the corridors of time'.

PART TWO:
DICTIONARY OF EGYPTOLOGY

Introduction

Egyptology, the study of ancient Egypt in all its aspects, is a subject of endless fascination that embraces the beginnings and early stages of human religion, architecture, government, art and organised society. This dictionary is conceived and planned as a non-expert's guide to the subject. The aim has been to keep entries as concise as possible, with cross-references to lead the reader to other topics that help to fill out a particular area of interest.

Egyptology is still very much a subject in which new discoveries are being made. These new discoveries are both pushing back the dates at which 'earliest' information is known and widening the range and adding to the detail of knowledge that we possess about later periods. It is far from being a static field in which everything is known and there are numerous areas in which experts disagree. This book has the straightforward aim of providing as clear an introduction as possible for people who not only want to find out, for example, what the pyramids were for and how they were built, but what sort of people built them and what their everyday life was like.

Overview and context

Egypt is one of the oldest, and by far the best documented, of the ancient civilisations. Evidence of an ordered human society here stretches back far into the Palaeolithic era. Writing was invented in Egypt more than five thousand years ago, and the Egyptians were the first people to develop a systematic calendar. The kingdom of United Egypt arose around 3150 BC and lasted until the very brink of the Christian era, in 34 BC. During this colossal span of time, the nature of the Egyptian state and of Egyptian society changed remarkably little. The Egyptians of the Later Period felt a strong kinship with their remote ancestors who had built the first pyramids. They were a remarkable people, with a deeply entrenched sense of national pride and identity. Literal believers in the divinity of their kings, they nevertheless also had a strong concept of law and justice, within which the kings should exercise their earthly power. They believed, with some reason, that their land was the most favoured one on earth. Its isolation from early neighbours, the stability of its climate and the annual regeneration of its soil by the River Nile all encouraged a settled disposition among the inhabitants, and once they had created for themselves a satisfactory explanation of their place in the universal scheme of things, they were content to lead their lives according to a set of beliefs and rituals that in essence remained unaltered for two and a half millennia.

A profound sense of the continuity of things was felt by the Egyptians. They lived among vast monuments built in the past, and were constantly adding to them and erecting new ones. To them the past was not dead and buried but lived on; previous generations gathered in an afterworld where each new generation would ultimately join them. The afterworld was not a separate place, and the spirits of the dead surveyed and influenced the lives of the living, and in turn had to be nourished and cared for. Their religious system, elaborated in and sustained by a culture based on (normally) secure agricultural prosperity and economic wealth, was the strong but flexible backbone of the nation, enabling it to preserve its resiliency through the unchanging years and many periods of turmoil and invasion. Such were the people whose culture, history and achievements are the subject of this dictionary.

To place ancient Egypt in its historical context, a brief look at the surrounding human world is illuminating. Throughout the entire period from the First Dynasty to the Thirtieth, there is no recorded history of Europe north of the Alps. As the centuries passed, the Stone Age gradually merged into the Bronze Age (introduced to northern Europe around 2000 BC). The people who first assembled the stone circles at Avebury and Stonehenge are unknown, their language a matter of surmise. They lived a pastoral existence in huts on the windy uplands whilst far away the Egyptians harvested their corn, made their wine, wrote down their thoughts, and made and decorated great and complex buildings. There were civilisations as old, or older, in Sumeria and China, in some ways more inventive and forward-looking than the Egyptians (who learned from Sumer), but they lacked the extraordinary stability of the Egyptian system. The civilisation of the Indus Valley rose, flourished and fell as Egypt proceeded (not without troubles) from Old Kingdom to Middle Kingdom. The Egyptians of the Middle and New Kingdoms watched the rise and fall of the Middle Eastern empires: Hurrian, Hittite, Mitannian, Babylonian, Assyrian and Persian, and survived conquest and occupation by the two last. The Trojan War was a distant flicker on Egypt's horizon in the spacious days of Rameses II, and two hundred years later, Solomon's glory was underlined by his marriage to a princess of Egypt. When a few pastoral communities banded together to make the first settlement at Rome, around 1000 BC, the Egyptian kingdom was more than two thousand years old. Its religion was ancient when the Greek pantheon was established, when Hinduism appeared and when Gautama Buddha was born, around 560 BC. During the centuries of Egypt's slow decline, the Celts migrated across Europe, bringing the Iron Age to Britain during the fourth century. It was as a still-functioning state that

Egypt passed into the last and greatest pre-Classical empire, that of Alexander the Great, in 333 BC. Even then it lived on, independent, although devoid of influence and glory, for another 300 years, until that upstart among empires, the Roman, gathered it in and turned it into a vast granary to feed the population of the metropolis.

A

AAHMES-NEFERTARI (1)
The queen of the EIGHTEENTH-DYNASTY pharaoh Amenophis I. After their deaths they were revered as deities.

AAHMES-NEFERTARI (2)
The queen of the EIGHTEENTH-DYNASTY pharaoh Thuthmosis I and mother of HATSHEPSUT.

AALU
In Egyptian mythology, the Osirian paradise in the west, the eventual goal of the soul after death and reached only by undergoing the journey in the sun barque and trial by Osiris in the hall of judgment (*see* Part One: Chapter 7).

AB
In Egyptian mythology, the 'spirit' of the heart (HATI), which signified the will and desires of an individual.

ABMERIRA *see* AKHTHOES.

ABRAHAM
The first of the patriarchs of the Old Testament who sojourned in Egypt as a result of famine in CANAAN.

ABU GHUROB
The site in the SAQQARA area, on the west bank of the NILE, south of Cairo, of the SUN TEMPLE of the Pharaoh Neuserre (FIFTH DYNASTY) and the best guide to the appearance of the now vanished sun temple of HELIOPOLIS.

ABU SIMBEL
The site in NUBIA of two rock-hewn temples, which are among the best-known images of Egypt ever since the campaign to preserve them when the ASWAN High Dam was under construction in the 1960s and the resulting lake (Lake Nasser)

threatened to submerge them. Placed on the west bank of the NILE, 760 miles (1,223 kilometres) south of MEMPHIS, they reflect the movement of grand-scale ARCHITECTURE into and beyond UPPER EGYPT as the dynasties wore on. They were constructed in the reign and at the behest of Pharaoh RAMESES II, and, although dedicated to HATHOR and HORUS, there is no doubt that they also were intended to proclaim the greatness of the god-king Rameses. Four COLOSSAL STATUES of the pharaoh are positioned outside the larger of the temples, rising to a height of 65 feet (20 metres). Behind the statues, a PYLON gate 100 feet (30 metres) high is cut from the cliff face, and the temple extends behind it, 180 feet (55 metres), into solid rock.

ABUSIR
A funerary site on the left bank of the NILE, close to MEMPHIS. There are a number of PYRAMIDS, including those of NEFERIRKARE and Neuserre (FIFTH DYNASTY).

ABYDOS
A site in UPPER EGYPT, to the west of the NILE, about 100 miles (160 kilometres) northwest of THEBES, which was the location of tombs from the earliest dynasties onwards. With stone quarries conveniently close, it became a major temple and funerary centre and was particularly famed, from the FIFTH DYNASTY onwards, as the cult centre of OSIRIS, whose heart was said to be buried there. During the FIRST INTERMEDIATE PERIOD, both Thebes and HERAKLEOPOLIS fought fiercely to gain control of Abydos and so obtain association with the prestige of Osiris. Temples, tombs and chapels were built at Abydos right up to the end of the dynastic period, particularly in the Nineteenth Dynasty when temples dedicated to Osiris were built by SETHOS and RAMESES II. The royal tombs were discovered by PETRIE.

ADON see ATEN.

ADORATRICE OF AMUN
During the Libyan rule (FIFTEENTH DYNASTY), the kings placed their own candidate in the position of high priest of AMUN-RA at THEBES, effectively creating a VICEROY in UPPER EGYPT. The tendency of these appointees to create their own power base was a problem that the kings sought to resolve by appointing a female chief PRIESTESS instead. These functionaries were known as the adoratrices, or divine worshippers, of AMUN-RA, and they held the role until the end of the THIRTIETH DYNASTY.

AFTERLIFE
The Egyptians maintained a firm belief in the afterlife. Indeed, the concept was

basic to their civilisation, with its tremendous emphasis on preparation for the life to come. DEATH was a staging point in the flow of existence – a difficult one, beset with dangers and unknown hazards. In the royal despotism of the OLD KINGDOM, there were two kinds of afterlife – the ascent to heaven and the gods, open only to the king and a select few, and an ill-defined, gloomy subterranean existence for everyone else. One of the products of the social disorder that accompanied the end of the Old Kingdom was a breakdown of this segregation. While kings retained a special place in heaven, eternity was also open to others who could afford the necessary rites. The concept of the afterlife became a kinder one, envisaged as a continuity of mortal life, with all its pleasures, activities, and privileges. *See also* UNDERWORLD.

AFRIT
In Egyptian mythology, a desert spirit embodied in the whirlwind summoned up by SETH.

AGRICULTURE
For all her GOLD and minerals, the chief wealth of Egypt lay in her 'black land', or *khemet*, the rich tillage fertilised each year by OSIRIS through the NILE flood or INUNDATION. After its end as an independent kingdom, Egypt became the granary of Rome, but throughout the dynasties, she had consumed this annual wealth herself. (There were instances of corn being supplied to Mesopotamian kingdoms when these suffered famine, but the quantities cannot have been large and were more likely to have been gifts to the court than to the mass of people.) During the OLD KINGDOM, it is likely that only one crop a year was raised. The grain crops were barley and the primitive wheat known as emmer, of more than one type as farmers evolved strains from the original wild crop. They sowed seed in November, with the onset of the mild winter season, scattering it from small wicker baskets suspended from their shoulders and using their flock of sheep or goats to tread it in, although as the PLOUGH came into general use it was ploughed in. The basic field tool was the hoe, made of wood, with the handle jointed to the wooden blade and further secured with fibre twine. During March the corn would ripen. Reapers would cut it with flint-bladed sickles unchanged from the PRE-DYNASTIC PERIOD, tie it up in sheaves and load the sheaves on to donkeys. Some tomb decorations record in hieroglyphic script the remarks of farm-workers, in a manner not unlike that of contemporary strip cartoons. The FIFTH-DY-NASTY tomb of Sekem-ankh-Ptah notes remarks like 'Jab him in the backside!' as advice given to a donkey-driver, or an overseer's call, 'Hurry up, our wheat is ready'. The cut corn was taken to a stone threshing floor and threshed by driving cattle or donkeys round and round over the sheaves. All these tasks were for men, but women took over for the winnowing process of separating the chaff,

either by shaking the grain in wooden sieves or by waving broad wooden winnowing fans to blow away the chaff. Finally, the grain was measured, the quantity recorded, perhaps with an official present if it were a large farm or yield, and it was stored in the granary or shipped off to a larger grain store. At the same time as the grain crop, flax was grown and harvested, and the dusty process of combing the fibres begun (*see* TEXTILES).

Cattle were bred in large numbers and provided the community with meat, milk and hides as well as draught oxen for ploughing and pulling. Cattle were of such economic importance that they formed part of the regular census. They were a source of anxiety in that they were subject to disease, and herds were often decimated by forms of foot and mouth disease, causing farmers to import breeds from outside Egypt to strengthen the stock. There were no grassy plains for animals to graze on, although grass was grown wherever possible, especially in the DELTA and on the slopes of the broad banks between the river and the flooded irrigation basins, so cattle had to be provided with fodder. On a large estate this was a major undertaking – herds could run into several hundreds.

Fruit and vegetables were grown in garden plots. These included salad plants, such as lettuce, and onions, garlic, cucumbers, beans, leeks, lentils and melons. Orchards were set aside for fig trees and vines. BEES were kept for their honey, which had many uses as a sweetener.

AH

In Egytian mythology, an ancient moon god, the son of Apet, considered to be symbolic of the male principle and the fighting principle. He developed into the later god KHONSU.

AHA

The second king of the Frist Dynasty (*see* FIRST AND SECOND DYNASTIES), the son of MENI and Neithhotep.

AHHOTEP

The queen of Seqenenre, a Theban king of the Seventeenth Dynasty (*see* FIFTEENTH, SIXTEENTH AND SEVENTEENTH DYNASTIES) in the SECOND INTERMEDIATE PERIOD. Her three sons reigned in succession and continued the war against the HYKSOS. The youngest was AHMOSIS, the first pharaoh of the Eighteenth Dynasty, the first dynasty of the New Kingdom.

AHMOSIS

The first king of the NEW KINGDOM and EIGHTEENTH DYNASTY, coming to power around 1550 BC. The first campaigns of his reign marked the end of the HYKSOS domination. He was a warrior king, keen to restore Egyptian prestige, which the

Hyksos dominion had severely undermined. He took Egyptian armies on expansionist campaigns through Palestine and also regained control of NUBIA, setting the pattern for the imperial style of the New Kingdom.

AHMOSIS II *see* AMASIS.

AHMOSIS OF EL KAB

A noble of the time of the EIGHTEENTH DYNASTY who took part in fighting the Hyksos under Pharaoh AHMOSIS and an invasion of Nubia under THUTHMOSIS I. In his tomb is recorded an account of a battle that took place between the second and third cataracts of the Nile.

AKER

In Egytian mythology, an ancient earth god who was depicted as a lion.

AKH

One of the five elements forming the human being seen as an aspect of the sun, the link between the human and the luminous life force. It left the body at DEATH to join the circumpolar stars. In HIEROGLYPHICS it is denoted by the crested ibis.

AKHENATEN *or* AMENOPHIS IV

EIGHTEENTH-DYNASTY king (ruled 1352–1338 BC). The son of AMENOPHIS III, after a period of co-regency with his father, he assumed sole reign, with NEFERTITI as his queen, and, from his second year as absolute monarch, set about a drastic revision of the time-honoured royal cult of AMUN-RA. He built a new temple at KARNAK to the ATEN, but in his fourth year as king began to build a completely new capital city and national cult centre, named Akhetaten ('horizon of the sun disc'), on the east bank of the Nile. Its site, AMARNA, is six miles (ten kilometres) south of present-day Mallawi. In size and splendour, he intended it to outdo THEBES or MEMPHIS. At this time he changed his names to affirm his god-identity with that of Aten. Amenophis means 'Amun is satisfied', whilst AKHENATEN means 'glory of the Aten'. All references to Amun were expunged, and the 'hidden' god was replaced by the 'visible' god. Like most revolutionary steps, this was the culmination of a trend, given pace by an all-powerful and determined individual. Its impact on the general population was slight, but the reaction of the conservative upper classes, and especially the priests, can be gauged by the ferocity with which all traces of Akhenaten's activities were wiped out after his death. It is possible to overestimate the extent of the changes he imposed. Even the great temple of the Aten, its open-air altar so unlike the classic Egyptian concept of the temple, with its inner recesses shrouded and mysterious, harked back to the SUN TEMPLES of the FIFTH DYNASTY. The king himself remained the high priest and intermediary between god and people. The administration of the country went on very much as before. Distinctive developments in the arts, although again part of a growing trend rather than a sudden change, reflect the tastes of the court. There was a move towards 'naturalism'. This was reflected in literature by an easing of the conventions that had kept MIDDLE KINGDOM Egyptian as the written language, ignoring the changes in everyday speech. Now the spoken language was allowed to be written in official documents, and the written language evolved rapidly at this time, a process that the anti-reformists who followed Akhenaten could not reverse. In ART, too, there was a greater freedom of line and realism of portrayal, notably in portrayals of the pharaoh himself.

Akhenaten reigned for some fourteen years, perhaps with a co-ruler forced on him at the end, when it had become apparent that his reforms could not be sustained. The image of a king preoccupied with his priest role and the arts is reinforced by the diplomatic letters left at the Amarna site, which testify to the erosion of the Asian empire created by his EIGHTEENTH DYNASTY predecessors. His successors returned to the old capital at MEMPHIS. El-Amarna was emptied of people and possessions and became a ghost city. Much of its stone was removed to form new buildings in the city of HERMOPOLIS MAGNA, facing it on the western bank. Official edicts announced the restoration of the cult of Amun-Ra and condemned the mistakes and crimes of Akhenaten. The monolithic power of tradition resumed its sway. *See also* TUTANKHAMUN. *SEE ALSO* PART ONE: CHAPTER 26.

AKHETATEN *see* AMARNA.

AKHTHOES *or* ABMERIRA
According to MANETHO, a name of Kheti, the first king of the Ninth Dynasty (*see* NINTH AND TENTH DYNASTIES).

ALABASTER
An easily worked white stone, quarried at a number of sites in MIDDLE EGYPT, notably at Alabastronpolis (Greek: 'city of alabaster') and used to make decorative bowls, vases and statues.

ALEXANDER THE GREAT (356–323 BC)
The Macedonian king who brought most of the Near East under his rule in an empire that reached from Greece to India. With his conquest of the Persians in 333 BC, he acquired Egypt, at that time under the SECOND PERSIAN OCCUPATION. It was as a result of Alexander's conquests that the Ptolemies ruled Egypt. On the death of Alexander, his enormous dominions were divided among his principal lieutenants, and PTOLEMY Lagos received Egypt and founded the last dynasty, whose kings were wholly Greek. *See also* MACEDONIAN DYNASTY.

ALEXANDRIA

The capital of Ptolemaic Egypt and the first really large city of Egypt. It was named in honour of ALEXANDER THE GREAT, who founded it. The great library at Alexandria was founded during the reign Ptolemy Philadelphus (283–247 BC), but it was nearly destroyed by fire during civil war between CLEOPATRA and her brother, Ptolemy.

AMARNA

This site (Tel el-Amarna) in MIDDLE EGYPT, downstream from THEBES, was chosen by the EIGHTEENTH-DYNASTY Pharaoh AKHENATEN as his new capital when, in a move unprecedented in Egypt's long history, he abandoned Thebes, where his ancestors had been kings, to found not only a new capital but a new centre of worship for a new, or at least newly invigorated, god. He commanded the building of the great temple of Aten, dedicated to the sun disc, as a replacement of the cult of AMUN-RA. The temple form was similar to the traditional one, except for one striking aspect: the sanctuary of the god, instead of being dark and mysterious, was open to the sky. The new city was named Akhetaten, and in the relatively brief span of Akhenaten's reign, it comprised a large number of ceremonial buildings and avenues, together with barracks of workers' houses on the periphery. The palaces and temples were constructed of relatively small stone blocks, which speeded up their building and, not long after, their demolition. A substantial number of inscribed clay tablets, the Amarna Letters, were found on the site in 1887, providing much information about international relations between the Middle Eastern empires around 1300 BC.

AMARNA LETTERS *see* AMARNA.

AMARNA PERIOD

A period of the New Kingdom, 1348–1336 BC, corresponding to the reign of Akhenaten, which was centred at his capital on the site of el-Amarna. The Amarna Period saw distinctive changes in the arts of sculpture and painting.

AMASIS *or* AHMOSIS II

A pharaoh (ruled 570–526 bc) of the Twenty-Sixth Dynasty who was a general of Apries, whom he overthrew to gain power. Amasis held off a Babylonian attack by Nebuchadnezzar and later formed alliances with former enemies, including Babylon to contain it.

AMENEMHET

The Egyptian form of the name of the AMMENEMES pharoahs.

AMENHOTEP (1)

The Egyptian form of the name of the AMENOPHIS pharoahs.

AMENHOTEP (2)

In the EIGHTEENTH DYNASTY, a favourite architect to AMENOPHIS III. He was regarded as a great magician by the people and was possibly the architect of the COLOSSI OF MEMNON.

AMENI

A NOMARCH of the Gazelle NOME during the reign of AMMENEMES I in the TWELFTH DYNASTY who had inscribed in his tomb an inscription that boasts of his good governorship and kind treatment to the people of his nome.

AMENOPHIS I

EIGHTEENTH-DYNASTY king (ruled 1526–1506 BC), son of AHMOSIS, who benefited from Ahmosis's conquests. His death marked a change in temple ARCHITECTURE; from now on, the king's MORTUARY TEMPLE was not linked to his tomb, which was physically distant from it. Royal mortuary temples were built on the west bank of the NILE in the Theban area, whilst the tombs were placed in the VALLEY OF THE KINGS.

AMENOPHIS II

EIGHTEENTH-DYNASTY king (ruled 1425–1401 BC). The successor to the great THUTHMOSIS III, he is remembered for his great physical strength and for a degree of cruelty unusual in Egyptian monarchs. Faced with a revolt in Egyptian-held Syria on his accession, he had seven Syrian princes slaughtered in front of the statue of AMUN-RA at THEBES, hanging six bodies on the city wall and sending the seventh to NAPATA, the Nubian capital, as a warning against rebellion. He conducted three military campaigns into Syria and is buried in the VALLEY OF THE KINGS. Some time after his death, his rock tomb was made a place of refuge for the mummies of six later monarchs to protect them from tomb robbers.

AMENOPHIS III

King of the EIGHTEENTH DYNASTY (ruled 1390–1352 BC) and a prodigious builder whose monuments span the country from Nubia to Bubastis and include the colossal baboon statues at Hermopolis and the gallery of the sacred Apis bulls at Saqqara. In the Temple of Mut of Asheru, south of Karnak, he had 600 statues of the lioness-goddess SEKHMET set up. He constructed a vast MORTUARY TEMPLE for himself on the west bank of the Nile at Malkata, which was later dismantled by Pharaoh Meneptah to provide stone for his own temple, leaving only the two colossal statues that once stood before the gate, the so-called COLOSSI OF MEMNON. Inheriting a strong empire from his predecessors, Amenophis did nothing to enlarge it and was content to lead a life of extreme opulence and luxury. One of his pleasures was to sail in his yacht, *Splendour of the Aten*, on an ornamental lake in the grounds of his palace. His reign was largely peaceful and he enjoyed great international prestige, more as a result of Egypt's status as the greatest power in the region than for his personal qualities. His mother was a Mitanni, and he himself acquired two other Mitanni princesses as wives, as well as two Babylonian princesses. Egypt was very much open to eastern influences in religion, art and other fields at this time. His principal wife, Tiy, mother of his successor, Akhenaten, was an Egyptian commoner whose father was Master of the Stud Farms. She was elevated to a special status as Great Royal Wife. *See also* Part One: Chapter 25.

AMENOPHIS IV *see* Akhenaten; Eighteenth Dynasty.

AMETSI *see* Weni.

AMMENEMES I

Middle Kingdom pharaoh of the Twelfth Dynasty (ruled 1991–1962 BC) who was assassinated as the result of a conspiracy that began in the women's quarters. The details of this are obscure, but it indirectly prompted one of the most popular literary texts, much used in schools, *The Story of* Sinuhe (*see also* Part One: Chapter 16 in Part One).

AMMENEMES II, III and IV *see* Twelfth Dynasty.

AMMIANUS MARCELLINUS (died after 390 AD)

Greek-born Roman historian who wrote on the institutions and manners of the Egyptians.

AMPHORA (*plural* AMPHORAE)

A tall pottery vase used to hold and conserve liquids, including wine and every kind of oil. They were given stoppers of hard mud and paste, marked with a seal to indicate content, ownership and age. The broken shards of amphorae, heaped in middens and tips, are among the most common relics of ancient times. These potsherds were often used by trainee scribes to write and draw on, and so can have added archaeological value.

AMSET

In Egyptian mythology, one of the four sons of Horus, who was depicted with a human face on one of the four canopic jars used in funerary practice. The stomach and large intestine were placed in this jar.

AMULET

A personal charm, often in the shape of an animal or animal-god, intended to procure the wearer certain benefits or to ward off evil spirits that might bring disease or bad luck. These could be simple clay objects or beautifully made, bejewelled ornaments.

AMUN and AMUN-RA

In the Hermopolitan COSMOLOGY, Amun was the 'hidden god', a member of the OGDOAD of creation. Despite this auspicious start, Amun remained a local Theban deity for many centuries, but THEBES was a royal city, and its god had wide prestige. Amun was taken up by the kings of Thebes as a war-god. This was during the troubled years of the FIRST INTERMEDIATE PERIOD, between the fall of the OLD KINGDOM and the establishment of the MIDDLE KINGDOM. Amun procured victory for them and was thereafter associated with RA as Amun-Ra. This assimilation with Ra, the supreme sun-deity, conferring national status, also served a useful theological purpose in giving the powerful but remote Ra a human-like persona, which could receive offerings and which could impregnate a queen with the divine seed and so ensure that a pharaoh was 'son of Ra'. Amun-Ra's own associate gods were the vulture-goddess, MUT, and their son, KHONSU. Throughout the Middle and the NEW KINGDOMS, his cult grew, and he had vast and lavish centres of worship at Thebes (LUXOR), KARNAK and MEDINET HABU. Kings of the EIGHTEENTH DYNASTY, most notably AKHENATEN, sought to reduce the power of the high priest of Amun-Ra, and the cult of Ra-ATEN, the 'visible sun', was propagated, but with no lasting success. By the end of the New Kingdom, Amun-Ra was the most powerful god in the Egyptian pantheon, his temples were hugely wealthy and his high priest correspondingly influential. During the THIRD INTERMEDIATE PERIOD, UPPER EGYPT became a theocracy ruled by the priesthood of Amun-Ra, who made their decisions according to the ORACLE of the god. *See also* Part One: Chapter 22.

AMYRTAEUS *see* TWENTY-EIGHTH DYNASTY.

ANATH *or* ANTA *or* ANTHAT

A goddess of love and war who was imported into Egyptian mythology in the Eighteenth Dynasty. In Arabia she was associated with the moon god Sin and in Asia Minor with Ashur. Thuthmosis III erected a shrine to her at Thebes. She is depicted as a goddess of war, holding a spear in one hand and swinging a battle-axe in the other, seated on a throne or armed with shield and club, riding on a horse.

ANDZTI *see* OSIRIS.

ANEDJIB *see* FIRST AND SECOND DYNASTIES; SED FESTIVAL.

ANI

The author of the *Maxims of Ani*, a widely copied text of the NEW KINGDOM period, drawing on earlier models, intended to lead the reader towards the harmonious life so much appreciated by the Egyptians.

ANIMAL CULTS

Animals are inextricably interwoven with Egyptian religion. Most of their oldest gods had animal features and probably began as wholly animal in form. This later underwent a degree of humanisation, with animal heads set upon human bodies. However, in addition to this, there were many instances of animal worship, either local or national. Bulls, rams, CROCODILES, ibex and falcons were all identified with gods, often, as with bulls and rams, with more than one deity. Such animals have a certain grandeur of their own, as well as a strong association with virility, wealth and fertility. Perhaps the jackal and the CAT fell into this category too. But far obscurer creatures, the BEE, the ichneumon fly and the dung beetle, were also treated with reverence and regarded as sacred. In the activities of these creatures, the Egyptians perceived a particular and intriguing aspect of the life force, linking insects to the gods in a striking and memorable way, like little living parables (*see* SCARAB). The Egyptians felt that the god might manifest itself on earth in the form of the locally worshipped animal, and these were consequently sacred within the NOME, with severe penalties for anyone who should harm or kill it. Such constraints applied only within the temple's area of influence. It is likely that the animal element in the Egyptian pantheon also makes a link with the ancient past of the peoples who came into the NILE Valley from central Africa, another region where animal cults were and, to some degree, still are maintained. Animal cults were far from exclusive to Egypt and existed in cultures with which the Egyptians had no contact, notably India. *See also* Part One: Chapter 5.

ANIMAL LIFE (1)

Domesticated the ancient Egyptians domesticated the wild ox, sheep and the goat. The ox stemmed from the long-horned wild ox (*Bos primigenius*) and was a common beast of burden long before it was ever hitched to a plough. The sheep was descended from the red-fleeced mouflon (*Ovis musimon*). Most common after the ox was the ass, also a beast of burden. Mule trains carried goods from the Red Sea coast or on portage round the Nile cataracts. The horse arrived in Egypt with the advent of the HYKSOS invasion, and the Egyptians adopted it with eagerness, especially for use with chariots, in sport, hunting and warfare. Dogs existed, both wild and tame. Dog breeding was practised, and the Saluki dog can already be seen in tomb paintings.

ANIMAL LIFE (2)

Wild in the PRE-DYNASTIC PERIOD and the OLD KINGDOM, when part of the NILE Valley remained untamed jungle, there was a wide variety of animal life, including elephant, hippopotamus, wild ox, giraffe, panther, leopard and okapi, as well as CROCODILE. Most of these animals were extinct in the region by the early centuries of the Old Kingdom, at least in LOWER EGYPT. In the desert areas there were lions, gazelles, ibex and jackals. For all their reverence for the life force and their appreciation of the divine in animals, the Egyptians were exuberant and skilful hunters, as much of their ART attests, hunting for pleasure as well as for the larder.

ANKH

A cross shaped like the Greek letter tau (T) with a loop on the top. In paintings it symbolises eternal life, and the word often appears in personal names, e.g. Tutankhamen.

ANPU (1) *see* ANUBIS.

ANPU (2)

In Egyptian mythology, the brother of Bata in the legend of 'The Peasant who became King' (*see* Part One: Chapter 4).

ANTA and ANTHAT *see* ANATH.

ANTI

In Egyptian mythology, a falcon-god, associated with war, worshipped in Upper Egypt, with his cult centre at Deir el-Gebrawi.

ANUBIS *or* ANPU

In Egyptian mythology, a god of the dead, portrayed as a man with the head of a jackal. Originally a deity of UPPER EGYPT, his cult was subsumed into that of OSIRIS (whose origins were in the DELTA) during the MIDDLE KINGDOM. He shared with Osiris the title of Prince of the West (i.e. the place where the dead were). *See also* UNDERWORLD.

ANUKET

In Egyptian mythology, the second of the two wifes of KHNUM. She is depicted as dark-skinned and wearing a crown of feathers. Like Sati, Khnum's first wife, she was a protective goddess of the CATARACTS.

ANZTI

In Egyptian mythology, an ancient DELTA god whose cult centre was at BUSIRIS. Uniquely among NOME deities, he was represented in human form, bearing the crook of a shepherd and the whip of a cowherd. He is depicted in the PYRAMID TEXTS but not later. His cult was absorbed into that of OSIRIS, who took over his emblems and his role, eventually on a national scale. The pyramid text depictions of Anzti are of interest for their display of him in 'mutilated' form – head, shoulders and arms only, with one attenuated leg. This was a precautionary measure. A portrayal of his entire body might risk his coming to life and harming the tomb's occupant. Wild animals were similarly rendered harmless.

APEP
In Egyptian mythology, a great serpent who lived in the depths of the celestial Nile and was the eternal enemy of Ra.

APEPA RA-AA-USER or APOPHIS I
The third HYKSOS king (see also FIFTEENTH, SIXTEENTH AND SEVENTEENTH DYNASTIES). A mathematical papyrus from his reign, known as the Rhind Papyrus and now in the British Museum, is evidence that their rule was not, as branded in the NEW KINGDOM, averse to culture.

APET see TAWARET.

APIRU
A tribe or tribes of displaced persons who lived in Egypt during the later New Kingdom, identified by some writers as the exiled Hebrews. See also EXODUS.

APIS
In Egyptian mythology, a bull-headed god, worshipped in MEMPHIS at the SERAPEUM. The Egyptian form is Hapi and the Greek form Serapis, from Asar-Hapi (Osiris-Apis).

APOPHIS
In Egyptian mythology, a god who personified the negative force of darkness against the light of RA, attacking the sun-god's sky-ship during the darkness of night but always repulsed by dawn. Certain HYKSOS kings also bore the name (see FIFTEENTH, SIXTEENTH AND SEVENTEENTH DYNASTIES).

APOPHIS I see APEPA RA-AA-USER.

APRIES see TWENTY-SIXTH DYNASTY.

APUIT
A queen of the SIXTH DYNASTY whose tomb was restored by a HYKSOS king.

APURA
A scribe of the TWELFTH DYNASTY who is believed to have been the author of a piece of LITERATURE in which is foretold a national disaster with civil war and the decline of agriculture followed by a conquest of evil and then conquest and rule by foreigners. See Part One: Part One: Chapter 17.

ARCHITECTURE

The materials available for building in Egypt were the reeds of the DELTA area, the muds and clays of the NILE valley, and the different bedrocks that lay beneath or rose up from the ground. Perhaps at a very early stage there was timber enough to have a timber architecture, of which almost nothing survives. It is notable that early rock-cut tombs in cliff faces show an attempt to imitate timber structures, with lintels and door jambs, something common in Asia Minor also. In the same way, the monumental curved cornices so typical of Egyptian temples have been traced back to the reed buildings of the Delta and marshes, where bundles of reed, assembled and tied together, produced a similar effect on a far smaller scale. Outside the Delta area, buildings from the PRE-DYNASTIC PERIOD onward were chiefly of mud brick. The durability of stone, which has preserved so many splendid monuments, should not obscure this fact. It was in the period of the kings, when central organisation and despotic rule made it possible to command a large labour force, that building in stone on a grand scale began. From its earliest beginnings, Egyptian stone architecture showed a quality of massiveness and bulk. This had some practical reasons. In a land prone to minor earthquake shocks, it was felt that large buildings should be of solid construction. Because of uncertainty on such matters as load-bearing, the distance between columns was at first deliberately small. The conservatism of Egyptian society tended to preserve such features, even after technical skill and knowledge could have achieved something different. The massive nature of the buildings was accentuated by the 'batter' of their design, i.e. they tended to be wider at the base than at the top, a pattern reflected also in doorways. Indeed, the essentially unchanging style of Egyptian architecture is one of its unique aspects. The superb achievements of the THIRD and the FOURTH DYNASTY seem to have attained the ideal expression of religious architecture, and once that was established, change might be dangerous. There were, however, inevitably some developments through the immense duration of the dynasties, caused by changing circumstances and tastes. The painstaking thoroughness of the early dynasties' workmanship, achieved by remorseless supervision, was only rarely equalled in later times.

Egyptian architecture as we know it is overwhelmingly the architecture of DEATH and religion. Aware that their lives on earth were short, the Egyptians spent more thought, resources and effort on the dwellings that were meant to see them through eternity. Our information on domestic dwelling houses prior to the NEW KINGDOM is limited and comes from models and pictures found in tombs, analogies with tombs and from a few ill-preserved remains. Even the PHARAOHS lived in houses less splendid than the tombs that awaited them. It was rare for a house to have more than two storeys. To the end of the ancient Egyptian period, the vast majority of houses had a ground storey only. The architecture associated with the OLD KINGDOM is chiefly that of the PYRAMIDS and of MASTABAS. The mastaba was the first true expression of Egyptian architecture. Originally it was a simple structure that marked and sealed the pit where an important person was buried. It developed into a building in its own right, made of stone by the time of the FOURTH DYNASTY rather than mud brick, with at first one room then eventually several rooms, all of them furnished and decorated. The earliest pyramids were of stepped construction, rising in a series of ledges and, like that of SAQQARA, which is oblong in plan, not always set on a square base. They owe their origin to the mastaba, which in its later form was often a very large construction. The later pyramids are true geometrical pyramids, rising smoothly to a point.

The architect was a court functionary whose job was not to innovate but to replicate, interpret and, under ambitious pharaohs, to do what had been done before, but bigger. The few truly original buildings that have come down the ages to us, like the Step Pyramid, stand out for their originality. Originality was not seen as a good thing by the Egyptians, at least after the period of the pyramids. Architecture was not prized in its own right as an ART, but as a means of expressing the liturgy and of praising the gods. As a result, long after thcy could have employed more daring designs and more sophisticated tools, the designers of Egyptian buildings followed tradition as slavishly as if they were walking a tightrope. Nevertheless, their work has remained a marvel to succeeding generations, and we still count the Great Pyramid among the Wonders of the World. *See also* HOUSE, TEMPLE, TOMB.

ARGO

An island near the third cataract of the River Nile on which Neferkhara-Sebekhotep, one of the Thirteenth Dynasty pharaohs erected two large granite statues.

ARMANT

An important PRE-DYNASTIC PERIOD site, cult centre of the god MONTU, in the heart of Theban territory.

ARMY

The Egyptians did not take readily to being soldiers, and during the OLD KINGDOM there was a very small standing army. Military leadership was considered as just one of the skills of a successful administrator (*see* WENI). The Egyptians brought in recruits from desert tribes as guards and law enforcers, on the basis that foreigners could be better relied on to serve the government. Corruption on a petty scale was endemic in Egypt, and local guards would have been unreliable. Conscription was necessary to gather a substantial army together. The system is seen at work when the TWELFTH-DYNASTY king, AMMENEMES I, appointed the

NOMARCH of the Oryx NOME as Great Director of Soldiers, in which capacity he had to bring up to 600 selected men to take part in an expedition into NUBIA. In the NEW KINGDOM and LATE PERIOD, when massive armies were common, a distinct military class appeared for the first time. Successful leaders on land and sea were rewarded with slaves and property. There were special decorations for distinguished military service. Pharaoh Rameses II, in his reproach to the soldiers who almost lost him the battle at Kadesh, said, 'There is not one man among you to whom I have not given a good portion on my land . . . I have relieved you of your taxes . . .', the implication being that there were privileges available to the common soldier as well. At this time the Egyptians also used foreign mercenaries on a large scale – Greek, Jewish, Libyan and Nubian. *See also* MILITARY ORGANISATION.

ART

Painting in ancient Egypt was a craft rather than an art, as art is understood in modern times. Its function was to display, inform and decorate, but the decoration invariably had a practical purpose, whether it was to demonstrate the greatness of a PHARAOH or to illustrate some simple process like fish-spearing. In effect, painting was the extension of hieroglyphic writing, on a larger surface, with different materials. The typical form of painting was the fresco, painted directly on to the inner walls of tombs, temples and large houses. The colours were sometimes applied directly to the wet plaster, but more often on to a specially prepared wall dressing of gypsum, or chalk plaster, mixed with gum in order to create a smooth surface. The paints were made from dry cakes of mineral-based pigment, mixed with water and a resinous gum. The colours were bright and strong, reflecting the sharp clarity and vivid colours of the sunlit landscape outside. Black, blue, brown, green, grey, red, white, yellow and pink were employed in the range, the last being a late NEW KINGDOM introduction. Application was made with a fibrous wood implement the ends of which could be teased into a brush-like formation. When planning the painting of a large surface, the painter, or master painter in charge of a team, divided the space into a series of registers, and within each, the figures and inscriptions were carefully plotted, with small squares marked out in red or black to act as guidelines for scale and content. This grid was unvarying through most of ancient Egyptian history, until the TWENTY-SIXTH DYNASTY (663–525 BC), when the proportions of the figures were altered to a taller, more slender schema. In the standard grid arrangement, every part of a figure had its specific and predetermined square. In the planning of decoration for a chamber, there were rules for which type of scene should go on each wall. The notion of artistic creativity was unknown to the Egyptians and, if suggested, would undoubtedly have horrified them. Excellence in art was excellence in reproducing the traditional design, the function of which was to assist and maintain the tomb occupant in the AFTERLIFE. Departure from the norm was as bad as laying faulty electrical wiring would be today, and an apprentice who sought to vary this would be whipped or dismissed rather than admired.

However, the choice of themes was very wide, from scenes of daily life in the fields and by the river, showing every form of agricultural and rustic activity, to daily life at home and on to battles, processions and feasts. The role of painting as a means of recording rather than of simply celebrating is shown by the literalness of approach. If a VIZIER's retinue consisted of 50 people, then 50 small figures would be depicted in a register, the vizier himself, as befitting his importance, being drawn to a much larger scale in the correct manner. Figures were clearly outlined and painted in the flat, bright colours, with no attempt to suggest shadow. The Egyptians did not discover, or need, perspective as part of their painting technique. The distinctive aspects of Egyptian figure portrayal are very familiar, and perhaps have become less strange to the modern eye during the twentieth century, when art sought to break free from the Renaissance tradition. The Egyptian portrait is drawn in profile, but the eye is drawn as if seen full-face. The torso also is facing the viewer, while the waist and legs again are presented in profile. The notion that the Egyptians knew no better is long defunct. Innumerable little figures in hieroglyph, and many SCULPTURES, display their capacity to render a shape with commanding visual realism. There were religious and cultural causes for this form of portrayal, set deep in the mental concrete of the Egyptian sense of tradition. The eye was always a symbol of the first importance, closely identified with HORUS. The artist's duty was to portray each part of the human body in its most 'characteristic' aspect and to combine them into a whole as an assemblage of different elements rather than as a single entity. The major figures are almost always shown in still or seated positions. Painting, especially in the tombs, was for eternity, and the fleeting nature of movement was entirely inappropriate both to the dignity of these figures and to their situation in time. As a result, Egyptian painting has a solemnity in its depiction of large figures that give it a somewhat static appearance. The eye has to look for the many lively details of smaller figures, especially in the painting of animals, where the artist had a freer reign and the capacity for cheerfulness, wit and humour of the Egyptian mind is revealed.

The revolution in religion and political life created by Akhenaten had a profound effect on Egyptian art. The pharaoh demanded realism and the painters struggled to oblige, and the frescoes of the AMARNA PERIOD have a quite different approach, with more vitality and movement than in the old tradition. With the end of the Amarna experiment, the old forms returned but never achieved the distinction of the interrupted tradition. *See also* WRITING.

ARTAXERXES I and II *see* TWENTY-SEVENTH DYNASTY.

ASENATH

The daughter of Potipherah, a priest of the sun temple at On (HELIOPOLIS), who, as told in the Bible in the Book of Genesis, married JOSEPH and had two sons.

ASHTAROTH and ASHTORETH *see* ASTARTE.

ASSURBANIPAL

King of the ASSYRIANS (ruled Egypt 669–640 BC), son of ESARHADDON, who had conquered LOWER EGYPT. The Pharaoh Taharqa retreated far into UPPER EGYPT and provoked rebellion among the northern puppet lords. Esarhaddon died before he could put them down, and Assurbanipal accomplished the task and also marched into Upper Egypt, whereupon Taharqa retreated into NUBIA. Assurbanipal left, only to find his collaborators change sides again. He returned to Egypt and had the DELTA lords and their families executed, sparing only his loyal supporter Necho, lord of SAIS, who was to found the TWENTY-SIXTH DYNASTY. When Taharqa's successor, Tantamani, reinvaded Egypt from Nubia to restore the TWENTY-FIFTH DYNASTY, the Assyrian king's response was swift and overwhelming. He came up the NILE with devastating force, and captured and pillaged Thebes. This put an end to the Twenty-fifth Dynasty, and Assurbanipal again controlled Egypt through the (temporarily) compliant Saites.

ASSYRIANS

One of the major peoples in the Near East in ancient times, with their capital at Nineveh. In 670 BC they invaded Egypt, subdued the DELTA area, and put the whole country under tribute. Unlike the Persians, their kings did not assume the style and dignities of pharaohs, but ruled through Egyptian collaborators. *See also* ASSURBANIPAL, ESARHADDON, TWENTY-SIXTH DYNASTY.

ASTARTE

A Phoenician fertility goddess who was imported into Egyptian mythology in the early Eighteenth Dynasty as a moon goddess and goddess of war. She was the most popular of the imported deities, and her worship became widespread during the later dynasties. She is the goddess of ill repute referred to in the Bible as Ashtaroth and Ashtoreth. She was depicted with the head of a lioness and stands in a chariot driving four horses over a fallen enemy.

ASTROLOGY *see* ASTRONOMY.

ASTRONOMY

The Egyptians were keen observers of the stars. The book list of the Temple of HORUS at EDFU notes books on such subjects as 'the periodical movement of the sun and moon'. The visible lights in the intensely black night sky were divided into three classes. The Unwearied Stars were the wandering planets: Jupiter, Saturn, Mars, Venus, Mercury. The Imperishable Stars were the circumpolar stars, believed to be the location of heaven. The Indestructible Stars were the fixed stars, of which the Egyptians chose thirty-six to identify the ten-day periods of the CALENDAR year. The constellations were picked out and given names, such as the Hippopotamus and the CROCODILE. The Egyptians did not turn ASTRONOMY into a science, and, like mathematics, it made little progress from the pyramid-building age onwards. They were more concerned with the application of astronomy to everyday life and made no distinction between astronomy and astrology. They believed that every month, day and hour were in the keeping of a particular god who could intervene favourably or unfavourably at the appropriate time. Episodes in the life of the gods fell on certain days, which were labelled as 'good' or 'bad', the bad days noted in texts in red, the colour of SETH. *See also* CALENDAR.

ASWAN

A settlement on the NILE and NOME capital, at the first cataract, now site of the High Dam. The Aswan quarries were the source of a prized red granite. There are important funerary sites nearby

ASYUT

A settlement in MIDDLE EGYPT, with large stone quarries nearby. A temple site and NOME capital, whose local deity, the jackal-headed WEPWAWET, became one of the guardians of the Osirian UNDERWORLD.

ATBARA

A tributary of the NILE, rising in Ethiopia and joining the main stream at Atbara, north of Khartoum.

ATEN *or* ATON *or* ADON

In Egyptian mythology, the disc of the sun, its brilliantly visible aspect, as distinct from its mystical, creative aspects, which are linked with AMUN, the 'hidden god'. Aten, on the other hand, was there for all to see and was taken by the AKHENATEN as a universal god. The EIGHTEENTH-DYNASTY cult of Aten was linked to solar cults in neighbouring countries. At this time, numerous temples to Aten were built, to be later demolished. *See also* RA.

ATET *or* MERSEKHNET

In Egyptian mythology, a goddess who was associated with HERSHEF. She was a cat goddess and in her cat form was called Maau. *See also* Part One: Chapter 14.

ATON *see* **ATEN**.

ATUM *or* **TUM**
In Egyptian mythology, the local god of the DELTA city of HELIOPOLIS, represented in human form and originally seen as creator of the world. He absorbed a primitive myth about KHEPERA, the beetle god. The priests of Heliopolis then joined his cult with that of RA, the universal sun-god, with the name of Atum-Ra, during the Second Dynasty. *See also* COSMOLOGY.

AVARIS
The site in the eastern DELTA, close to PIRAMESSE, where the HYKSOS kings established their first base before establishing themselves at MEMPHIS.

B

BA
An Egyptian term approximating to 'soul', one of the five elements constituting the human being. The ba was present at the weighing of its owner's heart after DEATH, and it was represented as a human-headed bird flying between the two worlds of life and AFTERLIFE.

BAAL
A creator god imported into Egyptian mythology from Asia in the Eighteenth Dynasty. 'Baal' means 'god', 'lord', 'owner' or 'master' and was applied to the chief or ruler of one of the primitive groups of nameless deities. In Egypt he was worshipped at Tanis and Memphis.

BACIS *see* BAKH.

BADARIAN PERIOD *see* PRE-DYNASTIC PERIOD.

BAKH
In Egyptian mythology, a bull that was worshipped in Upper Egypt. The Greek form of his name was Bacis.

BAKHTEN, PRINCE OF
An historical character (probably the Hittite king, HATTUSILIS) who features in a

legend that survived in a PAPYRUS of the Ramessid period, which relates the story of a miraculous cure brought about by KHONSU (*see* Part One: Chapter 15).

BAKING
Baking in the OLD KINGDOM was done in small ovens or by using heated stones. By the ELEVENTH and TWELFTH Dynasties, baking was practised on an almost industrial scale, with large bakeries, often with a brew house attached. Grain brought from the GRANARY was milled by hand, and dough was prepared in vats that were large enough for the maker to stand in and tread the dough with his feet. Loaves were baked both as flat cakes and in pottery moulds. In such places the arrival of raw material and the output of bread was carefully supervised and recorded, and from such establishments whole estates, or garrisons, would have been supplied.

BANEBTETTU
In Egyptian mythology, a ram god who was worshipped at MENDES. *See* Part One: Chapter 14.

BASTET *or* BAST
In Egyptian mythology, a CAT-headed goddess, guardian of the DELTA area, with her centre of cult at BUBASTIS.

BATA
In Egyptian mythology, the main protagonist in the legend of 'The Peasant who became King' (*see* Part One: Chapter 4).

BEE
The ancient emblem of LOWER EGYPT, associated with the DELTA town of BUTO.

BEER
The staple drink of the common people, taken at any time of day. The Egyptians made beer in various ways. One method was to allow lightly baked bread to ferment in water. Another method was based on the use of dates. The end-product was a thickish liquid, low in alcohol but high in food value.

BEN-BEN
A truncated OBELISK set on a podium in the temple of the sun-god at HELIOPOLIS, a fetish object representing the sun as creator and also set up in other SUN TEMPLES. This primitive object is the source of much of the symbolism of Egyptian architecture, including the PYRAMIDS.

BENI HASAN

The capital of the Oryx NOME in UPPER EGYPT, with large limestone deposits and tombs of governors. These rock tombs are among the finest of the MIDDLE KING-DOM period.

BENNU

In Egyptian mythology, a great bird deity that was worshipped as sacred at Herakleopolis. It is probably identified with the phoenix, the legendary Arabian bird that is said to set fire to itself and to rise from the ashes every five hundred years. It was depicted as resembling an eagle and had feathers of red and gold.

BENTRASH

A daughter of the Prince of Bakhten who features in a legend that survived in a papyrus of the Ramessid period, which relates the story of a miraculous cure brought about by KHONSU (*see* Part One: Chapter 15).

BERLIN SYSTEM *or* MINIMUM SYSTEM

A system of establishing the CHRONOLOGY of ancient Egypt, which favoured a shorter chronology than that established by Flinders PETRIE, who was very much influenced by MANETHO.

BES

A grotesque-looking war god who may have been introduced into Egyptian my-thology in the Twelfth Dynasty but came to prominence during the Eighteenth Dynasty. He was depicted as a dwarf with long arms and crooked legs and a broad, flat face with thick lips. In his other form as Sepd he was given a hand-some body and leonine face. *See also* Part One: Chapter 24.

BETHSHAMESH *see* ON.

BIRD LIFE

Egypt abounded in bird species, and certain birds play a key part in Egyptian mythology, especially the falcon, identified with HORUS, and the ibis, identified with THOTH. Geese and ducks were the prime domesticated species, kept in large numbers for their eggs and for their fat, flesh and feathers. Cranes were caught in the wild and kept for fattening with the geese. Wild birds were hunted or trapped. Hunters waited eagerly for the winter arrival of migratory species from northern latitudes. Swans and pelicans were known but do not appear to have been numer-ous as they do not feature in sacrificial offerings. Ostriches, found in the desert, were hunted for their feathers and became very rare.

BLEMMYES
A southern desert people, a source of troops for OLD KINGDOM rulers.

BLUE NILE
The right-hand branch (looking north) of the NILE, which rises in the mountains of Ethiopia and joins the WHITE NILE at Khartoum.

BOAT *see* SHIPS AND SHIPBUILDING.

BOAT PIT
Stone-lined pits, often found close to OLD KINGDOM pyramids. Boat pits are either boat-shaped, perhaps to provide the dead king with a sky vessel in which to accompany the sun-god, or rectangular pits containing dismantled wooden BOATS, for the same purpose.

BOCCHORIS *see* TWENTY-FOURTH DYNASTY.

BOOK OF CAVERNS
A set of religious illustrations and texts found on the walls of royal tombs of the NEW KINGDOM period. They show the progress of RA through the six caverns of the UNDERWORLD.

BOOK OF THE DEAD
A collection of New Kingdom and later funerary texts, on papyrus, found in tombs and often placed within the wrappings or between the legs of mummies. Based on the coffin texts, which go back to the Sixth Dynasty, these writings are spells intended to ease the transition of the dead person into the afterworld. There are some ninety 'chapters' altogether, and some versions are very finely written and beautifully illustrated, showing scenes of the dead undergoing judgement, worshipping the gods and at work in the fields of the underworld. Some of the texts are written on papyrus rolls up to 120 feet (37 metres) long, whilst others amount to a few scraps. The title, with its portentous ring, is inaccurate, and a better rendition would be the Book of Coming Forth By Day.

BOOK OF GATES
Another work of religious literature from the NEW KINGDOM, found on sarcophagi and tomb walls. It too is a collection of charms and spells to aid the deceased to get past WEPWAWET.

BOOK OF WHAT IS IN THE UNDERWORLD
The collective name for a set of funerary texts that originated in the MIDDLE

KINGDOM and reached their most definitive form during the NEW KINGDOM reign of AMENOPHIS I. They provide a description of the UNDERWORLD, showing the passage of the sun-god RA through the hours of the night, together with guidance as to the rituals that ensure safe passage into it. Versions of it are found in both royal and private tombs up to the end of the dynastic period.

BOOMERANG
The Egyptians possessed a throwing stick similar to the Australian boomerang and used for the same purposes – hunting and sport.

BRONZE
This metal, a compound of COPPER and tin, came into use in Egypt during the later MIDDLE KINGDOM, and Egypt remained a Bronze Age culture even when iron was in extensive use by neighbouring countries.

BUBASTIS
A religious site in the Nile Delta, nome capital and seat of the cult of the cat-goddess Bastet.

BUDGE, SIR [Earnest Alfred Thompson] WALLIS (1857–1934)
British Egyptologist who made sixteen official visits to Egypt from 1886, purchasing finds for the British Museum. He also worked at Aswan and translated the AMARNA Letters.

BUSIRIS
A religious site and nome capital in the Delta, a focus of the cult of Osiris, where a tree was kept as a fetish object, supposedly the tree against which his coffin was washed up. Eventually it was overshadowed by Abydos, where the god's heart was said to be buried.

BUTO
In Egyptian mythology, patron snake-goddess of LOWER EGYPT, to whom the cobra was sacred. Her original cult centre was the town and NOME capital of the same name, situated on a coastal lagoon in the northern DELTA. She was also called WADJET. Snake-goddesses were usually seen as benign, perhaps because of the snake's useful function of eating rats and other vermin.

BYBLOS
A port on the Syrian coast, which was used from early times by Egyptian sailors, and where numerous ancient Egyptian relics have been discovered. In the OSIRIS legend, his coffin chest was washed ashore there.

C

CALENDAR

From a very early time, the Egyptians had a form of calendar based on the phases of the moon. From around the end of the Second Dynasty (*see* FIRST AND SECOND DYNASTIES), they developed a more accurate calendar that divided the year into 365 days. Their new year began with the arrival of the INUNDATION at MEMPHIS, and was more precisely marked by the heliacal rising of the bright star SIRIUS (SOTHIS). It was divided into three seasons, each of four months lasting thirty days. There were five 'extra' days, designated as feast days and spread throughout the year. As they made no provision for a leap year, the calendar and the seasons drifted out of step, and by the end of the OLD KINGDOM there was a discrepancy of five months.

The invention of the calendar has been seen as one of the great Egyptian contributions to human knowledge. *See also* ASTRONOMY.

CAMBYSES

Persian king, the son of Cyrus the Great, who succeeded his father in 529 BC and invaded and conquered Egypt in 526 BC, thus establishing the TWENTY-SEVENTH DYNASTY (the first Persian occupation).

CANAAN

The ancient land that lay between the River Jordan and the Mediterranean Sea (modern coastal Israel and Syria), which was overcome by the Hebrews returning from Egypt about 1200 BC.

CANALS

Canals were relatively easy to dig in the alluvial soil of the NILE Valley and DELTA, but the Egyptians also attempted to cut canals through more intractable country, including the first cataract of the Nile, where evidence can still be seen of their effort to cut a channel through the rock. Sesostris III, in the MIDDLE KINGDOM, was able to proceed by BOAT all the way to the second cataract on his expedition to push back the Nubians. The most ambitious canal venture was the attempt made by the TWENTY-SIXTH-DYNASTY king, Necho II, to cut a waterway from the Mediterranean Sea, via the Damietta branch of the Nile, to the Red Sea, anticipating the Suez Canal by some 2,500 years. This work was completed under the Persian suzerainty of DARIUS I.

CANOPIC JAR

A jar sealed with a mud-paste cap in the OLD KINGDOM and with a cap carved like a human head in the MIDDLE KINGDOM, and with the heads of the four sons of HORUS (AMSET, HAAPI, DUAMUTEF and KEBEH-SENUF) in the later NEW KINGDOM. Four jars were used for preserving the entrails of the mummified dead. It was apparently so called from the town of Canopus, on the sea coast of the DELTA, but this is a modern connection without historical verification.

CAPITALS

Egyptian COLUMNS had two distinctive types of capital, whether carved or decorated. One is known as the bud-form or bell-form capital, based on the lotus bud, and the other the spreading capital, based on the open lotus flower. These two types can be seen clearly in the design of the HYPOSTYLE HALL at KARNAK, where the 'master' columns are of the open form and the 'minor' ones of the closed form. *See also* ARCHITECTURE, COLUMN, TEMPLE.

CARCHEMISH

An ancient city on the west bank of the Euphrates, which was held by the MITANNI and later the Hittites and was captured by THUTHMOSIS III and later by the Assyrians. It was the scene of the battle in 605 BC in which NEBUCHADNEZZAR defeated Necho II (*see* TWENTY-SIXTH DYNASTY) and destroyed Egyptian power in Asia.

CARNARVON, LORD [George Edward Stanhope Molyneux, 5th Earl of Carnarvon] (1866–1923)

British aristocrat and passionate amateur Egyptologist, who, on the advice of MASPERO, sponsored the excavations of Howard CARTER at THEBES. Before the First World War, these led to the discovery in 1908 of a 'king's son' of the Eighteenth Dynasty, in 1909 of a small funerary temple of Hatshepsut and in 1910 of a rich tomb of the Twelfth Dynasty containing a precious casket and gaming board. After the First World War, work at Thebes continued and culminated in the discover of the tomb of TUTANKHAMUN.

CARPENTRY

In the PRE-DYNASTIC and THINITE PERIODS, there may still have been woodlands with hardwood trees, but whether the timber used was native or imported, Egyptian woodworking reached a very high standard at an early stage. Wood was cut, jointed, shaped, inlaid and polished with techniques and results that rival anything achieved since. The Egyptians mastered the principle of concealed joints and could manufacture a form of plywood. A full range of household furniture was produced, from doors to beds, stools, tables and chests, as well as smaller wooden items like game boards. Many of the carpenter's implements were made of stone; the plane, for example, was not known and surfaces were levelled and smoothed with polishing stones. Axes, adzes and chisels, of stone or COPPER, were the main tools. Copper saws came into use during the early dynastic period, including large pull saws. Hand drills with FLINT blades were widely used. *See also* SHIPS AND SHIPBUILDING.

CARTER, HOWARD (1874–1939)

British painter and Egyptologist, who first went to Egypt at the age of seventeen. In 1892 he joned PETRIE at AMARNA and later worked at BENI HASAN. In 1893, he worked at DEIR EL-BAHRI, remaining there six years. In 1902 he began excavating in the VALLEY OF THE KINGS, where he discovered the tombs of HATSHEPSUT (as sovereign) and Thuthmosis IV. After working for five years as a watercolourist in England, he returned to Egypt in 1908 to supervise CARNARVON's excavations at THEBES. On 4 November 1922, he discovered the tomb of TUTANKHAMUN, with its treasures still intact. It took him ten years to record and transport down the Nile the extraordinary wealth of treasures he had found.

CARTOUCHE

Around the start of the THIRD DYNASTY, the practice arose of enclosing a king's name, and sometimes his whole set of ceremonial titles, in a cartouche, or drawn oval frame, set on a square base. To the Egyptians, this oval represented the elliptical course of the sun around the world and defined the limits of the kingdom that it lit. In the NEW KINGDOM the cartouche was also used as an amulet, evidently to prevent demons from devouring the name of the dead.

CAT

Cat cemeteries have been found at BUBASTIS in the DELTA and at Beni Hasan in UPPER EGYPT, where mummified cats were buried in very large numbers. These localities had CAT temples, and regarded the animals as sacred. *See also* ANIMAL CULTS.

CATARACTS

Sections of the River NILE where there are rapids and waterfalls created by hard bands of granitic rock and making obstructions to easy transport on the river. There were six sets of CATARACTS, stretching upriver from ASWAN, at the Nubian border, far into what is now SUDAN.

CHAMPOLLION, JEAN-FRANÇOIS (1790–1832)

French Egyptologist, who first analysed the hieroglyphic script of ancient Egypt in an epoch-making lecture to the Académie Française on 22 September 1822. His further work was published as *Monuments d'Egypte et Nubie*, and a *Grammaire Egyptien*, which was published posthumously in 1835.

CHANCELLOR

The Controller of the Seal – a very senior official of the royal court, whose responsibilities included tax levying and collection, and being paymaster general to the ARMY and navy. The two treasuries, the White House of UPPER EGYPT and the Red House of LOWER EGYPT, were under his supervision. At times both Lower and Upper Egypt would have separate chancellors. *See also* ECONOMY, TRADE.

CHEMISTRY

The derivation of the word has been traced by some back to the *khemet*, or 'black land', of Egypt. Drugs, perfumes and ointments were prepared in temple laboratories for all manner of purposes, from purifying and anointing statues to sweetening the breath. The Egyptians also became expert in the refining and combining of precious metals, developing processes for enamelling, gilding and casting.

CHEOPS *or* KHUFU

A PHARAOH of the FOURTH DYNASTY (between 2625 and 2510 BC) for whom the Great Pyramid at GIZA was constructed.

CHEPHREN *or* KHEPHREN *or* KHAFRA

A PHARAOH of the FOURTH DYNASTY (between 2625 and 2510 BC) whose PYRAMID is found close to that of CHEOPS, at GIZA. Chephren also had the Great SPHINX carved, as a guardian figure for his funerary site.

CHILDREN

There were many worse places to be a child than in ancient Egypt. The normal tenor of life was calm and peaceful, the DIET was usually varied and adequate, the climate encouraged a life out of doors, in the shade of a reed awning by a hut or the shady inner courtyard of a house with its tree-lined pool. The Egyptians were kind to their children, and in their society there were none of the rites of mutilation or ordeal that among many communities marked the passage into the adult world. Although boys enjoyed more status than girls, the Egyptians did not practise the killing of unwanted female children by exposure. Childhood was short, however. Puberty came early and a girl might be married and have her first child by the age of twelve or thirteen. By the age of sixteen, a boy came officially into manhood and could hold administrative and priestly positions. *See also* EDUCATION.

CHILDBIRTH

Since all recorded contemporary evidence from ancient Egypt is produced by men, the information on childbirth is scanty. Births took place within the family home, with the assistance of a midwife. A birthing stool was used for the mother to squat on, her baby passing through a hole in the seat into the hands of the midwife. The umbilical cord was cut with a knife of obsidian, and the placenta was sometimes buried at the doorstep but sometimes may also have been eaten, or partly eaten, by the mother.

CHRONOLOGY

Working out the time scale of ancient Egypt is a complex business. Our numbering of PHARAOHS as AMENOPHIS I or THUTHMOSIS I, II, and so on, was not practised by the Egyptians, who gave each of their kings a full and distinctive set of names. Egyptian scripts number the years from the start of the current king's reign, but we know nothing about their birth dates or the length of most reigns and so cannot simply use the kings' lives to count back to some original starting point. For early Egyptologists, the evidence of texts, combined with (for the LATE PERIOD) cross-references to the Bible, were the prime means of dating events in ancient Egypt. More recently, the contents of RUBBISH MOUNDS have been studied as closely as tomb walls. The scientific dating techniques of modern archaeology, based on measuring river erosion and deposits, on aerial photography, including infrared photography, and measuring the age of artefacts through radiocarbon dating and potassium-argon dating, have brought much greater precision into this area, but there are still uncertainties.

CIRCUMCISION

Male circumcision was practised throughout the OLD and MIDDLE KINGDOM periods, not in babyhood but between the ages of six and twelve. HERODOTUS reported that it was done for reasons of hygiene. There is no textual evidence of female circumcision, and no circumcised female mummies have been found.

CITIES

Ancient Egypt possessed no cities in the sense of great metropolitan centres with a mass of population, with the possible exception of THEBES and MEMPHIS, until the rise of ALEXANDRIA under Greek rule. The population was distributed throughout the long, narrow country, reflecting the agricultural basis of Egyptian life. The largest towns were the royal capitals like Memphis and Thebes, or major cult centres like HELIOPOLIS. But their growth was limited by the lack of transport other than river transport, the perishability of produce and the availability of good water. In the hot CLIMATE of Egypt, the close-packed network of narrow town streets, with the ubiquitous rubbish heaps picked over by dogs, donkeys and rats, must often have been smelly and unsalubrious.

CLEOPATRA (69–30 bc)

The last independent ruler of ancient Egypt (ruled 51–30 BC). She was not an Egyptian but a Greek, descended from Ptolemy Lago, the first Greek emperor. By her father's will she should have shared the throne with her brother but was ousted by his supporters. By this time Egypt had come within the sphere of influence of pre-Imperial Rome, and the dictator Julius Caesar took Cleopatra's side and restored her to the throne. She bore Caesar a son, Cesarion. Later she became the lover of Mark Antony and sided with him against Octavius, who defeated them at the naval battle of Actium. Cleopatra opened negotiations with Octavius (Emperor Augustus) but to no avail, and, after learning of Mark Antony's suicide, she took her own life. Egypt became a colony of Rome, as a fief of the emperor. *See also* PTOLEMAIC DYNASTY.

CLEOPATRA'S NEEDLE

The name given to two OBELISKS that were originally set up at HELIOPOLIS by THUTHMOSIS III. One was brought to England in 1878 and set up on the Thames Embankment in London. The other was taken to New York in 1880 and stands in Central Park.

CLIMATE

The climate of Egypt is generally hot and dry. The DELTA area, influenced by the Mediterranean Sea, has a mean summer temperature in the 25–35°C band, whilst in the NILE Valley proper, with arid desert on each side, it rises to 40°C and more. The days are typically clear and cloudless. As in all subtropical desert climates, nights can be cold, even below freezing in exposed regions. A beneficial aspect of the desert winds was that even in the marshy areas of the Delta and the Valley, malaria was unknown.

COFFIN TEXTS

Funerary inscriptions made on sarcophagi, usually formulae forming part of the ritual established to ensure that the spirit of the deceased passed successfully through to the AFTERWORLD. These date from the SIXTH DYNASTY, later than the PYRAMID TEXTS, and they are found not only on the tombs of kings, indicating that by this time knowledge of the precious, secret spells had spread to a wider, if still aristocratic, group. There are over 1,000 spells recorded. *See also* BOOK OF THE DEAD.

COLOSSAL STATUES

The origin of the vastly larger than life statues of PHARAOHS can be traced to their semi-godlike status and the political cult of kingship that made the most of this traditional view for the benefit of the ruling dynasty. Something comparable can be seen also in the 'perspective' of Egyptian painting, which accords greater stature to the most important personages depicted. This sense of scale based on status, together with the serenity exhibited by the colossal statues such as those of RAMESES II, prevent these superhuman sculptures from seeming completely megalomaniac in purpose and expression. Most statues were, if anything, smaller than life size.

COLOSSI OF MEMNON

Two COLOSSAL STATUES carved in the reign of Pharoah AMENOPHIS III of the EIGHT-EENTH DYNASTY as guardian figures to his MORTUARY TEMPLE at Malkata on the west bank of the NILE, at THEBES. The Greeks confused, or assimilated, Amenophis with their mythical hero Memnon, a king of Ethiopia who was killed by Achilles in the Trojan War and who figures in the *Iliad*, and believed that Memnon was buried there. An earthquake in 27 BC opened cracks in the stone, in which dew formed during the chilly night. With the heat of day the moisture evaporated and expanded, creating a moaning sound that impressed the superstitious Greeks and led to the name 'the vocal Memnon'. The moaning stopped when the Roman Emperor Septimius Severus had the monuments repaired.

COLUMNS

These were vital features of Egyptian ARCHITECTURE, essential for any building of size in order to support the weight of a roof or upper storey. Columns cut in the rock tombs of BENI HASAN have sometimes been taken to prefigure the Greek Doric column. Their faces have been planed to present first eight, then sixteen facets, and the facets have been hollowed out to give extra effect to the edges. Doric columns were still two thousand years in the future, but in the LATE PERIOD the Greeks were close observers of Egyptian detail. The standard Egyptian column decreases slightly in girth from base to top, sits on a plain flat stone base, and it terminates in an abacus, or square slab, of the same width as the beam that it supports (a feature that is unusual in later columnar structures). The great columns of KARNAK are 60 feet (18 metres) high and 12 feet (4 metres) in diameter; the blocks they support are 36 feet (11 metres) long and 4 feet (122 centimetres) thick. There is no contemporary indication of how these structures could have been erected, but one theory is that the temple building was filled with earth, or sandbags, so that the height of the working floor rose as the height of the columns rose, with the great blocks gradually raised to the working level by wedges. *See also* TEMPLE.

CONCUBINAGE

In addition to a chief wife and a number of subordinate wives, a wealthy man might have a number of concubines, in circumstances similar to the harem of later, Ottoman times. Although of lower status than the official wives, the concubines might have considerable power in the harem, and there are examples of concubines' sons who attained the kingship.

CONCEPTION AND CONTRACEPTION

On the whole, the Egyptians sought to have large families, partly because of the high infant mortality rate, which meant that only a few would survive, partly because a numerous progeny reflected credit on both parents, but perhaps especially the father. Fertility, the gift of OSIRIS, was prized, and sterility, by the same token, was considered more than unfortunate. A childless wife (the wife was invariably held responsible) was likely to be returned to her father. There were many more nostrums and prescriptions for aiding conception than for preventing it, and the Egyptians also developed their own forms of pregnancy tests to confirm the good news. Potency was regarded as necessary for full enjoyment of the AFTERLIFE as well as the present. Nevertheless, contraception was also practised, although the measures prescribed were more bizarre than efficacious, being based on magic rather than science, with considerable use of CROCODILE droppings.

COPPER

The principal metal used by the Egyptians. Copper was mined on the SINAI PENINSULA but in quite small quantities. Known from the beginning of the PRE-DYNASTIC PERIOD, it remained in short supply and was seen as a precious metal, but by the time of the pyramid-builders, it was common enough to be used for tools, although probably only the wealthiest or most talented of masons had copper chisels. Copper was used by sculptors in the SIXTH DYNASTY, from which we have a fine copper statue of PEPY I.

COPTIC

The language of the Egyptian Christians, in diminishing daily use until the eighteenth century and still preserved as a liturgical language. It has much altered elements of Egyptian, heavily admixed with ancient Greek, but was invaluable to the nineteenth-century Egyptologists in their efforts to decode the hieroglyphic script. *See also* CHAMPOLLION; LANGUAGE.

COPTOS *see* KOPTOS.

COSMETICS

Cosmetics were important both for decorative and for hygienic reasons. The Egyptians were especially concerned with emphasising the eyes, and kohl, made from the mineral galena, was used to lengthen the eyebrows and darken the eyelids, and to extend the outer corners of the eyes. It was used in powder form and applied with the finger or a flat instrument. Red ochre was used as rouge, and henna as a lightening dye for hair and nails. Scented oils and ointments were widely used. These were made and blended from a variety of ingredients, including almond oil, cinnamon, cardamoms, honey, olive oil, frankincense and myrrh, many of these imported down-river from NUBIA and Ethiopia as raw materials and refined and blended in Egyptian workshops. More basic pastes would also be made to help protect the skin of people who were obliged to work all day in the fields; it is unlikely that the Egyptians indulged in sunbathing. Cosmetics were used by both men and women. *See also* ORNAMENTATION.

COSMOLOGY

The ancient Egyptians' attitude to the heavens was not exploratory or analytical. They observed the patterns of the stars, moon and sun closely, and from the earliest times had framed legends and descriptions that sought to give the remote and unattainable sky some earthly parallels. Since the sky must have some support, they endowed it with four great pillars. These were seen sometimes as the legs of a cow, along the line of whose belly the sun travelled; sometimes as the arms and legs of the sky-goddess, NUT, whose naked form arched across the sky. The ancient Egyptian cosmologies, efforts to explain the source of the world, all start from the two immemorial aspects of life in Egypt – the annual flooding of the NILE, and the almost perpetual brilliance throughout the day of the sun. The first Egyptian cosmology is that of HELIOPOLIS, an ancient cult centre. In the beginning was the wild watery chaos called NUN, and from this the sun emerged, self-formed. He appeared on earth at Heliopolis in the form of a stone (the BENBEN stone was kept as a cult object in the temple there). This god was known as RA ('sun') or ATUM ('perfect being'). By the act of masturbation, Ra created from his own seed the god of air and dryness, SHU, and the goddess of wet, Tefnut. From their union came the god of earth, GEB, and the sky goddess, Nut. These in turn had four children, OSIRIS, ISIS, SETH and NEPHTHYS. These nine are known as the Great Ennead. Seth and Nephthys had no offspring, but Osiris and Isis were fertile.

The second great cosmology was that of Hermopolis (modern Ashmunein), a NOME capital of UPPER EGYPT about 210 miles (338 kilometres) south of Cairo. Again starting with a formless expanse of water, it endowed the water itself with creative power. Summoned by THOTH, the diety of Hermopolis, and at that very site, it brought forth four frogs and four serpents, which in combination produced an egg that they set upon a mound emerging from the water. From this egg was hatched the sun. The eight creatures formed an OGDOAD, a number of significance to the Egyptians. They were Nun (as in the Heliopolitan system) and his consort, Nunet, Heh and Hehet, flowing water, Keku and Keket, darkness, and AMUN and his consort, Amaunet, light.

Both the Heliopolitan and the Hermopolitan myths have ancient roots that reach far back into primitive and prehistoric African cultures. The third Egyptian cosmology is of a different sort. During the SECOND DYNASTY, when the rulers were based at MEMPHIS, a major effort was made to establish the local Memphite god, PTAH, as a major deity who should command the veneration of all the Egyptians. The Doctrine of Memphis asserted that Ptah was older than ATUM, coeval with the waters from which Atum emerged, and that he created Atum-Ra by a process of pure thought. This was an entirely political move, theologically unnecessary, and intended to supplant the supremacy of Heliopolis and Hermopolis. This cult of Ptah did not survive the THINITE PERIOD, though he remained a significant deity, patron especially of artists and writers, as suited his unusually abstract and intellectual theology. *See also* GODS, RELIGION, THEOLOGY.

COSTUME

The Egyptians had mastered the art of spinning cloth by the beginning of the dynastic period. Since they lived in a country that was almost always warm and often very hot, they did not need heavy garments. The basic garment was simply a loin cloth, worn originally by aristocrat and peasant alike, and many pictures suggest that nudity was not uncommon (although an observer of western art might make the same deduction, falsely). In the dynastic period, this evolved into a kilt-like garment for the nobility, whilst the great majority of the population continued to wear the loin cloth. For ceremonial occasions, priests or nobles wore a long robe, made of a single piece of cloth and reaching from the shoulder to the calf. From the MIDDLE KINGDOM on, they wore beneath it a close-fitting tunic. Women wore a more close-fitting robe that reached to the ankles. Very young CHILDREN wore no clothes; older children wore a version of adult costume. Linen was the prime dressmaking material; the Egyptians had been making it since the PRE-DYNASTIC PERIOD and brought its manufacture to a high art. Good clothes were consequently expensive, ranking high in the barter system, and were consequently often subject to theft. White was always the colour of formal clothing, and the Egyptians either did not master, or did not care to use, the techniques of dyeing linen. Instead they developed elaborate forms of pleating to display the quality of fine cloth. Personal ORNAMENTATION was important. This included wigs, as the heads, of men at least, were normally closely shaven during the OLD KINGDOM and later. Leatherwork was often very fine, with leather being used for sandals and belts, as well as being beaten and rolled out to provide a writing surface. Many people, however, went barefoot some or all of the time.

COURT LIFE

The court of a PHARAOH had many aspects, because every part of the country's life was here gathered into a single complex system and ultimately into a single personage, the pharaoh, the venerated god-king whose word was more than law, it was divine truth. The life of the court was stately and cermonious, with a number of religious services on each day and a procedure that, although in any one reign it may have seemed inflexible and unchanging, nevertheless evolved gradually as the dynasties passed, without, however, altering in its fundamental principles. The palace and its decorations and feasts were splendid and designed to overawe. Even although the pharaoh himself might be an ascetic, he lived in external magnificence in order to dramatise his difference to even the greatest of the nobility. The palace required a large staff to work effectively, but many of its higher functionaries were decorative, to provide society for the pharaoh and to add lustre to his retinue as he proceeded from place to place. The pharaohs divided their time between the two lands, with a residence in both LOWER and UPPER EGYPT, and the household was frequently on the move. Closest to the king, apart from his immediate family, were the HONOURED ONES, a circle of eminent advisers. Within this group some were awarded special titles of distinction, such as Unique Friend (*see* WENI). In the fixed hierarchical structure of the court, these titles were eagerly sought. Others bore titles of office, chief among them being the VIZIER, although his responsibilities were external rather than within the household. A formidable array of officials controlled all aspects of the PHARAOH'S DAY. His crown and jewels were looked after by the Lord of the Secret of the Royal House; his dress and ornamentation by the Director of the King's Dress, who in turn had a set of officials responsible for individual parts, like wigs, oils and footwear. The libraries, the kitchens, the gardens, all had their own hierarchy within the greater hierarchy. Each task, whether it was the washing of the pharaoh's hands or the tying of his shoes, must be performed by the appropriate functionary. The principal non-religious event of the day was the audience with the vizier, who reported on all matters relating to the administration of the kingdom. Each event was in charge of a master of protocol, whose business it was to see that tradition was not upset. In theory the king, as fountain of justice, was accessible to all his people, and his was the ultimate court of appeal. He alone could confirm a sentence of death.

The queen, the lesser queens and the royal harem had a staff of their own, just as elaborate as the king's but focused on the internal affairs of the women's quarters and the public role of the queens as consorts in attendance on all state occasions.

Despite the weight of protocol and tradition, there was scope for promotion within the ranks of the courtiers. Intelligence was useful, so long as it was not linked to subversiveness or excessive originality of mind. The ponderous framework of court life required a great deal of management and resourcefulness in crisis. An able courtier of fairly low beginnings might be given a number of tasks at different times, from leading a QUARRYING expedition and ensuring safe delivery of the stone to sitting in judgement on disputes among his peers or supervising a group of royal estates, or even acting as a general on a military raid. If he performed satisfactorily and showed himself to be thoroughly and utterly the king's man in every aspect of his life, he might end up as a Unique Friend, with his own royally provided tomb set in proximity to the ruler's own, so that in the AFTERLIFE he might continue to serve with the same devotion.

CREATION MYTH *see* PART ONE: CHAPTER 1.

CRIME AND PUNISHMENT
The need for civil order was instilled in the Egyptian consciousness from the very earliest times. The whole system of irrigation and cultivation required co-operation and harmony, and anything that disturbed the balance was deplored. Most crime was of a petty nature, punished by fines or by beating. Imprisonment was also used during the MIDDLE KINGDOM to punish those who evaded the annual forced labour. More serious crimes would be punished by mutilation or the infliction of a set number of wounds. No doubt these often led to death, but the death sentence itself was extremely rare in ancient Egypt. The most heinous crime was tomb robbing, which is by no means a modern activity. Its origins are almost as old as the practice of depositing valuable objects in the tomb, and all the Egyptians' reverence for the gods and the spirits of the departed did not deter tomb robbing. It was especially common in times of hardship and famine, and during the TWENTIETH and TWENTY-FIRST Dynasties it became an epidemic, and horrified priests were reduced to gathering up despoiled mummies and bundling them into secret caves. One such was discovered in the cliffs of the VALLEY OF THE KINGS in 1881 – there were 36 mummies piled in it. A TOMB ROBBER, if caught, could expect to have his ears and nose slit and to be impaled through the rectum on a pole.

CRIOSPHINX
A ram-headed Sphinx.

CROCODILE
This reptile lived in the NILE in substantial numbers, and the Egyptians treated it with great respect. One of the NOMES was called the Crocodile Nome. The god SETH was sometimes represented in crocodile form, but the crocodile is chiefly associated with the god SEBEK, who had a crocodile head, with a cult centre at Crocodilopolis (Greek: 'crocodile city') in the FAIYUM, set up in the course of the

MIDDLE KINGDOM. Sacred crocodiles were kept here, and preserved in a crocodile NECROPOLIS.

CROWN

The crown was an important part of the royal regalia, with strong symbolic value expressing the dualism and unity of the Egyptian kingdom. There were two crowns, the Red Crown of Lower Egypt and the White Crown of Upper Egypt, the colours corresponding to other things emblematic of the original division. They could be worn separately or combined in a single crown, the Double Crown.

CUBIT

A linear unit of MEASUREMENT. The Egyptian standard cubit was approximately 18 inches (46 centimetres), although there was also the royal cubit of approximately 20 inches (51 centimetres).

CURRENCY

Coinage was not used in ancient Egypt until the First Persian Occupation. *See also* TRADE, WEIGHTS AND MEASURES.

CYRUS THE GREAT

The founder of the Persian empire and its ruler 548–529 BC. He conquered Babylon and 539 BC. His son, Cambyses extended his empire into Egypt in 526 BC.

D

DAD

An amulet in the form of a fourfold altar that symbolised the backbone of Osiris and gave strength to the body and secured entrance to paradise. Amulets like the SCARAB, ANKH, etc, became increasingly popular during the NEW KINGDOM.

DAHSHUR

An important funerary site in the MEMPHIS area, on the west bank of the NILE, just south of SAQQARA. It has two PYRAMIDS built by SNOFRU (FIFTH DYNASTY) and the TWELFTH-DYNASTY pyramids of Ammenemes II, Sesostris III and Ammenemes III, who had another about 50 miles (80 kilometres) farther south, at Hawara.

DARIUS I

King of the Persians and, as suzerain of Egypt, the second pharaoh (522–486 BC) of the TWENTY-SEVENTH DYNASTY. During his reign coinage was introduced to Egypt. He visited Egypt to put down uprisings and completed the NILE-Red Sea CANAL. Darius also built temples in Egypt, re-opening the quarries at Wadi Hammamet in order to build a temple to AMUN-RA at the nearby el-Kargha oasis, and under his rule Egypt appears to have prospered.

DARIUS II *see* TWENTY-SEVENTH DYNASTY.

DEATH

The Egyptian attitude to death has fascinated every succeeding generation. So much of peoples' lives and energy in that sunlit, fertile land, so favoured by nature, was devoted to preparation for death and to the maintenance of entire towns of the dead, that the Egyptians were viewed as a morbid, gloomy, death-obsessed nation, stuck in a cul-de-sac of human thought and cosmological speculation. Yet there is ample evidence that the Egyptians were a cheerful people who appreciated and enjoyed the natural advantages their country possessed and who had time for the same celebrations and enjoyments of life as any other people, from harvest feasts to board games and dirty jokes. In a paradoxical way, their preoccupation with death may have stemmed from their enjoyment of life. Their awareness of life was exceptionally vivid and strong, not merely in the sense of being alive but in their perception of the sun-driven life force that animates the whole of nature. They were lovers of life, and because they loved it so much, life seemed all too brief. Just as they believed that certain creatures were born spontaneously from mud, created by the life force, so they also felt that the life force within themselves was not spent and exhausted on death; it carried on but in another form. Since they knew that life was short, and death was long, it seemed entirely reasonable to treat the brief period of life as the opportunity to prepare their long homes, where their spirits would reside for eternity.

The KA, or life force, was not the only element to constitute the human being. The Egyptians also distinguished the *AKH*, the link between the living person and the sun; the *HA*, an unbodied, independent entity that emanated from the power of its owner and was independent of the body (unlike the *ka*, which needed some physical form); and finally the name, which had a magic definitive power of its own that continued to identify the individual even after the body had disintegrated. All these attributes survived and had to be provided for in the tomb. *See also* AFTERLIFE, UNDERWORLD.

DEBEN

From the Ramessid time onwards, a standard weight, equivalent to about 3¹/4

ounces (91 grams), used for expressing values in trade. There was a COPPER, SIL-
VER and GOLD deben, in ascending order of value. *See also* MEASUREMENT.

DEDI

In Egyptian mythology, a wise old man and magician who features in the legend
of 'Dedi the Magician', which features Pharoah Khufu (CHEOPS) of the FOURTH
DYNASTY and also the birth of the first three kings of the FIFTH DYNASTY (*see* Part
One: Chapter 11).

DELTA

The great fan-shaped area of marshland intersected by waterways, over 100
miles (161 kilometres) long, between the two great arms into which the NILE di-
vides north of MEMPHIS before it eventually meets the sea. The Delta (so called
from its resemblance to the triangular shape of the Greek letter 'd') has been created through millennia by the soil and grit brought down by the river. As the river's speed drops, it can move less and less of this material, which sinks to the
river floor, and so the delta is gradually formed. Apart from the richness of the
soil, the region offered protection from overland raiding and ample building material in the form of the tall reeds used both for house and shipbuilding. It was in
the Delta area that Egyptian civilisation began, but the annual deposit of new soil
means that the earliest relics of life there are now far below ground level. *See
also* SHIPS AND SHIPBUILDING.

DEIR EL-BAHRI

The site of the EIGHTEENTH DYNASTY tomb of Queen HATSHEPSUT, and the PYRAMID
and temple of Mentuhotep, in the hills of the west bank of the NILE, opposite
THEBES.

DEIR EL-MEDINA

Dating from the Ramessid period, this is the site, a short distance south of DEIR
EL-BAHRI, of a well-preserved workmen's village for 120 artisans and their families. In the ELEVENTH DYNASTY it was a cemetery area, an extension of Deir el-
Bahri. When the VALLEY OF THE KINGS came into use as a place of burial, the village was set up, in the reign of THUTHMOSIS I. Its peak of activity was during the
NINETEENTH and TWENTIETH DYNASTIES, but activity continued until the TWENTY-
FIFTH DYNASTY, when a chapel to OSIRIS was erected. The site is of particular interest in what it reveals of the daily lives of skilled artisans and craftsmen, who
lived there and worked on the royal sites in ten-day shifts, with one day off. They
included scribes, draughtsmen, sculptors, wood-carvers, plasterers, masons and
stucco-workers, mostly Egyptian but with a leavening of foreigners from NUBIA,
Syria and LIBYA. The village was aligned on a north-south axis, with a guarded

gate at each end and a central roadway. The houses, set close to each other without gardens, were built of rough stone up to the 5-foot (1.5-metre) line, and then of mud brick, with mud plaster on a framework of wooden laths for a roof. The walls were painted white, the doors red. The front room had an altar built into the wall, for domestic rituals relating to ancestor cult and such deities as Bes, the god of fertility and CHILDBIRTH. The second room, larger and higher, was supported by a column, and its main piece of furniture was a couch. These were the 'public' rooms, with the family living quarters behind and a small subterranean storage room. The kitchen gave access to further cellar space and to the roof, which was substantial enough to be used as a terrace for relaxation in the evening. The kitchen had an oven, grindstones, mortars and jars, with stone knives and other implements. There was no water supply, no drainage, and water came by donkey from the nearest wells.

Adjoining the village at the north end are small cult chapels, each with space for a meeting room, then a little anteroom to the sanctuary and the sanctuary itself with a god's statue. Among the cults were those of HATHOR, AMUN and AMENOPHIS I. The workers had their own cemetery, with family tombs formed by an arched chamber of mud bricks. Later these were given a PYRAMID shape, which would have been seen as sacrilegious in the OLD KINGDOM. The tomb itself was underground, with a mortuary chapel above it. As far as they could, the workers reproduced the decoration, furniture and ornament of the royal tombs where they worked in the more modest tombs they built for themselves.

Provisions came from the store rooms of temples in the neighbourhood, and if these were inadequate, the workmen were liable to go on strike. Social life within the little community was introspective, and the records indicate a characteristic litany of minor crimes, adulteries and disturbances that suggest something other, and more normal, than a dedicated community where all is industry and harmony.

DEMOTIC

A speeded-up form of writing Egyptian (from Greek *demotikos*, 'popular'), introduced some 200 years after HIERATIC. Its characters are cursive and flowing, and far removed from the original pictorial basis of HIEROGLYPHICS.

DEN

A First-Dynasty king (ruled 3050–2995 BC), the first to be given the title 'he who belongs to the SEDGE and the BEE' (symbols of UPPER and LOWER EGYPT respectively). He was the first king to add a third name to his titulature. This was known as the *nsw-bity* name, or 'king of Upper and Lower Egypt' name, intended to emphasise his role as monarch of the entire country. He reclaimed swamp land in the FAIYUM. *See also* FIRST AND SECOND DYNASTIES.

DENDERA

The site in UPPER EGYPT, close to EDFU, of a major temple of the goddess HATHOR. A yearly festival linked the two sites, bringing the image of Hathor to Edfu to re-enact the conception of the young HORUS.

DENDROCHRONOLOGY

The science of dating timber and wooden structures.

DENG

A pygmy who was brought back to Egypt in the Sixth Dynasty from an expedition to Nubia. The pharoah, PEPY II, took a great interest in the Deng for he was believed to be able to charm the ferryman who transported the dead. *See also* Part One: Chapter 13.

DENTISTRY

Dentistry, in as far as it existed, was a department of medicine, not a separate science. The Egyptians' DIET, sugar-free and with quite a high fibrous content, was not injurious to the enamel of the teeth, and the dental problems that feature among the admittedly very sparse medical records left to us are more concerned with loose and missing teeth. The major dental problems were worn-down teeth and dental abscesses; few Egyptians can have avoided the pain of toothache. It is likely that the Egyptians cleaned their teeth with narrow 'brushes' made of fibry wood, or toothpicks, possibly with a paste whose aim would have been to sweeten the breath rather than to offer dental protection.

DIALOGUE OF A MAN WITH HIS SOUL, THE

A fragment of a PAPYRUS composition in which the lonely author bemoans his unhappy fate. *See* Part One: Chapter 18.

DIET

The Egyptians ate a single daily main meal at sunset. For the well-off, the diet was varied, with game of many sorts, such as the antelope, ibex and gazelle, and wild fowl from swamp or desert, although the staple meats were the farm-kept geese, beef, goat and mutton. Pork was regarded as unclean, with the pig placed in the realm of SETH. The rich also ate very little in the way of fish, which was also considered an unclean food, probably because of its rapid propensity to spoil. Among their vegetables were onions, leeks, garlic, beans, peas, lentils, carrots, turnips, spinach and radishes. Figs, dates, grapes and pomegranates were the principal fruits. Dried sea salt from the DELTA coast was shipped throughout the country, and there were rock-salt deposits also. Spices were widely used, then as now. Bread was baked in ovens or using specially heated flat stones. The diet of the peasants and serfs was less varied, with grains and pulses playing a major part, but they also ate fish without compunction.

DIODORUS SICULUS (*fl.* first century BC)
Greek historian who, in order to write a history of the world, travelled over a great part of Europe and Asia. His history, probably written after 8 BC, consisted of forty books, the first five of which mostly survive. They contain the early history of the Egyptians, Ethiopians and Greeks. The work has history, myth and fiction jumbled together.

DISEASE
The Egyptians were likely to meet their deaths through disease or the complications of disease rather than in any other way. Smallpox, leprosy and poliomyelitis were all uncurable killer diseases. Rheumatism and arthritis were common. The most common sexually transmitted disease was gonorrhea. Bilharzia and other waterborne diseases were passed on through contaminated NILE water, since all sorts of refuse, from the towns of NUBIA down, went into the river. Cuts, wounds and scrapes had a high likelihood of leading to sepsis and gangrene. *See also* MEDICINE.

DIVORCE *see* MARRIAGE CUSTOMS.

DJADJAT
A local council of elders and notables, advisers to the provincial governor as part of the LEGAL SYSTEM.

DJER
The second recorded pharoah of the First Dynasty (*see* FIRST AND SECOND DYNASTIES) who reigned at Memphis and maintained MENI's policies. His tomb at ABYDOS was one of great wealth.

DJOSER *or* **ZOSER**
THIRD-DYNASTY king who reigned at Memphis and for whom the Step PYRAMID at Saqqara was erected by IMHOTEP. Although little is known of this dynasty, Djoser probably waged war in the south, extended his territory below the first cataract and imposed rule firmly over the north.

DRINK
The Egyptians brewed BEER in various forms, notably by allowing specially made, part-cooked loaves of barley or wheat to ferment in water, and this formed the staple drink of the great mass of the people. Wine production, both red and

white, goes back to the origins of the OLD KINGDOM, and perhaps the PRE-DYNASTIC PERIOD, but the cost of production always made it a luxury item for the wealthy few. There were wine connoisseurs who appreciated a good wine and knew the best places to obtain it, although Egyptian wine contained resins for preservative or flavouring purposes

DROMOS
A processional way leading up to the entrance of a TEMPLE.

DUALISM
Egypt was formed from two kingdoms, and this fact was never forgotten. It became firmly imprinted on life and culture. The king wore the emblems of both, the BEE of LOWER EGYPT, and the lily (SEDGE) of UPPER EGYPT. The national institutions were duplicated, with a TREASURY (the Red House) for Lower Egypt, and another, the White House, for Upper Egypt. Similarly, each possessed a GRANARY, and the king had a palace in each. Kings from the THINITE PERIOD onwards usually had tombs built in each part of the country. The concept of opposites linked in a harmonious unity is also basic to much of Egyptian thought, as the story of OSIRIS and SETH shows. Such dualism does not imply an equal balance in the Egyptian mind. Horus would always triumph over Seth.

DUAMUTEF
In Egyptian mythology, one of the four sons of HORUS, who was depicted with a jackal's head on one of the four CANOPIC JARS used in FUNERARY PRACTICE. The lungs and heart were placed in this jar.

DUAT
A name for the UNDERWORLD. *See also* Part One: Chapter 12.

DYNASTY
A royal house, or a sequence of rulers, the successive families who inherited or took over the kingship. There were 30 dynasties, varying greatly in length, and some of them existing simultaneously with another. The reasons for separating the different dynasties are not always clear, and often there was at least some hereditary continuation from one to the next. Equally, there appear to be complete breaks of hereditary succession within certain dynasties. Location played a part, as the centre of power shifted up and down the NILE Valley. The dynasty lists have been handed down from the compilation of MANETHO and other contemporary sources, and as the science of Egyptology progresses, it may be that they will be discarded or revised as more accurate means of tracing the ruling families become available. *See individual entries.*

E

EARLY PRE-DYNASTIC PERIOD *see* PRE-DYNASTIC PERIOD.

ECONOMY

Egypt, especially in the formative period of the unitary state, was organised as a despotism. The king was all-powerful and, with a small group of his relatives and chosen administrators, imposed his will on every aspect of the people's lives. The entire country, its wealth and its population was his. His vast power was limited by the general respect for justice and the law, already a matter of ancient tradition, and religion, a matter of even more ancient tradition; and by the enduring political configuration of the country – the two Egypts, the NOMES, the regional and provincial loyalties of the population. Unlike later despots, the pharaoh did not have a large standing ARMY at his disposal, but he did have on his side custom, tradition and a more than earthly prestige. He was also owner of great estates in his own right, and of even more as high priest, since the temples came to be the second-greatest landowner after the crown, and also any unallocated or conquered land was in his gift. He controlled imports, exports, mining, quarrying and metalworking, and he levied taxes. Taxation was the responsibility of an official known as the CHANCELLOR, a deputy of the VIZIER, whose court title was Controller of the Seal, and he had two great central TREASURIES or storehouses, the Red Treasury of LOWER EGYPT, in the DELTA, and the White Treasury of UPPER EGYPT, at MEMPHIS. In a country with no coinage, taxation was a matter of payment in kind. The fiscal storehouses were extraordinary places that took in every kind of produce and manufactured article, although corn, dates, flour and hides must have formed the great bulk of it. A substantial and efficient distribution network was necessary in order to redistribute this hoard of goods, often perishable, to the court, the temples, the tomb cities and other recipients of the king's largesse. The chancellor and his staff computed the tax levels using a number of different criteria. By far the most important among these were the level of the last INUNDATION and the consequent agricultural yield that could be anticipated – an over-generous flood could be as disastrous as a meagre one. The chancellor's taxes had also to be enough to finance whatever plans the king might have, whether a foreign expedition or a PYRAMID to excel all others; and, as many projects lasted for many years, he had to think far ahead. He was aided by a well-established system of inspections and censuses, the Egyptian passion for making lists proving useful in such connections. His department needed extensive records, since many temples and funerary estates had tax privileges of one kind or another (*see* LAND OWNERSHIP).

Since the court, the government and the state were an indissolubly single entity, the government could never go bankrupt. Except in times of emergency, economic management was not a requirement, and in times of emergency it broke down. The chancellor and his army of clerks and inspectors set and supervised the rules for barter, and collected their quota of tax in every form. The economy, self-sufficient in so many respects, worked on almost independently, driven by the engine of the NILE and the apparently unlimited natural resources of the country. *See also* TRADE.

EDFU

An ancient site in UPPER EGYPT, south of THEBES, on the western bank of the NILE. Human habitation here has been dated far back into the Palaeolithic age. In dynastic times it was famed as a centre of the cult of HORUS, its temple the home of the TRIAD of Horus, Hathor and their child, Horus-Harakhte, the rising sun. At one time it was thought to be the source of the Horus cult, before that was traced back to the DELTA. The temple at Edfu was last reconstructed by the Ptolemaic kings in the post-dynastic period, and it remains exceptionally well preserved, with circuit wall, courtyard, HYPOSTYLE HALL and sanctuary. The Greeks called Edfu Apollinopolis, equating Horus with their own sun-god, Apollo.

EDUCATION

Most Egyptians had no formal education. They were illiterate and only basically numerate, as might be required by a particular trade. They acquired their skills and knowledge through handed-down wisdom and stories, through example and observation, and through personal experience. Among the wealthy, education in the intellectual sense would be provided only for the sons (although the deity of writing was a goddess, Seshat). The daughters, in the seclusion of the women's quarters, would learn domestic skills and graces, music and expressive dance, but not normally to read, write or deal with numbers. In the OLD and MIDDLE KINGDOMS, families normally employed tutors, trained scribes, to teach the boys, and this remained the norm for the upper levels of society. During the Middle Kingdom, schools were set up within the temples as part of the wide-ranging functions of these institutions. The pupils would be the sons of members of the official class, destined themselves to follow in their fathers' footsteps as clerks of works, tax inspectors or land surveyors. Their lessons were taken up with copying and re-copying classic texts, and chanting by rote, in a narrow curriculum that did not go beyond reading, writing and arithmetic. It was doubtless very tedious, and the trainee scribes were frequently beaten to encourage them, as well as being warned that if they failed to stay the course, manual labour, poverty and annual forced work on building sites awaited them. The methods of teaching explain the conventionality of much of Egyptian literary writing, the recurrence of identical phrases and word structures going straight back to the wearily assimilated thought patterns drubbed into the writers at school.

EGG

In Egyptian mythology, a symbol of the creation. *See also* Part One: Chapter 5.

EGYPT

The country occupying the NILE Valley, below the first cataract. Its extraordinary shape was dictated by the river: 750 miles (1,207 kilometres) long, but hardly more than 30 miles (48 kilometres) wide at its broadest, except on the Mediterranean coast, where the delta spread out to over 100 miles (161 kilometres). The Nile was both the country's reason for being and its defining feature. The word 'Egypt' is Greek, and in the *Iliad*, Homer takes it first to mean 'the great river' and secondarily the country, expressing the sense that the country was the gift of the river. The empty desert and scrub that stretched away for thousands of miles west and hundreds of miles east also helped in the formation of Egypt as a political unit, by creating a wide barrier between it and the states that arose simultaneously or later in the Near East and in Africa. The borders of ancient Egypt were never fully defined and shifted according to circumstances. The SINAI Peninsula, for example, was not at first regarded as Egypt but as an empty zone. In the imperial expansion of the NEW KINGDOM, the Egyptians boasted that their frontier was at the Euphrates, far off in Mesopotamia.

EGYPTIANS

The NILE Valley has been inhabited by man and his ancestors for more than a million years. Remains found near the temples of ABU SIMBEL in NUBIA date far back into the Old Stone (Palaeolithic) Age, some 700,000 years. Around 25,000 years ago, climatic changes were bringing about the vast growth of the Sahara Desert, and peoples who had lived in that region moved eastwards, in the process becoming fishers as well as hunters. Around 6000 BC permanent signs of AGRICULTURE can be traced. In the PRE-DYNASTIC PERIOD, it was occupied by early peoples both from North Africa and East Africa, followed by Semitic nomads from Asia.

EGYPTOLOGY

The scholarly study of ancient Egypt in all its aspects. For 1,700 years, the relics of ancient Egypt were disturbed only by tomb breakers in search of precious metals and by travellers, who admired or deplored but understood very little. In the seventeenth and eighteenth centuries, a number of European savants became interested in the fragmentary remains (still far more than we see today) and drew plans of certain sites. The English mathematician John Greaves published the first book devoted wholly to the PYRAMIDS in 1646. It was the French army's expedition to Egypt, under Napoleon Bonaparte, in 1799 that galvanised the process. Although it was part of a war campaign, a smaller ARMY of scholars, surveyors and scientists went with the main force, and the result of their work was the huge *Description de l'Egypte*. Masses of documents and artefacts were gathered and studied. By 1822, CHAMPOLLION had penetrated the secrets of HIEROGLYPHICS, and the ancient civilisation began to reveal itself in detail. The result was an ever-growing demand for Egyptian artefacts from the many new museums established in western capitals. The process by which these items were acquired was little short of looting, although in theory it was officially controlled. Since the Napoleonic expedition, France has been in the vanguard of Egyptological studies, and Auguste MARIETTE was the first great fieldworker, although his methods were crude and arbitrary. However, he persuaded the authorities to set up the National Antiquities Service, with the aim of stopping the flood of antiquities out of the country and of setting up a properly managed national collection. Mariette's successors, Brugsch and MASPERO, and the British archaeologist Sir Flinders PETRIE laid the basis of modern Egyptology around the turn of the nineteenth century. Major discoveries were still to be made, including AMARNA (1914), the tomb of TUTANKHAMUN (1922), the great boat of CHEOPS (1954), and more will undoubtedly follow. Egyptologists of all nations campaigned to prevent the immersion of some of the greatest monuments of NUBIA when the ASWAN High Dam was built in the 1960s. Egyptology is still a young science, and its true purpose is not to unearth fabulous, heroic monuments of the past but to use every modern technique, including radiocarbon dating, aerial photography, computer analysis and projection, to establish the details of the beginnings, progressive stages and end of the great civilisation. That beginning, with each new discovery, is pushed further and further into the remote past.

EIGHTEENTH DYNASTY

The first dynasty (1552–1314/1295 BC) of the NEW KINGDOM. The first king was AHMOSIS, who reigned 1552–1526 BC. Having driven the HYKSOS from Egypt, the king turned his attention southwards and set out to regain NUBIA from the local rulers. After three campaigns he succeeded, and then took his ARMY into Palestine, where he annexed the ports of the Phoenician coast, which were strategically placed for Egypt's timber imports. Ahmosis married his sister Nefertari, a popular queen whose cult was followed for some centuries after her death. Their son, AMENOPHIS I, succeeded in 1526 BC and continued the pushing outwards of Egypt's frontiers, and by the beginning of the following reign, it was stated that

Egypt's border was the River Euphrates. Amenophis I was followed by Thuthmosis I (reigned 1506–1493 BC), son of a concubine, who reinforced his claim to the throne by marrying his half-sister. His son, Thuthmosis II, had to fight down revolts in the occupied lands. He died, leaving a six-year-old son by a concubine and two daughters by his queen. The boy was Thuthmosis III, but the regency was assumed by his aunt, Hatshepsut (ruled 1478–1458 BC), wife and half-sister to Thuthmosis II. Hatshepsut proclaimed herself pharaoh and assumed the full honours of the position. During her rule, the focus of government was switched to internal administration, and the generals, who had gained a taste for campaigning abroad and accumulating rich tribute from the conquered tribesmen, became restive and hostile. On the death, or perhaps the deposition, of Hatshepsut, Thuthmosis III eventually acceded to the throne and became an extremely active military ruler, the greatest general among the kings of Egypt. His rule was spent almost entirely on campaign (17 in all) or on inspections of his growing empire. The record of his victories is found on the walls of Karnak, which received much of the booty. Under Thuthmosis III the conquests of the Egyptians became more organised. He brought the sons of Syrian noblemen back to Thebes, both as hostages for their fathers' good behaviour and to be taught the lifestyle and manners of the Egyptian nobility. As the power of Egypt spread farther, the opposition grew stronger. Thuthmosis III overcame numerous coalitions of enemy states and floated his army on rafts across the Euphrates to defeat the powerful Mitanni on their own territory. Egypt by this time was the greatest power in her own world (they were unaware of the existence of China). Tribute was received from Babylon, from Assyria, from the Hatti and Mitanni kingdoms, from Crete and other Mediterranean islands. Within Africa he pushed farther south than any pharaoh before him. No doubt remembering his own long frustration, he made his son, Amenophis II, co-ruler in the year before his death. Amenophis II (ruled 1425–1401 BC) was a man of great physical stature and as warlike as his father, maintaining the empire with a ferocity untypical of the Egyptians as a whole. He was followed by Thuthmosis IV (ruled 1401–1390 BC), who, in a break with tradition, took as his wife a foreign princess, Mutemuya, daughter of the Mitannian king. By now, with empires confronting each other (the Hittite power was growing rapidly in Anatolia), diplomacy was an essential part of statecraft and a diplomatic marriage was possible. Mutemuya was the mother of Amenophis III (ruled 1390–1352 BC). Perhaps the incorporation of other traditions into the royal household accounts for his style of kingship. Unlike his energetic predecessors, he pursued a life of luxury and leisure in the most opulent court that Egypt had ever known. He married a commoner, Tiy, who was given the new title of Great Royal Wife, although he also maintained a vast harem. In the course of this reign there is no doubt that Asiatic influences were strong, not only on dress and culture but also on religion, which remained at the heart of Egyptian life and thought. In the regions around, there was a growing emphasis on the worship of the sun as supreme, or even sole, deity. It was at this time that the cult of ATEN, rather than that of AMUN, began to grow, especially in court circles. But the priesthood of Amun-Ra at THEBES, whose wealth and power had grown with the absences of the warrior pharaohs and the indolence of Amenophis III, remained strong and jealous of its prestige and power. The Aten was championed by HELIOPOLIS, whose ancient predominance had long since been overtaken by Thebes.

With the reign of Amenophis IV (ruled 1352–1338 BC) the royal break to Aten was made complete. The king changed his name to AKHENATEN and moved the capital from Thebes to a new site, el-AMARNA, where he had a city built that he called Akhetaten, with a vast temple to Aten at its centre. Akhenaten's obsession with religion led him to ignore the fact that the empire was under serious threat. The Hittite king, Suppiliulumas, was forging alliances among the kingdoms and princedoms that paid tribute to Egypt. The prince of Kadesh invaded Syria, the Phoenician coast was lost to Amurru, and the Palestinians captured the fortresses of Megiddo and Jerusalem. The losses are chronicled in the Amarna Letters, stored carefully at Akhetaten and apparently ignored by the king. Akhenaten and his queen, NEFERTITI, had no son, although several daughters. His two immediate successors were legitimised by marrying royal daughters. The second of these was Tutankhaten. His name was altered to TUTANKHAMUN by the priests of AMUN-RA at Thebes, who busied themselves in rooting out the worship of the Aten and restoring the tradition. Tutankhamun's fame is wholly due to the fact that his tomb, uniquely among the pharaohs, was discovered intact in the twentieth century. He was an ineffectual and short-lived ruler. Authority lay with the priesthood and with the army leader, HOREMHEB, who had regained much of the territory lost in Asia. After Tutankhamun's early death, Horemheb assumed the throne (ruled c.1323–1295 BC). A member of the provincial nobility, he was an austere figure who dated his reign from the death of Amenophis III, as though the AMARNA PERIOD had never been. He held the frontier at the Lebanon and restored internal order. He may have married a princess of the Thuthmosid house to establish legitimacy as a ruler, but he left no son and, by pre-arrangement, on his death the kingship passed to another general, RAMESES I, the first king of the NINETEENTH DYNASTY.

EIGHTH DYNASTY

A dynasty (c.2200–2160 BC) of the FIRST INTERMEDIATE PERIOD. The kings were based at MEMPHIS and ruled only the area around Memphis. The DELTA area was occupied by invaders (described as 'Asiatics' by the Egyptians) who had come across SINAI. THEBES and HERAKLEOPOLIS were rival states to Memphis. All were determined to restore the unity of Egypt and to resurrect the grandeurs of the OLD

KINGDOM, but first they had one another to contend with. The Memphite kings claimed that theirs was the legitimate rule, but the other rulers were equally ready to proclaim their pedigrees. It was a confused and ill-recorded period with many brief reigns and no outstanding figures.

ELEPHANTINE

A site on the southern tip of Elephantine Island, in the NILE of Upper Egypt, a little way above the first CATARACT opposite Aswan. A NOME capital (of the Elephant nome), its history goes back to the early period of the OLD KINGDOM. The original brick shrine was covered by a succession of later temples, with much destruction of the preceding work, but even in the final EIGHTEENTH DYNASTY structure, the sanctuary is still linked to the original sanctuary through several successive levels and epochs of building. Many charms and votive objects have been recovered from the site, and the Elephantine papyri dating from the fifth century BC were discovered here in 1903.

ELEVENTH DYNASTY

The first dynasty of the MIDDLE KINGDOM. Known as the Theban Dynasty (2040–1991 BC), it was founded by Inyotef I, who gained control of UPPER EGYPT from HERAKLEOPOLIS. His successors contested Middle Egypt with KHETI III of the Tenth Dynasty (*see* NINTH AND TENTH DYNASTIES), as well as extending their dominion upriver into NUBIA. Under its rulers, the Eleventh Dynasty made steady gains until the final victory under MENTUHOTEP II, who defeated Herakleopolis to become undisputed king of Upper and Lower Egypt (ruled 2040–2009 BC). This dynasty marks the end of the FIRST INTERMEDIATE PERIOD and the start of the MIDDLE KINGDOM, which would last a further fifteen hundred years. At first there was considerable pacification to be done, and the power of the NOMARCHS, already broken in Lower Egypt by the TENTH DYNASTY, had to be reduced in Upper Egypt also. They ceased to be hereditary, except those of BENI HASAN, who had been allies of the Thebans.

Mentuhotep II revived the system of centralised administration but without the stifling absolutism of the OLD KINGDOM. The law considered all men to be equal, and the kings of the Middle Kingdom spent much time and thought on the administration of justice. With a return to regular floodings of the NILE, prosperity had already begun to climb, and the stability introduced under the Middle Kingdom accelerated the growth. At this time the cult of AMUN-RA, who had been the war-god of the Thebans in their victorious campaign, took its full form, encouraged by the monarchy and provided with a powerful priesthood and immensely rich endowments. With the death of Mentuhotep IV around 1991 BC, the dynasty comes to a rather sudden and obscure end for a line that had accomplished so much.

ELOQUENT PEASANT

An episode recorded in literature from the early MIDDLE KINGDOM, attesting the sense of humour of the Pharaoh Achthoes II. A peasant who had grounds for complaint against a greedy steward argued his case so forecefully and vividly, first before the VIZIER, finally before the pharaoh, that he had to restate it nine times. The tale makes a contrast with the far more ample evidence of procedural formality and heavy convention when the pharaoh met his people in the flesh. (*See* Part One: Chapter 9).

EMMER

The primitive wheat that was grown in ancient Egypt. Several strains were developed by farmers from the original wild crop. *See also* AGRICULTURE.

ENNEAD

In Egyptian mythology, a group of nine deities. The most famous ennead was the Heliopolitan based at HELIOPOLIS, comprising Ra-ATUM, SHU, Tefnut, GEB, NUT, OSIRIS, ISIS, NEPHTHYS and SETH. *See also* COSMOLOGY.

EROTICISM

The ancient Egyptians were no different from the rest of humanity in their interest in the erotic aspects of life. Throughout the dynasties there is evidence of intense interest. Pornographic pictures and writings were inscribed on valuable papyri. Love charms were universally believed in, and recipes for aphrodisiacs abounded. THEBES, MEMPHIS and no doubt other places of pilgrimage, had thriving brothels. The squat fertility god, MIN, whose cult centre was at KOPTOS, presided cheerfully over all this activity, but most major gods had some connection with the cult of fertility.

ESARHADDON

King of Assyria and conqueror of Egypt in 671 BC, defeating Pharaoh Taharqa of the Nubian Dynasty. He proclaimed, 'I laid siege to MEMPHIS, his royal residence, and captured it in half a day by means of mines, breaches and assault ladders. His queen, the women of his palace, his heir apparent, his other children, his possessions, horses, large and small, cattle beyond counting I carried away as plunder to Assyria.'

EUSEBIUS OF CAESAREA (AD 264–340)

Palestinian theologian and historian whose works include the *Chronicon*, a study of ancient history, including a sketch of several ancient nations, including Egypt. Much of this account was based on a work by JULIUS AFRICANUS and therefore MANETHO.

EXECRATION TEXTS

These texts, often found on magical figurines in the ELEVENTH and TWELFTH DYNASTIES, list foreign enemy peoples whom the rulers of Egypt wished to see dead. As was usually the case in such lists, they include both long-vanquished enemies as well as contemporary threats.

EXODUS

The Bibical exodus of the Jews may have occurred in the reign of RAMESES II, although no Egyptian written source refers to these events. There is archaeological evidence of an immigrant people, known as the APIRU, quarry workers and brick-makers, who may have been the Hebrew people.

EYE OF HORUS

In his epic battle with SETH, HORUS lost an eye, which was later reassembled by THOTH. This was the eye painted on the prow of Egyptian ships and much used as a protective AMULET. The eyes of Horus were regarded as being always vigilant to detect evil influences. The right eye was the sun and the left the moon so that protection was secured by day and night. It is also found used as a measure for grain – perhaps as a precaution against unfair dealing. It was divided into six portions – a half, a quarter, an eighth, a sixteenth, a thirty-second, and a sixty-fourth. A full barrel (approximately $8^{1}/_{2}$ pints/4 litres) was equivalent to a full Eye.

F

FAIENCE

Decorative pottery, made from a quartz paste with a glazed surface, sometimes inlaid with GOLD or other precious metals, used for dishes, jars, medallions, tiles, etc.

FAIYUM

A fertile area to the west of the NILE Valley, south of the DELTA, which was empty marshland during the OLD KINGDOM but was drained and exploited in the MIDDLE KINGDOM. The area is rich in archaeological objects and papyri.

FAMINE

A series of low INUNDATIONS, around the end of the SIXTH DYNASTY, coincided with political unrest and led to famine in UPPER EGYPT, with a contemporary record claiming that parents ate their own children and many other texts attesting to the hardship suffered by the people. The weakness of central government at this time exacerbated the problems caused by a temporary but drastic climatic change.

FEMALE KINGS *see* HATSHEPSUT, NITOCRIS, SOBEKNEFERU, TWOSRE.

FENKHU
A people of ancient Syria, many of whom were employed in Egypt in the New Kingdom in QUARRYING.

FESTIVAL
The Egyptian year was liberally punctuated by the festivals of gods and by other events, such as a king's jubilee (SED FESTIVAL), or a crown prince's wedding. The Sed Festival in theory celebrated 30 years, but an elderly man becoming king might hold his after a much shorter period of ruling. Particularly at important religious centres like ABYDOS, festivals came in almost constant succession and demanded careful administration. At MEDINET HABU in the time of Rameses III there were 60 festivals in the year, and a CALENDAR of feasts and offerings was kept in order to record what provision should be made for each. The feasting aspect was taken literally, and a major festival like the feast of the god Seker required 3,694 loaves, 410 cakes, and 905 jars of BEER for the celebrants.

Processions were a feature of festivals. The image of the god, escorted by other gods and by images of bygone kings, was brought forth on a boat-shaped vehicle (*see* SHIPS AND SHIPBUILDING) and taken on a ceremonial route, with regular stopping places, watched by huge crowds.

FIFTEENTH, SIXTEENTH AND SEVENTEENTH DYNASTIES
These span the SECOND INTERMEDIATE PERIOD (1675–1553 BC). The first king was Salatis (the dates of individual reigns at this time are unclear). He appears to have had total control of Lower and MIDDLE EGYPT, and the HYKSOS contacts extended to NUBIA, which had regained independence. Salitis and his successors took over the administrative and religious machine of Egypt and let it work for them with very little in the way of change. They assumed the pharaonic role. Based first of all at AVARIS in the DELTA, where they set up a SETH cult that identified Seth also with the foreign gods Baal and Teshub, the capital moved to MEMPHIS. The third Hyksos king, Apepa or Apophis I, ceded some of his power to a branch of the family that was classed as the Sixteenth Dynasty in MANETHO's list. The Hyksos dynasty took its pharaonic responsibilities seriously and encouraged building, the arts and crafts, and literature, although the upsurge of national feel-

ing in the NEW KINGDOM was to brand them as despoilers. The famous mathematical PAPYRUS, known as the Rhind Papyrus, now in the British Museum, dates from Apepa. It was a time of considerable technical innovation. The Hyksos brought Egypt the horse harness and the war chariot, and their military improvements were in due course to assist the later growth of the empire. In the south, some time after 1650 BC, an Egyptian dynasty emerged at THEBES, tracing its origins back to the THIRTEENTH Dynasty; its founder was Rahotep. With the apparent tolerance of the Hyksos (there may have been marriage links), they ruled UPPER EGYPT, in poorer circumstances than the northern kings, building themselves PYRAMIDS of mud brick. Eventually strife broke out between the two dynasties, under the Theban kings, Ta'a and his successors, Seqenenre (whose mummy shows evidence of a violent death) and Kamose. The Hyksos were being forced back on the Delta. Kamose, too, may have died in battle, but his successor, AHMOSIS, completed the task and drove the Hyksos out of Egypt, becoming the founder of the mighty EIGHTEENTH DYNASTY, the first in the NEW KINGDOM.

FIFTH DYNASTY

A dynasty (2510–2460 BC) of the OLD KINGDOM, which had strong hereditary links with the preceding one. The first king, Userkaf ('powerful is his KA') also retained officials from the previous reign. The Fifth-Dynasty kings traced their origins back to HELIOPOLIS and therefore were keen adherents of the sun-god cult. Userkaf built a SUN TEMPLE at ABUSIR. During his reign there were Egypt's first recorded contacts with the ancient Greek kingdoms, with luxury items including jars and furniture being exported. The Fifth Dynasty saw a growth in contact with the countries beyond Egypt to the north, east and south, including the first recorded expeditions to the tropical land of PUNT. Userkaf's successor, Sahure, employed warships on the Medierranean coast, although contacts on the whole were peaceful. The power and splendour of the pharaohs were becoming known to their neighbours, and Egypt was perceived as a source not only of marvellously made things but also of magic power and arcane knowledge. Relations were on a trading level rather than diplomatic – the era of empires had not yet come. Little is known about the kings Neferirkare-Kakai and Shepsesre, but Neferefre's MORTUARY TEMPLE, found with a great stock of papyri, inscribed plaques, model boats, carved figures of prisoners, and sculptures of the king himself, is an important source of knowledge on the period. It was during the later reigns of the Fifth Dynasty, with Pharaohs Neuserre, Isesi (Djedkare) and WENIS, that the iron hand of central control began gradually to slip. These kings are most closely identified with the sun cult, which rose to a peak unequalled until the EIGHTEENTH DYNASTY. As the personage of the monarch became evermore codified as divine, so the power of the provincial governors and the senior officials of the court became greater and more independent. Instead of being grouped in annexes to the king's tomb, important functionaries constructed their own mounuments, as seen in the great MASTABA of Ti at Saqqara. He was Chief Barber to the Royal Household and Controller of Lakes and Farmland. The peasantry remained heavily oppressed, depersonalised by the arbitrary conscription of the labour battalions, obliged to labour both for the king and the NOMARCH, and victims both of fighting between the rival power centres and of shortages caused by lack of administration.

FIRST AND SECOND DYNASTIES

During the five centuries of these two lines of kings, also known as the THINITE PERIOD, from the name of the city of This to which the first kings traced their origin, and lasting from 3150 to 2700 BC, ancient Egyptian society developed the basic form that was to continue throughout. The first king, MENI, is credited with achievements that may have both preceded and followed him, although he was certainly a strong ruler who set the pattern for the intensive control of land and people that was characteristic of the early dynasties of the OLD KINGDOM. There was warfare with LIBYA and NUBIA during his reign. He worked hard to promote the new-found unity of the two kingdoms, and had tombs at SAQQARA, close to MEMPHIS, at the southern extreme of LOWER EGYPT, and at ABYDOS in UPPER EGYPT. Although Meni had a son, Aha, the next recorded king is Djer, who continued to make war in NUBIA and Libya and otherwise maintained the policies set in motion by Meni. His principal residence was at Memphis, but his tomb was at Abydos. This king, whose tomb, surrounded by those of his courtiers, was clearly one of great wealth, may have been the source of the legend of OSIRIS's earthly reign. Osiris's heart was said to be buried at ABYDOS, and Djer's campaigns through Egypt and into Nubia can be compared to the scattering of Osiris's fragments through the country. The high point of the First Dynasty was reached with the lengthy reign of DEN, another energetic king whose attention seems to have been directed more across SINAI in the direction of Asia. Den, too, worked to placate Lower Egypt and establish full union. His rule may have lasted for as long as fifty years, and his is the first SED FESTIVAL of which we have a record. He is the first king to add the third name to his set of titles: the *nsw-bity*, or 'king of Upper and Lower Egypt name'. In his case it was Khasty, meaning 'man of the desert', a reference to his military excursions. His successor, Anedjib, initiated a further development of the pharaonic title, with the 'two lords' name', the name placed under the protection of both HORUS and SETH and so reconciling the dualism of the gods of north and south, field and desert, in the person of the king. It also underlines the king's possession of the destructive powers of SETH. During the First Dynasty, stoneworking was introduced into Upper Egypt, with a stone temple being built at Hierakonpolis and a granite floor laid in the tomb of the Pharoah Usephais. The last king of the First Dynasty was Ka'a. The reasons for the change of dynasty are obscure, although Ka'a's predecessor, Semerkhet, may have been considered illegitimate. In a practice that was often to be repeated by kings of dubious claim, he erased Anedjib's name from the commemorative vases produced for that king's *Sed* Festival.

The Second Dynasty located itself firmly at Memphis and built up strong contacts with the DELTA region. During this succession of kings, the cult of the sun-god RA gradually became established. Upper Egypt may have been neglected or developed a separatist tendency as a result of the fondness of the kings for northern deities like BASTET, the Delta CAT-goddess, and a separate line of priest-kings developed at ABYDOS. This political divide came to an end with the firm rule of Khasekhem, whose Horus name means 'the powerful one is crowned', later changed to Khesekemwy, 'the two powers are crowned'. His origins were from HERAKLEOPOLIS in Upper Egypt, and he imposed his rule on the north. This reign marks the beginning of substantial stone ARCHITECTURE, including his own tomb at Abydos, and opens the way to the achievements of the THIRD DYNASTY.

FIRST INTERMEDIATE PERIOD

The somewhat undescriptive title used to cover the transitional age between the OLD and the MIDDLE KINGDOMS (2200–2040 BC). As its vagueness suggests, there is not complete agreement among Egyptologists about the beginning or the duration of this period, taken by some to begin with the Seventh Dynasty and by others with the Ninth Dynasty. As the Seventh and Eighth Dynasties together only occupied a short span and presided over a state of growing confusion, there is good reason to take the Seventh Dynasty as the start of the First Intermediate Period, which continues for around 150 years and is characterised by a continuous internal struggle for power that went on until the accession of Mentuhotep II around 2040 BC. This struggle is essentially the rivalry between Herakleopolis and Thebes. The Eighth Dynasty, centred at Memphis, soon succumbed to the warlike rulers of Herakleopolis who supplied the Ninth and Tenth Dynasties, whose area of control fluctuated from Lower and Middle Egypt to almost the whole country. The Theban claimants established the Eleventh Dynasty at about the same time, and the two were locked in combat until the fifth Theban king, Mentuhotep II, defeated Herakleopolis and finally established the Theban kingship over the two lands.

The anguish and introspection forced on the Egyptians during the turbulent era of the First Intermediate Period are revealed in the writings of the time, which are sombre and pessimistic in tone. The age-old system had broken down. The individual Egyptian felt a greater responsibility for himself, and this altered his perception of the AFTERLIFE too. Everyone would now face the court of Osiris and defend his own record on earth, not in terms of good or bad but in terms of having upheld or disturbed the proper balance of life. This spiritual development paralleled the gradual improvements in the life of the peasantry, brought about the resumption of 'normal' floods, and by a less arbitrary and impersonal social policy following the revolts of the late OLD KINGDOM.

FIRST PERSIAN OCCUPATION *see* TWENTY-SEVENTH DYNASTY.

FLINT

Deposits of flint are found widely in Egypt and were extensively worked during the dynastic era. Even late on, flint-bladed implements were used by the poorer peasants and craftsmen.

FOURTEENTH DYNASTY *see* THIRTEENTH AND FOURTEENTH DYNASTIES.

FOURTH DYNASTY

The second dynasty of the OLD KINGDOM (2625–2510 BC). Its first king was SNOFRU who ruled 2625–2600 BC, or perhaps longer. He led an expedition into NUBIA to crush a revolt there, and also fought the Libyans, and extended Egyptian dominion into the SINAI PENINSULA. These campaigns all had an economic motivation, to secure access to valuable mineral reserves and quarries, and to protect trade routes. Snofru is credited with taking huge numbers of prisoners and cattle on his southern and eastern campaigns, whilst the Sinai expedition enabled Egypt to exploit the COPPER, malachite and turquoise of the region. Snofru was a shipbuilder and sent ships to Lebanon for timber; he was also a great builder in stone. Three PYRAMIDS are ascribed to him, the first at MAIDUM, near Saqqara, modelled on the step pyramid constructed by IMHOTEP for Djoser. He then built two more pyramids farther north, at DAHSHUR. Snofru was succeeded by CHEOPS (Khufu), whose name is linked to his own monument, the Great Pyramid, although his remains were robbed from it some time in antiquity. The actual details of Cheops's reign are not well known. By this time the central power of the kings was fully established and exercised in an absolute way. The desire to build ever greater funerary monuments drove the organisation of the state to an extreme of management, which dehumanised the bulk of the population and created the complex bureaucracy that overlooked every aspect of life. After Cheops the succession went first to his son, Djedefre, and then to Djedefre's half-brother, CHEPHREN. Chephren commissioned the sculpting of the Great SPHINX. He took a strong interest in theology and during his reign the combined diety RA-ATUM was fully developed. His son, MYCERINUS, is the occupant of the third and smallest pyramid of the GIZA complex. Shepseskaf, last king of the Fourth Dynasty, took as his queen Khentkawes, who was descended from Djedefre's other half-brother, Djedefhor, in what seems to have been a deliberate attempt to unify the strands of the royal family. He broke from the pyramid tradition for his own tomb, having it built in the form of a giant SARCOPHAGUS in the southern part of SAQQARA.

FUNERARY PRACTICE

The essence of Egyptian funerary practice at all times was to provide the best set of circumstances to perpetuate the dead person in the AFTERLIFE. Almost, if not entirely, alone among ancient peoples, they believed that the physical body was necessary after DEATH. The origins of this belief are unfathomable, although in PRE-DYNASTIC times, when burial was a matter of wrapping the corpse in an animal's hide and burying it, with accessories, in a pit in the sand, the corpse was often well preserved by the arid soil. Later, the preservation was assisted by the dismemberment of the corpse, which was placed in its grave in a tidy package of bony parts, with the skull set on top. With greater social cohesion, greater wealth and the tendency of all processes to become more elaborate in such circumstances, the funeral arrangements became more substantial. The MASTABA began to appear, in a simple form, as a monument above the grave, and a framework of mythology also arose, to provide explanation, reason and justification for the whole business (*see also* COSMOLOGY, OSIRIS, UNDERWORLD).

Alongside the accretion of myth directly related to death and the afterlife grew the concept of the god-king. In the OLD KINGDOM view, only the king achieved heaven, and the funeral of a god had to be of divine grandeur, so that when he joined RA in the sky, he would have sufficient retinue and provisions to be accepted as worthy. Such a view might have implied a hecatomb, with the death or suicide of wives and courtiers. This did not happen in Egypt, where respect for the life force was deeply ingrained. Instead, the king departed with a multitude of little figures whom the magic of religion would turn into servants and attendants. He was provided with furnishings, clothes, tools, weapons – everything that he used in life he would use again in death. Thus the ever larger tomb was filled with ever more objects. The STELE, or false door, that had originally carried only the king's name bore a list of all the offerings that should be presented to maintain the king suitably. Since the body, however well preserved, might decay eventually, effigies of the king were placed in the tomb, marked with his unique name in its CARTOUCHE. By the THIRD DYNASTY, the mastaba had evolved into the funerary complex of the PYRAMID, with satellite constructions functioning as MORTUARY TEMPLES, processional courts, store rooms, symbolic cenotaphs, tombs of courtiers and relatives, and dwellings for priest-attendants and guards. The point of entrance was the valley temple: this was equivalent to the quay at which the dead king embarked on a voyage, the final destination of which was the sky, although it was a place of reception rather than of departure. Every step from here to the tomb chamber was provided with a symbolic value. The valley temple itself was under the protection of the lion-goddess SEKHMET. In the tomb of the FIFTH-DYNASTY king, Neuserre, she is shown suckling him. A processional causeway led up to the MORTUARY TEMPLE; that of WENIS at SAQQARA is 700 metres (2,296 feet) long, roofed and decorated with scenes of life on the royal domains, scenes of the building of the temple itself and auspicious episodes of the king's life. The mortuary temple was placed at the north face of early pyramids, but from the FOURTH DYNASTY was set on the eastern face, towards the rising sun. This temple had a vestibule leading to a courtyard, with a sanctum beyond. Statues of the king and of his family were placed in the temple to receive offerings. The statues themselves were the object of considerable attention (*see* PHARAOH'S DAY). Hunting and warfare were the primary motifs of the mortuary temple's decoration. Close to the pyramid were the BOAT PITS, in which lay the wooden barques in which the king could travel with RA. The SARCOPHAGUS of the king was solemnly borne into the pyramid itself. The entrance was in the north face and led down to a vestibule, past three protective granite portcullises to an antechamber. On the east side was the SERDAB, where statues of the king were placed. On the west side was the tomb chamber. This relatively simple design lasted until the TWELFTH DYNASTY. The corridors of the last Fifth-Dynasty king, WENIS, and subsequent kings, were decorated with the PYRAMID TEXTS. These esoteric spells and charms, hidden within the pyramid, written by privileged scribes, preserved the ritual that would safely see the dead king past all obstacles and achieve his ascension to the sky, his assimilation with Ra and Osiris.

The coffin also evolved in use and significance. The Fourth Dynasty coffin appeared to represent a house for the deceased, decorated to resemble a palace facade and rectangular in shape, in effect another 'false door' through which the KA could pass. From the SIXTH DYNASTY it was inscribed with texts and its function became more clearly similar to that of the boat that conveyed the dead man through the dangerous region between life and death. From MIDDLE KINGDOM times, the shape of the coffin gradually became rounded and approximated the outline of the body. The coffin was also enclosed in the much larger and more substantial sarcophagus, made of stone or carved from the living rock. At the close of the funeral ceremony, the door to the coffin chamber was closed and sealed. It was intended never to be reopened.

By Middle Kingdom times, the view of the afterlife had changed. It was no longer the prerogative of the king and his HONOURED ONES. Tombs were erected by many others, equally anxious to provide for their long future. The tomb of a high functionary was a compressed version of his royal master's: a vestibule decorated with pictures of the properties of the dead man, a courtyard decorated with scenes of everyday life and of the preparation of the tomb. Store rooms are decorated with scenes of BAKING and brewing. The chapel would include family scenes, pictures of harvest and SACRIFICE, each with its allotted position in the overall design (*see* ART). In the Middle Kingdom, a tomb would also include finely detailed and painted models of the animals, slaves, boats and farm buildings belonging to or administered by the tomb's occupant.

The formalities of a funeral, as shown in the typical decorative scheme, include mourning the dead, with weeping mourners gathered around the corpse, then accompanying it to the house of embalmment. The next stages had to await the process of MUMMIFICATION. Then the body was brought to the NECROPOLIS, where its tomb had been prepared. Within the confines, ritual visits were enacted, to SAIS and to BUTO, with offerings made. Then the final offerings were made, and purifications performed with incense. A symbolic drama accompanied the drawing of the coffin into the tomb, with one priest striving to pull the coffin back towards life while another pulled it towards its tomb. This procedure was watched over by the *tekenu*, a human form wrapped in an animal skin, a protective spirit of the necropolis, as the coffin was drawn into the tomb, at whose entrance the funeral feast was laid out. The articles to serve the spirit of the dead were placed in position, and finally the coffin went in, with a statue of the deceased, representing him as a pilgrim to ABYDOS, burial place of OSIRIS. The rites of protection were enunciated, and then the chamber was sealed.

G

GAMES

The Egyptians enjoyed board and table games, and there is evidence of a variety of games from PRE-DYNASTIC times onwards. The oldest gaming board in the world was found in a Pre-dynastic cemetery at El-Mahasna, eight miles (13 kilometres) north of ABYDOS; it is made of clay. Actual games, like *han* (the jar game), can be traced back to the FIFTH DYNASTY. Games were among the diversions of the AFTERLIFE as well as daily life, and the tomb of TUTANKHAMUN yielded game boards, with lots and knucklebones to cast. Numerous temples have game boards carved or scratched in their stonework, clearly done for the entertainment of the workmen.

GARDNER, ERNEST ARTHUR (1862–1939)

British classical scholar and archaeologist. He took part with PETRIE in excavations at NAUCRATIS and later established a school of classical archaeology at University College, London.

GARSTANG, JOHN (1876–1956)

British archaeologist who worked with PETRIE at ABYDOS and later led expeditions to Negadeh, Hierakonpolis and BENI HASAN. He developed an interest in the Hittites and excavated in Asia Minor.

GEB *or* **SEB**

The earth-god in the Heliopolitan COSMOLOGY, from whose union with the sky-goddess, NUT, came the four children ISIS, OSIRIS, SETH and Nephthys. It is Geb who presides at the court of the gods that assigns the kingship of Egypt to HORUS rather than to Seth.

GEB EL-BARKAL

A temple site in Nubia, close to Napata. The temple had been dedicated to Amun by Thuthmosis III, and it was greatly enlarged by the Nubian king PIANKHY (TWENTY-FIFTH DYNASTY), who modelled it on KARNAK, with a HYPOSTYLE HALL, fronted by a PYLON, a PERISTYLE COURT fronted by another pylon, and an avenue of CRIOSPHINXES (these he removed from a temple of Amenophis III at Soleb).

GEORGIUS SYNCELLUS (*fl.* between AD 750 and 850)

The author of a chronicle that contains verbatim a considerable part of the *Chronicon* of EUSEBIUS.

GERZA

This site in UPPER EGYPT, important in PRE-DYNASTIC times, has given its name to a phase of Pre-dynastic culture, also known as Naqada, after another Upper Egypt site.

GERZEAN PERIOD *see* PRE-DYNASTIC PERIOD.

GEZER

An ancient city in CANAAN. Excavations here have revealed many cultures. Sesostris III of the Twelfth Dynasty fought a battle here.

GIZA

The site of the most spectacular PYRAMID complex, including the Great Pyramid, the Great SPHINX and many other monuments in a vast funerary complex spanning the range of dynastic history. Set on a plateau a few miles southwest of modern Cairo, it was originally selected because it had good stone for QUARRYING. The quarry faces themselves were then used for rock-cut tombs. The site was developed from early in the OLD KINGDOM.

GODS

There are more than 2,000 gods who were worshipped at some time or another, and in some place or another, by the ancient Egyptians. This vast array is further complicated by changings and mergings of identity. Gods originally were associated with specific areas and retained this association until the collapse of the whole Egyptian religious system. Each NOME had its protective god, from the PRE-DYNASTIC PERIOD on, and it was worshipped in the provincial capital. Sometimes it took on some of the attributes of a greater god, especially those of RA, the sun-god. All the gods were seen as having characteristics similar to those of people. They were subject to vanity, lechery, greed and drunkenness. Nor were they all-powerful; a strong man equipped with magic powers could influence the gods' behaviour. The gods were a higher manifestation of the same all-pervading life force that lived in man, bull and beetle, and in the richness of their own natures they could readily change or even share shapes. The Egyptians, who saw egg turn to tadpole and then to frog, saw nothing odd in a divinity being even more protean. They had a scanty knowledge of iron, derived mostly from the discovery of meteoritic fragments, and this may have been the cause of a supposition that the gods had bodies of iron. *See also* COSMOLOGY, RELIGION, THEOLOGY, INDIVIDUAL GOD NAMES.

GOLD

Gold was mined in parts of NUBIA and in the Eastern Desert, between the NILE Valley and the Red Sea. It was hammered and picked out of the veins in the rock. It was one of the most gruelling tasks in the Egyptian climate, and the labourers must often have been prisoners of war or criminals. Panning in that arid region, of course, was impossible. Gold was also obtained by military victory, and was the favourite form of tribute to be received by the conquering state from the defeated one. Egypt's gold became a matter of dreams and envy to neighbouring kingdoms. King Tushratta of MITANNI sent a message to the Egyptian king, saying 'In your land, my brother, gold is as common as dust'. *See also* JEWELLERY, METALWORK.

GOLDEN HORUS NAME

One of the five names making up the royal title, from the TWELFTH DYNASTY onwards. It characterised the king's personal qualities, as with RAMESES II, 'rich in years, great in victories'.

GRANARY

Egypt lived largely on the corn products of bread and BEER, and the annual grain crop had to be stored and made to last until the next harvest. OLD KINGDOM sources refer to two granaries, the Red Granary of LOWER EGYPT and the White

Granary of UPPER EGYPT, just as they do to the two treasuries, also in the same symbolic colours. As the country expanded southwards down the NILE and the population grew in Lower Egypt, these two great granaries must have been complemented by other subsidiary storage points. Their prime importance may have been to hold the buffer stocks – the reserves that could be used in time of shortage, and whose value in the commercial life of Egypt was as great as the GOLD reserves of a modern state.

GREAT ENNEAD
The nine gods – RA and the eight deities whom he formed: SHU, Tefnut, GEB, NUT, SETH, NEPHTHYS, OSIRIS and ISIS. *See also* COSMOLOGY.

GREAT PYRAMID *see* PYRAMID.

GREAT SPHINX *see* SPHINX.

GRENFELL, BERNARD PYNE (1869–1926)
British papyrologist who worked with PETRIE at KOPTOS 1893–4 and later at OXYRHINCHUS in the FAIYUM. They made many discoveries of Greek and Ptolemaic texts.

GREYWACKE
Extensively quarried at Wadi Hammamet, this hard grey-green stone, which can be polished to a fine sheen, was very widely used in building and also in sculpture, including some of the finest figure sculpture of the OLD KINGDOM period.

GRIFFITH, FRANCIS LLEWELLYN (1862–1936)
British Egyptologist who worked at Naucratis with Petrie. He latter accompanied Petrie on a journey through Upper Egypt that brought about discovers of tomb inscriptions and rock graffiti. His particular area of expertise was in translation of the inscriptions discovered by himself and others.

H

HAAPI (1)
In Egyptian mythology, the god of the River NILE. He was believed to live above the first cataract and to be hermaphrodite.

HAPPI (2)
In Egyptian mythology, one of the four sons of HORUS, who was depicted with a

dog's head on one of the four CANOPIC JARS used in FUNERARY PRACTICE. The small intestines were placed in this jar.

HAIU
In Egyptian mythology, a night serpent or snake who was said to chase the sun (interpreted as a wild ass) round the slopes of the mountains supporting the sky.

HALL, HARRY REGINALD HOLLAND (1873–1930)
British archaeologist who took part in excavations at DEIR EL-BAHRI and ABYDOS and later established an interest in the archaeology of Greece and the Middle East.

HAMTI
The greedy farmer in the tale of the ELOQUENT PEASANT. See Part One: Chapter 9.

HAPI *see* APIS.

HARAKHTE
In Egyptian mythology, a title of HORUS, identifying him with RA as god of the morning sun. The sun and moon were known as 'the two eyes of Horus'.

HARMAKHIS
In Egyptian mythology, the personification of the rising sun and the symbol of resurrection. It is the proper name of the Great SPHINX at GIZA built by CHEPHREN.

HATHOR
In Egyptian mythology, a major goddess, the Lady of Heaven, Earth and the UNDERWORLD, worshipped throughout Egypt and indeed beyond as far as Syria. Portrayed as a cow or as a woman with the horned head of a cow, she was perceived as a helpful and gentle deity, with women especially under her protection in pregnancy and CHILDBIRTH. Most other goddesses in the pantheon laid claim to some attributes of Hathor, but she was supreme, as her relationship with HORUS indicates. She was his wet-nurse and later his wife. Her cult was centred at DENDERA in UPPER EGYPT, although there were temples to her throughout the country. The Seven Hathors were the seven Egyptian Fates who presided at birth.

HATI
A term the ancient Egyptians used for the physical heart of an individual. It was considered to be the seat of the intelligence and its 'spirit' was named *ab*, which signified the will and desires.

HATSHEPSUT

A female king of the EIGHTEENTH DYNASTY (ruled 1478–1458 BC). Daughter of the Pharaoh Thutmosis I and of the widow of AMENOPHIS I, she married her half-brother who became king as Thuthmosis II. They had no son, but a daughter, Neferure. In 1478 BC her husband died, and Hatshepsut became regent to the six-year-old THUTHMOSIS III, a son of her husband by one of his concubines. After a short time she abandoned the regency and had herself proclaimed a king, with the names Maatkare Khnemet-Amun-Hatshepsut (MAAT is the *kha* of RA, 'she who embraces AMUN, foremost among women). As part of her claim to the throne, she associated her dead father with her rule and proclaimed herself the daughter of AMUN-RA. Hatshepsut was a competent ruler with no taste for warfare. The principal expedition of her reign was a peaceful commercial one to the land of PUNT. She reigned until 1458 BC, when THUTHMOSIS III at last regained the throne. There was no precedent for a queen regnant and Hatshepsut reigned as a female king, portrayed in some reliefs in male garments and without breasts. She was aided by a number of courtiers of relatively lowly origin, including SENMUT, who owed their position to her favour. After her death, the frustrated Thuthmosis III had her CARTOUCHE erased from her monuments.

HATTUSILIS

King of the Hittiies with whom Rameses II made the first recorded peace treaty in history in 1271 BC. The signing was said to be witnessed by a thousand Egyptian gods and a thousand Hittite gods. Hattusilis is believed to be the Prince of Bakhten, who features in a legend that survived in a papyrus of the Ramessid period, which relates the story of a miraculous curc brought about by KHONSU (*see* Part One: Chapter 15).

HEH AND HEHET *see* COSMOLOGY.

HEKT *or* HEKET

In Egyptian mythology, a goddess of the Hermopolitan COSMOLOGY. She is depicted as a frog or as a frog-headed woman and was associated with the decomposition and ermination of grain.

HELIOPOLIS

Now a suburb of Cairo, but once a great centre of Egyptian religion, seat of the cult of the sun-god RA and the centre of the most widely accepted COSMOLOGY. The doctrine of Heliopolis spelled out how creation originally occurred, and the BEN-BEN stone fetish in the temple was a symbol of that creation. In the Old Testament of the Bible Heliopolis is known as ON, and it was here that JOSEPH married the daughter of an Egyptian priest.

HENEB

In Egyptian mythology, a god of the vine worshipped at Herakleopolis. He was probably a form of Osiris.

HENU *see* MEASUREMENT.

HERAKLEOPOLIS

A settlement and NOME capital situated to the south of the FAIYUM region on a strategic north-south route. It was the home ground of the Herakleopolitan kings of the NINTH AND TENTH DYNASTIES, who rose from being NOMARCHS to kings who at times controlled the whole country, at times only parts of Middle and Lower Egypt.

HERIHOR

A high priest (first prophet) of AMUN, in the reign of Rameses XI. In effect, during this period of enfeebled monarchy, he was the ruler of UPPER EGYPT, and his decorations on the walls of the Temple of KHONSU at KARNAK indicate the growth of his status and authority. He inaugurated the line of independent 'priest-kings' at THEBES that was to last for almost 200 years, in parallel to the TWENTY-FIRST and TWENTY-SECOND Dynasties.

HERMOPOLIS MAGNA

(Latin and Greek: 'great city of Hermes', so called to distinguish it from the DELTA town of the same name) a temple city 187 miles (300 kilometres) south of Cairo and source of the Hermopolitan COSMOLOGY. Here the god SHU was said to have raised the sky above the earth. There are architectural remains here from many dynasties, including the last native Egyptian one.

HERODOTUS

A Greek traveller and historian who visited Egypt and recorded his impressions during the second half of the fifth century BC.

HERSHEF

In ancient Egyptian mythology, a ram-headed creation god who was worshipped from the First Dynasty and whose main sanctuary was at Herakleopolis – the Greeks identified him with Herakles. *See also* Part One: Chapter 14.

HERUPA-KAUT

In Egyptian mythology, a mother goddess who was represented as a woman with a fish on her head. She was displaced by Isis.

HIERAKONPOLIS

An ancient site in UPPER EGYPT, about 62 miles (100 kilometres) south of THEBES. Tomb finds here go back to the GERZA period, 400–3300 BC. It was here that two COPPER statues were discovered, of the OLD KINGDOM Pharaoh PEPY I and his heir, Merenra.

HIERATIC

A form of writing that was developed from HIEROGLYPHICS. Hieratic (from Greek *Hieroatiks*, 'priestly') was devised in order to have a faster means of writing for non-sacred documents. Later, by the time of NEW KINGDOM, hieratic script was also used for sacred texts. *See also* HIEROGLYPHICS, DEMOTIC, WRITING.

HIEROGLYPHICS

(From the Greek words *hieros*, 'sacred', and *glyphos*, 'sculpted') the word was coined by the Greeks to describe the Egyptian inscriptions. Hieroglyphic WRITING was practised in Egypt for over 3,500 years, from before the FIRST DYNASTY until after the time of Christ. From the evidence available, it seems clear that this form of writing was devised in Egypt and not imported, although other ancient civilisations also developed script at the same time or slightly earlier. In its earliest form, it was a useful means of identifying ownership by means of a recognisable and repeatable symbol. In such a primitive form, this can hardly be considered writing, if writing is taken to be a means of expressing LANGUAGE. But the Egyptians demonstrated their understanding of the linkage of writing to speech by setting down, in front of the little drawing, an alphabetic sign to denote its actual sound. The earliest known hieroglyphs are found as seals, or seal impressions, and as identifying marks on vases, clay tablets and wooden boards. The basic concept of hieroglyphic writing is to provide a picture of the object the writer is describing. This has its limitations as soon as more complex or abstract concepts are introduced. The simple pictogram, or visual sign, was soon reinforced by the phonogram, a mark intended to represent a particular sound, and by the ideogram, which is a picture that represents something other than the apparent image, e.g. to demonstrate anger the Egyptians used the stylised picture of a baboon, a creature notorious for its bad temper. A further development of this was the determinative symbol, used to avoid confusion between words that shared a common image. In hieroglyphics, a word could be a simple pictogram or a combination of ideogram, phonogram and determinative symbol. This process was complete by the beginning of the dynastic era, providing a splendid tool for the compilation of lists, always a necessity as a monarchy became centralised and sought to exert a bureaucratic control over land and people.

Hieroglyphic writing is an ART form in itself, and it is of interest here that in early Egyptian the term for 'to write' and 'to draw' was the same. There are a host of different images, many of them giving an insight into the social life, and the plants, animals and birds of the OLD KINGDOM period. Even when other forms of writing, HIERATIC and DEMOTIC, replaced it for more commercial or mundane purposes, the stately art of the hieroglyph continued to be employed in sacred inscription. The language that the hieroglyphs conveyed was slow to change and evolve. The rise of the Indo-German tongues and their evolution would seem like speeded-up film compared to the development of Egyptian. But language is a living thing and does change, even in the context of a profoundly conservative society with a rooted respect for the great past. The hieroglyphic script, which once reflected the spoken language, came gradually to be overtaken by developments in speech and to be left behind.

Hieroglyphs were normally written from right to left, with the symbols normally facing the beginning of the row. Vertically arranged symbols have also been found, on the walls of buildings. *See also* SCRIBES.

HITTITES

A dynamic and powerful people, centred in Anatolia, whose empire expanded southwards and came into conflict with that of Egypt during the NEW KINGDOM. Archaeology has revealed some of the first known diplomatic messages and peace treaties in official correspondence between the Hittite and Egyptian monarchs, Hattusilis and Rameses II. *See also* Part One: Chapter 20.

HOMOSEXUALITY

The NEW KINGDOM text *The Story of Horus and Seth* recounts an episode of mutual masturbation between the two gods, but there is little indication in the written or pictorial record of homosexuality. The *BOOK OF THE DEAD* encourages abstinence from homosexual acts. In a society founded on the concept of fertility, it may be that the cultural norms discouraged and repressed homosexuality without recourse to legal constraints. Certainly, in a culture as open in sexual matters as the Egyptian, if homosexuality were a frequent and tolerated occurrence, one would expect to read a great deal more about it.

HONOURED ONES

The group forming a king's closest advisers. They lived at court and formed a leading part of his retinue at all ceremonial occasions. Their functions would continue after the king's and their own deaths, as they received the right to have a tomb in proximity to the king's own and were provided with the materials to build and decorate it. *See also* COURT LIFE, PHARAOH'S DAY.

HOPHRA

The name in the Bible given to Pharoah Apries of the TWENTY-SIXTH DYNASTY.

HORDADEF

A son of CHEOPS (Khufu) who features in a legend concerning Dedi. *See* Part One: Chapter 11.

HOREMHEB

A NEW KINGDOM pharaoh, the last king of the EIGHTEENTH DYNASTY (ruled 1323–1295 BC). Although with no hereditary connection to his predecessor, he was a soldier who escorted TUTANKHAMUN on a demonstrative campaign in Palestine and who took the throne on the young king's death. Taking as his HORUS NAME 'powerful bull with wise decisions', he set about restoring order within the kingdom. The AMARNA PERIOD, with its religious controversies, had witnessed a form of iconoclasm in some temples of AMUN-RA, and Horemheb made amends to the re-established deity. He began the HYPOSTYLE HALL at KARNAK and constructed three pylons, using the stonework of the nearby Aten temples. He superintended the introduction of a conservative programme of worship and reformed the legal system, which had become slack and excessively corrupt. He had no heir of his own, and passed the crown to a fellow-general, RAMESES I.

HORUS

In Egyptian mythology, the hawk-god, seen as the special protector of kings. Horus was normally incorporated into the king's name, and the hawk motif was widely used as a royal seal. Horus was the son and avenger of OSIRIS, and was also known as 'son of RA' (a title also used by kings). The oldest HIEROGLYPHICS to portray the concept of 'god' use a falcon, indicating that the same word stood for both. Many PRE-DYNASTIC localities had falcon-gods, and the history of Horus is a palimpsest in which these many local origins come together and continue to develop into the complicated entity of the classical Horus. At LETOPOLIS in the DELTA, there was an ancient cult of a Horus known as *Hor-khent-irti*, 'Horus of the two eyes' (sun and moon). The priests of HELIOPOLIS took this as the supreme Horus and named four others as subordinate to him, 'the four young ones who sit in the shadow of the lofty one' (the sons of Horus – AMSET, HAAPI, DUAMUTEF and KEBEH-SENUF). This was Horus the Elder, who was later to be assimilated in another Horus, Horus the Child, who was born to ISIS and OSIRIS and who avenged the death of Osiris and became king of Egypt, ancestor of all the pharaohs. Horus was thus a deity of great significance, linked both to the light-giving sky and the life-giving earth. His divine struggles found all sorts of practical significances, as with the EYE OF HORUS, but his principal identification was with kings. There is a splendid statue of the FOURTH-DYNASTY Pharaoh CHEPHREN with the Horus-falcon seated protectively on his shoulders.

HORUS EYES *see* EYE OF HORUS.

HORUS LOCK
A long twist of hair in a single lock on an otherwise close-shaven scalp, worn by CHILDREN of the nobility.

HORUS NAME
The first of the royal set of names denoting a particular king; also the first in time. It associates the king with a particular aspect of the hawk-god.

HOUSES
In the PRE-DYNASTIC PERIOD, houses were little more than tents: skins and textile spread over a wood frame, or made of wattle and daub. These perishable structures are preserved in early HIEROGLYPHICS. A headman's house would have a stockade around it, of sharpened sticks. By the THINITE PERIOD, wood-framed houses of a more substantial sort were built, with a mud-plaster outer covering. A pillared hall behind a portico was their main feature. By the MIDDLE KINGDOM there was an external stair leading to the roof and sometimes a proper second storey. Throughout the ancient period, however, most houses were single-storey. The hall remained the principal room of the house, where the great man received guests, tenants, seekers after justice and criminals for judgement. There were private rooms for the master of the house, for his womenfolk and CHILDREN, and for guests. His servants lived outside the house but in their own meagre dwelling inside the fenced-off compound. Around the house would be ornamental gardens and flower beds. Shade and coolness were among the prime concern of the house-builder, and the garden would contain a pool surrounded by trees, overlooked from a broad portico supported by two rows of wooden pillars. A large house would have its own bakehouse, brewhouse, grain stores and workshops for weaving and CARPENTRY.

HYGIENE
The Egyptians set store by cleanliness, although their culture did not develop the bath house and its accompanying customs and rituals. They relied chiefly on cleansing oils, waxes and ointments to keep themselves clean and sweet-smelling. Men at least often kept their hair shaved off, except perhaps for one lock. At least partly for hygienic reasons, it was normal in both sexes to remove all bodily hair. *See also* SANITATION.

HYKSOS
A dynasty of foreign rulers from Asia, including peoples from the Hitttite and Hurrian empires, who established themselves in the eastern DELTA around 1600 BC and controlled Lower and MIDDLE EGYPT for 100 years until Egyptian rule from THEBES was re-established. Their name is from the Egyptian *hekaw-*

khasut, 'chiefs of foreign lands'. The struggle against the Hyksos was responsible for introducing many innovations to the Egyptians' methods of warfare, particularly the use of horses and chariots. Hyksos kings supplied the Fifteenth and Sixteenth Dynasties (*See* FIFTEENTH, SIXTEENTH AND SEVENTEENTH DYNASTIES). Although there is little evidence of their having a dynamic foreign policy, the period does show an increase of Asiatic influence on Egyptian arts, crafts and religion, which was an enduring feature of the NEW KINGDOM despite its ebullient nationalist spirit. *See also* Part One: Chapter 20.

HYPOSTYLE HALL

A temple hall, supported by rows of COLUMNS, in which there were two levels of ceiling, supported by columns of different heights, creating a high central nave flanked by two lower aisles.

I

IAN *or* KHIAN *or* IANIAS

A ruler of the Hyksos period whose name appears on relics found at Knossos in Crete and Baghdad. Manetho called him Ianias.

IARSU *see* NINETEENTH DYNASTY; TWOSRE.

IBIS

A wading bird similar to the stork, which was saced to the ancient Egyptians.

IDEOGRAM *see* HIEROGLYPHICS.

IMHOTEP

The VIZIER of the THIRD-DYNASTY Pharaoh DJOSER, credited with commissioning the first PYRAMID, the Step Pyramid at Saqqara. He was a man of great consequence as an administrator and architect. He was deified in the course of the MIDDLE KINGDOM.

INAROS *see* PEDUBASTIS.

INCENSE

Incense was widely used in temple and tomb ceremonies, where it helped to create a mystical, perhaps at times even hallucinatory, atmosphere. It was burned in small decorative FAIENCE cups to give off an aromatic smoke.

INUNDATION

The annual rise of the NILE in the August-November period, caused by the monsoon rains falling in the mountains of Ethiopia and southern SUDAN. Much land in the Nile Valley and the DELTA remained flooded for about 10 weeks. The levels varied from year to year, and there was a long and difficult period of low inundation during the OLD KINGDOM. At the first cataract the average rise was about 50 feet (15 metres); at the edge of the DELTA it was about 25 (7.5). The flood came in stages and was carefully observed and measured by the Egyptians. A green wave, laden with vegetable matter from the equatorial swamps, heralded the waters of the WHITE NILE. Two to four weeks later came the red wave, the waters of the BLUE NILE, stained by the red ferrous soil of the Ethiopian mountains and speeding up the pace of the inundation. The PYRAMID TEXTS of the SIXTH DYNASTY express the awe felt by the inhabitants at the spectacle: 'They tremble, who see Hapi when he beats his waves; but the meadows smile, the banks blossom, the offerings of the gods come down; men do homage; the hearts of the gods are lifted up.'

INYOTEF I *see* ELEVENTH DYNASTY.

ISESI *see* FIFTH DYNASTY.

ISIS

In Egyptian mythology, the prime goddess of the Egyptian pantheon, sister and wife of OSIRIS, mother of HORUS and a potent divinity in her own right. She is normally depicted in human form. Her origin was as the protective goddess of Perhebit, north of Busiris in the DELTA. The ruins of her temple, the Iseium, still exist. Isis was famed for her magic skills, which enabled her to resurrect the re-assembled body of Osiris and make it copulate with her in order to produce Horus. Isis was often depicted as a midwife, and the moments of birth and death are both closely associated with her. Motherhood became a part of the Isis cult in the LATE PERIOD and gradually led to her being linked with the Mother Goddess of eastern religion. Her cult was still maintained at PHILAE long after the advent of Christianity.

ISLE OF ENCHANTMENT

A legend in Egyptian LITERATURE, also known as *The Tale of the Shipwrecked Sailor*. *See* Part One: Chapter 19.

ITRU *see* MEASUREMENT.

J

JEHOIAKIM

The third and last king of Judah, son of Josiah and puppet king of the TWENTY-SIXTH DYNASTY pharaoh Necho II, who put him on the throne of Jerusalem after the battle of Megiddo in 605 BC.

JEWELLERY

This was a high ART in ancient Egypt, which was well endowed with precious stones and metals, and imported others. The jewellers used a wide range of materials, including agate, amethyst, beryl, calcite, carnelian, chalcedony, coral, garnet, jade, jasper, lapis lazuli, malachite, onyx, pearl, sardonyx and turquoise, with GOLD, SILVER and COPPER for settings. Gold itself was formed into ornamentation both by melting and casting and by hammering. Gold wire and gold leaf were extensively used. Perhaps the highest point of jewellery design was in the TWELFTH DYNASTY, including objects found by PETRIE in the pyramid of Sesostris II, which included a pectoral and coronet of great technical skill and design. Exquisite work was done on all sorts of personal adornments and accoutrements, including BRONZE hand mirrors whose reflective power associated them with the magic of the gods. *See also* ORNAMENTATION.

JOSEPH

The Biblical character, one of the two sons of the patriarch Jacob by his favourite wife, Rachel. His father's preference for him drew down the enmity of his elder brothers, who sold him to slave traders by whom he was sold to Potiphar, a high-ranking Egyptian official. The story of his elevation to the position of vice-regent of Egypt and the settlement of his father and brothers there is told in the Book of Genesis 37–50. Authorities still differ as to the period in Egyptian history to which Joseph's life belongs, some placing it before, others under, and others after the time of the HYKSOS. *See also* ON; Part One: Chapter 21.

JOSEPHUS (AD 37–*c*.100)

Jewish historian and soldier who took part in the defence of Galilee against the Roman army and held the fortified town of Jotapata for forty-seven days. He was captured when the city fell and was with the Roman army at the destruction of Jerusalem in AD 70. He then went to Rome where he adopted the family name of his patron, Flavius, and wrote his histories of the Jews and of Egypt, in which he quotes verbatime some passages from MANETHO's history.

JULIUS AFRICANUS (*fl.* beginning of third century AD)
Christian writer whose chief work was a *Chronicon*, now lost, but a considerable part of which is contained in the *Chronicon* of EUSEBIUS. Many fragments are also preserved by GEORGIUS SYNCELLUS.

JUVENAL (AD *c*.55–*c*.140)
Roman lawyer and satirist whose satirical works in verse annoyed the authorities who appointed him, although an old man of eighty, to the command of a body of troops in a remote district of Egypt, where he died shortly afterwards.

K

KA
A term used for the life force or spirit of an individual, which continued to reside inside the tomb, passing through the 'false door' into the chapel to receive offerings. One of the five elements constituting the human being, its HIEROGLYPHIC is two raised arms.

KADESH (1) *or* **QUEDESH**
A Hittite goddess who was imported into Egyptian mythology in the EIGHTEENTH DYNASTY as another form of ASTARTE. She was depicted as a moon goddess, standing naked on the back of a lioness, holding lotus flowers and what appears to be a mirror in one hand and two snakes in the other. She formed a TRIAD with MIN and RESHEP.

KADESH (2)
An ancient city on the River Orontes, which was possibly a HYKSOS centre. It was captured by THUTHMOSIS III after MEGIDDO and was the scene of an indecisive battle between the Hittites and RAMESES II.

KA'A *see* FIRST AND SECOND DYNASTIES.

KAKAI *see* NEFERIRKARE-KAKAI.

KAMOSE *see* FIFTEENTH, SIXTEENTH AND SEVENTEENTH DYNASTIES.

KARNAK

The site of a group of colossal temples, including the greatest of the Egyptian temples, that of AMUN-RA. The location is immediately north of THEBES, on the east bank of the NILE. The great temple complex was not all built at one time but was adapted and added to over no less than seven centuries. The granite-built sanctuary is the oldest portion and was complete before HYKSOS rule. In the reign of AMENOPHIS I, first king of the EIGHTEENTH DYNASTY, this was surrounded by a temple court, and in the reign of THUTHMOSIS I the grand facade was built in what became the standard Egyptian plan, two vast pylons of masonry, narrowing as they rose, crowned by wide curved cornices, another typically Egyptian feature. Between these two great structures was the gateway, at a lower level, also corniced. Two further such gateways were erected, one in front of the other. The hall between them was built in the reign of THUTHMOSIS III. Later kings added major sections, notably the great HYPOSTYLE HALL of COLUMNS, credited to SETHOS I and RAMESES II. There are 14 rows of PAPYRUS-bud columns, with two central rows of columns having capitals carved to resemble the open papyrus. These are 69 feet (21 metres) high and almost 12 feet (3.5 metres) round. Around 980 BC, during the TWENTY-SECOND Dynasty, the ninth and last pylon and the square forecourt in front of the hall of columns were added. The complete building is about 1200 feet (366 metres) long by 350 feet (107 metres) wide at its broadest and remains one of the largest buildings in the world. A ceremonial avenue lined by SPHINXes joined Karnak to THEBES, where further Eighteenth and NINETEENTH DYNASTY buildings rise, with OBELISKS, pylons, pillared courts and arcades, in honour of the Theban TRIAD, Amun-Ra, MUT and KHONSU. *See also* ARCHITECTURE, TEMPLE.

KEBEH-SENUF

In Egyptian mythology, one of the four sons of HORUS, who was depicted with a hawk's head on one of the four CANOPIC JARS used in FUNERARY PRACTICE. The liver and gall bladder were placed in this jar.

KEKU KEKET *see* COSMOLOGY.

KENBET *see* LEGAL SYSTEM.

KERMA

A site in NUBIA, above the third cataract of the NILE, and centre of a local kingdom.

KHABRI

The name of a tribe mentioned in the AMARNA Letters, who are believed to have been the Hebrews.

KHAFRA
The Egyptian form of CHEPHREN. In this form it appears in the legend of Dedi, *see* Part One: Chapter 11.

KHAIN *see* IAN.

KHASEKEM
A warrior king of the Second Dynasty (see FIRST AND SECOND DYNASTIES) conqueror of NUBIA, *c*.2700 BC. His HORUS NAME means 'the powerful one is crowned', later changed to Khesekemwy, 'the two powers are crowned'. His origins were from HERAKLEOPOLIS in Upper Egypt, and he imposed his rule on the north. This reign marks the beginning of substantial stone ARCHITECTURE, including his own tomb at Abydos, and opens the way to the achievements of the THIRD DYNASTY

KHAT
A term used for the body of an individual, one of the five elements constituting the human being. It formed a triad with the KA and the KHU.

KHAYBET
A term for the shadow of an individual and another manifestation of the KA. It formed a tria with the ka and the SAHU.

KHENENSU
The Egyptian name for HERAKLEOPOLIS.

KHENSU *see* KHONSU.

KHEPERA *or* KHEPRI
In Egyptian mythology, the beetle god identified with the SCARAB. At HELIOPOLIS he was a sun god who was absorbed by ATUM. He formed a sun triad with RA and Atum, with Khepera appearing as the sun at dawn, Ra at high noon and Atum in the evening.

KHEPHREN *see* CHEPHREN.

KHET
A standard unit of MEASUREMENT of area, 100 square CUBITS.

KHETI I AND II *see* NINTH AND TENTH DYNASTIES.

KHETI III
The last king of the Tenth (Herakleopolitan) Dynasty (*see* NINTH AND TENTH DYNASTIES) in the FIRST INTERMEDIATE PERIOD (2200–2040 BC); an active and effective king who drove the Asiatic colonisers out of the Nile DELTA, reintroduced

NOMES as local government districts and renewed irrigation systems. His dynasty was, however, to be eclipsed by the ELEVENTH DYNASTY (Theban), which ultimately triumphed in the long war with HERAKLEOPOLIS that characterised the First Intermediate Period of Egyptian history.

KHNUM

In Egyptian mythology, a ram-headed god whose cult was centred in the city of ELEPHANTINE. A potter, he was believed to have shaped the world and men upon his wheel in another version of the Creation myth. At Memphis, where Ptah was worshipped in the FIRST AND SECOND DYNASTIES as the creator of the world, he was assisted by eight earth gnomes called Khnum.

KHONSU *or* KHENSU

A war-god of the later period, worshipped at Thebes, son of Amun and Mut. *See also* Part One; Chapter 15.

KHU

A term used for the soul of an individual, one of the five elements constiting the human being. It formed a triad with the KA and the KHAT and was depicted as a bird.

KHUFU *see* CHEOPS.

KING *see* PHARAOH.

KING LIST

Lists of PHARAOHS' names inscribed on temple walls, as at KARNAK and ABYDOS, or on PAPYRUS, as in the TURIN CANON. Although incomplete and sometimes mutually contradictory, they remain an important guide for the student of Egyptology.

KINGSHIP

The king, or PHARAOH, was seen as a semi-divine figure. Metaphorically, and literally to many, he was son of RA, the sun-god, and would ultimately rejoin his divine parent in the sky. His role on earth was to intercede on behalf of the country with the gods. To help make this effective, his life was encased in a set of ritual practices and religious ceremonies. He was high priest, above all others. But all strands of Egyptian life ultimately came together in the person of the king. He also had a decisive secular role; in his person the divine and the mortal came together. In the OLD KINGDOM period, it was believed that only the pharaoh, his immediate family and a few favoured others could attain to heaven. Justice was done in his name, and his word was law as well as sacred. The unchanging aspects of Egyptian life over centuries meant that kings were not required to be creative lawmakers or agents of change, which no doubt made AKHENATEN's religious revolution all the more shocking. But circumstances arose that required the king's decision or action, invasions, FAMINES, disputes between great men. Despite the official climate of adoration and fulsome praise, pharaohs were not immune from court plots, and several were assassinated as a result of conspiracies hatched in the harem, where rival queens were seeking the succession for their sons or nephews.

KIOSK
A small, open-roofed chapel in which a god's statue was placed during a festival. One has been restored at KARNAK.

KOHL *see* COSMETICS; ORNAMENTATION.

KOPTOS *or* COPTOS
A settlement on the River NILE, at the entrance to the Wadi Hammamet, with evidence of OLD and MIDDLE KINGDOM temples. It was particularly a cult centre of the fertility god MIN.

KUSH
The Egyptian term for Nubia.

KUSHITE DYNASTY *see* TWENTY-FIFTH DYNASTY.

L

LAND OWNERSHIP
In principle, the king owned the land as well as everything else; others held it by his leave. From the Second Dynasty (*see* FIRST AND SECOND DYNASTIES) onwards, the king held a census every two years of land (immovable property) as well as movable goods. At this time there was still a distinction between the royal domain – the king's vineyards, orchards, fields, and woodlands – and the estates of private individuals; but as the royal power swiftly expanded, the entire area of Egypt came under royal control. The king granted land and could take it away. Land held under the king could be passed on by will but was subject to certain

constraints. Under normal tenure, inherited land was divisible among all members of a family; but land given as a royal donation, to a successful soldier, for example, was transmissible without subdivision directly to the eldest son and therefore highly prized. A case is recorded in which one Mesmen appealed to the VIZIER at Heliopolis, and records of a land donation to his ancestor four hundred years previously were produced in his favour.

LANE, EDWARD WILLIAM (1801–76)
British Arabic scholar and illustrator whose great-uncle was the painter Thomas Gainsborough. In 1925 Lane travelled up the Nie to the second cataract and in 1826 went to Thegbes, making sepia drawing of the monuments. He wrote two books on his travels.

LANGUAGE
The language of the ancient Egyptians was brought by the Semitic peoples who moved into the Nile Valley from the Asiatic deserts. In its oldest forms it also shows traces of the African languages of the first inhabitants. It forms one of the languages of the Afro-Asiatic group (also known as the Hamito-Semitic group) that numbers over 200 living languages. The parent language of this vast and ancient group was spoken in the seventh millennium BC in Africa or the Middle East. Egyptian is now extinct, although in a much debased form, and heavily mixed with Greek, it can still be traced in COPTIC, a language that developed in Egypt from the second century AD and is still used as a liturgical language by Christian communities in Egypt. It was in everyday use until the eighteenth–nineteenth centuries. The language of modern Egypt is Arabic.

LATE PERIOD
The era between the THIRD INTERMEDIATE PERIOD and the MACEDONIAN DYNASTY (747–333 BC). For nearly half of this period, Egypt was ruled by the Nubian or Kushite Dynasty (the TWENTY-FIFTH), when the former colony, which had become independent during the THIRD INTERMEDIATE PERIOD, displaying a vigour that Egypt itself had lost, overran and conquered its once predominant northern neighbour. This incursion first halted then stifled an Egyptian drive by the lords of SAIS in the western DELTA to unite the country under their own rule. Their descendants finally succeeded in 664 BC, when the Kushite kingdom fell before the invading Assyrians. The Saites formed the TWENTY-SIXTH DYNASTY, beginning as a puppet regime for the Assyrians. Under both the Kushite and the Saite kings, the country enjoyed a degree of stability and prosperity, given a firm central rule and a 'good Nile', Egypt could make a rapid recovery from any vicissitude, because of the size of her population and the potential for agricultural wealth if the state were well managed. The latter part of the Late Period was marked by two

periods of Persian conquest, the first of which, 525–404 BC, signalled the end of the Saite revival. The period between 404 and the SECOND PERSIAN OCCUPATION in 343 was characterised by sporadic warfare and strenuous efforts to maintain alliances with the volatile Greek states in the almost constant effort to hold off the Persians. Despite this, especially under king NECTANEBO I, the last of the Egyptian PHARAOHS maintained the dignities, styles and practices of their predecessors, until the invasion of Artaxerxes III Ochos brought the Second Persian Occupation in 343 BC. This lasted for ten years until Alexander's destruction of the Persian empire. *See also* TWENTY-NINTH AND THIRTIETH DYNASTIES.

LATE PRE-DYNASTIC PERIOD *see* PRE-DYNASTIC PERIOD.

LAY OF THE HARPIST
An ancient poem in Egyptian LITERATURE. *See* Part One: Chapter 18.

LEGAL SYSTEM
At the administrative head of the legal system was the VIZIER, who dispensed and administered justice in the king's name. At a local level, each city possessed a council of elders, called the Saru in the OLD KINGDOM and the Kenbet from the MIDDLE KINGDOM onwards. This was an advisory body, and an active tribunal known as the DJADJAT was responsible to it for maintaining public order. Only minor cases could be dealt with locally, and anything of a serious nature was referred upwa rds to the Great Kenbet of MEMPHIS or that of THEBES. The vizier's was the supreme court. He alone could pronounce a death sentence, although only with the express permission of the pharaoh. His jurisdiction applied both to civil and criminal cases. In keeping with the whole Egyptian philosophy of life, law was given on a basis of precedent. The division between right and wrong was 'What Pharaoh loves' and 'What Pharaoh hates'. The vizier gave his judgements under very close scrutiny by his master, and a famous injunction by the Pharaoh THUTHMOSIS III to his vizier Rekhmara says, 'When a man is an official he should act according to the rules laid down for him. Happy is the man who does what he is told. Never swerve from the letter of justice. . . .' *See also* CRIME AND PUNISHMENT.

LETOPOLIS
A settlement in LOWER EGYPT, a NOME capital on the west bank of the Rosetta arm of the NILE, an early source of the HORUS legend. Its deity was a mummified falcon.

LIBYA
The country to the west of the DELTA, exercising a strong influence on the west-

ern side and sometimes invading and overrunning it. There was traditional enmity between Egypt and Libya, extending back into PRE-DYNASTIC times, and warfare or punitive expeditions were frequent. Egypt also used Libyan mercenaries, and descendants of these provided the FIFTEENTH and Sixteenth Dynasties.

LIBYAN DYNASTY *see* TWENTY-SECOND AND TWENTY-THIRD DYNASTIES.

LILY
One of the symbols of the kingdom of UPPER EGYPT.

LITERATURE
The literature of the Egyptians is found in written form from the NINTH DYNASTY onwards, although there can be no doubt that, as with the legend of OSIRIS, there was a long-established oral tradition that related and passed on folk tales, folk humour and folk wisdom from generation to generation, both in literate and illiterate society. The survival of the oldest literary writings is often due to copies made by scribes in later periods. OLD KINGDOM literature is primarily religious, the expression particularly of the priests of HELIOPOLIS. The PYRAMID TEXTS fall into this category. Other inscriptions of a less ritualistic sort are occasionally found in the Old Kingdom tombs at MEMPHIS, including short fragments of songs or popular sayings. PAPYRUS sources are found from the FIRST INTERMEDIATE PERIOD, when the anxieties of the time prompted some scribes to put their thoughts down in writing and to comment sourly or pessimistically on the spirit of the age.

There are several long stories from the MIDDLE KINGDOM, including *The Tale of* SINUHE, *The Tale of the* ELOQUENT PEASANT and *The Tale of the Shipwrecked Sailor* (or *The Isle of Enchantment*). These stories have a strong element of fantasy. From the same period comes the new religious literature, on sarcophagi, temple walls and papyri, spreading the previously esoteric formulae that enabled all good people to enter the UNDERWORLD. From this time also come collections of proverbs and wise maxims. Few poems have been preserved from this period, apart from a collection of hymns in praise of the Pharaoh Sesostris III. Altogether, the MIDDLE KINGDOM remnants suggest a wide variety of literature, both narrative, lyrical and didactic.

The writings of the NEW KINGDOM are more realistic in tone and sometimes display a brutally down-to-earth attitude. They include such stories as *The Tale of the Doomed Prince*, *The Tale of the Two Brothers*, *The Tale of Truth and Falsehood*, *The Voyage of Wenamon*, and *The Tale of* HORUS *and* SETH. From this period we also have poetry in the form of AKHENATEN's hymns to the sun-god Ra-Aten, a love-poem cycle similar to the Song of Songs, and sundry official poems addressed to PHARAOHS and gods. The counter-reformation of ATUM also has its hymns to the god.

A favourite form of writing for the Egyptians was the collection of maxims, giving guidance on how to lead a life of such poise and virtue that would ensure an easy passage at the trial of Osiris. Egyptian prose writing, even at its most creative, has a stilted and repetitive feeling, with a formulaic quality and an artificiality of style and tone that were accepted and appreciated by the contemporary reader in a way with which we find it hard to empathise. But writing, like every other form of ART and craft, was expected to serve the purposes of the state. The works are anonymous, following fixed forms and canons and produced for specific purposes. Literature was not for its own sake, it was essentially utilitarian.

LOWER EGYPT

The area of the Nile DELTA between MEMPHIS and the Mediterranean coast. Below Memphis, the Nile splits into two great arms, the western (Rosetta) arm and the eastern (Damietta) arm. The area between them, despite its marshiness and propensity to flood at the time of the INUNDATION (although here the rise was far less because of the width and number of the streams), was densely inhabited from an early period. It was later subdivided into 17 NOMES, each of which indicates the presence of a distinct tribal group or clan with its own chieftain and its own protective deity. Much of Egyptian religion was evolved in this region, with major cult centres such as BUSIRIS (for ANZTI/OSIRIS), BUBASTIS (BASTET), BUTO (the cobra goddess of the same name), HELIOPOLIS (RA), LETOPOLIS (HORUS the Elder).

Apart from Memphis, which was a later settlement despite its eventual status as capital, its major centres were the cities of TANIS, on the eastern side, and SAIS, on the western, as well as the cult centres. Both Tanis and Sais, as well as Memphis, were to provide Egypt with royal dynasties. Lower Egypt, open to the sea on its north front, and with empty desert stretching to LIBYA on the east and to Palestine in the west, was always more open to influence and attack from outside than was UPPER EGYPT. The initiative in the joining of the two kingdoms came from here, and the archaeological evidence of PRE-DYNASTIC times indicates the spreading of advanced culture up the Nile Valley rather than downstream. In the NEW KINGDOM and LATE PERIOD its population became increasingly mixed, with strong influxes of Libyans, Greeks, Jews and Assyrians.

LUXOR

A site in Upper Egypt, on the east bank of the Nile, immediately south of, and often equated with, Thebes. The name comes from Arabic and refers to Roman camps built on the site. Amenophis III built a splendid temple here, partly on top of older buldings, which was enlarged and decorated by later kings, forming a uniquely impressive linked site with the temple of Amun-Ra at Thebes.

M

MAADIT BARQUE
In Egyptian mythology, the boat occupied by RA in the morning on his journey through the UNDERWORLD.

MAAT
In Egyptian mythology, the goddess of truth. She presided over the judgement of the dead, which controlled entry to the UNDERWORLD. Human-faced, she is a later addition to the pantheon.

MAAU *see* ATET.

MACEDONIAN DYNASTY
The dynasty (332–304 BC) that followed the Thirtieth Dynasty (*see* TWENTY-NINTH AND THIRTIETH DYNASTIES), with which the numbering system ceases, and the SECOND PERSIAN OCCUPATION. The Persian satrap of Egypt resigned his satrapy to ALEXANDER THE GREAT, with the consent of the people, as expressed by the ORACLE of AMUN-RA at THEBES, which hailed Alexander as Master of the Universe. The Macedonians, Alexander himself (ruled Egypt 333–323 BC), Philip Arrhidaeus (323–316 BC) and Alexander IV (316–304 BC), all preserved the forms of Egyptian life and society. Like the Persian empire, Alexander's was too vast and disparate for it to live under one set of laws. Egypt, with its immemorial tradition and the inherent stability of its systems, could function as a state within the greater empire. The key to this lay with the priesthood. Religion and the AFTERLIFE remained an obsession with the Egyptians, and the gods and their priests remained a constant factor in the life of the country, whoever held the crown. In the peace that followed Alexander's conquest, the priesthood kept or renewed its privileges, and temple reconstruction and temple-building went on at a rapid pace.

MAGIC
The Egyptians made some distinction between magic and religion. The household of the PHARAOH contained magicians as well as priests. The priestly function was to venerate the gods and make supplications. The magician's function was to use his wiles to circumvent the gods' will or to compel them towards certain actions. His power, too, devolved from the gods themselves, particularly from ISIS,

the great magician who resurrected OSIRIS, and THOTH, the keeper of records, including divine spells. Talismans and spells were the armoury of the magician. The talismans, AMULETS of wood, metal, clay or pottery, depict HIEROGLYPHIC signs for such attributes as long life, health, strength, fertility, beauty, etc. They are linked to the power of a particular god, and a spell would be recited to increase their efficacy. The magician could exorcise a malign spirit that was causing illness or misfortune if he knew its name (*see* NAMES). The magicians were close observers of the stars and made prophecies relating to their conjunctions. Much of the later continuing tradition of 'black magic' stems from the pratices of the Egyptian magicians, who used wax figures of their intended victims and created love potions and elixirs of life. Even Pharaoh Rameses III had to take protective action against a magician who 'had stolen the secret books of the king, to bewitch and destroy the people of the court'. The 'wise men' had to be taken account of. They were numbered among the king's advisers, and the king himself would proclaim that he had been taught the secret knowledge of things by THOTH and that he, like Thoth, was also the Great Magician.

MAIDUM

A site on the west bank of the NILE, about 30 miles (50 kilometres) south of SAQQARA, where the Pharaoh SNOFRU of the FOURTH DYNASTY erected a PYRAMID, which, initially a step pyramid like that of Djoser, was altered to form a uniform-slope pyramid cased in limestone masonry, the first of its type. Maidum was also the site of the first valley temple, a temple separated from the pyramid complex, at which the dead king's FUNERARY rites were carried out.

MANETHO

An Egyptian priest from the time of Greek rule (around 250 BC), who compiled a kind of history of Egypt together with a list of kings and dynasties. Lost in the original, his text is known through other writers' quotations and comments. It has been a vexation almost as much as a blessing to Egyptologists, since so much of it has been lost and so much of what survives is flimsy legend and obviously false or misleadingly phrased information, such as his reference to 'seventy kings in seventy days' during the FIRST INTERMEDIATE PERIOD.

MARIETTE, AUGUSTE (1821–81)

French Egyptologist who became Keeper of Monuments to the Egyptian government. He excavated the SPHINX and uncovered many other monuments, including the SERAPEUM.

MARRIAGE CUSTOMS

Marriage was an important institution in Egyptian life, and on the whole, among the general population, it seems to have been a voluntary affair rather than a matter of purchase or arrangement. There was no special wedding ceremony, no dowry or bride price, and no marriage contract was necessary; such contracts often came later in a marriage, when impending death or perhaps divorce meant that assets had to be counted and apportioned. As with the royal families, it appears that there was no bar against incestuous marriages. Men could have more than one wife, but the status of the chief wife was protected by law. In practice, the vast bulk of the population was monogamous, if only for economic reasons; very few men could support more than one wife, especially as they may have had other female relations to support. Husband and chief wife lived together on equal terms, and she had considerable rights of her own. Her eldest son, even if not the eldest son of the husband, would normally be the chief heir. Divorce was provided for, and seems to have been as relatively unregulated as marriage, apart from the property aspect. Husbands could repudiate a wife whom they regarded as unsatisfactory, and there is some evidence to suggest that wives had a reciprocal right, although much less likely to exercise it because of social custom and the difficulty of maintaining an independent existence. Adultery was considered a serious crime, particularly in women, but despite various accounts of severe penalties like nose-slitting or even death, it was most commonly settled by divorce, and an adulterous wife might lose her legal rights to a share of the family goods. *See also* WOMEN.

MASONRY
The Egyptians became highly skilled stonemasons at an early stage, although the conservatism of design meant that their skill showed itself in perfection of technique rather than in inventiveness. Their tools were made of the hardest stone or of COPPER, with BRONZE tools developed in the course of the NEW KINGDOM. With such rudimentary equipment they cut, chiselled and shaped huge blocks of stone and fitted them together with minute precision. They knew the principle of the arch but never employed it, sticking to the ancient column-and-lintel style of the first structures. A distinctive characteristic of the Egyptian stonemason was to cut some of his blocks at an oblique rather than a vertical angle. This was not a decorative feature, as all temples were coated with a thin layer of white plaster, concealing the stone from view.

MASPERO, GASTON (1846–1916)
French Egyptologist, discoverer of the PYRAMID TEXTS, who first went to Egypt in 1880. He served as Director of the Antiquities service, made valuable discoveries at SAQQARA and DAHSHUR, and was instrumental in saving the royal mummies at THEBES from tomb robbers.

MASTABA

A structure of brick, later of stone, with decorative niches, to indicate and to seal a tomb. The name is from an Arabic word, meaning 'bench', which was how the mastabas seemed to the Arab workers employed by nineteenth-century archaeologists. The original mastabas, in the First Dynasty (*see* First and Second Dynasties), were solid. In the Second (and later) Dynasties they became steadily larger and more elaborate, with a room or rooms inside, and eventually they were a whole group of intersecting rooms above a substantial underground plan. By the late Second Dynasty, mastabas were of sufficient size to prompt the notion of the step pyramid, with the mastaba as its base storey.

MATHEMATICS

Like many other aspects of intellectual life, mathematics in Egypt appears to have been developed in the Pre-dynastic and Thinite Periods, and to have progressed little from the period of the pyramids. With their aversion to speculative and abstract thought, mathematics was not a congenial subject to the Egyptians, who pursued it not for its own sake but for the practical application it had to their needs. This related chiefly to architecture and building. Like all subjects that had to be taught, mathematics was in the province of the priests, who were fearful of making their knowledge too widely known, since it was perceived as magic. The mathematical formulae were more akin to spells than general truths to them. The decimal system was employed, with multiples of 100 up to one million. There was no zero. *See also* measurement.

MAYOR

The headman of a town or settlement, although, of course, he was appointed, very often as a hereditary official, not elected. He would be among the wealthiest inhabitants of the settlement and had local powers to maintain order and settle disputes. Many of his duties would involve preparing for visits from more important state officials and ensuring that they were suitably lodged and entertained.

MEASUREMENT

The social organisation of the Nile Valley was dependent on a universal system of measurement. The standard measures were taken from the human form. The unit of short measure, used by painters and sculptors in particular, was the foot. The unit of long measure was the cubit, which subdivided into two spans, six hands or 24 fingers. The standard cubit was about 46 centimetres, with the royal cubit being some four centimetres longer. Longer distances were measured by the *itru*, around 5,000 cubits. The royal surveyors measured land in squares of 100 royal cubits (the khet). The standard unit of capacity was the *henu*, of about one-third of a litre (11 fluid ounces). The basic unit of weight, the DEBEN, was about 3¼ ounces (91 grams).

MEDICINE

Occupying a position somewhere between empirical science and superstitious magic, medicine was greatly respected, and Egyptian doctors had a high reputation in the ancient world. Medical inscriptions date back to the MIDDLE KINGDOM, although they often claim to be copies of documents originating from the OLD KINGDOM. Given the Egyptian respect for traditional knowledge, this may well be true, or it may be a means of giving authority to more recent treatments. Medicine, like every other form of knowledge, lived under the umbrella of the priesthood. Early doctors appear to have been priests chiefly of Serket and of NEITH. Temples had their herb gardens to provide a supply of medicaments, and among the gods who sponsored the art of curing were RA-ATUM himself, Neith (whose temple at SAIS had a medical school adjacent to the school of the Wise Magicians) and ANUBIS. The most reliable and effective medical treatments were those that were applied to external solutions. The Egyptians were good bone-setters. They also practised amputation successfully. Wounds and cuts were treated with bandages and poultices impregnated with antiseptic herbs and ointments. Internal illness was far more of a mystery, and the doctor reverted to spells and potions, as his successors would do in other lands, too, for centuries after the end of the Egyptian kingdom. These frequently involved the use of odd products like lizard's blood, the excrement of various animals and mother's milk. Incantations accompanied the administration of the medicine. Prescriptions were adapted to the age of the patient and the time of the year: a medicine that cured in the first month of summer might not do so in the second. Doctors knew the importance of the heart but had a strange ignorance of the softer organs of the human body, considering that their own society also practised a sophisticated form of embalming that involved the removal of the viscera. But the doctors were not embalmers, and the embalmers were not doctors.

A number of papyri on medical topics have come down to us, showing among other things that the Egyptians were students of gynaecology. Much of this interest centred on infertility and its supposed cures, often bizarre if not harmful, and again there was no serious anatomical study. Cosmetic medicine was also extensively practised. One surviving treatise is entitled *Book for Turning an Old Man into a Youth of Twenty*. Medical materials were chiefly plant-based, and the Egyptians knew the uses of castor oil, mandragora, dill, cumin, hartshorn and coriander, among others. HERODOTUS noted the degree of specialisation among Egyptian doctors, as healers of the eyes, the head, the belly, and so on, and observed, 'The Egyptians look after their health with emetics and purgatives, and clear themselves out for three days running, once a month, considering that all the ailments of men come from the food they eat.' *See also* DISEASE, HYGIENE, SANITATION, TEMPLE.

MEDINET HABU

The site of numerous temples on the west bank of the NILE, facing THEBES, and in the vast funerary region that includes Malqata and DEIR EL-BAHRI. It includes the MORTUARY TEMPLE of TUTANKHAMUN (EIGHTEENTH DYNASTY) and the great palace-temple of RAMESES III (TWENTY-SECOND DYNASTY).

MEDJAY

A desert tribe from whom the Egyptians recruited soldiers, including internal guards: an early application of the principle that a district should not provide its own policemen.

MEGIDDO

A very ancient fortress city in northern Palestine (modern Israel). Because of its strategic site, guarding the pass at the entrance to the plain of Jezreel through which ran the only trade and military road from Egypt to Mesopotamia, it was the site of several battles. THUTHMOSIS III defeated the Syrians here, and in 609 BC the TWENTY-SIXTH DYNASTY king Necho II defeated the army of Judah under Josiah (who was killed) and installed Jehoiakim as a puppet king. The Armageddon of the New Testament Book of Revelation ('the hill of Megiddo') is the place where the final battle between good and evil will be fought.

MEMPHIS

Close to modern Cairo, and strategically placed at the apex of the Nile DELTA, ancient MEMPHIS was the capital during the period of the THIRD to the SIXTH DYNASTIES (2980–2475 BC), the most brilliant period of the OLD KINGDOM. It was founded on a reclaimed flood plain by AHA at the start of the FIRST DYNASTY as the 'city of the white wall'. As a new foundation it had no tutelary god from prehistoric times and took over PTAH from a nearby settlement. It was the prestige of HELIOPOLIS, north of Memphis, that drew the kings to move steadily northwards, incorporating the name of RA into their titles. The name changed to Memphis under the reign of PEPY I, who established a new royal district and called it Menefer, 'good harbour', later transliterated into Greek as Memphis. Always a place of high prestige, Memphis became capital again with the TWELFTH DYNASTY and again with the HYKSOS invaders of the FIFTEENTH DYNASTY. The location of Memphis as a point controlling both the DELTA and the Valley made it attractive to invaders. Libyan, Nubian, Assyrian and Persian armies all headed for Memphis, and the captor of Memphis was in effect the captor of Egypt. When

Cambyses took Memphis in the first Persian conquest, the reigning PHARAOH, Psammetichus II, committed suicide. The funerary sites of Memphis, SAQQARA and DAHSHUR are among the richest and most splendid of ancient Egypt. *See also* Part One: Chapters 6 and 9.

MENDES

A site on the southern side of the DELTA, NOME capital and capital of the Thirtieth Dynasty kings (*see* TWENTY-NINTH AND THIRTIETH DYNASTIES).

MENEPTAH *see* NINETEENTH DYNASTY.

MENI

The first known king of a unified Egypt, from around 3150 BC. His reign marks the beginning of the dynasties. He is also known as Meni and Narmer. *See also* FIRST AND SECOND DYNASTIES.

MYCERINUS *or* MENKAURE

A FOURTH-DYNASTY (2625–2510 BC) PHARAOH, builder of the smallest of the three PYRAMIDS of GIZA.

MENTU *or* MONT

In Egyptian mythology, the god of war worshipped at Thebes. The Greeks iden-tified him with Apollo. Several Eleventh-Dynasty kings took their name from him, Mentuhotep, 'Mentu is satisifed'. He is depicted as a falcon-headed man with a solar disc and two plumes. He was later overshadowed and absorbed by AMUN-RA.

MENTUHOTEP II

ELEVENTH-DYNASTY king (ruled 2040–2009 BC) and first king of the MIDDLE KINGDOM, who came to the throne of the Theban kingdom and later extended his kingship over all Egypt with the military defeat of the Herakleopolitans. To mark this he took a new title, Nebhepetre ('son of RA'), and later took a new HORUS NAME, Sematawy ('he who unifies the two lands'). Setting up his capital at THEBES, he restored many of the functions and systems of the OLD KINGDOM, in-cluding the VIZIERSHIP, and built numerous temples, including that of HATHOR at Gebelein, and added to the complex of buildings serving OSIRIS at ABYDOS. After a lengthy reign he died in 2009 BC, leaving a far more united and prosperous kingdom behind him. His tomb is in the rock cliffs of DEIR EL-BAHRI.

MENTUHOTEP III

ELEVENTH-DYNASTY king (ruled 2009–1997 BC). The son of MENTUHOTEP II, he was another strong king who continued internal reforms, consolidated the defences of the DELTA region and sent a large trading expedition to PUNT.

MENTUHOTEP IV *see* ELEVENTH DYNASTY.

MERENRA *see* PEPY I; SIXTH DYNASTY; WENI.

MERITENSA
The fair-minded judge in *The Tale of the* ELOQUENT PEASANT. *See* Part One: Chapter 9.

MERKHET
A surveying instrument used by the Egyptians in laying out the ground for a temple or PYRAMID.

MERMENFATIU *see* THIRTEENTH AND FOURTEENTH DYNASTIES.

MERSEKHNET *see* ATET.

MERWER *see* MNEUIS.

MESHKHENT
In Egyptian mythology, a goddess of CHILDBIRTH. She is a depicted as a woman with a heraddress consisting of two palms curved at the ends. She features in a FIFTH-DYNASTY legend about the birth of the first three kings of that dynasty (*see* Part One: Chapter 11).

METAL-WORKING
On the wall of a passage leading to the PYRAMID temple of the SIXTH-DYNASTY King Teti at SAQQARA there is the relief depiction of a metal-working shop. The metals being worked are electrum, 'white gold', an alloy of GOLD and SILVER, and COPPER. Four men are shown hammering sheets of metal with stone hammers. Two others are blowing through long tubes to raise the fire under a crucible of electrum. Another scene shows a craftsman shaping or polishing a metal bowl round a wooden modelling core, while others are putting the finishing touches to handled water jugs. Other scenes show the weighing of metal ingots and the sharpening of an adze blade. Such establishments were not large and were workshops rather than factories, employing a relatively small number of skilled craftsmen. There was a royal monopoly on the working of metal, and such workshops would be under the administration of an official ultimately responsible through a long hierarchic chain to the VIZIER.

The Egyptians knew iron at first only through meteorite fragments, which would be viewed as god-sent and used only for sacred ornamentation, and the occasional gift from a foreign king. COPPER remained the foundation of Egyptian metalwork, although by the NEW KINGDOM it was being alloyed with tin to make

BRONZE. Tin was not accessible in Egypt, and bronze remained in limited use. Copper was used in many different ways apart from tools. Copper pipes were used to carry water, and even drainage, and many of the jugs, bowls and drinking vessels of the wealthy were made of it.

MIDDLE EGYPT

A geographical term applied to the Nile Valley between ASYUT and Cairo.

MIDDLE KINGDOM

The period of the ELEVENTH to the FOURTEENTH DYNASTIES (2040–1675 BC), a distinctive epoch between the chaotic conditions of the FIRST INTERMEDIATE PERIOD and the first instance of foreign rule. With a succession of strong and determined kings in its first two dynasties, the early Middle Kingdom represents perhaps the peak of Egyptian prosperity and internal security. It was a time of relative peace, in which trading overseas and overland was widely practised. In the conversion of the FAIYUM region from marshland to irrigated farmland, a vast public work was achieved whose purpose owes nothing either to death or defence, which hitherto had been the principal objects of such expense. Not that funerary ARCHITECTURE was neglected, as the Middle Kingdom PHARAOHS once again had the resources to build PYRAMIDS. In this and in many other ways they looked back to the time of the OLD KINGDOM for inspiration and example. They wanted to feel that they were perpetuating the ancient traditions of the country; that there was a continuing link back to the days of such figures as SNOFRU and IMHOTEP, both of whom were deified during the Middle Kingdom. It was a rich period for Egyptian literature, in some repects a 'classical' period, in which the writers praised the circumstances of their own time and looked back into the heroic past for parallels or examples. But it was also in the Middle Kingdom that the great mythological accounts, such as *The Tale of* HORUS *and* SETH, were set down. The later dynasties were less distinguished, but the continuity of religion, culture and work went on almost changelessly through a succession of pharaohs of whom little is known. *See also* ELEVENTH TO FOURTEENTH DYNASTIES.

MIDDLE PRE-DYNASTIC PERIOD *see* PRE-DYNASTIC PERIOD.

MILITARY ORGANISATION

In the OLD KINGDOM, the isolation of Egypt was such that an organised ARMY was not normally required. At need, an army of sorts could be levied from the peasantry. During the FIRST INTERMEDIATE PERIOD internal warfare as well as greater contact with other states brought about a swift increase in the number of trained soldiers and a regular army came into being. Many of the soldiers were mercenaries from other lands; the Egyptian tradition and lifestyle was anything but militaristic, and they did not take to warfare with any enthusiasm. By the time the NEW KINGDOM had established an Egyptian empire, however, the army was very large and possessed considerable prestige, aided by the efforts of the priesthood to instil enthusiasm for the cause of Egyptian arms.

MIN

In Egyptian mythology, a fertility god whose cult centre was KOPTOS, where he was also worshipped as god of roads and desert travellers. Popular especially in MIDDLE EGYPT, and with many chapels attached to the temples of other gods, he was portrayed as a rotund figure with a large penis. In the NEW KINGDOM he formed a TRIAD with RESHEP and KADESH (1). In Akhmin (Panopolis) he was identified with the Greek god Pan and games were celebrated in his honour. Statues and charms featuring Min were very common. He is depicted standing with a flail in his right hand behind his head.

MINIMUM SYSTEM *see* BERLIN SYSTEM.

MITANNI

An Indo-European people of relatively advanced skills in social organisation and in warfare. Coming from farther east, they imposed themselves on the Hurrian kingdom in Mesopotamia as an aristocratic ruling class, and confrontation with Egypt followed. Egyptian relations with Mitanni were to fluctuate violently between savage war and peaceful alliance. Under THUTHMOSIS III the Egyptians defeated the Mitanni on their own territory and put them under tribute. The Mitanni, faced with a nearer and more hostile kingdom, as the HITTITE power increased, sought friendship and alliance with Egypt in its phase of Thuthmosid imperial power.

MNEUIS *or* MERWER

In Egyptian mythology, a bull who was worshipped at Heliopolis, where he was sacred to Ra-Atum. Mneuis was the Greek for of his name, Merwer, 'the bull of Meroe', the Egyptian form. He was evidently a rival of APIS.

MOERIS, LAKE

An ancient lake which was drained in the MIDDLE KINGDOM and became the fertile FAIYUM.

MONT *see* MENTU.

MORTUARY TEMPLE

The temple in which the religious cult of a dead king was celebrated. Statues of the deceased would be placed in its sanctum, together with those of gods with whom he had been especially associated. Its store rooms would contain votive offerings and the walls were decorated with testaments to his greatness and his fitness for the AFTERLIFE. It was to the mortuary temple that the KA of the dead king or queen would come to inspect and receive the offerings placed there by the priests of the cult and, on anniversaries, by the royal successors. In the OLD and MIDDLE KINGDOMS, the mortuary temple was immediately adjacent to the PYRAMID or tomb. In the NEW KINGDOM period it was in a separate location.

MUMMIFICATION

The first evidence of this practice, so firmly identified with ancient Egypt, is on a tablet from the reign of Djer, last of the FIRST-DYNASTY kings, although in popular legend the first Egyptian to be embalmed and consequently reincarnated was OSIRIS himself. The word 'mummy' comes from the Arabic *mumiyah*, meaning bitumen. Until the popularising of the Osiris cult, mummification was only practised on kings and those closest to them, but from the MIDDLE KINGDOM onwards it was made available to all who could afford it. The business of embalming and mummifying was managed by a special guild of craftsmen, recognised by law. The dry sandy soil of Egypt had a natural tendency to preserve dead bodies, allowing the fluids to drain away and preventing the flesh from rotting. In the PRE-DYNASTIC millennia, the inhabitants of Egypt must have become well aware of this and regarded the preservation of a corpse as something natural and, by extension, desirable, willed by the gods. When their burial practice became more elaborate than the simple earthen pit, it must have soon become apparent that in a stone-lined cell beneath a MASTABA the process of desiccation did not happen and putrefaction was much more likely. Embalming and mummification emerged as the answer to this problem. After death, the corpse was taken to a special house of purification. It was laid out on a slab, and the brain was removed, drawn out through the nose aperture with a hook after a process of maceration. A FLINT knife was used to cut open the left side, and the internal organs, stomach, liver, intestines, etc, were extracted. The maker of the initial cut might run away, with the other undertakers in mock pursuit, in a ritualised enactment of guilt and expiation. The soft parts were given separate treatment; embalmed, wrapped and placed in the four so-called 'CANOPIC JARS'. The heart was left in the body, as it had to be weighed on the entry into the UNDERWORLD. The body was then packed in NATRON for from 35 to 70 days to dry it out. Pieces of material were then soaked in gums, sweetened with herbs and placed in the abdominal cavity. The wound made by the dissector was covered with a plaque that conferred the protection of the four sons of HORUS. The body was then ritually cleaned and purified before the wrapping began. Each individual member, including the fingers and the penis in the case of males, was wrapped in linen, over which went a piece of material that covered the torso. Selected charms and AMULETS were placed at particular parts of the body or inserted between the layers of bandaging. The number of layers varied. The mummy of TUTANKHAMUN had 16. Finally, a mask was prepared to go over the face, and the mummy was ready for its interment. *See* FUNERARY PRACTICE.

MUSIC
Music was present in Egyptian life in many different ways. Workers in the fields sang folk songs and love songs to traditional tunes. Many work activities were carried out to a strong rhythm, produced by percussion, rowing, marching, pulling and heaving. Music played a large part in social life. It was an essential accompaniment to the many feasts and parties, and professional musicians were well paid. Musicians were often women; indeed, perhaps there were more women musicians than there were male ones. Percussion was basic to the orchestra, with various types of rattles and clappers in use as well as drums of different sizes and construction. There were also wind and stringed instruments, forms of the flute, clarinet and harp. In the NEW KINGDOM period, the lute and the lyre were brought in from Asia, with foreign performers. There was also an early form of bagpipe. Temples used music to please the gods, who loved feasts at least as much as mortal men did, and there were corps of sacred musicians, singers and dancers. A number of high-ranking women became religious singers. Among the gods, music was mostly a perquisite of the female deities, with HATHOR in particular closely identified with the sistrum, an instrument whose use was restricted to women. It was a rattle-type instrument with a long handle, decorated with the cow-head of the goddess. Music was also associated with the brothel, and prostitutes are often depicted with a lute or lyre. In those temples where sacred prostitutes practised, there was no dividing line between the prostitute, the dancer and the musician.

MUT
In Egyptian mythology, wife to AMUN-RA, the goddess-mother, a vulture-headed goddess local to THEBES and so given this elevated status and provided there with a splendid temple but little worshipped elsewhere.

MUTALLU
The Hittite king who organised an army of allies to defend KADESH from the army of RAMESES II. *See also* Part One: Chapter 27.

MYCERINUS *see* MENKAURE

MYTHOLOGY *see* COSMOLOGY, GODS, RELIGION, THEOLOGY.

N

NAMES

Egyptian gradually ceased to be a living language after the Roman occupation. During the period of the Greek kings, Greek had become the official language, and many Egyptian names come to us through their Greek form, taken from the lists left by MANETHO. Since, in Egyptian writing, the consonants in a word only were set down, the vowel sound is sometimes a matter of conjecture. Even so short a name as that of RA is spelled Re by some writers. By the time they have been rendered again from Greek to English, they are likely to be phonetically and alphabetically remote from the Egyptian original. The pronunciation of Egyptian can only be guessed at. Consequently, different Egyptologists have spelt names in different ways, and there has been much debate and argument about how a 'correct' orthography for ancient Egyptian names could be set up. The picture is further complicated by the number of names each PHARAOH possessed. In recent years, there has been movement towards a degree of standardisation, with the former -en ending now much more often seen as -on or -un. Since the Hellenised (Greek) forms are the most established and most widely found in the literature on ancient Egypt, these chiefly are used in this dictionary with cross-references to alternative forms when these are relatively common, as with Thuthmosis and Thotmes, Sesostris and Senusert, and others.

NAMING

The possession of a name was of literally vital importance to the Egyptians. A baby was given its name immediately after birth, so that it should have a name even if it died in post-birth trauma. There is a close connection between the power of naming and the magic element in Egyptian religious thought. Not to have a name was to be in a form of limbo. Knowledge of a name might confer some secret power over that named person. To obliterate the name inscribed on a king's CARTOUCHE was to jeopardise his continuing existence in the AFTERLIFE. For such reasons, the naming of PHARAOHS was a complicated business, hedged about with precautions. In the early dynasties, the king was given three names. These were later added to as the concept of the god-king grew. By the NINTH DYNASTY the final form was established. The names of the NINETEENTH-DYNASTY king RAMESES II were as follows. His HORUS NAME was 'mighty bull, beloved of justice'. His Lord of the Two Lands (*nbty*) name was 'defender of Egypt, binder of

405

foreign lands'. His GOLDEN HORUS NAME was 'rich in years, great in victories'. His king of Upper and LOWER EGYPT name (also known as the TWO LADIES NAME) was 'rich in the justice of RA, chosen of Ra' (this was his coronation name, shown on the first CARTOUCHE designating him). His Son of Ra name was 'beloved of AMUN, Ramses' (his birth name, inscribed on the second CARTOUCHE designating him). By contrast, most ordinary Egyptians had only a single personal name, perhaps with a reference to the father added.

NAOS
A shrine or niche in the innermost part of a temple or chapel, where a divine statue was placed.

NAPATA
The capital city of NUBIA, situated just below the third cataract of the NILE. Following the end of the Nubian Dynasty (the TWENTY-FIFTH DYNASTY), the capital moved farther into the hinterland, at Meroe.

NAQADAL PERIOD *see* PRE-DYNASTIC PERIOD.

NARMER *see* MENI.

NATRON
A mineral produced by combining sodium carbonate and bicarbonate and naturally found as deposits of sesquicarbonate of soda, this was an important element in MUMMIFICATION as a drying and an antiseptic agent. It had many other uses, including the manufacture of FAIENCE and glassware, and in soldering metal. It was used with salt to preserve meat, and, when mixed with oil and scented unguents, produced a kind of soap.

NAUCRATIS
An ancient Greek city in the Nile Delta in northern Egypt. Founded in the seventh century BC, it was the site of excavations by PETRIE in the twentieth century AD.

NEBUCHADNEZZAR *or* NEBUCHADREZZAR
Babylonian emperor who in 605 BC defeated the Egyptian army of Necho II (*see* Twenty-sixth Dynasty) at Carchemish on the Eurphrates and therefore gained power over the whole of the Middle East.

NECHO I and II *see* TWENTY-SIXTH DYNASTY.

NECROPOLIS
An area set aside for tombs (Greek: 'city of death'). Tomb areas were generally

to the west of cities and settlements, as the west was seen as the direction in which the dead travelled, towards the sunset.

NECTANEBO I

A PHARAOH (ruled 380–362 BC) of the final dynastic period, the Thirtieth (*see* TWENTY-NINTH AND THIRTIETH DYNASTIES), whose reign was dominated by efforts to keep the Persians from reclaiming Egypt as a satrapy. There was intensive diplomacy and shifting of alliances between Egypt and the Greek states, with Egypt in a very weak negotiating position. Nectanebo organised defences against invasion, but a Greek-Persian fleet evaded these by attacking the western DELTA. The way to MEMPHIS was open, but they delayed, waiting for Persian reinforcements, and, aided by the July INUNDATION and the Egyptians' mastery of the waterways, Nectanebo was able to drive them out. Even at this time, the traditional pharaonic activities were maintained. During Nectanebo's 18-year rule, a vast programme of temple restoration was carried out. He also began the temple of ISIS at PHILAE, and made endowments to temples at SAIS, EDFU and elsewhere.

NECTANEBO II

The last Egyptian-born king of ancient Egypt (ruled 360–343 BC). Displaced by the SECOND PERSIAN OCCUPATION, he retreated southwards and eventually took refuge in NUBIA, where he maintained a government in exile for few years. *See* TWENTY-NINTH AND THIRTIETH DYNASTIES.

NEFERIRKARE-KAKAI *or* NEFEREFRE

The third pharaoh of the OLD KINGDOM, FIFTH DYNASTY (2510–2460 BC). His MORTUARY TEMPLE at Abusir was excavated in the 1980s AD and revealed one of the most valuable collections of PAPYRUS scrolls relating to the Old Kingdom, inscribed plaques, statues of the king's prisoners and sculptures of the king himself. He also features in the legend (*see* Part One: Chapter 11).

NEFERT (1)

A royal princess of the OLD KINGDOM, a limestone statue of whom has survived and is now in Cairo.

NEFERT (2)

A favourite wife of the TWELFTH-DYNASTY pharoah Sesostris II and mother of Ammenemes III.

NEFERTARI (1)

The queen of the EIGHTEENTH DYNASTY pharoah AHMOSIS and mother of AMENOPHIS I.

NEFERTARI (2)

The queen of the NINETEENTH-DYNASTY pharoah RAMESES II to whom he dedicated the Small Temple at ABU SIMBEL, the Great Temple being dedicated to himself.

NEFERTITI

Queen consort of AKHENATEN. Her fine painted portrait bust (in the Berlin Museum) has been very well preserved. Nefertiti, who may have been of Asiatic origin, perhaps from MITANNI, shared her husband's enthusiasm for the worship of ATEN. When his failure to sustain the cult compelled him to compromise with the priests of AMUN, she separated from him to live in a house named 'fortress of the Aten' at AKHETATEN. After Akhenaten's death, she asked the HITTITE king to send her one of his sons as a husband. There may have been an ambitious dynastic and religious scheme behind this, but the prince was killed by agents of the priests of Amun-Ra on his way to Egypt; and with the eradication of Aten-worship, Nefertiti fell into obscurity.

NEFERURE

The daughter of the EIGHTEENTH-DYNASTY female king HATSHEPSUT. Her mother selected her as her successor, but after THUTHMOSIS III regained the throne she disappeared from history.

NEHEB-KAU

In Egyptian mythology, a serpent goddess whose was worshipped at HERAKLEOPOLIS. She is depicted as a flying serpent or as a serpent with a human head, arms and legs.

NEITH

In Egyptian mythology, a goddess whose origins go into the PRE-DYNASTIC PERIOD. She was a huntress and a major goddess of the TWENTY-SIXTH DYNASTY, which was centred on her cult centre of SAIS, in the western DELTA.

NEITHHOTEP

A princess of the royal house of the city of Sais, whom MENI of the FIRST DYNASTY made his wife, thus legitimatising the succession. Her name means 'Neith is pleased'.

NEKHEBAT

In Egyptian mythology, a goddess of Upper Egypt who was worshipped at El Kab. She is depicted with a vulture's head or wearing a crown in the shape of a vulture.

NEMES HEADDRESS

A royal headdress, made of cloth, knotted at the back and with two prominent side lappets.

NEOLITHIC PERIOD

This era of human development begins at the end of the seventh millennium BC. It leads in to the PRE-DYNASTIC PERIOD of Egyptian history, over a period of some 2000 years, a time of significant cultural development. Although stone was by far the most important source of tools and weapons, metals were gradually being introduced. Society evolved with settled agricultural practice, based on crop growing and animal husbandry.

NEPHTHYS

In Egyptian mythology, an ancient but relatively unimportant goddess, sister and wife of SETH but nevertheless devoted to both OSIRIS and ISIS. She assisted Isis to find the body of Osiris.

NESHI *see* THIRTEENTH AND FOURTEENTH DYNASTIES.

NETER

According to BUDGE, the word used in ancient Egyptian texts for the one god, self-created and almighty.

NETHERWORLD *see* UNDERWORLD.

NEUSERRE *see* FIFTH DYNASTY; FUNERARY PRACTICE.

NEWBERRY, PERCY EDWARD (1869–1949)

British Egyptologist who led the expedition that unearthed tombs at BENI HASAN and other sites.

NEW KINGDOM

From around 1552–1070 BC, the period of the EIGHTEENTH to the TWENTIETH DYNASTIES. Some sources take it as lasting until the end of dynastic Egypt (*see* LATE PERIOD). The New Kingdom showed the underlying resilience of Egyptian institutions after the SECOND INTERMEDIATE PERIOD, with its rule by the foreign HYKSOS kings. Under a succession of strong kings, Egypt was turned into the most powerful state in the world, its frontiers extending from NUBIA to the Euphrates. Wealth poured in from client kingdoms in the form of GOLD, luxury goods and slaves. International diplomacy developed, and many aspects of life and ART were influenced by Asian examples. For the first time, there was intermarriage between kings of Egypt and foreign princesses. The internal situation was less secure than at the high point of the MIDDLE KINGDOM, with tensions between the kings and the powerful high priests of AMUN-RA, reflected in the religious controversy that reached its height when AKHENATEN attempted to supplant Amun-Ra with ATEN. The New Kingdom's ARCHITECTURE was as ambitious as its foreign policy and reached a peak of grandiloquence under RAMESES II. The final century of the New Kingdom was one of gradual decline after the brilliant early period, and it ended with Egypt's prestige at a low ebb and the kingdom itself again divided in two. *See also* NINETEENTH DYNASTY.

NILE

The great river, whose BLUE NILE branch rises in the mountains of Equatorial Africa, and whose longer WHITE NILE branch rises in Lake Victoria, south of the Equator. It flows for some 4,000 miles (6,500 kilometres) to reach the Mediterranean Sea through its many streamed DELTA. The Nile has always been the spine and lifeline of Egypt, the great common possession of the two lands. Its fertile valley, varying in width from 12 to 31 miles (19 to 50 kilometres), was renewed each year by the INUNDATION, which prevented the soil from being worked out and enabled a continuity of human occupation. It was the chief means of communication, with a complex network of CANALS leading from it to important towns and temples. Strangely perhaps, considering its overwhelming importance in their lives, the Egyptians never saw the river itself as a god, and the river deity HAAPI is a relatively minor figure in their pantheon. They never discovered the source of the river. The name Nile is first found in the writings of the Greek Hesiod; its derivation is obscure. The Egyptians called it *itr-da*, 'the great river', or even referred to it as the sea. *See also* LOWER EGYPT.

NINE BOWS

In Egyptian ART, the PHARAOH is sometimes depicted with his foot placed upon the Nine Bows, which represent the peoples subject to his rule. These included the Egyptians themselves as well as neighbouring peoples like the Libyans and Nubians.

NINETEENTH DYNASTY

The second dynasty (1295–1188 BC) in the NEW KINGDOM. The first king was RAMESES I (ruled 1295–1294 BC), already an elderly man when he assumed the kingship. He was probably of HYKSOS descent and was succeeded after two years by his son, SETHOS I (ruled 1294–1279 BC). Early in his reign he was challenged by a powerful alliance of Amorites and Aramaeans with the prince of Hamath. He sent three separate armies, those of RA, AMUN and SETH, and defeated all three opponents before they could combine. Like other warrior kings, Sethos was also a prolific builder. The Temple of OSIRIS at ABYDOS dates from his reign, and he continued the building at KARNAK that his father had started. His tomb is in the VALLEY OF THE KINGS. His son, RAMESES II (ruled 1279–1212 BC), was called 'the great' by early Egyptologists, on account of his monuments rather than his performance as a ruler, although both were formidable. He completed the great HYPOSTYLE HALL at Karnak, had temples built in the SUDAN, set up many buildings in THEBES and also rebuilt the city of TANIS, from where his family had originated. Reputedly, Rameses II fathered over fifty daughters and one hundred sons. In his reign there was direct confrontation with the HITTITE empire, which hitherto had encouraged buffer states to attack, or revolt against, Egypt. There was a long and hard battle at Kadesh, beyond the Orontes River, in which the Egyptians fought back bravely after a surprise attack and which ended in a stalemate. Rameses's temple walls proclaim it as a major victory, won by the king himself after rallying his broken and disheartened troops. Sporadic warfare continued, with Rameses managing to hold his boundaries. At this time, the power of Assyria was growing, and the kingdom of MITANNI was swallowed up by the rulers of Nineveh. In the face of this threat to both their kingdoms, Egypt and the Hittites made a peace treaty, the earliest of which a written record exists. This was to last for almost 50 years, and the Hittite king paid a state visit to Egypt, bringing his daughter to be Rameses's bride. Rameses died, reputedly aged a hundred years, and his son, Meneptah (ruled 1212–1202 BC), faced a rapidly deteriorating international situation. To the east and north the old order was crumbling. There were revolts in Palestine, which he put down. The Hittites were in dire trouble, and he sent them a supply of corn. From the west came the double threat of the ever-hostile Libyans, and the PEOPLE OF THE SEA. They invaded Egypt and attacked MEMPHIS, but Meneptah drove them back. Already an old man, he died after a short reign, leaving a complicated succession problem brought about by the prolific number of cadet branches of the Ramessid royal house. With no clear or undisputed successor, there was a series of usurpations and short reigns during some twelve years, and the state fell into some disarray. For a time the land was ruled by a queen, TWOSRE (c.1196–1188 BC), during the minority and again after the death of, her son, Siptah. Contemporary with Twosre was a CHANCELLOR, Iarsu, of Syrian origin, said to have been her lover and accused by a PAPYRUS of the time as plundering the treasury. *See also* Part One: Chapter 27.

NINTH AND TENTH DYNASTIES
Dynasties (2160–c.2140 BC) in the FIRST INTERMEDIATE PERIOD. Following the strife-torn EIGHTH DYNASTY, the emergence of the Ninth saw a new power appear. This was the Herakleopolitan dynasty, whose first king was the NOMARCH Kheti I, who seized control of the MEMPHIS kingdom and defeated the forces of UPPER

EGYPT at KOPTOS, establishing a somewhat fragile unity maintained by his own ARMY and energy. HERAKLEOPOLIS also provided the Tenth Dynasty, effectively a continuation of the Ninth, with Kheti II as king. The Herakleopolitans cleared the Asiatic invaders from the DELTA, but during the reign of Kheti III the parallel ELEVENTH DYNASTY emerged in THEBES. The Herakleopolitan army invaded Theban territory and captured ABYDOS but was unable to stamp out the rival house. Fighting continued indecisively over a period of about a century.

NITOCRIS
The first example in Egyptian history of a female king, i.e. a ruling queen. She is shown on MANETHO's list and in the TURIN CANON as a king. There is no archaeological evidence of her reign, which is said to have been at the end of the SIXTH DYNASTY, around 2200 BC, a time of confusion and upheaval.

NO
The name in the Old Testament of the Bible for THEBES.

NOMARCH
The governor of a NOME, or province, a leader of a provincial aristocracy, with power as administrator, judge and high priest of the nome's own local deity. In the tightly centralised days of the OLD KINGDOM, nomarchs were royal appointees, but from the SIXTH DYNASTY onwards they became increasingly independent and hereditary. They absorbed an ever greater share of the nome's wealth and constructed tombs for themselves on a splendid scale. Their rivalry and refusal to respond to the demands of the central government contributed to the later weakness and eventual decline into chaos of the OLD KINGDOM. During the FIRST INTERMEDIATE PERIOD, there was rivalry and warfare between nomarchs and super-nomarchs who had gained power over their neighbours. With the establishment of the MIDDLE KINGDOM, the role of the nomarchs was systematically reduced, there was a return to central control, and greater rights were granted to peasants and craftsmen, reducing the petty despotism of the nomarch. The last contribution of the nomarchs was to break the rule of the HYKSOS invaders and to bring about the NEW KINGDOM, but with the re-establishment of Egyptian rule, the nomarchs again lost independent power, although the office and title remained up to the end of the dynastic era.

NOME
The two Egypts were subdivided into 42 provinces, or nomes, based at least in part on the territories of the tribes who had inhabited the DELTA and NILE Valley in PRE-DYNASTIC times. To this can be traced the continuation of the nome's own local deity, with a god or fetish set up in the temple of the main town, which attracted the loyalty of the inhabitants and at the same time bound it into the

greater national COSMOLOGY. The nome was identified by its emblematic god, as in the Elephant Nome (capital Abu, now ELEPHANTINE), the Wolf Nome (This), the Hare Nome (HERMOPOLIS MAGNA) the Two Arrows Nome (SAIS, with its hunter-goddess NEITH). Loyalty to the nome and its god was always strong, and cities such as HERAKLEOPOLIS, TANIS and Sais profited greatly from the elevation of their local lords into the founders of dynasties.

NOMEN

One of the five names in a king's formal set of titles. The nomen is the king's birth name and is the second in the sequence. It was normally accompanied by the designation 'son of Ra'. This is the name that Egyptologists use to identify PHARAOHS, and it is modern Egyptology that has added the sequential number (e.g. Thuthmosis II) to designate a particular king.

NOPH

The name given in the Old Testament to MEMPHIS

NSW-BTY NAME *see* PRE-NOMEN.

NU *or* NUN

In Egyptian mythology, the pre-Creation, a primordial shapeless ocean out of which the sun-god RA emerged. *See* COSMOLOGY.

NUBIA

The country south of the first NILE cataract, south of present-day ASWAN, known to the Egyptians as Kush. Important as a source of building stone and timber and precious metals. In OLD KINGDOM times it was incorporated as part of the Egyptian kingdom, and in the NEW KINGDOM a VICEROY was appointed to rule it, but in the disturbed period of the TWENTY-SECOND to the TWENTY-FOURTH Dynasties it became a separate kingdom and its rulers achieved a reverse takeover of rule in Egypt, between 722–663 BC, the short-lived and unstable Nubian or Kushite Empire. The capital of Nubia was NAPATA, seat at various times of an Egyptian viceroy, of the exiled Theban priests of AMUN-RA and of an imperial PHARAOH.

NUBIAN DYNASTY *see* TWENTY-FIFTH DYNASTY.

NUN *see* NU.

NUNET

In Egyptian mythology, the consort of Nun. *See* COSMOLOGY.

NUT

In Egyptian mythology, the sky goddess, paired in the original OGDOAD with the earth-god GEB. Nut came later to be fused with HATHOR.

O

OBELISK

A tall monolithic four-sided shaft of stone, usually granite, tapering from base to top and surmounted by a small PYRAMID shape (PYRAMIDION). Originally they formed part of the sun cult at HELIOPOLIS, but became widely used as part of the processional entrance to temple complexes from MIDDLE KINGDOM times onwards.

OGDOAD

In Egyptian mythology, a group of eight deities. The most famous is the Hermopolitan, comprising four pairs of male frogs and female snakes, personifying the primeval forces of creation. The term is preserved in the modern town of Asmunein, on the west bank of the NILE opposite AMARNA, the ancient Khmunu or Eight-Town. *See* COSMOLOGY.

OLD KINGDOM

The greatest epoch of the history of the Egyptian kingdom, *c.* 2658–2185 BC. Its five-hundred-year history spans four dynasties, from the THIRD DYNASTY to the SIXTH. Initially maintaining the pace of development set during the immediately preceding THINITE PERIOD, there was rapid development in many walks of life during the Third Dynasty. For many commentators, the Third Dynasty, that of the first PYRAMID builders, represents a high point of culture and achievement that was never attained again. Up to that point, Egypt had shown an inventiveness, an energy and a technical development that brought many advances of civilisation into being. From the FOURTH DYNASTY onwards, a reaction set in. It was as if, to many Egyptians, a pinnacle had been reached that simply needed to be maintained. Stasis was everything. The years, the INUNDATIONS, the crops, would repeat themselves as a regular pattern, and human life and human activity, in an equally regular and predictable pattern, would fit together with the natural process in a divine harmony. The scale and quality of the early PYRAMIDS presented an unanswerable challenge. In the MIDDLE and the NEW KINGDOMS there were periods of comparable lustre and greater international renown, but the OLD KINGDOM was always the yardstick for comparison. Particularly for a people so passionately concerned with tradition and with the past, the shadow of the Old Kingdom and the purity of its rituals and practices during its most brilliant period lay far over the future. When the structures and systems of the Old Kingdom finally collapsed, it was felt to be like the end of the world. It had lasted for so long, had seemed so solid, had left such an enduring imprint upon the soil and the soul of Egypt – how could it perish? After the anarchy, FAMINE and disturbance of the FIRST INTERMEDIATE PERIOD, it was inevitable that the reunified Kingdom should model itself on its mighty predecessor. *See also* FIFTH DYNASTY.

OLD PRE-DYNASTIC PERIOD *see* PRE-DYNASTIC PERIOD.

ON
In the Old Testament of the Bible, the name used in the book of Genesis for HELIOPOLIS. In On JOSEPH married Asenath, daughter of Potipherah, priest of On, and Moses was educated at On.

ONOMASTICON (plural onomastica)
A categorised list of HIEROGLYPHIC words, listing animals, towns, plants, etc.

OPET FESTIVAL
The annual processional journey of AMUN-RA, down-river from THEBES to LUXOR and back again.

ORACLE
Some of the Egyptian gods had an oracular function, especially in the NEW KINGDOM and LATE PERIOD, when the power of the priests was at its height. This was notably the case with AMUN-RA at his temple in THEBES, where the figure of the deity was capable of movement when articulated by an unseen hand.

ORNAMENTATION
Aristocratic Egyptians of both sexes had time, opportunity and a definite taste for personal ornamentation. Women gilded their breasts, painted their nipples blue, curled their hair, plucked hair away from places where it was considered unsightly, shadowed their eyes with kohl and painted their palms and feet with henna. They wore anklets, earrings, necklaces and broad-neck collars, bracelets and SCARAB charms. The broad collar, made of rows of differently coloured and sized beads, arranged in a variety of patterns, was the main ornamentation. Throughout the dynastic period, both sexes wore wigs, sometimes with a little conical vessel set on top of the elaborate headdress, which slowly dripped a pleasant-smelling oil down on to the wearer's head. SILVER, GOLD, ivory and precious stones were worn by aristocrats, but shells and clay beads were available to everyone. Dancers wore bead girdles that clicked and rattled as they moved. Much ornamentation was of a prophylactic type, charms worn to ward off specific evils or diseases, or to venerate a particular deity. Other ornaments denoted

status, like the scarab seal rings worn on the third finger of the left hand by senior officials or the earrings awarded by the PHARAOH to long-serving courtiers. Earrings were worn by men and women TUTANKHAMUN had pierced ears, although no earrings in place. There were also FAIENCE earplugs, designed to fit into the lobes of the ears. Tattooing was common among female acrobats, dancers and prostitutes, whose work required partial or complete nudity. Often they featured the squat god Bes, a powerful fertility charm. *See also* COSMETICS; COSTUME.

OSIRIAN MYSTERIES

These rites were celebrated at the temple of OSIRIS at ABYDOS but also in other places. HERODOTUS records witnessing them at SAIS. The temples of other gods often had an Osirian chapel attached, for the festival of Osiris, which was a re-enactment of the god's death, burial and resurrection. A number of books have been found containing details of the ritual, including the *Book of the Wrapping of the Mummy* and the *Book of the Opening of the Mouth and Eyes for the Statue in the Golden Building*. A STELE from Abydos, set up in the reign of the TWELFTH DYNASTY king Sesostris III by the Chief of the Secrets of the Divine Sayings, records a royal command 'My Majesty has ordered that you should be taken up to Abydos in the NOME of Taur, to make a monument to my father, Osiris Khyent-Amenti, to adorn every sanctuary with electrum, which he has permitted my Majesty to bring from Nubia, as conqueror and a Justified One.' This text goes on to record the stages of the Mysteries, including a struggle to rescue the dead Osiris from evil spirits, the procession led by Anubis and THOTH to Osiris's tomb, the vengeance and the ultimate triumph of Horus. It is clear that these rites were performed by the very highest officials under the king.

OSIRIS

In Egyptian mythology, the most popularly worshipped of all the Egyptian gods, closely identified with the fertile 'black land' of the NILE Valley. The cycle of his life and death, and rebirth, corresponded to the annual cycle of flooding and new growth in the valley. Among his many attributes was to be the god of the dead, and he was believed to have been the first to undergo the process of MUMMIFICATION before his resurrection. Before admission to the UNDERWORLD, the dead were judged at the court of Osiris. Unlike such deities as PTAH or AMUN-RA, who were essentially gods of the ruling class, Osiris lived within the heart and soul of the people, and his legend is one of the great fundamental tales of Egyptian civilisation. He provides the essential link between the far-off sky-gods and the human condition, especially in terms of the AFTERLIFE. References to Osiris are not found in the early dynastic records, and his legend emerges from association with the DELTA god Andzti at BUSIRIS and a later assimilation with Khentiamentiu, god of the NECROPOLIS at ABYDOS, during the course of the FIFTH DYNASTY. The cults of such gods as Horus, Isis and Anubis were all originally independent of Osiris and appear to have preceded, and been absorbed by, him.

There are four key elements in the Osiris legend – his life, his death, his rebirth and his transfer of power to his son Horus. Osiris, first king of Egypt, taught his people many arts and sciences, including Agriculture, and so gave the Egyptians their staple fare of bread, beer and wine. He also gave them laws and taught them to honour the gods. His wife and queen was the sorceress Isis. Thoth was his vizier and brought the art of writing. Anubis and Wepwawet attended Osiris on his journeys of conquest across the world. Osiris was treacherously murdered by his brother, Seth. Seth produced a splendid casket at court and offered it to the man who would best fit it. After others had tried, Osiris did, and it was found to fit him perfectly. But Seth and his helpers shut down the lid of the casket, sealed it and sent it floating down the river. Seth then seized the throne of Egypt. But Isis, wife and sister to Osiris, aided by Nephthys, wife and sister to Seth, searched for the dead king, and they found the chest with his corpse inside it, washed up on the seashore at Byblos. Isis brought her husband's body to the holy city of Buto, but Seth discovered it there and hacked it into many pieces. The parts of Osiris's dismembered body were then distributed all over Egypt, but Isis found them all and reconstituted them with the help of Anubis, the jackal-headed god (said in the legend to have been the product of adulterous love between Osiris and Nephthys), who embalmed the dead king's body. In this mummified form, Osiris lived again, although apart from the mortal world, as ruler of the Kingdom of the Dead. Isis then gave birth to Horus, the posthumous son of Osiris, following a magical impregnation, and hid the baby from Seth amidst the marshes of the Delta, aided by the cow-goddess Hathor as wet-nurse. Horus eventually grew up to claim his inheritance and, after a long struggle against Seth, defeated him in battle. In the violence, Seth plucked out one of Horus's eyes and Horus tore off Seth's genitals. Seth appealed to the gods, claiming Horus to be illegitimate, but Horus's claim was found to be valid by a divine council presided over by Geb, and he became king of Egypt.

Thus it was that Osiris and Horus were ancestors of all the pharaohs, endowing them with godlike qualities. It can be seen how the Horus of the Osiris legend, Horus the Child, is different from the old sky-god of Letopolis. Osiris himself, with his original fetish object a tree, is in his beginning an agricultural god. The time of his death was the time when the full Nile began to sink. His legend appears in the pyramid texts, but its source is unknown. It was brought to the Delta region from elsewhere, and Osiris absorbed the older Delta cult of Andzti, 'the protector', at Busiris. His prestige spread through the two Egypts, he was back-absorbed into the cosmologies, annexed other gods to himself, including Anubis and Wepwawet, and remained the most omnipresent Egyptian deity until Egyptian religion itself was extinguished by Christianity.

Although the Osiris legend can be seen as a metaphor of the Egyptian cycle of flood, growing season, harvest, dry season, with the opposition of wet and dry, fertile and desert, and always the humanly vital aspect of regeneration, commentators have also seen the distant reflection of real social events and conditions within the myth. These events are the abandonment of a nomadic life and the settlement of a kingdom whose agriculture was arable rather than pastoral. There are hints of a culture in which the blood feud was a feature. With the change in settlement patterns came a change in marriage customs, with men seeking brides from within the community (endogamy) rather than from outside (exogamy) – hence the sister-wives of the god-kings. *See also* Part One: Chapter 2.

OSORKON *see* TWENTY-FIFTH DYNASTY.

OSTRACON (*plural* **OSTRACA**)
A potsherd, or fragment, of a pottery, clay or stone vessel, featuring a written or painted symbol or a piece of script.

OXYRHYNCHUS
An archaeological site in the FAIYUM where ancient papyri were discovered in 1897 and 1903.

P

PALACE
The king had separate residences in LOWER and UPPER EGYPT and progressed regularly between the two. Although imposing mansions, they were made of mud brick and wood rather than stone, with stone decorative features at the entrance, like SPHINXES and OBELISKS, and were less splendid than the funerary sites.

PALERMO STONE
A piece of a black stone slab, now in Palermo, Sicily. Where it came from in Egypt is not known. It bears a list of kings from Meni in the FIRST DYNASTY to NEFERIRKARE in the FIFTH, but the list is not complete. Other fragments have appeared since 1877, when the Palermo Stone was bequeathed to the museum there, but their connection with the Palermo Stone and, in some cases, their authenticity is not confirmed.

PALESTINE

The ancient land, co-extensive with the modern state of Israel and somewhat larger, which was conquered by Pharoah Necho II of Egypt in 609 BC but was seized by Nebuchadnezzar in 605 BC following his defeat of the Egyptians at Carchemish. *See also* TWENTY-SIXTH DYNASTY.

PALETTE ART

Palettes are small flat stone tools used to grind COSMETICS but also produced simply as votive objects and found in large numbers in PRE-DYNASTIC tombs. These are of archaeological importance in the period before written records for tracing the southwards push of cultural trends from the north, suggestive of a political development also going on in which the kingdom of LOWER EGYPT gained supremacy over that of UPPER EGYPT. These palettes, along with contemporary items such as mace heads, show how the Pre-dynastic Egyptians had already developed a very fine, small-scale ART of stone carving, which in the best examples shows an appreciation of the shape of the slate or stone, fitting the design to the form, as well as a delicacy of effect and sharpness of finish that can only have been accomplished by the finest of FLINT tools.

PANTHEON

In mythology, all the gods worshipped by a people.

PAPYROLOGY

The science of examining and dating the papyrus rolls on which the ancient Egyptians wrote.

PAPYRUS (*plural* PAPYRI)

Papyrus was always expensive, and its use was normally restricted to important documents. Papyrus paper was made from the plant of the same name, a tall, sedge-like marsh plant. The fresh green stems of the papyrus reed were chopped down and cut into manageable lengths. The outer rind was stripped away, exposing the soft and moist inner pith. The pith was cut out and the long slivers laid crosswise on top of one another on a stone surface. They were then pounded and rolled into long flat sheets, pressed and dried. Papyrus rolls up to 120 feet (36.5 metres) in length have been discovered. *See also* WRITING.

PEASANTRY

The great majority of the Egyptian population. They lived in small huts made out of mud brick or reeds smeared with a muddy paste, whose structure varied little with the centuries. Their possessions were very few. The gulf between this labouring multitude and the small number of upper-class priests and nobles was very great. The social division was at its worst during the first dynasties of the OLD KINGDOM, when the PHARAOHS were still extending their power and dominion against a deeply entrenched tradition of local rule. Joined in their family units, and sometimes outside them into 'battalions' supervised by foremen, the peasants were bound to the land in a permanent and hereditary serfdom. During the period of the INUNDATION, when field work was impossible, they were used as forced labour in the construction of monumental ARCHITECTURE. Armies of up to 10,000 toiled at individual sites, supplying by force of numbers the deficiencies of engineering science. At the end of the OLD KINGDOM there was revolt, when the peasantry at last found their lot so intolerable that the inbred respect for the status quo was forgotten. Reforms followed, and although the peasants remained without any share in the country's wealth, their social conditions were improved. By the NEW KINGDOM, SERFDOM was declining and there were little landholdings worked by single families, trading their flax for foodstuffs or their grain for cloth. Also, the great religious burden that denied heaven to all but the king and a chosen few had been lifted. From the end of the OLD KINGDOM it was accepted that a pleasant AFTERLIFE was open to all. This must have spread a spiritual relief through the entire nation. In periods of peace and a 'good NILE' their lives, al;though montonous, were not wretched or miserable. On the whole, the owners of the land were not cruel or heartless, and the workload was not so great that social pleasures and enjoyment were impossible. The year had its festivals and rituals, and it can be said that the Egyptian peasant was more fortunate than his contemporaries in other parts of the world.

PEDUBASTIS

A local DELTA king during the turbulent period of the Assyrian war, who opposed and was executed by ASSURBANIPAL. The Pedubastis Cycle is a collection of LATE PERIOD writings, in the DEMOTIC script, relating the exploits of the legendary hero Inaros and others against the Assyrians. There was a TWENTY-THIRD-DYNASTY PHARAOH of the same name.

PELUSIUM

A strategic town in the eastern DELTA region, one of the first to face any invader from Asia, and the location of several sieges and battles in the LATE PERIOD.

PEOPLE OF THE SEA

A loose term to cover the Indo-European peoples who migrated through the Middle East and across the Mediterranean during the late second millennium BC. A shifting confederation, constantly seeking land to occupy and practising piracy at sea, they made ferocious efforts to invade Egypt during the late NINE-TEENTH and early TWENTIETH Dynasties but were repulsed.

PEPY I

An OLD KINGDOM PHARAOH of the SIXTH DYNASTY. His reign was lengthy, suggesting that he acceded when very young. He undertook much building in northern NUBIA, and it was at HIERAKONPOLIS that the fine COPPER statue of him was found (now in the Egyptian Museum, Cairo). It was in his reign that the harem conspiracy referred to in WENI's memoir occurred, and he married again, late on, two sisters of a noble family from ABYDOS, one of whom produced his successor, Merenra.

PEPY II

An OLD KINGDOM PHARAOH of the SIXTH DYNASTY. He is believed to have reigned for longer than any other king of Egypt, and may have attained the age of a hundred. He took a great interest in NUBIA from childhood, writing to the governor of ASWAN, who had brought a pygmy back from an expedition, 'When you arrive at the Residence and this pygmy is with you, live and in good condition, my Majesty will do great things for you' – an unusual note of enthusiasm amidst the platitudinous phrases of official correspondence. The early confidence and prosperity of Pepy II's rule degenerated during the king's old age, and perhaps senility, into the administrative and social decay and upheavals that produced the FIRST INTERMEDIATE PERIOD.

PERISTYLE COURT

A temple or palace courtyard with a pillared arcade on all four sides.

PETRIE, SIR [William Matthew] FLINDERS (1853–1942)

British Egyptologist who, after spending two winters making accurate measures of the Great PYRAMID at GIZA, from what he saw of the excavations there, he advocated a quite different technique of painstaking, careful research. 'The true line,' he wrote, 'lies ias much in the careful noting and comparison of small details as in more wholesale and off-hand clearances.' This approach was justified when, during the course of exploratory work at Tanis, he discovered an early Greek trading station at NAUCRATIS. There were no sculptures at this site and therefore no inscriptions to provide information. Instead, Petrie and his colleagues, GRIFFITH and GARDNER, had to reconstruct the history of the site from its broken pottery.

For fifty years Petrie worked independently, funded by what was eventually called the British School of Archaeology in Egypt, founded by himself. He was Surveyor of the PYRAMIDS and temples of GIZA, and author of many books on ancient Egypt.

His discoveries in Egypt include the early royal tombs at ABYDOS, but even more important were the methods he introduced, including sequence-dating for

Egyptian pottery and a chronological framework for prehistoric antiquities for which there could be no dating in terms of years. His contribution to practical Egyptology was enormous, but he clung to his own 'long' chronology, despite general agreement among other Egyptologists on a shorter date.

PHARAOH

The Egyptian king, also known, among many other honorific titles, as 'the double lord' because of the original two kingdoms. The word is derived from the words *per aa*, meaning 'great house'. This is a typical circumlocution, reflecting the awe in which the king was held, by which the chief inhabitant of the palace became known by the name of the building itself. On accession, the pharaoh received five NAMES, beginning with his HORUS NAME, then his *nbty* names, taken from the tutelary goddesses of the two kingdoms, the vulture goddess Nekhebet of UPPER EGYPT and the cobra goddess BUTO of LOWER EGYPT. His third name was called the GOLDEN HORUS NAME. The fourth name was his principal name, to be used on official records, and finally his own family name, or his private name prior to assuming the kingship. Names were of prime importance, and this is why tombs and the objects that they contained were so liberally marked with the occupant's name and also why a usurper, or restored king of a legitimate line, might seek to expunge the AFTERLIFE of the king by erasing all mentions of his name (*see* THUTHMOSIS III).

The king lived at the absolute pinnacle of human life, at the point where he was partly a god. Even the most exalted of his subjects would be expected to lie prostrate before him until invited to stand. His role was to intercede with the gods for the welfare of the people, and thus he combined the secular aspects of kingship with the active role of high priest. The communion of pharaoh and the gods was a matter of ritual, of formulaic utterance, of giving offerings, all rich in symbolism and performed with a religious solemnity and a sense of human attunement to the cosmic life force that transcended the often (to modern eyes at least) puerility of the charms and spells that were inscribed and uttered.

Normally but not invariably the eldest son of his father's senior queen, the king-to-be was brought up after infancy in full awareness of his ultimate role. He would be solemnly married whilst still a child to a sister, half-sister or cousin. He would be thoroughly tutored in the subjects that it was felt proper for the king to know, including reading and writing, and always he would be taught the gods, their lives, their natures, their part in his ancestry, their multifarious influence on the life of Egypt, their rule of the AFTERLIFE. One day, he would be the master of the spells and incantations by which these immortal and capricious beings could be addressed, placated, thanked and venerated. In his teens he would learn the duties of a soldier, and, in the expansionist periods of the MIDDLE and NEW KINGDOMS, might go on a real campaign or even act as head of an expedition out of

Egypt. As crown prince he would have an honoured place in the household, his life less controlled by ceremony than the king's, with opportunities for hunting in the swamps and the desert and still treated as a fellow-mortal. On his accession to the throne, he was and would forever remain separate, invested with the qualities of a god. *See also* KINGSHIP.

PHARAOH'S DAY

The king's day began at dawn, with the rising of his father-patron, the sun. He was greeted with a song of good omen, ushering in the new day. In the temples, singers and musicians were awakening the gods in just the same way. The king's ablutions, bathing, shaving and massage, were performed by servants, he was dressed in his royal garments and took the first meal of the day. The secular side of his life was conducted in the palace, with his chief SCRIBE, assistant scribes, his VIZIER, his CHANCELLOR, and the HONOURED ONES who made up his council. The king took note of letters and reports, and dictated or himself wrote replies, orders, commissions and declarations. These were rolled, sealed with the great seal and despatched via waiting messengers. Accounts were dealt with, a scribe recording in the *Book of the God* (i.e. the king) items of receipt and outgoing. Problems might be discussed with the councillors, most of whom would be members of his own family, including his heir. For public audience, he sat on his throne before the palace door for the two royal offices of judging and commanding. Wearing the CROWN and holding the symbolic crook and flail, he announced decrees or listened to a herald (some of the oldest court offices were designated as The Mouth, The Tongue, etc) perform the task on his behalf and gave judgement on issues. There was no debate or dissension. Those who wished audience of the king 'nosed' the ground before him and kissed it; a specially favoured individual might be allowed to kiss his feet.

The predominant item in the king's routine was religion. Every day had its special religious significance, marking the feast of a particular god or an episode in the life of a major god. Borne on a palanquin, for gods did not walk in public view, he proceeded to the temple. There he was ritually washed and anointed, and the sanctum itself was purified by incense-burning. Then he opened the seals that closed off the shrine of the god and lay prostrate before it as the hymn of worship was chanted. He purified and anointed the figure, took it in his arms and offered it food. Further purifications and anointings followed; the statue was decorated with ornaments and dressed in symbolic bandages before it was returned to the shrine, the doors were closed and the seals replaced. The king left the sanctuary walking backwards, with the traces of his footsteps being sent away. Details of such ritual varied from day to day and evolved with the passage of the dynasties. Often a SACRIFICE was made, with wild animals like gazelles preferred for the purpose over domesticated ones.

The king did not spend all his time on official duties. There was opportunity for leisure pursuits, including hunting. Palace and temple both possessed singers and dancers, entertainers and magicians to amuse the court. His meals were elaborate and symbolic, preceded by rinsings and anointings. The original determinative sign for a meal is composed of a cone-shaped loaf, a beer pot and a round cake. A king's ceremonial meal comprised loaves and cakes, but also as many as ten kinds of meat, many different vegetables and an assortment of drinks, including red and white wine.

PHILAE
A site on the NILE, just north of ELEPHANTINE, centre of the cult of ISIS. The Philae temples have been resited in modern times on the island of Agilkia because of the building of the ASWAN High Dam.

PIANKHY
A PHARAOH of the TWENTY-FIFTH DYNASTY (ruled 747–716 BC). King of NUBIA, he stormed through Egypt with an invasion that took the country by surprise and, having obtained the surrender of UPPER and LOWER EGYPT, returned to his capital, NAPATA, as unexpectedly as he had come. He had been brought up in the tenets of the Egyptian religion and was a devout worshipper of the Egyptian gods. His court and society at Napata set out to follow the example of the Egyptian capital, including the construction of PYRAMIDS and MORTUARY TEMPLES.

PINUDJEM I *see* TWENTY-FIRST DYNASTY.

PIRAMESSE
A site in the eastern DELTA, selected as capital by RAMESES II and used until the end of the Ramessid era, about 200 years later. Its monumental buildings were later used as quarries to extend the new capital at nearby TANIS.

PLOUGH
The ox-drawn plough, which had a huge impact on AGRICULTURE and on society, appeared in Egypt around the time of the FIRST DYNASTY and at the same time as it appeared in Mesopotamia. Previously, a hand-pushed plough or a digging stick or a copper-bladed hoe had been used. The ox-drawn plough, primitive as it was, was incomparably more efficient. It had the effect of 'freeing' labour from the fields, which was speedily transferred to building projects.

PLUTARCH (AD *c.* 46–*c.*120)
Greek philosopher, biographer and historian who recorded the myth of Osiris.

POPULATION

In the late PRE-DYNASTIC PERIOD it has been estimated at around 1,000,000. By the THIRD DYNASTY it may have been three times as much or even more. It seems likely that throughout the OLD and MIDDLE KINGDOMS, the population was around 5,000,000, except when there was civil disorder and FAMINE, when it dropped rapidly through a combination of early death and high infant mortality. By Roman times, at least during peace, it had attained some 7,000,000. Life expectancy in Egypt was low. Even for a member of the leisured class, the average life span was around 36 years.

POTIPHAR *see* JOSEPH.

POTIPHERAH *see* ASENATH; ON.

PRE-DYNASTIC PERIOD

Corresponding to the New Stone Age, the era between the Palaeolithic civilisation of Egypt (*see* PRE-HISTORY) and the rise of the FIRST Dynasty of kings, approximately from 5500 BC to 3500 BC. This lengthy period saw the gradual but steady development of AGRICULTURE and a settled way of life. The majority of settlements were in the areas of MIDDLE and UPPER EGYPT, although they extend from the apex of the DELTA area as far as the second cataract, at Wadi Halfa. Although writing was invented during the Pre-dynastic Period, its lack of written texts made it initially less accessible or attractive to archaeologists and Egyptologists. It was only in the latter part of the twentieth century that it became appreciated as not simply a 'prehistoric' preparation but a period of intense interest and great richness. It is now subdivided into separate phases. The Early Pre-dynastic (sixth–fifth millennium BC) or Badarian Period (from the Badari site in Upper Egypt) is still Stone Age, although at the highest point of development. Pottery was being made, often of a sophisticated design. Already the development of the tomb as a monument is detectable, the medium of its construction being mud brick, although the corpse was simply wrapped in an animal's hide. The Old Pre-dynastic or Naqadal Period, named after the Naqada site in the centre of the Nile's huge bend north of LUXOR, from about 4500 BC, is traced chiefly by means of its highly developed clay pottery, notably in terracotta statuettes. The third phase, the Middle Pre-dynastic, Naqadal or Gerzean Period, takes its name from later finds at Naqada and the discovery of tombs, pottery items and other artefacts at el-GERZA, near MAIDUM. This shows increasing evidence of an intermingling of styles from north and south. Pottery is decorated not only with representations of birds and animals but with devices that may be the symbols of gods. The tombs were substantial, often containing several chambers. The final phase is the Late Pre-dynastic, blending imperceptibly into the dynastic period. By this time the population had grown considerably and there were substantial communities that were fully aware of one another, exchanged goods and shared a common culture and language. The process of political agglomeration had also begun, with larger and more successful communities drawing neighbouring settlements into their own spheres of influence.

If the development of ancient Egypt is imagined in graph form, then the Predynastic Period would be a long, very shallow curve but beginning to rise much more sharply in the last few hundred years of its two-and-a-half millennia duration. Mobile tribal units with ill-defined frontiers were being replaced by agricultural communities organised in larger groups, with enough internal organisation to create communal grain stores, manage the division of land after the INUN-DATION and engage in mutual and even foreign trade. In time, the tribal units, whilst maintaining much of their own identities and local loyalties, were drawn into two kingdoms. These corresponded to the DELTA area and to the NILE Valley stretching southward from it. The concept of duality, deeply rooted in the ancient Egyptians' minds and ideas, can be at least partly ascribed to this early division.

PREHISTORY

The human race appears to have originated on the African continent, where its most ancient remains have been found. A million years ago the geographical configuration of the landscape and the climatic conditions were very different from now and, indeed, very different from those of the historical period of ancient Egypt. There was greater rainfall in the area, and the Sahara depression was a vast lake. The course and size of the NILE were different, following a course well to the west of the present stream. There is evidence of pre-human habitation in the area of ABU SIMBEL from around 700,000 years ago, and *homo sapiens* has been in the region for at least 100,000 years, as is shown by archaeological evidence from the depressions in the Eastern Desert which once held lakes. A number of cultural phases have been identified, some suggesting regression as well as progress. The peoples of the region had to adapt to climatic change, however slow, as the Sahara assumed its desert aspect and the Nile assumed its present form. The dwellers in the regions that are now arid moved towards the Nile Valley, maintaining a combined riverine and savannah hunting style, living in separate groups. AGRICULTURE was practised at a very early stage, and the use of stone implements displayed skills and tools akin to those of the NEOLITHIC PE-RIOD. Around the middle of the sixth millennium BC, the practice of AGRICULTURE took firm hold and with it settled communities and a way of life that was dependent on the natural cycle of sowing, tilling and reaping, with all the skills that these activities require.

PRE-NOMEN

One of the five names making up the king's formal title. Written inside a

CARTOUCHE, it is also known as the *nsw-bty* name, from the accompanying phrase meaning 'He of the SEDGE and the BEE', or *neb tawy* name 'Lord of the Two Lands', both expressing the dual kingship.

PRIEST

Every priest, from the grandest to the most rustic craftsman-attendant of a minor tomb, was merely a deputy of the chief priest, the PHARAOH. They were the keepers of ritual, they knew the formulae appropriate to their own rank and department, but they did not partake of the pharaoh's unique and indivisible power. The Egyptian term for the priesthood was the 'pure ones'. There were two major divisions, with a superior group known as Prophets and an inferior group of Ordinary priests. Reflecting the structure of the court, there was a distinct hierarchy within the temple, with many gradations between the neophyte and the chief prophet. Whilst the priest was of course aware of and respectful to the entire pantheon of gods and their complex and changing interrelations, he was nevertheless especially a priest of the god to whom his temple was dedicated and served his rite in particular. As the year passed, each major and local deity had its own time of festival.

The status of priests varied according to the prestige of their god, their proximity to the court, their birth and their ability. Many of the priests in MORTUARY TEMPLES were part-timers, who were also craftsmen who kept the site in good repair. These men would provide the regular offerings but would command few of the secrets relating to the AFTERLIFE which were the source of the priesthood's vast prestige. But the priesthood, in charge of education and of the magic art of reading and writing, had great power and influence over the secular life of Egypt, although it was a country where the religious and the secular are unusually hard to separate. Doctors, jurists, administrators, architects, could achieve their professional status only through the priesthood. Priests could marry. They had many social privileges, including exemption from the forced labour that was inflicted on most adult males at the time of the INUNDATION. Normally they were free of taxation, as were their temples and tomb cities. Their symbol was a staff of office.

PRIESTESS

The priesthood was largely male, with the role of the female priest confined chiefly to ceremonial dance and the provision of music. Allied with this was the role of the sacred prostitutes, found in many temples where the god had a fertility connection but especially those of Min. See also adoratrice of Amun.

PRISSE D'AVENNES, EMILE (1807–79)

French Egyptologist who went to Egypt as a civil engineer but after 1836 devoted himself entirely to archaeology. He made numerous finds at KARNAK and in Nubia and Ethiopia, including papyri of the Fifth and Fourteenth Dynasties.

PROSTITUTION

In a male-dominated society, where fertility and its display were encouraged, prostitution will flourish. There was nothing furtive or underhand about it in ancient Egypt, where most of the major gods had a strong link with fertility. The prostitute, whether practising under the patronage of the temple or not, had her place in the scheme of things in this cashless society, and there is no suggestion of stigma attaching itself to the profession.

PSAMMETICHUS I

A PHARAOH of the TWENTY-SIXTH DYNASTY in the LATE PERIOD. At this time Egypt was under Assyrian domination, and Psammetichus began his rule by permission of ASSURBANIPAL as a client king. He was king of SAIS, and his rule was at first effective only in LOWER EGYPT. Even here, local lords had considerable independence. He eventually gained control of THEBES, obtaining the surrender of Mentuemhet, who had ruled there as VIZIER of the Nubian kings. Using a composite ARMY of Egyptians and displaced Phoenicians, Syrians and Jews, he gradually established full control. His reign was lengthy, occupying almost half the entire period characterised as the Saite Dynasty in which Egypt once again flourished as a unified state, and a determined, consciously nationalist, effort was made to return to the religious and artistic traditions of earlier times.

PSAMMETICHUS II and III *see* TWENTY-SIXTH DYNASTY.

PSUSENNES I *see* TWENTY-FIRST DYNASTY.

PTAH

In Egyptian mythology, the local god of MEMPHIS. When Memphis became a royal capital during the FIRST AND SECOND DYNASTIES, Ptah's status grew accordingly. The Memphis priesthood developed a cult of Ptah, which claimed he was the oldest god and had himself created RA-ATUM by pure thought. All other gods and created things were similarly the product of the mind of Ptah. HORUS was claimed to be his heart and THOTH his tongue. The concept of Ptah, although a profound one, was too abstract and abstruse for him to become a true deity of the people. In the course of the OLD KINGDOM, the worship of Ptah, with revivals whenever Memphis was dominant, gradually declined and Ra-Atum became established as the principal god. *See also* TANEN.

PTAHHOTEP

A hereditary royal official of the Pharaoh WENIS (FIFTH DYNASTY), grandson of a

VIZIER of the same name. He is credited with the authorship of a celebrated set of maxims, *The Instruction of Ptahhotep* (see Part One: Chapter 13), setting out rules for leading a well-ordered and balanced life. These were much copied during the MIDDLE and NEW KINGDOM periods.

PTOLEMAIC PERIOD

The period (304–30 BC) that most Egyptologists take to be outside the study of ancient Egypt and more properly part of the study of the Greek and Roman era. But the Ptolemies in their turn assumed the dignities and titles of pharaohs, accepted their status as semi-divine and took up such Egyptian traditions as incestuous marriage. They restored many temples and built others. But throughout the country the Greeks formed a kind of upper class, controlling official posts to the exclusion of Egyptians, who resented and despised the Greeks as 'Ionian dogs'. The many immigrant Greeks were contemptuous of Egyptian religion and tradition. During this period the indigenous peasant population, performing their daily tasks as their ancestors had done for thousands of years, were increasingly exploited and impoverished as Greek merchants and magnates took control of production. The Ptolemies could not regenerate Egypt's greatness, as had been done so many times in the past. Egypt was inexorably drawn more and more into the international politics of the Graeco-Roman world, and in 30 BC even the shadow of a kingdom came to an end with the suicide of Cleopatra, last of the Ptolemies to reign in Egypt.

PTOLEMY

The family name of the last independent rulers of Egypt (304–30 BC).

PUNT

A land south of NUBIA, situated inland from the Somali coast, and a source of myrrh and other resins and ointments, also GOLD, ivory, ebony and leopard skins. Exploratory visits to Punt were made during the FIFTH and SIXTH DYNASTIES, and the young king PEPY II was very excited by the arrival of a pygmy tribesman, brought back by the governor of ASWAN. Numerous large expeditions were despatched in MIDDLE and NEW KINGDOM times. Such ventures were major undertakings. The route taken was not overland into the interior of the continent but across the Eastern Desert to the Red Sea and by ship to a safe haven on the east coast of tropical Africa. During the LATE PERIOD, the trade eventually died out and Punt lapsed into a place of myth.

PYLON

An architectural term referring to a monumental gateway rising above the surrounding construction, formed of two great towers with a gateway between them, all their outer sides sloping inwards, and crowned with a wide, upturned cornice.

PYRAMID

The pyramid evolved from the MASTABA during the THIRD DYNASTY, as ever more imposing tombs were desired. There was a further reason, which explains the specific shapes adopted for these vast monuments. Pyramid is a Greek word, not Egyptian, possibly derived from a term meaning 'wheat cake', a comestible whose shape may have been pyramidal. The oldest-dated pyramid is the Step Pyramid at Saqqara, dating back to about 2800 BC, and the first great stone monument of the world. It was built as a tomb for the PHARAOH, Djoser, of the Third Dynasty, by his VIZIER, IMHOTEP. Its stepped formation may be seen as a succession of mastabas built on top of one another, and the specific intention, as revealed by the PYRAMID TEXTS, was to assist the dead ruler's progress skywards by providing him with a gigantic staircase. Secondary reasons can also be provided. As early as this, there would still have been a wish to prevent the depredations of the tomb robber, and also the sheer size and complexity of this structure must have given satisfaction to the great man who commissioned it. At this point in the kingdom's development, the necessary elements of a huge labour force, the raw materials and the constructional skills could all be brought together. The pyramid did not stand alone but was the centrepiece of a group of buildings set around courtyards. The functions of these were to provide a processional route for the KA, or the statue, of the king to promenade, to house priests and to store votary objects, in addition to the MORTUARY TEMPLE and chapels. In one of the latter would be housed the jars holding the preserved entrails of the mummified pharaoh. Just as the living pharaoh moved from room to room within his earthly residences, so his abode in DEATH provided a range of chambers for different rites. His statue in the SERDAB faced two eyeholes in the wall separating it from the mortuary temple, enabling him to see the offerings made to him. A great wall was built around the whole site, itself of ornamental construction and with a single gate.

The Step Pyramid itself stands well preserved, but its facing has been lost, and it no longer reflects the gleaming light of the sun as it did when new and for long afterwards. But the architectural details of the interior, and of the whole site, are lively and finely carved and shaped, with a vitality that lightens the massively monumental nature of the construction. The surviving COLUMNS are elegantly slender, with beautifully executed leaf-shaped capitals. The columns take various shapes, some resembling the papyrus stem, some ribbed or fluted, forms that would be reused and adapted many times over in the succeeding millennia. This instant leap into a sophisticated ARCHITECTURE in stone has long been wondered at, but much of its design is owed to imitation of wooden forms. There may have been many more wooden buildings in the PRE-DYNASTIC and THINITE PERIODS than was once thought possible, with their architecture providing inspiration when the use of dressed and carved stone really got under way.

The pyramid of SNOFRU at MAIDUM shows the culmination of the next phase of pyramid-building. Square in plan, it probably began as a mastaba-style construction, with the step formation as at Saqqara, but the steps were filled in with limestone masonry to form a smooth-sided pyramid that reached a peak. Snofru constructed two more pyramids, including the oddly shaped 'bent' or rhomboidal pyramid at Dabshur.

The art of pyramid construction was perfected in the FOURTH DYNASTY with the pyramid of CHEOPS at GIZA, the 'Great Pyramid', a superb feat of engineering, architecture and masonwork. Each side measures 230 metres (754$\frac{1}{2}$ feet), to an accuracy of 25 centimetres (10 inches), and the sides are oriented to the points of the compass. It slopes at 51 or 52 degrees and reaches a height of 146.59 metres (481 feet). Its heaviest stone blocks weigh over forty tonnes, and the total number of blocks has been estimated at 2,700,000. Within the structure, entered from the northern face, are chambers, galleries, shafts and air vents, including the 'grand gallery', 48 metres (157$\frac{1}{2}$ feet) in length, 5.4 metres (17$\frac{3}{4}$ feet) wide and 8.5 metres (27$\frac{7}{8}$ feet) high. The method of construction has been long debated, but it seems most likely that temporary earth ramps were built up against the rising structure of the pyramid, enabling the massive blocks of stone to be slowly hauled up and set into position.

The work was carried out over a number of years, perhaps as many as twenty for a major work like the Great Pyramid, with a work force of 10,000 or more peasants drafted in during the period of the INUNDATION, accommodated and fed in barracks set up close by – remains of these can still be seen at Giza. The Fourth-Dynasty kings CHEPHREN and MENKAURE also erected pyramids at Giza, and pyramid construction continued in the FIFTH and SIXTH and subsequent dynasties, several Fifth-Dynasty ones at ABUSIR, the Sixth-Dynasty at Saqqara. But the later pyramids have not survived the storm of time nearly so well as the Great Pyramid; their stone casings have largely gone and they have been subject to erosion by natural and human agencies. From the Fourth Dynasty onwards, pyramids for queens were also constructed, in the vicinity of the king's pyramid and on a smaller scale.

All the pyramids were looted by tomb robbers in ancient times. The Old Dynasty Pyramids were robbed during the FIRST INTERMEDIATE PERIOD, and efforts were made to restore some of them during the MIDDLE KINGDOM. We only know Cheops to be the 'owner' of the Great Pyramid by the fact that his symbol is cut into some of the stone blocks: all trace of his occupancy, the statues, the furnishings, the reliefs, were long gone when western visitors first penetrated its mysterious and awe-inspiring interior. *See also* FUNERARY PRACTICE.

PYRAMIDION

The pyramid-shaped apex of an OBELISK. It represents the BEN-BEN stone: the rays of the sun caught in stone, set on the primeval mound that rose from the waters.

PYRAMID TEXTS

Texts engraved on the passage walls of FIFTH- and SIXTH-DYNASTY pyramids at Saqqara, concerned with securing entry into the AFTERLIFE for the deceased. These texts, often repeated from tomb to tomb, are a mixture of PRE-DYNASTIC writings, preserved by tradition, and the later OSIRIS legend, and the conflation of the two gives rise to a certain amount of confusion. The pyramid texts also give an indication of the thinking behind the development of the pyramid itself. The ultimate destination of the dead king was the sky, where he would join the gods. The pyramid, in its original form of the step pyramid, provided him with a stair-case (the HIEROGLYPHIC symbol for the step pyramid was also the determinative sign of the verb 'to climb'). In its later smooth-sided form, the pyramid symbolised the sun's rays, petrified – another means by which the king could climb to heaven. The placing of the texts symbolised the two journeys made by the deceased. Those reading inwards to the burial chamber corresponded to the stages by which the corpse was borne to its last resting place. Those reading outwards from the SARCOPHAGUS chamber follow the journey of resurrection, as the king leaves his sarcophagus in its actual and symbolic UNDERWORLDS and attains heaven through his transit of the various chambers and doors, and finally by means of the pyramid itself, reflecting the sun's rays back to their source. *See also* BOOK OF THE DEAD, COFFIN TEXTS.

Q

QUARRYING

Egypt is rich in stone, and when the development of society in the OLD KINGDOM brought about the rise of stone buildings and a stone-based ARCHITECTURE, quarrying became an important industry. It was necessary to find workable outcrops of good building stone, to quarry it, to cut it into movable blocks and to transport it, sometimes many miles, to the building site. To quarry the stone, slots were first cut into it, then hardwood wedges were driven in and hammered down. The technique of using dry wood and soaking it so that it expanded and forced the stone apart may also have been used. The new-cut block was then shaped with hammers of a harder stone; and copper saws may have been used also, in con junction with an abrading agent to assist the cutting. Rollers and sledges were used with thick ropes made of fibre to drag the blocks, some of them weighing more than thirty tonnes, into position for further working. The Egyptians were prepared to travel far in search of the right stone for their purposes and knew of deposits far out in the desert areas. Expeditions would be mounted to open up such quarries, following an order from the king or high priest. All this large-scale quarrying activity was carried out without the use of iron tools or of the block and tackle. Time, patience and a huge labour force made up for the deficiency in equipment.

QUEDESH *see* KADESH (1).

R

RA *or* **RE**
The oldest and one of the greatest of the gods, with a complex history of development. He is also known as ATUM, or Ra-Atum. A sky-god identified with the sun, he arose out of NUN, the primeval water, and through his own creation created the elements to sustain life on Earth, with SHU the air-god, NUT the sky-god, GEB the earth-god, Tefnut, the goddess of moisture, NEPHTHYS, OSIRIS and ISIS. The centre of Ra's cult was HELIOPOLIS (Greek: 'sun city') in the DELTA. Ra was perceived in different ways, according to whether the sun was blazing at the zenith or setting in the western sky: this latter was its Atum persona. *See also* AMUN.

RADADEF
A possible king of the Fourth Dynasty in the line of Khufu (Cheops), who cannot be placed with any certainty.

RAHOTEP *see* FIFTEENTH, SIXTEENTH AND SEVENTEENTH DYNASTIES.

RAMESES I
The first PHARAOH of the NINETEENTH DYNASTY in the NEW KINGDOM. Like HOREMHEB, his predecessor, he was not of the royal line but had been a general and VIZIER.

RAMESES II
A PHARAOH of the NINETEENTH DYNASTY (ruled 1279–1212 BC) in the NEW KING-

DOM. Until the sudden twentieth-century fame of TUTANKHAMUN, he was the best-known pharaoh to posterity. The early years of his reign were marked by foreign campaigns, culminating in the battle at Kadesh between the Egyptians and the HITTITES. The king recorded this battle in temples at ABYDOS, KARNAK (in three different parts of the temple of AMUN-RA) and at his great temple at ABU SIMBEL, among others, proclaiming the doubtful result as a resounding victory. In the twenty-first year of his reign he made the first recorded peace treaty between two states, with King Hattusilis of the Hittites. Copies were kept in both capitals, transliterated in the languages of both countries. The treaty did actually inaugurate a lasting peace, and Rameses acquired two Hittite princesses in his collection of wives. He set up his capital at PIRAMESSE, close to AVARIS in the eastern DELTA, a convenient location for his eastern interests – at this time the Egyptian dominions stretched from NUBIA to Syria. In the course of his lengthy reign, RAMESES II built some of the most grandiose of Egyptian monuments. These include the Great and Small Temples at Abu Simbel, the Great Temple being dedicated to the king himself in association with Amun-Ra, PTAH and Ra-Horakhty ('the rising sun') and the Small Temple dedicated to his queen, Nefertari, linked with HATHOR, the RAMESSEUM at Thebes, and many others. Unlike his long-reigning predecessor, PEPY II, Rameses II appears to have been vigorous to the end, and his successor inherited a state that was the major world power. *See also* Part One: Chapter 27.

RAMESES III *see* TWENTIETH DYNASTY.

RAMESSEUM
One of the vast monuments erected by RAMESES II in the NEW KINGDOM period, a palace-cum-MORTUARY TEMPLE on the grandest scale in the centre of the great 'dead city' on the west bank of the NILE at THEBES. Among the elements it retains are a PYLON, HYPOSTYLE HALL, COLOSSAL STATUE and sanctuary. Opinions among Egyptologists on its style vary from condemnation as outright vulgarity to praise for its purity. The palace consisted of an audience chamber and throne room, with apartments behind. From this a ramp flanked by two colossi led through a pylon to a PERISTYLE COURT, lined on two sides with further colossi. A hypostyle hall led through to the sanctuary area. Subsidiary temples at each side were dedicated to the Theban TRIAD (AMUN, MUT, KHONSU), and to OSIRIS.

RAMMAN *see* SUTEKH.

RAN
The personal name of an individual (*see* NAMING). *See also* Part One: Chapter 1.

RE *see* RA.

RED CROWN *see* CROWN; REGALIA.

REDDEDET

In Egyptian mythology, the mother of the first three kings of the FIFTH DYNASTY. *See also* Part One: Chapter 11.

RED GRANARY *see* GRANARY; TRADE.

RED HOUSE OR RED TREASURY *see* CHANCELLOR; TREASURY.

REGALIA

The prime item in the royal regalia was the CROWN. The White Crown of UPPER EGYPT was a tall, elegant conical hat. The Red Crown of LOWER EGYPT was a flat-topped hat with a high projection at the back and a long forward-curling feather. These two were combined as the Double Crown. In the NEW KINGDOM there was also the Blue Crown, or War Crown, made of blue leather and studded with sequins of GOLD. Around the crown was placed the URAEUS, the ancient cobra symbol of the Lower Kingdom goddess BUTO. Since Buto was also represented as a vulture, and the Upper Kingdom goddess Nekhbet was a vulture-goddess, the uraeus had significance in both lands. In its centre was placed the sun disc. The king's other accoutrements included a crook and a flail, the two instruments signifying his role as guide and shepherd on the one hand (and a reminder of his ancient responsibility for securing the harvest) and as chastiser and source of justice on the other.

RENENUTET

In Egyptian mythology, a cobra-headed goddess, a protector of households and the harvest. Traces of her worship have been found at Deir el-Medina.

RESHEP *or* **RESHPU**

A Phoenician creator god imported into Egyptian mythology during the EIGHTEENTH DYNASTY. He was depicted as a bearded man in profile, carrying a club and spear or a spear and the ANKH (the symbol of life), with the head and neck of a gazelle, one of the holy animals associated with ASTARTE, projecting from his helmet. In Egypt he formed a triad with MIN and KADESH.

RHAMPSINITUS

A possible king of the THIRD DYNASTY. He features in a legend as related by Herodotus (see Part One: Chapter 11).

RHIND PAPYRUS *see* FIFTEENTH, SIXTEENTH AND SEVENTEENTH DYNASTIES.

RIMMON *see* SUTEKH.

ROCK TOMBS

The earliest Egyptian rock tombs are FOURTH DYNASTY, cut in the rock of the GIZA plateau. Their layout was similar to that of the MASTABA, with anteroom, chapel and SERDAB. The tomb chamber was beneath, reached by a shaft from the chapel or from a special antechamber. The entrance, in the rock face, was carved to resemble the structure of a mastaba. The most elaborate rock tombs are in the VALLEY OF THE KINGS.

ROSETTA STONE

A milestone in the decipherment of ancient Egyptian texts was the discovery in 1799, by members of Napoleon's expedition, of an inscribed slab of black basalt at Rosetta (now Rashid), at the mouth of the Nile. A piece of late Egyptian work, it carries the text of a decree of Ptolemy V Epiphanes, in the official Greek but also in DEMOTIC Egyptian and HIEROGLYPHICS. The fragment measures 114 by 72 centimetres ($44^7/_8$ by $28^3/_8$ inches). The Egyptian text was translated and published by both [Young] and CHAMPOLLION. The Rosetta Stone is in the British Museum in London.

ROYAL MARRIAGE

In religious legend OSIRIS had married his sister, ISIS, who gave birth to HORUS. This sanctified the practice of a future PHARAOH marrying, while still a child, one of his sisters or another close female relation. Later he might take further wives and mistresses, but the Egyptians strongly believed that the pharaoh should have as much royal (and so divine) blood as possible. Kings regularly married their own daughters. Despite this legitimised and holy incest, there seems to have been little of the adverse affects of inbreeding. The extent to which the practice occurred outside the royal family is uncertain, but since it was an effective way of retaining titles and possessions within a family, it may well have been practised by the baronial class.

RUBBISH MOUNDS

Every Egyptian settlement had rubbish mounds, or communal middens, into which all kinds of waste and debris were pitched. They relied on the heat of the sun, and on scavenging birds and animals to keep the tips from becoming too noisome. Even so, they cannot have been nice to be near. These midden heaps are treasuries for the archaeologist, who can find out an immense amount about people's culture, DIET and living habits from the things they throw away, with the different layers assisting in the dating process.

S

SACRIFICE

Offerings were routinely presented to the gods and to the dead in their MORTUARY
TEMPLES. Meat offerings usually constituted the head, legs, ribs or offal. Wild animals were regarded as superior to domestic animals for sacrificial purposes. It
does not seem that animals were slaughtered on a large scale for sacrificial purposes, although FIFTH-DYNASTY SUN TEMPLES have slaughter yards attached,
which suggests that there may have been exceptions.

SAHU

A term for the mummy (*see* MUMMIFICATION) of an individual. It formed a TRIAD
with the KHAYBET and the KA.

SAHURE

The second king of the Fifth Dynasty. He used seagoing warships to harry the
Phoenician coast (*see* SHIPS AND SHIPBUILDING). He features in the legend of the
birth of the first three kings of the dynasty (*see* Part One: Chapter 11).

SAIS

A settlement and NOME capital in the eastern DELTA region, centre of the cult of
NEITH and the source of two of the later dynasties, the brief TWENTY-FOURTH and
the more splendid TWENTY-SIXTH. See also PSAMMETICHUS.

SAITE DYNASTY *see* TWENTY-SIXTH DYNASTY.

SALATIS *see* FIFTEENTH, SIXTEENTH AND SEVENTEENTH DYNASTIES.

SANITATION

In NEW KINGDOM houses of the gentry there is some evidence of small bathrooms
and lavatories, but only in larger houses and only adjacent to the master bed-
room. The bathroom had a bath place in the corner, a shallow tub of stone in
which the bather stood and had water poured over him by a servant. The water
was carefully drained off to the outside or into a collecting vessel; water and mud
brick were best kept apart. Lavatories were a luxury furnishing, a stone or
wooden seat above a collecting pot that would be taken to the rubbish heap for

emptying. Egyptian cities had no drainage. Most people simply used the fields, although houses in towns and villages may also have had trays of earth and sand.

SAQQARA

A major funerary site of the OLD KINGDOM, at the southern end of the vast funerary district that extends from GIZA, on the west bank of the NILE, south of Cairo. North Saqqara has the Step Pyramid of Djoser (the first pyramid) and numerous others; among those at south Saqqara are the pyramids of PEPY I and II. Saqqara is rich in other monuments, MORTUARY TEMPLES and MASTABAS

SARCOPHAGUS (*PLURAL* SARCOPHAGI)

The chest, made of stone or wood and equipped with a lid, in which the coffin of the mummified corpse was laid. Sarcophagi, especially royal ones, were often extremely elaborate. As the closest thing to the body, apart from the wrappings themselves and the coffin, the spells painted on or incised into the sarcophagus were among the most important and powerful.

SARU *see* LEGAL SYSTEM.

SATI *or* SATET

In Egyptian mythology, one of the two wives of KHNUM. She was a protective goddess of the cataracts of the Nile, and her title, Lady of the Heavens, links her with NUT and HATHOR. She is depicted as a stately woman wearing a cow's horns and the white CROWN of Upper Egypt. Khnum's other wive was ANUKET.

SCARAB

Close observers of every form of life, the Egyptians developed a special feeling for the humble scarab, a species of dung beetle. This tiny creature was linked to the majestic sun-god and became the symbol of resurrection. The female lays her eggs in a ball of dung, which she then rolls in front of her through the dust and sand until it is as large as she is. To the observer, this was the same process as that of RA rolling the sun's disc across the sky. In addition, the beetle's young emerged from this ball, in a manner parallel to the god's own creation of life. The scarab was considered sacred, and millions of representations of it were made, from little lumps of clay to semi-precious stones like jasper. There were many inlaid pottery scarabs. All were inscribed with a charm or marked with the CARTOUCHE of a king or god. The scarab might be pierced to wear round the neck or was mounted on a ring. Scarabs were inserted between the linen folds of the mummified corpse.

SCRIBE

WRITING, in its origins, was closely identified with MAGIC, and the scribe was a respected figure, perhaps even feared on occasion. Eminent men often had themselves sculpted, sitting with pen, paper and ink palette. Despite the general rule that said a son should follow his father's occupation, the role of a scribe was one way in which clever boys from the ranks of the peasantry or unskilled labourers could rise to positions of power and authority. The scribes' functions were closely linked with the priesthood, and the apprentice scribe would be a pupil at a priestly college. Once his training was complete, he would be attached to the staff of the local NOMARCH or a high priest or, if he were well connected, the VIZIER himself. As the role of government expanded, much of the scribes' work was of a secular nature, making lists, setting out regulations, reporting on the work of courts or expeditions, compiling the 'wisdom texts' that helped to regulate social behaviour or reproducing the tale sequences of Egyptian literature. Such work would be done in the HIERATIC or DEMOTIC scripts, while the priestly scribe, at a higher level within the hierarchy, pursued the slower but vastly more prestigious art of HIEROGLYPHIC script. In the same way as 'priest', the term 'scribe' denotes a role that could go far beyond that of writing. Scribes might also be architects, doctors or senior officials of any sort. *See also* EDUCATION.

SCULPTURE

Small-scale decorative stone carving goes far back beyond recorded history. In the PRE-DYNASTIC era, carved palettes were created for ritual and MAGIC purposes. By the time of the SECOND DYNASTY, large-scale stone sculpture was being undertaken, with the first of the superb statues that, with the shape of the PYRAMID, most strongly typify Egyptian ART in modern times. By the FOURTH DYNASTY, contemporary with the construction of the pyramids, sculpture had reached a high point both of achievement and of production. The Egyptians appreciated the plastic possibilities of sculpture, which developed quite differently from painting; it was far more lifelike in appearance. But, like every other department of Egyptian art, sculpture had a function in the scheme of things, and its purpose was religious. The pharaohs and queens who formed its subjects were gods on earth, and even the lesser subjects of their work were attributes or possessions of these same godly figures. If the subject were a lion, for example, although the master sculptor would draw out its lion-like qualities, he would also ensure that its mane resembled the headdress of the king, so that the connection was plain. The sculptor set to work with a definite system in view. His block of stone was a cube, and the cube shape determined the form of his work. Having received his commission, he set about cutting into the cube from the front and sides, leaving the back untouched. Egyptian sculpture was not intended to be seen in the round, and the statue would normally be placed against a wall or column, so that a back view would be impossible. Many sculptures were intended never to be seen by anyone other than the spirit residing in the tomb and the gods. Likewise, many of the finest reliefs were set up in the darkest recesses of temples, where they would never be viewed. To be seen and admired was not part of their purpose. The inscriptions on sculpture were of primary importance to those who commissioned the work: these, rather than the likeness, constituted the identification of the king with the statue and would enable him, when returning in spirit form, to recognise his own earthly image. Later tombs often show evidence of a CARTOUCHE having been erased and a later name added, thereby taking over possession of the figure.

Although sculpture set out to be lifelike, and is often arrestingly so, it did not necessarily attempt to be true to life in the sense of reproducing an actual set of features. The sculptor sought an element of idealisation in his work, expressive of the role and status of the figure whom he was portraying. The figures are strong, well shaped, serene, as godlike mortals should be. In the finest examples, their faces and bodies express immense calm and reposeful dignity. Originally, many of the statues would have been painted to add to the lifelike effect. Eyes were made out of quartz, crystal and copper and carefully inserted in position.

Throughout the millennia, the state of sculpture varied. The Fourth Dynasty was a high point, and later OLD KINGDOM sculpture does not possess that combination of crisp vigour and sedate monumentality that defines the best early Egyptian work. At different times, there are differences between Upper and Lower Kingdom work. Later, there were two distinct phases of development, in the AMARNA PERIOD and the Saite Dynasty (the TWENTY-SIXTH). Amarna tended towards naturalism, sometimes almost extreme, as in a famous sculpture of king AKHENATEN himself (in Cairo) which shows him with the emblems of royalty but a less than heroic physique. During the Saite Dynasty, a determined effort was made to put away foreign influences and return to the sculptural style of the MIDDLE and OLD KINGDOMS. This resulted, not in feeble imitation but in a concern for form, material and expression that produced sculpture of a high order.

SEB *see* GEB.

SEBEK
In Egyptian mythology, a deity associated with SETH. Crocodile-headed, his cult was in the Faiyum region.

SEBEKHOTEP *see* THIRTEENTH AND FOURTEENTH DYNASTIES.

SECOND DYNASTY *see* FIRST AND SECOND DYNASTIES.

SECOND INTERMEDIATE PERIOD
The period (1675–1553 BC) after the MIDDLE KINGDOM had dwindled to a confused end, its great glories far in the past, under a succession of undistinguished

PHARAOHS of whom little is known. Some writers on Egypt even date the next 'Intermediate' period from the end of the TWELFTH DYNASTY. The peasant population continued to till the soil and maintain the traditional way of life. But the ethnic and political maps were changing, step by step. Already in Egypt there were substantial communities who had come in from the Asian continent, and these increased in size and number as more flowed in, pushed outwards by the pressure of expanding empires, the Hittites in Anatolia, the Hurrians in Mesopotamia (who were ruled by another migrant people, the MITANNI). These peoples possessed skills that the Egyptians had never found it necessary to acquire, including ironwork and the mastery of the horse. They fought from chariots, giving them a speed and mobility that the Egyptian infantry had no way of countering. Gradually, the Asiatic communities coalesced and spread until they constituted an invasion force with its own hierarchy and plans. The process took some fifty years, down to 1675 BC, by which time the invaders had taken control of the kingdom of Egypt. For the first time, the Egyptians found themselves under foreign rule. In fact, the THIRTEENTH Dynasty did not disappear for a further twenty years, but it controlled less and less of the land, becoming less and less consequential, until it simply faded out of history to be followed by a brief, local FOURTEENTH Dynasty (*see* THIRTEENTH AND FOURTEENTH DYNASTIES) based at XOIS, in the DELTA.

The FIFTEENTH and Sixteenth Dynasties were thus foreign ones, founded by one Salitis. They did not impose a foreign system of government and assimilated themselves to the existing Egyptian system. This extended to keeping records in Egyptian script, using Egyptian royal titles and copying Egyptian styles in their art. It indicates, as with the Gothic kingdoms that followed the Roman empire, that the nomadic HYKSOS recognised a superior degree of civilisation among the people they had, somewhat surprisingly, conquered. Their kings called themselves 'son of Ra' and they followed a cult of SETH, although they also brought in the worship of the Near Eastern deities Baal and Teshub, who became assimilated with Seth. They also worshipped the moon goddess Astarte. Their first capital was AVARIS, on the Delta shore, then they moved to MEMPHIS. The Egyptian resistance began in THEBES, around 1680 BC, where a branch of the Thirteenth Dynasty arose, which became the Seventeenth Dynasty (*see* FIFTEENTH, SIXTEENTH AND SEVENTEENTH DYNASTIES), existing simultaneously with the Hyksos Dynasty for almost 100 years before warfare broke out on a large scale under the Theban monarch Seqenenre, who was killed in battle, and his son, Kamose. Kamose had little help from the other NOMARCHS and employed mercenary tribesmen of the MEDJAY. He gained some ground from the Hyksos king Apophis, but it was his successor, AHMOSIS I, who broke the Hyksos, storming first Memphis and then AVARIS. By then the Egyptians had learned the art of chariot warfare.

The Hyksos occupancy had a psychological effect on the Egyptians for two main reasons: they had never been conquered; and they were somewhat shamed by conquest by an opportunistic army of nomadic tribesmen. The imperialism of the NEW KINGDOM can be traced back to this sense of national humiliation.

SECOND PERSIAN OCCUPATION

The period (343–333 BC) when the double CROWN of Egypt was firmly in the possession of Artaxerxes III Ochos (ruled Egypt 341–338 BC), who had overrun the DELTA with an army of more than a quarter of a million men. There ensued a brutal and vengeful rule, in which the Egyptian population was terrorised and much of the country's wealth, in tomb and temple, TREASURY and GRANARY, was looted and despoiled. Artaxerxes III was followed by Arses (338–336 BC) and by Darius III Codoman (336–332 BC). In the shadow of the Persian rule, in the deep south, perhaps with Nubian support, there is some scanty evidence of an effort to maintain a native dynasty against the day when independence would return, as it had done on so often before. The name of a 'pharaoh' named Khababash is preserved from this time. He appears to have enacted some laws, and a Ptolemaic tradition states that he was fighting the Persians in the Delta in 336/335 BC. But he was not the king in any substantive sense, nor did he found a dynasty. In 334 BC, ALEXANDER THE GREAT finally destroyed the Persian empire at Issus and took Persepolis. In the following year the Persian satrap surrendered Egypt to the Macedonian who had become Lord of the World.

SED FESTIVAL

A king's jubilee festival, supposedly held to mark thirty years of rule but often held after a much shorter time. The FIRST-DYNASTY king Anedjib celebrated his soon after coming to the throne, probably because he was already an elderly man. The word *sed* means a bull's tail ('mighty bull' was a regular description of a king). There was also a deity called Sed, a dog-headed god who was an associate of WEPWAWET, the 'opener of the ways' to the UNDERWORLD. The festival was a re-enactment of the coronation ritual, with processions to the temples of the principal gods and a lavish production of commemorative objects. Its various rituals were intended to demonstrate the continuing vigour of the king.

SEDGE

The lily emblem of UPPER EGYPT. The king of the two lands was known, in the allusive style preferred by the Egyptians, as 'He of the sedge and the BEE'.

SEKER *see* SOKAR.

SEKHEM

The term for the controlling force or 'vital spark' of an individual.

SEKHMET

In Egyptian mythology, the lion-headed goddess of war and sickness, originally associated with MEMPHIS and a figure to be placated.

SEKTI BARQUE

In Egyptian mythology, the boat occupied in the afternoon by Ra on his voyage through the UNDERWORLD.

SEMERKHET *see* FIRST AND SECOND DYNASTIES.

SENEFRU *see* SNOFRU.

SENMUT

A favourite courtier of the EIGHTEENTH-DYNASTY female king, HATSHEPSUT. He and several fellow courtiers were probably executed by THUTHMOSIS III.

SEPD *see* BES.

SEQENENRE *see* FIFTEENTH, SIXTEENTH AND SEVENTEENTH DYNASTIES; SECOND INTERMEDIATE PERIOD.

SERAPEUM

Among the most imposing of ancient Egypt's monuments, the underground galleries at SAQQARA where the sacred APIS bulls were buried, from the EIGHTEENTH DYNASTY onwards. These bulls were the personification of the KA of PTAH, god of MEMPHIS. The name comes from the ground-level temple of Serapis, a composite deity who combined aspects of OSIRIS and APIS in the PTOLEMAIC PERIOD. In the dynastic period, the sacred bulls were worshipped during their lifetime and on their deaths solemnly buried in gigantic granite sarcophagi.

SERAPIS

The Greek name for the APIS bull worshipped at the SERAPEUM.

SERDAB

A tomb chamber in which statues of the deceased were placed (from the Arabic word for 'cellar'). It was usually adjacent to the chapel and sometimes eye holes were made in the dividing wall so that the KA could observe the daily offerings.

SERFDOM

The condition of the bulk of the Egyptian people during the OLD KINGDOM was not unlike medieval serfdom. They laboured as work groups whose selection cut across family ties, and their rights were very few. Following the easing of social conditions after the collapse of the Old Kingdom, matters improved, with families working together and being granted land for their own cultivation.

SESOSTRIS

A mythical pharaoh recorded by Greek writers who credited him with the achievements of Sesostris III of the TWELFTH DYNASTY, THUTHMOSIS III of the EIGHTEENTH DYNASTY and RAMESES II of the NINETEENTH DYNASTY.

SESOSTRIS I

A PHARAOH of the MIDDLE KINGDOM, TWELFTH DYNASTY (ruled 1962–1928 BC). He was an energetic ruler who went farther beyond Egypt's bounds than any predecessor, invading NUBIA as far as the third cataract, acquiring much GOLD and territory. He promoted trading contacts into the Mediterranean and with the land of PUNT, and sponsored many building projects, including a rebuilding of the temple of RA-Atum at HELIOPOLIS. The restored SED FESTIVAL kiosk (the White Chapel) at KARNAK dates back to Sesostris I.

SESOSTRIS II and III *see* TWELFTH DYNASTY.

SETH

In Egyptian mythology, one of the principal gods, murderer of his brother, OSIRIS, identified with the dry desert areas to east and west of the NILE Valley. Seth has sometimes been seen as a Satan figure, but this is not right. In the long-established Egyptian notion of duality, he was necessary, as a counter to OSIRIS, just as the desert was opposed to the valley, and the north to the south, and the dark to the light. The desert had its riches and its charms; and Seth too had his votaries. He was seen as a power who required respect and placation, not at all as the abhorrent entity that Satan was to become. Thunder, storms, whirlwind and hail were all instruments of Seth. The waning of the moon and the occasional lunar and solar eclipses showed that, although defeated by HORUS, he had not lost his powers. He was also a war god. Unlike Horus, his great rival, Seth remained the same unchanging figure in the Egyptian pantheon from beginning to end. He was chiefly identified with UPPER EGYPT, the land of desert, and one tradition had him as the ancestor of the kings of Upper Egypt. As the patron deity of NOMES in both Upper and LOWER EGYPT, he took on a number of animal forms, including that of the hawk but also the dog, CROCODILE, hippopotamus and Oxyrrinchus (the fish that consumed Osiris's genitals, the only part of him which Isis could not retrieve). The oldest centre of SETH's cult is Nubt, on the west bank of the Nile in Upper Egypt, opposite KOPTOS. *See also* COSMOLOGY, GODS.

SETIINAKHTE *see* TWENTIETH DYNASTY; TWOSRE.

SETHOS

A PHARAOH of the NEW KINGDOM, NINETEENTH DYNASTY (ruled 1294–1279 BC). A military leader and former VIZIER, he rewrote the KING LISTS in order to provide himself with a pharaonic pedigree. It was he who restored the prestige of Egypt in the Middle East after the neglect of the later EIGHTEENTH-DYNASTY kings, leading successful forays into Palestine and LIBYA, and subduing the Bedouin. His TWO LADIES NAME echoes his success: 'The strong-armed one who renews births and recaptures the NINE BOWS'. His tomb in the VALLEY OF THE KINGS and his MORTUARY TEMPLE at ABYDOS are both well preserved and show ART of a high quality, still very much of the liberated style of the AMARNA PERIOD.

SEVEN HATHORS *see* HATHOR.

SEVENTEENTH DYNASTY *see* FIFTEENTH, SIXTEENTH AND SEVENTEENTH DYNASTIES; SECOND INTERMEDIATE PERIOD.

SEVENTH DYNASTY

In the FIRST INTERMEDIATE PERIOD, from 2200 to around 2160 BC, MANETHO's text describes the Seventh Dynasty as 'seventy kings in seventy days', a sufficient comment on the turbulence that followed the decline of the SIXTH DYNASTY. A contemporary document known as the *Admonitions*, written by a SCRIBE called Ipuwer, bemoans the disasters of the age and especially the lack of a strong central kingship. A temporary climatic change in eastern Africa at this time, around 2100 BC, caused a succession of low NILES, with a diminution in the crops that eventually led to protests, riots and insurrections by a starving people. Coinciding with the decline of central authority, the stable world of Egypt found itself in a state of imminent collapse, apparently deserted by the gods and deprived of their royal interlocutor. At this time, trading contact with the countries beyond seems to have come to a halt, while Bedouin raided into the DELTA from SINAI and NUBIA relapsed into independent chiefdoms. The successive kings of the Seventh Dynasty (seventeen in six years) were unable to control developments, and it is doubtful how much of Egypt they actually ruled.

SHABAKA AND SHABITKU *see* TWENTY-FIFTH DYNASTY.

SHABTI

A small figure in the form of a mummy, made of stone, wood or pottery. They were placed in tombs, and their function was to work for the deceased in the AFTERLIFE, performing necessary tasks like dredging silt from waterways.

SHADUF

The ancient Egyptian device for raising water from one level to a higher one by means of a pole set on a pivot, with a leather bucket at one end and a stone counterweight to balance it at the other. Introduced to Egypt by the HYKSOS, it is seen from the EIGHTEENTH DYNASTY onwards.

SHENDYR KILT *or* SKIRT

The pleated linen kilt-like garment seen on many representations of kings, with a flat central tab.

SHEPSESKAF *see* FOURTH DYNASTY.

SHESH

The mother of the FIRST DYNASTY king MENI. She is reputed to have invented a hair wash that is recorded in a medical PAPYRUS.

SHIPS AND SHIPBUILDING

The oldest-known pictures of boats come from Egypt. From PRE-DYNASTIC times the Egyptians built boats, out of two basic materials: reeds in LOWER EGYPT and wood in UPPER EGYPT. In the DELTA marshes particularly, boats were a necessity, and from basic rafts made of bundled reeds, the Egyptians evolved more sophisticated vessels capable of seagoing voyages as well as being paddled about the calm waterways of the marshland. Models of reed boats found in OLD-KINGDOM tombs reveal the style of construction, with the reeds bundled together in long cylindrical forms with fibre ropes and extending from a narrow, high prow to a stout waist, then narrowing again to the raised stem. More reed bundles formed the core of the vessel, providing a level deck on which a basket-work deckhouse, on the model of the terrestrial hut, could be set. Most of these boats were propelled by paddles. The mast, on a larger vessel, was formed of two braced poles supported by fibre rigging, and with a broad yardarm to hold a sail in place. Heavy-duty cloth was woven to make sails that could withstand the pressure of wind and the pull of ropes without splitting. Whilst the seagoing capacity of reed vessels has been successfully tested in modern times, it seems more likely that they were used for river and canal work (by far the most common requirement for boats) and that foreign trade was undertaken by wooden craft. The indigenous woods, chiefly sycamore and acacia, do not produce long planks, and Egyptian wooden boats were constructed, without ribs, of short, thick wooden blocks, joined by a combination of pegs and hour-glass-shaped pieces of wood that locked into adjoining pieces. The mast was two-legged, as on the reed vessel; set well forward, it was probably only fitted with a sail when the wind was directly astern. Quite substantial fleets were in existence during the OLD KINGDOM. The Pharaoh SNOFRU (FOURTH DYNASTY) sent 40 ships to BYBLOS to carry back cedar logs. In the FIFTH DYNASTY, Sahure used seagoing warships to harry the Phoenician coast. These ships had no keel and were kept rigid by a stout rope stretched from stern to stern. By then the concept of the rowlock had been developed and ships were rowed rather than paddled. A set of steering oars was fitted at the stern, three on each side. By the ELEVENTH DYNASTY, an official might have at his disposal a whole range of specialised vessels. The tomb of the CHANCELLOR Meket-Ra illustrates his range of river-boats. It includes travelling boats, of different sizes, equipped with a deck-house, kitchen tenders, lightly built yachts with open decks or awnings, a sporting boat and canoe-like fishing vessels. By the NEW KINGDOM, shipbuilding had advanced somewhat. The ships of HATSHEPSUT's expedition to PUNT, which sailed down the Red Sea to the Somali coast, were quite substantial vessels, around 90 feet (27 metres) in length. They had a single mast, stepped amidships on a keel plank that projects forward as a ram. There is no sign of ribbing, but lateral deck beams are in use, assisting stability. Specialisation continued. Hatshepsut's tomb shows a substantial barge specially designed for the transport of OBELISKS. It was almost 200 feet (61 metres) long and 70 feet (21 metres) broad, and could support two obelisks with a combined weight of 700 tonnes. To control this mammoth, 27 smaller boats, each manned by 30 oarsmen, were used. One of the obelisks borne by this vessel survives in front of the temple of AMUN-RA at KARNAK. At the other extreme of specialisation, the EIGHTEENTH-DYNASTY Pharaoh AMENOPHIS III had a luxury yacht for use on a great ornamental lake within his palace grounds. As with many other aspects of technology, Egyptian shipbuilding made relatively little technical progress and contributed little or nothing to the wider development of the craft.

SHOSHENQ *see* TWENTY-SECOND AND TWENTY-THIRD DYNASTIES.

SHU
In Egyptian mythology, in the COSMOLOGY of HELIOPOLIS, Shu was the air-god (dry), a member of the original OGDOAD, whose partner was Tefnut, goddess of moisture.

SILVER
Always a rare metal in Egypt, by contrast with the relatively plentifully available GOLD. As a result, silver was more highly regarded than gold.

SINAI PENINSULA
The peninsula to the northeast of Egypt which was strategically important as the land route to the Middle Eastern kingdoms. It was also a source of precious stones, referred to by the Egyptians as 'turquoise land'. It was a desert region, inhabited by roving bands of Bedouin, who were liable to ambush any travellers who were not part of well-armed groups.

SINUHE

The Story of Sinuhe, dating from the reign of SESOSTRIS I, became one of the most widely copied texts, much used in the schools for SCRIBES during the NEW KINGDOM period. It told the story of the harem official Sinuhe, who ran away from his post in fear at the assassination of Sesostris's father, Anemmenes. He crossed SINAI and eventually reached Syria, where he managed to establish himself as a chief among the Bedouin. But he pined for his own country and regretted his disloyalty. He made application to Sesostris for a pardon, which was granted, and he returned to Egypt to serve the pharaoh faithfully until his death. There was a clear propaganda message in the tale, salted by picaresque detail of Sinuhe's adventures in outlandish places. See Part One: Chapter 00.

SIRIUS

The Dog Star, the brightest star in the sky and one of the closest to earth. The Egyptians used it in the establishment of their CALENDAR. The goddess allocated to it was SOTHIS.

SISTRUM *see* MUSIC.

SIXTEENTH DYNASTY *see* FIFTEENTH, SIXTEENTH AND SEVENTEENTH DYNASTIES; SECOND INTERMEDIATE PERIOD.

SIXTH DYNASTY

A dynasty in the OLD KINGDOM, 2322–2151 BC. WENIS, last king of the FIFTH DYNASTY, left no son but was succeeded by the first Sixth-Dynasty king, Teti, who married Wenis' daughter, Iput, and thus acquired legitimacy as king. Teti was an active legislator, and, as his HORUS NAME ('he who pacifies the two lands') indicates, his rule was mainly focused on internal affairs. He appears to have died by assassination, an indication of growing disorder in the state. The next notable reign was that of PEPY I, who was king for at least 40 years, inheriting as a young boy. Pepy worked hard to maintain the unity of the state, with much building in UPPER EGYPT at sites such as ABYDOS, HERAKLEOPOLIS and ELEPHANTINE. Conspiracy within the royal household, centring on the harem, disturbed his reign (*see* WENI). Under Pepy's son Merenra, Egypt carried out invasions into Palestine and Syria and also struggled successfully to retain control of NUBIA against the increasing assertiveness of local chieftains. PEPY II, who followed Merenra, was fascinated by the exotic remoteness of the Upper Nile. His reign was a very long one, between fifty and seventy years, and its momentum steadily decreased, whilst the ambitions of provincial governors grew. It also produced a succession crisis, resulting in two brief and uncertain reigns before the collapse of the Sixth Dynasty and the emergence of the SEVENTH. By the end of Pepy II's reign, the decline can clearly be seen. The court was vast and filled with members of the nobility who enjoyed sinecure positions and who assisted in the intense ceremonial that surrounded the pharaoh. The civil service struggled to maintain the administration, its drills and regulations now centuries old. The principal NOMARCHS, treating their functions as hereditary in a way that would have been impossible in earlier dynasties, were behaving like petty kings, even to the erection of their own NECROPOLISES on a royal scale. The no-man's land of desert around Egypt, although still a protection, was less and less of a deterrent to her increasingly powerful and curious neighbours.

SLAVERY

Native Egyptians were not slaves, however much their condition might resemble slavery. From the late MIDDLE KINGDOM until the end of the dynasties, Egypt had a slave population consisting partly of prisoners of war and partly of purchased slaves. Slaves had few rights in society and were not allowed to practise religion except for the cult of the local fetish. The poorest, who could not afford burial, placed their dead in the river, where the CROCODILES ate them. The better-off slaves had the opportunity become freedmen, at the discretion of the owner, who was also under a responsibility to ensure that they were housed, fed and clothed.

SMENDES *see* TWENTY-FIRST DYNASTY.

SNOFRU *or* SENEFRU

A king of the FOURTH DYNASTY (2625–2510 BC). He is the first king, and one of the few from the OLD KINGDOM, of whom some personal characteristics were preserved. He is said to have been a genial and popular figure. Certainly his memory was well preserved, and in the course of the MIDDLE KINGDOM he was deified. In a manner prodigal even among kings of Egypt, Snofru had three successive pyramids built for himself.

SOBEKNEFERU

One of the three certain examples (with HATSHEPSUT and TWOSRE) of a woman who performed the functions of king. She ruled at the end of the TWELFTH DYNASTY, around 1790–1785 BC. Sister and perhaps also wife of the Pharaoh Ammenemes IV, her titles announce her as a woman king. Her rule has been attributed to difficulties over the succession, with no satisfactory male claimant available. Her femaleness does not seem to have been resented, and she is included as a she-king in KING LISTS. Statues of her, recovered in the DELTA area, show her in women's dress, unlike Hatshepsut. Sobekneferu built a PYRAMID at Mazghuna, close to DAHSHUR.

SOKAR *or* SEKER

In Egyptian mythology, one of the oldest deities. He was an UNDERWORLD god with three human heads, the body of a serpent and a mighty wings between which appeared his hawk form.

SOTHIC CYCLE

A period of 1,460 years, each year being a fixed Sothic year of 365 days and 6 hours, each year beginning when the star SIRIUS appeared on the eastern horizon at dawn, heralding the annual INUNDATION of the NILE. The fixed nature of the Sothic cycle did not allow for a leap year so gradually the seasons drifted out of step. *See also* CALENDAR.

SOTHIS

In Egyptian mythology, goddess of the star SIRIUS. The heliacal (before the sunrise) rising of Sirius was incorporated into the Egyptian CALENDAR. *See also* SOTHIC CYCLE.

SPEOS

A temple cut into rock, like those at ABU SIMBEL and BENI HASAN.

SPHINX

The word may derive from Egyptian *shesep ankh* ('living image'). The first and by far the most formidable of such statues is that of the Great Sphinx at GIZA (proper name Harmakhis), carved from an outcrop of rock left after quarrying operations and some 60 metres (197 feet) in length. It shows the body of a lion with the head of a man, whose headcloth shows him to be a king. It was intended as a guardian figure to the funerary area of the Pharaoh CHEPHREN. There is no evidence that the Sphinx itself was worshipped, although legends and fables were to build up around it, including the Greek myth of 'Oedipus and the Riddle of the Sphinx'.

STELE (*PLURAL* STELAE)

An engraved slab, set up in a temple or tomb, made of stone, although early wooden examples have also been found. In PRE-DYNASTIC and THINITE tomb sites, the steles might well be the only stone items in constructions of mud brick, their function being to indicate the place where offerings should be made, their text often listing the appropriate items. In later tombs, steles were often employed as 'false doors', imitation doors through which the KA of the deceased could pass in order to find sustenance from the offerings in the mortuary chapel.

STONE

The preferred building stone was sandstone or limestone, both of which are relatively easy to cut into clean-edged masonry blocks that fit finely together. Harder rock, like granite, was used for OBELISKS but rarely in buildings, although there is one small granite temple in the vicinity of the SPHINX and the Great Pyramid. The Egyptians explored widely in search of good stone, especially for the fine-grained limestone that would be used for outer surfaces. One of the prime sources for this was TURA in the Mokattam Hills. Hard stone like dolerite was searched out and used for hammers and cutting equipment.

SUDAN
The land of Nubia, or Kush, corresponds to modern Sudan, although the frontier is farther south than in ancient times, when it was at Aswan.

SUN TEMPLE
During the period of the FIFTH DYNASTY, and coinciding with the high point of Heliopolitan theology, a new type of temple was built. Compared to the conventional Egyptian temple, which preserved its mysteries in the scented dusk of the inner sanctuary, this was the temple turned inside out. Its holiest place was open to the sky, as befitted a temple dedicated to the sun. The best preserved sun temple is that of King Neuserre at ABU GHUROB. Its nodal point was a representation of the BEN-BEN stone, which was faced by four interlinked altars carved from the same block of ALABASTER. SACRIFICE was an important part of the ritual, and the temple had a stockyard attached, from which the animals were led up to the place of oblation. In other respects the sun temples conformed to the basic temple layout. The sun temple reappears much later, in the NEW KINGDOM, with the rise of the ATEN cult, and the priests of Aten took much interest in the temple forms and worship of Neuserre, Menkauhor and the other Fifth-Dynasty kings. *See also* TEMPLE.

SUTEKH
A Hyksos warrior of the Hyksos god imported into Egyptian mythology during the EIGHTEENTH DYNASTY. By the NINETEENTH DYNASTY he was identified with SETH. He is shown on a SCARAB with wings and a horned cap, standing on the back of a lion. In his form as Tark or Tarku he is depicted carrying a hammer in one hand and in the other three wriggling flahes of lightning. He is also shown grasping a mace and trident or a double battle-axe. He was adopted in Babylon after the Hittite conquest as Ramman, (Biblical Rimmon), with double horns and bearing an axe and three thunderbolts.

SYCAMORE
The sycamore was a sacred tree in ancient Egypt. THOTH at one time must have been considered as a tree spirit as in the NINETEENTH DYNASTY he is shown recording the name of a pharoah on a sycamore.

T

TA'A *see* FIFTEENTH, SIXTEENTH AND SEVENTEENTH DYNASTIES.

TACHOS I *see* TWENTY-NINTH AND THIRTIETH DYNASTIES.

TAHARQA *see* ASSURBANIPAL; ESARHADDON; TWENTY-FIFTH DYNASTY.

TALATAT BLOCKS
The small blocks of sandstone used for rapid building during the AMARNA PERIOD (the word 'talatat' comes rom Arabic and means 'three hand-widths'). They were reused on later buildings on other sites.

TALE OF THE SHIPWRECKED SAILOR, THE
A tale in Egyptian LITERATURE, also known as *The Isle of Enchantment*. *See* Part One: Chapter 19.

TANEN *or* **TATUNEN**
In Egyptian mythology, an earth god who resembles GEB and was united with PTAH in order to make the originally elfin Ptah a giant.

TANIS
A settlement and NOME capital in the eastern DELTA region, home town of the Ramessides of the NINETEENTH and TWENTIETH DYNASTIES. Much building was carried out at these times.

TANTAMINI *see* ASSURBANIPAL; THEBES.

TARK *or* **TARKU** *see* SUTEKH.

TATUNEN *see* TANEN.

TAWERET *or* **APET** *or* **OPET**
In Egyptian mythology, a goddess with a hippopotamus head, credited with bringing babies to childless women and thus often portrayed on charms and AMULETS.

TEFNAKHT *see* TWENTY-FIFTH DYNASTY; TWENTY-FOURTH DYNASTY.

TEFNUT

In Egyptian mythology, the goddess of moisture, created by RA. She was also a sun deity and was depicted as a lioness or a lion-headed woman.

TEKENU *see* FUNERARY PRACTICE.

TEMPLE

The centre of the cult of a particular god or gods. In the OLD and MIDDLE KINGDOMS, temples in inhabited areas were relatively modest structures, to a scale similar to that of the other buildings. Very large temples were built on open sites. In the NEW KINGDOM, massive stone temples became a feature of the towns, although they were by no means open to all the people. It was typical of the temple to have an imposing doorway; that of AMUN-RA at KARNAK had 10 sets of PYLON gates, fronting on to an avenue of SPHINXES. Apart from the gate, the whole temple compound was separated from the outside world by a high brick wall, sometimes fortified with towers and crenellations. On festival days, a gorgeous procession would emerge through the gate, priests dressed and decorated in robes and headdresses, bearers carrying the painted and gilded boats in which the figure of the god rode for its public progress. This was the only time at which the outside population had any contact with life inside the temple. The great temples were important centres of economic life. They owned land, they owned and jealously guarded mineral rights, their income was substantial, and they were exempt from taxation. They required every kind of service from the most basic to the most luxurious, and they provided many other services, like EDUCATION and medicine. The temple site normally included substantial gardens, with flowers and shrubs, and also herb gardens, tended for the practical purpose of providing medical and culinary herbs. They had schools and workshops, cattle pens and grain stores attached.

The architectural form of temples often appears complicated, since many temples, of which KARNAK is merely the best-known example, were added to, rebuilt or restored through successive dynasties, and often with lengthy lapses between building phases. The alterations were often on a totally different scale from the original buildings, as with the sudden growth in the cult of NEITH during the Saite Dynasty (the TWENTY-SIXTH). The New Kingdom temple had a set form. It was surrounded by a high blank wall, so that none of its splendour was seen from outside, apart from the entrance-way. Here there was a PYLON, usually approached from the direction of the Nile by an avenue lined with SPHINXES or lions and terminating in a pair of OBELISKS. The temple was set on an east-west axis, with the pylon positioned centrally in the east-facing wall so that the rising sun shone directly on its towers, dedicated to Isis and Nephthys. Masts could be fitted into it, supporting banners. Within the gateway was a forecourt, with a pillared arcade surrounding it. Opening on to the court was the HYPOSTYLE HALL, a stately construction of massive columns in rows, creating up to four aisles and lit by clerestory windows cut in the upper walls of the high central nave. This hall gave access, sometimes through a further, smaller hall, to the sanctuary area. As the hierophant proceeded from the bright light of the outside world into the recesses of the temple, the interior of the building became ever darker, more hushed, more full of the odours of incense, more an abode of sacred mysteries. The floor level was raised, to symbolise the primordial mound of earth. Only the priests came this far. The statue of the god was in the NAOS, or sanctuary, with further sanctuaries on either side where other divinities might also reside. (This feature was common in a king's temples, where his own cult would be glorified by association. The temple of Sethos I at ABYDOS had seven sanctuaries.) Such was the essential temple; often they were set on rising ground, where ramps leading from court to court added to the grandeur of the plan. Around it spread an agglomeration of all the auxiliary buildings necessary to preserve the life of the temple and its daily ritual. In the dusk of the interior, the walls were lined with reliefs and paintings, with statues placed against pillars and in niches. Outside the temple, if its grounds were extensive enough, there might be a sacred lake, like the lake of Asheru that partially surrounded the Temple of MUT at Karnak. *See also* ARCHITECTURE, KARNAK, SUN TEMPLE.

TENTH DYNASTY *see* HERAKLEOPOLIS; NINTH AND TENTH DYNASTIES.

TESHUB
An Asian god of the tempest imported by the Hyksos into Egyptian mythology.

TET
An amulet that was a symbol of the blood of Isis and protected the dead against demons. Amulets like the SCARAB, ANKH, etc, became increasingly popular during the NEW KINGDOM.

TETI *see* SIXTH DYNASTY.

TEXTILES
Flax was a major crop, grown in large quantities in designated areas. It was harvested at the same time as the grain crop, and the bundles of stems were forced through large combs in order to remove the bolls. Linseed oil was then extracted from the bolls. The bast fibres were separated by the retting process, steeping the stems in pools, and then spun by use of the simple spindle-whorl into threads of

varying fineness. From these, linen was woven on a horizontal loom. Fine linen was highly prized and often stolen, both from houses and tombs.

The Egyptians also produced wool, but it was not used in the tombs. The degree of its use is not known, but it was used for cloaks and shawls for night-time and the cool time of winter.

THEBAN DYNASTY *see* ELEVENTH DYNASTY.

THEBES
(Modern LUXOR) in the decline of the OLD KINGDOM, in the period after 2475 BC, Thebes became a capital city, controlling a great area of the NILE Valley and sometimes the entire country. The ELEVENTH and TWELFTH DYNASTIES ruled from here, and presided over many advances in cultural and economic life. As the home of the kings who reinvigorated Egypt at the start of the NEW KINGDOM and after the HYKSOS dominion, and as the cult centre of AMUN-RA, Thebes enjoyed prestige unequalled by any other city in Egypt. It was with the EIGHTEENTH DYNASTY that it became in effect an imperial capital (1580–1350 BC), its domains extending beyond Egypt into Syria. To the whole ancient world it was a place of legend and wonder, for its wealth, its importance and its unique range of buildings. The Nile divided Thebes in two in a typically Egyptian manner, the living city on the east bank, with its royal residence, its government offices, its close-packed houses and the great temple compounds. On the west bank was the city of the dead, the NECROPOLISES and MORTUARY TEMPLES of kings, queens and nobles, spread out as lavishly as the bustling metropolis on the opposite bank. In the AMARNA PERIOD, Thebes lost its role, although not its prestige, until the restoration under HOREMHEB. With the end of the TWENTIETH DYNASTY, Egypt once more was politically divided into Upper and Lower, and in UPPER EGYPT the High Priests of AMUN-RA ruled as kings in effect, and sometimes actually in name, for more than a century. But with the advent of Greek alliances and the threats from Persia and Assyria, the nerve centre of Egypt shifted down-river to MEMPHIS and the DELTA towns. Thebes was left with its temples and its glorious past. When in 664 BC the last Kushite pharaoh, Tantamani, fled back to his home country in the face of the Assyrians under ASSURBANIPAL, Thebes was left open to the invaders, who looted, burned and destroyed the city that had been one of the marvels of the world.

THEOLOGY
The Egyptians were profoundly aware of their gods, from the local fetish stone to the brilliant, life-giving splendour of RA-ATUM and the annual fertilisation symbolised by OSIRIS. The GODS existed, but in a non-personal sense. Aloof from the everyday aspects of human life and behaviour, they did not demand or set out

a code of moral conduct or supervise the morality of the people. They could be angered and could inflict punishment, but this would be on account of neglect, or an improper ritual, or an insufficient offering. Egyptian RELIGION existed for man to celebrate and safeguard his own place in the universe by worshipping and appeasing the gods; it was not an ethical system. The polarity of good and evil so fundamental in Christianity is not at all present in Egyptian religion, which is based upon the harmony of duality. HORUS and SETH are both necessary, not as crude counter-balances to each other but as part of a more subtly arranged, more fluid harmony, in which good and evil are not extremes and gods may have elements of both. Although gods controlled the AFTERLIFE (OSIRIS as King of the Dead), the next world contained no mutually opposed heaven and hell. Entry to it was not influenced by a person's moral behaviour but by his or her possession of the right information, the magic formulae that were the key. Egyptian religion retained potent elements of primitive magic until its eventual decline and disappearance. *See also* COSMOLOGY, DEATH.

THINITE PERIOD

The era (3150–2700 BC) of the first two dynasties, from the name of the kings' city of origin, This, near ABYDOS. Perhaps the most creative period of Egyptian history, in which the basic tenets that were to govern life for many centuries afterwards were formed or confirmed. *See also* FIRST AND SECOND DYNASTIES.

THIRD DYNASTY

With the Third Dynasty (2700–2625 BC) we come to the period of the Old Kingdom. This dynasty endured for a period of less than a century and is dominated by the Pharaoh DJOSER, or Zoser, and his vizier, IMHOTEP. Imhotep, priest and architect, was himself to be deified by admiring later generations. He was the constructor of the first pyramid. Despite its massive legacy in stone, the history of the Third Dynasty is obscure.

THIRD INTERMEDIATE PERIOD

The period (1069–715 BC) spanning the TWENTY-FIRST to the TWENTY-FOURTH Dynasties (*see also* TWENTY-SECOND AND TWENTY-THIRD DYNASTIES), this era opens the final millennium of ancient Egypt's history and corresponds to the Biblical period of David and Solomon. Apart from a brief time of unified rule by the Theban priest-king Pinudjem I, it was marked by divisions within the kingdom, with pharaohs in control only of LOWER EGYPT and UPPER EGYPT ruled by the hereditary chief priests at THEBES, sometimes as crowned kings. The Theban rule was a theocracy, with AMUN-RA at its head. The statue of the god was turned into an ORACLE and manipulated by the priest to provide appropriate answers. Thebes had no foreign policy, and the pharaohs of Memphis were incapable of firm rule.

The international standing of Egypt sank to a low level until the assumption of power by Shoshenq I and the commencement of the Twenty-second, or Libyan, Dynasty. The Libyans ruled for a century and a half, with their base in the north, until a branch set up a separate kingdom at Thebes, the Twenty-third Dynasty, whose succession of five kings co-existed with the parent branch until the uprising of Tefnakht at SAIS, and the invasion of the Nubians, which brought the era to a close.

THIRTEENTH AND FOURTEENTH DYNASTIES

These two dynasties (1785–c.1675 BC) in the MIDDLE KINGDOM are little known, and the KING LISTS of the time are confused and sometimes contradictory. It was a lengthy period in which no individual reign stands out among some twenty-five pharaohs, many of whom bore the name Sebekhotep ('SEBEK is pleased'), including Neferkhara-Sebekhotep, who erected two large granite statues on the island of Argo in the Nile near the third CATARACT. During this period, the unity and cohesion of the state were maintained. In the later stages there is evidence of social unrest and of incursions in the south by Neshi, a Nubian, and in the north by Mermenfatiu, 'commander of soldiers'. The unrest and the uncertainty of central rule allowed the more dynamic immigrant HYKSOS community first to extend its own area of control in the DELTA and then take over the monarchy of the whole country, with the imposition of the FIFTEENTH DYNASTY.

THIRTIETH DYNASTY *see* TWENTY-NINTH AND THIRTIETH DYNASTIES.

THIS *see* FIRST AND SECOND DYNASTIES; THINITE PERIOD.

THOTH

An early rival to RA, the sun-god, as creator of Egypt (and hence the world). In the dark before the sun, Thoth summoned the gods who produced the egg from which the sun hatched. These were animal gods, four frogs and four snakes, known collectively as the OGDOAD. Thoth, depicted as a man with the head of an ibis, or sometimes entirely as an ibis, was the SCRIBE of the gods, the inventor of WRITING, language and MAGIC. His wife was Seshat, who wrote the details of every human life on the leaves of the Tree of Heaven. There was considerable animosity between the priesthood of Thoth and that of Ra. The centre of Thoth's cult were the cities of Hermopolis (Greek: 'city of Hermes'), one in the DELTA, one in MIDDLE EGYPT.

THUTHMOSIS I

A NEW KINGDOM pharaoh of the EIGHTEENTH DYNASTY (ruled 1506–1493 BC). An able soldier who held the frontier of the Egyptian empire against the Mitanni, he also began the transformation of the temple of AMUN-RA at KARNAK. Thuthmosis I inaugurated the practice of royal burial in the VALLEY OF THE KINGS. The definitive version of the BOOK OF WHAT IS IN THE UNDERWORLD was found on the walls of his burial chamber.

THUTHMOSIS II *see* EIGHTEENTH DYNASTY; HATSHEPSUT.

THUTHMOSIS III

A NEW KINGDOM pharaoh of the EIGHTEENTH DYNASTY (ruled 1479–1425 BC). One of the great kings of Egypt, who acceded at the age of six but whose career was frustrated at its start by the usurpation of the throne by his redoubtable aunt, Queen HATSHEPSUT, who was acting as regent. Thuthmosis finally regained his position around 1458 BC, and immediately found himself involved in warfare with MITANNI. It took 17 campaigns to make good the boast of his predecessor, THUTHMOSIS I, that Egypt's border was on the Euphrates. Thuthmosis III took his army across the Euphrates on rafts to win victory in the Mesopotamian heartland. The walls of the Temple of AMUN-RA at KARNAK bear the legend of his conquests. He made Egypt the supreme power in the Middle East, and tribute was sent to him from as far away as Adana in present-day Turkey. Thuthmosis tried hard but in vain to obliterate all mentions of the name of Hatshepsut in the many buildings she had erected. His own record as a builder includes further work on the temple of AMUN-RA at KARNAK (the colonnade), as well as at DEIR EL-BAHRI and MEDINET HABU. The SO-CALLED Cleopatra's Needles, THE OBELISKS on the Thames Embankment in London and in Central Park, New York, were originally set up by Thuthmosis III at HELIOPOLIS. He was buried in the VALLEY OF THE KINGS; his mummy has been preserved and shows him to have been a short man, like some other great military leaders.

THUTHMOSIS IV *see* EIGHTEENTH DYNASTY.

TI *see* FIFTH DYNASTY.

TIME

The Egyptians measured the day into twelve hours of light and twelve of darkness, whatever the real duration of daylight. In the tropics, the division of light and dark is more constant than farther north or south. They used sundials to measure the passage of time, and in the NEW KINGDOM the water clock was developed. However, a glance at the position of the sun would have been enough to tell any Egyptian what the time of day was. By night, for religious or magical purposes, the hour could be told by observing the positions of the stars. *See also* CALENDAR.

TIRHAKAH
The name by which TAHARQA is known in the Bible.

TIY
A notable queen of the NEW KINGDOM, principal wife to the Pharaoh AMENOPHIS III and mother of AKHENATEN (EIGHTEENTH DYNASTY). She was a commoner, although her father was a court official of some importance, Master of the Stud Farm. *See also* Part One: Chapter 25.

TOMB
From PRE-DYNASTIC times up to the end of the dynastic period, the vast majority of the population were buried in pits, with a few possessions that could be spared to equip them for the AFTERLIFE. Tombs were not for them. In the OLD KINGDOM, tombs were for the king and his closest family and advisers, but by the NEW KINGDOM, people well down the social scale were building tombs (*see* DEIR EL-MEDINA). For the wealthy Egyptian, his tomb was a more important consideration than his dwelling house during his life. It would reflect his wealth and prestige, and should contain a suitable range of artefacts in order to maintain these throughout the long, long future, and above all it would perpetuate his name. It should be made durable for the same reason. Its position was important, preferably close to the main PYRAMID of the pharaoh or a great man whom he had served or, failing that, in some particularly sacred site such as ABYDOS, where, according to legend, the head of OSIRIS was buried. Pharaohs had more than one tomb, usually having one provided in LOWER and one in UPPER EGYPT. One of these was a cenotaph, or empty tomb, since the mummified body could only be in one place. *See also* ARCHITECTURE, DEATH, MASTABA, PYRAMID.

TOMB ROBBERS
Somewhat on the analogy of safe-builders and safe-blowers, the constructors of tombs, particularly PYRAMIDS, sought to make them secure against intruders, with false doors and entrances, decoy corridors and massive portcullis-type barriers, whilst the tomb robbers sought for new ways of getting in to reach the tomb chamber and its adjacent rooms. During times of FAMINE and political unrest, when public order had broken down or was only sporadically imposed, the lure of the riches of the tombs outweighed the ingrained respect for the dead, and tomb robbing became rife. The desperation of the rulers is shown by the EIGHTEENTH DYNASTY's decision to build concealed tombs in the VALLEY OF THE KINGS. During the incompetent reigns of the later TWENTIETH-DYNASTY kings, tomb robbing was practised on such a scale as to scandalise the entire country, and it was clear that often the robbers were workmen who knew exactly where to go and what to look for. As a result of despoliation of the tombs, only one royal tomb,

that of TUTANKHAMUN, reached the twentieth century AD without being ransacked. There was also a degree of official tomb robbing. Certain kings found it more convenient to annex a tomb rather than to construct one. Statues from older tombs were also removed, their CARTOUCHES obliterated and new ones incised in their place since it was only the name that counted. *See also* CRIME AND PUNISHMENT.

TRADE (1)

Internal trading trading is so old a practice that its origins are lost. Ever since human communities began to talk to one another, trade has probably been practised, first of all in the form of ceremonial exchanges, soon followed by bartering. Barter and payment in kind remained the basis of trading within Egypt right up until the time of the Persian conquest. Until the MIDDLE KINGDOM, individual communities tended to be self-sufficient. An estate, whether crown land, under a provincial baron, or attached to a temple or royal tomb, could cater for virtually all its everyday needs. The existence of the two granaries (*see* GRANARY), the Red Granary of the DELTA and the White Granary of UPPER EGYPT, indicates some central provision for the storing of surpluses and for distribution in time of shortages. Property could be acquired, by barter or exchange, and there were set standards to establish the value of transactable items. Profit and loss would seem to be excluded from this system, but many lawsuits reflect the disappointment of buyers who found that the goods for which they had made exchange did not live up to the vendor's description.

TRADE (2)

External trading virtually all Egypt's imports, with the exception of long timber, could be described as luxury goods. The wood came from Lebanon and Syria by sea. There were also land trading routes in that direction, more hazardous because of the hostile Bedouin, and other items coming from or through the Middle Eastern lands include lapis lazuli and wine. Caravan routes linked Egypt, through NUBIA and the lands beyond, with the tropical African regions. Ebony, ivory, hides, exotic beasts, ostrich feathers and GOLD all came that way, or by sea from round the Horn of Africa to a port on the Red Sea coast, and then by a toilsome mule train across the Eastern Desert. The PALERMO STONE records commodities brought from the land of PUNT, including 80,000 measures of myrrh, 6,000 units of ELECTRUM, 2,900 units of wood and 23,020 measures of unguents. The value of these must have been immense. Much of what came in from the south may have been the result of raids, or simply taking, rather than trade, but in the later centuries some form of exchange was practised about which little is known. Other items came into Egypt in the form of tribute, during the periods of imperial expansion, or as gifts from friendly or anxious neighbours. Much Egyptian GOLD went on the outward journey for the same reason. Actual exports from Egypt reflected the country's capacity for manufacture of luxury goods. They included made-up medicines, fine furniture and pottery, oils, and cloth. *See also* ECONOMY.

TRANSPORT

The principal artery of travel was the NILE. Many of the CANALS that drew water from the main river were navigable, and for any major building project within a reasonable distance of the stream, it was easiest to construct a canal through the soft earth in order to transport the tonnages of stone and the major timbers required. A wide variety of shipping was developed. Vessels had to cope with the upstream way, against the flow of the river, as well as the easy downstream passage. Movement up and down the river was highly organised. For the benefit of the court, rest houses were built on the riverbanks, with a permanent staff and farmland. *See also* SHIPS AND SHIPBUILDING.

Roads were few and rudimentary. As with canals, a road might be made for a specific purpose and then revert to cultivated fields. Although the wheel was known to the Egyptians, they made no serious use of it, at least until the HYKSOS period, when the war chariot became an important part of military equipment. Wheeled vehicles might have sunk in the lightweight road surfaces, where traditional vehicles spread their weight widely and with an even pressure. Hauliers used sleds, often of massive construction, which were pulled by oxen and slid along trackways that had been specially watered so that the runners moved easily along, supported by a thin layer of mud. Freight that could be readily broken up into smaller packages would be carried overland by mule trains. Over shorter distances, many burdens were carried by the peasants themselves, with yokes with leather water buckets, bundles of faggots, baskets of fish and grain. Along and between the irrigation canals and ditches were pathways formed by the regular imprint of human feet and animal hooves.

TREASURY

The kingdom possessed two great treasuries, the White Treasury of UPPER EGYPT and the Red Treasury of LOWER EGYPT. Under the control of the CHANCELLOR or a deputy, these were repositories of the GOLD and precious metal mined in and around Egypt or brought into the country as a result of trade and tribute. Although there was no CURRENCY, gold by weight was used as a medium of exchange by those who had it. All precious metal was under direct royal control. The gold of Egypt was legendary in the ancient world, and by the NEW KINGDOM, friendly kings did not hesitate to ask for it in gifts, and it was also extensively used to pay the salaries of the vast numbers of mercenary soldiers employed during the LATE PERIOD. *See also* ECONOMY.

TRIAD

In Egyptian mythology, a traditional triple grouping of deities, usually father, mother and son (as in AMUN, MUT and KHONSU).

TUM *see* ATUM.

TURA

Much of the best building limestone came from the famous quarries at this site at the apex of the DELTA, on the eastern bank from Saqqara.

TURIN CANON

A KING LIST, written on a fragmentary papyrus roll, now preserved in the Egyptian Museum, Turin.

TUTANKHAMUN

This EIGHTEENTH-DYNASTY king (ruled 1336–1327 BC), who died at eighteen, has enjoyed more fame in recent times than he did when alive. He was an ineffectual ruler, of somewhat obscure origins, his name originally Tutankhaten until the discrediting of the ATEN cult, when the priests of AMUN – the real power in the land – changed it. He was buried in the VALLEY OF THE KINGS, and his tomb survived unviolated until 1922, when it was discovered and opened by Howard CARTER. Its magnificence stunned the world, brought ancient Egypt to public attention and made Egyptologists speculate wistfully on what might have been found in the tomb of a great pharaoh, a Thuthmosis or Sesostris. In the antechamber were found a wide range of objects, gilded and jewelled chairs, stools, model boats, chariots, different sorts of weaponry, chests containing items of clothing, and mummified birds. Two life-size statues of the king stood by the sealed door into the burial chamber. The mummy of the king, its face covered by a superb mask, perhaps the best-known single piece of Egyptian ART, lay within the innermost of three coffins, made of solid GOLD and profusely ornamented with turquoise, lapis lazuli, carnelians and other jewels. The outer coffin, of stone, lay within a series of shrines made of gold. In another chamber were found the chest containing the king's entrails, a large quantity of votive objects and, among other things, an ivory fan, its feathers still perfectly preserved.

TWELFTH DYNASTY

A dynasty (1991–1785 BC) in the Middle Kingdom, the so-called Golden Age of ancient Egypt. The first king was Ammenemes I, who had been vizier to the previous Eleventh-Dynasty king. There were other claimants to the throne, who had to be fought down, and the king, who was the son of a priest named Sesostris, was keen to prove his legitimacy, and had a literary work composed, set in the reign of Snofru, to foretell his own reign: 'A king will come from the south. He will take the white crown, he will take the red crown; he will join the two mighty ones'. Ammenemes moved the capital from Thebes to a site in Middle Egypt, although Thebes, with the temple of Amun-Ra, remained a place of major importance. He introduced a new element into the kingship, which most of his successors were to follow, by bringing his crown prince, Sesostris I, in as co-regent. This enabled the king to go on campaign while having less fear of the same kind of coup that had brought himself to power, and also introduced the heir to the responsibilities of the kingship. In 1962 BC Ammenemes was murdered after a conspiracy in the harem; Sesostris was on campaign in the Libyan desert and presumably not involved. He acceded to the throne and maintained a vigorous rule, finally reconquering Lower Nubia and extending fortresses up to the third cataract. His son, Ammenemes II, inherited (1928 BC) and duly passed on a stable and wealthy kingdom, with extensive trading and cultural links into the whole eastern Mediterranean and Near East. Sesostris II (ruled 1895–1878 BC) began a major reclamation work in the Faiyum, which was not completed until the reign of his grandson, Ammenemes III. Sesostris II set up his own tomb complex in the region, at el-Lahun. Wth prolonged peace and prosperity, the provincial aristocracy again became powerful and threatened the effectiveness of central administration. Sesostris III (ruled 1878–1842 BC) tackled this problem resolutely, reducing the power of the nobles and appointing civil servants under three viziers for Lower Egypt, Upper Egypt and Lower Nubia. The long reign of Ammenemes III (1842–1797 BC) saw the peak of the Middle Kingdom. The vast work of transforming the Faiyum from marsh to crop land was complete, opening up a great tract of land for the expanding population and bringing a vast increase to the national yield. Many foreign workers crowded into Egypt at this time as economic migrants, bringing a large Asiatic element into the population. Such opulence was inevitably translated into stone. Ammenemes III had two colossal granite figures of himself set up on limestone bases at Biahmu and constructed one pyramid at Dahshur and another at Hawara, beside which are the remains of his mortuary temple. Many other temples and fortifications were constructed at the time.

Despite the great wealth of the land and the peacefulness of the times, decline was setting in. After the short reign of Ammenemes IV (1797–1790 BC), there was a brief period of disputed succession that brought the dynasty to an end. At this time, a queen came to exercise supreme power, SOBKNEFERU ('the beauty of Sobek'), who was Ammenemes' sister and perhaps wife. Her rule was brief and may have ended with her assassination. *See also* Part One: Chapter 17.

TWENTIETH DYNASTY

A dynasty (1188–1069 BC) in the New Kingdom. The first king was Sethnakhte (ruled 1188–1186 BC). In this brief time he reimposed a firm central rule after the collapse of the Nineteenth Dynasty. His son, Rameses III (ruled 1186–1154 BC), was another pharaoh of great ability. Internal reforms were made, defining the status and rights of every member of the community. The imperial tribute was exacted from client kings once again, trading expeditions went out, mining was resumed in areas where banditry had made it impossible, and a great building programme was launched. The long process of building the temple at Karnak continued, and Rameses III also built at Thebes and set up his own great temple at Medinet-Habu. All this was achieved against a state of almost permanent warfare. The Libyans attacked again and were repulsed again. The PEOPLE OF THE SEA attempted a direct invasion by sea and land, and a great sea battle was fought off the Delta, with archers firing from the ships and the vessels then ramming the enemy. Fought off, the invaders returned four years later and were again heavily defeated. A period of peace ensued, but Rameses III's reign was troubled by a plot, which originated in the harem but appears to have involved numerous officials, to manipulate the succession. The affair was discovered, and the chief plotters, including the king's son, compelled to commit suicide; others had their ears and noses slit. The Twentieth Dynasty continued under a further eight Rameses in a state of steady decline. The priesthood of Amun-Ra, whose temple had received much of Rameses' plunder, was the main power in the state, but its attention was focused on its own cult and the preservation of its oligarchic status, without concern for civil order. With a lack of firm central government, civil unrest grew. Food supplies were inefficiently distributed, and there was a situation similar, although less drastic, to that so deplored by Ipuwer in his admonitions during the FIRST INTERMEDIATE PERIOD.

TWENTY-EIGHTH DYNASTY

A dynasty (404–399 BC) in the Late Period that consisted of the reign of a single king, Amyrtaeus, a lord of Sais in the Delta, who drove out the residual Persian garrison in 404 BC. Little is known about his actual reign.

TWENTY-FIFTH DYNASTY

A dynasty (747–656 BC) in the Late Period, also known as the Nubian Dynasty. Under the Libyan kings, Nubia had ceased to be an Egyptian possession or dependency, but it retained some of the character of a colony. During the Eighteenth Dynasty, a viceroyalty had been set up in Nubia, centred on the city of Napata, and its court had reproduced all the main features of the royal court of Thebes. The cult of Amun-Ra was celebrated there and took a strong hold on the Nubian population. When the priest-kings of Thebes were supplanted by the Libyan Dynasty, many of the priesthood took refuge in Nubia. The temple at Napata became a sort of Thebes in exile, and the cult was carried on even when

Nubia slipped entirely out of the control of the rulers of Egypt. For two centuries of Libyan domination the tradition was maintained. Egyptian was the official language of government, and in some ways, as Egypt appeared to have lost its imperial pride, the Nubians prided themselves on being more Egyptian than the Egyptians.

In a surprise move, their king, PIANKHY, launched an invasion of Egypt from the south, transporting his army down the NILE in a huge flotilla of boats. They encountered Tefnakht, the local prince or governor of SAIS, at Thebes and defeated him there, then fought their way on down-river, taking Hermopolis, MEMPHIS and finally overrunning the DELTA. The Egyptians made submission to Piankhy, and Tefnakht on his surrender was treated honourably by the Nubian king. Then, his conquest complete, Piankhy and his army abandoned Egypt and returned up the Nile to their distant capital. No attempt was made to leave an administration. The last king of the Libyan Dynasty, Osorkon, reoccupied Thebes and set up his own rule again. Tefnakht resumed his control of Memphis and the Delta (see TWENTY-FOURTH DYNASTY). Piankhy's motives for invasion remain obscure. He may have been prompted by an ORACLE of Amun-Ra, transmitted through the priests, anxious to return to their ancient sanctuary at Thebes. It does not appear to have been for gain or for empire. But the Nubians had not finished with Egypt. Piankhy's son and successor, Shabaka (ruled 716–702 BC), invaded Egypt, brought the Libyan Dynasty and the Twenty-fourth Dynasty to an end, and set up his capital at Thebes. He shared the piety of his father despite his reputation for cruelty, as with the death of Bocchoris (see TWENTY-FOURTH DYNASTY). During his reign temples were renovated throughout the country. He treated with the Assyrians, avoiding war on that front. His successor was Shabitku (ruled 702–690 BC), during whose reign confrontation with Assyria could not be avoided, and an alliance was made with the kingdom of Judah. His uncle, Taharqa, led an army into Palestine, where Sennacherib, king of Assyria, was besieging Jerusalem. At this time the Assyrians were struck by the mysterious plague described in the Biblical Book of Kings, and war was again delayed. In 690 BC, Taharqa had Shabitku murdered and assumed the throne himself. He moved his capital to TANIS, in the eastern Delta, from which forward position he hoped to mount an empire-building campaign into the Near East. Taharqa was an efficient administrator and planner. Military governors were installed at Thebes and Napata, and the priests of Amun-Ra were forbidden to participate in civil affairs. In 671 BC the Assyrian King ESARHADDON finally launched a direct attack on Egypt. Whilst Taharqa awaited him in the Delta, the Assyrian marched directly on Memphis, capturing the city and cutting the Egyptians' lines of communication. Taharqa's family was captured by the Assyrians and the pharaoh himself fled back to Nubia. His governor at Thebes duly surrendered to Esarhaddon. Esarhaddon, by now overlord of a vast extent of the Middle East, did not remain in Egypt. He left a garrison and obtained the dubious allegiance of many Egyptian lords, especially those of the Delta. On the Assyrian king's departure, Taharqa returned and retook Memphis. His possession was only for a few years before Esarhaddon's successor, ASSURBANIPAL, came with a vast force and captured Memphis and Thebes. Taharqa died in 664 BC and was followed by Tantamani (ruled 664–656 BC). He invaded Egypt from Napata in order to drive out the Assyrians, but Assurbanipal forced him back into Nubia. The Nubian Dynasty was at an end. The kings retreated deep into their vast country, setting up a new capital at Meroe, between the fifth and sixth cataracts. Gradually the land of Kush was to acquire a mythic status for the Egyptians.

TWENTY-FIRST DYNASTY

A dynasty (1069–945 BC) in the THIRD INTERMEDIATE PERIOD. The result of the feeble rule of the last Ramessids was a lapse into the division of the two lands. The first king was Smendes (ruled 1069–1043 BC), a vizier of Lower Egypt, who set up his capital in the Delta city of Tanis. Upper Egypt was ruled from Thebes, where Herihor, who combined the offices of high priest of Amun and vizier of Upper Egypt, was installed as effective king. Unity was briefly restored when his grandson, Pinudjem I, who at first had 'reigned' as high priest, formally assumed the kingship and ruled at Tanis (1054–1042 BC). But Tanis was an outstation of Thebes rather than a Delta power at that point. In the reign of Pinudjem I the royal mummies that had been violated and robbed in the Valley of the Kings were rewrapped and reinterred in a secret place behind the temple of Hatshepsut, where they were found in modern times. After his death, power fluctuated between Tanis and Thebes; sometimes, as with Psusennes I (ruled 1039–993 BC), under a single king, more often under a combination of king in the north and high priest in the south, operating in uneasy coalition. The strings were generally pulled from Thebes, despite the royal status of Tanis. The priests were the real rulers, using the oracular powers of Amun-Ra to deal with all questions.

TWENTY-FOURTH DYNASTY

A brief dynasty (727–715 BC) of two kings in the Third Intermediate Period. Its founder was Tefnakht, the local prince or governor of the Delta city of Sais, who made himself master of the Delta, taking Bubastis and Tanis, and then moved on Upper Egypt, capturing Hermopolis and Memphis, and laying siege to Herakleopolis, when the Nubian invasion brought his venture to a sudden halt (see Twenty-fifth Dynasty). On the departure of the Nubians, he regained control of Lower Egypt and was succeeded by his son, Bocchoris, who ruled well, playing a careful diplomatic game with the Assyrians under Sargon II. He was favourably remembered, but his rule ended with the return of the Nubians, who are reputed to have captured him and burned him alive.

TWENTY-NINTH AND THIRTIETH DYNASTIES

Two dynasties (399–343 BC) in the LATE PERIOD. For a period of almost half a century there was a succession of somewhat shadowy kings, none of whom was able to take a grasp of affairs in the way that many predecessors had done when the country's affairs seemed to be distracted. Egypt as a state was embarked on an inexorable decline. Mercenary generals and captains exercised influence, formed competing factions, and sought to make their own fortunes. The Twenty-ninth Dynasty, centred on MENDES, in the DELTA between Busiris and TANIS, comprised Nepherites I, Psammuthis, Achoris and Nepherites II. In international affairs, Egypt played a subsidiary part, with the brunt of opposition to Persia being taken by the Greek states. Indeed, the Persians simply regarded Egypt as a rebelled satrapy, to be brought back into line as soon as possible, and not as an independent state. The first king of the Thirtieth Dynasty, NECTANEBO I, lord of Sebennytos (modern Sammanud), made a valiant effort to restore the form of the Saite kingdom and encouraged Greek mercenaries to leave the country. Nectanebo I was clearly in control of the whole country, since his buildings can be found from PHILAE down to BUBASTIS in the Delta. During his reign there was a serious attempt by the Persians – using Athenian help – to regain Egypt, which was thwarted by dissension between the Persians and their Greek allies, delaying their march on MEMPHIS and enabling Nectanebo to rally his forces. In the ensuing period of peace, Nectanebo's Egypt saw a revival of the arts, on the Saite model but on a lesser scale. The temple precincts at KARNAK were restored and the temple of ISIS at PHILAE begun. Nectanebo's son, Tachos (ruled 362–360 BC), renewed alliance with the Greek states and invaded Syria with an army composed of Egyptians, Athenians and Spartans. To finance this expedition, he levied heavy taxes and suffered consequent unpopularity. He was abandoned in mid-campaign by his grandson, NECTANEBO II, who defected back to Egypt, leaving Tachos to surrender to the Persians. NECTANEBO assumed the throne, putting down a rebellion from MENDES, where the lord still aspired to the kingship, with the help of Sparta. His building record surpassed that of NECTANEBO I, with over 100 sites showing evidence of building work from his reign. He was a particular adherent of bull cults, propagating the Buchis bull cult at ARMANT as well as the APIS cult at Memphis. He held out against increasing Persian pressure until 343 BC, when the Persians returned in overwhelming force and resumed their overlordship. Nectanebo fled south and kept up an appearance of rule in exile, probably in Lower NUBIA, for at least two years, but Egypt was again a satrapy.

TWENTY-SECOND AND TWENTY-THIRD DYNASTIES

Two dynasties (945–715 BC) in the THIRD INTERMEDIATE PERIOD. The first king was Shoshenq (Bibilical Shishak), a Libyan by descent. He was a leader of the Libyan community that had first come to Egypt partly as slave-prisoners from the armies defeated by Rameses III, partly as mercenaries hired by the Egyptians. His power centre was HERAKLEOPOLIS, in MIDDLE EGYPT, between THEBES and the DELTA, and he found it easy to extend his power northwards, eventually making his capital at BUBASTIS. Under the Libyans, kingship was a military dictatorship, and the Egyptian peasantry went about their daily work just as they had done under the rule of the HYKSOS. Shoshenq became wealthy by a raid on the kingdom of Judah in which he sacked the Temple at Jerusalem and departed with the riches of Solomon. The descendants of Shoshenq reigned undisturbed until 825 BC, when another branch set up the Twenty-third Dynasty, based at Thebes. These ruled in parallel, but the division was a sign of weakness in the structure, and local governors once again claimed hereditary and independent power.

TWENTY-SEVENTH DYNASTY

A dynasty (525–404 BC) under the first Persian occupation. Egypt became a satrapy of the vast empire, under the control of a satrap or governor. As it was the richest satrapy by far, the Persian monarchs took a considerable interest in its affairs and government. They assumed the title and style of pharaohs, as legitimate monarchs of Egypt, and did not attempt to alter the institutions and customs of the country. Cambyses (ruled Egypt 525–522 BC) was regarded as the founder. Although Egyptian propaganda after the Persian period depicts him as an impious and savage invader, he seems in fact to have behaved with restraint, and there is evidence of his having supported local cults and having built and added to temples. He invaded Nubia in a catastrophic campaign in which his entire army perished. He was followed by Darius I (522–486 BC). The Egyptians were not quiescent under the Persian rule, and Darius came in person in 518 BC to put down an uprising. This seems to have been caused by reaction to a heavy-handed and over-ambitious satrap, Aryandes, whom Darius had executed. Darius introduced a number of reforms. By now coinage was in use in Egypt, introduced by the Persians, although the trading ports had probably been using money for some time before. He built a temple to Amun-Ra in the oasis of el-Kharga. Four years after the Greeks defeated Persia at Marathon, the Egyptians again rebelled, and Darius's successor, Xerxes I (ruled 486–465 BC), arrived to crush it. The continuing struggle between Greeks and Persians encouraged the Egyptians in further efforts at resistance, and there was a large-scale rising against Artaxerxes I (ruled 465–424 BC), with a temporary victory won at Pepremis in the Delta, with the help of the Athenians. The satrap was killed, but the satrap of Syria was despatched with a large army to regain control, and Persian rule continued through the reign of Darius II (424–405 BC) and into that of Artaxerxes II (405–359 BC). In 404 BC, with the Persian empire under threat at its very heart, a Saite lord, Amyrtaeus, succeeded in expelling the Persian satrap and his garrison (*see* TWENTY-EIGHTH DYNASTY).

TWENTY-SIXTH DYNASTY

A dynasty (672–525 BC) in the Late Period that assumed power under the shadow of Assyrian domination. The first king was Necho I (ruled 672–664 BC), a descendant of the resolute Tefnakht. As a Delta lord, he had collaborated with Sennacherib and Assurbanipal and had been rewarded with gold and honours. He has been criticised for this, but he had no reason to support the Nubians. The capital was Sais, and this dynasty is often referred to as the Saite Dynasty. His son, Psammetichus I, shook off the dominion of the Assyrians and re-established a wholly independent Egypt. He penetrated Assyria as far as their fortress of Ashdod, with an army composed very largely of Greek mercenaries. Upper Egypt was under the control of the governor, Mentuemhat, a diplomatist who in his time had seen Nubian and Assyrian overlords come and go. Psammetichus made careful and pacific moves in order to establish his own control in Upper Egypt, whose spiritual leader, the chief priestess of Amun (*see* ADORATRICE OF AMUN) was a daughter of the great PIANKHY. The national spirit revived rapidly, and the Saite Dynasty presided over a renaissance of artistic and religious life which, in typical Egyptian manner, manifested itself in a determined return to the traditional ways and imitation of the splendours of the past. After the long foreign domination there was a degree of xenophobia, and foreign ways and foreign gods were abandoned in the search for a return to a true Egyptian identity. The cult of Ptah became prominent, as did that of the Saite protective goddess Neith. The Old Kingdom was looked to as a model, and the PYRAMID TEXTS were favoured over the more recent *Book of the Dead* as a reliable passport to the afterlife. Psammetichus's son, Necho II (ruled 610–595 BC), pursued an ambitious foreign policy. The situation in the Near East had altered dramatically. The Assyrians had been broken by the Medes, and the Egyptian king now became their ally against the Babylonians. In 609 BC Necho II destroyed the army of Judah under Josiah at MEGIDDO, set up Jehoiakim as a puppet king, then marched into Syria. Briefly it seemed as if the empire was restored. But in 605 BC, Necho's army was routed by Nebuchadnezzar, king of Babylon, at Carchemish, and Palestine was annexed by Babylon. Necho's successor, Psammetichus II (ruled 595–589 BC), directed his attention southwards, sending an expedition as far as the second cataract. His successor, Apries (ruled 589–570 BC), made war on the Phoenician cities of Tyre and Sidon, perhaps more in the pursuit of trading disputes than with any thought of re-establishing a Palestinian empire. Many Jewish refugees entered Egypt at this time (the period of the Babylonian Captivity). Apries was ultimately overthrown by his own general, Amasis (ruled 570–526 BC), who held off a Babylonian attack by Nebuchadnezzar and kept the state in prosperity. For all the vicissitudes of changing rulers and dynasties, the Egyptian state had continued in being for far longer than any other and had already seen empires such as those of the Hittites and Assyrians rise and fall. Now, from beyond Babylon, a new empire was flexing its muscles. Amasis observed the rise of Persia and formed alliances with old enemies, including Babylon, to contain it. But the Persians, under Cyrus, defeated the Babylonians and the Lydians, and then turned their attention to Egypt. A new pharaoh, Psammetichus III (ruled 526–525 BC), had just assumed the throne when, under Cambyses, guided across Sinai by the Bedouin and assisted by the treachery of Greek mercenaries, the Persians utterly defeated the Egyptians at Pelusium. When Cambyses took Memphis, Psammetichus killed himself.

TWENTY-THIRD DYNASTY *see* TWENTY-SECOND AND TWENTY-THIRD DYNASTIES.

TWO LADIES' NAME

One of the sequence of five NAMES denoting the title of a particular king. The Two Ladies are the vulture goddess Nekhbet (UPPER EGYPT) and the cobra-goddess WADJET (LOWER EGYPT).

TWOSRE

The last female king of Egypt (ruled 1196–1188 BC), she took power in the turbulent and anarchic period at the end of the NINETEENTH DYNASTY, after the death of her stepson, Siptah. Twosre had the support of the VIZIER, a shadowy figure named Bay or Iarsu, who has left a sinister reputation as a plunderer of the TREASURY he was supposed to safeguard. Documents relating to the reign are few, but Twosre appears to have sent expeditions to SINAI and Palestine, and to have built or added to temples at Heliopolis and Thebes. Her successor, Sethnakhte, described her as a usurper (not necessarily because of her gender) and appropriated for himself the tomb she had built in the VALLEY OF THE KINGS.

U

UNDERWORLD

During the OLD KINGDOM, life after death for the vast majority of the population was assumed to be located in the underworld, a vast, gloomy, ill-defined region where spirits wandered, deprived both of the splendour of heaven and the material pleasures of life on earth. Although it contrasted with the fate of a dead king, who ascended to the sky to join the gods, it was not a hell in the later Christian sense, as entry there was inevitable and not governed by any kind of choice or moral practice; nor was it a place of punishment. By the end of the OLD KINGDOM, this concept of the underworld began to lose its force. The slight 'democratisation' of society was a factor, as was the growing independence of NOMARCHS, who were building greater tombs for themselves and associating them with local as well as national deities. The development and popularity of the OSIRIS legend played a part, although here cause and effect are difficult to distinguish. The old idea was replaced by the notion of an underworld open to all, although not to be entered without some difficulty. Situated beneath the valley of the NILE and parallel to it, it could only be entered through a narrow gorge in a mountain range. This intermediate area was a dangerous and fearful place, inhabited by demons and monsters. Safe passage for the traveller, in his spirit-boat, was not guaranteed. He passed through a succession of gates where the correct phrases must be uttered, or entry would be refused. In such a situation, the correct phrases on papyrus scrap, tomb wall or coffin lid could drive off the demons and make the passage easy. At last he reached the realm of OSIRIS, but his ordeals were not yet over. He must undergo the Judgement of the Dead, which took place in the Hall of MAAT, goddess of truth and harmony. In the scales of Maat, the deceased's heart was weighed against her divine feather. While the heart was being weighed, and its owner prayed for a good result and for his heart not to traduce him, a varied company looked on. This included THOTH himself, who wrote down the result of the Judgement, whilst ANUBIS, assisted by WEPWAWET, adjusted the scales. A devouring monster, with a CROCODILE head and a body composed of lion and hippopotamus, waited nearby in case the judgement should be adverse. The candidate had to make a form of 'negative' confession, enumerating a list of 42 bad or undesirable actions that he had not committed in his lifetime. This was read out to a court of 42 assessor-gods (the same number as the total of the NOMES). When the Judgement was complete and satisfactory (as the papyri and murals show it to have always been), the dead person was ushered by HORUS into the presence of Osiris, prince of the underworld, and was free to pursue his future existence. The realm of the underworld was assumed to be like that of Egypt, with the reeds and fields, the houses and temples, the waterways, and all the pleasures and pursuits of mortal life, including work. But work in the underworld was a pleasure, not a duty. *See also* AFTERLIFE, DEATH.

UPPER EGYPT
The long, narrow valley of the NILE from MEMPHIS to the first cataract, forming one of the original two lands that comprised the ancient Egyptian kingdom. Its chief centre was THEBES. Its ancient emblem was the SEDGE or LILY.

URAEUS
An ornamental serpent worn on the brow, emblematic of the snake-goddess WADJET or BUTO, and symbol of kingship from the early LOWER EGYPT kingdom. *See also* REGALIA.

USERKAF

The first king of the FIFTH DYNASTY. In Egyptian mythology he features in the legend of the first three kings of the dynasty, the sons of RA and Reddedet. *See* Part One: Chapter 11.

USEPHAIS *see* FIRST AND SECOND DYNASTIES.

USERT

In Egyptian mythology, an earth goddess who was identified with ISIS and closely resembled NEITH. Worship of her may have been closely associated with worship of SEBEK, the crocodile god, who was the son of an earth goddess.

USHEBTIU

In FUNERARY PRACTICE little figures, inscribed with magic formulae, which would obey the dead person and perform whatever duties were required in paradise. Ultimately they were shaped in mummy form and in later dynasties were made of glazed ware instead of wood, which was destroyed by white ants.

V

VALLEY OF THE KINGS

A steep-sided, rocky valley in the arid hills on the west bank of the NILE, opposite THEBES. The EIGHTEENTH-DYNASTY king THUTHMOSIS I inaugurated the practice of royal burial here in an effort to protect the tombs against the depredations of TOMB ROBBERS, and it was used for 400 years. A barrier was built across the entrance to the valley and was put under permanent guard. Rock-cut tombs go back to early times, and there were superb MIDDLE-KINGDOM examples at BENI HASAN. The tombs in the Valley of the Kings were much more ambitious. That of Thuthmosis I was a three-chambered one, but the later ones are more complex. The general plan comprised a steep descending entrance stair, ending in an anteroom. Beyond this was a large pillared hall with store rooms for the funerary items and accessories. The entrances were concealed at first, but since this did not save the tombs from robbery, reliance was placed later on formidable defences and secret passages. The Ramessid pharaohs sought to outdo all others with their tombs, as with other constructions. That of Sethos I has a great hall nearly 200 metres (650 feet) long.

A consequence of the decision to place royal tombs in this remote valley was that the tomb and the MORTUARY TEMPLE were inevitably far apart from each other.

Previously, the temple had been placed immediately adjacent to the PYRAMID or MASTABA. Now the KA of the dead king had to travel a long way to inspect and receive its offerings in the mortuary chapel.

VALLEY OF THE QUEENS
A funerary site at THEBES, in the hills above MEDINET HABU and close to DEIR EL-MEDINA, where queens' tombs were situated.

VALLEY TEMPLE *see* FUNERARY PRACTICE.

VICEROY
From the EIGHTEENTH DYNASTY the office of viceroy of NUBIA was created, assuring the rule of Egypt as far as the fourth cataract. The viceroy's court was a replica of that of the imperial capital but with authority on civil matters only.

VIZIER
The highest office under the king. The post goes back to the Second Dynasty in the OLD KINGDOM. The vizier's duties were chiefly concerned with the administration of justice, but he was head of all administration and had a vast staff, with ramifications all over the country. Often the vizier was a member of the royal family, perhaps the son of a junior queen, who had shown special ability.

W

WADI *or* WADY
A watercourse that dries out in the dry season.

WADI HALFA
An important archaeological site in what is now northern Sudan. In 1971 it was partly submerged by Lake Nasser as a result of the building of the ASWAN High Dam.

WADJET
In Egyptian mythology, a serpent-goddess, protector of the UPPER EGYPT nome called after her, with the cult centre at BUTO.

WASTE DISPOSAL
Every Egyptian settlement was liberally supplied with RUBBISH MOUNDS, which

may have been a nuisance at the time as well as a convenience but which have proved to be treasuries for the archaeologist, even though every object in them, other than the very smallest, is broken. They reveal much about the everyday life of the town, the utensils and equipment used, even the DIET of the people.

WATER CLOCK

This was invented in the reign of AMENOPHIS I (EIGHTEENTH DYNASTY) by one Amenemmes, virtually the only inventor recorded by name in dynastic history. It is a device for measuring the passage of time by the flow of water from a marked vessel. *See also* TIME.

WATER SUPPLY

The inhabited NILE Valley stretched for several miles on each side of the river, and settlements that could not draw directly on the stream had to make other arrangements. In some cases, in the NEW KINGDOM, wells were sunk, sometimes to considerable depth, and were equipped with a spiral stair to enable water-carriers with their pottery jars to reach the water level, up to 50 metres (164 feet) below ground level. Wells were not found everywhere; many places depended on a supply of water brought in by donkey from a well or water hole beyond the boundary.

WENI

A courtier and high official of the SIXTH DYNASTY. He served under the first three pharaohs of the dynasty but is particularly associated with PEPY I. In his tomb at ABYDOS was found a form of autobiography that sheds much light on the career of a royal official in the OLD KINGDOM. The autobiographical details are incidental to the main purpose of the work, which is to praise Weni and show to the AFTERLIFE that he had an exemplary career. Beginning as an administrator on the royal estates, he was brought into the palace as a groom of the bedchamber of King Pepy I. Promoted to the rank of King's Friend, he was given the task of superintending the construction of Pepy's PYRAMID city. He was then made a judge and worked closely with the VIZIER, proclaiming that he often discussed secret matters with the vizier alone. He was given the high status of Unique Friend and employed on the delicate and secret task of investigating a plot in the harem involving the queen, Ametsi. 'His Majesty made me go in to hear it alone. No chief judge and vizier, no official was there, only I alone, because I was worthy, because I was rooted in His Majesty's heart, because His Majesty filled his heart with me . . . Never before had one like me heard a secret of the king's harem.' Having performed this task satisfactorily, Weni was then made a general and put at the head of a punitive expedition sent eastwards against the Bedouin and Libyans. This was successful, and he led a further raid into southern Palestine. Describing this, Weni records, 'His Majesty sent me at the head of this army, there being counts, royal seal-bearers, sole companions of the palace, chieftains and MAYORS of towns of UPPER and LOWER EGYPT, companions, leaders of scouts, chief priests of Upper and Lower Egypt, from the villages and towns that they governed and from the Nubians of those foreign lands'. Outliving his master, Pepy, he also served Merenra I, who created a governorship for him. His final task was to supervise the gathering of ALABASTER for the decoration of Merenra's PYRAMID at Saqqara. One of the many marks of royal favour that he notes was that Pepy provided him with a splendid SARCOPHAGUS of fine TURA limestone. Weni's narrative reveals the different tasks that a career official might be asked to undertake and demonstrates the resourcefulness and energy of such men. Above all it reveals the utter and complete worshipful loyalty he felt to the kings he served. Although couched in the conventional phraseology of all such 'autobiographical' texts, there is no reason to doubt its sincerity.

WENIS
The last pharaoh of the Fifth Dynasty, his rule ending around 2460 BC. It is generally taken to mark the end of the classic period of the Old Kingdom. Wenis's funerary complex at northern Saqqara, restored in the reign of Rameses II, was so grand as to give him the status of a local deity in later times.

WEPWAWET
In Egyptian mythology, a deity of the UNDERWORLD, a jackal- or wolf-headed god, the 'opener of the ways'. His origin was as the NOME deity of ASYUT, and, with ANUBIS, he was recognised as protector of the NECROPOLIS at ABYDOS.

WESTCAR PAPYRUS
A PAPYRUS manuscript in which is recorded the legend of the birth of the children who were to become the first three kings of the FIFTH DYNASTY. *See also* Part One: Chapter 11.

WHITE CHAPEL *see* SESOSTRIS I.

WHITE CROWN *see* CROWN; REGALIA.

WHITE GRANARY *see* GRANARY; TRADE.

WHITE HOUSE or Treasury *see* CHANCELLOR; TREASURY.

WHITE NILE
The longer of the two branches of the NILE, rising in Lake Victoria in Central Africa.

WHITE WALLS
An early name for the site that was later called MEMPHIS.

WILKINSON, SIR JOHN GARDNER (1797–1875)
British explorer and Egyptologist who spent twelve years in Egypt from 1821, twice ascending the NILE as far as the second CATARACT. He carried out excavations at THEBES and uncovered many of the tombs at KARNAK and the RAMESSEUM.

WOMEN
The dynastic world was male-oriented government, the priesthood, the learned professions, were male preserves. Whatever her natural abilities and her ambitions, very few women could break this established order of things. Occasionally one such, finding herself in a strategic situation, could manoeuvre events to her own will. Queen HATSHEPSUT was one, but there were few others of similar stature. Women's rights were ranked below men's, but they were not negligible, and women were not their husband's chattels. The status of women in ancient Egypt was higher than in any comparable empire or culture of the ancient world. In the eyes of the law, it appears that women and men, at least within the same social grouping, were equal. A woman could make her own will, which demonstrated that she had property that was her own. She could sell this property or buy more (including slaves). She could live on her own, without a male 'guardian'. Certain trades, not only in those areas of activity always entrusted to women, midwifery, COSMETICS, child-caring, were pursued largely by women; this seems to have included the economically important business of milling corn. But generally, women were relegated to supporting or subservient roles in public life, as MUSICIANS, dancers and sacred or secular PROSTITUTES. *See also* ADORATRICE OF AMUN, CHILDBIRTH, PRIESTESSES.

WRITING
The Egyptians evolved their own style of writing over a lengthy period, beginning far back in the Naqada phase of the PRE-DYNASTIC era. Study of decorated pottery remains reveals a progression of illustration from representation towards greater stylisation and finally the emergence of pure symbol, as in the emblems denoting particular gods. It was a slow and gradual process, and there was no single moment at which it could be said, 'today writing has been invented'. Rather, writing crept up on society, as the increasingly intricate and stylised ART of design was found to be capable of containing and passing on more complex messages. The initial purpose was the utilitarian one of keeping records and assigning property. Egyptian writing omitted the vowel sounds and rendered consonants only, causing speculation about which vowels were in use in certain words or names, hence the alternative spellings of RA as Re, and many other ex-

amples. There were two additional forms of writing to supplement the original HIEROGLYPHICS. HIERATIC was a cursive form of hieroglyphics, used in accounting and administration and for annotating hieroglyphics, in use from the late OLD KINGDOM period. DEMOTIC was a later version of hieratic, from the seventh century BC. In the schools, hieratic was the first form of writing to be taught. The pupil would learn by copying symbols with a reed pen on to an OSTRACON, or occasionally with a stylus on a clay tablet. Writing on papyrus was reserved for the more important documents.

WRITING MATERIALS
PAPYRUS was the principal writing material but beaten-out leather sheets and wooden boards were also used, as were clay tablets, in which the letters would be scratched with a stylus. Ink was not a liquid but was manufactured in the form of little cakes of paste and pigment, similar to modern watercolour paints, and held on a small rectangular palette. The most common colours are black and red, although writing is also found in yellow, blue, green and white on variously coloured backgrounds. The writing instrument was a fibrous reed brush, its tip filed or shaped according to the degree of fineness required.

XYZ

XERXES I *see* TWENTY-SEVENTH DYNASTY.

XOIS
A settlement in the Nile DELTA, between BUSIRIS and BUTO; the home of the FOURTEENTH DYNASTY.

YOUNG, THOMAS (1773–1829)
British physician, physicist and Egyptologist who in 1815 published a comparison of the translations of the DEMOTIC and Greek texts of the ROSETTA STONE in which he pointed out the phonetic rather than symbolic character of the hieroglyphs, which he found to be royal names. This approach to the whole text was taken up by CHAMPOLLION.

ZARU
A Pre-Dynastic ruler who extended his kingdom to the frontier of the Faiyum, unting several smaller kingdoms in the process so that there remained only two – Upper Egypt and Lower Egypt.

ZEDEKIAH

The last king of Judah and brother of JEHOIAKIM. When NEBUCHADNEZZAR seized Jerusalem in 597 BC, he made Zedekiah a vassal king. Eleven years later, Zedekiah rebelled and Nebuchadnezzar besiged Jerusalem, which fell finally in 587 BC. Zedekiah's eyes were put out and he was led away to captivity in Babylon.

ZOAN

The name given in the Bible to TANIS.

ZOSER *see* DJOSER.

The Periods and Dynasties of Ancient Egypt

Pre-Dynastic   5500–3500 BC

Thinite Period   3150–2700 BC
First Dynasty
Second Dynasty

Old Kingdom   c.2658–2185 BC
Third Dynasty
Fourth Dynasty
Fifth Dynasty
Sixth Dynasty

First Intermediate Period   2200–2040 BC
Seventh Dynasty
Eighth Dynasty
Ninth Dynasty
Tenth Dynasty

Middle Kingdom   2040–1675 BC
Eleventh Dynasty (Theban Dynasty)
Twelfth Dynasty
Thirteenth Dynasty
Fourteenth Dynasty

Second Intermediate Period   1675–1553 BC
Fifteenth Dynasty
Sixteenth Dynasty
Seventeenth Dynasty

New Kingdom   1552–1071 BC
Eighteenth Dynasty
Nineteenth Dynasty
Twentieth Dynasty

Third Intermediate Period   1069–715 BC
Twenty-first Dynasty
Twenty-second Dynasty (Libyan Dynasty)
Twenty-third Dynasty
Twenty-fourth Dynasty

Late Period   747–333 BC
Twenty-fifth Dynasty (Nubian Dynasty)
Twenty-sixth Dynasty (Saite Dynasty)
Twenty-seventh Dynasty
Twenty-eighth Dynasty
Twenty-ninth Dynasty
Thirtieth Dynasty

Macedonian Dynasty   332–304 BC

Ptolemaic Period   304–30 BC